# Revenue Statistics in Latin America and the Caribbean

## 1990-2013

# Estadísticas tributarias en América Latina y el Caribe

## 1990-2013

IDB
OECD
BETTER POLICIES FOR BETTER LIVES
UNITED NATIONS
ECLAC

**Please cite this publication as:**
OECD/ECLAC/CIAT/IDB (2015), *Revenue Statistics in Latin America and the Caribbean*, OECD Publishing, Paris.
*http://dx.doi.org/10.1787/rev_lat-2015-en-fr*

**Por favor, cite esta publicación de la siguiente manera:**
OCDE/CEPAL/CIAT/BID (2015), *Estadísticas tributarias en América Latina y el Caribe*, OECD Publishing, Paris.
*http://dx.doi.org/10.1787/rev_lat-2015-en-fr*

ISBN 978-92-64-22938-9 (print/*impresa*)
ISBN 978-92-64-22939-6 (PDF)

Corrigenda to OECD publications may be found on line at: *www.oecd.org/publishing/corrigenda*.
Las erratas de las publicaciones de la OCDE se encuentran en línea en *www.oecd.org/publishing/corrigenda*.

# *Foreword*

*Revenue Statistics in Latin America and the Caribbean* is a joint publication by the OECD Centre for Tax Policy and Administration, the OECD Development Centre, the United Nations Economic Commission for Latin America and the Caribbean (ECLAC), the Inter-American Centre of Tax Administrations (CIAT) and the Inter-American Development Bank (IDB). It presents detailed, internationally comparable data on tax revenues for 20 Latin American and Caribbean economies, 2 of which are OECD members. Its approach is based on the well-established methodology of the OECD Revenue Statistics database (OECD, 2014), which has become an essential reference source for OECD member countries. Comparisons are also made with the average for OECD economies.

The term "taxes" in this publication is confined to compulsory, unrequited payments to general government. As outlined in the Interpretative Guide to the Revenue Statistics, taxes are "unrequited" in the sense that benefits provided by government to taxpayers are not normally in proportion to their payments. The OECD methodology classifies a tax according to its base: income, profits and capital gains (classified under heading 1000), payroll (heading 3000), property (heading 4000), goods and services (heading 5000) and other taxes (heading 6000). Compulsory social security contributions paid to general government are treated as taxes, and classified under heading 2000. Much greater detail on the tax concept, the classification of taxes and the accrual basis of reporting is set out in the Interpretative Guide in Annex A.

Extending the OECD methodology to Latin America and the Caribbean countries makes possible comparisons of tax systems on a consistent basis both across this region and between them and OECD and countries. However, in a few cases this methodology is different from the approach used by ECLAC, CIAT and IDB. In these cases the differences are noted in the text and in the tables, either with a footnote or an extra row.

The report provides an overview of the main taxation trends in Latin America and the Caribbean. It examines changes in both the level and the composition of taxation plus the attribution of tax collection by sub-level of government between 1990 and 2013.

# *Presentación*

La publicación *Estadísticas tributarias en América Latina y el Caribe* ha sido elaborada conjuntamente por el Centro de Política y Administración Tributaria de la OCDE, el Centro de Desarrollo de la OCDE, la Comisión Económica de las Naciones Unidas para América Latina y el Caribe (CEPAL), el Centro Interamericano de Administraciones Tributarias (CIAT) y el Banco Interamericano de Desarrollo (BID). Esta publicación presenta datos detallados comparables a escala internacional sobre los ingresos tributarios de 20 economías latinoamericanas y caribeñas, 2 de las cuales son miembros de la OCDE. Su enfoque se basa en la metodología consagrada de la base de datos Revenue Statistics de la OCDE (OCDE, 2014), que se ha convertido en un referente esencial para los países miembros de la OCDE. Se presentan también comparaciones con la media de la OCDE.

En la presente publicación, el término "impuestos" se circunscribe exclusivamente a los pagos obligatorios sin contraprestación efectuados al gobierno general. Tal y como lo subraya la Guía de interpretación de Revenue Statistics, los impuestos carecen de contraprestación en el sentido en que, normalmente, las prestaciones proporcionadas por el gobierno a los contribuyentes no guardan relación directa con los pagos realizados por estos. La metodología de la OCDE clasifica los impuestos según la base sobre la que recaen: renta, utilidades y ganancias del capital (categoría 1000); nómina (categoría 3000); propiedad (categoría 4000); bienes y servicios (categoría 5000); y otros impuestos (categoría 6000). Las contribuciones obligatorias a la seguridad social abonadas al gobierno general se tratan aquí como impuestos (categoría 2000). Para mayor detalle sobre el concepto de impuesto, su clasificación y su registro según el criterio de devengo, véase la Guía de interpretación que figura en el Anexo A.

Aplicar la metodología de la OCDE a América Latina y el Caribe posibilita la comparación de sistemas tributarios a partir de una base coherente en la region, entre los países latinoamericanos, y con los países de la OCDE. Sin embargo, en algunas ocasiones, esta metodología difiere de la empleada por la CEPAL, el CIAT y el BID; en esos casos, las diferencias se han indicado en el texto y los cuadros, sea con una nota a pie de página, o en una línea adicional.

El informe ofrece un panorama general de las principales tendencias en materia tributaria en América Latina y en el Caribe. A tal efecto, examina los cambios registrados entre 1990 y 2013 en el nivel y la composición de la tributación, así como en la atribución de la recaudación tributaria a los diversos subsectores de gobierno.

# *Acknowledgements*

*Revenue Statistics in Latin America and the Caribbean* has been jointly produced by the Organisation for Economic Co-operation and Development (OECD) Centre for Tax Policy and Administration, the OECD Development Centre, the United Nations Economic Commission for Latin America and the Caribbean (ECLAC), the Inter-American Centre of Tax Administrations (CIAT) and the Inter-American Development Bank (IDB). The staff from these organisations with responsibility for producing the publication were: René Orozco and Daniel Adshead of the OECD Development Centre under the supervision of the Director Mario Pezzini and the Head of the Latin American and Caribbean Unit Angel Melguizo; Maurice Nettley and Emmanuelle Modica of the OECD Centre for Tax Policy and Administration under the supervision of the Director Pascal Saint-Amans, Deputy Director Grace Perez-Navarro and the Head of the Tax Policy and Tax Statistics Division David Bradbury; Juan Pablo Jiménez and Michael Hanni of the Economic Development Division of UN-ECLAC under the supervision of the Director Daniel Titelman and the Chief of the Fiscal Affairs Unit Ricardo Martner; Julio Alberto López from the CIAT Tax Studies and Research Directorate, under the supervision of Director, Miguel Eduardo Pecho; and Juan Carlos Benítez and Agnes Rojas under the supervision of Principal Technical Leader in Fiscal Economics, Alberto Barreix of the IDB.

The authors would like to thank other staff at the OECD Development Centre, the OECD Centre for Tax Policy and Administration and the IDB for their invaluable help in completing this fourth edition of the publication. Rosaura Quinones, from the OECD Latin American and Caribbean Unit, provided substantial support and feedback for the special chapters. Elizabeth Nash and Delphine Grandrieux from the OECD Development Centre's Communications and Publications team ensured the production of the publication, in both paper and electronic form. Gerardo Reyes-Tagle, from the IDB, provided key inputs for the publication.

Finally, the Centre for Tax Policy and Administration and the Development Centre are also very grateful to our colleagues working in national entities with whom we have consulted regularly. These institutions include the finance ministries and national tax agencies of Argentina, Barbados, Bolivia, Brazil, Chile, Colombia, Costa Rica, Dominican Republic, Ecuador, El Salvador, Guatemala, Honduras, Jamaica, Mexico, Nicaragua, Panama, Paraguay, Peru, Uruguay and Venezuela, the Ministry of Economy and Production of Argentina, the Central Bank of Barbados and the Central Reserve Bank of Peru. In addition, CIAT would like to thank their Network of Tax Studies and Research.

# *Agradecimientos*

La publicación *Estadísticas tributarias en América Latina y el Caribe* ha sido elaborada conjuntamente por el Centro de Política y Administración Tributaria de la Organización para la Cooperación y el Desarrollo Económicos (OCDE), el Centro de Desarrollo de la OCDE, la Comisión Económica de las Naciones Unidas para América Latina y el Caribe (CEPAL), el Centro Interamericano de Administraciones Tributarias (CIAT) y el Banco Interamericano de Desarrollo (BID). Las personas de esas organizaciones responsables de redactar la presente publicación han sido: René Orozco y Daniel Adshead del Centro de Desarrollo de la OCDE, bajo la supervisión del director, Mario Pezzini y del Jefe de la Unidad de América Latina y el Caribe Angel Melguizo; Maurice Nettley y Emmanuelle Modica del Centro de Política y Administración Tributaria de la OCDE, bajo la supervisión del director, Pascal Saint-Amans, sub-directora Grace Perez-Navarro y el Jefe de la División de Políticas y Estadísticas Tributarias David Bradbury; Juan Pablo Jiménez y Michael Hanni de la División de Desarrollo Económico de la CEPAL, bajo la supervisión del director Daniel Titelman y del jefe de la Unidad de Asuntos Fiscales Ricardo Martner; Julio Alberto López de la Dirección de Estudios e Investigaciones Tributarias del CIAT, bajo la supervisión del Director, Miguel Eduardo Pecho; y Juan Carlos Benítez y Agnes Rojas bajo la supervisión del Líder Técnico Principal en Economia Fiscal Alberto Barreix del BID.

Los autores desean agradecer a otras personas del Centro de Desarrollo de la OCDE, del Centro de Política y Administración Tributaria de la OCDE y BID su incalculable contribución a la finalización de la quarta edición de esta publicación. En particular, Rosaura Quinones, de la Unidad de América Latina y el Caribe del Centro de Desarrollo realizó aportes significativo a los capítulos especiales, Elizabeth Nash y Delphine Grandrieux, del equipo de Comunicaciones y Publicaciones del Centro de Desarrollo de la OCDE, que aseguraron la producción de la publicación, tanto fisica como en formato electrónico y Gerardo Reyes-Tagle del BID, quien aporto elementos clave para la publicación.

Por último, el Centro de Política y Administración Tributaria y el Centro de Desarrollo de la OCDE hacen partícipes de nuestro agradecimiento a nuestros colegas de entidades nacionales, a los que hemos consultado con frecuencia. Entre esas instituciones, se cuentan los ministerios de finanzas y las agencias tributarias nacionales de Argentina, Barbados, Bolivia, Brasil, Chile, Colombia, Costa Rica, Ecuador, El Salvador, Guatemala, Honduras, Jamaica, México, Nicaragua, Panamá, Paraguay, Perú, República Dominicana, Uruguay y Venezuela, así como el Ministerio de Economía y Producción de Argentina, el Banco Central de Barbados (CBB) y el Banco Central de Reserva del Perú. Asimismo, CIAT también desea agradecer La Red de Estudios e Investigaciones Tributarias.

# Table of contents

Executive summary....12

Part I. Tax revenue trends 1990-2013....19
A. Tax ratios....20
B. Tax structures....24
C. Taxes by level of government....26
D. Comparative charts....29
References....33

Special Feature S1: Features of fiscal pressure in Latin America and the Caribbean....34
Special Feature S2: Fiscal revenues from non-renewable natural resources in Latin America....46

Part II. Tax levels and tax structures, 1990-2013....85
A. Comparative tables, 1990-2013....86
B. Comparative charts....104

Part III. Country tables, 1990-2013 – Tax revenues....109

Part IV. Tax revenues by sub-sectors of general government....149

Annex A....173
The OECD classification of taxes....174
The OECD Interpretative Guide....176
A. Coverage....176
B. Basis of reporting....178
C. General classification criteria....179
D. Commentaries on items of the list....181
E. Conciliation with National Accounts....191
F. Memorandum item on the financing of social security benefits....191
G. Memorandum item on identifiable taxes paid by government....191
H. Relation of OECD classification of taxes to national accounting systems....191
I. The OECD classification of taxes and the International Monetary Fund (GFS) system....192
J. Comparison of the OECD classification of taxes with other international classifications....192
K. Attribution of tax revenues by sub-sectors of general government....194
L. Provisional classification of revenues from bank levies and payments to deposit insurance and financial stability schemes....197
Notes....198

# *Índice de materias*

Resumen ejecutivo ..... 14

Parte I. Tendencias tributarias, 1990-2013 ..... 53
A. Niveles de recaudación ..... 54
B. Estructuras impositivas ..... 58
C. Impuestos por nivel de gobierno ..... 61
Referencias ..... 64

Sección especial S1: Características de la presión fiscal en América Latina y el Caribe ..... 65
Sección especial S2: Ingresos fiscales provenientes de recursos naturales no renovables en América Latina ..... 78

Parte II. Niveles impositivos y estructuras tributarias, 1990-2013 ..... 85
A. Cuadros comparativos, 1990-2013 ..... 86
B. Gráficos comparativos ..... 104

Parte III. Cuadros país, 1990-2013 – Ingresos tributarios ..... 109

Parte IV. Ingresos tributarios por sub-sectores de gobierno general ..... 149

Anexo A ..... 199
Clasificación de impuestos de la OCDE ..... 200
Guía de Interpretación de la OCDE ..... 202
A. Cobertura ..... 202
B. Principios de registro ..... 205
C. Criterios generales de clasificación ..... 206
D. Comentarios sobre ítems de la lista ..... 208
E. Conciliación con las cuentas nacionales ..... 219
F. Partida informativa sobre el financiamiento de las prestaciones sociales ..... 220
G. Partida informativa sobre impuestos identificables pagados por el gobierno ..... 220
H. Relación de la clasificación de impuestos de la OCDE con el Sistema de Cuentas Nacionales ..... 220
I. Relación de la clasificación de impuestos de la OCDE con el sistema de estadísticas de finanzas públicas del Fondo Monetario Internacional ..... 221
J. Comparación de la clasificación de impuestos de la OCDE con otras clasificaciones internacionales ..... 221
K. Atribución de ingresos tributarios por subsectores del gobierno general ..... 223
L. Clasificación provisional de los ingresos tributarios procedentes de gravámenes bancarios y pagos a sistemas de seguro de depósitos y de estabilidad financiera ..... 226
Notas ..... 227

## List of tables/Índice de cuadros

### Part I/Parte I
Tax revenue trends 1990-2013/Tendencias tributarias, 1990-2013


Table A. Total tax revenue as percentage of GDP ....22
Cuadro A. Total de recaudación tributaria como porcentaje del PIB ....56
Table B. Value added taxes as percentages of GDP ....23
Cuadro B. Impuesto al valor agregado en porcentaje del PIB ....57
Table C. Tax structures in a group of Latin American and Caribbean countries ....24
Cuadro C. Estructuras impositivas en un grupo de países de América Latina y del Caribe ....58
Table D. Attribution of tax revenues to sub-sectors of general government as percentage of total tax revenue ....28
Cuadro D. Atribución de los ingresos tributarios en los sub-sectores del gobierno general como porcentaje del ingreso tributario total ....63
Table S1.1. Features of social security systems in LAC ....39
Cuadro S1.1. Características de los sistemas de seguridad social en ALC ....71
Table S2.1. Fiscal instruments considered within the framework of fiscal revenues from non-renewable natural resources ....51
Cuadro S2.1. Los instrumentos considerados dentro del marco de los Ingresos fiscales provenientes recursos naturales no renovables ....84


### Part II/Parte II
Tax levels and tax structures, 1990-2013/Niveles impositivos y estructuras tributarias, 1990-2013


Table 1. Total tax revenue as percentage of GDP
Cuadro 1. Total de ingresos tributarios en porcentaje del PIB ....87
Table 2. Tax revenue of main headings as percentage of GDP, 2013
Cuadro 2. Ingresos tributarios en las principales partidas en porcentaje del PIB, 2013 ....89
Table 3. Tax revenue of main headings as percentage of total taxation, 2013
Cuadro 3. Ingresos tributarios en las principales partidas en porcentaje del total de ingresos tributarios, 2013 ....90
Table 4. Taxes on income and profits (1000) as percentage of GDP
Cuadro 4. Impuestos sobre la renta y las utilidades (1000) en porcentaje del PIB ....91
Table 5. Taxes on income and profits (1000) as percentage of total taxation
Cuadro 5. Impuestos sobre la renta y las utilidades (1000) en porcentaje del total de ingresos tributarios ....92
Table 6. Social security contributions (2000) as percentage of GDP
Cuadro 6. Contribuciones a la seguridad social (2000) en porcentaje del PIB ....93
Table 7. Social security contributions (2000) as percentage of total taxation
Cuadro 7. Contribuciones a la seguridad social (2000) en porcentaje del total de ingresos tributarios ....94
Table 8. Taxes on property (4000) as percentage of GDP
Cuadro 8. Impuestos sobre la propiedad (4000) en porcentaje del PIB ....95
Table 9. Taxes on property (4000) as percentage of total taxation
Cuadro 9. Impuestos sobre la propiedad (4000) en porcentaje del total de ingresos tributarios....96

Table 10. Taxes on goods and services (5000) as percentage of GDP
Cuadro 10. Impuestos sobre bienes y servicios (5000) en porcentaje del PIB ..... 97
Table 11. Taxes on goods and services (5000) as percentage of total taxation
Cuadro 11. Impuestos sobre bienes y servicios (5000) en porcentaje del total de ingresos tributarios ..... 98
Table 12. Taxes on general consumption (5110) as percentage of GDP
Cuadro 12. Impuestos generales sobre el consumo (5110) en porcentaje del PIB ..... 99
Table 13. Taxes on general consumption (5110) as percentage of total taxation
Cuadro 13. Impuestos generales sobre el consumo (5110) en porcentaje del total de ingresos tributarios ..... 100
Table 14. Taxes on specific goods and services (5120) as percentage of GDP
Cuadro 14. Impuestos específicos sobre bienes y servicios (5120) en porcentaje del PIB ..... 101
Table 15 Taxes on specific goods and services (5120) as percentage of total taxation
Cuadro 15. Impuestos específicos sobre bienes y servicios (5120) en porcentaje del total de ingresos tributarios ..... 102
Table 16. Gross domestic product for tax reporting years at market prices, in billions of national currency units
Cuadro 16. Producto interno bruto para los años fiscales a precios de mercado, en millardos de moneda local ..... 103

## Part III/Parte III

### Country tables 1990-2013 - Tax revenues/Cuadros país, 1990-2013 - Ingresos tributarios

Tables 17-36. Latin American countries in alphabetical order
Cuadros 17-36. Países latinoamericanos clasificados por orden alfabético en inglés ..... 110

## Part IV/Parte IV

### Tax revenues by sub-sectors of general government
### Ingresos tributarios por sub-sectores de gobierno general

Table 37. Attribution of tax revenues to sub-sectors of general government as percentage of total tax revenue
Cuadro 37. Atribución de los ingresos tributarios en los sub-sectores del gobierno general como porcentaje del ingreso tributario total ..... 150
Tables 38-57. Latin American countries in alphabetical order
Cuadros 38-57. Países latinoamericanos clasificados por orden alfabético en inglés ..... 151

## List of charts/ Índice de gráficos

## Part I/Parte I

### Tax revenue trends 1990-2013/Tendencias tributarias, 1990-2013

Chart A. Total tax revenues as percentage of GDP in Latin America and the Caribbean, and OECD, 1990-2013 ..... 21
Gráfico A. Total de recaudación tributaria como porcentaje de PIB en América Latina y el Caribe, y la OCDE, 1990-2013 ..... 55

Chart B. Tax structures in Latin America and the Caribbean, and the OECD, 2012 .......... 26
Gráfico B. Estructuras impositivas en América Latina y el Caribe, y la OCDE, 2012 .......... 60
Chart C. Total tax revenues as percentage of GDP, 2013
Gráfico C. Total de recaudación tributaria como porcentaje del PIB, 2013 .......... 29
Chart D. Tax to GDP ratios in Latin American and Caribbean countries in 1990 and 2013
Gráfico D. Recaudación tributaria como porcentaje del PIB en países de América Latina y el Caribe en 1990 y 2013 .......... 30
Chart E. Tax to GDP ratios in Latin American and Caribbean countries in 1990 and 2000
Gráfico E. Recaudación tributaria como porcentaje del PIB en países de América Latina y el Caribe en 1990 y 2000 .......... 31
Chart F. Tax to GDP ratios in Latin American and Caribbean countries in 2000 and 2013
Gráfico F. Recaudación tributaria como porcentaje del PIB en países de América Latina y el Caribe en 2000 y 2013 .......... 32
Figure S1.1 Equivalent Fiscal Pressure, 1990-2013 .......... 35
Gráfico S1.1. Presión Fiscal Equivalente, 1990-2013 .......... 66
Figure S1.2. Equivalent Fiscal Pressure, per capita and as % of GDP .......... 36
Gráfico S1.2. Presión Fiscal Equivalente, per cápita y como % del PIB .......... 67
Figure S1.3. Public and private social security contributions .......... 38
Gráfico S1.3. Contribuciones y aportes públicos y privados a la seguridad social .......... 70
Figure S1.4. EFP and Adjusted Commodity Price Index .......... 41
Gráfico S1.4. PFE e Índice de Precios de Commodities, América Latina el Caribe .......... 73
Figure S2.1 Fiscal revenues from non-renewable natural resources, 2013 .......... 46
Gráfico S2.1 Ingresos fiscales provenientes recursos naturales no renovables, 2013 .......... 78
Figure S2.2. Change in fiscal revenues from non-renewable natural resources, 2012-13 .......... 47
Gráfico S2.2 Cambio en los ingresos fiscales provenientes recursos naturales no renovables, 2012-13 .......... 79
Figure S2.3. Fiscal revenues from non-renewable natural resources, by selected product groups, 2000-14 .......... 50
Gráfico S2.3 Ingresos fiscales provenientes recursos naturales no renovables, por grupos seleccionados de materias primas, 2000-14 .......... 82

## Part II/Parte II

### Tax levels and tax structures, 1990-2013/Niveles impositivos y estructuras tributarias, 1990-2013

Chart 1. Tax revenue of main headings as percentage of total tax revenue, 2013
Gráfico 1. Ingresos tributarios de categorías principales como porcentaje del ingreso tributario total, 2013 .......... 104
Chart 2. Tax structures in Latin American and Caribbean countries, 1990-2013
Gráfico 2. Estructuras impositivas en países de América Latina y el Caribe, 1990-2013 .......... 105

## Part IV/Parte IV

### Tax revenues by sub-sectors of general government
### Ingresos tributarios por sub-sectores de gobierno general

Chart 3. Attribution of tax revenues to sub-sectors of general government, 2012
Gráfico 3. Atribución de los ingresos tributarios en los sub-sectores del gobierno general, 2012 ... 171

# *Executive summary*

Tax revenues as a proportion of national incomes in Latin American and Caribbean countries rose slightly in 2013. This followed a period of steady increases since the 1990s that was only interrupted during the financial crisis in 2009. In the group of 20 Latin American and Caribbean (LAC) countries covered by the Report the average tax to GDP ratio increased to 21.3% in 2013, compared with 21.2% in 2012 and 20.5% in 2011. Between 1990 and 2013, this average rose more quickly than the OECD equivalent – by 6.9 percentage points compared with 1.9. However at 21.3% in 2013 it is still well below the corresponding OECD figure of 34.1%.

There are wide national variations in the tax ratio across both OECD and Latin American and Caribbean countries. In 2013, the LAC countries covered by the Report range from 35.7% in Brazil (above the OECD average) to 13.0% in Guatemala. The corresponding range amongst OECD countries was from 48.6% in Denmark to 19.7% in Mexico.

The Report provides internationally comparable data on tax levels and tax structures for the group of 20 Latin American and Caribbean (LAC) countries. It is a joint publication by the Inter-American Development Bank (IDB), the Inter-American Centre for Tax Administrations (CIAT), the Economic Commission for Latin America and the Caribbean (ECLAC) and the OECD. Using the same methodology as the *OECD Revenue Statistics* database, it presents cross-country comparisons between LAC economies and between LAC and OECD economies. The LAC countries covered are Argentina, Barbados, Bolivia, Brazil, Chile, Colombia, Costa Rica, Dominican Republic, Ecuador, El Salvador, Guatemala, Honduras, Jamaica, Mexico, Nicaragua, Panama, Paraguay, Peru, Uruguay and Venezuela. Barbados and Jamaica have been added since the third edition. The Revenue Statistics in Latin America figure for the tax to GDP ratio in Mexico is different from those presented in ECLAC and CIAT publications because the former includes fees levied on hydrocarbon production as tax revenues.

The term “taxes” in this publication refers to compulsory, unrequited payments to general government. Taxes are “unrequited” in the sense that the benefits provided by governments to taxpayers are not normally allocated in proportion to their payments, as outlined in the Interpretative Guide to the Revenue Statistics. The OECD methodology classifies a tax according to its base: income, profits and capital gains; payroll; property; goods and services; and other taxes. Compulsory social security contributions paid to general government are also treated as taxes, and are classified under a separate heading. Detailed information on the tax concept, the classification of taxes and the accrual basis of reporting is set out in the Interpretative Guide in Annex A of this report. The Report also analyses the share of tax revenue attributed to the various levels of government; federal or central; state (regional); local and social security funds.

There are two special features in this edition. The first considers an alternative approach to the way government fiscal revenues are accounted for. In particular it examines the usefulness of taking into account two additional sources of revenues or “revenue equivalent” in addition to the tax revenues traditionally considered. The second describes trends in revenues from non-renewable natural resources in some Latin American countries since the year 2000.

## Key findings

### *Tax to GDP ratios*

- The average tax burden in the group of 20 LAC countries increased to 21.3% in 2013. This followed rises of 0.7 percentage points in both 2012 and 2011, reversing the decline from 20.1% to 19.5% between 2008 and 2009.
- In 2013, the ratio of tax revenues to GDP compared to 2012 rose in 12 of the LAC countries, fell in 7 and stayed the same in 1.
- The difference between the OECD average tax to GDP ratio and that for the 20 LAC countries fell from 18 to 13 percentage points between 1990 and 2013.
- Increases in revenue from taxes on income and profits, taxes on goods and services and social security contributions contributed to the recovery in tax-to-GDP ratios between 2010 and 2013.
- The largest increases in tax to GDP ratios in 2013 were in Bolivia (2.1 percentage points), Argentina (1.7), Costa Rica (1.2) and El Salvador (0.7).
- The largest falls in 2013 were in Barbados (4.2 percentage points) and Paraguay (1.3) points.
- There is considerable variation in trends over time for individual LAC countries. The countries with the largest increases between 1990 and 2013 were Bolivia (20.6 percentage points) Argentina (18.8), Ecuador (12.2), Colombia (11.1) and Paraguay (11.0). There was a decline of 4.5 percentage points in Venezuela.

### *Tax structures*

- Following strong growth over the past twenty years, general consumption taxes (mainly VAT and sales taxes) accounted for 32.3% of tax revenues in the LAC countries in 2012 compared with 20.2% in OECD countries whereas the share of specific consumption taxes (such as excises and taxes on international trade) declined to 17.6% (in OECD it is 10.7%)
- In 2012, taxes on income and profits accounted for 26.6% of revenues on average in the Latin American and Caribbean countries and social security contributions represented 16.5% (in OECD the corresponding figures are 33.6% and 26.2% respectively).

### *Tax revenues attributed to local governments*

- The share of tax revenues collected by local governments in Latin America and the Caribbean is small in most countries and has not increased, reflecting the relatively narrow range of taxes under their jurisdictions compared with OECD countries.

# *Resumen ejecutivo*

Los ingresos tributarios como proporción del PIB se incrementaron ligeramente en 2013 en las economias de América Latina y el Caribe, siguiendo un periodo de constantes aumentos desde 1990, solo inerrumpido por la crisis financiera del 2009. En el grupo de 20 países de América Latina y el Caribe (LAC) objeto del informe, el ratio medio de recaudación tributaria sobre PIB se elevó hasta un 21.3% en 2013, frente al 21.2% de 2012 y el 20.5% en el 2011. Entre 1990 y 2013, dicho ratio medio subió más rápidamente que su homólogo de la OCDE – en 6.9 puntos porcentuales frente a 1.9 puntos porcentuales. Sin embargo, con un 21.3% en 2013 se sitúa aún muy por debajo del 34.1%, último dato disponible de la OCDE.

Existen amplias diferencias entre los ratios de ingresos tributarios tanto en los países latinoamericanos como en los de la OCDE. En 2013, en los países de América Latina y el Caribe incluidos en el informe, dichos ratios oscilan entre el 35.7% de Brasil (por encima de la media de la OCDE) y el 13.0% de Guatemala. Entre los países de la OCDE, el rango varía entre el 48.6% de Dinamarca y el 19.7% en México.

El informe presenta datos internacionalmente comparables sobre los niveles y estructuras tributarios para el grupo de 20 países de América Latina y el Caribe (ALC). Es una publicación elaborada conjuntamente por el Banco Interamericano de Desarrollo (BID), el Centro Interamericano de Administraciones Tributarias (CIAT), la Comisión Económica para América Latina y el Caribe (CEPAL) y la OCDE. Utilizando la misma metodología que la base de datos Revenue Statistics de la OCDE, ofrece comparaciones por países entre las economías de América Latina y el Caribe, y las economías de la OCDE. Los países de América Latina y el Caribe objeto de examen son Argentina, Barbados, Bolivia, Brasil, Chile, Colombia, Costa Rica, República Dominicana, Ecuador, El Salvador, Guatemala, Honduras, Jamaica, México, Nicaragua, Panamá, Paraguay, Perú, Uruguay y Venezuela. Desde la tercera edición se han incluido a Barbados y a Jamaica. En las Estadísticas Tributarias en América Latina, el dato de recaudación tributaria como porcentaje del PIB de México difiere del presentado en las publicaciones de la CEPAL y el CIAT, esto se debe a que las citadas Estadísticas Tributarias incluyen los derechos sobre la producción de hidrocarburos como ingresos tributarios.

En la presente publicación, el término "impuestos" se refiere a pagos obligatorios sin contraprestación efectuados al gobierno general. Los impuestos carecen de contraprestación en el sentido que, normalmente, las prestaciones que los gobiernos proporcionan a los contribuyentes no guardan relación directa con los pagos realizados por estos, tal como se señala en la Guía de Interpretación de las Estadísticas Tributarias. La metodología de la OCDE clasifica los impuestos según la base sobre la que recaen: renta, utilidades y ganancias del capital; nóminas; propiedad; bienes y servicios; y otros impuestos. Las contribuciones obligatorias a la seguridad social abonadas al gobierno general se tratan también como impuestos y se clasifican dentro de una categoría distinta. Para obtener información más pormenorizada sobre el concepto de impuesto, y su clasificación y registro según el criterio de devengo, véase la Guía de Interpretación que figura en el Anexo A de este informe. El informe también analiza la parte de ingresos tributarios que se atribuye a los distintos niveles de gobierno; federal o central; estatal (regional); local y fondos de seguridad social.

Incluye asimismo dos capítulos especiales. En el primero se considera una metodología diferente para contabilizar los ingresos fiscales. De manera más específica se examina la utilidad de incluir dos fuentes adicionales de ingreso o de "ingresos equivalentes" además de la recaudación impositiva tradicional. En el Segundo se exponen las tendencias de los ingresos procedentes de recursos naturales no renovables en países latinoamericanos y se estudian los factores que han impulsado su crecimiento desde el año 2000.

## Principales conclusiones

***Recaudación tributaria como porcentaje del PIB***

- La carga fiscal media en el grupo de los 20 países de América Latina y el Caribe represento el 21.3% del PIB en 2013. Esto tuvo lugar después de los incrementos de 0.7 puntos porcentuales en 2012 y 2011, que revirtieron el descenso del 20.1% al 19.5% recaudado entre 2008 y 2009.
- En 2013, el ratio de recaudación tributaria sobre PIB subió, con respecto a 2012, en 12 países de América Latina y el Caribe, se redujo en 7 y permaneció constante en 1.
- La diferencia entre el ratio medio de recaudación tributaria sobre PIB de la OCDE y el correspondiente a los 20 países de América Latina y el Caribe se redujo de 18 a 13 puntos porcentuales entre 1990 y 2013.
- Los aumentos de recaudación de los impuestos sobre la renta y las utilidades y los impuestos sobre bienes y servicios fueron los que más contribuyeron a la recuperación de los ratios de recaudación tributaria sobre PIB entre 2010 y 2013.
- En 2013, los mayores incrementos de estos ratios de recaudación tributaria sobre PIB correspondieron a Bolivia (2.1 puntos porcentuales), Argentina (1.7), Costa Rica (1.2) y El Salvador (0.7).
- Las mayores caídas se produjeron en Barbados (4.2 puntos porcentuales) y Paraguay (1.3 puntos porcentuales).
- Existe una considerable disparidad entre las tendencias descritas a lo largo del tiempo para cada uno de los países de América Latina y el Caribe. Entre 1990 y 2013, los países que experimentaron mayores incrementos fueron Bolivia (20.6 puntos porcentuales), Argentina (18.8), Ecuador (12.2), Colombia (11.1) y Paraguay (11.0). Venezuela sufrió un descenso de 4.5 puntos porcentuales.

***Estructuras tributarias***

- Luego del sólido crecimiento de los últimos veinte años, los impuestos generales sobre el consumo (principalmente el IVA y los impuestos sobre las ventas) representan un 32.3% de los ingresos tributarios de los países de América Latina y el Caribe en 2012, frente al 20.2% de los países de la OCDE, mientras que el peso de los impuestos específicos sobre el consumo (como los impuestos selectivos o los impuestos sobre el comercio internacional) se ha reducido hasta un 17.6% (en la OCDE es de un 10.7%).
- En el 2012, los impuestos sobre la renta y las utilidades representaron, en promedio, un 26.6% de la recaudación, mientras que las contribuciones a la seguridad social alcanzaron un 16.5% para los países latinoamericanos y caribeños (en la OCDE, dichos porcentajes son de un 33.6% y 26.2% respectivamente).

***Ingresos tributarios atribuidos a gobiernos locales***

- La parte de los ingresos tributarios recaudada por los gobiernos locales es pequeña y no se ha elevado en la mayoría de los países de América Latina y el Caribe, debido al reducido abanico de impuestos sobre el que tienen competencia en contraste con los países de la OCDE.

# PART I

# TAX REVENUE TRENDS 1990-2013

# PARTE I

# TENDENCIAS TRIBUTARIAS, 1990-2013

# PART I

# TAX REVENUE TRENDS 1990-2013

## A. Tax ratios

Tax revenues as a proportion of gross domestic product (GDP) have increased considerably in Latin America and the Caribbean during the last two decades. Both Chart A and Table A show how revenues, including social security contributions, for these Latin American and Caribbean countries have, with the exception of 2009, risen almost continuously from 14.4% of GDP in 1990 to 21.3% of GDP (unweighted averages) in 2013. This growth in the relative importance of tax revenues is a reflection of favourable macroeconomic conditions, changes in the tax systems design and strengthening of tax administrations.

This trend contrasts with that in the OECD area where the ratio has been relatively stable – in 2013 it stood at 34.1% – just over one percentage point above its level in 1990. As a result, the gap between the averages for the two areas started to narrow after 2000. This difference was around 18 percentage points in 1990 but had fallen to around 13 percentage points by 2010 and has remained steady since then.

Tax to GDP ratios in Latin America and the Caribbean increased in each year from 2010 to 2013 following the interruption of the long-term rising trend in 2009, as a result of the fall in economic activity and commodity prices due to the international financial crisis. The average tax ratio increased slightly in 2013 to 21.3% compared with 21.2% in 2012. In 2013, the tax ratio rose in 12 of 20 countries and fell in 7 compared with 2012, while it remained the same in Nicaragua. The corresponding figures for 2012 compared with 2011 were an increase in 18 countries, a fall in 1 and no change in 1. The average in OECD countries, however, rose by 0.4 percentage points in 2013 to 34.1% but still remained 0.1 percentage points below the pre-crisis tax-to-GDP level of 34.2% in 2007.

The average tax to GDP ratio in OECD countries is much higher than the one for Latin American and Caribbean countries in the sample (34.1% compared with 21.3% in 2013, respectively). However, there is a wide range between the highest and lowest tax to GDP ratios across countries in Latin America and the Caribbean. Amongst the sample countries the highest levels in 2013 were in Brazil and Argentina (35.7% and 31.2% respectively) whereas the lowest levels were observed in Guatemala (13.0%) and Dominican Republic (14.0%). In the same way, the characteristics of the OECD economies show a wide variation. In 2013, the OECD tax to GDP ratios ranged from 48.6% in Denmark down to 19.7% in Mexico (this figure is different from the ones presented in ECLAC and CIAT publications because of the inclusion of fees levied on hydrocarbon production as tax revenues). The implications of these wide ranges are that differences in tax to GDP ratios between OECD and Latin America & the Caribbean should be interpreted with caution given that they include economies that are widely different in character.

There are many factors that determine what should be the appropriate ratio for an individual country, but one of them is the extent of goods and services provided by the State. From the 1980s onwards many Latin American and Caribbean countries to greater or lesser degrees privatised healthcare, education and social security (ECLAC, 2010). This regional position stands in contrast to the substantial public provision of these services, and the corresponding need for revenue receipts, in many OECD countries, particularly in Europe. There are also high levels of informality that exclude many from paying taxes in Latin American and Caribbean countries (OECD, 2008 and Gómez Sabaini et al. 2010), something which has a particular incidence in the case of SMEs. However the issue of non-payment of taxes generally has a significant impact on tax revenues in all countries.

Table A shows considerable variation in trends over time for individual countries. Irrespective of the wide range of tax levels, widespread strengthening of public revenues can be observed since 1990. The countries with the largest increases between 1990 and 2013 were Bolivia (20.6 percentage points) Argentina (18.8), Ecuador (12.2), Columbia (11.1) and Paraguay (11.0). The majority of the countries showed increases of between 3 and 8 percentage points. The exceptions were Jamaica and Honduras with respective increases of 2 and 1.8 percentage points and Venezuela, where a decline of 4.5 percentage points was observed over the same period.

Chart A. **Total tax revenues as percentage of GDP in Latin America and the Caribbean, and OECD, 1990-2013**

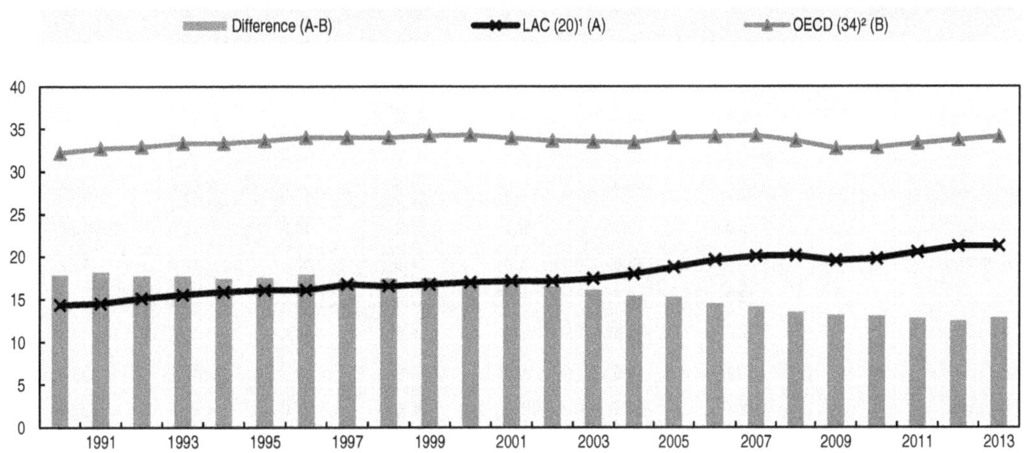


1. Represents a group of 20 Latin American and Caribbean countries. These are Argentina, Barbados, Bolivia, Brazil, Chile, Colombia, Costa Rica, Dominican Republic, Ecuador El Salvador, Guatemala, Honduras, Jamaica, Mexico, Nicaragua, Panama, Paraguay, Peru, Uruguay and Venezuela. Chile and Mexico are also part of the OECD (34) group.

2. Represents the unweighted average for OECD member countries.

*Source*: Table 1 in Part II.

StatLink http://dx.doi.org/10.1787/888933189652

The background to the rise in tax revenues that started in the early 1990s was the period of macroeconomic instability occurring in Latin American and Caribbean countries during the previous decade. During the 1980s, countries ran large fiscal imbalances and at the same time some recoursed to alternative ways to finance their spending (borrowing or printing money). This caused rapid inflation across the region, which eroded the real value of their tax revenues. As a result, the reforms in the 1990s focused on fighting this inflation and imposing fiscal discipline.

Most Latin American and Caribbean governments responded by both cutting public expenditure and implementing policies aimed at increasing tax revenues with budget management and fiscal balance improving considerably. On the revenue side of the equation, tax policy and administration reforms contributed considerably in achieving this goal. As part of that, the impact of inflation on revenues forced policy makers to find ways to render tax systems less vulnerable to inflationary episodes by shortening collection lags and indexing tax liabilities.

## Table A. Total tax revenue as percentage of GDP[1]

| | 1990 | 2000 | 2008 | 2009 | 2010 | 2011 | 2012 | 2013 |
|---|---|---|---|---|---|---|---|---|
| Argentina | 12.4 | 18.0 | 24.7 | 25.6 | 26.7 | 27.7 | 29.5 | 31.2 |
| Barbados | 23.0 | 30.2 | 31.5 | 30.6 | 30.7 | 32.3 | 34.0 | 29.8 |
| Bolivia[2] | 7.0 | 14.7 | 20.1 | 22.3 | 20.4 | 23.8 | 25.5 | 27.6 |
| Brazil | 28.2 | 30.1 | 33.8 | 33.1 | 33.2 | 35.0 | 35.6 | 35.7 |
| Chile | 17.0 | 18.8 | 21.4 | 17.2 | 19.5 | 21.2 | 21.4 | 20.2 |
| Colombia | 9.0 | 14.6 | 18.8 | 18.6 | 18.0 | 18.9 | 19.6 | 20.1 |
| Costa Rica | 16.1 | 18.2 | 22.7 | 21.2 | 20.8 | 21.3 | 21.2 | 22.4 |
| Dominican Republic | 8.3 | 12.4 | 15.0 | 13.1 | 12.8 | 12.9 | 13.5 | 14.0 |
| Ecuador | 7.1 | 10.1 | 14.0 | 14.9 | 16.3 | 17.3 | 19.4 | 19.3 |
| El Salvador | 10.5 | 12.2 | 15.1 | 14.4 | 14.8 | 14.9 | 15.1 | 15.8 |
| Guatemala | 9.0 | 12.4 | 12.9 | 12.2 | 12.4 | 12.7 | 12.8 | 13.0 |
| Honduras | 16.2 | 15.3 | 18.9 | 17.1 | 17.3 | 16.9 | 17.5 | 18.0 |
| Jamaica | 23.0 | 22.8 | 25.0 | 24.8 | 25.0 | 24.5 | 24.5 | 25.0 |
| Mexico[3,4] | 15.5 | 16.5 | 20.7 | 17.2 | 18.5 | 19.5 | 19.6 | 19.7 |
| Nicaragua | .. | 13.0 | 16.8 | 16.9 | 17.6 | 18.6 | 19.2 | 19.2 |
| Panama | 14.7 | 16.7 | 16.9 | 17.4 | 18.1 | 18.1 | 18.7 | 18.9 |
| Paraguay[2,5] | 5.4 | 14.5 | 14.6 | 16.1 | 16.5 | 16.8 | 17.7 | 16.4 |
| Peru | 12.1 | 14.5 | 19.0 | 17.0 | 18.0 | 18.5 | 18.8 | 18.3 |
| Uruguay[2] | 19.6 | 21.6 | 26.1 | 26.8 | 27.0 | 26.8 | 27.4 | 27.1 |
| Venezuela[2] | 18.7 | 13.6 | 14.1 | 14.1 | 11.4 | 13.1 | 13.9 | 14.2 |
| Unweighted average: | | | | | | | | |
| LAC (20)[6] | 14.4 | 17.0 | 20.1 | 19.5 | 19.8 | 20.5 | 21.2 | 21.3 |
| OECD (34)[7] | 32.2 | 34.3 | 33.6 | 32.7 | 32.8 | 33.3 | 33.7 | 34.1 |

1. The figures exclude local government revenues for Argentina (but include provincial revenues), Barbados, Bolivia, Costa Rica (up to 1997), Dominican Republic, Ecuador, El Salvador, Honduras, Jamaica, Nicaragua, Panama (up to 1998), Paraguay (up to 2004 and 2013), Peru (up to 2004), Uruguay (2013)and Venezuela as the data are not available.
2. Estimated figures from 2011 to 2013 (Bolivia and Venezuela) and for 2013 (Uruguay and Paraguay).
3. In ECLAC and CIAT data, fees levied on hydrocarbon production are treated as non tax revenues.
4. Estimated figure for 2013 including expected revenues for state and local governments.
5. ECLAC does not consider contributions to certain social security pension funds, such as those for railway, bank, and power (ANDE) companies, to be tax revenue.
6. Represents a group of 20 Latin American and Caribbean countries. Chile and Mexico are also part of the OECD (34) group.
7. Represents the unweighted average for OECD member countries. Calculated by applying the unweighted average percentage change for 2013 in the 30 countries providing data for that year to the overall average tax to GDP ratio in 2012.

StatLink http://dx.doi.org/10.1787/888933189749

The tax burden in the group of 20 Latin American and Caribbean countries increased by 6.9 percentage points of GDP between 1990 and 2013. The introduction of VAT was the most significant tax reform in Latin America and the Caribbean in the 1980s and early 1990s. Subsequent reforms relating to the tax have concentrated on extending and strengthening it by increasing the tax rate and widening the tax base. In the 1990s the VAT to GDP ratio increased by 2.4 percentage points and then by a further 1.3 points up to 2013 (see Table B).

Between 2000 and 2013, the increase in revenue from taxes on income taxes and profits – mainly corporate income tax – (by 1.7 percentage points of GDP) became a more important contributor than VAT to the rise in tax revenues. One of the elements that contributed to this result was the commodity prices' boom period following 2003, which was very important for some countries in the region (see the Special Feature S2 for more information). Other tax reforms also included the introduction or development of simplified regimes for small taxpayers and the taxation of property based on presumed incomes. In addition, during the past few years various income tax reforms were introduced in Latin America and the Caribbean, which have included rate hikes and increases in the tax base. These measures have had a positive effect thanks to the expansion of taxation to all labour and capital income, including dividends (Colombia, Dominican Republic, Guatemala, El Salvador, Nicaragua, Panama, Peru). Additionally, they have also included the establishment of minimum taxes, reductions in exemptions, a tightening of deductable expenses, the gradual reduction in the real income level taxed at the top marginal rate and additional controls on transfer prices (ECLAC, 2013).

Table B. **Value added taxes as percentages of GDP**

| | 1990 | 2000 | 2008 | 2009 | 2010 | 2011 | 2012 | 2013 |
|---|---|---|---|---|---|---|---|---|
| Argentina | 1.9 | 5.4 | 6.0 | 6.0 | 6.3 | 6.5 | 6.9 | 7.3 |
| Barbados | .. | 8.0 | 9.0 | 7.4 | 8.5 | 10.3 | 10.7 | 9.7 |
| Bolivia | 3.2 | 5.1 | 7.0 | 6.3 | 6.7 | 7.3 | 7.6 | 7.8 |
| Brazil | 10.4 | 8.6 | 8.1 | 7.7 | 7.8 | 7.8 | 8.2 | 8.2 |
| Chile | 6.3 | 7.9 | 8.4 | 7.3 | 7.6 | 7.9 | 8.1 | 8.1 |
| Colombia | 2.0 | 4.1 | 5.6 | 5.1 | 5.3 | 5.7 | 5.5 | 4.9 |
| Costa Rica | 3.2 | 4.5 | 6.0 | 4.9 | 4.8 | 4.9 | 4.9 | 4.7 |
| Dominican Republic | 1.3 | 2.6 | 4.7 | 4.2 | 4.3 | 4.2 | 4.0 | 4.5 |
| Ecuador | 2.0 | 4.6 | 4.6 | 4.8 | 5.6 | 5.3 | 6.2 | 6.4 |
| El Salvador | 0.0 | 5.4 | 6.8 | 6.1 | 6.7 | 6.8 | 6.7 | 6.8 |
| Guatemala | 2.4 | 4.7 | 5.5 | 4.9 | 5.1 | 5.2 | 5.3 | 5.2 |
| Honduras | 2.7 | 4.8 | 6.3 | 5.2 | 5.4 | 5.7 | 5.6 | 5.5 |
| Jamaica | 0.0 | 3.4 | 4.0 | 3.8 | 3.9 | 3.9 | 3.9 | 4.0 |
| Mexico | 3.2 | 3.1 | 3.7 | 3.4 | 3.8 | 3.7 | 3.7 | 3.5 |
| Nicaragua | .. | 4.5 | 5.5 | 5.2 | 5.4 | 5.8 | 6.0 | 6.0 |
| Panama | 1.3 | 0.6 | 2.3 | 2.3 | 2.9 | 3.3 | 3.3 | 3.1 |
| Paraguay | 0.0 | 4.7 | 5.5 | 5.6 | 6.3 | 6.5 | 6.5 | 6.3 |
| Peru | 1.5 | 5.3 | 7.1 | 6.3 | 6.8 | 6.7 | 6.7 | 6.8 |
| Uruguay | 5.5 | 6.5 | 9.2 | 8.9 | 8.9 | 8.7 | 8.7 | 8.6 |
| Venezuela | 0.0 | 4.1 | 4.6 | 5.9 | 5.5 | 6.2 | 6.8 | 7.4 |
| Unweighted average: | | | | | | | | |
| LAC (20)[1] | 2.5 | 4.9 | 6.0 | 5.6 | 5.9 | 6.1 | 6.3 | 6.2 |
| OECD (34)[2] | 5.2 | 6.4 | 6.4 | 6.2 | 6.5 | 6.5 | 6.6 | .. |

1. Represents a group of 20 Latin American and Caribbean countries. Chile and Mexico are also part of the OECD (34) group.
2. Represents the unweighted average for OECD member countries.

StatLink http://dx.doi.org/10.1787/888933189753

Changes in revenue from taxes on goods and services, taxes on income and profits and social security contributions have contributed to the recovery in tax-to-GDP ratios since 2010. These increases in tax revenues are partly due to the recovery of Latin American and Caribbean economic activity (ECLAC-OECD, 2012).

## B. Tax structures

At the same time that tax levels have been rising in Latin America and the Caribbean, the tax structure (defined as the share of major taxes in total tax revenue) also changed significantly between 1990 and 2013. Table C illustrates the several trends on "tax mix" that emerge from the data. The most important trends are those related to consumption taxes and taxes on income and profits.

The overall share of consumption taxes remained fairly stable over the period but within the total, the share of general consumption taxes increased considerably by 11 percentage points between 1990 and 2013, while specific consumption taxes saw their share decline by 14 percentage points over the same period.

Table C. **Tax structures in a group of Latin American and Caribbean countries**[1]

| | 1990 | 2000 | 2010 | 2011 | 2012 | 2013 |
|---|---|---|---|---|---|---|
| Taxes on income and profits | 23 | 22 | 26 | 26 | 27 | 27 |
| Social security contributions | 14 | 16 | 16 | 16 | 17 | 17 |
| Payroll taxes | 1 | 1 | 1 | 1 | 1 | 1 |
| Property taxes | 5 | 4 | 4 | 4 | 4 | 4 |
| General consumption taxes | 21 | 31 | 33 | 33 | 32 | 32 |
| Specific consumption taxes | 31 | 24 | 19 | 18 | 18 | 17 |
| Other taxes[2] | 5 | 3 | 2 | 2 | 2 | 2 |
| Total | 100 | 100 | 100 | 100 | 100 | 100 |

1. Represents the percentage shares of major tax categories in total tax revenue. The group of 20 countries is listed in Table A.
2. Including certain taxes on goods and services (heading 5200) and stamp taxes.

StatLink http://dx.doi.org/10.1787/888933189760

These two opposing trends within consumption taxes are due to the rising importance of VAT and the diminishing role of specific consumption taxes, such as excises and taxes on international trade. Although VAT was adopted early by the economies of the region (most countries had already introduced it in some form by the late 1970s), its expansion in revenue terms has been relatively recent. From the early 1990s, it has represented a growing source of revenue for Latin American and Caribbean countries and has been consolidated by the implementation of cumulative adjustments to the tax base and statutory rates, as well as strengthening of tax administrations. The reforms also focused on the simplification of tax systems, with most countries reducing the number of items with zero or reduced rates, moving towards single-rate VAT schemes in several cases.

In contrast, the decline in the share of specific consumption taxes is associated with the processes of trade liberalisation generating a consequent reduction in import tariffs and the elimination of taxes on exports in a considerable number of Latin American and Caribbean countries (one important exception being Argentina where taxes on exports were re-established in 2002). Additionally, the range of goods and services subject to excises has been narrowed to focus mainly on products and services with a relatively inelastic demand, such as alcoholic beverages, fuel and tobacco.

At the same time, revenues from incomes and profits grew from 23% to 27% of total tax revenues from 1990 to 2013, mainly as a result of much higher collection levels in the late 2000s. Corporate income tax shares are generally larger than those from personal income tax in Latin American and Caribbean countries and this growth reflects the sizeable increase in revenues from the former category, especially from companies in the natural–resources sector. The income and profits share actually peaked over the years from 2008 to 2009 at a level of 27% before declining to 25.6% in 2010, probably due to the impact of the global crisis on the generation of income and profits. It has subsequently risen back to 26.7% in 2013 (Table 5).

On average the revenues from social security contributions as a percentage of GDP increased from 2.1% in 1990 to 3.8% in 2013 (Table 6), while their share in total tax revenues increased from 13.9% to 17.1% in this period (Table 7). This reflects two major factors working simultaneously. Firstly, rising personal incomes have had an upward impact on the amounts collected. But this is partially counter-balanced, and sometimes more than off-set, by the varying processes of full or partial privatisation that occurred in many countries in the region. There has been a wide variation in the ways that countries have implemented and reformed their social-security schemes. Some countries like Chile, Mexico and Peru rely heavily on private, personally funded schemes, explaining the relatively low levels of tax revenues used to finance social security. In countries with public or mixed schemes, including Barbados, Brazil, Costa Rica Ecuador, Nicaragua, Panama, Paraguay and Uruguay, social-security contributions still have a significant weight (more than 20% of total tax revenues). In Argentina, the figures reflect the introduction of funded schemes in 1994 and their subsequent nationalisation in 2008.

Turning to the comparison between OECD and Latin American and Caribbean countries, the main difference between the tax-structures of the two groups is immediately apparent. Relative to the OECD, Latin America and the Caribbean exhibit a relatively low direct-tax take counterbalanced by high indirect-tax receipts (see Chart B). In particular, Latin America and the Caribbean rely heavily on taxes on goods and services, which make up about half of overall tax revenues compared with around 30% in OECD economies. By comparison less than 45% of tax revenues in Latin America and the Caribbean come from the combination of taxes on income and profits and social security contributions compared with around 60% in OECD economies. This greater reliance on indirect taxes may imply a more regressive tax system.

In 2012, the average ratio of the combined tax revenue from income and profits and social security contributions to GDP in the Latin American and Caribbean countries was 9.3% compared with 20.4% in OECD countries. As a result, these taxes play a secondary role as a source of revenue in Latin America and the Caribbean compared with the OECD area. The share of social security contributions in total tax revenues was about 10 percentage points lower in Latin America and the Caribbean than in the OECD (16.5% compared with 26.2%). As noted above, the tendency towards privately-oriented provision of social security in many countries in the Latin American and Caribbean region explains some of the differences for this category. The corresponding figures for taxes on income and profits were 7 percentage points lower (26.6% compared with 33.6%).

Revenues from personal income taxes contributed as much as to 25% of the aggregate tax collection in the OECD area in 2012, while this category has a considerably lower share in Latin American and Caribbean countries. Previous OECD studies (OECD, 2008 and Daude, Melguizo and Neut, 2010) suggest that this has two main drivers: the share of labour income in GDP is substantially lower in Latin American and Caribbean countries than in OECD countries; and its distribution means that there are relatively fewer taxpayers, given the concentration of income earners at low income levels. Moreover, several ECLAC studies (ECLAC, 2010 and Gómez Sabaini et al., 2010) mention two additional factors: the high income tax gap in Latin American and Caribbean countries and a more limited taxable base that is comprised primarily of wages, given the tax privileges granted to returns on capital.

### Chart B. **Tax structures in Latin America and the Caribbean and the OECD, 2012**

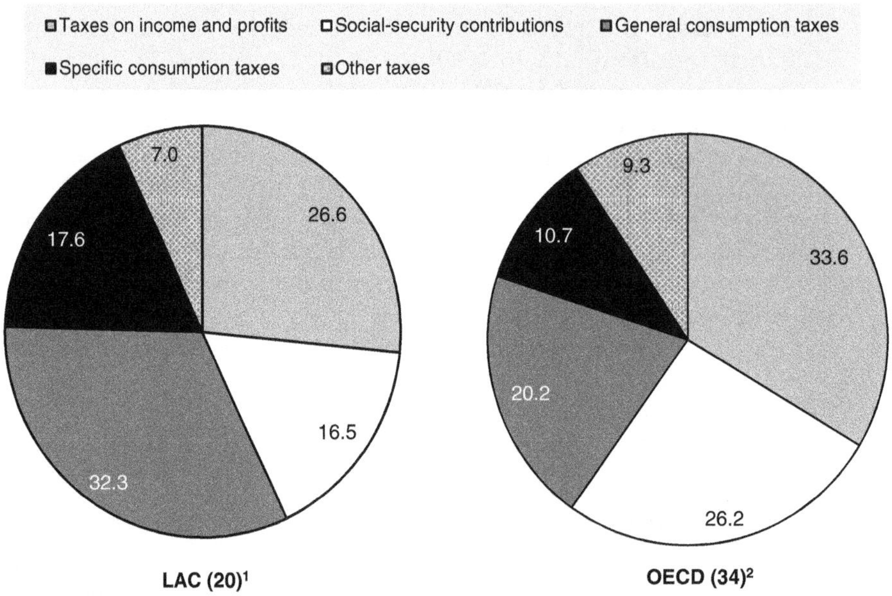


1. Represents a group of 20 Latin American and Caribbean countries listed in Table A. Chile and Mexico are also part of the OECD (34) group.
2. Represents the unweighted average for OECD member countries.
*Source*: Table 2 and Tables 5-15 in Part II.

StatLink http://dx.doi.org/10.1787/888933189667

As a counterpart of a lower share of direct taxes, general consumption taxes represent a significant portion of total tax collection. In 2012, this category accounted for 32.3% of the total tax revenues in the region whereas the corresponding figure in the OECD area is only 20.2% .However, the ratio of general consumption taxes to GDP in the countries of Latin America and the Caribbean was the same in the OECD (6.8%).

Finally, taxes on immovable property and payroll (comprised within the category "Other taxes" in Chart B) are not important sources of revenues for Latin American and Caribbean countries. The difficulties that sub-national governments have in collecting their own taxes are exemplified by the weak revenue-generating capacity of property taxes, which are usually the main source of revenue for local governments in the region (Brossio and Jiménez, 2012). The share of payroll taxes has been negligible over the whole period, partly because these types of schemes are not very well developed in Latin America and the Caribbean. Nevertheless, it must be pointed out that missing data at the sub-national level makes the analysis of this category difficult. The shares of property and payroll taxes as a proportion of total tax revenue in the Latin American and Caribbean countries are similar on average to those in OECD countries.

## C. Taxes by level of government

Since the mid-1980s the Latin American and Caribbean countries have generally experienced reforms involving the transfer of government functions from the central government to sub-national entities. In the first stage, this wave of decentralisation mainly focused on strengthening the democratic role of local authorities. This has been followed by a gradually increasing trend towards a higher share of public expenditure being executed at sub-national level.

In contrast, the scope of the sub-national tax policies in the region has been relatively modest and focuses on a limited number of taxes. The available data suggests that most Latin American and Caribbean countries have not been concentrated on the strengthening of the revenues received by the sub-national entities. Between 1995 and 2012, the share of revenue raised by sub-national levels of government declined by between 0.8 and 3.9 percentage points in Argentina, Brazil and Uruguay and rose by 0.9 and 0.4 percentage points respectively in Mexico and Colombia. In the other countries where trends in sub-national revenue data are available, the share changed by less than one percentage point. At the same time the share of social security funds has fallen in 9 of the 20 Latin American and Caribbean countries sometimes due to full or partial privatisation. The largest falls were in Colombia and Panama (by around 14 and 6 percentage points respectively). The largest increases in the share of Social Security contributions were in Nicaragua and Barbados (7 and 4 percentage points respectively) (see Table D).

There are two statistical issues to be taken into account when comparing the attribution of revenues for these Latin American and Caribbean countries with that of OECD members. First, the revenues of both groups have been attributed to the different levels of government according to the revised guidelines set out in to the final version of the 2008 System of National Accounts (SNA). This means that revenues are generally attributed to the level of government that exercises the authority to impose the tax or has the final discretion to set and vary the tax rate. This has implications for situations where one level of government collects tax revenues and transfers them in whole or in part to other levels. Regional examples of this type of mechanism are the Co-participation Law in Argentina, federal participations in Mexico mandated in the Fiscal Co-ordination Law, and participation funds in Brazil defined in Article 159 of the Constitution. The second issue is that the data for some of the Latin American and Caribbean countries are affected by the lack of tax-revenue statistics at sub-national level.

Notwithstanding these points, the attribution of tax revenues appears to be highly skewed towards central or federal entities with sub-national activities relying more heavily on a system of transfers from upper to lower levels of administration compared with OECD members. In all but one of the Latin American and Caribbean countries, receipts by central governments accounted for about two thirds or more of the total collected whereas the corresponding figure for OECD countries was about 60%. Brazil is a notable exception with less than 50% of revenues attributed to the Federal administration, and where a large part of the VAT (ICMS – *imposto sobre operações relativas à circulação de mercadorias e prestação de serviços de transporte interestadual e intermunicipal e de comunicação*) is collected at the sub-national state level. To a lesser extent, Argentina has a significant collection at state level, which is explained in part by the provincial sales tax (*impuesto sobre los ingresos brutos*).

These figures reflect the fact that sub-national governments in Latin America and the Caribbean tend to have a relatively narrow range of taxes under their jurisdiction. The taxes most frequently assigned to sub-national entities are property taxes, motor-vehicle licenses, taxes on specific services and municipal fees and the revenue generation potential of these instruments is relatively limited compared with the tax bases under central jurisdiction, such as VAT and income taxes. In OECD member countries, sub-national entities on average tend to have much broader potential tax bases. A substantial proportion of the revenue collection for sub-national governments in OECD countries is through income taxes and profits (representing more than a third of the total collected amount at sub-national level). In contrast, none of the Latin American and Caribbean countries with available data recorded any collection of income taxes by sub-national governments.

Table D. **Attribution of tax revenues to sub-sectors of general government as percentage of total tax revenue**[1]

| | Central government | | | State or regional government | | | Local government | | | Social Security funds | | |
|---|---|---|---|---|---|---|---|---|---|---|---|---|
| | 1995 | 2000 | 2012 | 1995 | 2000 | 2012 | 1995 | 2000 | 2012 | 1995 | 2000 | 2012 |
| **Federal countries** | | | | | | | | | | | | |
| Argentina | 59.0 | 66.4 | 62.7 | 17.5 | 17.8 | 15.1 | .. | .. | .. | 23.4 | 15.8 | 22.2 |
| Brazil | 44.7 | 47.8 | 45.1 | 26.8 | 25.3 | 24.3 | 3.7 | 3.4 | 5.4 | 24.8 | 23.5 | 25.9 |
| Mexico | 80.1 | 80.7 | 81.0 | 2.1 | 2.0 | 2.9 | 1.1 | 0.8 | 1.2 | 16.6 | 16.5 | 14.9 |
| Venezuela | 94.6 | 94.6 | 95.8 | .. | .. | .. | .. | .. | .. | 5.4 | 5.4 | 4.2 |
| OECD[2,3] | 53.3 | 56.5 | 54.5 | 15.9 | 15.3 | 16.5 | 7.7 | 6.9 | 7.6 | 22.9 | 21.1 | 21.3 |
| **Regional countries** | | | | | | | | | | | | |
| Colombia[4] | 63.2 | 68.6 | 76.4 | 5.5 | 5.6 | 4.2 | 8.6 | 9.4 | 10.3 | 22.7 | 16.4 | 9.0 |
| OECD[5] | 50.4 | 49.0 | 22.3 | 4.8 | 7.6 | 32.2 | 8.5 | 9.1 | 9.9 | 35.8 | 33.8 | 35.1 |
| **Unitary countries** | | | | | | | | | | | | |
| Barbados | 85.3 | 84.3 | 81.6 | | | | .. | .. | .. | 14.7 | 15.7 | 18.4 |
| Bolivia | 100.0 | 91.2 | 94.0 | | | | .. | .. | .. | .. | 8.7 | 6.0 |
| Chile | 89.9 | 87.8 | 88.2 | | | | 6.5 | 7.9 | 6.7 | 3.6 | 4.4 | 5.1 |
| Costa Rica | 66.2 | 65.3 | 61.7 | | | | .. | 2.1 | 3.0 | 33.8 | 32.6 | 35.3 |
| Dominican Republic | 99.3 | 99.0 | 99.6 | | | | .. | .. | .. | 0.7 | 1.0 | 0.4 |
| Ecuador | 73.9 | 87.7 | 72.1 | | | | .. | .. | .. | 26.1 | 12.3 | 27.9 |
| El Salvador | 85.9 | 83.6 | 89.3 | | | | .. | .. | .. | 14.1 | 16.4 | 10.7 |
| Guatemala | 83.8 | 83.6 | 83.0 | | | | 0.6 | 0.9 | 1.5 | 15.6 | 15.5 | 15.6 |
| Honduras | 90.1 | 89.4 | 82.9 | | | | .. | .. | .. | 9.9 | 10.6 | 17.1 |
| Jamaica | 100.0 | 99.3 | 95.5 | | | | .. | 0.7 | 0.9 | .. | .. | 3.6 |
| Nicaragua | 84.0 | 80.1 | 77.1 | | | | .. | .. | .. | 16.0 | 19.9 | 22.9 |
| Panama | 62.0 | 59.6 | 66.1 | | | | .. | 2.2 | 1.6 | 38.0 | 38.2 | 32.4 |
| Paraguay | 100.0 | 82.7 | 80.6 | | | | .. | .. | 3.0 | .. | 17.3 | 16.4 |
| Peru | 88.2 | 87.7 | 86.7 | | | | .. | .. | 3.1 | 11.8 | 12.3 | 10.1 |
| Uruguay | 62.0 | 62.5 | 70.0 | | | | 7.8 | 7.9 | 3.9 | 30.1 | 29.6 | 26.1 |
| OECD[2,6] | 65.8 | 66.4 | 62.9 | | | | 10.7 | 11.0 | 12.0 | 23.2 | 22.3 | 24.8 |

1. The figures exclude local government revenues for Argentina (but include provincial revenues), Barbados, Bolivia, Costa Rica (up to 1997), Dominican Republic, Ecuador, El Salvador, Honduras, Jamaica, Nicaragua, Panama (up to 1998), Paraguay (up to 2004 and 2013), Peru (up to 2004), Uruguay (2013) and Venezuela as the data are not available.
2. Chile and Mexico are also part of the OECD group.
3. Represents the unweighted average for OECD federal member countries.
4. Colombia is constitutionally a unitary country with high autonomy of its territorial entities.
5. Represents Spain, which is constitutionally a non-federal country with a highly decentralised political structure.
6. Represents the unweighted average for OECD unitary countries.

StatLink http://dx.doi.org/10.1787/888933189778

## D. Comparative charts

Chart C. **Total tax revenues as percentage of GDP, 2013**[1]
Gráfico C. **Total de recaudación tributaria como porcentaje del PIB, 2013**[1]

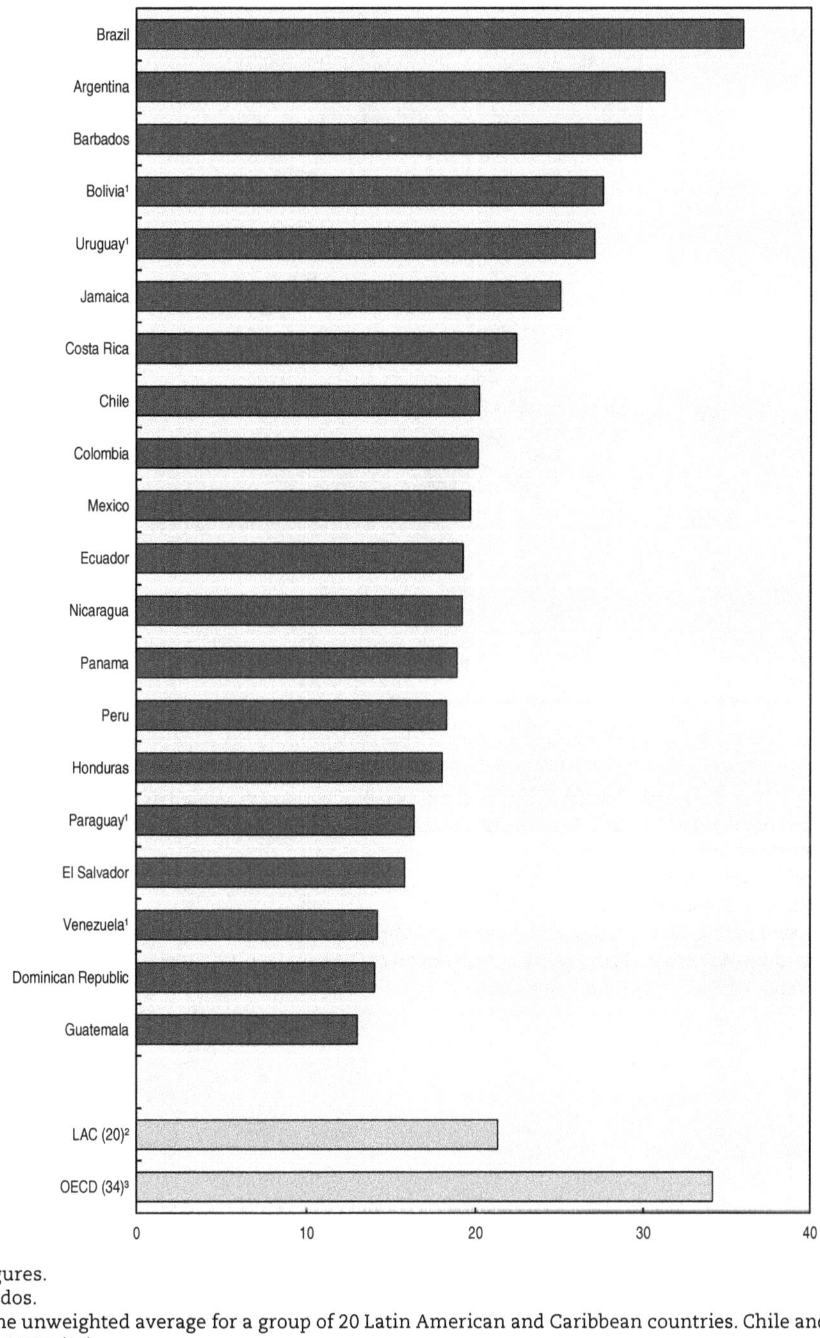


1. Estimated figures.
1. Datos estimados.
2. Represents the unweighted average for a group of 20 Latin American and Caribbean countries. Chile and Mexico are also part of the OECD (34) group.
2. Representa el promedio no ponderado para un grupo de 20 países de América Latina y el Caribe. Chile y México son también parte del grupo OCDE (34).
3.Represents the unweighted average for OECD member countries. Calculated by applying the unweighted average percentage change for 2013 in the 30 countries providing data for that year to the overall average tax to GDP ratio in 2012.
3. Calculado aplicando el promedio no ponderado en el cambio porcentual para el 2013 en los 30 países con datos disponibles para ese año en el total de ingreso tributario en porcentaje del PIB.
*Source*: Table 1 in Part II. Cuadro 1 en Parte II.

StatLink http://dx.doi.org/10.1787/888933189805

## Chart D. Tax to GDP ratios in Latin American and Caribbean countries in 1990 and 2013[1]
## Gráfico D. Recaudación tributaria como porcentaje del PIB en países de América Latina y el Caribe en 1990 y 2013[1]

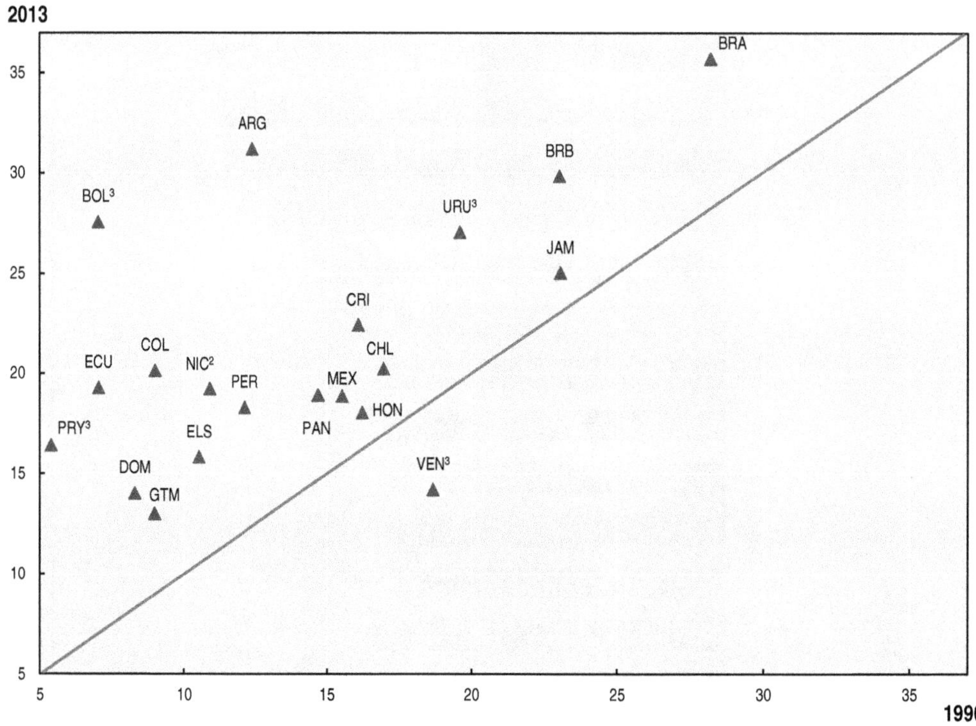


1. In ECLAC and CIAT data, fees levied on hydrocarbon production are treated as non tax revenues.

1. En los datos de CEPAL y CIAT, los derechos sobre la producción de hidrocarburos son tratados como ingresos no tributarios.

2. Figures for 1991 are used.

2. Se utilizan datos para el 1991.

3. Estimated figures from 2011 to 2013 (Bolivia and Venezuela) and for 2013 (Uruguay and Paraguay).

3. Datos estimados desde el 2011 hasta el 2013 (Bolivia y Venezuela) y 2013 (Uruguay y Paraguay).

*Source*: Table 1 in Part II. Cuadro 1 en Parte II.

StatLink http://dx.doi.org/10.1787/888933189819

Chart E. **Tax to GDP ratios in Latin American and Caribbean countries in 1990 and 2000**[1]

Gráfico E. **Recaudación tributaria como porcentaje del PIB en países de América Latina y el Caribe en 1990 y 2000**[1]

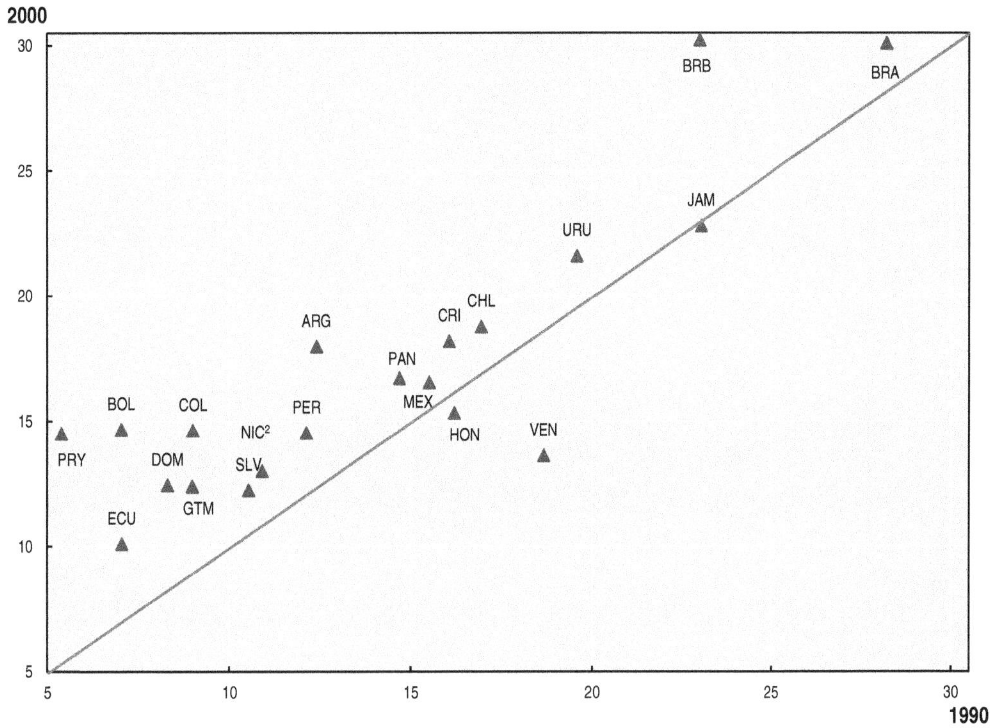


1. In ECLAC and CIAT data, fees levied on hydrocarbon production are treated as non tax revenues.

1. En los datos de CEPAL y CIAT, los derechos sobre la producción de hidrocarburos son tratados como ingresos no tributarios.

2. Figures for 1991 are used.

2. Se utilizan datos para el 1991.

*Source:* Table 1 in Part II. Cuadro 1 en Parte II.

StatLink http://dx.doi.org/10.1787/888933189823

Chart F. **Tax to GDP ratios in Latin American and Caribbean countries in 2000 and 2013**[1]

Gráfico F. **Recaudación tributaria como porcentaje del PIB en países de América Latina y el Caribe en 2000 y 2013**[1]

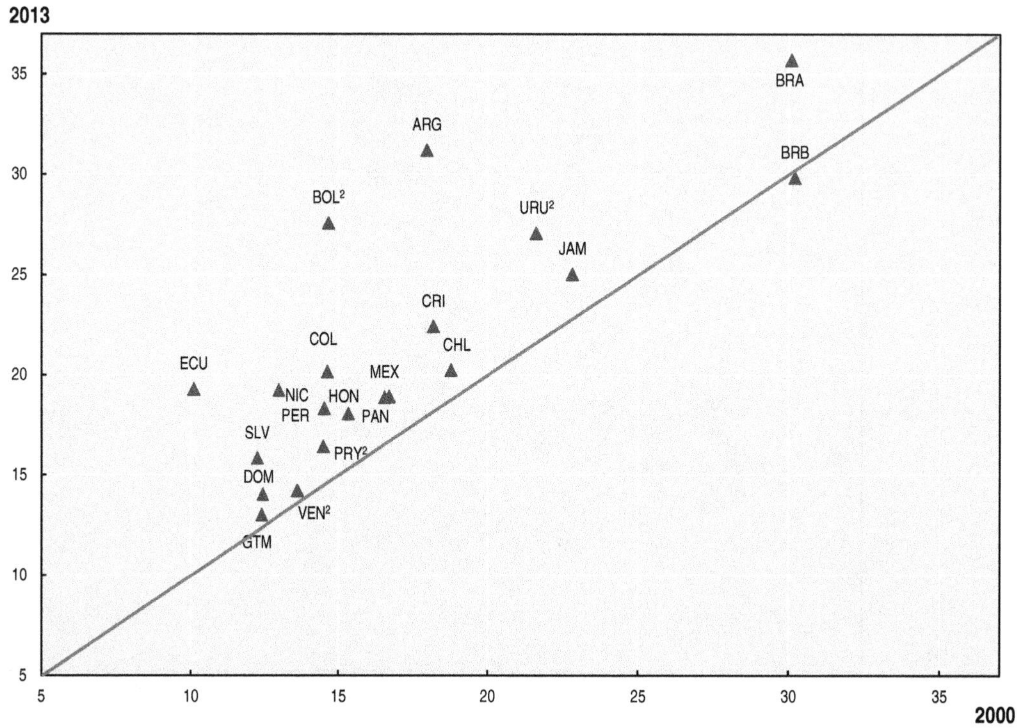


1. In ECLAC and CIAT data, fees levied on hydrocarbon production are treated as non tax revenues.

1. En los datos de CEPAL y CIAT, los derechos sobre la producción de hidrocarburos son tratados como ingresos no tributarios.

2. Estimated figures from 2011 to 2013 (Bolivia and Venezuela) and for 2013 (Uruguay and Paraguay).

2. Datos estimados desde el 2011 hasta el 2013 (Bolivia y Venezuela) y 2013 (Uruguay y Paraguay).

*Source*: Table 1 in Part II. Cuadro 1 en Parte II.

StatLink http://dx.doi.org/10.1787/888933189835

## *References*


Brossio, G. and J.P. Jiménez (2012), *Decentralization and Reform in Latin America: Improving Intergovernmental Relations*, Edward Elgar, in press, Cheltenham, UK and Northampton, MA.

Daude, C., A. Melguizo and A. Neut (2010), "Fiscal Policy in Latin America: Countercyclical and Sustainable at Last?", *OECD Development Centre Working Paper* No. 291, OECD Development Centre, Paris.

ECLAC (2013), *Fiscal Panorama of Latin America and the Caribbean: tax reform and renewal of the fiscal covenant*, ECLAC, Santiago de Chile

ECLAC (2011), *Economic Survey of Latin America and the Caribbean 2010-2011*, ECLAC, Santiago, Chile.

ECLAC (2010), "La Hora de la igualdad. Brechas por cerrar, caminos por abrir", (LC/G.2432(SES.33/3)), Santiago, Chile, ECLAC.

ECLAC-OECD (2012), *Latin American Economic Outlook 2013: SME Policies for Structural Change*, OECD Publishing, Paris. http://dx.doi.org/10.1787/leo-2013-en.

Gómez Sabaini, J.C., J.P. Jiménez and A. Podestá (2010), "Evasión y equidad en América Latina", *Project documents*, No. 309 (LC/W.309/ Rev.1), Santiago, Chile, ECLAC.

OECD (2014), *Revenue Statistics 1965-2013*, OECD Publishing, Paris, http://dx.doi.org/10.1787/rev_stats-2014-en-fr.

OECD (2008), *Latin American Economic Outlook 2009*, OECD Publishing, Paris, http://dx.doi.org/10.1787/leo-2009-en.

# SPECIAL FEATURE S1
# Features of fiscal pressure in Latin America and the Caribbean[1]

## Introduction

Standardisation initiatives are essential in a globalised and heterogeneous world, since they enable a wealth of comparisons and analytical possibilities. In the fiscal arena, the Organisation for Economic Co-operation and Development (OECD) has been a pioneer in defining the way in which tax revenues are classified and measured, not only by OECD member countries[2] but also by other nations around the world.

At the heart of the OECD's work on tax revenues is the classification that defines taxes as "compulsory, unrequited payments to the general government sector". This definition has three distinct elements, each with a sound rationale. That taxes are "compulsory" payments is generally accepted. Equally, if tax statistics are to reflect the state's efforts to collect revenue from its citizens, it is difficult to characterise a payment as a tax unless it is paid "to the government". Finally, in OECD's view, as there is a wide range of circumstances where governments provide services in return for a fee, such circumstances should be distinguished from those where payment is "unrequited" and simply required as an incident of one's personal or corporate residence.

There have been several other attempts at defining and standardising how we account for a government's fiscal revenues. Under all these frameworks, international comparisons have consistently emphasised the low levels of tax revenues in Latin America, and to a lesser extent the Caribbean, relative to more developed countries. As is often the case, however, the reality is more complex. Governments everywhere raise revenues differently in their structures and dimensions. In the case of Latin American and Caribbean (LAC) countries, additional insights into the nature of the interaction between governments and their citizens can be gleaned from a broader comparison of fiscal revenues. For example, it is widely known that LAC countries derive significant revenues from permitting the exploitation of natural resources. Moreover, private and public arrangements to finance social security co-exist in Latin America to a much greater extent than in OECD countries, a circumstance that is not completely addressed in international definitions and comparisons.

In this regard, it may be useful to take into account those two additional sources of revenue or "revenue equivalent" besides the tax revenues traditionally considered. In this special feature we incorporate the sum of these sources into the theoretical construct known as the Equivalent Fiscal Pressure (EFP). For that purpose, it is important to establish the basic concepts that comprise the EFP (Barreix et al, 2013a). The first is the traditional revenue from taxes, consisting of all sorts of direct and indirect taxes levied on residents at all levels of government. The second comprises the social security contributions made to all mandatory pension and healthcare systems, both private and public. The third part of our construct consists of all the non-tax revenues derived from the exploitation of renewable and non-renewable natural resources – that is, fees, royalties, dividends paid and net profits that (totally or partially) state-owned public enterprises engaged in the exploitation of natural resources transfer to national treasuries.

EFP = general government tax revenues + all mandatory social security contributions + non-tax revenue from the exploitation of natural renewable and non-renewable resources

This fiscal-revenue indicator may offer a more comprehensive picture for LAC countries, both from the perspective of the revenues available to the state and from the viewpoint of the effort demanded of citizens. Figure S1.1 shows that components 2 and 3 of the EFP are not only significant but also widespread in the region.

Figure S1.1. **Equivalent Fiscal Pressure (1990-2013)**

Share of GDP (both left and right axes)

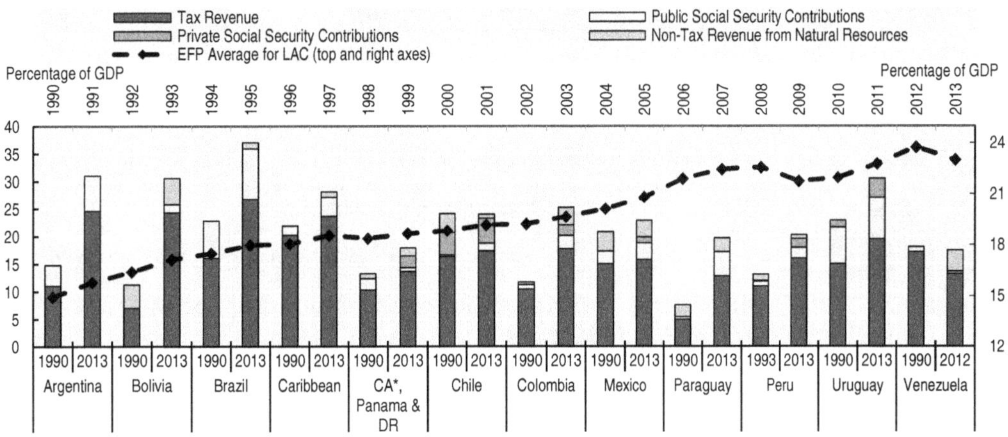


*Note:* Values for the Caribbean, *CA (Central America), Panama and the Dominican Republic are unweighted averages.

*Sources:* Tables 1 and 4 and IDB-CIAT Database 2014.[3]

StatLink http://dx.doi.org/10.1787/888933189676

Figure S1.1 distinguishes between the three components of the EFP: tax revenues, mandatory public and private social security contributions, and revenues from renewable and non-renewable natural resources. It also highlights the effects that the 12 structural social security reforms, occurring in the LAC countries between 1981 and 2008, had on the landscape of fiscal revenues, as well as the significant proportion of revenues derived from natural resources in 10 countries of the region.

It should be noted that despite the considerable fiscal effort of LAC countries during the past two decades, there persists a substantial revenue gap between the region and more developed countries. This is clear from a calculation of the differences in absolute collection. For that purpose, the weighted average of the OECD and LAC countries' per capita collection was calculated in 2011 US dollars at purchasing power parity (PPP), to reflect the relative levels of spending capacity.

The differences are noteworthy, as Figure S1.2 shows. The weighted average per capita collection (at PPP) for the OECD in the period 2011–13 was three times that of LAC, and almost seven-fold that of Central America, Panama and the Dominican Republic (CA-PA-DR). The gap is narrower if the comparison is with the aggregate of MERCOSUR, Chile and Mexico, which have the region's largest per capita income. They achieved a per capita collection close to a third of the OECD average. This substantial revenue gap highlights the significant revenue differential to finance public services, and the critical need to improve tax policy and administration in LAC countries.

Figure S1.2. **Equivalent Fiscal Pressure, per capita and as % of GDP**[a]

PPP, constant 2011 international USD

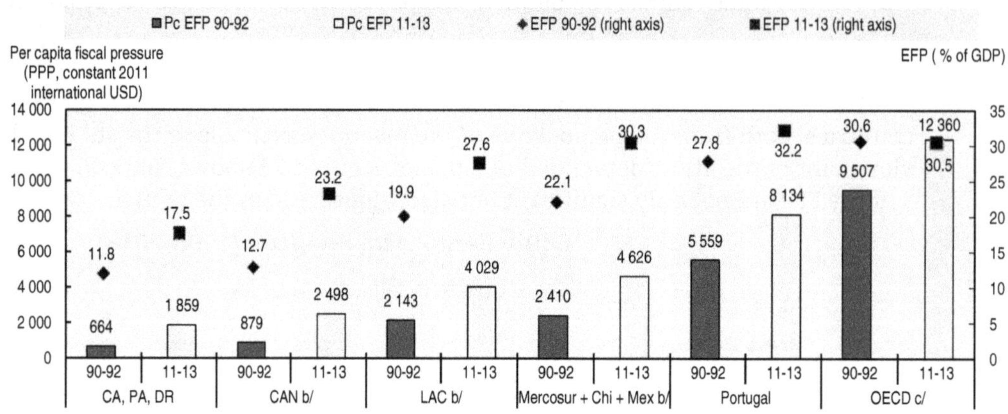


*Notes:*

a/ Average and per capita fiscal pressure weighted by PPP-GDP, in constant 2011 USD . b/ LAC and subregions do not include Argentina and Ecuador. Mercosur includes Brazil, Paraguay, and Uruguay. c/ OECD excludes Chile, Slovak Republic, Slovenia, Estonia, Israel, Mexico and Czech Republic.

*Sources:* IDB-CIAT (2014), World Bank (2014).

StatLink http://dx.doi.org/10.1787/888933189686

The following sections provide a more in-depth explanation of the alternative fiscal revenue equation for LAC countries.

## The social security *revolution* in Latin America

In the early 1980s, the so-called "lost decade", Latin America experienced a series of reforms to its social security systems that, arguably, have come to shape the way in which fiscal revenues can be accounted for in LAC. The main feature of the pioneering Chilean reform was the introduction in 1981 of privately managed individual capitalisation accounts. This was the first experiment of its kind, allowing the free market to finance public pensions while slowly phasing out the traditional pay-as-you-go system. At the time, supporters of the reform championed it on the assumption that individual responsibility would promote national savings and labour formality, contribute to the development of capital markets and the subsequent returns on capital, and insulate pension funds against political prying (Uthoff, 2001; Gill, Packard and Yermo, 2005; Bosch, Melguizo and Pagés, 2013).

Following Chile's example, several other countries embarked on a quest to overhaul their national public pension systems through structural reforms. These shifts, while diverse and complex in their own ways, have been broadly grouped into three categories:

- "The replacement model" (Chile, 1981; Bolivia, 1997, reversed in 2010; El Salvador, 1998; and Mexico, 1997), whereby the public pension programme is completely replaced by a fully funded, mostly privately managed pension system financed through individual capitalisation accounts.
- "The parallel model" (Peru, 1993; Colombia, 1994), which ends the state's monopoly by introducing a new private alternative. In this model, the public and the private pension programmes coexist and compete, and employees can choose between them when they enter the labour market.
- "The mixed model" (Argentina, 1994, reversed in 2008; Uruguay, 1996; Costa Rica, 2001; Dominican Republic, 2003; Panama 2005–2007), in which the provision of a basic universal service is complemented by compulsory contributions to individual

capitalisation accounts run by privately managed pension funds. Under this model, the non-contributory and the contributory schemes meet in a single programme (Mesa-Lago, 2000; Bonilla and Conte-Grand, 1998; Rofman, Apella and Vezza, 2013).

The most recent wave of structural reforms, dubbed the "re-reforms" (Mesa-Lago, 2009), sought to instill stability and adapt pension systems to the particular socio-economic context of each country. For instance, Argentina (2008) decided to end the private pillar by which citizens saved for retirement, and returned to a pay-as-you-go system. It also extended coverage to those previously excluded from the system. Bolivia (2007) nationalised its pensions system once again and established three branches: a contributory branch for the elderly, the disabled and survivors; a semi-contributory branch to serve as a solidarity fund; and a non-contributory pillar to finance the "Dignidad" bond.

On a different note, in 2008 Chile introduced a supplementary, non-contributory pillar to the private pillar already in place. In 2009, both El Salvador and Peru introduced minimum pension guarantees for low-income citizens who did not reach the established threshold of contributions. This latter group of countries filled the gaps but did not change the nature of the private system.

As discussed above, the focus of the OECD Revenue Statistics is to measure the value of tax revenues paid to government and establish the sources of these payments. However, from the individual's perspective, whether the payment is made to the public or private sector is of less consequence in the short term to the employer or the employee. Both types of payment equally affect the overall cost of labour. The size of the fiscal burden – that is, the fiscal effort demanded of contributors – will be affected, given the compulsory nature of social security contributions, which clearly resemble a tax in the eyes of the taxpayer – whether actually defined as a tax or not. A critical issue, then, is to understand the state's fiscal responsibilities and liabilities arising from these reforms.

In this regard, the last two models described above involve active participation by the state. In the replacement model the state's participation was curbed, but it still played an important role as a regulator and guarantor of the private system. In most cases the state financed the transition, which entails a substantial fiscal cost that is still being paid by most countries that underwent reforms. Additionally, several studies have shown that pensions paid through traditional public systems tend to be regressive which raises questions regarding the solidarity component claimed by public social security programmes (Barreix, Bès and Roca, 2009; Barreix, Roca and Villela, 2006; Lustig, 2013).

Furthermore, the system of social security contributions comprises several public programmes, especially health insurance, which makes it a complex and indivisible system as a whole. Data also indicate that, contrary to intuition (see Figure S1.3), social security contributions paid to the public sector did not decline sharply in countries where replacement models were enforced. In fact, public social contributions increased in Mexico, where the public pillar was closed to new entrants and where a large share of contributors to the public scheme were required to switch to the newly created private pension fund. But even in countries that did experience a decline in public contributions (Argentina, Uruguay and El Salvador), the fall was not dramatic despite the increase in contributions to the private pillars. This might be explained by the intrinsic link between pensions schemes and healthcare systems (sickness, maternity, excluding paid benefits, and occupational hazards), wherein the main goal of the reforms was to increase coverage and thereby reassert solidarity[4] within the system. In this regard, virtually all Latin American countries reformed their healthcare systems (Mesa-Lago, 2013). These health reforms, however, did not greatly affect the role of private providers in this type of insurance market, at least, not in the same way that structural pension reforms substantially changed the landscape of public finances in the region.

### Figure S1.3. Public and private social security contributions

Percentage of GDP

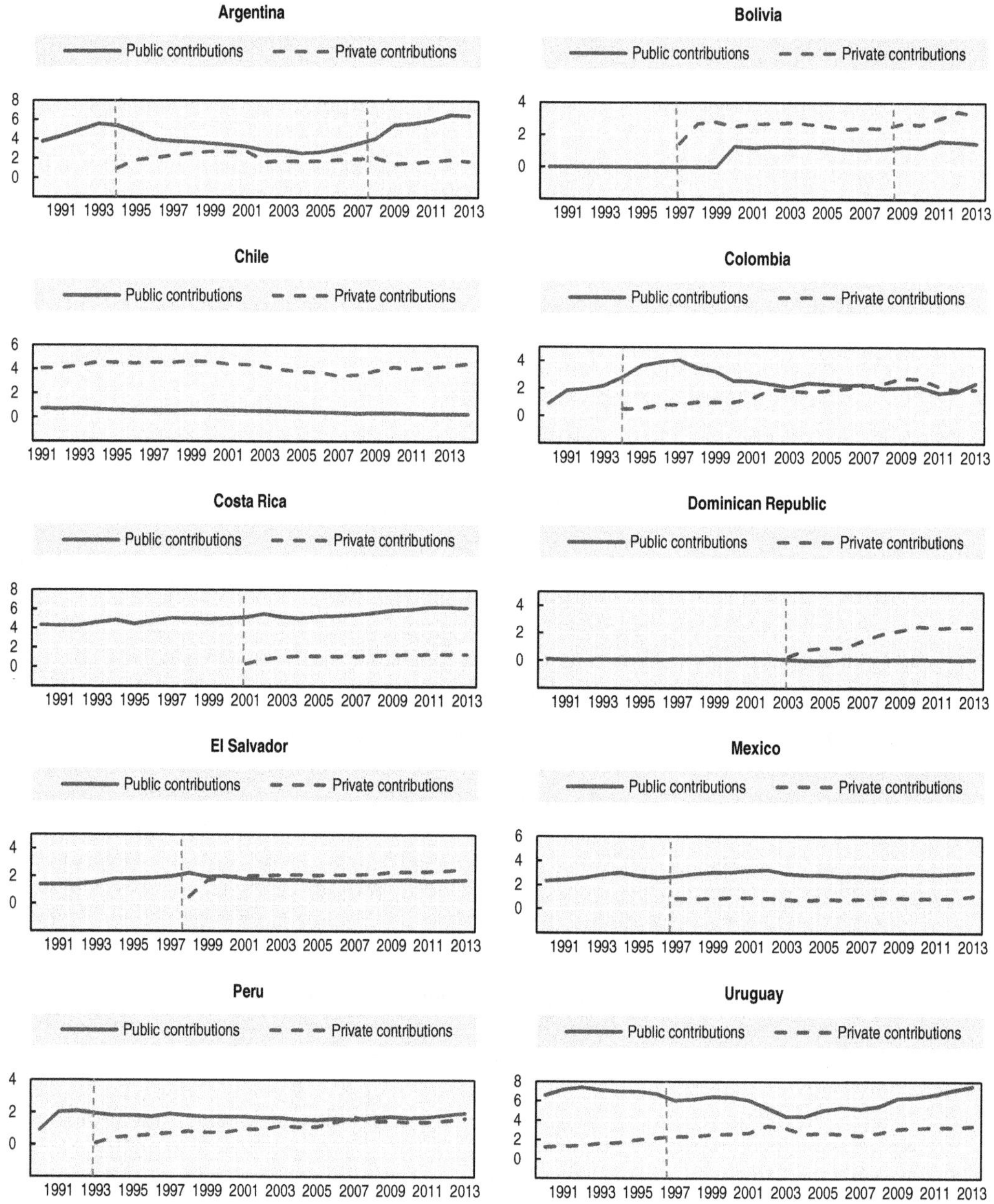


*Note*: Vertical lines indicates year of reform.

*Sources*: Table 4 and IDB-CIAT (2014).

StatLink http://dx.doi.org/10.1787/888933189699

Granted, some important responsibilities have been transferred to private actors, but this has not entailed complete separation from government even in the replacement model. In most cases, governments have regulated private pension funds' portfolio allocations, requiring these private entities to purchase government bonds up to a certain extent. Indeed, the separation of government and private pension schemes comes into question.

### Table S1.1. Features of social security systems in LAC

| Country | Mandatory private insurance | Social security contributions as % of GDP 2013 | | Administered Funds 2013 (% of GDP) | Invested in Government Holdings 2013 (%Total Administered Funds) |
|---|---|---|---|---|---|
| | | Public | Private | | |
| Argentina[a] | - | 6.5 | | | |
| Barbados | - | 6.0 | | | |
| Bolivia[b] | X | 1.5 | | 31.34 | 36.42 |
| Brazil | - | 9.2 | | | |
| Chile | X | 0.3 | 4.5 | 58.85 | 21.47 |
| Colombia | X | 2.4 | 1.9 | 17.96 | 40.48 |
| Costa Rica | X | 6.2 | 1.3 | 11.15 | 77.86 |
| Dominican Republic | X | 0.1 | 2.4 | 7.45 | 65.46 |
| Ecuador | - | 4.9 | | | |
| El Salvador | X | 1.7 | 2.5 | 30.18 | 81.13 |
| Guatemala | - | 2.0 | | | |
| Honduras | - | 3.3 | | | |
| Jamaica | - | 1.0 | | | |
| Mexico | X | 3.0 | 1.1 | 13.02 | 46.05 |
| Nicaragua | - | 4.6 | | | |
| Panama | - | 6.6 | | 1.59 | 0.00 |
| Paraguay | - | 1.3 | | | |
| Peru | X | 2.0 | 1.6 | 17.51 | 13.47 |
| Trinidad and Tobago | - | 1.9 | | | |
| Uruguay | X | 7.5 | 3.4 | 18.65 | 70.74 |
| Venezuela | - | 0.4 | | | |

*Notes:*

a In 2008, the pension reform enforced a universal social insurance. Before this, and after 1993, employees contributed to an individual account managed by a private fund chosen by the employee.

b In 2010, Bolivia's Pensions Act No. 065 created the Comprehensive Pension System (SIP). Under this law the two privately managed pension funds relinquished responsibility for administration. The law established a new state agency, the Public Management of Long-Term Social Security (GSS), within the Ministry of Economy and Public Finance; this is in charge of administering the funds. The pension fund administrators (AFPs) are still in a transition period during which they continue to operate.

*Sources:* Table 4, FIAP (2014); IDB-CIAT (2014); and SSA (2014).

StatLink http://dx.doi.org/10.1787/888933189782

In other cases, the separation between the public and private schemes is also diffuse. In Colombia, for example, individuals are allowed to switch from the private pension scheme to the public one every five years and one last time, ten years before retirement. This requires an individual's contributions to the private scheme to be transferred to the public pillar, and thus to be regarded as tax revenue in the EFP. Mexico is a similar case: the Mexican Institute of Social Security (IMSS) collects citizens' contributions and subsequently transfers these to the Institute of the National Housing Fund for Workers (INFONAVIT) and to each contributor's personal savings account in the Retirement Funds Administrators (AFOREs). To complicate matters further, the collected funds transferred to the AFOREs are invested in specialised retirement investment funds known as SIEFORES, in which government "authorities determine the criteria for the composition of the portfolio, indicating the type and characteristics of the permitted financial instruments and the accepted limits" (Rofman, Apella and Vezza, 2013). Furthermore,

Mexico allows a significant share of its citizens – those who were working before the reform – to choose between receiving the pension they would have received under the public programme or to collect the defined benefit pension they are entitled to under the private scheme (Mesa-Lago, 2000; Rofman, Apella and Vezza, 2013). In both these cases, the funds are fungible in either the private or public pillars of the broader social security system. Moreover, Argentina did not record as tax revenue the contributions made to the then-existing private pillar. However, after the 2008 "counter-reform" nationalised the social security system, those contributions were regarded as taxes, although the bases and the contribution rates were not altered.

At any rate, in several LAC countries, contributions to private pension[5] schemes account for such a share of GDP that they are hard to ignore in terms of the burden on taxpayers, especially when making international comparisons (Table S1.1).

### Non-tax revenues from natural resources

"National accounts are always evolving" (Piketty, 2014). Until half a decade ago, environmental accounting was a concept unknown to most. This significantly changed with the publication of the report by Stiglitz, Sen and Fitoussi (2009), which argued that comprehensive wealth served as a useful indicator to measure a nation's overall wellbeing. Since then, significant efforts have been made to measure the value of natural capital[6] (World Bank, 2011) as a component of much larger wealth accounts, and as a means of gauging development sustainability.

A parallel from the foregoing example can be drawn to the third component of the EFP. The OECD Revenue Statistics classification focuses on those government revenues which are defined as taxes. Countries also receive non-tax revenue incomes, and in LAC, many countries have a stream of income derived from their ability to exploit natural economic rents, sometimes through monopolies. Including this non-tax component in the aggregate measure of fiscal revenue offers a different perspective of the fiscal resources available to a large number of LAC countries. First, it is difficult to conceive public finances in the region without considering the importance of natural resources. The tax structure, the tax effort demanded of citizens, fiscal rules, macroeconomic performance, and several other aspects of public policies are all deeply affected by countries' natural endowments. In this regard, it has been noted repeatedly that LAC countries rely on consumption taxes to a greater extent than other regions, because these taxes have a limited impact on export activities (OECD IDB, 2014) and because consumption taxes are easier to collect than income taxes – consumption and income being the largest national account aggregates. In the past decade, substantial progress has been made on macroeconomic performance because of the introduction of fiscal frameworks that saved rents from commodities and provided the necessary leeway to manage public expenditures and liabilities. Similarly, stabilisation funds have assuaged the effects on the region of volatility in commodity prices. Further, the fact that the impact of the recent international financial crisis was brief and mild in several LAC countries can mostly be explained by the macroeconomic resilience that revenues from natural resources helped to strengthen.

Revenue from natural resources differs in both source and nature, a circumstance that complicates its accounting. For instance, Panama has been endowed with a privileged geographical feature that has turned it into a unique logistical platform. The fees paid by clients to use the canal have accounted for an average of 2.4% of GDP during the past 20 years and they are expected to increase more than 50% with its expansion. While technically this revenue stream cannot be characterised as a tax, these funds are not a negligible amount relative to tax revenues, excluding social security contributions, which accounted for only 11.2% of GDP on average in the same period. Similarly, Paraguay sells electricity generated by its two central hydroelectric dams, Itaipú and Yacyretá, to neighboring Brazil and Argentina. On average, this institutional arrangement has reported revenues of 2.7% of GDP during the past two decades. A common feature of these two countries is that both have a national enterprise that exploits the use of natural resources and afterwards transfers the net proceeds to the national treasury.

This sort of institutional arrangement is ubiquitous throughout the region. For example, the Mexican federal government received substantial amounts in payments and transfers from Pemex, the state-owned oil company, year after year. During the past two decades these accounted, on average, for 2.7% of GDP.[7] Similar situations prevail in countries like Chile, Bolivia, Colombia, Ecuador, Trinidad and Tobago, and Venezuela, where a state-run institution holds some form of monopoly or has significant market power over the exploitation of natural resources and transfers a portion of its net profits to the national treasury. It is likely that Argentina, which has the world's second biggest shale oil and gas reserves, and Brazil with its unique pre-salt oil production, will soon join the club.

Furthermore, it should come as no surprise that there is such a strong relationship between shifts in commodity prices and the revenues available to LAC countries. In most countries an overwhelming share of exports is accounted for by commodities, approximately 70% on average during 2010-12 (Barreix et al, 2013b), which makes the region's revenue collection susceptible to the volatility of international market prices. Figure S1.4 shows the direct relationship between the average EFP, weighted by GDP, and an adjusted commodity price index. This index was built under the methodological premise that commodity price fluctuations greatly affect our countries. Hence, this particular index controls for the export structure of each country, which later collapses into a single commodity price index average, weighted by GDP.[8]

Figure S1.4. **EFP and Adjusted Commodity Price Index**

Latin America and the Caribbean

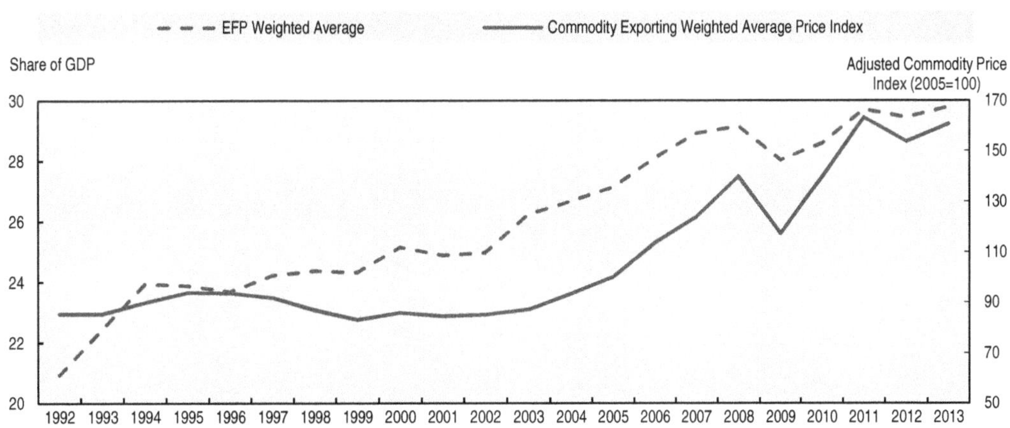


*Sources*: Prepared by authors on the basis of Barreix et al. (2013a), Table 1, IDB-CIAT (2014), IMF (2014), and WTO (2014).

StatLink http://dx.doi.org/10.1787/888933189706

Finally, the flow of government-appropriated non-tax revenues from natural resources can be traced back several decades in many countries. In some cases, this has been a very significant source of revenue. The period of extraordinarily high commodity prices only accentuated the importance of these resources and the need to increase the rents that governments appropriated from the exploitation of natural endowments by private or public actors.

## Conclusion

From the perspective of the authors, appraisals of revenues in LAC that include the components of the EFP methodology could give greater insight into fiscal revenues in the region and provide a broader view of the extent of domestic resource mobilisation occurring in LAC.

There can be little discussion that governments impose a fiscal burden upon employers and employees when they require individuals to contribute to social security schemes, be they public or private. Undeniably, from the individual's perspective, the financial effort exerted is the same, regardless of the type of institutional arrangement established by the government to ensure people's financial independence during their old age. In addition, the rounds of reforms and re-reforms in both the pension and healthcare systems have effectively created an intricate system in which the limits of state and private participation are not clearly determined.

Also, revenues from natural resources generate a wide range of institutional arrangements in LAC countries, and those revenues have been increasing significantly in the past decade. This not only demonstrates that this component has been resilient in providing substantial – albeit fluctuating – revenues, but also highlights the fact that these countries have to tax it better and improve the management of its macroeconomic impacts, through fiscal-prudence instruments such as fiscal rules or stabilisation funds.

## Notes

1. The authors of this special feature are Alberto Barreix, Juan Carlos Benítez, Martin Bès, Miguel Pecho, Agnes Rojas and Fernando Velayos. The opinions expressed and arguments employed herein are the views of the authors and do not necessarily represent the official views of the Inter-American Development Bank (IDB), the Inter-American Center of Tax Administrations (CIAT), and the Organisation for Economic Co-operation and Development (OECD) or the governments of its member countries.
2. The OECD has presented internationally comparable tax data in a common format for all OECD countries since 1965. Available at: www.oecd-ilibrary.org/taxation/data/oecd-tax-statistics_tax-data-en.
3. The IDB-CIAT Fiscal Revenue Dataset is available at: www.iadb.org/en/research-and-data/publication-details,3169.html?pub_id=IDB-DB-101. This dataset distinguishes among revenues collected through each kind of tax for every level of government. It also presents data on compulsory private and public social security contributions and non-tax resources from renewable and non-renewable natural resources. The data was compiled from finance and economy agencies, statistical institutions, state owned enterprises, the OECD (Revenue Statistics in Latin America 2014), and information provided to the IDB-CIAT partnership by local authorities. The profiles for each country have been verified by local fiscal authorities.
4. Average premiums are based on collective risk; hence the contribution bears no relationship to an individual's risk. There are transfers among generations and benefits are standardised to some extent. A much more detailed account of healthcare reforms can be found in Mesa-Lago (2013), chapters 7–10.
5. As with pensions, the precedent set by the US government with the Patient Care and Affordable Care Act, popularly known as "Obamacare", whereby the US Supreme Court considered the introduction of mandatory healthcare, should contribute to the debate about whether contributions paid to private providers ought to be regarded as tax revenue. Our estimates give an increase of about 16% in the US tax burden in 2014.
6. Comprises economic rents or profits derived from agricultural lands, protected areas, forests, minerals, and energy. $V_t = \sum_{i=t}^{t+T-1} \left(\frac{\pi_i q_i}{(1+r)^{(1-t)}}\right)$. where $\pi_i q_i$ is the economic profit or total rents derived from natural resources at time i, r is the social discount rate and T is the expected lifetime of the natural resource.
7. Also, it is worth noting that during some previous years before the recent fiscal and energy reforms, Mexico subsidised much of its citizens' internal oil consumption during periods of high prices.
8. To build this adjusted index, the exporting structures by commodity for each country were calculated using data from the World Trade Organization (http://stat.wto.org/Home/WSDBHome.aspx?Language=E). These structures served as weights to estimate the effects of changes in commodity prices (IMF monthly data, aggregated by year: www.imf.org/external/np/res/commod/index.aspx) for each country. For the final series, these resulting sub-indices were averaged using each country's GDP as weights.

## *References*


Barreix, A., J. Roca and L. Villela (2006), editors, "Fiscal Equity in the Andean Community: Distributive Impact of Main Taxes and Public Expenditures", *IDB Fiscal Equity Series*, Andean Community. 2006, www.comunidadandina.org/public/libro_EquidadFiscal.pdf.

Barreix, A., M. Bès and J. Roca (2009), editors, "Fiscal Equity in Central America, Panama and the Dominican Republic", *IDB Fiscal Equity Series*, EUROsociAL and Inter-American Development Bank, Washington, DC.

Barreix, A, M. Bès, J. C. Benitez, M. Pecho and F. Velayos (2013a). "Equivalent Fiscal Pressure in Latin America and the Caribbean: Concept, Development and International Comparisons", *Working Paper* 9/2013, Institute of Fiscal Studies (Spain), www.ief.es/documentos/recursos/publicaciones/papeles_trabajo/2013_09.pdf.

Barreix, A., C. Garcimartín and F. Velayos (2013b), "The Corporate Income Tax: The art of competing for investment and increasing tax revenue" in Corbacho, A., V. Fretes and E. Lora (Editors) (2013), *More than Revenue: Taxation as a Development Tool*, Inter-American Development Bank, Washington, DC.

Bonilla-Garcia, A. and A. Conte-Grand (comps.) (1998), *Pensiones en América Latina. Dos Décadas de Reformas*, International Labour Office, Geneva.

Bosch, M., A. Melguizo and C. Pagés (2013). *Mejores Pensiones, Mejores Trabajos. Hacia la cobertura universal en América Latina y el Caribe*, Inter-American Development Bank, Washington, DC.

Cetrángolo, O and A. Goldschmit (2009), "Metodología, experiencia comparada y recomendaciones", in O. Cetrangolo (ed.), *La seguridad social en América Latina y el Caribe. Una propuesta metodológica para su medición y aplicación a los casos de Argentina, Chile y Colombia*. Economic Commission for Latin America and the Caribbean, Santiago, Chile.

Gill, I., T. Packard and J. Yermo (2005), *Keeping the Promise of Social Security in Latin America*. World Bank, Washington, DC. Available at: https://openknowledge.worldbank.org/bitstream/handle/10986/7391/344330PAPER0LA101official0use0only1.pdf?sequence=1. Accessed on 19 September 2014.

IDB-CIAT (2014), *Equivalent Fiscal Pressure Database* 2014. Available at: www.iadb.org/en/research-and-data/publication-details,3169.html?pub_id=IDB-DB-101.

FIAP (2012), *Informe Semestral* No. 33, Federación Internacional de Administradoras de Fondos de Pensiones 31.12.2012', International Federation of Pension Fund Administrators. Available at: www.fiap.cl/prontus_fiap/site/artic/20130818/asocfile/20130818182859/informe_semestral_n__33.pdf. Accessed on 20 August 2014.

Lustig, et al. (2013), "The Impact of Taxes and Social Spending on Inequality and Poverty in Argentina, Bolivia, Brazil, Mexico, Peru and Uruguay: An Overview", *ECINEQ WP* 2013-15. ECINE Society for the Study of Economic Inequality.

Machinea, J. L. (2014), "En Busca de un Marco Fiscal para América Latina", *Colección de Estudios* 4 Programa Eurosocial, Madrid.

Mesa-Lago, C. (2013), *Reassembling Social Security: A Survey of Pensions and Health Care Reforms in Latin America*, Oxford University Press, Oxford.

Mesa-Lago, C. (2009), "Re-reform of Latin American Private Pensions System: Argentinean and Chilean Models and Lessons", *The Geneva Papers* 34 (602–617).

Mesa-Lago, C. (2000), "Estudio Comparativo de los Costos Fiscales en la Transición de Ocho Reformas de Pensiones en América Latina", *Financiamiento del desarrollo series* 93, ECLAC, Santiago, Chile.

OECD-ECLAC-CIAT (2014), *Revenue Statistics in Latin America* 2014, OECD Publishing, Paris, http://dx.doi.org/10.1787/9789264207943-en-fr.

OECD-IDB (2014), *Government at a Glance: Latin America and the Caribbean 2014*, OECD Publishing, Paris. Available at: http://dx.doi.org/10.1787/9789264209480-en.

Piketty, T. (2014), *Capital in the Twenty-First Century*, Harvard University Press, Cambridge, MA.

Rofman, R., I. Apella and E. Vezza (eds.) (2013), *Más Allá de las Pensiones Contributivas. Catorce experiencias en América Latina*, World Bank, Buenos Aires.

Ruezga Barba, A. (1995), "Administración Pública y Privada de los Seguros Sociales en América Latina" *Serie Estudios* 16, Conferencia Interamericana de Seguridad Social.

Social Security Administration, SSA (2014), "Social Security Programs throughout the World: The Americas, 2013", *SSA Publication* 13-11804, Social Security Administration, Washington, DC. Available at: www.ssa.gov/policy/docs/progdesc/ssptw/2012-2013/americas/ssptw13americas.pdf.

Stiglitz, J., A. Sen and J. P. Fitoussi (2009), "Report by the Commission on the Measurement of Economic Performance and Social Progress", Mimeographed document. Available at: www.stiglitz-sen-fitoussi.fr/documents/rapport_anglais.pdf.

Uthoff, A. (2001) "La Reforma del Sistema de Pensiones en Chile: Desafíos pendientes", *Financiamiento del desarrollo series* 112, ECLAC, Santiago, Chile.

World Bank (2014), *World Development Indicators*, Available at: http://data.worldbank.org/data-catalog/world-development-indicators. Accessed on 19 September 2014.

World Bank (2011), *The Changing Wealth of Nations. Measuring Sustainable Development in the New Millennium*, World Bank, Washington, DC.

World Trade Organization (2014), *Statistics Database*. Available at: www.wto.org/english/res_e/statis_e/data_pub_e.htm.

## SPECIAL FEATURE S2
## Fiscal revenues from non-renewable natural resources in Latin America

### Revenues from non-renewable natural resources, relative to GDP, remained stable in 2013

Public revenues from non-renewable natural resources held steady in 2013, relative to GDP, reflecting the relative stability of international petroleum prices during the year and strong profits realised in 2012. Revenue from hydrocarbons rose from an average of 7.4% of GDP in 2012 to 7.8% in 2013 among the seven principal producing countries in the region. Mining revenues, however, continued to slide, from a regional average of 1.1% of GDP in 2012 to only 0.7% in 2013. These trends notwithstanding the value of non-renewable natural resource public revenues, as measured in current US dollars, in nine Latin America countries rose to a record USD 258.6 billion (Figure S2.1).

Figure S2.1. **Fiscal revenues from non-renewable natural resources, 2013**

USD billion and percentage of GDP

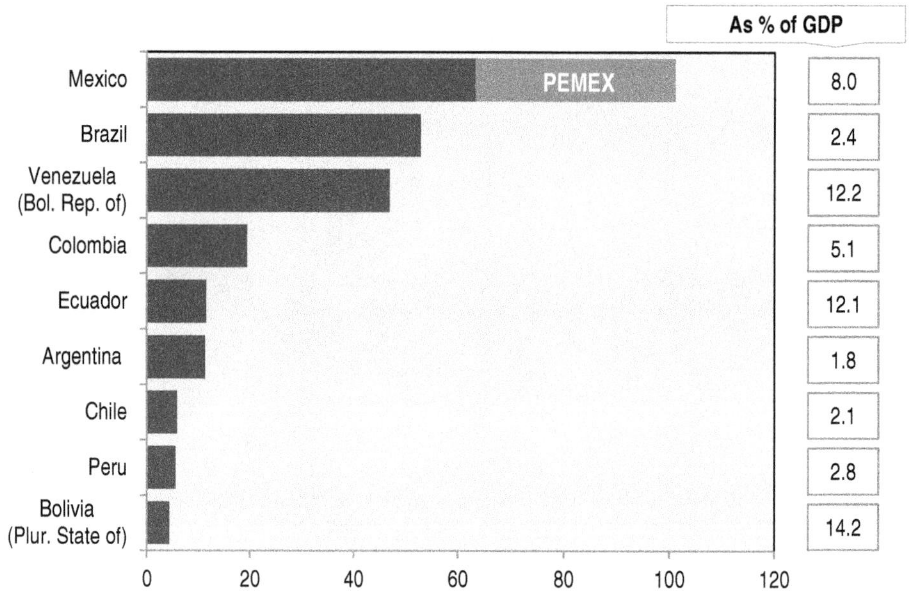


*Source*: ECLAC.

StatLink http://dx.doi.org/10.1787/888933189718

The relative stability of non-renewable natural resource revenues in 2013, however, belies the much more heterogeneous results registered by the region's countries during the year (Figure S2.2). Among the nine countries under consideration five registered an increase relative to GDP, in general of the order of less than 1% of GDP, though Venezuela was a clear exception. Revenues fell in four countries, with Ecuador posting the largest decline relative to GDP. Rising revenues were largely associated with countries who are principally hydrocarbons producers. Mining revenues, on the other hand, fell in nearly all countries.

Figure S2.2. **Change in fiscal revenues from non-renewable natural resources, 2012-13**

Percentage of GDP

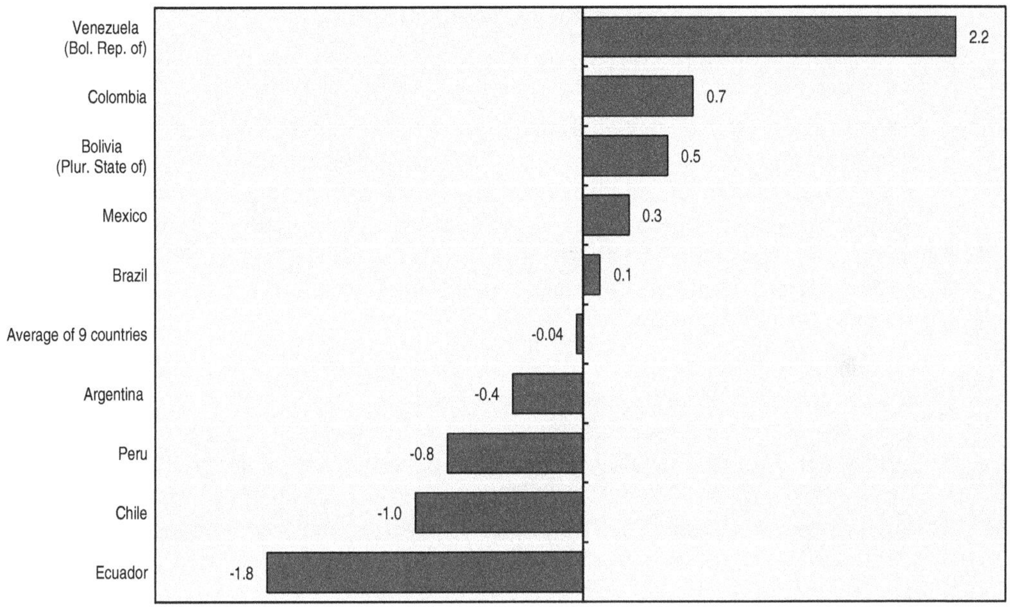


*Source:* ECLAC.

StatLink http://dx.doi.org/10.1787/888933189723

The sharp rise of oil revenues in Venezuela, with an increase of 2.2% of GDP, was largely due to the devaluation of the country's currency and a significant jump in extraordinary non-tax revenues. Nevertheless, oil revenues as a share of GDP remained significantly below the average registered in 2005-07 of 14.6%. During the year Petróleos de Venezuela S.A. (PDVSA) paid dividends of VEF 69 billion (Venezuelan bolivar) to the central government, thanks to a one-off exchange rate gain and the sale of a 40% stake in PDVSA's fully owned subsidiary Empresa Nacional Aurífera S.A. to the Central Bank. The company's corporate income tax contribution, which largely reflected its 2012 pre-devaluation results, was muted as production fell. Central government revenues from the production tax, extraction tax, and export registration tax rose 39.5% as a result of the devaluation and the government's amendment in February of the special contribution for extraordinary prices and exorbitant prices in the international hydrocarbons market. This measure raised the ceiling for their calculation from USD 70 to USD 80 per barrel as well as restructuring the payment structure of the windfall tax – which forms the basis of PDVSA's contribution to FONDEN, an extra-budgetary development fund – above that amount. The net effect of this measure for central government revenues will likely be limited as higher production costs – royalties and extraction taxes – will reduce operating profits and in turn corporate income tax payments.

Colombia's non-renewable natural resource revenues rose in 2013 due to high inflows of non-tax revenues from the hydrocarbons sector. In particular, dividends transferred by Ecopetrol to the central government nearly doubled as a result of the payment of an extraordinary dividend and the reduction of liabilities carried over from previous years. Royalty payments in 2013 decreased slightly as the average price per barrel of Colombian crude declined. Revenues from corporate income tax fell slightly reflecting the 3.7% fall in operating profits in 2012 due to lower sales volumes and higher costs. Colombia's recent tax reform, which lowered the corporate income tax to 25% but created an additional tax for equity of 9% (for the period 2013-15 and of 8% thereafter) served to increase Ecopetrol's effective tax rate, with its full impact on central government receipts only being felt from calendar year 2014. Mining revenues, mainly in the form of royalties from the production of coal which is the country's principal mineral export, fell in line with falling prices in international markets.

Revenues from natural gas exploitation in Bolivia continued to grow strongly in 2013. This growth was mainly attributed to rising exports to Argentina, as the gas pipelines to Brazil – the country's principal purchaser of natural gas – have reached capacity. During the year revenues from the Direct Tax on Hydrocarbons (IDH) as well as those from corporate income tax on companies in the hydrocarbons sector rose by 28% and 30% respectively. These gains were offset somewhat by a sharp decline in mining revenues, which fell from 1.3% of GDP in 2012 to 0.6% in 2013. Falling prices in 2012 and 2013 – especially of tin, silver and zinc – contributed to a 69.3% fall in the sector's corporate income tax contribution.

Hydrocarbons revenues in Mexico rose slightly as a share of GDP in 2013 due to a substantial decline in the "negative" Special Production and Services Tax (IEPS) on gasoline and diesel that offsets a decline in other oil revenues. The fiscal cost of this tax, which acts as a subsidy when international prices of specific hydrocarbon products are high, fell from 1.3% of GDP in 2012 to 0.5% in 2013. Oil production by PEMEX and its subsidiaries declined 1.0% in volume during the year, with exports registering a steeper decline of 5.3% – or 8.7% in terms of value. These trends, coupled with a slight decline in the average sale price of Mexican crude, resulted in a 6.7% fall in public revenues from hydrocarbons duties – and a 47.4% decline in the extraordinary duty for the export of crude oil – in nominal peso terms. Mining revenues, relative to GDP, registered little change in the year.

Brazil's non-renewable natural resource revenues held roughly steady, with a slight decrease in hydrocarbons revenues being offset by a rise in those from mining activities. Public revenues from hydrocarbons were principally affected by a decline in Petrobras' income tax payments, including both corporate income tax (IRPJ) and social contribution on net corporate profits (CSLL), and slow growth in non-tax hydrocarbons revenues due to a drop in upstream production. Downstream revenues rose sharply reflecting domestic demand and additional production of refined oil products by Petrobras for the local market. Mining revenues rebounded in 2013 on the back of higher international prices, principally of iron ore, and the settlement of a long-standing tax case between Vale S.A. and the Brazilian government. The company agreed to pay USD 9.6 billion in taxes on profits from its foreign operations over a period of 15 years. By year's end the company had paid USD 2.6 billion in income taxes, which included a significant upfront payment from the settlement.

Oil revenues of the non-financial public sector in Ecuador registered a notable decline of 1.8% of GDP in 2013. Despite rising production and higher exports volumes, the value of crude oil exports rose only 2.3% compared with the previous year as the price of Ecuadorean crude fell from an average price per barrel of USD 98.2 to USD 95.6. It is important to highlight that as a dollarised economy Ecuador does realise gains – or losses – due to changes in exchange rates. Mining revenues in Ecuador are currently insignificant, with royalties and licenses accounting for a mere USD 57.2 million in 2013. The government is seeking to develop this sector and in June the Congress approved a reform with the aim of increasing private investment while at the same time increasing the State's take of any resulting revenues.

Mining revenues in Chile and Peru were affected by the continued slide in copper prices, which fell a further 8% in 2013. The case of Peru is illustrative of the situation faced by many countries with revenues from mining. Non-tax revenues in the form of royalties, which represented 26.6% of mining revenues in 2013, experienced a 13.1% decline in line with the fall of international prices. Tax revenues, comprising the sector's corporate income tax contribution as well as the special tax on mining, dropped 47% as profit margins narrowed as prices fell and production costs remained high. Similarly in Chile the corporate tax contribution of private mining companies fell 27.5% and that of CODELCO fell 70.4% – though the latter was offset somewhat by an increase in dividend payments.

Falling hydrocarbons exports dragged on oil revenues from customs duties in Argentina, pushing overall non-renewable natural revenues down 0.4% of GDP in 2013. Crude oil exports, which fell 37.2% in volume terms compared with the previous year, have been affected by slowing production, rising domestic demand and increased governmental control of exports. Furthermore, due to price controls in the local market, profits – and thus corporate income tax revenues – have grown at rates slower than that of the economy as a whole. In response to declining production the government decreed in July the creation of the Investment Promotion Scheme for the Exploitation of Hydrocarbons. This measure allows for unimpeded exports – free of customs duties – of up to 20% of the hydrocarbons produced from projects with an investment of USD 1 billion or more. The decree also allows participating companies to use at their discretion the foreign exchange deriving from qualifying exports.

## Falling crude oil prices in the second half of 2014 will drag down revenues for the year and beyond

International reference prices for crude oil, which had remained stable between 2011 and 2013, began to decline in the third quarter of 2014. To some extent this reflected an imbalance between international supply and demand. Higher oil production in the United States was not offset by a decline in that of other traditional producers, including the region's principal exporters. Demand for oil, however, remained soft due to modest growth in developing countries and stagnant demand in developed countries. This declining price trend accelerated in the fourth quarter when the members of OPEC decided to maintain their production levels for the foreseeable future. Between the last week of June and the first week of December the spot prices of Brent and West Texas Intermediate (WTI) fell roughly 40%. As a consequence government forecasts as well as projections carried out by ECLAC suggest a decline in oil revenues of at least 1% of GDP on average in 2014 (Figure S2.3). Nevertheless, if prices remain below USD 70 the decline in hydrocarbons revenues will be greater.

Revenues from hydrocarbons in Bolivia, Ecuador and Mexico – which include those from both upstream and downstream activities – are projected to decline by 1% to 1.5% of GDP. Oil revenues in Venezuela, which represented 46.6% of the central government's overall revenues in 2013, may climb in nominal terms but fall relative to GDP as nominal GDP growth is forecast to far outstrip that of revenues. For these countries, the affect of falling prices will be coupled with slowing or even declining production. Colombia and Peru are also projected to register declines relative to GDP, though of 0.5% of GDP or less, despite rising production of oil and natural gas, respectively.

Figure S2.3. **Fiscal revenues from non-renewable natural resources, by selected product groups, 2000-14**

Percentage of GDP

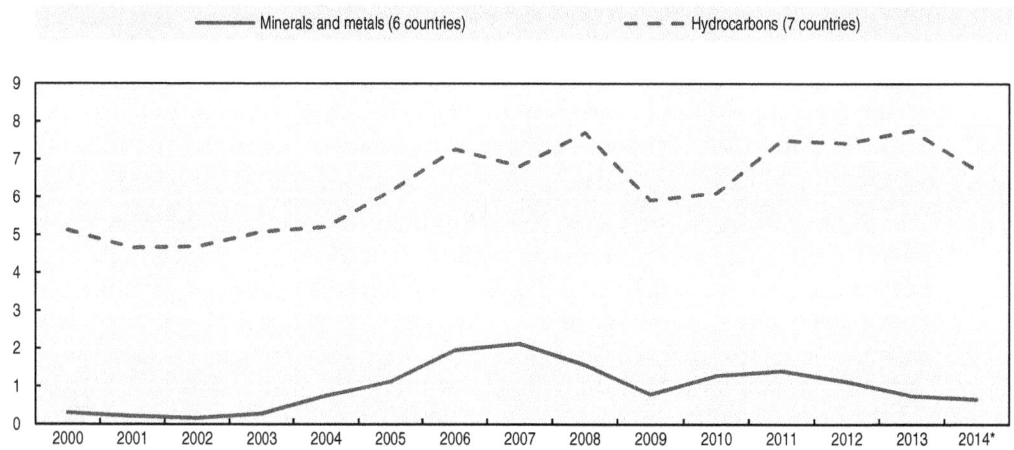


*Note*: Data for 2014 from government estimates or based on forecasted changes in commodity prices and nominal exchange rates holding production constant. Commodities price forecasts from EIU (2014) and IMF (2014), exchange rate forecasts from national budgets, and nominal GDP from ECLAC. Disaggregated data for Argentina was not available thus it is not included in this figure.

*Source*: ECLAC.

StatLink http://dx.doi.org/10.1787/888933189733

Mining revenues, in contrast, are estimated to either hold steady or decline slightly on average as a share of GDP in 2014. This largely reflects the fact that the corporate income tax contribution of mining enterprises, which accounted for the bulk of the rise in mining revenues during the decade, has returned to its pre-boom level. Non-tax revenues, mainly royalties related to production levels, have held steady at roughly 0.2% of GDP on average since 2005. Among the countries under consideration the largest decline is forecast in Chile, with a fall of 0.2% of GDP.

The year also witnessed a series of significant reforms, especially in the mining sector, that will have an impact on revenues in 2015 and beyond. Bolivia enacted a new mining and metallurgy law in 2014 after overcoming significant resistance by mining cooperatives. The new legal framework removes certain privileges that they enjoyed under the previous system, namely the right to associate with private firms. It also created a new government regulatory body for the mining sector which will oversee the renegotiation of any concessions that are not in line with the new regulations. Peru amended its General Mining Law in July to expand tax stability agreements – effectively locking in the current fiscal regime – for up to 15 years for new investments of USD 500 million or greater.

Mexico also undertook a series of important measures impacting both the hydrocarbons and mining sectors. In January the reformed fiscal regime of the mining sector took effect. The new regime includes a 7.5% tax on net profits from mining operations and an environmental levy of 0.5% on the gross value of gold, silver and platinum sales. The measure also created an additional levy on concessions where exploration or production has not occurred. In August the President signed into law the "secondary laws" of the energy reform of 2013, which opened the hydrocarbons sector to private participation for the first time since nationalisation in 1938. The new legal framework defines the mechanisms for issuing entitlements for exploration and extraction of hydrocarbons as well as the contractual forms for private participation.

Additionally the measure defines the fiscal obligations of private firms operating in the sector and streamlines those of PEMEX to bring them in line with international best practices.

In October the Argentine Congress approved an amendment of the Federal Hydrocarbons Law with the aim of further bolstering investment in the hydrocarbons sector. In particular, the measure targets the exploitation of non-conventional sources through the creation of a separate concession structure with longer terms and lower royalties. Additionally, all hydrocarbons concessionaires will now have the right to request multiple extensions without limit, though the State reserves the right to increase the royalty rate by 3% increments – to a maximum rate of 18% – for the first two extensions. The amendment also curtailed the use of other fiscal instruments by subnational governments, defining royalties as their only means of participation in hydrocarbons exploitation. The Investment Promotion Scheme for the Exploitation of Hydrocarbons – which was decreed in 2013 – was also modified to extend its benefits to projects with an initial investment value of USD 250 million or greater, down from the original USD 1 billion.

### Box S2.1. **The definition of fiscal revenues from non-renewable natural resources**

The data presented in this article come from a database that ECLAC maintains for the countries of the region. Both tax revenues and non tax revenues – such as royalties, dividends, etc – are considered (Table S2.1). Data for mining revenues refer specifically to the exploitation of the resources. Hydrocarbons revenues, in contrast, include both upstream and downstream activities. ECLAC continuously updates this database to improve its coverage of countries as well as the disaggregation of the data. For more information over the fiscal instruments used by each country please see the special feature in Revenues Statistics of Latin America 2014.

Table S2.1. **Fiscal instruments considered within the framework of fiscal revenues from non-renewable natural resources**

| | | | Hydrocarbons | | |
|---|---|---|---|---|---|
| | Mining | | Upstream | | Downstream |
| | Tax revenues | Non tax revenues | Tax revenues | Non tax revenues | Tax revenues |
| Argentina | • | • | • | • | • |
| Bolivia (Plur. State of) | • | • | • | • | • |
| Brazil | • (Vale S.A.) | • | • (Petrobras) | • | • |
| Chile | • | • | ... | ... | ... |
| Colombia | • | • | • (Ecopetrol) | • (Ecopetrol) | • |
| Ecuador | ... | ... | • | • | ... |
| Mexico | • | • | • | • | • |
| Peru | • | • | • | • | • |
| Venezuela (Bol. Rep. of) | ... | ... | • | • | • |

*Source:* ECLAC.

StatLink http://dx.doi.org/10.1787/888933189794

# PARTE I

# TENDENCIAS TRIBUTARIAS, 1990-2013

## A. Niveles de recaudación

Los ingresos tributarios como proporción del producto interno bruto (PIB) han aumentado considerablemente en América Latina y el Caribe en los dos últimos decenios. Tanto el cuadro A como el gráfico A plasman cómo los ingresos de los países latinoamericanos y caribeños objeto de este estudio, incluidas las contribuciones a la seguridad social, han venido incrementándose casi ininterrumpidamente, con excepción de 2009, y han pasado del 14.4% del PIB en 1990 al 21.3% del PIB (promedios no ponderados) en 2013. La mayor importancia relativa de los ingresos tributarios es reflejo de unas condiciones macroeconómicas favorables, así como de los cambios en el diseño de los sistemas tributarios y del fortalecimiento de las administraciones tributarias.

Esta tendencia contrasta con la registrada en la zona de la OCDE, donde la proporción ha permanecido relativamente estable y en 2013, arrojaba un valor del 34.1% del PIB, menos de un punto porcentual por encima de su nivel de 1990. Como resultado, la brecha entre los promedios de las dos zonas comenzó a disminuir a partir del año 2000. Esta diferencia era de unos 18 puntos porcentuales en 1990 y para 2010 había caído a 13 puntos porcentuales, nivel al que se ha mantenido relativamente constante.

Los ingresos tributarios como proporción del PIB en América Latina y el Caribe aumentaron cada año desde 2010 a 2013, continuando con la tendencia expansiva que se venía dando desde hace muchos años pero que se había visto interrumpida en 2009 como consecuencia de la caída del nivel de actividad y de los precios de los materias primas debido a la crisis financiera internacional. El ratio de ingresos tributarios sobre el PIB se incremento ligeramente en 2013 y representó un 21.3%, comparado con 21.2% en el 2012. En 2013 este ratio, comparado con 2012, creció en 12 de los 20 países analizados de la región, se mantuvo igual en Nicaragua, y cayó en los 7 países restantes. Si se compara el ratio de 2012 con el del 2011, sólo en 18 países ha experimentado un crecimiento, mientras que en uno disminuyo y en otro se mantuvo constante. La media de los países OCDE creció en 0.4 puntos porcentuales en 2013, dejando el ratio en un nivel de 34.1%, todavía 0.1 puntos porcentuales por debajo del nivel precrisis de 2007, 34.2%.

La proporción media de los impuestos en relación con el PIB es mucho mayor en los países de la OCDE que en los países latinoamericanos de la muestra (34.1% frente al 21.3%, respectivamente, en 2013). Sin embargo, cabe señalar que entre los países latinoamericanos y caribeños, existe una amplia variación entre las proporciones más altas y más bajas de impuestos en relación con el PIB. Las cifras más elevadas en 2013 correspondieron a Brasil y Argentina (35.7% y 31.2%, respectivamente), mientras que Guatemala (13.0%) y República Dominicana (14.0%) registraron los niveles más bajos. Del mismo modo, se evidencia una gran disparidad entre las economías de la OCDE. Así, en 2013, la proporción de los impuestos en el PIB oscilaba entre el 48.6% de Dinamarca y el 19.7% de México (esta cifra difiere de las presentadas en las publicaciones de CEPAL y CIAT debido a la inclusión de derechos sobre la producción de hidrocarburos como ingresos tributarios). La interpretación de las diferencias aparentes entre las proporciones de impuestos en relación con el PIB de la OCDE y América Latina debe realizarse con cautela, dado que en estas regiones se incluyen economías de naturaleza muy dispar.

Entre los numerosos factores que determinan cuál debería ser la proporción de impuestos adecuada para cada país, se encuentra el volumen de provisión de bienes y servicios por parte del Estado. A partir de los años 1980, muchos países latinoamericanos privatizaron, en mayor o menor medida, los servicios de atención sanitaria, educación y seguridad social (CEPAL, 2010). Esta característica regional contrasta con la provisión sustancialmente pública de esos servicios, y la consiguiente necesidad de ingresos fiscales, en múltiples países de la OCDE, en particular en Europa. Además, en los países latinoamericanos, los elevados niveles de informalidad hacen que muchas personas queden al margen de la imposición (OCDE, 2008; Gómez Sabaini et al., 2010), algo que además tiene especial importancia en el entorno de las pymes. Con todo, la cuestión del incumplimiento en el pago de impuestos suele tener un impacto significativo en los ingresos tributarios en todo tipo de países.

El cuadro A muestra una considerable disparidad entre las tendencias de los diversos países considerados a lo largo del tiempo. Pero, independientemente de la amplia variedad de niveles impositivos, se observa un reforzamiento de los ingresos tributarios desde el 1990. Los países que registraron mayores incrementos entre 1990 y 2013 fueron Bolivia (20.6 puntos porcentuales), Argentina (18.8), Ecuador (12.2), Colombia (11.1) y Paraguay (11.0). En el mismo periodo, en la mayoría de los países restantes los aumentos oscilaron entre 3 y 8 puntos porcentuales, con la excepción de Jamaica y Honduras, con un aumento respectivo de 2 y 1.8 puntos porcentuales y Venezuela, que sufrió un descenso de 4.5 puntos porcentuales.

Gráfico A. **Total de recaudación tributaria como porcentaje de PIB en América Latina y el Caribe y la OCDE, 1990-2013**

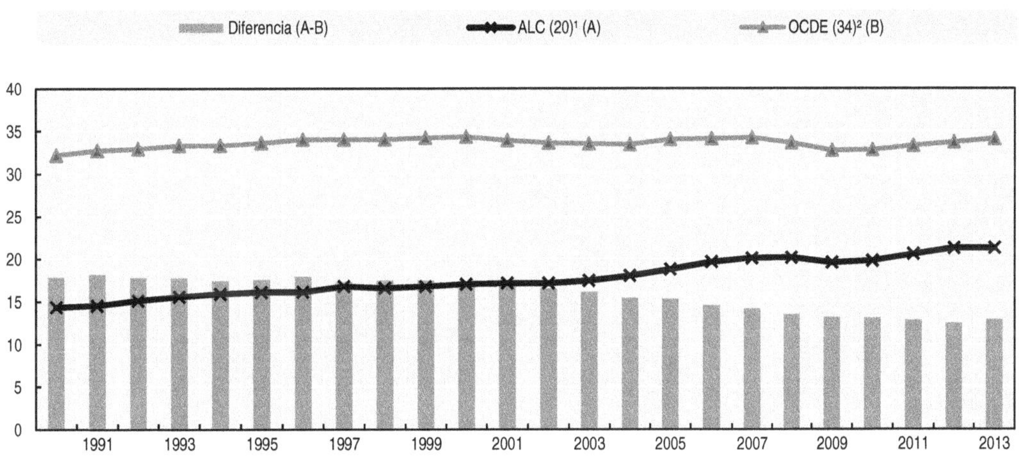


1.Representa un grupo de 20 países de América Latina y el Caribe. Estos son Argentina, Barbados, Bolivia, Brasil, Chile, Colombia, Costa Rica, República Dominicana, Ecuador, El Salvador, Guatemala, Honduras, Jamaica, México, Nicaragua, Panama, Paraguay, Perú, Uruguay y Venezuela. Chile y México son también parte del grupo OCDE (34).

2.Representa el promedio no ponderado de los países miembros de la OCDE.

*Fuente*: Cuadro 1 en Parte II.

StatLink http://dx.doi.org/10.1787/888933189873

El contexto en el que se produjo el incremento de los ingresos tributarios registrado a partir de los años 1990 fue uno de inestabilidad macroeconómica vivida por los países latinoamericanos en la década anterior. Durante los años 1980, los países de la región padecieron fuertes desequilibrios fiscales y, al mismo tiempo, algunos recurrieron a vías alternativas para financiar su gasto (tomando préstamos o imprimiendo moneda), lo que generó una inflación que se extendió rápidamente por toda la región y erosionó el valor real de los ingresos tributarios. Como resultado de ello, las reformas de los años 1990 se centraron en controlar dicha inflación y en imponer disciplina fiscal.

## Cuadro A. Total de recaudación tributaria como porcentaje del PIB[1]

| | 1990 | 2000 | 2008 | 2009 | 2010 | 2011 | 2012 | 2013 |
|---|---|---|---|---|---|---|---|---|
| Argentina | 12.4 | 18.0 | 24.7 | 25.6 | 26.7 | 27.7 | 29.5 | 31.2 |
| Barbados | 23.0 | 30.2 | 31.5 | 30.6 | 30.7 | 32.3 | 34.0 | 29.8 |
| Bolivia[2] | 7.0 | 14.7 | 20.1 | 22.3 | 20.4 | 23.8 | 25.5 | 27.6 |
| Brasil | 28.2 | 30.1 | 33.8 | 33.1 | 33.2 | 35.0 | 35.6 | 35.7 |
| Chile | 17.0 | 18.8 | 21.4 | 17.2 | 19.5 | 21.2 | 21.4 | 20.2 |
| Colombia | 9.0 | 14.6 | 18.8 | 18.6 | 18.0 | 18.9 | 19.6 | 20.1 |
| Costa Rica | 16.1 | 18.2 | 22.7 | 21.2 | 20.8 | 21.3 | 21.2 | 22.4 |
| Ecuador | 7.1 | 10.1 | 14.0 | 14.9 | 16.3 | 17.3 | 19.4 | 19.3 |
| El Salvador | 10.5 | 12.2 | 15.1 | 14.4 | 14.8 | 14.9 | 15.1 | 15.8 |
| Guatemala | 9.0 | 12.4 | 12.9 | 12.2 | 12.4 | 12.7 | 12.8 | 13.0 |
| Honduras | 16.2 | 15.3 | 18.9 | 17.1 | 17.3 | 16.9 | 17.4 | 18.0 |
| Jamaica | 23.0 | 22.8 | 25.0 | 24.8 | 25.0 | 24.5 | 24.5 | 25.0 |
| México[3,4] | 15.5 | 16.5 | 20.7 | 17.2 | 18.5 | 19.5 | 19.6 | 19.7 |
| Nicaragua | .. | 13.0 | 16.8 | 16.9 | 17.6 | 18.6 | 19.2 | 19.2 |
| Panamá | 14.7 | 16.7 | 16.9 | 17.4 | 18.1 | 18.1 | 18.7 | 18.9 |
| Paraguay[2,5] | 5.4 | 14.5 | 14.6 | 16.1 | 16.5 | 16.8 | 17.7 | 16.4 |
| Perú | 12.1 | 14.5 | 19.0 | 17.0 | 18.0 | 18.5 | 18.8 | 18.3 |
| República Dominicana | 8.3 | 12.4 | 15.0 | 13.1 | 12.8 | 12.9 | 13.5 | 14.0 |
| Uruguay[2] | 19.6 | 21.6 | 26.1 | 26.8 | 27.0 | 26.8 | 27.4 | 27.1 |
| Venezuela[2] | 18.7 | 13.6 | 14.1 | 14.1 | 11.4 | 13.1 | 13.9 | 14.2 |
| Promedio no ponderado: | | | | | | | | |
| ALC (20)[6] | 14.4 | 17.0 | 20.1 | 19.5 | 19.8 | 20.5 | 21.2 | 21.3 |
| OCDE (34)[7] | 32.2 | 34.3 | 33.6 | 32.7 | 32.8 | 33.3 | 33.7 | 34.1 |

1. Las cifras excluyen los ingresos de gobiernos locales en Argentina (pero incluye ingresos de las provincias), Barbados, Bolivia, Costa Rica (hasta 1997), República Dominicana, Ecuador, El Salvador, Honduras, Jamaica, Nicaragua, Panamá (hasta 1998), Paraguay (hasta 2004 y 2013), Perú (hasta 2004), Uruguay (2013) y Venezuela dado que los datos no están disponibles.
2. Datos estimados desde el 2011 hasta el 2013 (Bolivia y Venezuela) y 2013 (Uruguay y Paraguay).
3. En los datos de CEPAL y CIAT, los derechos sobre la producción de hidrocarburos son tratados como ingresos no tributarios.
4. La data estimada incluye ingresos esperados a nivel estatal y local para el 2012.
5. CEPAL no incluye como ingresos tributarios las contribuciones a cajas de jubilaciones y pensiones de ciertos sectores como el ferroviario, el bancario y el de la Administracion Nacional de la Electricidad (ANDE).
6. Representa un grupo de 20 países de América Latina y el Caribe. Chile y México son también parte del grupo OCDE (34).
7. Representa el promedio no ponderado para los países miembros de la OCDE.

StatLink http://dx.doi.org/10.1787/888933189966

La mayor parte de los gobiernos latinoamericanos y caribeños reaccionaron tanto recortando el gasto público como instaurando políticas destinadas a incrementar la recaudación, obteniendo así una notable mejora de la gestión presupuestaria y del saldo fiscal. En la parte recaudatoria de la ecuación, las reformas fiscales y de las administraciones tributarias contribuyeron notablemente a alcanzar ese objetivo. Como parte de este proceso, el impacto de la inflación en los ingresos obligó a los responsables de dictar políticas (policy-makers) a hallar soluciones para hacer que el sistema fuera menos vulnerable a episodios inflacionistas, tales como disminuir los plazos para el pago de impuestos e indexar las obligaciones tributarias.

De esta forma, la carga fiscal del grupo de 20 países de América Latina y el Caribe aumentó cerca de 6.9 puntos porcentuales del PIB entre 1990 y 2013. Pero la reforma fiscal más significativa en América Latina y el Caribe en los años 1980 y principios de los 1990 vino constituida por la introducción del IVA. Las subsiguientes reformas relacionadas con este impuesto se han centrado en extenderlo y reforzarlo mediante la subida de la tasa impositiva y la ampliación de la base tributaria. En los años 1990, el porcentaje del IVA en el PIB aumentó 2.4 puntos porcentuales y, posteriormente, 1.3 puntos más hasta 2013 (véase el cuadro B).

Cuadro B. **Impuesto al valor agregado en porcentaje del PIB**

| | 1990 | 2000 | 2008 | 2009 | 2010 | 2011 | 2012 | 2013 |
|---|---|---|---|---|---|---|---|---|
| Argentina | 1.9 | 5.4 | 6.0 | 6.0 | 6.3 | 6.5 | 6.9 | 7.3 |
| Barbados | .. | 8.0 | 9.0 | 7.4 | 8.5 | 10.3 | 10.7 | 9.7 |
| Bolivia | 3.2 | 5.1 | 7.0 | 6.3 | 6.7 | 7.3 | 7.6 | 7.8 |
| Brasil | 10.4 | 8.6 | 8.1 | 7.7 | 7.8 | 7.8 | 8.2 | 8.2 |
| Chile | 6.3 | 7.9 | 8.4 | 7.3 | 7.6 | 7.9 | 8.1 | 8.1 |
| Colombia | 2.0 | 4.1 | 5.6 | 5.1 | 5.3 | 5.7 | 5.5 | 4.9 |
| Costa Rica | 3.2 | 4.5 | 6.0 | 4.9 | 4.8 | 4.9 | 4.9 | 4.7 |
| Ecuador | 2.0 | 4.6 | 4.6 | 4.8 | 5.6 | 5.3 | 6.2 | 6.4 |
| El Salvador | 0.0 | 5.4 | 6.8 | 6.1 | 6.7 | 6.8 | 6.7 | 6.8 |
| Guatemala | 2.4 | 4.7 | 5.5 | 4.9 | 5.1 | 5.2 | 5.3 | 5.2 |
| Honduras | 2.7 | 4.8 | 6.3 | 5.2 | 5.4 | 5.7 | 5.6 | 5.5 |
| Jamaica | 0.0 | 3.4 | 4.0 | 3.8 | 3.9 | 3.9 | 3.9 | 4.0 |
| México | 3.2 | 3.1 | 3.7 | 3.4 | 3.8 | 3.7 | 3.7 | 3.5 |
| Nicaragua | .. | 4.5 | 5.5 | 5.2 | 5.4 | 5.8 | 6.0 | 6.0 |
| Panamá | 1.3 | 0.6 | 2.3 | 2.3 | 2.9 | 3.3 | 3.3 | 3.1 |
| Paraguay | 0.0 | 4.7 | 5.5 | 5.6 | 6.3 | 6.5 | 6.5 | 6.3 |
| Perú | 1.5 | 5.3 | 7.1 | 6.3 | 6.8 | 6.7 | 6.7 | 6.8 |
| República Dominicana | 1.3 | 2.6 | 4.7 | 4.2 | 4.3 | 4.2 | 4.0 | 4.5 |
| Uruguay | 5.5 | 6.5 | 9.2 | 8.9 | 8.9 | 8.7 | 8.7 | 8.6 |
| Venezuela | 0.0 | 4.1 | 4.6 | 5.9 | 5.5 | 6.2 | 6.8 | 7.4 |
| Promedio no ponderado: | | | | | | | | |
| ALC (20)[1] | 2.5 | 4.9 | 6.0 | 5.6 | 5.9 | 6.1 | 6.3 | 6.2 |
| OCDE (34)[2] | 5.2 | 6.4 | 6.4 | 6.2 | 6.5 | 6.5 | 6.6 | .. |

1. Representa un grupo de 20 países de América Latina y el Caribe. Chile y México son también parte del grupo OCDE (34).
2. Representa el promedio no ponderado para los países miembros de la OCDE.

StatLink http://dx.doi.org/10.1787/888933189971

Entre 2000 y 2013, el incremento de los ingresos procedentes de los impuestos sobre la renta (principalmente, el impuesto sobre la renta de las sociedades), cercano a 1.7 puntos porcentuales del PIB, hizo de este tipo de tributos el principal motor del aumento de los ingresos tributarios, por delante del IVA. Uno de los elementos que contribuyó a este resultado fue el periodo de auge de los precios de las materias primas que se inició tras 2003, que resultó particularmente importante para algunos países de la región (ver la Sección especial S2 para más información). Otras reformas fiscales incluyeron la introducción o el desarrollo de regímenes simplificados para pequeños contribuyentes y la imposición de la propiedad sobre la base de ingresos presuntos. Además, en el último quinquenio se han impulsado varias reformas del impuesto sobre la renta en América Latina y el Caribe, donde ha predominado el efecto positivo de ampliaciones de las bases imponibles del impuesto debido a la extensión de la tributación al conjunto de ingresos del trabajo y de las rentas de capital, incluida la aplicación de impuestos a dividendos

(Colombia, Guatemala, El Salvador, Nicaragua, Panamá, Perú, República Dominicana), además de otras medidas que han incluido el establecimiento de impuestos mínimos, la reducción de exenciones, la precisión de gastos deducibles para acotarlos, la gradual reducción del nivel de ingreso real al cual es aplicada la máxima tasa marginal y cierto control de los precios de transferencia (CEPAL, 2013).

El cambio en la recaudación procedente de los impuestos sobre los bienes y servicios, los impuestos sobre la renta y las utilidades, y las contribuciones a la seguridad social contribuyó principalmente a la recuperación de la participación de los ingresos tributarios en el PIB desde el 2010. Estos aumentos en los ingresos tributarios se deben parcialmente a la recuperación de la actividad económica en América Latina y el Caribe, y en cierta medida, también a la recuperación de los precios de las materias primas (CEPAL-OCDE, 2012).

## B. Estructuras impositivas

A medida que los niveles impositivos han ido aumentando en América Latina y el Caribe, la estructura impositiva (esto es, la proporción de las principales categorías de impuestos respecto al total de ingresos tributarios) ha venido transformándose también significativamente entre 1990 y 2013. El cuadro C plasma las diversas tendencias registradas en la "combinación tributaria" (tax mix) que se desprenden de los datos. Las tendencias más destacadas se han observado en relación con los impuestos sobre el consumo y los impuestos sobre la renta y las utilidades.

Cuadro C. **Estructuras impositivas en un grupo de países de América Latina y del Caribe**[1]

| | 1990 | 2000 | 2010 | 2011 | 2012 | 2013 |
|---|---|---|---|---|---|---|
| Impuestos sobre ingresos y utilidades | 23 | 22 | 26 | 26 | 27 | 27 |
| Contribuciones a la seguridad social | 14 | 16 | 16 | 16 | 17 | 17 |
| Impuesto sobre la nómina | 1 | 1 | 1 | 1 | 1 | 1 |
| Impuestos sobre la propiedad | 5 | 4 | 4 | 4 | 4 | 4 |
| Impuestos generales sobre el consumo | 21 | 31 | 33 | 33 | 32 | 32 |
| Impuestos específicos sobre el consumo | 31 | 24 | 19 | 18 | 18 | 17 |
| Otros impuestos[2] | 5 | 3 | 2 | 2 | 2 | 2 |
| Total | 100 | 100 | 100 | 100 | 100 | 100 |

1. Representa la proporción de las principales categorías de impuesto en el total de ingresos tributarios. El grupo de 20 países está listado en el cuadro A.
2. Incluye algunos impuestos sobre bienes y servicios (partida 5200) e impuestos de timbres.

StatLink http://dx.doi.org/10.1787/888933189983

La proporción global de los impuestos (generales y específicos) sobre el consumo permaneció bastante estable durante el periodo de referencia, pero el peso de los impuestos generales sobre el consumo aumentó considerablemente, 11 puntos porcentuales, entre 1990 y 2013, mientras que la incidencia de los impuestos específicos sobre el consumo cayó 14 puntos en ese mismo periodo.

Estas dos tendencias antagónicas en el seno de los impuestos sobre el consumo se explican por la creciente incidencia del IVA y la pérdida de importancia de impuestos específicos sobre el consumo tales como los impuestos selectivos o los impuestos sobre el comercio internacional. Aunque el IVA fue introducido tempranamente en las economías de la región (la mayoría de los países ya lo habían adoptado de alguna forma a finales de los años 1970), su expansión en términos de ingresos tributarios es relativamente reciente. Desde principios de los años 1990, este impuesto ha venido constituyendo una fuente creciente de ingresos para los países latinoamericanos y caribeños y se ha consolidado mediante sucesivas ampliaciones de la base tributaria y de las tasas impositivas oficiales así como también a través del fortalecimiento de las administraciones tributarias. Las reformas se han enfocado también en la simplificación de los sistemas tributarios, con la mayoría de los países reduciendo el número de bienes con tasa nula o reducida, encaminándose así a un sistema de tasa única para el IVA en muchos casos.

En contraste, el declive del peso de los impuestos específicos sobre el consumo tiene que ver con los procesos de liberalización del comercio, y la consiguiente reducción de los derechos de aduanas sobre las importaciones, y la supresión de los impuestos sobre las exportaciones en numerosos países latinoamericanos y caribeños (con la destacable salvedad de Argentina, donde los impuestos sobre las exportaciones se reestablecieron en 2002). Además, se ha acotado el conjunto de bienes y servicios sujetos a impuestos selectivos, que hoy se limitan principalmente a productos y servicios con una demanda relativamente inelástica, tales como bebidas alcohólicas, combustible y derivados, y tabaco.

Al mismo tiempo, han crecido los ingresos procedentes de la renta y las utilidades, que han pasado del 23% al 27% del total de ingresos tributarios entre 1990 y 2013, esencialmente como resultado de niveles de recaudación mucho más elevados a finales de los años 2000. Por lo general, en los países latinoamericanos y caribeños, la participación del impuesto sobre la renta de las sociedades es superior a la del impuesto sobre la renta personal, y el incremento general de esta categoría refleja el notorio aumento de los ingresos generados por la tributación de las sociedades, especialmente las empresas del sector de los recursos naturales. Sin embargo, el peso de los impuestos sobre la renta y utilidades en el total de la recaudación cayó entre 2009 y 2010, probablemente debido al impacto de la crisis sobre los ingresos y utilidades, para posteriormente crecer hasta 26.8% en 2013 (Cuadro C).

En cuanto a las contribuciones a la seguridad social, en promedio, la proporción de los ingresos procedentes de esta categoría en el PIB aumentó entre 1990 y 2013, pasando de un 2.1% a un 3.8% en ese periodo (Cuadro 6). Su peso en los ingresos tributarios totales pasó de un 13.9% a un 17.1% en ese mismo período (Cuadro 7). Este resultado traduce en realidad la actuación de dos fuerzas contrapuestas. En primer lugar, el incremento de las rentas personales ha empujado al alza las cantidades recaudadas. Pero este efecto se ha visto contrarrestado y, a menudo, más que compensado, por los variados procesos de privatización total o parcial registrados en numerosos países de la región. En este sentido, ha habido gran heterogeneidad en la forma en que los países han instaurado y reformado sus regímenes de seguridad social. Algunos países, como Chile, México y Perú, se basan en gran medida en regímenes privados de capitalización individual, lo que explica los niveles relativamente bajos de la recaudación por contribuciones a la seguridad social. En los países con sistemas públicos o mixtos, tales como Barbados, Brasil, Costa Rica, Ecuador, Nicaragua, Panamá, Paraguay y Uruguay, las contribuciones a la seguridad social aún mantienen una significativa importancia (más del 20% del total de ingresos tributarios). En Argentina, las cifras reflejan la introducción de sistemas de capitalización en 1994 y su posterior nacionalización en 2008.

Si se comparan los países de la OCDE y de América Latina y el Caribe, salta a la vista la principal diferencia de estructura impositiva entre estos dos grupos: en relación con la OCDE, América Latina y el Caribe registra una incidencia de los impuestos directos relativamente baja, compensada por ingresos fiscales elevados en concepto de impuestos indirectos (véase el gráfico B). En concreto, América Latina y el Caribe dependen significativamente de los impuestos sobre los bienes y servicios, que representan aproximadamente la mitad de los ingresos tributarios totales, en comparación con el

30% en el caso de las economías de la OCDE. A título comparativo, obsérvese que, en América Latina y el Caribe, cerca del 40% de los ingresos tributarios procede de la suma de los impuestos sobre la renta y las utilidades y de las contribuciones a la seguridad social, frente al 60% en la OCDE. Esta mayor dependencia de los impuestos indirectos puede acarrear que el sistema tributario sea más regresivo.

Gráfico B. **Estructuras impositivas en América Latina y la OCDE, 2012**

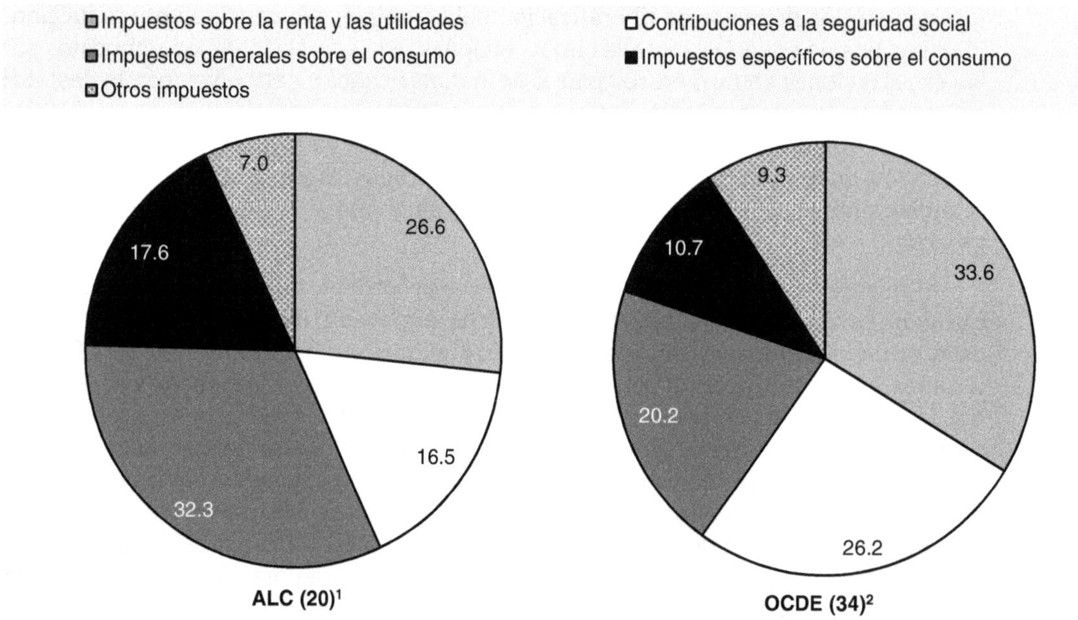


1. Representa un grupo de 20 países de América Latina y el Caribe. Chile y México son también parte del grupo OCDE (34).

2. Representa el promedio no ponderado de los países miembros de la OCDE.

*Fuente:* Cuadro 2 y Cuadros 5-15 en Parte II.

StatLink http://dx.doi.org/10.1787/888933189885

En 2012, la proporción media, en relación con el PIB, de los ingresos tributarios procedentes de la suma de los impuestos sobre la renta y las utilidades y de las contribuciones a la seguridad social era del 9.3% en el grupo de países latinoamericanos y caribeños, mientras alcanzaba el 20.4% en los países de la OCDE. Cabe señalar que, en América Latina y el Caribe, esos impuestos desempeñan una función secundaria como fuente de ingresos en comparación con la zona de la OCDE. La proporción de las contribuciones a la seguridad social sobre el total de ingresos tributarios era 10 puntos porcentuales menor en América Latina y el Caribe que en la OCDE (el 16.5% frente al 26.2%). Tal y como se ha apuntado anteriormente, la tendencia hacia una provisión privada de servicios de seguridad social en numerosos países latinoamericanos explica parte de las diferencias en esta categoría. Por su parte, la proporción de los impuestos sobre la renta y las utilidades era 7 puntos porcentuales inferior (26.6% frente al 33.6%).

Los ingresos procedentes de los impuestos sobre la renta personal contribuyeron en un 25% a la recaudación tributaria agregada de la zona de la OCDE en 2012, mientras que esta categoría representa una proporción considerablemente menor en los países latinoamericanos y caribeños. Anteriores estudios de la OCDE (OCDE, 2008; Daude, Melguizo y Neut, 2010) parecen sugerir que esto viene condicionado principalmente por dos factores: en primer lugar, la participación de la renta procedente del trabajo en el PIB es sustancialmente más débil en América Latina y el Caribe que en los países de la OCDE; y, en segundo lugar, su distribución implica que hay relativamente menos contribuyentes, dada la concentración de los perceptores en los niveles de renta inferiores. Además, varios estudios de la CEPAL (CEPAL, 2010; Gómez Sabaini et al., 2010) añaden dos factores: la elevada brecha de incumplimiento del impuesto sobre la renta en los países latinoamericanos y una base imponible más limitada, compuesta fundamentalmente por salarios, dados los privilegios fiscales otorgados a las ganancias del capital.

Como contrapartida de la menor importancia de los gravámenes directos, los impuestos generales sobre los bienes y servicios representan una significativa parte de la recaudación tributaria total. En 2012, esta subpartida supuso en la región el 32.3% del total de los ingresos tributarios mientras la cifra correspondiente en la zona de la OCDE fue sólo del 20.2%. Sin embargo, el peso de los impuestos generales sobre bienes y servicios como proporción del PIB es bastante similar tanto en América Latina y el Caribe como en la OCDE, con porcentajes del 6.8%.

Por último, los impuestos sobre la propiedad inmueble y la nómina (incluidos en "Otros impuestos" en el gráfico B) no constituyen importantes fuentes de ingresos para los países latinoamericanos y caribeños. Las dificultades que encuentran los gobiernos subnacionales para recaudar sus propios tributos quedan ejemplificadas por la escasa capacidad de generar ingresos que tienen los impuestos sobre la propiedad, que suelen ser la principal fuente de entradas de los gobiernos locales de la región (Brossio y Jiménez, 2012). Por su parte, los impuestos sobre la nómina han sido insignificantes durante todo el periodo, en parte porque este tipo de mecanismos no está muy desarrollado en América Latina y el Caribe. Sin embargo, conviene señalar que la falta de datos a escala subnacional dificulta el análisis de estas categorías. Las proporciones de los impuestos sobre la propiedad y la nómina en la recaudación tributaria total de los países latinoamericanos son similares, en promedio, a las de los países de la OCDE.

## C. Impuestos por nivel de gobierno

Desde mediados de los años 1980, las economias de América Latina y el Caribe han experimentado de forma generalizada reformas que implican la transferencia de funciones gubernamentales desde el gobierno central a entidades subnacionales. En su primera fase, la ola de descentralización se centró principalmente en reforzar el carácter democrático de las autoridades locales. A esto siguió una creciente tendencia a que, paulatinamente, una parte cada vez mayor del gasto público se ejecutase a escala subnacional.

Pese a ello, el alcance de las políticas tributarias subnacionales de la región ha permanecido relativamente modesto y se concentra en un reducido número de impuestos. Los datos disponibles parecen apuntar que la mayoría de los países latinoamericanos y caribeños no se han ocupado de reforzar los ingresos que reciben las instancias subnacionales. Entre 1995 y 2012, la parte de ingresos recaudada por los niveles de gobierno subnacional descendió entre 0.8 y 3.9 puntos en Argentina, Brasil y Uruguay y aumentó en 0.9 y 0.4 puntos porcentuales en México y Colombia. En los otros países con datos disponibles sobre las tendencias en los ingresos subnacionales, la proporción varió menos de un punto porcentual. Al mismo tiempo, la proporción de los fondos de seguridad social cayó en 9 de los 20 países latinoamericanos y caribeños estudiados, a veces debido a su privatización total o parcial. Las caídas más nítidos en este ámbito se registraron en Colombia y Uruguay (con descensos de casi 14 y 6 puntos porcentuales, respectivamente). Los mayores incrementos a la seguridad social se llevaron acabo en Nicaragua y Barbados (7 y 4 puntos porcentuales, respectivament) (véase el cuadro D).

A fin de comparar la atribución de los ingresos en los países latinoamericanos y caribeños con la de los miembros de la OCDE, cabe tener en cuenta previamente dos cuestiones estadísticas. En primer lugar, los ingresos de ambos grupos se han atribuido a los diferentes niveles de gobierno de acuerdo con lo recogido en la versión final 2008 del Sistema de Cuentas Nacionales (SCN), según el cual, los ingresos se atribuyen por lo general al nivel de gobierno que ejerce la facultad de aplicar el impuesto o que puede a su discreción establecer y modificar la tasa del impuesto. Esto tiene claras implicaciones para aquellas situaciones en que un nivel de gobierno recauda los ingresos tributarios y los transfiere, en todo o en parte, a otros niveles. Ejemplos regionales de este tipo de mecanismos son la Ley de Coparticipación de Argentina; el Fondo General de Participación de México establecido en la Ley de Coordinación Fiscal; y los Fondos de Participación de Brasil definidos en el artículo 159 de la Constitución de este país. La segunda cuestión está relacionada con el hecho de que los datos para algunos países latinoamericanos y caribeños se ven afectados por la falta de estadísticas de ingresos tributarios en la esfera subnacional.

Considerando las dos acalaraciones anteriores, la atribución de los ingresos tributarios en América Latina y el Caribe, en comparación con la OCDE, parece estar muy orientada hacia las entidades centrales o federales, mientras que las actividades subnacionales dependen más claramente de las transferencias que reciben de niveles superiores de la Administración. En todos los países latinoamericanos, menos en uno, las entradas de los gobiernos centrales representaron cerca de dos tercios o más de la recaudación total, mientras los países de la OCDE arrojan un resultado aproximado del 60%. Brasil constituye la notable excepción a la regla, ya que atribuye menos del 50% a la Administración federal, entre otras, porque en este país una gran parte del IVA (ICMS – imposto sobre operações relativas à circulação de mercadorías e prestação de serviços de transporte interestadual e intermunicipal e de comunicação) se recauda en la esfera subnacional. Aunque en menor medida, Argentina cuenta también con una significativa recaudación a nivel estatal, que se explica en parte por la existencia del impuesto sobre los ingresos brutos, un impuesto provincial sobre las ventas.

Todo lo anterior pone de manifiesto que los gobiernos subnacionales latinoamericanos y caribeños tienden a tener competencia sobre un abanico de impuestos restringido. Los impuestos que más frecuentemente se atribuyen a las instancias subnacionales son aquellos que gravan la propiedad, las licencias de vehículos automotores, las tasas por servicios específicos, así como ciertas tasas municipales, y no cabe duda de que el potencial de generación de ingresos de esos instrumentos es relativamente limitado en comparación con las bases tributarias atribuidas a los órganos centrales, tales como el IVA o los impuestos sobre la renta. En los países miembros de la OCDE, las entidades subnacionales tienden a disponer en promedio de bases tributarias potenciales mucho más amplias. De hecho, una proporción sustancial de la recaudación tributaria de los gobiernos subnacionales de los países de la OCDE se obtiene de los impuestos sobre la renta y utilidades, que representan más de un tercio de la cantidad total recaudada a nivel sub-nacional. Por el contrario, ninguno de los países latinoamericanos o caribeños para los que se dispone de datos registra recaudación alguna en concepto de impuestos sobre la renta por parte de los gobiernos subnacionales.

## Cuadro D. Atribución de los ingresos tributarios en los sub-sectores del gobierno general como porcentaje del ingreso tributario total[1]

| | Gobierno central | | | Gobierno estatal o regional | | | Gobierno local | | | Fondos de seguridad social | | |
|---|---|---|---|---|---|---|---|---|---|---|---|---|
| | 1995 | 2000 | 2012 | 1995 | 2000 | 2012 | 1995 | 2000 | 2012 | 1995 | 2000 | 2012 |
| **Países federales** | | | | | | | | | | | | |
| Argentina | 59.0 | 66.4 | 62.7 | 17.5 | 17.8 | 15.1 | .. | .. | .. | 23.4 | 15.8 | 22.2 |
| Brasil | 44.7 | 47.8 | 45.1 | 26.8 | 25.3 | 24.3 | 3.7 | 3.4 | 5.4 | 24.8 | 23.5 | 25.9 |
| México | 80.1 | 80.7 | 81.0 | 2.1 | 2.0 | 2.9 | 1.1 | 0.8 | 1.2 | 16.6 | 16.5 | 14.9 |
| Venezuela | 94.6 | 94.6 | 95.8 | .. | .. | .. | .. | .. | .. | 5.4 | 5.4 | 4.2 |
| OCDE[2,3] | 53.3 | 56.5 | 54.5 | 15.9 | 15.3 | 16.5 | 7.7 | 6.9 | 7.6 | 22.9 | 21.1 | 21.3 |
| **Países regionales** | | | | | | | | | | | | |
| Colombia[4] | 63.2 | 68.6 | 76.4 | 5.5 | 5.6 | 4.2 | 8.6 | 9.4 | 10.3 | 22.7 | 16.4 | 9.0 |
| OCDE[5] | 50.4 | 49.0 | 22.3 | 4.8 | 7.6 | 32.2 | 8.5 | 9.1 | 9.9 | 35.8 | 33.8 | 35.1 |
| **Países unitarios** | | | | | | | | | | | | |
| Barbados | 85.3 | 84.3 | 81.6 | | | | .. | .. | .. | 14.7 | 15.7 | 18.4 |
| Bolivia | 100.0 | 91.2 | 94.0 | | | | .. | .. | .. | .. | 8.7 | 6.0 |
| Chile | 89.9 | 87.8 | 88.2 | | | | 6.5 | 7.9 | 6.7 | 3.6 | 4.4 | 5.1 |
| Costa Rica | 66.2 | 65.3 | 61.7 | | | | .. | 2.1 | 3.0 | 33.8 | 32.6 | 35.3 |
| Ecuador | 73.9 | 87.7 | 72.1 | | | | .. | .. | .. | 26.1 | 12.3 | 27.9 |
| El Salvador | 85.9 | 83.6 | 89.3 | | | | .. | .. | .. | 14.1 | 16.4 | 10.7 |
| Guatemala | 83.8 | 83.6 | 83.0 | | | | 0.6 | 0.9 | 1.5 | 15.6 | 15.5 | 15.6 |
| Honduras | 90.1 | 89.4 | 82.9 | | | | .. | .. | .. | 9.9 | 10.6 | 17.1 |
| Jamaica | 100.0 | 99.3 | 95.5 | | | | .. | 0.7 | 0.9 | .. | .. | 3.6 |
| Nicaragua | 84.0 | 80.1 | 77.1 | | | | .. | .. | .. | 16.0 | 19.9 | 22.9 |
| Panamá | 62.0 | 59.6 | 66.1 | | | | .. | 2.2 | 1.6 | 38.0 | 38.2 | 32.4 |
| Paraguay[6] | 100.0 | 82.7 | 80.6 | | | | .. | .. | 3.0 | .. | 17.3 | 16.4 |
| Perú | 88.2 | 87.7 | 86.7 | | | | .. | .. | 3.1 | 11.8 | 12.3 | 10.1 |
| República Dominicana | 99.3 | 99.0 | 99.6 | | | | .. | .. | .. | 0.7 | 1.0 | 0.4 |
| Uruguay | 62.0 | 62.5 | 70.0 | | | | 7.8 | 7.9 | 3.9 | 30.1 | 29.6 | 26.1 |
| OCDE[2,6] | 65.8 | 66.4 | 62.9 | | | | 10.7 | 11.0 | 12.0 | 23.2 | 22.3 | 24.8 |

1. Las cifras excluyen los ingresos de gobiernos locales en Argentina (pero incluye ingresos de las provincias), Barbados, Bolivia, Costa Rica (hasta 1997), República Dominicana, Ecuador, El Salvador, Honduras, Jamaica, Nicaragua, Panamá (hasta 1998), Paraguay (hasta 2004 y 2013), Perú (hasta 2004), Uruguay (2013) y Venezuela dado que los datos no están disponibles.
2. Chile y México son también parte del grupo OCDE.
3. Representa el promedio no ponderado para los países federales miembros de la OCDE.
4. Colombia es constitucionalmente un país unitario con una estructura política descentralizada.
5. Representa a España, que es constitucionalmente un país no federal con una estructura política altamente descentralizada.
6. Representa el promedio no ponderado para los países unitarios miembros de la OCDE.

StatLink http://dx.doi.org/10.1787/888933189999

## Referencias

Brossio, G. y J. P. Jiménez (2012), *Decentralization and Reform in Latin America: Improving Intergovernmental Relations*, Edward Elgar, próxima publicación, Cheltenham, UK y Northampton, MA.

CEPAL (Comisión Económica para América Latina y el Caribe) (2013), *Panorama fiscal de América Latina y el Caribe: reformas tributarias y renovación del pacto fiscal*, Santiago de Chile.

CEPAL (2011), *Estudio económico de América Latina y el Caribe 2010-2011*, CEPAL, Santiago de Chile.

CEPAL (2010), "La Hora de la igualdad. Brechas por cerrar, caminos por abrir", (LC/G.2432(SES.33/3)), CEPAL, Santiago de Chile.

CEPAL-OCDE (2012), *Perspectivas Económicas de América Latina 2013: Políticas de pymes para el cambio estructural*, CEPAL y OCDE, http://dx.doi.org/10.1787/leo-2013-es.

Daude, C., A. Melguizo y A. Neut (2010), "Fiscal Policy in Latin America: Countercyclical and Sustainable at Last?", *Documentos de trabajo*, No. 291, Centro de Desarrollo de la OCDE, París.

Gómez Sabaini, J.C., J.P. Jiménez y A. Podestá (2010), "Evasión y equidad en América Latina", *Documentos de proyectos*, No. 309 (LC/W.309/ Rev.1), CEPAL, Santiago de Chile.

OCDE (2014), *Revenue Statistics 1965-2013*, OCDE, París, http://dx.doi.org/10.1787/rev_stats-2014-en-fr

OCDE (2008), *Perspectivas Económicas de América Latina 2009*, OCDE, París, http://dx.doi.org/10.1787/leo-2009-es

# SECCIÓN ESPECIAL S1
# Características de la presión fiscal en América Latina y el Caribe[1]

## Introducción

Las iniciativas de estandarización son esenciales en un mundo heterogéneo y globalizado, ya que permiten una variedad de comparaciones y posibilidades analíticas. En el área fiscal, la Organización para la Cooperación y el Desarrollo Económicos (OCDE) ha sido una institución pionera en la manera en que los ingresos tributarios son clasificados y cuantificados, no solo para países miembros de la OCDE[2] sino para otros países del mundo.

Como punto central de la clasificación que la OCDE hace sobre los ingresos fiscales está la definición de impuestos como "pagos obligatorios al gobierno general que no conllevan una contraprestación". Esta definición tiene tres elementos distintivos, cada uno con una base sólida. En primer lugar, es generalmente aceptado que los impuestos son pagos "obligatorios". En segundo término, si las estadísticas fiscales deben reflejar los esfuerzos del Estado para cobrar impuestos a sus ciudadanos, es difícil de catalogar a un pago como impuesto a menos que sea pagado "al gobierno". Por último, desde la perspectiva de la OCDE, ya que hay una amplia gama de circunstancias en las que los gobiernos prestan servicios a cambio de un pago, tales casos deben distinguirse de aquellos en los que el pago "no tiene contraprestación" y simplemente se da como consecuencia de la residencia personal o corporativa del individuo.

Ha habido numerosos intentos para definir y normalizar la forma en la que los ingresos fiscales deben contabilizarse. Todas estas comparaciones han resaltado de manera consistente los bajos niveles de recaudación tributaria en América Latina y, en menor medida, en el Caribe, relativos a países más desarrollados. Sin embargo, como suele ser el caso, la realidad es mucho más compleja. Los sistemas utilizados por los gobiernos para recaudar ingresos varían en su estructura y dimensiones. En el caso de los países de América Latina y el Caribe (ALC), es posible tener una mejor perspectiva acerca de la naturaleza y magnitud de la interacción entre los ciudadanos y el gobierno cuando se hace un análisis más profundo de los ingresos fiscales. Éstos deben reflejar, por ejemplo, el hecho ampliamente conocido que los países de ALC obtienen ingresos significativos de la explotación de recursos naturales. Por otra parte, existen arreglos públicos y privados para el financiamiento de los programas de seguridad social que no están reflejados integralmente en las comparaciones y definiciones internacionales.

En este sentido, es útil tomar en consideración las fuentes adicionales de ingresos o "ingresos equivalentes" además de la recaudación impositiva tradicional. En este artículo especial, la incorporación de estos dos rubros resulta en la construcción teórica del concepto denominado Presión Fiscal Equivalente (PFE). Para este fin, es importante establecer los conceptos básicos que componen la PFE (Barreix et al. 2013a). El primero es la recaudación impositiva tradicional, que comprende todos los impuestos directos e indirectos que gravan a los ciudadanos en todos los niveles de gobierno. El segundo viene dado por los aportes y contribuciones sociales obligatorias, ya sean públicos o privados, a los sistemas de pensiones y salud. Finalmente, la tercera parte está dada por todos los ingresos no-tributarios derivados de la explotación de recursos naturales, renovables y no renovables; es decir, cánones, royalties, dividendos pagados y ganancias netas que empresas públicas (de propiedad total o parcial del Estado) que explotan recursos naturales, transfieren a las arcas del Estado.

PFE = ingresos impositivos del gobierno general + aportes y contribuciones obligatorias a los sistemas de seguridad social + ingresos no-tributarios derivados de la explotación de recursos naturales renovables y no renovables

Este indicador de ingresos fiscales podría brindar un panorama más amplio para ALC, tanto desde la perspectiva de los recursos a disposición de un Estado, como del esfuerzo fiscal demandado a los ciudadanos. En efecto, el gráfico S1.1 demuestra que los componentes 2 y 3 de la PFE son comunes y significativos para la región.

Gráfico S1.1. **Presión Fiscal Equivalente (1990-2013)**

Porcentaje del PIB (ejes izquierdo y superior)

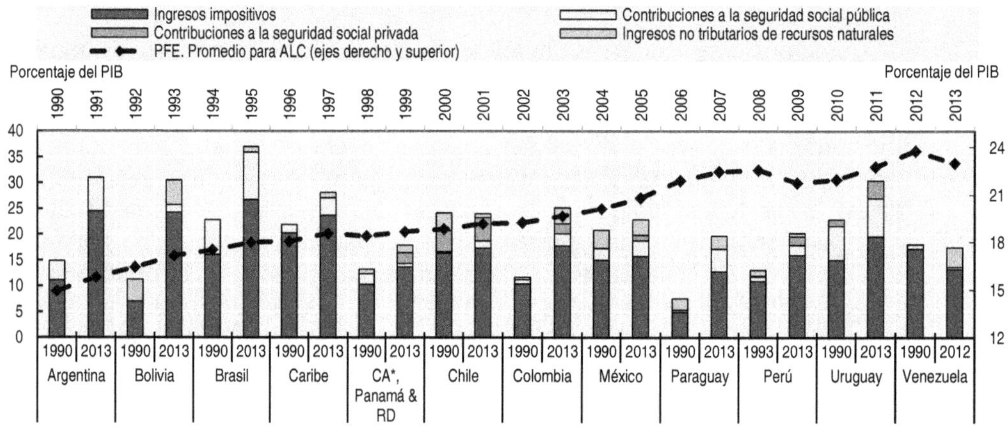


*Nota*: Los valores para el Caribe, *CA (Centroamérica), Panamá y República Dominicana son promedios simples.
*Fuentes*: Cuadros 1 y 4 y Base de datos BID-CIAT 2014.[3]

StatLink http://dx.doi.org/10.1787/888933189890

El gráfico S1.1 distingue todos los conceptos considerados por la PFE, a saber: ingresos impositivos, aportes y contribuciones obligatorias a la seguridad social pública y privada e ingresos provenientes de la explotación de recursos naturales renovables y no renovables. Por otra parte, resalta los efectos que las doce reformas estructurales a la seguridad social, que se dieron entre 1981 y 2008, han tenido sobre el panorama fiscal regional, así como la importante participación de los ingresos derivados de recursos naturales para diez países de la región.

Cabe señalar que pese al considerable esfuerzo fiscal de ALC durante las últimas dos décadas, aún persiste una brecha significativa en sus ingresos relativa a otros países más desarrollados. Estas diferencias son evidentes cuando se compara la recaudación en términos absolutos. Para ello, se calculó el ingreso per cápita promedio ponderado de la OCDE y ALC en dólares estadounidenses medidos en poder de paridad de compra del año 2011, para reflejar los niveles relativos en la capacidad de consumo.

Las diferencias son notorias como lo muestra el gráfico S1.2. El promedio ponderado del recaudo per cápita (en paridad de poder adquisitivo) para la OCDE para el período 2011-13 fue tres veces superior al de ALC, y aproximadamente siete veces más al de Centroamérica, Panamá y la República Dominicana (CA-PA-RD). La brecha es menor cuando se compara con el promedio agregado de los países que componen el Mercosur, México y Chile, los que exhiben el ingreso per cápita más alto de la región. Este grupo alcanzó un recaudo per cápita cercano a un tercio del promedio de la OCDE. Esta brecha pone de relieve el significativo diferencial de ingresos para financiar servicios públicos, y la necesidad imperativa de mejoras en las áreas de política y administración tributaria en la región.

Gráfico S1.2. **Presión Fiscal Equivalente, per cápita y como % del PIB**[a]

PPP, US dólares internacionales constantes de 2011

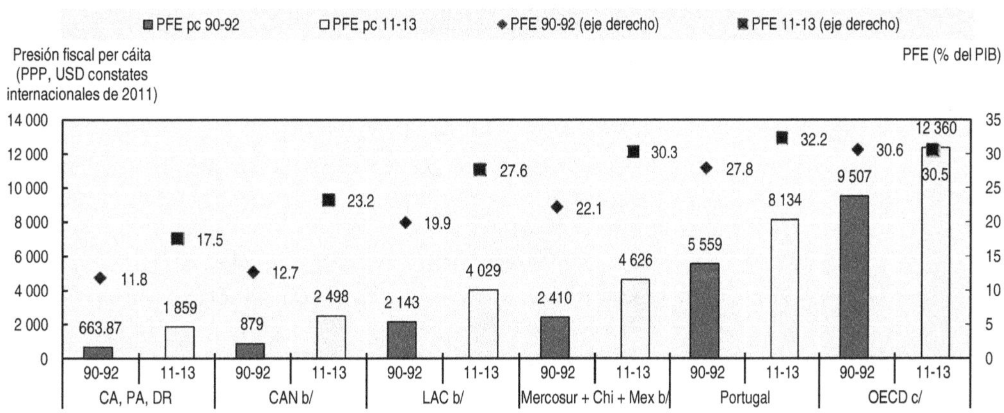


*Notas*: a/ Los promedios y la presión fiscal per cápita fueron ponderados por el PIB en poder de paridad de compra, en dólares estadounidenses constantes del año 2011. b/ LAC y las distintas subregiones no incluyen Argentina y Ecuador. Mercosur incluye a Brasil, Paraguay y Uruguay. c/. OCDE no incluye a Chile, Eslovaquia, Eslovenia, Estonia, Israel, México y República Checa.

*Fuente*: BID-CIAT (2014), Banco Mundial (2014).

StatLink http://dx.doi.org/10.1787/888933189903

Las siguientes secciones proveen una explicación más detallada de las nuevas variables en la ecuación de la presión fiscal equivalente para los países de América Latina y el Caribe.

## La *revolución* de la seguridad social en América Latina

A principios de la década de los ochenta, en la denominada "década perdida", América Latina experimentó una serie de reformas a sus sistemas de seguridad social que, indiscutiblemente, han influido en la forma en la que los ingresos fiscales pueden ser contabilizados en América Latina. La característica principal de la reforma liderada por Chile en 1981, fue la introducción de cuentas de capitalización individual del ahorro previsional administradas por el sector privado. Este fue el primer experimento de este tipo, bajo el que se permitió al libre mercado financiar los sistemas de pensiones a la vez que se desfasó gradualmente el tradicional sistema de reparto. En dicho momento, los partidarios de la reforma la defendieron bajo el supuesto de que la responsabilidad individual promovería el ahorro nacional y la formalidad laboral, contribuiría al desarrollo de mercados de capitales y los subsiguientes retornos al capital, así como protegería los fondos previsionales de intromisiones políticas (Uthoff, 2001; Gill, Packard y Yermo, 2005; Bosch, Melguizo y Pagés, 2013).

Siguiendo el ejemplo chileno, varios otros países indujeron reformas estructurales en sus sistemas nacionales de pensiones. Estos cambios, si bien diversos y complejos, han sido agrupados en tres categorías:

- "El modelo sustitutivo" (Chile, 1981; Bolivia, 1997 revertido en el 2010; El Salvador, 1998; y México, 1997), en el cual el sistema público es sustituido por uno totalmente financiado a través de aportes a cuentas de capitalización individual y administrado de forma privada.

- "El modelo paralelo" (Perú, 1993; Colombia, 1994), el cual termina con el monopolio estatal mediante la introducción de una alternativa privada. En este modelo, los sistemas de jubilación públicos y privados coexisten y compiten, y los trabajadores pueden elegir entre ambos sistemas al ingresar al mercado laboral.
- "El modelo mixto" (Argentina, 1994, revertido en 2008; Uruguay, 1996; Costa Rica, 2001; República Dominicana, 2003; Panamá 2005-2007), en el que la provisión de un servicio de pensión básico y universal es complementado por aportes obligatorios a cuentas individuales de capitalización administradas por fondos de pensiones privados. Bajo este modelo, los esquemas no contributivos y contributivos se unen en un único programa (Mesa-Lago, 2000; Bonilla y Conte-Grand, 1998; Rofman, Apella y Vezza, 2013).

La ola más reciente de reformas estructurales, denominada como "las re-reformas" (Mesa-Lago, 2009), buscó instaurar estabilidad en los sistemas de pensiones y adaptarlos al contexto socio-económico de cada país. Por ejemplo, Argentina (2008) decidió suprimir el pilar privado de jubilación, dejando únicamente el sistema de reparto tradicional, a la vez que amplió la cobertura al incluir a los que quedaban fuera del sistema. De forma similar, Bolivia (2007) nacionalizó su sistema de pensiones una vez más y estableció tres pilares: uno contributivo para la vejez, discapacidad y sobrevivientes; uno semi-contributivo que funge como un fondo de solidaridad; y finalmente un pilar no contributivo para financiar el bono Dignidad.

En una línea diferente, en el año 2008 Chile introdujo un pilar no-contributivo como complemento del pilar privado existente. En 2009, tanto El Salvador como Perú introdujeron garantías de pensión mínima para empleados de bajos ingresos que no alcanzaran el mínimo de contribuciones establecido por la legislación. Este último grupo de países completó vacíos en sus sistemas pero no cambió la naturaleza del sistema privado.

Como se mencionó anteriormente, el enfoque de las Estadísticas de Recaudación Tributaria de la OCDE es el de medir el monto de los impuestos pagados al gobierno y el establecer las fuentes de estos ingresos. Sin embargo, desde la perspectiva del empleador o el empleado, el que el pago sea realizado al sector público o privado es de poca consecuencia en el corto plazo, ya que ambos afectan el costo laboral total. El tamaño de la carga fiscal, es decir, el esfuerzo fiscal demandado a los ciudadanos, se verá afectado dada la naturaleza obligatoria de las contribuciones sociales, las cuales claramente se asemejan a un impuesto a los ojos del contribuyente, independientemente de que estén definidos como impuestos o no. El elemento crítico es entonces entender las responsabilidades y obligaciones fiscales para el Estado que surgieron de estas reformas.

En este sentido, las dos últimas categorías de sistemas de pensiones indicadas arriba requieren la participación activa del Estado. Si bien es cierto que su participación se redujo en el modelo sustitutivo, éste todavía desempeña un papel importante como regulador y garante del sistema privado. En la mayoría de los casos el Estado financió la transición, la cual ha representado un sustancial costo fiscal que todavía está siendo pagado por la mayoría de países que atravesaron esas reformas. Adicionalmente, varios estudios han demostrado que las pensiones pagadas a través de los sistemas de reparto tradicionales tienden a ser regresivas, lo que genera dudas sobre la solidaridad de los programas de seguridad social públicos (Barreix, Bès y Roca, 2009; Barreix, Roca y Villela, 2007; y Lustig et al., 2013).

Asimismo, los sistemas de seguridad social abarcan una serie de programas públicos, especialmente en seguros de salud, que los hacen complejos e indivisibles. Los datos también indican que, contrariamente a la intuición (ver gráfico S1.3), las contribuciones al pilar público no se redujeron significativamente en los países en los que se instauraron modelos sustitutivos. De hecho, los aportes al sistema público en México se incrementaron, pese a que en este país el pilar público fue cerrado a nuevos entrantes y una gran parte de sus contribuyentes fue obligada a migrar al nuevo sistema previsional privado. Pero incluso en aquellos países que sí experimentaron un declive en las contribuciones al sector público (Argentina, Uruguay y El Salvador) la caída no fue importante, a pesar del incremento en los aportes al pilar privado. Esto quizá pueda ser explicado por el vínculo intrínseco entre los sistemas de pensiones y salud (enfermedad, maternidad, excluyendo el pago de beneficios, y riesgos del trabajo) y a que el principal objetivo de las reformas fue aumentar la cobertura y con ello reafirmar la solidaridad[4] dentro del sistema. En este ámbito, prácticamente todos los países latinoamericanos reformaron sus sistemas de salud (Mesa-Lago, 2013). Este tipo de reformas, sin embargo, no alteró el rol del sector privado en este mercado de seguros, al menos no en la misma forma en el que las reformas estructurales en los sistemas de pensiones cambiaron fundamentalmente el panorama de las finanzas públicas en la región.

Igualmente, la transferencia de responsabilidades importantes hacia el sector privado no representó una separación total del sistema por parte del gobierno, inclusive bajo el modelo sustitutivo. En la mayoría de los casos, los gobiernos han regulado los destinos de inversión dentro de la cartera de las administradoras privadas de pensiones, requiriendo en no pocas ocasiones que estas entidades adquieran bonos estatales hasta un tope fijado legalmente. Con ello, la separación del gobierno de la gestión de los sistemas de pensiones es discutible.

La separación entre los sistemas públicos y privados es también difusa por otros motivos. En Colombia, por ejemplo, los individuos pueden elegir cambiar entre el sistema privado o público cada cinco años, y una última vez diez años antes de su retiro. Esto implica que en caso que los aportes efectuados al sector privado sean transferidos al pilar público, éstos son ahora considerados como ingresos tributarios. México es un caso similar. El Instituto Mexicano del Seguro Social (IMSS) recauda las contribuciones de los ciudadanos y las transfiere al Instituto del Fondo Nacional de la Vivienda para los Trabajadores (INFONAVIT) y a las cuentas individuales dentro del sistema de ahorro administrado por las Administradoras de Fondos para el Retiro (AFOREs). Inclusive, se aumenta el grado de complejidad porque los recursos administrados por las AFOREs son invertidos en fondos de inversión para el retiro especializados llamados SIEFORES, en los cuales las "autoridades federales determinan el criterio para la composición de la cartera de inversiones, indicando el tipo y las características de los distintos instrumentos financieros, así como los límites aceptados" (Rofman, Apella y Vezza, 2013). Asimismo, en México se permite a una porción significativa de ciudadanos, aquellos que estaban trabajando previo a la reforma, escoger entre recibir la pensión que habrían recibido bajo el régimen anterior bajo un esquema de reparto o el beneficio definido correspondiente bajo el régimen privado (Mesa-Lago, 2000; Rofman, Apella y Vezza, 2013). En ambos casos, los fondos son fungibles entre los pilares público y privado del sistema. Por otra parte, Argentina no contabilizaba los aportes al pilar privado. Sin embargo, luego de la contra-reforma de 2008 que nacionalizó el sistema de jubilación, dichos aportes fueron registrados como tributos, aunque las bases y tasas de aportes y contribuciones no cambiaran.

## Gráfico S1.3. **Contribuciones y aportes públicos y privados a la seguridad social**

Porcentaje del PIB

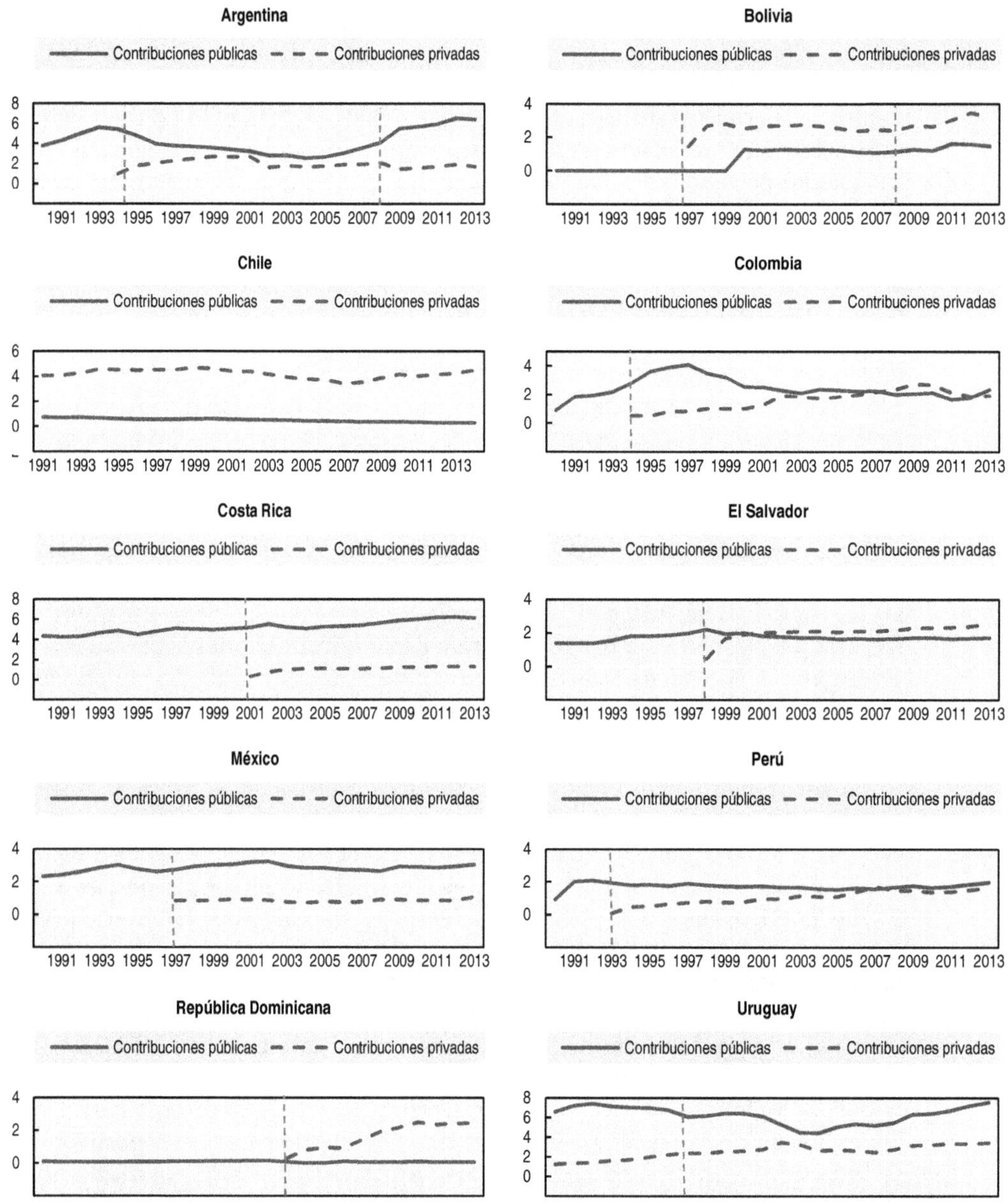


*Notas*: Líneas verticales indican año de reforma.
*Fuente*: Cuadro 4 y IDB-CIAT (2014).

StatLink http://dx.doi.org/10.1787/888933189918

Cualquiera sea el análisis, para muchos países de ALC los recursos de los esquemas privados de pensiones[5] son de tal magnitud que son difíciles de ignorar, especialmente en el marco de comparaciones internacionales (Cuadro S1.1).

## Cuadro S1.1. Características de los sistemas de seguridad social en ALC

| País | Seguros Privados Obligatorios | Contribuciones a la Seguridad Social 2013 (% del PIB) | | Fondos Privados Administrados 2013 (% del PIB) | Invertidos en Títulos Nacionales de Gobierno (% Del Total de los Fondos Administrados 2013) |
|---|---|---|---|---|---|
| | | Público | Privado | | |
| Argentina[a] | - | 6.5 | | | |
| Barbados | - | 6.0 | | | |
| Bolivia[b] | X | 1.5 | | 31.34 | 36.42 |
| Brasil | - | 9.2 | | | |
| Chile | X | 0.3 | 4.5 | 58.85 | 21.47 |
| Colombia | X | 2.4 | 1.9 | 17.96 | 40.48 |
| Costa Rica | X | 6.2 | 1.3 | 11.15 | 77.86 |
| República Dominicana | X | 0.1 | 2.4 | 7.45 | 65.46 |
| Ecuador | - | 4.9 | | | |
| El Salvador | X | 1.7 | 2.5 | 30.18 | 81.13 |
| Guatemala | - | 2.0 | | | |
| Honduras | - | 3.3 | | | |
| Jamaica | - | 1.0 | | | |
| México | X | 3.0 | 1.1 | 13.02 | 46.05 |
| Nicaragua | - | 4.6 | | | |
| Panamá | - | 6.6 | | 1.59 | 0.00 |
| Paraguay | - | 1.3 | | | |
| Perú | X | 2.0 | 1.6 | 17.51 | 13.47 |
| Trinidad y Tobago | - | 1.9 | | | |
| Uruguay | X | 7.5 | 3.4 | 18.65 | 70.74 |
| Venezuela | - | 0.4 | | | |

*Notas:* a En el 2008, la reforma pensional aplicó un sistema universal de seguro social. Antes de este año y luego de 1993, los empleados aportaban a una cuenta de capitalización individual administrada por un fondo de pensiones privado escogido por el empleado. b En 2010, la Ley de Pensiones N°065 de Bolivia creó el Sistema Integral de Pensiones (SIP). Bajo esta ley, los fondos administradores de pensiones renuncian a la responsabilidad de administración. La ley establece una nueva agencia pública, la Gestora Pública de la Seguridad Social de Largo Plazo (GSS) dentro del Ministerio de Economía y Finanzas Públicas. Las Administradoras de Fondos de Pensiones (AFPs) se encuentran en un período de transición dentro del cual todavía operan.
*Fuentes:* Cuadro 4, FIAP (2014), BID-CIAT (2014), y SSA (2014).

StatLink http://dx.doi.org/10.1787/888933190001

### Ingresos no tributarios provenientes de recursos naturales

"Las cuentas nacionales se encuentran en constante evolución" (Piketty, 2014). Hasta hace media década, el concepto de contabilidad ambiental era desconocido para la mayoría. Esto cambió de forma fundamental con la publicación del reporte de Stiglitz, Sen y Fitoussi (2009), el cual plantea que el nivel de riqueza agregado sirve como un indicador útil para medir el bienestar general de un país. Desde entonces, se han hecho esfuerzos importantes para medir el valor del capital natural[6] (Banco Mundial, 2011) como un componente de cuentas más amplias de riqueza y como una forma de medir el desarrollo sostenible.

Se puede hacer una analogía con el ejemplo anterior para el tercer componente de la PFE. La clasificación de las Estadísticas de Recaudación Tributaria de la OCDE se enfoca en aquellos ingresos gubernamentales catalogados como impuestos. Sin embargo, los países también reciben ingresos no tributarios, y en América Latina y el Caribe, muchos tienen una fuente de ingreso derivada de su capacidad de explotación de rentas económicas naturales, en ocasiones mediante monopolios estatales. La inclusión de estos ingresos no tributarios al agregado de ingresos fiscales permite un cómputo diferente de los recursos fiscales que están a disposición de un número significativo de países de ALC. Primero, es difícil concebir las finanzas públicas de la región sin considerar la importancia de los recursos naturales. La estructura tributaria, el esfuerzo fiscal demandado a los ciudadanos, las reglas fiscales, el desempeño macroeconómico, y otros aspectos de las políticas públicas son impactadas por las riquezas naturales de los países. En este sentido, se ha señalado reiteradamente que los países de ALC dependen de los impuestos sobre el consumo en mayor medida que otras regiones, porque estos impuestos tienden a tener un impacto limitado en actividades exportadoras (OCDE-BID, 2014) y porque los impuestos al consumo son más fáciles de recaudar que los impuestos a la renta, siendo los ingresos por consumo y renta los agregados tributarios más grandes. En la década pasada, se han registrado mejoras significativas en el desempeño macroeconómico por la introducción de reglas fiscales que capturan las rentas de commodities y que han provisto un suficiente margen para el manejo del gasto y del pasivo público. De forma similar, los fondos de estabilización han mitigado los efectos de la volatilidad derivada de las fluctuaciones de los precios de los commodities. Además, el hecho de que la crisis financiera internacional reciente haya sido breve y leve en varios países de ALC puede ser explicado en gran parte por la fortaleza macroeconómica generada por el ahorro de buena parte de los ingresos provenientes de recursos naturales.

Los ingresos provenientes de recursos naturales difieren tanto por su fuente como por su naturaleza, lo cual complica su contabilización. Por ejemplo, Panamá dispone de una privilegiada situación geográfica que lo ha convertido en una plataforma logística única. Las tarifas pagadas por los clientes que usan el canal han significado un promedio de 2.4 puntos del PIB durante los últimos 20 años y se espera que incrementen un 50% más con la expansión. Si bien, técnicamente, esta fuente de ingresos no puede catalogarse como un impuesto, este flujo no es despreciable en relación a los ingresos tributarios, excluyendo las contribuciones a la seguridad social, los cuales únicamente sumaron 11.2% del PIB en el mismo período. De forma similar, Paraguay vende la electricidad generada por sus dos centrales hidroeléctricas, Itaipú y Yacyretá, a sus vecinos Argentina y Brasil. Esto le reportó ingresos anuales de 2.7% del PIB, en promedio, durante las últimas dos décadas. Una característica común de estos países es que ambos explotan los recursos naturales mediante una empresa nacional que luego transfiere sus ganancias netas al tesoro nacional.

Este tipo de arreglos institucionales es común en la región. Por ejemplo, el gobierno federal de México recibió sustanciales pagos y transferencias de Pemex, la empresa petrolera estatal, año tras año. Durante las últimas dos décadas estas transferencias alcanzaron, en promedio, 2.7 puntos del PIB.[7] Una situación similar se da en países como Chile, Bolivia, Colombia, Ecuador, Trinidad y Tobago y Venezuela, países en los que una empresa estatal posee algún tipo de monopolio o ejerce poder de mercado sobre la explotación de los recursos naturales y transfiere una porción de sus ingresos netos a las arcas del tesoro nacional. Es muy probable que Argentina, que posee la segunda reserva mundial más grande de gas de esquistos, y Brasil, con su producción única de petróleo "pre-sal", se unan pronto al club.

Tampoco debería sorprender que exista una relación tan fuerte entre las fluctuaciones de precios de commodities y los recursos fiscales disponibles en ALC. En la mayoría de los países, una proporción abrumadora de las exportaciones totales se concentra en cinco productos por lo cual su recaudación es susceptible a la volatilidad de los precios internacionales. El gráfico S1.4 muestra la relación directa entre el promedio de la PFE, ponderado por el PIB, y un índice de precios de commodities ajustado. Este índice ha sido construido bajo la premisa metodológica de que las variaciones en los precios de materias primas afectan significativamente a los países de LAC. Este índice está definido por el peso de cada materias primas en la estructura exportadora de cada país en forma de índice de precios promedio, y es ponderado por el PIB de cada país.[8]

Gráfico S1.4. **PFE e Índice de Precios de Commodities, América Latina y el Caribe**

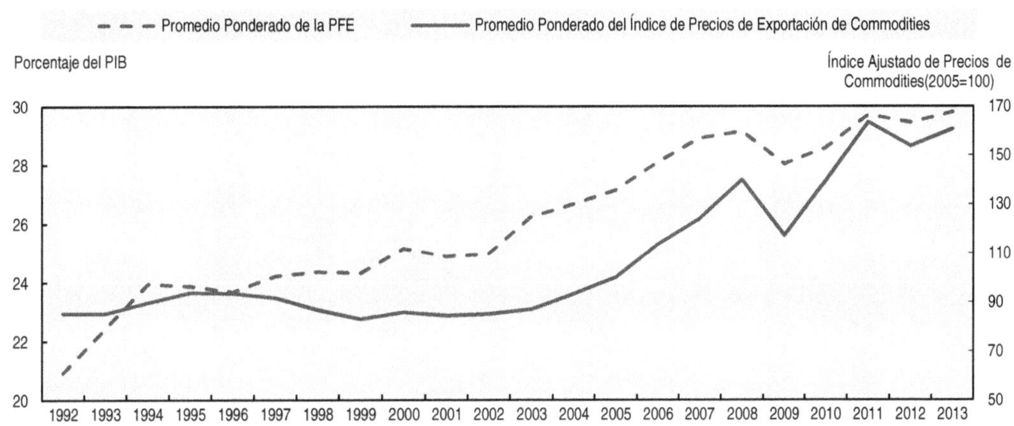


*Fuente*: Preparado por los autores con base en Cuadro 1, Barreix et al. (2013a), BID-CIAT (2014), FMI(2014) y OMC(2014).

StatLink http://dx.doi.org/10.1787/888933189929

Finalmente, el flujo de ingresos no tributarios apropiados por el gobierno proveniente de recursos naturales se remonta varias décadas atrás para muchos países. En algunos casos, éstos han representado una fuente importante de recursos fiscales. El período de precios extraordinariamente altos de commodities únicamente ha acentuado la importancia de estos recursos y la necesidad de incrementar las rentas que los gobiernos obtienen de la explotación de estas dotaciones naturales, ya sea por actores públicos o privados.

## Conclusión

Desde la perspectiva de los autores, el análisis de los ingresos fiscales en ALC que incluyen los componentes de la metodología de cómputo de la PFE podría proporcionar una visión más integral del grado de movilización doméstica de recursos que se da en ALC.

Es difícilmente rebatible que los gobiernos imponen una carga fiscal a los empleadores y empleados cuando se les exige contribuir a los sistemas de seguridad social, ya sean éstos públicos o privados. Sin duda, desde la perspectiva del individuo, el esfuerzo fiscal realizado es el mismo, independientemente del tipo de arreglo institucional establecido por el gobierno para asegurar la independencia financiera de las personas en sus años de vejez. Así, las rondas de reformas y "re-reformas" de los sistemas de pensiones, y también los de salud, han creado modelos de gestión de elevada complejidad en el cual los límites de la participación privada y estatal no están claramente determinados pero que sí pueden y deben contabilizarse que es lo que propone la PFE.

Adicionalmente, los ingresos provenientes de la explotación de recursos naturales se han incrementado significativamente en la última década. Esto catalizó la puesta en marcha de una amplia gama de arreglos institucionales para la apropiación de los mismos en los países de ALC. La robustez que ha tenido este componente en la provisión de recursos fiscales – aunque fluctuante – se refleja en la PFE. A su vez, así se destaca la necesidad de mejorar tanto la manera en que se apropian y gravan estos flujos como la gestión de sus impactos macroeconómicos, a través de instrumentos de prudencia fiscal como reglas fiscales o fondos de estabilización.

## Notas

1. Los autores de esta Sección Especial son Alberto Barreix, Juan Carlos Benítez, Martin Bès, Miguel Pecho, Agnes Rojas y Fernando Velayos. Las opiniones y argumentos utilizados en el presente documento son de sus autores y no representa necesariamente las del Banco Interamericano de Desarrollo (BID), del Centro Interamericano de Administraciones Tributarias (CIAT), de la Organización de Cooperación y Desarrollo Económicos (OCDE) ni de los gobiernos de los países miembros.
2. La OCDE presenta estadísticas tributarias comparables internacionalmente en un formato estándar para todos sus países miembros desde 1965. Disponible en: www.oecd-ilibrary.org/taxation/data/oecd-tax-statistics_tax-data-en.
3. La base de datos BID-CIAT 2014 de ingresos fiscales está disponible en: www.iadb.org/en/research-and-data/publication-details,3169.html?pub_id=IDB-DB-101. Esta base de datos detalla la recaudación por tipo de impuesto a cada nivel de gobierno. También presenta cifras de los aportes privados y públicos obligatorios a la seguridad social e ingresos procedentes de recursos naturales. Los datos han sido compilados a partir de las agencias tributarias y hacendarias de los países, institutos estadísticos y empresas públicas, OCDE (2014, Estadísticas Tributarias para América Latina) e información provista a la sociedad BID-CIAT por autoridades locales. Los perfiles de cada país han sido contrastados con las autoridades fiscales locales.
4. El promedio de las primas está basado en el riesgo colectivo. Por lo tanto, la contribución no guarda relación con el riesgo de un individuo en particular. Existen transferencias entre generaciones y los beneficios están estandarizados en cierta medida. Un detalle mucho más pormenorizado de las reformas a los sistemas de salud puede encontrarse en Mesa-Lago (2013), capítulos 7–10.
5. De forma similar a lo que ocurrió con las pensiones, el precedente que sentó el Gobierno de Estados Unidos con la Ley de Protección al Paciente y Cuidado de la Salud Asequible, popularmente conocida como "Obamacare", por la cual la Corte Suprema de Estados Unidos aprobó la obligatoriedad de contar con un seguro de salud, debería abonar al debate sobre si los pagos hechos a proveedores privados deben ser considerados como impuestos. Nuestras estimaciones arrojan un incremento de aproximadamente 16 por ciento de la carga fiscal para los Estados Unidos en 2014.
6. Comprende rentas económicas o ganancias derivadas de tierras agrarias, áreas protegidas, bosques, minerales y energía. $V_t = \sum_{i=t}^{t+T-1} \left(\frac{\pi_i q_i}{(1+r)^{(1-t)}}\right)$, donde $\pi_i q_i$ es la ganancia económica o rentas totales derivadas de recursos naturales en el período i, r es la tasa de descuento social y T es el tiempo de vida esperado del recurso natural.
7. Además, es importante hacer notar que en México, en los años previos a la reciente reforma fiscal y energética, se subsidiaba mucho el consumo interno de combustibles durante épocas de precios altos.
8. Para la construcción de este índice ajustado se estimó la estructura exportadora de commodities de cada país usando los datos disponibles en la Organización Mundial del Comercio. (http://stat.wto.org/Home/WSDBHome.aspx?Language=E). Estas estructuras sirvieron de ponderadores para reflejar los cambios que los precios de commodities (FMI data mensual, agregada por año: www.imf.org/external/np/res/commod/index.aspx) representaron para cada país. Para el resultado de la serie final, los sub-índices resultantes fueron promediados ponderando por el PIB de cada país.

## *Referencias*


Banco Mundial (2014), *World Development Indicators*. Available at: http://data.worldbank.org/data-catalog/world-development-indicators. Consultado en Septiembre 19, 2014.

Banco Mundial (2011), *The Changing Wealth of Nations. Measuring Sustainable Development in the New Millennium*, Banco Mundial, Washington, DC.

Barreix, A., J. Roca y L. Villela, editores (2006), "Equidad Fiscal en la Comunidad Andina: Impacto Redistributivo de los Impuestos y Gastos Públicos". *Serie de Equidad Fiscal del BID*; Comunidad Andina, www.comunidadandina.org/public/libro_EquidadFiscal.pdf.

Barreix, A., M. Bès y J. Roca (2009), editores, "Fiscal Equity in Central America, Panama and the Dominican Republic", *Serie de Equidad Fiscal del BID*; EUROsociAL y Banco Interamericano de Desarrollo, Washington, DC.

Barreix, A, M. Bès, J. C. Benitez, M. Pecho y F. Velayos. (2013), "Equivalent Fiscal Pressure in Latin America and the Caribbean: Concept, Development and International Comparisons", *Working Paper* 9/2013, Instituto de Estudios Fiscales de España, www.ief.es/documentos/recursos/publicaciones/papeles_trabajo/2013_09.pdf.

BID-CIAT (2014), *Dataset de Presión Fiscal Equivalente* 2014. Disponible en: www.iadb.org/en/research-and-data/publication-details,3169.html?pub_id=IDB-DB-101.

Bonilla-García, A. y A. Conte-Grand (comps.) (1998), *Pensiones en América Latina. Dos Décadas de Reformas*, Oficina Internacional del Trabajo, Ginebra.

Bosch, M., A. Melguizo y C. Pagés (2013), *Mejores Pensiones, Mejores Trabajos. Hacia la cobertura universal en América Latina y el Caribe*, Banco Interamericano de Desarrollo. Washington, DC.

Cetrángolo, O y A. Goldschmit (2009), "Metodología, experiencia comparada y recomendaciones", en O. Cetrangolo (ed.), *La seguridad social en América Latina y el Caribe. Una propuesta metodológica para su medición y aplicación a los casos de Argentina, Chile y Colombia*, Economic Commission for Latin America and the Caribbean, Santiago, Chile.

Federación Internacional de Administradores de Pensiones, FIAP (2012), "Informe Semestral No. 33, Federación Internacional de Administradoras de Fondos de Pensiones 31.12.2012". Disponible en: www.fiap.cl/prontus_fiap/site/artic/20130818/asocfile/20130818182859/informe_semestral_n__33.pdf. Consultado en Agosto 20, 2014.

FMI (2014), *World Economic Outlook*, Fondo Monetario Internacional, Washington, DC. Disponible en: www.imf.org/external/pubs/ft/weo/2014/01/.

Gill, I., T. Packard y J. Yermo (2005), *Keeping the Promise of Social Security in Latin America*, Banco Mundial, Washington, DC. Disponible en: https://openknowledge.worldbank.org/bitstream/handle/10986/7391/344330PAPER0LA101official0use0only1.pdf?sequence=1. Consultado en Septiembre 19, 2014.

Lustig, et al. (2013), "The Impact of Taxes and Social Spending on Inequality and Poverty in Argentina, Bolivia, Brazil, Mexico, Peru and Uruguay: An Overview", *ECINEQ WP* 2013-15, ECINE Society for the Study of Economic Inequality.

Machinea, J. L. (2014), "En Busca de un Marco Fiscal para América Latina", *Colección de Estudios* 4. Programa Eurosocial, Madrid.

Mesa-Lago, C. (2013), *Reassembling Social Security: A Survey of Pensions and Health Care Reforms in Latin America*, Oxford University Press, Oxford.

Mesa-Lago, C. (2009), "Re-reform of Latin American Private Pensions System: Argentinean and Chilean Models and Lessons", *The Geneva Papers* 34 (602–617).

Mesa-Lago, C. (2000), "Estudio Comparativo de los Costos Fiscales en la Transición de Ocho Reformas de Pensiones en América Latina", *Financiamiento del desarrollo series* 93, CEPAL. Santiago, Chile.

OCDE-BID (2014), *Government at a Glance: Latin America and the Caribbean 2014*, OECD Publishing, Disponible en: http://dx.doi.org/10.1787/9789264209480-en.

OECD-ECLAC-CIAT (2014), *Revenue Statistics in Latin America* 2014, OECD Publishing, Paris, http://dx.doi.org/10.1787/9789264207943-en-fr.

Organización Mundial del Comercio – OMC (2014), Base de Datos estadística. Disponible en: www.wto.org/english/res_e/statis_e/data_pub_e.htm.

Piketty, T. (2014), *Capital in the Twenty-First Century*, Harvard University Press, Cambridge, MA.

Rofman, R., I. Apella y E. Vezza (eds.) (2013), *Más Allá de las Pensiones Contributivas. Catorce experiencias en América Latina*, Banco Mundial. Buenos Aires.

Ruezga Barba, A. (1995), "Administración Pública y Privada de los Seguros Sociales en América Latina", *Serie Estudios* 16, Conferencia Interamericana de Seguridad Social.

Social Security Administration, SSA (2014), "Social Security Programs throughout the World: The Americas, 2013". SSA *Publication* 13-11804, Social Security Administration, Washington, DC. Disponible en: www.ssa.gov/policy/docs/progdesc/ssptw/2012-2013/americas/ssptw13americas.pdf.

Stiglitz, J., A. Sen and J. P. Fitoussi (2009), "Report by the Commission on the Measurement of Economic Performance and Social Progress", Documento mimeografiado. Disponible en: www.stiglitz-sen-fitoussi.fr/documents/rapport_anglais.pdf.

Uthoff, A. (2001), "La Reforma del Sistema de Pensiones en Chile: Desafíos pendientes", *Financiamiento del desarrollo series* 112, CEPAL, Santiago, Chile.

# SECCIÓN ESPECIAL S2
# Ingresos fiscales provenientes de recursos naturales no renovables en América Latina

## Los ingresos por recursos naturales no renovables, con respecto al PIB, se mantuvieron estables en 2013

En 2013, los ingresos públicos por recursos naturales no renovables en América Latina se mantuvieron constantes, con respecto al PIB, reflejando la estabilidad relativa de los precios internacionales del petróleo crudo y las altas ganancias realizadas en 2012. El promedio de los ingresos por hidrocarburos en los siete principales productores de la región aumentaron de 7.4% del PIB en 2012 a 7.8% en 2013. En cambio, los ingresos por minería siguieron cayendo, de un promedio regional de 1.1% del PIB en 2012 a 0.7% en 2013. No obstante, el valor de los ingresos por recursos naturales no renovables, medido en dólares corrientes, alcanzó un nuevo record de USD 258 600 millones (Gráfico S2.1).

Gráfico S2.1. **Ingresos fiscales provenientes recursos naturales no renovables, 2013**

En miles de millones de dólares y porcentajes del PIB

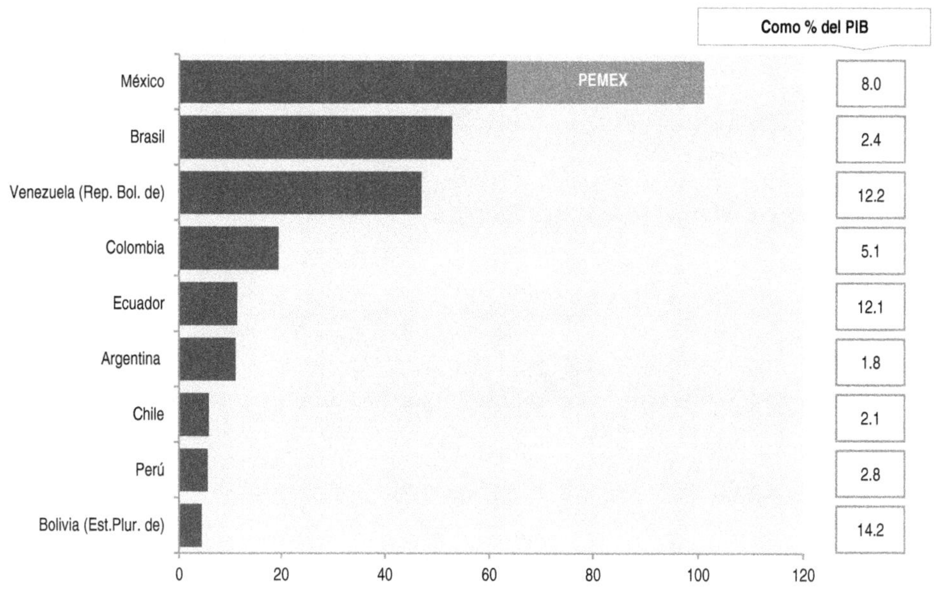


*Fuente:* CEPAL.

StatLink http://dx.doi.org/10.1787/888933189938

La estabilidad relativa de los ingresos por recursos naturales no renovables en 2013 en su promedio regional oculta una heterogeneidad en los resultados al nivel de los países (Gráfico S2.2). Entre los nueve países considerados en el presente trabajo, cinco países registraron un aumento de sus ingresos con respecto al PIB. En general este incremento fue menor al 1% del PIB, con Venezuela como clara excepción. Estos ingresos cayeron en cuatro países, con Ecuador registrando la caída más significativa como porcentaje del PIB. Generalmente los aumentos en ingresos se asocian con aquellos provenientes de la explotación de los hidrocarburos. En cambio, los ingresos por minería cayeron en casi todos los países.

Gráfico S2.2. **Cambio en los ingresos fiscales provenientes recursos naturales no renovables, 2012-13**

En porcentajes del PIB

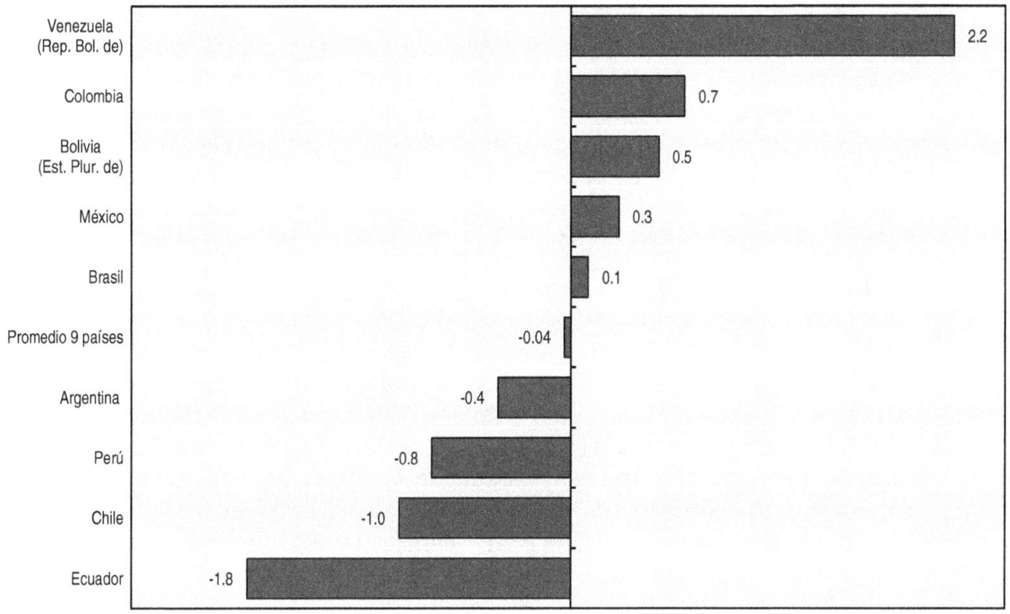


*Fuente:* CEPAL.

StatLink http://dx.doi.org/10.1787/888933189942

El alza en los ingresos petroleros en Venezuela, que aumentaron 2.2% del PIB, se explica en mayor parte por la devaluación de la moneda nacional en el año y por un aumento significativo de los ingresos no tributarios extraordinarios. Sin embargo, cabe mencionar que los ingresos petroleros como porcentaje del PIB siguen estando por debajo del promedio de 14.6% del PIB que habían logrado entre 2005-07. Los dividendos pagados de Petróleos de Venezuela S.A. (PDVSA) al gobierno central en el año alcanzaron VEF 69 mil millones (bolívares fuentes), gracias la ganancia cambiaria y la venta de una participación de 40% de su filial Empresa Nacional Aurífera al Banco Central. Los ingresos petroleros del gobierno central por concepto del impuesto sobre la renta, que a su vez refleja en buena parte las utilidades obtenidas en 2012 antes de la devaluación, disminuyó como porcentaje del PIB dado que aún no incluyen el impacto de la devaluación del tipo de cambio. En cambio, los ingresos no tributarios del dominio petrolero – sobre la producción, la extracción y las exportaciones – aumentaron 39.5% como resultado de la devaluación y la revisión en febrero de la Contribución Especial por Precios Extraordinarios y Precios Exorbitantes en el Mercado Internacional de Hidrocarburos. Esta medida incrementó el límite máximo del cálculo de estos ingresos de USD 70 a USD 80 por barril y reformuló la estructura del pago de la contribución – que sirve como el aporte de PDVSA al FONDEN, un fondo de desarrollo extrapresupuestario – sobre este valor. El efecto neto de este cambio para los ingresos fiscales del gobierno central probablemente será limitado dado que un aumento en los costos de producción – a través de regalías e impuestos sobre la extracción – reducirá las utilidades operacionales y a su vez la contribución del impuesto sobre la renta.

En Colombia los ingresos por recursos naturales no renovables aumentaron debido al alza en los ingresos no tributarios del sector hidrocarburo. En particular, los dividendos pagados por Ecopetrol al gobierno central casi se duplicaron como resultado del pago de un dividendo extraordinario y de la reducción en pasivos pendientes desde años anteriores. La disminución del precio promedio de crudo colombiano resultó en un leve declive en el pago de regalías. Los ingresos por concepto del impuesto sobre la renta de Ecopetrol, que refleja en parte los resultados del año anterior, también disminuyeron siguiendo la caída de 3.7% en las utilidades operacionales en 2012 como resultado del menor volumen de ventas y de un aumento en los costos operacionales. La reciente reforma tributaria en Colombia que redujo la tasa del impuesto sobre la renta de sociedades al 25% pero creó un nuevo impuesto para equidad (CREE) de 9% sirvió para aumentar la tasa efectiva que Ecopetrol pagará aunque su impacto total sobre los ingresos tributarios del gobierno central se manifestará en 2014. Los ingresos por minería, básicamente en la forma de regalías de la extracción de carbón, que es el principal producto mineral que exporta el país, cayeron conforme a la reducción en los precios internacionales.

Los ingresos por la explotación del gas natural en el Estado Plurinacional de Bolivia continuaron creciendo fuertemente en 2013. Se explica esta alza por el aumento de las exportaciones a la Argentina, dado que la capacidad ociosa de los gasoductos a Brasil – el principal comprador – se ha agotado. Durante el año tanto los ingresos por concepto del Impuesto Directo a los Hidrocarburos (IDH) como los del impuesto sobre la renta del sector registraron avances del 28% y del 30%, respectivamente. El aumento en los ingresos por hidrocarburos se vio atenuado por una caída en los del sector minero, que bajaron de 1.3% del PIB en 2012 a 0.6% en 2013. La reducción en los precios internacionales – especialmente de estaño, plata y zinc – en 2012 y 2013 provocó un declive de 69.3% del pago del impuesto sobre la renta del sector durante el año.

En México los ingresos por hidrocarburos con respecto al PIB subieron ligeramente debido a la reducción significativa en el valor del "negativo" Impuesto Especial sobre Producción y Servicios (IEPS) de gasolinas y diesel que compensó la baja en los otros ingresos petroleros. El costo fiscal de este impuesto, que funciona como un subsidio cuando el precio internacional de ciertos productos de hidrocarburos está alto, cayó de 1.3% del PIB en 2012 a 0.5% en 2013. La producción del petróleo crudo de PEMEX y sus filiales descendió 1.0% en términos de volumen durante el año, con una reducción mayor de 5.3% en sus volúmenes exportados – o de 8.7% en términos de valor. Estas tendencias junto con una leve bajada en el precio del crudo mexicano, resultaron en un descenso de 6.7% en los ingresos públicos por concepto de los derechos sobre hidrocarburos. Cabe mencionar que el valor del derecho extraordinario sobre la exportación del petróleo crudo registró un declive de 47.4%. En cuanto a los ingresos públicos del sector minero, se mantuvieron estables en el año con respecto al PIB.

Una caída en los ingresos por hidrocarburos, como porcentaje del PIB, en Brasil fue contrarrestada por un aumento de los ingresos por minería. En el primer caso, se explica la reducción por una menor contribución del impuesto sobre la renta (IRPJ y CSLL) de Petrobras y por una disminución de los ingresos no tributarios como consecuencia de un descenso en la extracción de hidrocarburos en el año. Se destaca un alza en los ingresos por las actividades de "downstream" en hidrocarburos que a su vez refleja una fuerte demanda interna y una mayor producción de refinados por parte de Petrobras. Los ingresos por minería registraron un repunte en 2013 a causa del alza en el precio internacional de hierro y por el cierre de un acuerdo tributario entre Vale S.A. y el Estado. La empresa aceptó pagar por retroactivo un total de USD 9 600 millones en impuestos sobre las utilidades de sus filiales extranjeras durante un periodo de 15 años. A finales del año el valor del impuesto sobre la renta pagado por la empresa había ascendió a USD 2 600 millones, que incluyó un cobro inicial significativo establecido en el acuerdo.

En Ecuador los ingresos petroleros del sector público no financiero registraron un declive de 1.8% del PIB en 2013. A pesar del aumento en la producción y de un mayor volumen de exportaciones, el valor de las exportaciones solo aumentó 2.3% como resultado de la caída del precio del crudo ecuatoriano de USD 98.2 por barril a USD 95.6. Dado que la economía de Ecuador es dolarizada el país no obtiene beneficios – o pérdidas – por fluctuaciones en el tipo de cambio. Los ingresos por minería todavía son bastante pequeños: los pagos por regalías y licencias solo alcanzaron USD 57.2 millones en 2013. Con el fin de desarrollar este sector en junio el Congreso aprobó una reforma para potenciar la inversión privada y, al mismo tiempo, aumentar la participación del Estado en los ingresos resultantes.

Los ingresos mineros en Chile y en el Perú se vieron afectados por la caída continua del precio de cobre, cuyo valor se redujo 8% en 2013. El caso del Perú es ilustrativo de la situación que enfrentan muchos países en la región con ingresos por minería. Por un lado, los ingresos no tributarios en la forma de regalías, que constituyó 26.6% de los ingresos mineros en 2013, bajó 13.1% siguiendo la caída de los precios internacionales. Por otro lado, los ingresos tributarios, que reflejan la contribución de las empresas productoras a través del impuesto sobre la renta y del impuesto especial a la minería, cayeron 47% debido a la reducción de los márgenes de beneficio en el sector. Asimismo, en Chile la tributación de la minería privada registró una baja de 27.5%. La contribución tributaria de CODELCO también se redujo durante el año, con una caída de 70.4%, pero eso fue atenuado por un mayor rendimiento en términos de dividendos.

Una caída importante de las exportaciones petroleras en la Argentina redujo los ingresos petroleros por los derechos de exportación y a su vez los ingresos fiscales provenientes recursos naturales no renovables en general. El volumen de las exportaciones del petróleo crudo cayó 37.2% en 2013 como resultado del dinamismo de la demanda interna por productos petroleros y por el mayor control de las exportaciones por parte del gobierno. Adicionalmente, los controles de precios en el mercado doméstico impactaron las ganancias del sector resultando en un menor crecimiento en los ingresos por concepto del impuesto a las ganancias de sociedades. En respuesta a la declinación de la producción el gobierno decretó en julio la creación del Régimen de Promoción de Inversión para la Explotación de Hidrocarburos. Esta medida permite la exportación sin restricción y libre del pago del derecho de exportación de hasta 20% de los hidrocarburos producidos de proyectos con un valor de inversión de USD 1 000 millones o más. También se permite el uso libre de las divisas que provienen de estas exportaciones a las empresas que se conformen al régimen.

## El derrumbe del precio internacional del petróleo crudo en el segundo semestre de 2014 perjudicará los ingresos para ese año y los siguientes

En el tercer trimestre del año los precios internacionales referentes del petróleo crudo, que se habían mantenido estables entre 2011 y 2013, empezaron a caer. Se explica este cambio en parte por un desequilibrio en la oferta y en la demanda internacional. En el primer caso, la oferta mundial sigue siendo alta dado que el alza en la producción de hidrocarburos en los Estados Unidos no ha sido compensada por una reducción de la parte de los productores tradicionales, incluyendo los principales productores de la región. Por otro lado, la demanda por petróleo crudo se ha visto afectada por el crecimiento modesto de los países en desarrollo y la reducción en la demanda de petróleo en los países desarrollados. Esta tendencia a la baja en el precio se aceleró en el cuarto trimestre del año cuando los países miembros de la OPEP decidieron mantener sus niveles de producción para el futuro previsible. Entre la última semana de junio y la primera semana de diciembre los precios del Brent y del West Texas Intermediate (WTI) cayeron alrededor de 40%. Como resultado las previsiones por parte de los gobiernos de la región para sus ingresos petroleros así como las estimaciones de la CEPAL sugieren una caída en promedio de al menos 1% del PIB (Gráfico S2.3). Sin embargo, si los precios siguen estando por debajo de USD 70 la reducción en los ingresos petroleros será aún mayor.

Gráfico S2.3. **Ingresos fiscales provenientes recursos naturales no renovables, por grupos seleccionados de materias primas, 2000-14**

En porcentajes del PIB

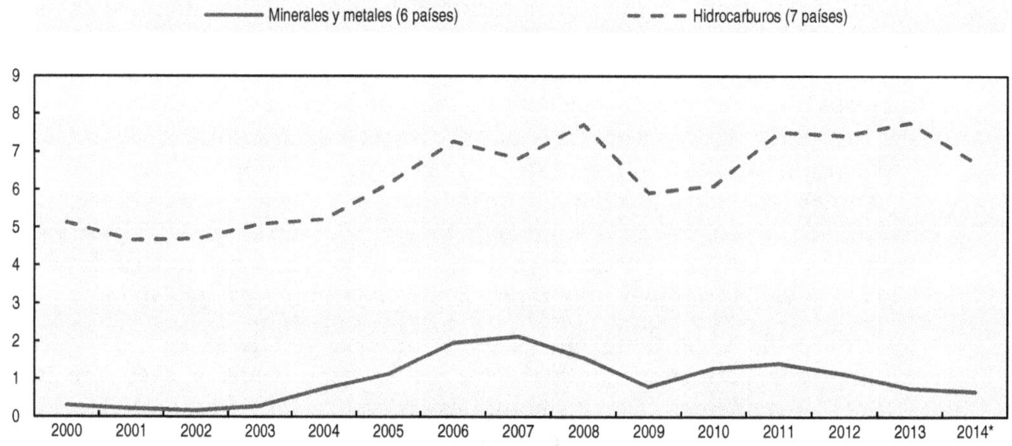


*Nota*: Los datos para 2014 provienen de previsiones gubernamentales o de estimaciones de la CEPAL basadas en las previsiones de los precios de commodities y del tipo de cambio nominal, manteniendo la producción constante. Las previsiones provienen de: los precios de commodities de EIU y el FMI; los tipos de cambio nominal de los presupuestos nacionales; y el PIB nominal de la CEPAL. Los datos desagregados para la Argentina no estaban disponibles por lo que el país no se incluye es este gráfico.

*Fuente*: CEPAL.

StatLink http://dx.doi.org/10.1787/888933189951

Se prevé una caída en los ingresos fiscales provenientes de hidrocarburos en el Estado Plurinacional de Bolivia, Ecuador y México – incluyendo los ingresos de las actividades "upstream" y "downstream" – de entre 1% y 1.5% del PIB. Los ingresos petroleros en la República Bolivariana de Venezuela, que representaron 46.6% de los ingresos totales del gobierno central en 2013, podrían aumentar algo en valor corriente pero bajarán como porcentaje del PIB dado al fuerte crecimiento previsto en el PIB nominal en 2014. En estos países el efecto del declive en los precios se combina con un crecimiento lento, o incluso una reducción, en la producción. En Colombia y en el Perú se estima una reducción en los ingresos por hidrocarburos con respecto al PIB, a pesar de un aumento en la producción de petróleo crudo y de gas natural respectivamente.

En cambio, los ingresos por minería se mantendrán o registrarán una leve disminución como porcentaje del PIB en 2014. Este resultado refleja el hecho de que la contribución del sector por el impuesto sobre la renta, que representó la mayoría del alza en los ingresos por minería durante la década, ha regresado a su nivel de antes del "boom". Los ingresos no tributarios, principalmente el pago de regalías sobre la producción, se han mantenido estables con un promedio de alrededor de 0.2% del PIB desde 2005. Cabe mencionar que entre los países bajo consideración, Chile prevé la mayor caída de alrededor de 0.2% del PIB.

Se destaca la aprobación de varias medidas importantes en 2014, especialmente con respecto al sector minero, que afectarán los ingresos por recursos naturales no renovables en 2015 y más adelante. En el Estado Plurinacional de Bolivia el gobierno logró promulgar la Ley de Minería y Metalurgia después de superar la resistencia de las cooperativas mineras. El nuevo marco regulatorio elimina ciertos privilegios de lo que habían disfrutado antes, principalmente el derecho de subscribir contratos con empresas privadas. La ley estableció un nuevo órgano para regular el sector que a su vez supervisará la renegociación de concesiones que no se acuerden con los nuevos reglamentos. En el Perú se aprobó en julio una modificación de la Ley General de Minería que expandió los convenios de estabilidad tributaria hasta 15 años para nuevas inversiones de USD 500 millones o más.

México adoptó una serie de medidas significativas en las áreas de minería y de hidrocarburos. En enero el nuevo marco fiscal para el sector minero entró en vigor. Desde esa fecha las empresas en el sector empezaron a pagar un derecho especial sobre la minería del 7.5% sobre la utilidad neta que derive de su actividad minera y un derecho extraordinario sobre la minería que corresponde al 0.5% sobre el valor bruto de la venta del oro, plata y platino. La medida también creó un derecho adicional sobre la minería que grava las concesiones sin exploración o explotación. En agosto el presidente firmó las leyes secundarias de la reforma energética de 2013, que abrió el sector de los hidrocarburos a la participación de empresas privadas por primera vez desde la nacionalización en 1938. El nuevo marco define el mecanismo de otorgar asignaciones para la exploración y la explotación de hidrocarburos así como los contratos que a los que las empresas privadas pueden suscribirse. Adicionalmente, la medida define las obligaciones fiscales de las empresas privadas que operan en el sector y al mismo tiempo racionaliza los aportes fiscales de PEMEX en conformidad con las mejores prácticas internacionales.

En octubre el Congreso de la Argentina aprobó una modificación de la Ley de Hidrocarburos con la intención de fomentar la inversión en el sector. En particular la medida tiene como propósito incentivar la exploración y la explotación de los recursos no convencionales a través de un nuevo tipo de concesión con plazos más largos y menores tarifas de regalías. Adicionalmente, todas las concesiones de hidrocarburos tienen el derecho de pedir extensiones múltiples sin límite, aunque el Estado se reserva el derecho de aumentar la tarifa de regalía por incrementos de 3% – hasta una límite de 18% – durante las primeras dos extensiones. La medida restringió el uso de otros instrumentos fiscales de los gobiernos subnacionales, dejando las regalías como la única forma de participar en la explotación de hidrocarburos en su territorio. Se modificó también el Régimen de Promoción de Inversión para la Explotación de Hidrocarburos, que había decretado en 2013, extendiendo sus beneficios a proyectos con inversiones con un valor de USD 250 millones o más, en vez del valor original de USD 1 000 millones.

### Recuadro S2.1. Los instrumentos considerados dentro del marco de los Ingresos fiscales provenientes de recursos naturales no renovables

Los datos que se presentan en este artículo provienen de una base de datos que la CEPAL mantiene para los países de la región. Se considera tanto los ingresos tributarios como los no tributarios (Cuadro S2.1). Para los ingresos de minería los datos se refieren a la explotación de los recursos. En el caso de los hidrocarburos, las estadísticas intentan capturar no solo los ingresos por la explotación de los recursos sino también los ingresos que provienen del uso del recurso en el propio país. Para más información sobre los instrumentos fiscales de cada país véase el resumen de la sección especial en Estadísticas Tributarias en América Latina 2014. Cabe mencionar que esta base de datos se actualiza constantemente con la intención de mejorar la cobertura de países así como la desagregación de los datos.

#### Cuadro S2.1. Los instrumentos considerados dentro del marco de los Ingresos fiscales provenientes de recursos naturales no renovables

| | | | Hidrocarburos | | |
|---|---|---|---|---|---|
| | Minería | | Upstream | | Downstream |
| | Tributarios | No tributarios | Tributarios | No tributarios | Tributarios |
| Argentina | • | • | • | • | • |
| Bolivia (Est. Plur. de) | • | • | • | • | • |
| Brasil | • (Vale S.A.) | • | • (Petrobras) | • | • |
| Chile | • | • | ... | ... | ... |
| Colombia | • | • | • (Ecopetrol) | • (Ecopetrol) | • |
| Ecuador | ... | ... | • | • | ... |
| México | • | • | • | • | • |
| Perú | • | • | • | • | • |
| Venezuela (Rep. Bol. de) | ... | ... | • | • | • |

*Fuente*: CEPAL.

StatLink http://dx.doi.org/10.1787/888933190010

# PART II

# TAX LEVELS AND TAX STRUCTURES 1990-2013

# PARTE II

# NIVELES IMPOSITIVOS Y ESTRUCTURAS TRIBUTARIAS, 1990-2013

# Part II / Parte II

## A. Comparative Tables, 1990-2013

In all of the following tables a ('') indicates not available or not applicable. The main series in this volume cover the years 1990 to 2013.

Figures referring to 1991-94 in Table 1 and figures relating to 1991-99, 2001-04 and 2006 in Tables 3 to 16 have been omitted because of lack of space. Complete series are, however, available on line at www.latameconomy.org.

## A. Cuadros comparativos, 1990-2013

En todos los cuadros siguientes, ('') indica no aplicable o dato indisponible. Las principales series de datos de esta sección cubren el periodo que va de 1990 a 2013.

Las cifras relativas a 1991-94 en Cuadro 1 y las cifras relativas a 1991-99, 2001-04 y 2006 en Cuadros 3 hasta 16 a se han omitido por falta de espacio. Sin embargo, las series completas están disponibles en línea en www.latameconomy.org.

## Table 1. Total tax revenue as percentage of GDP, 1990-2003
## Cuadro 1. Total de ingresos tributarios en porcentaje del PIB, 1990-2003

| | 1990 | 1995 | 1996 | 1997 | 1998 | 1999 | 2000 | 2001 | 2002 | 2003 |
|---|---|---|---|---|---|---|---|---|---|---|
| Argentina | 12.4 | 16.9 | 16.5 | 17.2 | 17.6 | 17.7 | 18.0 | 17.5 | 16.7 | 19.6 |
| Barbados | 23.0 | 27.1 | 26.7 | 30.8 | 29.1 | 28.8 | 30.2 | 31.2 | 29.6 | 31.2 |
| Bolivia[1,2] | 7.0 | 10.9 | 11.7 | 11.9 | 12.7 | 11.8 | 14.7 | 12.8 | 14.3 | 13.0 |
| Brazil / Brasil | 28.2 | 27.0 | 26.4 | 26.6 | 27.4 | 28.7 | 30.1 | 31.0 | 31.7 | 31.2 |
| Chile | 17.0 | 18.4 | 19.6 | 19.1 | 18.8 | 18.1 | 18.8 | 19.0 | 19.0 | 18.7 |
| Colombia | 9.0 | 13.8 | 14.7 | 15.6 | 15.0 | 15.0 | 14.6 | 16.3 | 16.2 | 16.7 |
| Costa Rica | 16.1 | 16.3 | 17.8 | 17.9 | 18.3 | 17.7 | 18.2 | 19.3 | 19.8 | 19.8 |
| Dominican Republic / República Dominicana | 8.3 | 10.6 | 10.4 | 11.7 | 11.7 | 12.0 | 12.4 | 13.8 | 13.7 | 12.0 |
| Ecuador | 7.1 | 7.9 | 7.4 | 8.3 | 8.8 | 8.7 | 10.1 | 11.5 | 12.3 | 11.4 |
| El Salvador | 10.5 | 13.0 | 12.3 | 12.2 | 12.3 | 12.2 | 12.2 | 12.3 | 12.9 | 13.3 |
| Guatemala | 9.0 | 10.4 | 11.3 | 11.4 | 11.5 | 12.3 | 12.4 | 12.7 | 13.7 | 13.5 |
| Honduras | 16.2 | 18.1 | 16.6 | 16.0 | 18.7 | 19.4 | 15.3 | 15.4 | 15.6 | 16.2 |
| Jamaica | 23.0 | 24.7 | 22.8 | 22.4 | 21.1 | 22.2 | 22.8 | 21.6 | 22.1 | 25.0 |
| Mexico / México[3,4] | 15.5 | 14.9 | 15.0 | 15.6 | 14.8 | 15.5 | 16.5 | 16.8 | 16.2 | 17.1 |
| Nicaragua | .. | 10.9 | 11.2 | 12.3 | 13.0 | 12.8 | 13.0 | 12.6 | 13.3 | 14.7 |
| Panama / Panamá | 14.7 | 17.1 | 17.4 | 17.1 | 16.5 | 17.2 | 16.7 | 15.6 | 15.1 | 15.0 |
| Paraguay[2] | 5.4 | 13.6 | 12.7 | 12.7 | 12.6 | 14.2 | 14.5 | 14.2 | 13.4 | 11.6 |
| Peru / Perú | 12.1 | 15.9 | 16.3 | 16.7 | 16.3 | 15.0 | 14.5 | 14.8 | 14.3 | 15.0 |
| Uruguay[2] | 19.6 | 21.0 | 21.2 | 21.9 | 22.0 | 21.6 | 21.6 | 22.0 | 21.1 | 21.5 |
| Venezuela[2] | 18.7 | 13.3 | 14.2 | 17.6 | 12.9 | 13.8 | 13.6 | 12.2 | 11.2 | 11.9 |
| *Unweighted average / Moyenne non pondérée* | | | | | | | | | | |
| **LAC / ALC[5]** | **14.4** | **16.1** | **16.1** | **16.8** | **16.6** | **16.7** | **17.0** | **17.1** | **17.1** | **17.4** |
| **OECD / OCDE[6]** | **32.2** | **33.6** | **34.0** | **34.0** | **34.0** | **34.2** | **34.3** | **33.9** | **33.6** | **33.5** |

*Note:* The figures exclude local government revenues for Argentina (but include provincial revenues), Barbados, Bolivia, Costa Rica (up to 1997), Dominican Republic, Ecuador, El Salvador, Honduras, Jamaica, Nicaragua, Panama (up to 1998), Paraguay (up to 2004 and 2013), Peru (up to 2004), Uruguay (2013) and Venezuela as the data are not available.

1. In ECLAC data the excise tax on hydrocarbons is treated as non tax revenues.
2. Estimated figures from 2011 to 2013 (Bolivia and Venezuela) and for 2013 (Uruguay and Paraguay).
3. In ECLAC and CIAT data, fees levied on hydrocarbon production are treated as non tax revenues.
4. Estimated figure for 2013 including expected revenues for state and local governments.
5. Represents a group of 20 Latin American and Caribbean countries. Chile and Mexico are also part of the OECD (34) group.
6. Calculated by applying the unweighted average percentage change for 2013 in the 30 countries providing data for that year to the overall average tax to GDP ratio in 2012.

*Nota :* Las cifras excluyen los ingresos de gobiernos locales en Argentina (pero incluye ingresos de las provincias), Barbados, Bolivia, Costa Rica (hasta 1997), República Dominicana, Ecuador, El Salvador, Honduras, Jamaica, Nicaragua, Panamá (hasta 1998), Paraguay (hasta 2004 y 2013), Perú (hasta 2004), Uruguay (2013) y Venezuela dado que los datos no están disponibles.

1. En los datos de CEPAL, el Impuesto Directo sobre Hidrocarburos (IDH) es considerado como regalía en los ingresos no tributarios.
2. Datos estimados desde el 2011 hasta el 2013 (Bolivia y Venezuela) y 2013 (Uruguay y Paraguay).
3. En los datos de CEPAL y CIAT, los derechos sobre la producción de hidrocarburos son tratados como ingresos no tributarios.
4. La data estimada incluye ingresos esperados a nivel estatal y local para el 2013.
5. Representa un grupo de 20 países de América Latina y el Caribe. Chile y México son también parte del grupo OCDE (34).
6. Calculado aplicando el promedio no ponderado en el cambio porcentual para el 2013 en los 30 países con datos disponibles para ese año en el total de ingreso tributario en porcentaje del PIB.

## Table 1. Total tax revenue as percentage of GDP, 2004-2013 *(cont.)*
## Cuadro 1. Total de ingresos tributarios en porcentaje del PIB, 2004-2013 *(cont.)*

| | 2004 | 2005 | 2006 | 2007 | 2008 | 2009 | 2010 | 2011 | 2012 | 2013 |
|---|---|---|---|---|---|---|---|---|---|---|
| Argentina | 22.0 | 22.1 | 22.2 | 23.0 | 24.7 | 25.6 | 26.7 | 27.7 | 29.5 | 31.2 |
| Barbados | 31.2 | 29.5 | 30.5 | 30.4 | 31.5 | 30.6 | 30.7 | 32.3 | 34.0 | 29.8 |
| Bolivia[1,2] | 14.3 | 18.9 | 21.6 | 22.3 | 20.1 | 22.3 | 20.4 | 23.8 | 25.5 | 27.6 |
| Brazil / Brasil | 32.1 | 33.1 | 33.1 | 33.4 | 33.8 | 33.1 | 33.2 | 35.0 | 35.6 | 35.7 |
| Chile | 19.1 | 20.7 | 22.0 | 22.8 | 21.4 | 17.2 | 19.5 | 21.2 | 21.4 | 20.2 |
| Colombia | 17.5 | 18.1 | 19.1 | 19.1 | 18.8 | 18.6 | 18.0 | 18.9 | 19.6 | 20.1 |
| Costa Rica | 19.6 | 20.1 | 20.6 | 22.0 | 22.7 | 21.2 | 20.8 | 21.3 | 21.2 | 22.4 |
| Dominican Republic / República Dominicana | 12.9 | 14.7 | 15.0 | 16.0 | 15.0 | 13.1 | 12.8 | 12.9 | 13.5 | 14.0 |
| Ecuador | 11.4 | 11.7 | 12.4 | 12.8 | 14.0 | 14.9 | 16.3 | 17.3 | 19.4 | 19.3 |
| El Salvador | 13.2 | 14.1 | 15.1 | 15.2 | 15.1 | 14.4 | 14.8 | 14.9 | 15.1 | 15.8 |
| Guatemala | 13.4 | 13.1 | 13.8 | 13.9 | 12.9 | 12.2 | 12.4 | 12.7 | 12.8 | 13.0 |
| Honduras | 17.0 | 16.9 | 17.6 | 19.0 | 18.9 | 17.1 | 17.3 | 16.9 | 17.5 | 18.0 |
| Jamaica | 24.7 | 23.3 | 24.1 | 24.9 | 25.0 | 24.8 | 25.0 | 24.5 | 24.5 | 25.0 |
| Mexico / México[3,4] | 16.8 | 17.7 | 17.9 | 17.6 | 20.7 | 17.2 | 18.5 | 19.5 | 19.6 | 19.7 |
| Nicaragua | 15.3 | 16.1 | 17.1 | 17.3 | 16.8 | 16.9 | 17.6 | 18.6 | 19.2 | 19.2 |
| Panama / Panamá | 14.7 | 14.6 | 16.0 | 16.7 | 16.9 | 17.4 | 18.1 | 18.1 | 18.7 | 18.9 |
| Paraguay[2] | 13.1 | 13.8 | 14.2 | 13.9 | 14.6 | 16.1 | 16.5 | 16.8 | 17.7 | 16.4 |
| Peru / Perú | 15.3 | 16.7 | 18.1 | 18.7 | 19.0 | 17.0 | 18.0 | 18.5 | 18.8 | 18.3 |
| Uruguay[2] | 22.7 | 23.8 | 25.4 | 25.0 | 26.1 | 26.8 | 27.0 | 26.8 | 27.4 | 27.1 |
| Venezuela[2] | 13.3 | 15.9 | 16.3 | 16.8 | 14.1 | 14.3 | 11.4 | 13.1 | 13.9 | 14.2 |
| *Unweighted average / Moyenne non pondérée* | | | | | | | | | | |
| **LAC / ALC[5]** | **18.0** | **18.7** | **19.6** | **20.0** | **20.1** | **19.5** | **19.8** | **20.5** | **21.2** | **21.3** |
| **OECD / OCDE[6]** | **33.4** | **34.0** | **34.1** | **34.2** | **33.6** | **32.7** | **32.8** | **33.3** | **33.7** | **34.1** |

*Note:* The figures exclude local government revenues for Argentina (but include provincial revenues), Barbados, Bolivia, Costa Rica (up to 1997), Dominican Republic, Ecuador, El Salvador, Honduras, Jamaica, Nicaragua, Panama (up to 1998), Paraguay (up to 2004 and 2013), Peru (up to 2004), Uruguay (2013) and Venezuela as the data are not available.

1. In ECLAC data the excise tax on hydrocarbons is treated as non tax revenues.
2. Estimated figures from 2011 to 2013 (Bolivia and Venezuela) and for 2013 (Uruguay and Paraguay).
3. In ECLAC and CIAT data, fees levied on hydrocarbon production are treated as non tax revenues.
4. Estimated figure for 2013 including expected revenues for state and local governments.
5. Represents a group of 20 Latin American and Caribbean countries. Chile and Mexico are also part of the OECD (34) group.
6. Calculated by applying the unweighted average percentage change for 2013 in the 30 countries providing data for that year to the overall average tax to GDP ratio in 2012.

*Nota :* Las cifras excluyen los ingresos de gobiernos locales en Argentina (pero incluye ingresos de las provincias), Barbados, Bolivia, Costa Rica (hasta 1997), República Dominicana, Ecuador, El Salvador, Honduras, Jamaica, Nicaragua, Panamá (hasta 1998), Paraguay (hasta 2004 y 2013), Perú (hasta 2004), Uruguay (2013) y Venezuela dado que los datos no están disponibles.

1. En los datos de CEPAL, el Impuesto Directo sobre Hidrocarburos (IDH) es considerado como regalía en los ingresos no tributarios.
2. Datos estimados desde el 2011 hasta el 2013 (Bolivia y Venezuela) y 2013 (Uruguay y Paraguay).
3. En los datos de CEPAL y CIAT, los derechos sobre la producción de hidrocarburos son tratados como ingresos no tributarios.
4. La data estimada incluye ingresos esperados a nivel estatal y local para el 2013.
5. Representa un grupo de 20 países de América Latina y el Caribe. Chile y México son también parte del grupo OCDE (34).
6. Calculado aplicando el promedio no ponderado en el cambio porcentual para el 2013 en los 30 países con datos disponibles para ese año en el total de ingreso tributario en porcentaje del PIB.

StatLink http://dx.doi.org/10.1787/888933190426

## Table 2. Tax revenue of main headings as percentage of GDP, 2013
## Cuadro 2. Ingresos tributarios en las principales partidas en porcentaje del PIB, 2013

| | 1000 Income & profits / Renta & utilidades | 2000 Social security / Seguridad social | 3000 Payroll / Nómina | 4000 Property / Patrimonio | 5000 Goods and services / Bienes & servicios | 6000 Others / Otros |
|---|---|---|---|---|---|---|
| Argentina | 5.6 | 7.1 | 0.0 | 2.9 | 15.5 | 0.2 |
| Barbados | 7.1 | 6.1 | 0.0 | 1.5 | 14.8 | 0.4 |
| Bolivia[1] | 3.9 | 1.4 | 0.0 | 1.9 | 18.8 | 1.5 |
| Brazil / Brasil | 7.4 | 9.2 | 0.7 | 2.0 | 15.2 | 1.2 |
| Chile | 7.2 | 1.4 | 0.0 | 0.8 | 10.7 | 0.0 |
| Colombia | 6.8 | 2.4 | 0.5 | 2.1 | 7.3 | 1.1 |
| Costa Rica | 4.1 | 7.6 | 1.0 | 0.4 | 9.1 | 0.2 |
| Dominican Republic / República Dominicana | 3.5 | 0.1 | 0.8 | 0.9 | 8.8 | 0.0 |
| Ecuador | 4.1 | 4.8 | 0.0 | 0.0 | 10.3 | 0.1 |
| El Salvador | 5.3 | 1.7 | 0.0 | 0.1 | 8.7 | 0.0 |
| Guatemala | 3.8 | 2.0 | 0.0 | 0.2 | 6.9 | 0.1 |
| Honduras | 5.2 | 3.3 | 0.0 | 0.1 | 9.5 | 0.0 |
| Jamaica | 9.1 | 1.0 | 0.0 | 0.4 | 13.6 | 0.9 |
| Mexico / México[2] | 5.2 | 2.9 | 0.3 | 0.3 | 10.7 | 0.2 |
| Nicaragua | 5.2 | 4.6 | 0.0 | 0.1 | 9.3 | 0.0 |
| Panama / Panamá | 5.4 | 6.6 | 0.2 | 0.8 | 5.6 | 0.2 |
| Paraguay[1] | 2.5 | 4.1 | 0.0 | 0.3 | 9.4 | 0.1 |
| Peru / Perú | 7.3 | 2.0 | 0.0 | 0.3 | 8.2 | 0.5 |
| Uruguay[1] | 6.3 | 7.5 | 0.0 | 1.9 | 11.4 | 0.0 |
| Venezuela[1] | 4.2 | 0.5 | 0.0 | 0.0 | 9.3 | 0.2 |
| *Unweighted average / Moyenne non pondérée* | | | | | | |
| **LAC / ALC[3]** | **5.5** | **3.8** | **0.2** | **0.8** | **10.6** | **0.3** |
| **OECD / OCDE[2,4]** | **11.4** | **9.0** | **0.4** | **1.8** | **10.8** | **0.2** |

*Note:* The figures exclude local government revenues for Argentina (but include provincial revenues), Barbados, Bolivia, Costa Rica (up to 1997), Dominican Republic, Ecuador, El Salvador, Honduras, Jamaica, Nicaragua, Panama (up to 1998), Paraguay (up to 2004 and 2013), Peru (up to 2004), Uruguay (2013) and Venezuela as the data are not available.

1. Estimated figures.
2. Data for 2012.
3. Represents a group of 20 Latin American and Caribbean countries. Chile and Mexico are also part of the OECD (34) group.
4. Represents the unweighted average for OECD member countries.

*Nota :* Las cifras excluyen los ingresos de gobiernos locales en Argentina (pero incluye ingresos de las provincias), Barbados, Bolivia, Costa Rica (hasta 1997), República Dominicana, Ecuador, El Salvador, Honduras, Jamaica, Nicaragua, Panamá (hasta 1998), Paraguay (hasta 2004 y 2013), Perú (hasta 2004), Uruguay (2013) y Venezuela dado que los datos no están disponibles.

1. Datos estimados.
2. Se utilizan los datos 2012.
3. Representa un grupo de 20 países de América Latina y el Caribe. Chile y México son también parte del grupo OCDE (34).
4. Representa el promedio no ponderado para los países miembros de la OCDE.

StatLink http://dx.doi.org/10.1787/888933190433

## Table 3. Tax revenue of main headings as percentage of total taxation, 2013
## Cuadro 3. Ingresos tributarios en las principales partidas en porcentaje del total de ingresos tributarios, 2013

| | 1000 Income & profits / Renta & utilidades | 2000 Social security / Seguridad social | 3000 Payroll / Nómina | 4000 Property / Patrimonio | 5000 Goods and services / Bienes & servicios | 6000 Others / Otros |
|---|---|---|---|---|---|---|
| Argentina | 17.8 | 22.6 | 0.0 | 9.2 | 49.5 | 0.8 |
| Barbados | 23.9 | 20.3 | 0.0 | 5.0 | 49.6 | 1.2 |
| Bolivia[1] | 14.1 | 5.1 | 0.0 | 6.9 | 68.3 | 5.5 |
| Brazil / Brasil | 20.9 | 25.7 | 2.0 | 5.7 | 42.5 | 3.3 |
| Chile | 35.8 | 7.1 | 0.0 | 4.0 | 53.1 | -0.1 |
| Colombia | 33.5 | 11.7 | 2.5 | 10.6 | 36.4 | 5.2 |
| Costa Rica | 18.2 | 33.7 | 4.5 | 1.8 | 40.8 | 1.1 |
| Dominican Republic / República Dominicana | 25.0 | 0.4 | 5.4 | 6.3 | 62.8 | 0.0 |
| Ecuador | 21.1 | 25.0 | 0.0 | 0.0 | 53.2 | 0.7 |
| El Salvador | 33.6 | 10.6 | 0.0 | 0.5 | 55.3 | 0.0 |
| Guatemala | 29.2 | 15.7 | 0.0 | 1.4 | 52.9 | 0.8 |
| Honduras | 28.8 | 18.4 | 0.0 | 0.4 | 52.4 | 0.0 |
| Jamaica | 36.3 | 4.1 | 0.0 | 1.6 | 54.5 | 3.5 |
| Mexico / México[2] | 26.3 | 14.9 | 1.6 | 1.5 | 54.5 | 1.2 |
| Nicaragua | 27.1 | 23.9 | 0.0 | 0.6 | 48.2 | 0.1 |
| Panama / Panamá | 28.8 | 35.0 | 1.1 | 4.4 | 29.5 | 1.3 |
| Paraguay[1] | 15.1 | 25.2 | 0.0 | 1.6 | 57.5 | 0.6 |
| Peru / Perú | 39.9 | 10.9 | 0.0 | 1.9 | 44.5 | 2.7 |
| Uruguay[1] | 23.1 | 27.9 | 0.0 | 6.9 | 42.0 | 0.1 |
| Venezuela[1] | 29.8 | 3.2 | 0.0 | 0.2 | 65.3 | 1.6 |
| *Unweighted average / Moyenne non pondérée* | | | | | | |
| **LAC / ALC[3]** | **26.7** | **17.1** | **0.8** | **3.5** | **50.5** | **1.5** |
| **OECD / OCDE[2,4]** | **33.6** | **26.2** | **1.1** | **5.5** | **32.8** | **0.6** |

*Note:* The figures exclude local government revenues for Argentina (but include provincial revenues), Barbados, Bolivia, Costa Rica (up to 1997), Dominican Republic, Ecuador, El Salvador, Honduras, Jamaica, Nicaragua, Panama (up to 1998), Paraguay (up to 2004 and 2013), Peru (up to 2004), Uruguay (2013) and Venezuela as the data are not available.

1. Estimated figures.
2. Data for 2012.
3. Represents a group of 20 Latin American and Caribbean countries. Chile and Mexico are also part of the OECD (34) group.
4. Represents the unweighted average for OECD member countries.

*Nota :* Las cifras excluyen los ingresos de gobiernos locales en Argentina (pero incluye ingresos de las provincias), Barbados, Bolivia, Costa Rica (hasta 1997), República Dominicana, Ecuador, El Salvador, Honduras, Jamaica, Nicaragua, Panamá (hasta 1998), Paraguay (hasta 2004 y 2013), Perú (hasta 2004), Uruguay (2013) y Venezuela dado que los datos no están disponibles.

1. Datos estimados.
2. Se utilizan los datos 2012.
3. Representa un grupo de 20 países de América Latina y el Caribe. Chile y México son también parte del grupo OCDE (34).
4. Representa el promedio no ponderado para los países miembros de la OCDE.

StatLink http://dx.doi.org/10.1787/888933190449

## Table 4. Taxes on income and profits (1000) as percentage of GDP
## Cuadro 4. Impuestos sobre la renta y las utilidades (1000) en porcentaje del PIB

| | 1990 | 2000 | 2005 | 2007 | 2008 | 2009 | 2010 | 2011 | 2012 | 2013 |
|---|---|---|---|---|---|---|---|---|---|---|
| Argentina | 0.5 | 3.3 | 4.5 | 4.3 | 4.3 | 4.0 | 4.3 | 4.8 | 5.1 | 5.6 |
| Barbados | 6.2 | 9.2 | 8.2 | 9.7 | 9.1 | 10.2 | 8.6 | 8.9 | 8.8 | 7.1 |
| Bolivia | 0.8 | 1.9 | 2.7 | 3.0 | 3.8 | 3.9 | 3.9 | 3.8 | 4.0 | 3.9 |
| Brazil / Brasil | 5.1 | 5.8 | 7.0 | 7.2 | 7.7 | 7.2 | 6.9 | 7.6 | 7.3 | 7.4 |
| Chile | 3.9 | 4.4 | 7.5 | 10.4 | 8.0 | 5.4 | 7.5 | 8.5 | 8.3 | 7.2 |
| Colombia | 2.7 | 3.4 | 5.1 | 5.6 | 5.1 | 5.6 | 4.8 | 5.4 | 6.6 | 6.8 |
| Costa Rica | 1.8 | 2.6 | 3.4 | 3.9 | 4.4 | 4.1 | 3.9 | 4.0 | 3.9 | 4.1 |
| Dominican Republic / República Dominicana | 2.2 | 1.8 | 2.3 | 3.3 | 3.0 | 2.5 | 2.1 | 2.3 | 3.3 | 3.5 |
| Ecuador | 0.9 | 1.6 | 2.3 | 2.5 | 3.8 | 4.0 | 3.4 | 3.8 | 3.8 | 4.1 |
| El Salvador | 2.0 | 3.3 | 3.9 | 4.6 | 4.7 | 4.6 | 4.4 | 4.4 | 4.8 | 5.3 |
| Guatemala | 1.6 | 2.5 | 2.9 | 3.3 | 3.3 | 3.2 | 3.1 | 3.4 | 3.4 | 3.8 |
| Honduras | 3.4 | 2.8 | 4.1 | 5.1 | 5.1 | 4.6 | 4.7 | 5.1 | 4.8 | 5.2 |
| Jamaica | 11.7 | 10.2 | 10.0 | 11.1 | 11.5 | 11.7 | 10.3 | 9.9 | 9.6 | 9.1 |
| Mexico / México | 4.2 | 4.5 | 4.3 | 4.9 | 5.1 | 4.9 | 5.2 | 5.3 | 5.2 | 6.0 |
| Nicaragua | .. | 1.8 | 3.7 | 4.2 | 4.3 | 4.6 | 4.4 | 5.0 | 5.2 | 5.2 |
| Panama / Panamá | 3.6 | 4.2 | 3.6 | 4.7 | 4.8 | 5.3 | 5.0 | 4.3 | 5.5 | 5.4 |
| Paraguay | 1.1 | 1.9 | 1.7 | 1.8 | 1.9 | 2.8 | 2.2 | 2.5 | 2.7 | 2.5 |
| Peru / Perú | 0.7 | 2.9 | 5.0 | 7.6 | 7.4 | 6.2 | 6.8 | 7.8 | 8.0 | 7.3 |
| Uruguay | 0.9 | 2.0 | 2.8 | 3.4 | 5.4 | 5.6 | 5.7 | 5.6 | 5.7 | 6.3 |
| Venezuela | 15.6 | 5.9 | 6.1 | 7.6 | 5.8 | 5.5 | 3.6 | 3.9 | 4.3 | 4.2 |
| *Unweighted average / Moyenne non pondérée* | | | | | | | | | | |
| **LAC / ALC[1]** | **3.6** | **3.8** | **4.6** | **5.4** | **5.4** | **5.3** | **5.0** | **5.3** | **5.5** | **5.5** |
| **OECD / OCDE[2]** | **12.2** | **12.2** | **11.9** | **12.4** | **12.0** | **11.0** | **11.0** | **11.2** | **11.4** | **11.6** |

*Note:* The figures exclude local government revenues for Argentina (but include provincial revenues), Barbados, Bolivia, Costa Rica (up to 1997), Dominican Republic, Ecuador, El Salvador, Honduras, Jamaica, Nicaragua, Panama (up to 1998), Paraguay (up to 2004 and 2013), Peru (up to 2004), Uruguay (2013) and Venezuela as the data are not available.

1. Represents a group of 20 Latin American and Caribbean countries. Chile and Mexico are also part of the OECD (34) group.
2. Represents the unweighted average for OECD member countries. The OECD average for 2013 is estimated by applying the unweighted average percentage change for 2013 in the 31 countries providing data for that year to the OECD average for 2012.

*Nota :* Las cifras excluyen los ingresos de gobiernos locales en Argentina (pero incluye ingresos de las provincias), Barbados, Bolivia, Costa Rica (hasta 1997), República Dominicana, Ecuador, El Salvador, Honduras, Jamaica, Nicaragua, Panamá (hasta 1998), Paraguay (hasta 2004 y 2013), Perú (hasta 2004), Uruguay (2013) y Venezuela dado que los datos no están disponibles.

1. Representa un grupo de 20 países de América Latina y el Caribe. Chile y México son también parte del grupo OCDE (34).
2. Representa el promedio no ponderado para los países miembros de la OCDE . El promedio OCDE del 2013 es calculado aplicando el promedio no ponderado en el cambio porcentual para el 2013 en los 31 países con datos disponibles para ese año al promedio OCDE del 2012.

StatLink http://dx.doi.org/10.1787/888933190455

## Table 5. Taxes on income and profits (1000) as percentage of total taxation
## Cuadro 5. Impuestos sobre la renta y las utilidades (1000) en porcentaje del total de ingresos tributarios

| | 1990 | 2000 | 2005 | 2007 | 2008 | 2009 | 2010 | 2011 | 2012 | 2013 |
|---|---|---|---|---|---|---|---|---|---|---|
| Argentina | 3.7 | 18.5 | 20.4 | 18.7 | 17.2 | 15.8 | 16.2 | 17.3 | 17.3 | 17.8 |
| Barbados | 27.0 | 30.5 | 27.8 | 31.9 | 29.0 | 33.2 | 28.0 | 27.7 | 25.9 | 23.9 |
| Bolivia | 11.3 | 12.7 | 14.1 | 13.5 | 18.7 | 17.3 | 19.0 | 16.0 | 15.9 | 14.1 |
| Brazil / Brasil | 18.1 | 19.3 | 21.0 | 21.7 | 22.8 | 21.9 | 20.7 | 21.7 | 20.6 | 20.9 |
| Chile | 23.2 | 23.3 | 36.3 | 45.7 | 37.5 | 31.1 | 38.4 | 40.1 | 39.0 | 35.8 |
| Colombia | 29.9 | 23.3 | 28.2 | 29.2 | 27.1 | 29.9 | 26.7 | 28.6 | 33.4 | 33.5 |
| Costa Rica | 11.1 | 14.4 | 16.9 | 17.8 | 19.3 | 19.3 | 18.8 | 18.7 | 18.4 | 18.2 |
| Dominican Republic / República Dominicana | 26.0 | 14.6 | 16.0 | 20.8 | 20.2 | 19.2 | 16.6 | 18.1 | 24.2 | 25.0 |
| Ecuador | 12.8 | 15.9 | 19.3 | 19.4 | 27.0 | 27.0 | 20.7 | 22.1 | 19.5 | 21.1 |
| El Salvador | 18.9 | 26.7 | 27.7 | 30.5 | 31.0 | 32.0 | 29.6 | 29.6 | 31.5 | 33.6 |
| Guatemala | 18.1 | 19.9 | 22.2 | 23.8 | 25.4 | 25.8 | 25.1 | 27.0 | 26.7 | 29.2 |
| Honduras | 21.2 | 18.3 | 24.1 | 27.0 | 27.1 | 26.8 | 27.0 | 30.1 | 27.7 | 28.8 |
| Jamaica | 50.9 | 44.8 | 42.8 | 44.5 | 45.9 | 47.1 | 41.2 | 40.4 | 39.2 | 36.3 |
| Mexico / México | 27.1 | 27.3 | 24.1 | 27.7 | 24.8 | 28.6 | 27.8 | 27.3 | 26.3 | 31.6 |
| Nicaragua | .. | 13.6 | 22.9 | 24.1 | 25.3 | 27.1 | 24.8 | 27.1 | 27.2 | 27.1 |
| Panama / Panamá | 24.3 | 25.0 | 24.9 | 28.0 | 28.2 | 30.7 | 27.4 | 23.8 | 29.6 | 28.8 |
| Paraguay | 21.1 | 13.1 | 12.6 | 12.7 | 13.4 | 17.2 | 13.4 | 14.7 | 15.1 | 15.1 |
| Peru / Perú | 5.7 | 19.8 | 29.8 | 40.7 | 39.2 | 36.4 | 37.5 | 42.3 | 42.5 | 39.9 |
| Uruguay | 4.8 | 9.4 | 11.8 | 13.6 | 20.7 | 20.8 | 21.2 | 20.8 | 21.0 | 23.1 |
| Venezuela | 83.7 | 43.2 | 38.4 | 45.2 | 41.4 | 38.6 | 31.7 | 29.9 | 31.1 | 29.8 |
| *Unweighted average / Moyenne non pondérée* | | | | | | | | | | |
| **LAC / ALC[1]** | **23.1** | **21.7** | **24.1** | **26.8** | **27.1** | **27.3** | **25.6** | **26.2** | **26.6** | **26.7** |
| **OECD / OCDE[2]** | **37.2** | **35.0** | **34.4** | **36.0** | **35.4** | **33.6** | **33.2** | **33.5** | **33.6** | .. |

*Note:* The figures exclude local government revenues for Argentina (but include provincial revenues), Barbados, Bolivia, Costa Rica (up to 1997), Dominican Republic, Ecuador, El Salvador, Honduras, Jamaica, Nicaragua, Panama (up to 1998), Paraguay (up to 2004 and 2013), Peru (up to 2004), Uruguay (2013) and Venezuela as the data are not available.

1. Represents a group of 20 Latin American and Caribbean countries. Chile and Mexico are also part of the OECD (34) group.
2. Represents the unweighted average for OECD member countries.

*Nota :* Las cifras excluyen los ingresos de gobiernos locales en Argentina (pero incluye ingresos de las provincias), Barbados, Bolivia, Costa Rica (hasta 1997), República Dominicana, Ecuador, El Salvador, Honduras, Jamaica, Nicaragua, Panamá (hasta 1998), Paraguay (hasta 2004 y 2013), Perú (hasta 2004), Uruguay (2013) y Venezuela dado que los datos no están disponibles.

1. Representa un grupo de 20 países de América Latina y el Caribe. Chile y México son también parte del grupo OCDE (34).
2. Representa el promedio no ponderado para los países miembros de la OCDE.

StatLink http://dx.doi.org/10.1787/888933190460

## Table 6. Social security contributions (2000) as percentage of GDP
## Cuadro 6. Contribuciones a la seguridad social (2000) en porcentaje del PIB

| | 1990 | 2000 | 2005 | 2007 | 2008 | 2009 | 2010 | 2011 | 2012 | 2013 |
|---|---|---|---|---|---|---|---|---|---|---|
| Argentina | 3.1 | 2.8 | 2.7 | 3.6 | 4.1 | 5.5 | 5.7 | 6.0 | 6.6 | 7.1 |
| Barbados | 3.3 | 4.7 | 5.2 | 5.4 | 5.8 | 5.7 | 5.9 | 6.0 | 6.3 | 6.1 |
| Bolivia[1] | 0.0 | 1.3 | 1.2 | 1.1 | 1.1 | 1.2 | 1.2 | 1.6 | 1.5 | 1.4 |
| Brazil / Brasil | 6.8 | 7.1 | 7.8 | 8.1 | 8.1 | 8.4 | 8.4 | 8.8 | 9.2 | 9.2 |
| Chile | 1.5 | 1.4 | 1.4 | 1.3 | 1.4 | 1.4 | 1.3 | 1.3 | 1.4 | 1.4 |
| Colombia | 0.7 | 2.4 | 2.3 | 2.2 | 2.0 | 2.0 | 2.1 | 1.7 | 1.8 | 2.4 |
| Costa Rica | 4.4 | 5.1 | 5.5 | 5.7 | 5.9 | 6.2 | 6.3 | 6.5 | 6.5 | 7.6 |
| Dominican Republic / República Dominicana | 0.1 | 0.1 | 0.0 | 0.1 | 0.1 | 0.1 | 0.1 | 0.1 | 0.1 | 0.1 |
| Ecuador | 1.6 | 1.2 | 2.7 | 3.5 | 3.4 | 3.3 | 3.7 | 5.0 | 5.4 | 4.8 |
| El Salvador | 1.4 | 2.0 | 1.7 | 1.6 | 1.7 | 1.7 | 1.7 | 1.7 | 1.6 | 1.7 |
| Guatemala | 1.4 | 1.9 | 2.0 | 2.0 | 1.9 | 1.9 | 1.9 | 1.9 | 2.0 | 2.0 |
| Honduras | 1.4 | 1.6 | 2.4 | 2.6 | 2.8 | 2.9 | 2.9 | 2.1 | 3.0 | 3.3 |
| Jamaica | 0.0 | 0.0 | 0.7 | 0.8 | 0.7 | 0.6 | 0.8 | 0.9 | 0.9 | 1.0 |
| Mexico / México | 2.1 | 2.7 | 2.8 | 2.7 | 2.6 | 2.9 | 2.8 | 2.8 | 2.9 | 3.1 |
| Nicaragua | .. | 2.6 | 3.2 | 3.6 | 3.7 | 4.0 | 4.2 | 4.3 | 4.4 | 4.6 |
| Panama / Panamá | 4.5 | 6.4 | 5.4 | 5.6 | 5.8 | 5.7 | 6.2 | 6.5 | 6.0 | 6.6 |
| Paraguay | 0.4 | 3.7 | 3.0 | 3.3 | 3.4 | 3.9 | 3.7 | 3.8 | 4.5 | 4.1 |
| Peru / Perú | 0.9 | 1.8 | 1.6 | 1.6 | 1.7 | 1.8 | 1.7 | 1.8 | 1.9 | 2.0 |
| Uruguay | 6.0 | 6.4 | 5.0 | 5.2 | 5.5 | 6.2 | 6.4 | 6.6 | 7.1 | 7.5 |
| Venezuela[1] | 0.9 | 0.7 | 0.6 | 0.9 | 0.8 | 1.0 | 0.5 | 0.5 | 0.6 | 0.5 |
| *Unweighted average / Moyenne non pondérée* | | | | | | | | | | |
| **LAC / ALC[2]** | **2.1** | **2.8** | **2.9** | **3.0** | **3.1** | **3.3** | **3.4** | **3.5** | **3.7** | **3.8** |
| **OECD / OCDE[3]** | **7.4** | **8.6** | **8.6** | **8.5** | **8.7** | **8.9** | **8.9** | **8.9** | **9.0** | .. |

*Note:* The figures exclude local government revenues for Argentina (but include provincial revenues), Barbados, Bolivia, Costa Rica (up to 1997), Dominican Republic, Ecuador, El Salvador, Honduras, Jamaica, Nicaragua, Panama (up to 1998), Paraguay (up to 2004 and 2013), Peru (up to 2004), Uruguay (2013) and Venezuela as the data are not available.

1. Estimated figures for 2011 to 2013.
2. Represents a group of 20 Latin American and Caribbean countries. Chile and Mexico are also part of the OECD (34) group.
3. Represents the unweighted average for OECD member countries.

*Nota :* Las cifras excluyen los ingresos de gobiernos locales en Argentina (pero incluye ingresos de las provincias), Barbados, Bolivia, Costa Rica (hasta 1997), República Dominicana, Ecuador, El Salvador, Honduras, Jamaica, Nicaragua, Panamá (hasta 1998), Paraguay (hasta 2004 y 2013), Perú (hasta 2004), Uruguay (2013) y Venezuela dado que los datos no están disponibles.

1. Datos estimados del 2011 al 2013.
2. Representa un grupo de 20 países de América Latina y el Caribe. Chile y México son también parte del grupo OCDE (34).
3. Representa el promedio no ponderado para los países miembros de la OCDE.

StatLink http://dx.doi.org/10.1787/888933190473

## Table 7. Social security contributions (2000) as percentage of total taxation
## Cuadro 7. Contribuciones a la seguridad social (2000) en porcentaje del total de ingresos tributarios

| | 1990 | 2000 | 2005 | 2007 | 2008 | 2009 | 2010 | 2011 | 2012 | 2013 |
|---|---|---|---|---|---|---|---|---|---|---|
| Argentina | 25.3 | 15.8 | 12.2 | 15.5 | 16.6 | 21.4 | 21.2 | 21.5 | 22.2 | 22.6 |
| Barbados | 14.2 | 15.7 | 17.8 | 17.7 | 18.4 | 18.6 | 19.3 | 18.6 | 18.4 | 20.3 |
| Bolivia[1] | 0.0 | 8.7 | 6.4 | 4.8 | 5.6 | 5.6 | 5.9 | 6.7 | 6.0 | 5.1 |
| Brazil / Brasil | 24.0 | 23.5 | 23.7 | 24.2 | 24.0 | 25.5 | 25.1 | 25.0 | 25.9 | 25.7 |
| Chile | 9.0 | 7.3 | 6.5 | 5.6 | 6.4 | 8.3 | 6.9 | 6.3 | 6.5 | 7.1 |
| Colombia | 7.9 | 16.4 | 12.8 | 11.8 | 10.7 | 11.0 | 11.7 | 8.8 | 9.0 | 11.7 |
| Costa Rica | 27.2 | 28.0 | 27.6 | 25.9 | 26.0 | 29.3 | 30.3 | 30.5 | 30.6 | 33.7 |
| Dominican Republic / República Dominicana | 0.8 | 1.0 | 0.0 | 0.4 | 0.4 | 0.5 | 0.8 | 0.5 | 0.4 | 0.4 |
| Ecuador | 22.5 | 12.3 | 22.9 | 27.4 | 24.2 | 22.1 | 22.5 | 28.9 | 27.9 | 25.0 |
| El Salvador | 13.3 | 16.4 | 11.7 | 10.8 | 11.0 | 12.1 | 11.6 | 11.1 | 10.7 | 10.6 |
| Guatemala | 15.6 | 15.5 | 15.0 | 14.2 | 14.4 | 15.4 | 15.6 | 15.2 | 15.6 | 15.7 |
| Honduras | 8.8 | 10.6 | 14.2 | 13.6 | 14.7 | 17.2 | 16.7 | 12.3 | 17.1 | 18.4 |
| Jamaica | 0.0 | 0.0 | 3.1 | 3.2 | 2.8 | 2.6 | 3.2 | 3.8 | 3.6 | 4.1 |
| Mexico / México | 13.4 | 16.5 | 15.7 | 15.3 | 12.7 | 16.7 | 15.4 | 14.5 | 14.9 | 16.2 |
| Nicaragua | .. | 19.9 | 19.8 | 20.6 | 21.7 | 23.6 | 24.1 | 22.9 | 22.9 | 23.9 |
| Panama / Panamá | 30.4 | 38.2 | 36.7 | 33.5 | 34.3 | 33.0 | 34.0 | 36.0 | 32.4 | 35.0 |
| Paraguay | 8.3 | 25.6 | 21.4 | 23.4 | 23.7 | 24.5 | 22.7 | 22.4 | 25.1 | 25.2 |
| Peru / Perú | 7.8 | 12.3 | 9.7 | 8.7 | 9.2 | 10.7 | 9.5 | 9.6 | 10.1 | 10.9 |
| Uruguay | 30.5 | 29.6 | 21.1 | 20.7 | 20.9 | 23.3 | 23.7 | 24.5 | 26.1 | 27.9 |
| Venezuela[1] | 4.9 | 5.4 | 3.9 | 5.1 | 5.3 | 6.7 | 4.8 | 4.2 | 4.2 | 3.2 |
| *Unweighted average / Moyenne non pondérée* | | | | | | | | | | |
| **LAC / ALC[2]** | **13.9** | **15.9** | **15.1** | **15.1** | **15.1** | **16.4** | **16.2** | **16.2** | **16.5** | **17.1** |
| **OECD / OCDE[3]** | **22.0** | **24.6** | **25.0** | **24.6** | **25.3** | **26.5** | **26.4** | **26.2** | **26.2** | .. |

*Note:* The figures exclude local government revenues for Argentina (but include provincial revenues), Barbados, Bolivia, Costa Rica (up to 1997), Dominican Republic, Ecuador, El Salvador, Honduras, Jamaica, Nicaragua, Panama (up to 1998), Paraguay (up to 2004 and 2013), Peru (up to 2004), Uruguay (2013) and Venezuela as the data are not available.

1. Estimated figures from 2011 to 2013.
2. Represents a group of 20 Latin American and Caribbean countries. Chile and Mexico are also part of the OECD (34) group.
3. Represents the unweighted average for OECD member countries.

*Nota :* Las cifras excluyen los ingresos de gobiernos locales en Argentina (pero incluye ingresos de las provincias), Barbados, Bolivia, Costa Rica (hasta 1997), República Dominicana, Ecuador, El Salvador, Honduras, Jamaica, Nicaragua, Panamá (hasta 1998), Paraguay (hasta 2004 y 2013), Perú (hasta 2004), Uruguay (2013) y Venezuela dado que los datos no están disponibles.

1. Datos estimados del 2011 al 2013.
2. Representa un grupo de 20 países de América Latina y el Caribe. Chile y México son también parte del grupo OCDE (34).
3. Representa el promedio no ponderado para los países miembros de la OCDE.

StatLink http://dx.doi.org/10.1787/888933190486

## Table 8. Taxes on property (4000) as percentage of GDP
## Cuadro 8. Impuestos sobre la propiedad (4000) en porcentaje del PIB

| | 1990 | 2000 | 2005 | 2007 | 2008 | 2009 | 2010 | 2011 | 2012 | 2013 |
|---|---|---|---|---|---|---|---|---|---|---|
| Argentina | 1.6 | 1.1 | 2.5 | 2.3 | 2.4 | 2.4 | 2.4 | 2.5 | 2.6 | 2.9 |
| Barbados | 1.0 | 1.5 | 1.6 | 1.3 | 1.3 | 1.7 | 1.3 | 1.3 | 1.8 | 1.5 |
| Bolivia | 1.3 | 1.8 | 2.7 | 2.2 | 2.2 | 1.9 | 1.8 | 1.9 | 1.9 | 1.9 |
| Brazil / Brasil | 1.8 | 2.4 | 2.6 | 2.9 | 1.9 | 1.9 | 2.0 | 2.1 | 2.1 | 2.0 |
| Chile | 1.0 | 1.3 | 1.3 | 1.1 | 1.2 | 0.8 | 0.7 | 0.8 | 0.9 | 0.8 |
| Colombia | 0.2 | 1.0 | 1.4 | 1.5 | 1.9 | 1.6 | 1.5 | 2.1 | 2.0 | 2.1 |
| Costa Rica | 0.1 | 0.3 | 0.3 | 0.3 | 0.3 | 0.3 | 0.3 | 0.3 | 0.4 | 0.4 |
| Dominican Republic / República Dominicana | 0.1 | 0.1 | 0.6 | 0.7 | 0.7 | 0.7 | 0.7 | 0.7 | 0.8 | 0.9 |
| Ecuador | 0.0 | 0.0 | 0.0 | 0.0 | 0.0 | 0.0 | 0.0 | 0.0 | 0.0 | 0.0 |
| El Salvador | 0.5 | 0.1 | 0.1 | 0.1 | 0.1 | 0.1 | 0.1 | 0.1 | 0.1 | 0.1 |
| Guatemala | 0.1 | 0.1 | 0.2 | 0.2 | 0.2 | 0.2 | 0.2 | 0.2 | 0.2 | 0.2 |
| Honduras | 0.1 | 0.2 | 0.1 | 0.1 | 0.1 | 0.1 | 0.1 | 0.1 | 0.1 | 0.1 |
| Jamaica | 0.2 | 0.2 | 0.2 | 0.2 | 0.2 | 0.2 | 0.2 | 0.2 | 0.2 | 0.4 |
| Mexico / México[1] | 0.2 | 0.2 | 0.3 | 0.3 | 0.3 | 0.3 | 0.3 | 0.3 | 0.3 | 0.0 |
| Nicaragua | .. | 0.0 | 0.0 | 0.0 | 0.0 | 0.0 | 0.1 | 0.1 | 0.1 | 0.1 |
| Panama / Panamá | 0.7 | 0.5 | 0.7 | 0.8 | 0.7 | 0.7 | 0.8 | 0.7 | 0.7 | 0.8 |
| Paraguay[1] | 0.3 | 0.0 | 0.0 | 0.3 | 0.3 | 0.3 | 0.3 | 0.3 | 0.3 | 0.3 |
| Peru / Perú | 1.9 | 0.0 | 0.5 | 0.6 | 0.6 | 0.6 | 0.5 | 0.4 | 0.4 | 0.3 |
| Uruguay | 1.6 | 2.2 | 2.8 | 2.5 | 2.4 | 2.4 | 2.2 | 2.1 | 2.0 | 1.9 |
| Venezuela | 0.1 | 0.5 | 0.9 | 0.5 | 0.9 | 0.0 | 0.0 | 0.0 | 0.0 | 0.0 |
| *Unweighted average / Moyenne non pondérée* | | | | | | | | | | |
| **LAC / ALC[2]** | **0.7** | **0.7** | **0.9** | **0.9** | **0.9** | **0.8** | **0.8** | **0.8** | **0.8** | **0.8** |
| **OECD / OCDE[3]** | **1.8** | **1.8** | **1.8** | **1.9** | **1.7** | **1.7** | **1.7** | **1.7** | **1.8** | **..** |

*Note:* The figures exclude local government revenues for Argentina (but include provincial revenues), Barbados, Bolivia, Costa Rica (up to 1997), Dominican Republic, Ecuador, El Salvador, Honduras, Jamaica, Nicaragua, Panama (up to 1998), Paraguay (up to 2004 and 2013), Peru (up to 2004), Uruguay (2013) and Venezuela as the data are not available.

1. Estimated figures for 2013.
2. Represents a group of 20 Latin American and Caribbean countries. Chile and Mexico are also part of the OECD (34) group.
3. Represents the unweighted average for OECD member countries.

*Nota :* Las cifras excluyen los ingresos de gobiernos locales en Argentina (pero incluye ingresos de las provincias), Barbados, Bolivia, Costa Rica (hasta 1997), República Dominicana, Ecuador, El Salvador, Honduras, Jamaica, Nicaragua, Panamá (hasta 1998), Paraguay (hasta 2004 y 2013), Perú (hasta 2004), Uruguay (2013) y Venezuela dado que los datos no están disponibles.

1. Datos estimados para el 2013.
2. Representa un grupo de 20 países de América Latina y el Caribe. Chile y México son también parte del grupo OCDE (34).
3. Representa el promedio no ponderado para los países miembros de la OCDE.

StatLink http://dx.doi.org/10.1787/888933190493

## Table 9. Taxes on property (4000) as percentage of total taxation
## Cuadro 9. Impuestos sobre la propiedad (4000) en porcentaje del total de ingresos tributarios

| | 1990 | 2000 | 2005 | 2007 | 2008 | 2009 | 2010 | 2011 | 2012 | 2013 |
|---|---|---|---|---|---|---|---|---|---|---|
| Argentina | 12.7 | 6.4 | 11.2 | 10.1 | 9.7 | 9.2 | 9.0 | 9.0 | 9.0 | 9.2 |
| Barbados | 4.2 | 4.9 | 5.5 | 4.2 | 4.2 | 5.5 | 4.2 | 4.0 | 5.2 | 5.0 |
| Bolivia | 19.1 | 12.4 | 14.4 | 9.7 | 10.7 | 8.7 | 9.1 | 8.0 | 7.6 | 6.9 |
| Brazil / Brasil | 6.5 | 8.1 | 7.9 | 8.6 | 5.6 | 5.7 | 5.9 | 6.0 | 5.9 | 5.7 |
| Chile | 6.2 | 7.0 | 6.3 | 4.9 | 5.4 | 4.8 | 3.6 | 4.0 | 4.3 | 4.0 |
| Colombia | 2.2 | 6.6 | 7.9 | 7.8 | 9.9 | 8.8 | 8.5 | 11.1 | 10.4 | 10.6 |
| Costa Rica | 0.3 | 1.4 | 1.3 | 1.4 | 1.3 | 1.3 | 1.6 | 1.6 | 1.7 | 1.8 |
| Dominican Republic / República Dominicana | 0.7 | 1.0 | 4.4 | 4.5 | 4.8 | 5.0 | 5.2 | 5.6 | 6.0 | 6.3 |
| Ecuador | 0.0 | 0.0 | 0.0 | 0.0 | 0.0 | 0.0 | 0.0 | 0.0 | 0.0 | 0.0 |
| El Salvador | 5.1 | 0.7 | 0.7 | 0.7 | 0.5 | 0.5 | 0.5 | 0.5 | 0.5 | 0.5 |
| Guatemala | 1.6 | 1.0 | 1.3 | 1.2 | 1.3 | 1.5 | 1.5 | 1.4 | 1.5 | 1.4 |
| Honduras | 0.8 | 1.2 | 0.5 | 0.7 | 0.5 | 0.5 | 0.5 | 0.5 | 0.5 | 0.4 |
| Jamaica | 0.9 | 0.7 | 0.9 | 0.8 | 0.9 | 0.7 | 1.0 | 0.8 | 0.9 | 1.6 |
| Mexico / México[1] | 1.5 | 1.4 | 1.6 | 1.7 | 1.4 | 1.7 | 1.6 | 1.5 | 1.5 | 0.0 |
| Nicaragua | .. | 0.0 | 0.0 | 0.0 | 0.0 | 0.2 | 0.4 | 0.5 | 0.5 | 0.6 |
| Panama / Panamá | 4.9 | 3.2 | 4.8 | 4.7 | 4.1 | 4.2 | 4.4 | 4.0 | 3.9 | 4.4 |
| Paraguay[1] | 4.9 | 0.0 | 0.0 | 2.1 | 2.2 | 2.0 | 1.7 | 1.6 | 1.6 | 1.6 |
| Peru / Perú | 15.3 | 0.0 | 3.2 | 3.2 | 3.2 | 3.3 | 3.0 | 2.2 | 2.0 | 1.9 |
| Uruguay | 8.4 | 10.2 | 11.9 | 10.2 | 9.1 | 9.0 | 8.1 | 7.8 | 7.4 | 6.9 |
| Venezuela | 0.3 | 3.7 | 5.9 | 3.3 | 6.5 | 0.2 | 0.2 | 0.2 | 0.2 | 0.2 |
| *Unweighted average / Moyenne non pondérée* | | | | | | | | | | |
| **LAC / ALC[2]** | **5.0** | **3.5** | **4.5** | **4.0** | **4.1** | **3.6** | **3.5** | **3.5** | **3.5** | **3.5** |
| **OECD / OCDE[3]** | **5.7** | **5.5** | **5.6** | **5.6** | **5.4** | **5.5** | **5.5** | **5.4** | **5.5** | .. |

*Note:* The figures exclude local government revenues for Argentina (but include provincial revenues), Barbados, Bolivia, Costa Rica (up to 1997), Dominican Republic, Ecuador, El Salvador, Honduras, Jamaica, Nicaragua, Panama (up to 1998), Paraguay (up to 2004 and 2013), Peru (up to 2004), Uruguay (2013) and Venezuela as the data are not available.

1. Estimated figures for 2013.
2. Represents a group of 20 Latin American and Caribbean countries. Chile and Mexico are also part of the OECD (34) group.
3. Represents the unweighted average for OECD member countries.

*Nota :* Las cifras excluyen los ingresos de gobiernos locales en Argentina (pero incluye ingresos de las provincias), Barbados, Bolivia, Costa Rica (hasta 1997), República Dominicana, Ecuador, El Salvador, Honduras, Jamaica, Nicaragua, Panamá (hasta 1998), Paraguay (hasta 2004 y 2013), Perú (hasta 2004), Uruguay (2013) y Venezuela dado que los datos no están disponibles.

1. Datos estimados para el 2013.
2. Representa un grupo de 20 países de América Latina y el Caribe. Chile y México son también parte del grupo OCDE (34).
3. Representa el promedio no ponderado para los países miembros de la OCDE.

StatLink http://dx.doi.org/10.1787/888933190504

## Table 10. Taxes on goods and services (5000) as percentage of GDP
## Cuadro 10. Impuestos sobre bienes y servicios (5000) en porcentaje del PIB

| | 1990 | 2000 | 2005 | 2007 | 2008 | 2009 | 2010 | 2011 | 2012 | 2013 |
|---|---|---|---|---|---|---|---|---|---|---|
| Argentina | 6.9 | 10.2 | 12.0 | 12.5 | 13.6 | 13.3 | 14.0 | 14.2 | 14.9 | 15.5 |
| Barbados | 10.3 | 14.4 | 14.2 | 13.7 | 14.4 | 12.2 | 14.0 | 15.6 | 16.8 | 14.8 |
| Bolivia | 5.1 | 10.0 | 12.6 | 16.5 | 16.4 | 14.1 | 14.5 | 16.4 | 17.0 | 18.8 |
| Brazil / Brasil | 13.5 | 13.9 | 14.8 | 14.3 | 14.8 | 13.8 | 14.3 | 14.7 | 15.1 | 15.2 |
| Chile | 10.7 | 12.0 | 10.7 | 10.0 | 10.8 | 9.6 | 10.0 | 10.5 | 10.7 | 10.7 |
| Colombia | 4.8 | 6.4 | 7.6 | 8.1 | 8.2 | 7.5 | 7.7 | 7.9 | 7.6 | 7.3 |
| Costa Rica | 7.9 | 9.3 | 9.9 | 11.1 | 11.1 | 9.5 | 9.2 | 9.4 | 9.3 | 9.1 |
| Dominican Republic / República Dominicana | 5.8 | 9.3 | 10.9 | 11.0 | 10.5 | 9.2 | 9.2 | 9.0 | 8.6 | 8.8 |
| Ecuador | 4.4 | 7.3 | 6.8 | 6.8 | 6.8 | 7.2 | 8.8 | 8.5 | 10.1 | 10.3 |
| El Salvador | 5.4 | 6.9 | 8.5 | 8.8 | 8.7 | 8.0 | 8.7 | 8.8 | 8.7 | 8.7 |
| Guatemala | 5.5 | 7.7 | 7.9 | 8.3 | 7.5 | 6.8 | 7.0 | 7.0 | 7.0 | 6.9 |
| Honduras | 11.2 | 10.7 | 10.4 | 11.1 | 10.9 | 9.5 | 9.7 | 9.6 | 9.6 | 9.5 |
| Jamaica | 9.8 | 11.6 | 11.2 | 11.5 | 11.4 | 11.4 | 12.9 | 12.6 | 13.0 | 13.6 |
| Mexico / México[1] | 8.6 | 8.8 | 10.0 | 9.3 | 12.3 | 8.6 | 9.7 | 10.6 | 10.7 | 9.7 |
| Nicaragua | .. | 8.6 | 9.2 | 9.6 | 8.9 | 8.3 | 8.9 | 9.2 | 9.5 | 9.3 |
| Panama / Panamá | 5.5 | 4.9 | 4.5 | 5.2 | 5.3 | 5.2 | 5.7 | 6.0 | 5.9 | 5.6 |
| Paraguay[1] | 2.8 | 8.4 | 8.0 | 8.4 | 8.7 | 8.9 | 10.0 | 10.2 | 10.2 | 9.4 |
| Peru / Perú | 7.9 | 8.8 | 8.8 | 8.2 | 8.6 | 7.7 | 8.3 | 8.0 | 8.0 | 8.2 |
| Uruguay[1] | 11.1 | 11.2 | 13.1 | 13.9 | 12.9 | 12.6 | 12.7 | 12.6 | 12.5 | 11.4 |
| Venezuela[1] | 2.1 | 6.5 | 8.2 | 7.8 | 6.6 | 7.8 | 7.2 | 8.0 | 8.7 | 9.3 |
| *Unweighted average / Moyenne non pondérée* | | | | | | | | | | |
| **LAC / ALC[2]** | **7.3** | **9.3** | **10.0** | **10.3** | **10.4** | **9.6** | **10.1** | **10.4** | **10.7** | **10.6** |
| **OECD / OCDE[3]** | **10.2** | **11.0** | **11.0** | **10.7** | **10.5** | **10.4** | **10.7** | **10.8** | **10.8** | .. |

*Note:* The figures exclude local government revenues for Argentina (but include provincial revenues), Barbados, Bolivia, Costa Rica (up to 1997), Dominican Republic, Ecuador, El Salvador, Honduras, Jamaica, Nicaragua, Panama (up to 1998), Paraguay (up to 2004 and 2013), Peru (up to 2004), Uruguay (2013) and Venezuela as the data are not available.

1. Estimated data for 2013.
2. Represents a group of 20 Latin American and Caribbean countries. Chile and Mexico are also part of the OECD (34) group.
3. Represents the unweighted average for OECD member countries.

*Nota :* Las cifras excluyen los ingresos de gobiernos locales en Argentina (pero incluye ingresos de las provincias), Barbados, Bolivia, Costa Rica (hasta 1997), República Dominicana, Ecuador, El Salvador, Honduras, Jamaica, Nicaragua, Panamá (hasta 1998), Paraguay (hasta 2004 y 2013), Perú (hasta 2004), Uruguay (2013) y Venezuela dado que los datos no están disponibles.

1. Datos estimados para el 2013.
2. Representa un grupo de 20 países de América Latina y el Caribe. Chile y México son también parte del grupo OCDE (34).
3. Representa el promedio no ponderado para los países miembros de la OCDE.

StatLink http://dx.doi.org/10.1787/888933190515

## Table 11. Taxes on goods and services (5000) as percentage of total taxation
## Cuadro 11. Impuestos sobre bienes y servicios (5000) en porcentaje del total de ingresos tributarios

| | 1990 | 2000 | 2005 | 2007 | 2008 | 2009 | 2010 | 2011 | 2012 | 2013 |
|---|---|---|---|---|---|---|---|---|---|---|
| Argentina | 55.7 | 56.5 | 54.6 | 54.3 | 55.2 | 52.2 | 52.4 | 51.2 | 50.5 | 49.5 |
| Barbados | 44.8 | 47.6 | 47.9 | 44.9 | 45.8 | 40.0 | 45.7 | 48.4 | 49.5 | 49.6 |
| Bolivia | 72.2 | 68.4 | 66.5 | 73.8 | 81.7 | 63.1 | 71.3 | 69.1 | 66.6 | 68.3 |
| Brazil / Brasil | 47.7 | 46.3 | 44.7 | 42.7 | 43.8 | 41.7 | 43.1 | 42.2 | 42.4 | 42.5 |
| Chile | 62.9 | 63.8 | 51.5 | 43.8 | 50.6 | 55.9 | 51.3 | 49.3 | 50.1 | 53.1 |
| Colombia | 53.8 | 43.8 | 42.1 | 42.2 | 43.4 | 40.6 | 42.9 | 41.7 | 38.5 | 36.4 |
| Costa Rica | 49.0 | 51.1 | 49.4 | 50.4 | 48.7 | 45.1 | 44.3 | 44.2 | 43.8 | 40.8 |
| Dominican Republic / República Dominicana | 69.9 | 74.6 | 74.4 | 69.1 | 70.0 | 69.9 | 72.0 | 70.0 | 64.0 | 62.8 |
| Ecuador | 62.1 | 71.8 | 57.8 | 53.2 | 48.3 | 48.4 | 54.2 | 48.8 | 51.9 | 53.2 |
| El Salvador | 51.3 | 56.2 | 60.0 | 57.9 | 57.5 | 55.5 | 58.3 | 58.8 | 57.3 | 55.3 |
| Guatemala | 61.0 | 62.4 | 60.3 | 59.8 | 57.9 | 55.7 | 56.5 | 55.1 | 54.6 | 52.9 |
| Honduras | 69.1 | 70.0 | 61.2 | 58.6 | 57.6 | 55.4 | 55.8 | 57.1 | 54.6 | 52.4 |
| Jamaica | 42.5 | 50.9 | 47.8 | 46.2 | 45.5 | 46.1 | 51.6 | 51.4 | 53.1 | 54.5 |
| Mexico / México[1] | 55.3 | 53.0 | 56.7 | 53.1 | 59.2 | 50.2 | 52.6 | 54.1 | 54.5 | 51.3 |
| Nicaragua | .. | 66.3 | 57.2 | 55.2 | 52.9 | 49.1 | 50.7 | 49.5 | 49.4 | 48.2 |
| Panama / Panamá | 37.6 | 29.5 | 30.7 | 31.0 | 31.2 | 30.1 | 31.4 | 33.4 | 31.7 | 29.5 |
| Paraguay[1] | 51.4 | 58.0 | 58.0 | 60.1 | 59.9 | 55.5 | 60.5 | 60.6 | 57.5 | 57.5 |
| Peru / Perú | 65.6 | 60.9 | 52.9 | 43.9 | 45.1 | 45.3 | 46.1 | 43.6 | 42.4 | 44.5 |
| Uruguay[1] | 56.7 | 51.8 | 55.1 | 55.5 | 49.3 | 46.9 | 47.1 | 46.9 | 45.6 | 42.0 |
| Venezuela[1] | 11.1 | 47.7 | 51.8 | 46.5 | 46.8 | 54.6 | 63.4 | 60.8 | 62.3 | 65.3 |
| *Unweighted average / Moyenne non pondérée* | | | | | | | | | | |
| **LAC / ALC[2]** | **53.7** | **56.5** | **54.0** | **52.1** | **52.5** | **50.1** | **52.6** | **51.8** | **51.0** | **50.5** |
| **OECD / OCDE[3]** | **32.9** | **33.1** | **33.2** | **32.0** | **32.1** | **32.5** | **33.1** | **32.9** | **32.8** | .. |

*Note:* The figures exclude local government revenues for Argentina (but include provincial revenues), Barbados, Bolivia, Costa Rica (up to 1997), Dominican Republic, Ecuador, El Salvador, Honduras, Jamaica, Nicaragua, Panama (up to 1998), Paraguay (up to 2004 and 2013), Peru (up to 2004), Uruguay (2013) and Venezuela as the data are not available.

1. Estimated data for 2013.
2. Represents a group of 20 Latin American and Caribbean countries. Chile and Mexico are also part of the OECD (34) group.
3. Represents the unweighted average for OECD member countries.

*Nota :* Las cifras excluyen los ingresos de gobiernos locales en Argentina (pero incluye ingresos de las provincias), Barbados, Bolivia, Costa Rica (hasta 1997), República Dominicana, Ecuador, El Salvador, Honduras, Jamaica, Nicaragua, Panamá (hasta 1998), Paraguay (hasta 2004 y 2013), Perú (hasta 2004), Uruguay (2013) y Venezuela dado que los datos no están disponibles.

1. Datos estimados para el 2013.
2. Representa un grupo de 20 países de América Latina y el Caribe. Chile y México son también parte del grupo OCDE (34).
3. Representa el promedio no ponderado para los países miembros de la OCDE.

StatLink http://dx.doi.org/10.1787/888933190520

## Table 12. Taxes on general consumption (5110) as percentage of GDP
## Cuadro 12. Impuestos generales sobre el consumo (5110) en porcentaje del PIB

| | 1990 | 2000 | 2005 | 2007 | 2008 | 2009 | 2010 | 2011 | 2012 | 2013 |
|---|---|---|---|---|---|---|---|---|---|---|
| Argentina | 3.0 | 7.2 | 7.7 | 8.3 | 8.6 | 8.8 | 9.1 | 9.6 | 10.2 | 11.2 |
| Barbados | 4.8 | 8.0 | 7.8 | 8.5 | 9.0 | 7.4 | 8.5 | 10.3 | 10.7 | 9.7 |
| Bolivia | 3.2 | 5.1 | 5.9 | 6.5 | 7.0 | 6.3 | 6.7 | 7.3 | 7.6 | 7.8 |
| Brazil / Brasil | 13.4 | 13.1 | 13.7 | 13.2 | 13.7 | 13.1 | 13.5 | 13.8 | 14.2 | 14.3 |
| Chile | 6.3 | 7.9 | 7.8 | 7.5 | 8.4 | 7.3 | 7.6 | 7.9 | 8.1 | 8.1 |
| Colombia | 2.3 | 4.6 | 5.9 | 6.2 | 6.5 | 6.0 | 6.1 | 6.4 | 6.3 | 5.7 |
| Costa Rica | 3.2 | 4.5 | 5.1 | 5.9 | 6.0 | 4.9 | 4.8 | 4.9 | 4.9 | 4.7 |
| Dominican Republic / República Dominicana | 1.3 | 2.6 | 4.1 | 4.9 | 4.7 | 4.2 | 4.3 | 4.2 | 4.0 | 4.5 |
| Ecuador | 2.0 | 4.6 | 4.8 | 4.9 | 4.6 | 4.8 | 5.6 | 5.3 | 6.2 | 6.4 |
| El Salvador | 2.8 | 5.4 | 6.5 | 6.9 | 6.8 | 6.1 | 6.7 | 6.8 | 6.7 | 6.8 |
| Guatemala | 2.4 | 4.7 | 5.2 | 5.9 | 5.5 | 4.9 | 5.1 | 5.2 | 5.3 | 5.2 |
| Honduras | 2.7 | 4.8 | 5.2 | 6.1 | 6.3 | 5.2 | 5.4 | 5.7 | 5.6 | 5.5 |
| Jamaica | 0.0 | 3.4 | 3.9 | 4.1 | 4.0 | 3.8 | 3.9 | 3.9 | 3.9 | 4.0 |
| Mexico / México | 3.2 | 3.1 | 3.4 | 3.6 | 3.7 | 3.4 | 3.8 | 3.7 | 3.7 | 3.5 |
| Nicaragua | .. | 4.5 | 5.3 | 5.8 | 5.5 | 5.2 | 5.4 | 5.8 | 6.0 | 6.0 |
| Panama / Panamá | 1.3 | 0.6 | 0.9 | 1.0 | 2.3 | 2.3 | 2.9 | 3.3 | 3.3 | 3.1 |
| Paraguay | 0.0 | 4.7 | 4.6 | 5.0 | 5.5 | 5.6 | 6.3 | 6.5 | 6.5 | 6.3 |
| Peru / Perú | 1.5 | 5.4 | 6.0 | 6.2 | 7.1 | 6.3 | 6.8 | 6.7 | 6.7 | 6.8 |
| Uruguay | 5.5 | 6.5 | 8.2 | 9.3 | 9.2 | 8.9 | 8.9 | 8.7 | 8.7 | 8.6 |
| Venezuela | 0.0 | 4.1 | 6.4 | 5.6 | 4.6 | 5.9 | 5.5 | 6.2 | 6.8 | 7.4 |
| *Unweighted average / Moyenne non pondérée* | | | | | | | | | | |
| **LAC / ALC[1]** | **3.1** | **5.2** | **5.9** | **6.3** | **6.4** | **6.0** | **6.3** | **6.6** | **6.8** | **6.8** |
| **OECD / OCDE[2]** | **5.7** | **6.7** | **6.8** | **6.8** | **6.6** | **6.5** | **6.7** | **6.7** | **6.8** | .. |

*Note:* The figures exclude local government revenues for Argentina (but include provincial revenues), Barbados, Bolivia, Costa Rica (up to 1997), Dominican Republic, Ecuador, El Salvador, Honduras, Jamaica, Nicaragua, Panama (up to 1998), Paraguay (up to 2004 and 2013), Peru (up to 2004), Uruguay (2013) and Venezuela as the data are not available.

1. Represents a group of 20 Latin American and Caribbean countries. Chile and Mexico are also part of the OECD (34) group.
2. Represents the unweighted average for OECD member countries.

*Nota :* Las cifras excluyen los ingresos de gobiernos locales en Argentina (pero incluye ingresos de las provincias), Barbados, Bolivia, Costa Rica (hasta 1997), República Dominicana, Ecuador, El Salvador, Honduras, Jamaica, Nicaragua, Panamá (hasta 1998), Paraguay (hasta 2004 y 2013), Perú (hasta 2004), Uruguay (2013) y Venezuela dado que los datos no están disponibles.

1. Representa un grupo de 20 países de América Latina y el Caribe. Chile y México son también parte del grupo OCDE (34).
2. Representa el promedio no ponderado para los países miembros de la OCDE.

StatLink http://dx.doi.org/10.1787/888933190532

## Table 13. Taxes on general consumption (5110) as percentage of total taxation
## Cuadro 13. Impuestos generales sobre el consumo (5110) en porcentaje del total de ingresos tributarios

| | 1990 | 2000 | 2005 | 2007 | 2008 | 2009 | 2010 | 2011 | 2012 | 2013 |
|---|---|---|---|---|---|---|---|---|---|---|
| Argentina | 23.9 | 40.2 | 34.7 | 35.9 | 34.7 | 34.5 | 34.1 | 34.5 | 34.7 | 36.0 |
| Barbados | 20.9 | 26.6 | 26.6 | 27.9 | 28.6 | 24.1 | 27.7 | 31.8 | 31.6 | 32.6 |
| Bolivia | 45.7 | 34.8 | 31.4 | 29.3 | 34.6 | 28.4 | 33.1 | 30.7 | 29.9 | 28.3 |
| Brazil / Brasil | 47.4 | 43.4 | 41.4 | 39.4 | 40.4 | 39.5 | 40.5 | 39.4 | 39.9 | 40.0 |
| Chile | 37.4 | 41.8 | 37.8 | 32.9 | 39.4 | 42.5 | 38.7 | 37.0 | 37.7 | 40.2 |
| Colombia | 26.1 | 31.4 | 32.4 | 32.7 | 34.4 | 32.1 | 33.8 | 34.1 | 31.9 | 28.4 |
| Costa Rica | 20.0 | 24.9 | 25.3 | 26.7 | 26.3 | 23.3 | 23.1 | 23.2 | 23.2 | 21.2 |
| Dominican Republic / República Dominicana | 15.2 | 21.1 | 27.6 | 30.7 | 31.5 | 31.7 | 33.6 | 32.8 | 29.7 | 31.9 |
| Ecuador | 28.1 | 45.2 | 40.7 | 38.3 | 32.6 | 32.4 | 34.3 | 30.6 | 31.8 | 33.3 |
| El Salvador | 26.2 | 44.4 | 45.7 | 45.5 | 45.1 | 42.2 | 45.1 | 45.7 | 44.6 | 43.2 |
| Guatemala | 27.2 | 37.9 | 39.6 | 42.3 | 42.3 | 39.9 | 41.2 | 41.4 | 41.5 | 39.8 |
| Honduras | 16.9 | 31.5 | 30.7 | 32.0 | 33.2 | 30.5 | 31.0 | 33.6 | 31.8 | 30.3 |
| Jamaica | 0.1 | 14.9 | 16.7 | 16.3 | 16.1 | 15.4 | 15.7 | 15.7 | 15.8 | 16.1 |
| Mexico / México | 20.8 | 18.7 | 19.1 | 20.4 | 18.0 | 19.7 | 20.5 | 19.0 | 19.0 | 18.4 |
| Nicaragua | .. | 34.8 | 32.9 | 33.7 | 32.5 | 30.7 | 30.8 | 31.3 | 31.5 | 31.3 |
| Panama / Panamá | 9.0 | 3.6 | 6.1 | 6.2 | 13.6 | 13.3 | 15.9 | 18.4 | 17.7 | 16.6 |
| Paraguay | 0.0 | 32.1 | 33.3 | 36.2 | 37.5 | 34.6 | 38.3 | 38.9 | 37.0 | 38.3 |
| Peru / Perú | 12.1 | 36.8 | 35.8 | 33.2 | 37.2 | 36.8 | 37.9 | 36.4 | 35.5 | 37.0 |
| Uruguay | 28.1 | 30.2 | 34.2 | 37.0 | 35.0 | 33.3 | 33.0 | 32.6 | 31.8 | 31.8 |
| Venezuela | 0.0 | 30.2 | 40.4 | 33.5 | 32.8 | 41.2 | 48.2 | 47.3 | 48.9 | 52.4 |
| *Unweighted average / Moyenne non pondérée* | | | | | | | | | | |
| **LAC / ALC[1]** | **21.3** | **31.2** | **31.6** | **31.5** | **32.3** | **31.3** | **32.8** | **32.7** | **32.3** | **32.3** |
| **OECD / OCDE[2]** | **18.1** | **19.7** | **20.2** | **19.8** | **19.8** | **20.0** | **20.5** | **20.4** | **20.2** | .. |

*Note:* The figures exclude local government revenues for Argentina (but include provincial revenues), Barbados, Bolivia, Costa Rica (up to 1997), Dominican Republic, Ecuador, El Salvador, Honduras, Jamaica, Nicaragua, Panama (up to 1998), Paraguay (up to 2004 and 2013), Peru (up to 2004), Uruguay (2013) and Venezuela as the data are not available.

1. Represents a group of 20 Latin American and Caribbean countries. Chile and Mexico are also part of the OECD (34) group.
2. Represents the unweighted average for OECD member countries.

*Nota :* Las cifras excluyen los ingresos de gobiernos locales en Argentina (pero incluye ingresos de las provincias), Barbados, Bolivia, Costa Rica (hasta 1997), República Dominicana, Ecuador, El Salvador, Honduras, Jamaica, Nicaragua, Panamá (hasta 1998), Paraguay (hasta 2004 y 2013), Perú (hasta 2004), Uruguay (2013) y Venezuela dado que los datos no están disponibles.

1. Representa un grupo de 20 países de América Latina y el Caribe. Chile y México son también parte del grupo OCDE (34).
2. Representa el promedio no ponderado para los países miembros de la OCDE.

StatLink http://dx.doi.org/10.1787/888933190543

## Table 14. Taxes on specific goods and services (5120) as percentage of GDP
## Cuadro 14. Impuestos específicos sobre bienes y servicios (5120) en porcentaje del PIB

| | 1990 | 2000 | 2005 | 2007 | 2008 | 2009 | 2010 | 2011 | 2012 | 2013 |
|---|---|---|---|---|---|---|---|---|---|---|
| Argentina | 3.8 | 2.7 | 4.2 | 4.0 | 4.9 | 4.3 | 4.7 | 4.4 | 4.4 | 4.0 |
| Barbados | 5.5 | 4.7 | 4.7 | 3.8 | 4.2 | 3.6 | 3.8 | 3.9 | 4.0 | 3.8 |
| Bolivia | 1.9 | 4.9 | 6.6 | 9.9 | 9.5 | 7.8 | 7.8 | 9.1 | 9.4 | 11.0 |
| Brazil / Brasil | 0.0 | 0.7 | 0.9 | 0.8 | 0.9 | 0.7 | 0.9 | 1.0 | 0.9 | 0.9 |
| Chile | 3.9 | 3.5 | 2.3 | 2.0 | 1.9 | 1.7 | 1.9 | 2.0 | 2.0 | 2.0 |
| Colombia | 2.5 | 1.8 | 1.7 | 1.8 | 1.7 | 1.6 | 1.6 | 1.4 | 1.3 | 1.6 |
| Costa Rica | 4.3 | 4.3 | 4.4 | 4.8 | 4.6 | 4.1 | 3.9 | 4.0 | 3.6 | 3.5 |
| Dominican Republic / República Dominicana | 4.4 | 6.5 | 6.7 | 6.0 | 5.6 | 4.9 | 4.8 | 4.7 | 4.5 | 4.2 |
| Ecuador | 2.4 | 2.6 | 1.8 | 1.8 | 2.0 | 2.2 | 3.0 | 2.9 | 3.7 | 3.6 |
| El Salvador | 2.6 | 1.4 | 2.0 | 1.9 | 1.9 | 1.9 | 2.0 | 2.0 | 1.9 | 1.9 |
| Guatemala | 2.9 | 2.9 | 2.6 | 2.3 | 1.9 | 1.8 | 1.7 | 1.6 | 1.4 | 1.3 |
| Honduras | 8.5 | 5.9 | 5.2 | 5.1 | 4.6 | 4.3 | 4.3 | 4.0 | 4.0 | 4.0 |
| Jamaica | 9.6 | 8.0 | 7.1 | 7.3 | 7.2 | 7.4 | 8.8 | 8.6 | 9.0 | 9.4 |
| Mexico / México | 5.3 | 5.5 | 6.5 | 5.6 | 8.4 | 5.1 | 5.8 | 6.7 | 6.8 | 6.2 |
| Nicaragua | .. | 4.1 | 3.9 | 3.7 | 3.4 | 3.1 | 3.5 | 3.4 | 3.4 | 3.2 |
| Panama / Panamá | 2.3 | 4.0 | 3.3 | 3.8 | 2.7 | 2.6 | 2.7 | 2.6 | 2.5 | 2.3 |
| Paraguay[1] | 2.8 | 3.8 | 3.4 | 3.2 | 3.1 | 3.2 | 3.4 | 3.4 | 3.4 | 3.0 |
| Peru / Perú | 6.5 | 3.5 | 2.9 | 2.0 | 1.5 | 1.4 | 1.5 | 1.3 | 1.3 | 1.4 |
| Uruguay | 5.1 | 3.7 | 4.3 | 3.9 | 3.1 | 3.1 | 3.3 | 3.4 | 3.3 | 2.4 |
| Venezuela | 2.1 | 2.4 | 1.8 | 2.2 | 2.0 | 1.9 | 1.7 | 1.8 | 1.9 | 1.8 |
| *Unweighted average / Moyenne non pondérée* | | | | | | | | | | |
| **LAC / ALC[2]** | **4.0** | **3.9** | **3.8** | **3.8** | **3.7** | **3.3** | **3.6** | **3.6** | **3.6** | **3.6** |
| **OECD / OCDE[3]** | **4.0** | **3.7** | **3.6** | **3.4** | **3.3** | **3.3** | **3.4** | **3.4** | **3.4** | .. |

*Note:* The figures exclude local government revenues for Argentina (but include provincial revenues), Barbados, Bolivia, Costa Rica (up to 1997), Dominican Republic, Ecuador, El Salvador, Honduras, Jamaica, Nicaragua, Panama (up to 1998), Paraguay (up to 2004 and 2013), Peru (up to 2004), Uruguay (2013) and Venezuela as the data are not available.

1. Estimated data for 2013.
2. Represents a group of 20 Latin American and Caribbean countries. Chile and Mexico are also part of the OECD (34) group.
3. Represents the unweighted average for OECD member countries.

*Nota :* Las cifras excluyen los ingresos de gobiernos locales en Argentina (pero incluye ingresos de las provincias), Barbados, Bolivia, Costa Rica (hasta 1997), República Dominicana, Ecuador, El Salvador, Honduras, Jamaica, Nicaragua, Panamá (hasta 1998), Paraguay (hasta 2004 y 2013), Perú (hasta 2004), Uruguay (2013) y Venezuela dado que los datos no están disponibles.

1. Datos estimados para el 2013.
2. Representa un grupo de 20 países de América Latina y el Caribe. Chile y México son también parte del grupo OCDE (34).
3. Representa el promedio no ponderado para los países miembros de la OCDE.

StatLink http://dx.doi.org/10.1787/888933190557

## Table 15. Taxes on specific goods and services (5120) as percentage of total taxation
## Cuadro 15. Impuestos específicos sobre bienes y servicios (5120) en porcentaje del total de ingresos tributarios

| | 1990 | 2000 | 2005 | 2007 | 2008 | 2009 | 2010 | 2011 | 2012 | 2013 |
|---|---|---|---|---|---|---|---|---|---|---|
| Argentina | 30.6 | 15.0 | 19.0 | 17.6 | 19.7 | 16.8 | 17.6 | 16.0 | 15.0 | 12.7 |
| Barbados | 23.9 | 15.5 | 15.8 | 12.3 | 13.2 | 11.7 | 12.5 | 12.2 | 11.8 | 12.8 |
| Bolivia | 26.6 | 33.6 | 35.0 | 44.5 | 47.1 | 34.7 | 38.2 | 38.5 | 36.7 | 40.0 |
| Brazil / Brasil | 0.0 | 2.4 | 2.6 | 2.5 | 2.6 | 2.2 | 2.6 | 2.7 | 2.5 | 2.5 |
| Chile | 23.0 | 18.8 | 10.9 | 8.7 | 8.7 | 10.1 | 9.8 | 9.4 | 9.4 | 9.7 |
| Colombia | 27.8 | 12.4 | 9.7 | 9.5 | 9.0 | 8.4 | 9.1 | 7.6 | 6.5 | 8.0 |
| Costa Rica | 26.8 | 23.9 | 22.1 | 21.7 | 20.3 | 19.3 | 18.6 | 18.9 | 16.8 | 15.8 |
| Dominican Republic / República Dominicana | 53.6 | 51.9 | 45.6 | 37.3 | 37.7 | 37.2 | 37.5 | 36.2 | 33.2 | 30.0 |
| Ecuador | 33.8 | 26.1 | 15.8 | 13.7 | 14.6 | 14.7 | 18.6 | 17.0 | 18.9 | 18.8 |
| El Salvador | 25.0 | 11.8 | 14.2 | 12.5 | 12.4 | 13.3 | 13.3 | 13.1 | 12.7 | 12.1 |
| Guatemala | 32.8 | 23.4 | 19.6 | 16.6 | 14.6 | 14.6 | 14.0 | 12.4 | 11.3 | 10.3 |
| Honduras | 52.2 | 38.5 | 30.4 | 26.7 | 24.5 | 24.9 | 24.9 | 23.5 | 22.8 | 22.1 |
| Jamaica | 41.6 | 35.1 | 30.5 | 29.2 | 28.7 | 29.9 | 35.3 | 35.0 | 36.5 | 37.6 |
| Mexico / México | 34.0 | 33.4 | 36.6 | 31.6 | 40.3 | 29.4 | 31.2 | 34.3 | 34.9 | 32.9 |
| Nicaragua | .. | 31.5 | 24.3 | 21.5 | 20.4 | 18.4 | 19.9 | 18.3 | 17.9 | 16.9 |
| Panama / Panamá | 15.5 | 23.8 | 22.3 | 22.9 | 15.9 | 15.1 | 14.7 | 14.2 | 13.2 | 12.1 |
| Paraguay[1] | 51.4 | 25.9 | 24.6 | 22.7 | 21.1 | 19.9 | 20.8 | 20.4 | 19.3 | 18.1 |
| Peru / Perú | 53.5 | 24.1 | 17.1 | 10.7 | 7.9 | 8.4 | 8.1 | 7.2 | 7.0 | 7.5 |
| Uruguay | 25.9 | 17.3 | 17.9 | 15.8 | 11.7 | 11.5 | 12.2 | 12.6 | 12.2 | 8.7 |
| Venezuela | 11.1 | 17.5 | 11.4 | 13.0 | 14.0 | 13.4 | 15.1 | 13.4 | 13.4 | 12.9 |
| *Unweighted average / Moyenne non pondérée* | | | | | | | | | | |
| **LAC / ALC[2]** | **31.0** | **24.1** | **21.3** | **19.5** | **19.2** | **17.7** | **18.7** | **18.1** | **17.6** | **17.1** |
| **OECD / OCDE[3]** | **13.2** | **11.5** | **11.1** | **10.4** | **10.5** | **10.6** | **10.8** | **10.7** | **10.7** | .. |

*Note:* The figures exclude local government revenues for Argentina (but include provincial revenues), Barbados, Bolivia, Costa Rica (up to 1997), Dominican Republic, Ecuador, El Salvador, Honduras, Jamaica, Nicaragua, Panama (up to 1998), Paraguay (up to 2004 and 2013), Peru (up to 2004), Uruguay (2013) and Venezuela as the data are not available.

1. Estimated data for 2013.
2. Represents a group of 20 Latin American and Caribbean countries. Chile and Mexico are also part of the OECD (34) group.
3. Represents the unweighted average for OECD member countries.

*Nota :* Las cifras excluyen los ingresos de gobiernos locales en Argentina (pero incluye ingresos de las provincias), Barbados, Bolivia, Costa Rica (hasta 1997), República Dominicana, Ecuador, El Salvador, Honduras, Jamaica, Nicaragua, Panamá (hasta 1998), Paraguay (hasta 2004 y 2013), Perú (hasta 2004), Uruguay (2013) y Venezuela dado que los datos no están disponibles.

1. Datos estimados para el 2013.
2. Representa un grupo de 20 países de América Latina y el Caribe. Chile y México son también parte del grupo OCDE (34).
3. Representa el promedio no ponderado para los países miembros de la OCDE.

StatLink http://dx.doi.org/10.1787/888933190568

## Table 16. Gross domestic product for tax reporting years at market prices, in billions of national currency units
## Cuadro 16. Producto interno bruto para los años fiscales a precios de mercado, en millardos de moneda local

| | 1990 | 2000 | 2005 | 2007 | 2008 | 2009 | 2010 | 2011 | 2012 | 2013 |
|---|---|---|---|---|---|---|---|---|---|---|
| Argentina | 82 | 340 | 647 | 1 027 | 1 284 | 1 412 | 1 810 | 2 303 | 2 745 | 3 342 |
| Barbados | 4 098 | 6 239 | 7 783 | 9 026 | 9 083 | 9 185 | 8 867 | 8 738 | 8 450 | 8 456 |
| Bolivia | 15 | 52 | 77 | 103 | 121 | 122 | 138 | 166 | 187 | 211 |
| Brazil / Brasil | 0 | 1 179 | 2 147 | 2 661 | 3 032 | 3 239 | 3 770 | 4 143 | 4 392 | 4 845 |
| Chile | 10 482 | 42 095 | 68 883 | 90 429 | 93 848 | 96 444 | 111 008 | 121 403 | 129 601 | 137 212 |
| Colombia | 28 651 | 208 531 | 340 156 | 431 072 | 480 087 | 504 647 | 544 924 | 619 894 | 665 441 | 706 677 |
| Costa Rica | 664 | 4 915 | 9 539 | 13 598 | 15 702 | 16 845 | 19 087 | 20 852 | 22 819 | 24 799 |
| Dominican Republic / República Dominicana | 77 | 388 | 1 020 | 1 364 | 1 576 | 1 679 | 1 902 | 2 119 | 2 317 | 2 534 |
| Ecuador | 15 | 18 | 42 | 51 | 62 | 63 | 70 | 79 | 88 | 94 |
| El Salvador | 5 | 13 | 17 | 20 | 21 | 21 | 21 | 23 | 25 | 25 |
| Guatemala | 31 | 133 | 208 | 262 | 296 | 308 | 333 | 371 | 395 | 423 |
| Honduras | 13 | 107 | 184 | 234 | 262 | 276 | 299 | 335 | 362 | 378 |
| Jamaica | 34 | 385 | 700 | 885 | 997 | 1 066 | 1 154 | 1 241 | 1 316 | 1 430 |
| Mexico / México | 825 | 6 132 | 9 425 | 11 399 | 12 257 | 12 073 | 13 267 | 14 509 | 15 561 | 16 049 |
| Nicaragua | .. | 65 | 106 | 138 | 164 | 170 | 191 | 222 | 251 | 278 |
| Panama / Panamá | 6 077 | 11 621 | 15 465 | 19 794 | 23 002 | 24 163 | 26 590 | 31 316 | 35 938 | 40 467 |
| Paraguay | 6 474 | 24 737 | 53 962 | 69 426 | 80 735 | 79 117 | 94 934 | 105 203 | 108 832 | 124 853 |
| Peru / Perú | 5 | 178 | 247 | 320 | 356 | 365 | 420 | 470 | 508 | 547 |
| Uruguay | 12 | 276 | 425 | 549 | 636 | 687 | 780 | 912 | 1 016 | 1 141 |
| Venezuela | 2 | 80 | 304 | 495 | 678 | 707 | 1 017 | 1 357 | 1 635 | 2 212 |

*Source:* OECD National Accounts data for Chile and Mexico and official National Accounts data for the other countries. The World Economit Outlook (IMF) was used for the 2013 estimation of Panama and Venezuela.

*Fuente :* Datos de Cuentas Nacionales de la OCDE para Chile y México y estadísticas oficiales de Cuentas Nacionales para el resto de países. Para el año 2013 en Panamá y Venezuela se utilizó el World Economit Outlook (FMI).

StatLink http://dx.doi.org/10.1787/888933190574

## B. Comparative Charts / B. Gráficos comparativos

### Chart 1. Tax revenue of main headings as percentage of total tax revenue, 2013
### Gráfico 1. Ingresos tributarios de categorías principales como porcentaje del ingreso tributario total, 2013

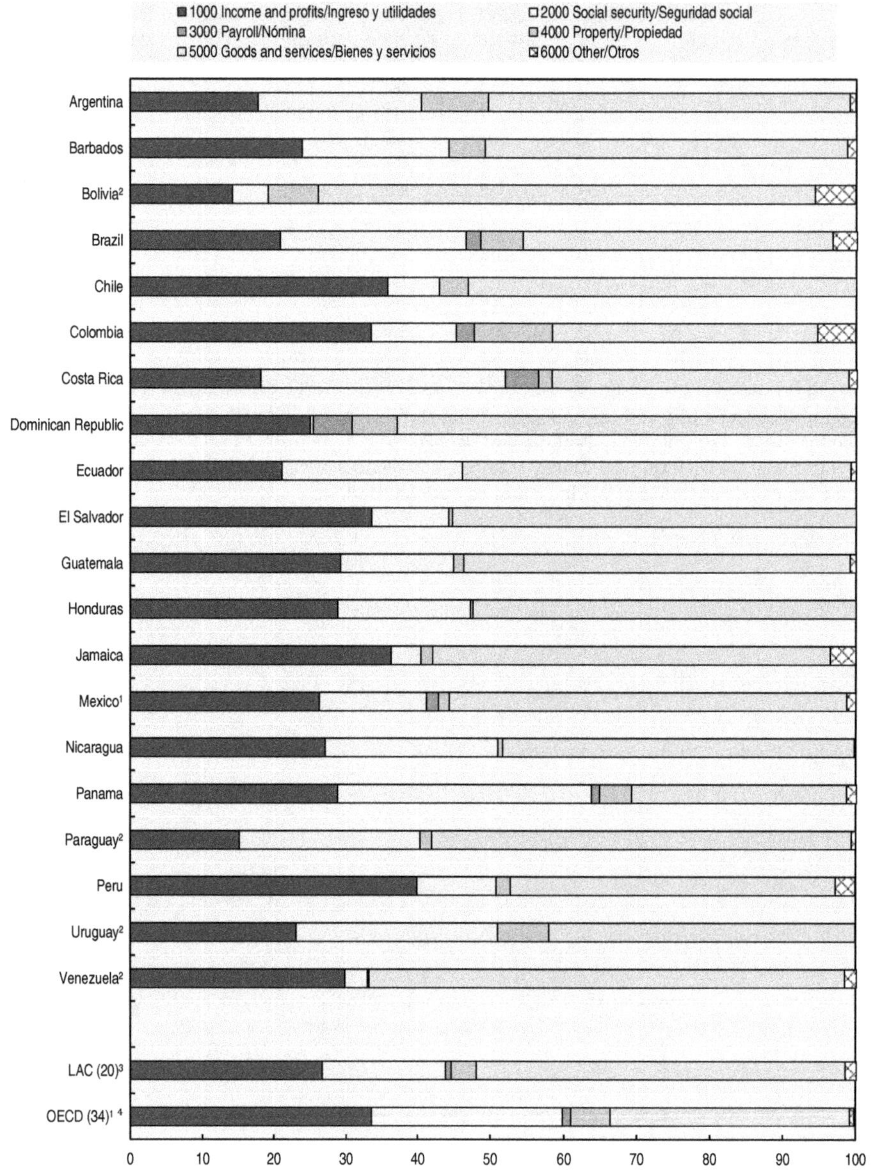


1. Data for 2012 is used.
1. Se utilizan datos del 2012.
2. Estimated data.
2. Datos estimados.
3. Represents the unweighted average for a group of 20 Latin American and Caribbean countries. Chile and Mexico are also part of the OECD (34) group.
3. Representa el promedio no ponderado para un grupo de 20 países de América Latina y el Caribe. Chile y México son también parte del grupo OCDE(34).
4. Represents the unweighted average for OECD member countries.
4. Representa el promedio no ponderado para los países miembros de la OCDE.

*Source:* Table 3 in Part II. Cuadro 3 en Parte II.

StatLink http://dx.doi.org/10.1787/888933189844

## Chart 2. Tax structures in Latin American and Caribbean countries, 1990-2013

Receipts as percentage of total tax revenues

## Gráfico 2. Estructuras impositivas en países de América Latina y el Caribe, 1990-2013

Ingresos como porcentaje de los ingresos tributarios totales

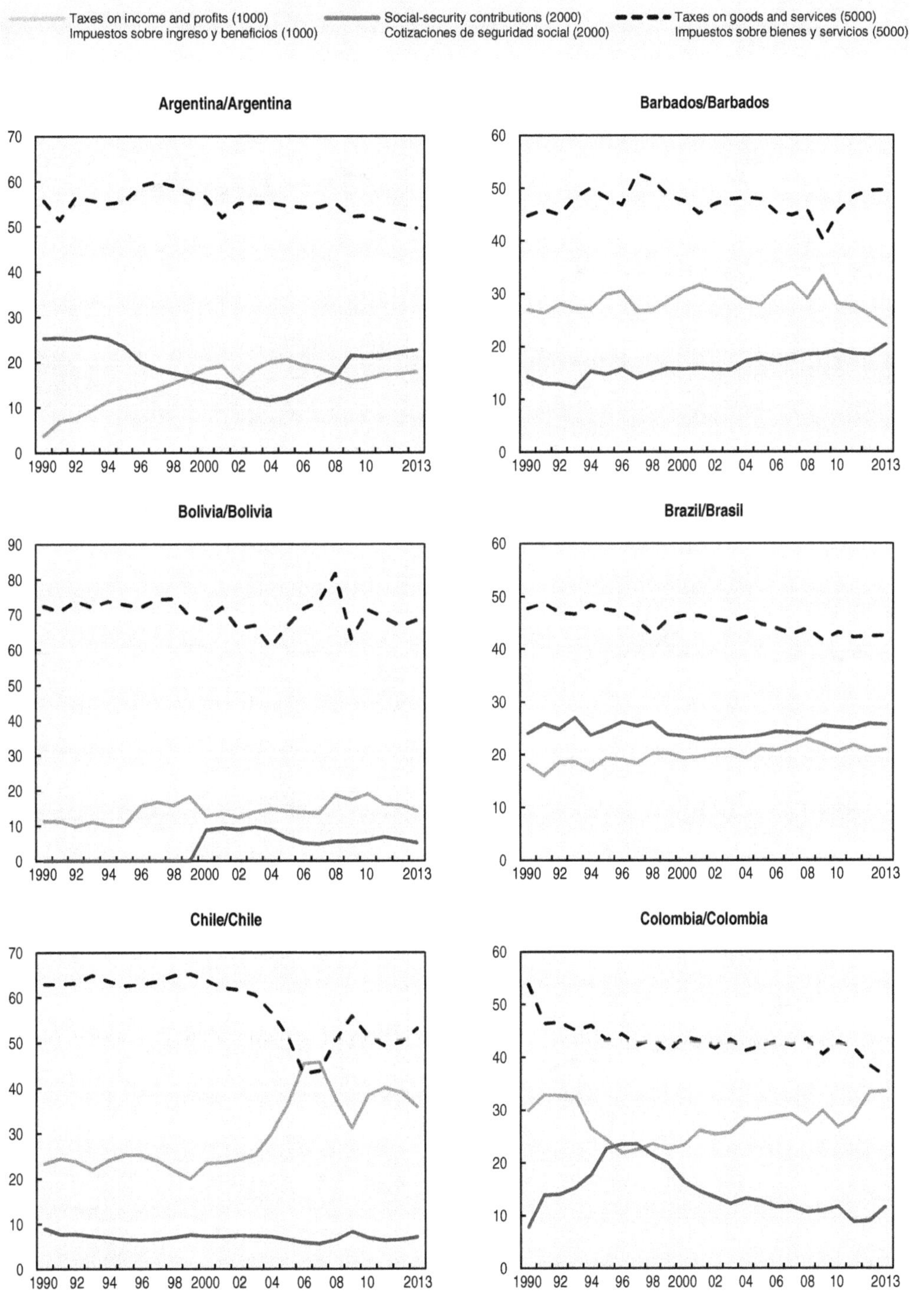

## Chart 2. **Tax structures in Latin American and Caribbean countries, 1990-2013** *(cont.)*

Receipts as percentage of total tax revenues

## Gráfico 2. **Estructuras impositivas en países de América Latina y el Caribe, 1990-2013** *(cont.)*

Ingresos como porcentaje de los ingresos tributarios totales

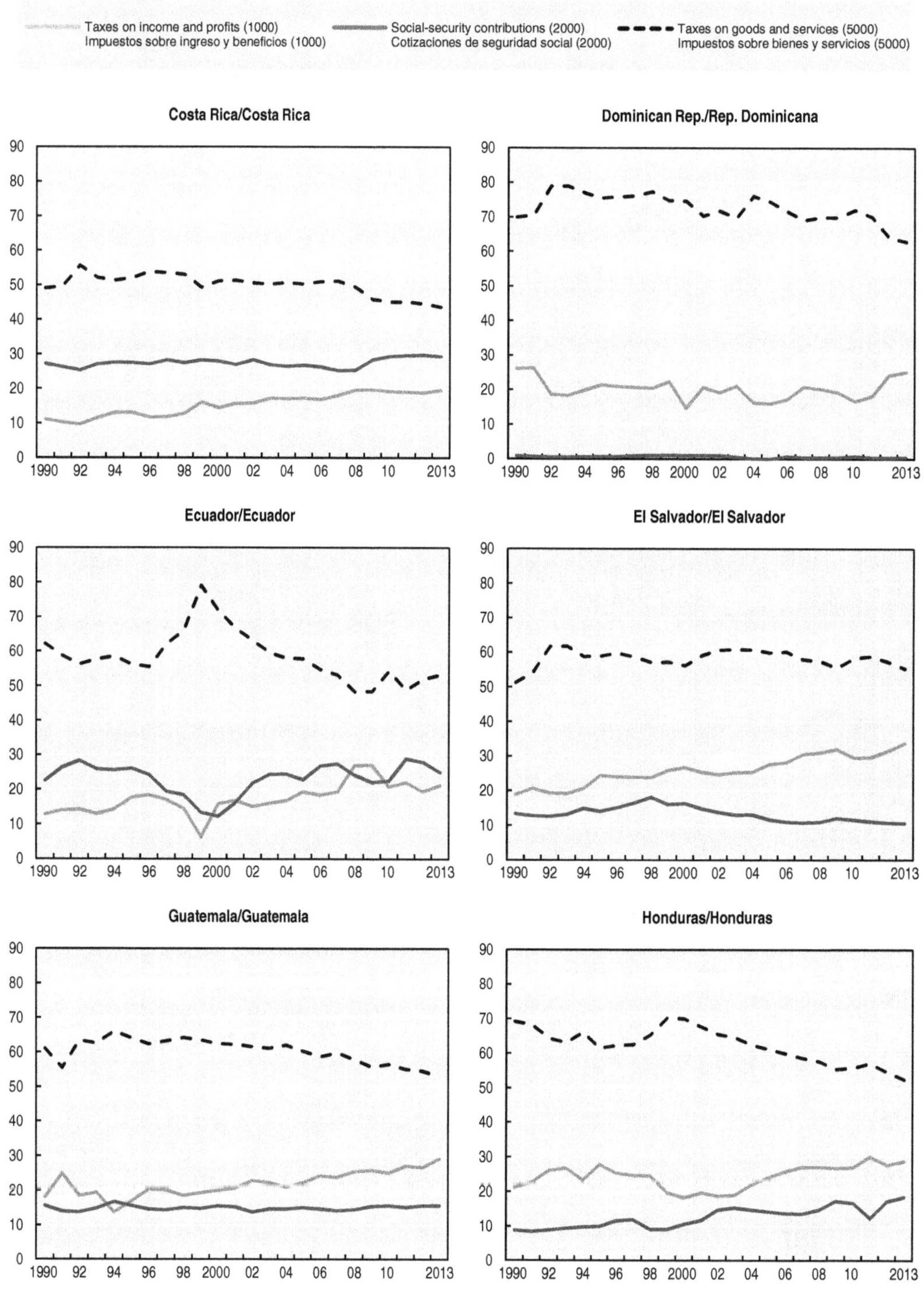

## Chart 2. **Tax structures in Latin American and Caribbean countries, 1990-2013** *(cont.)*

Receipts as percentage of total tax revenues

## Gráfico 2. **Estructuras impositivas en países de América Latina y el Caribe, 1990-2013** *(cont.)*

Ingresos como porcentaje de los ingresos tributarios totales

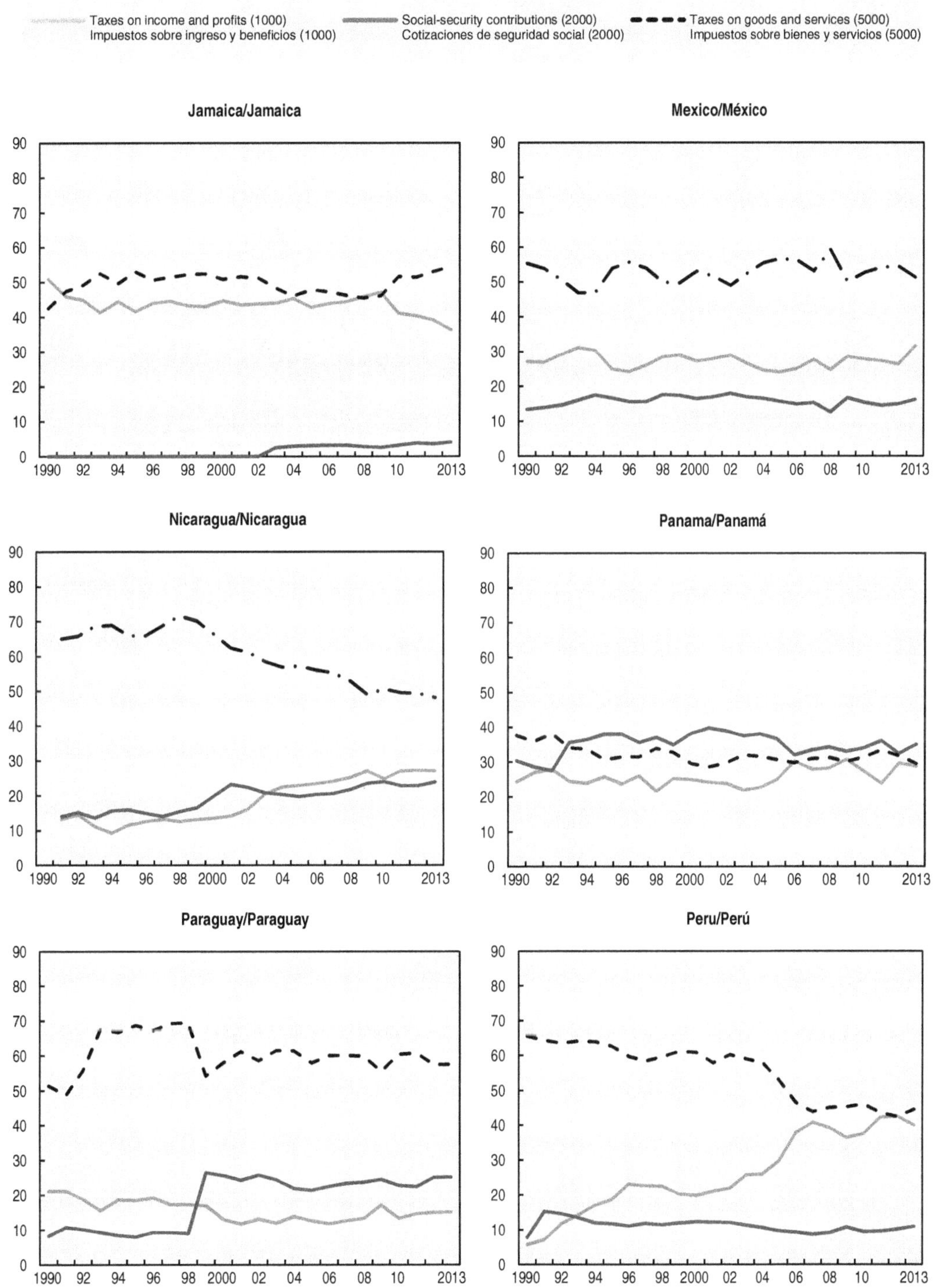

Chart 2. **Tax structures in Latin American and Caribbean countries, 1990-2013** *(cont.)*

Receipts as percentage of total tax revenues

Gráfico 2. **Estructuras impositivas en países de América Latina y el Caribe, 1990-2013** *(cont.)*

Ingresos como porcentaje de los ingresos tributarios totales

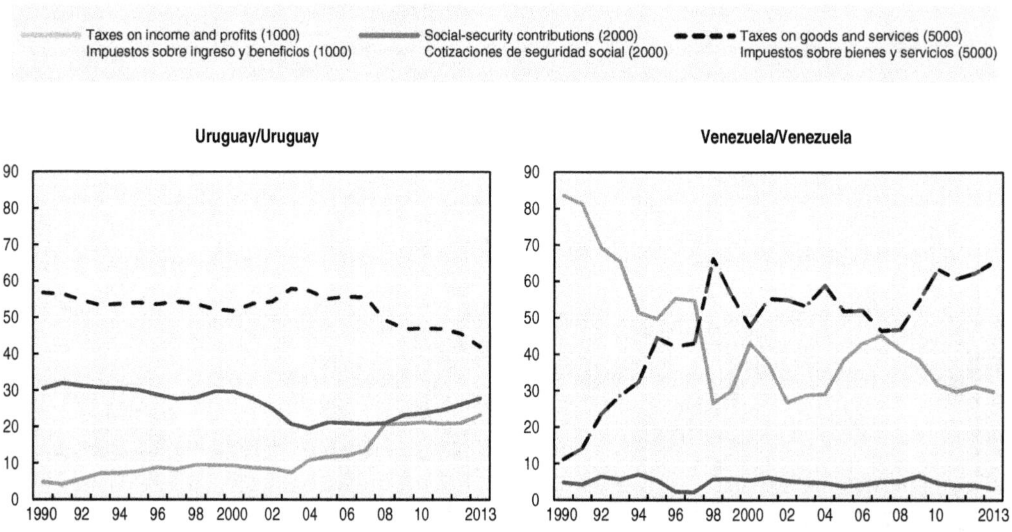


StatLink http://dx.doi.org/10.1787/888933189852

# PART III

# COUNTRY TABLES 1990-2013 – TAX REVENUES

# PARTE III

# CUADROS PAÍS, 1990-2013 – INGRESOS TRIBUTARIOS

## Table 17. Argentina / Argentina
Details of tax revenue / Ingresos tributarios detallados

*Million ARS*

| | 1990 | 2000 | 2005 | 2007 | 2008 | 2009 | 2010 | 2011 | 2012 | 2013 |
|---|---|---|---|---|---|---|---|---|---|---|
| **Total tax revenue** | **10 218** | **61 085** | **142 905** | **236 512** | **317 585** | **360 951** | **483 015** | **638 355** | **808 848** | **1 043 048** |
| **1000 Taxes on income, profits and capital gains** | **382** | **11 304** | **29 202** | **44 226** | **54 722** | **56 887** | **78 428** | **110 118** | **140 108** | **185 688** |
| 1100 Of individuals | 12 | 3 937 | 8 192 | 12 777 | 17 614 | 19 574 | 23 981 | 35 436 | 54 498 | 79 582 |
| 1110 On income and profits | .. | 3 855 | 8 151 | 12 715 | 17 534 | 19 460 | 23 859 | 35 279 | 54 283 | 79 228 |
| 1120 On capital gains | 12 | 82 | 41 | 62 | 80 | 114 | 122 | 157 | 215 | 354 |
| 1200 Corporate | .. | 6 575 | 19 601 | 29 145 | 34 026 | 33 921 | 50 664 | 70 717 | 81 934 | 99 470 |
| 1210 On profits | .. | 6 575 | 19 601 | 29 145 | 34 026 | 33 921 | 50 664 | 70 717 | 81 934 | 99 470 |
| Corporate income taxes | .. | 5 956 | 18 494 | 27 837 | 33 031 | 32 702 | 49 012 | 69 356 | 80 486 | 97 739 |
| Tax on assets | .. | 19 | 5 | 9 | 7 | 6 | 4 | 4 | 5 | 3 |
| Tax on assumed minimum income | .. | 600 | 1 102 | 1 299 | 988 | 1 213 | 1 648 | 1 357 | 1 443 | 1 728 |
| 1220 On capital gains | .. | .. | .. | .. | .. | .. | .. | .. | .. | .. |
| 1300 Unallocable between 1100 and 1200 | 371 | 792 | 1 409 | 2 304 | 3 082 | 3 392 | 3 783 | 3 965 | 3 676 | 6 636 |
| Non resident taxpayers | 0 | 792 | 1 409 | 2 304 | 3 082 | 3 392 | 3 783 | 3 965 | 3 676 | 6 636 |
| Other | 371 | 0 | 0 | 0 | 0 | 0 | 0 | 0 | 0 | 0 |
| **2000 Social security contributions** | **2 583** | **9 670** | **17 400** | **36 606** | **52 565** | **77 230** | **102 460** | **137 187** | **179 777** | **236 072** |
| 2100 Employees | .. | 2 486 | 3 690 | 7 052 | 12 917 | 28 871 | 37 990 | 51 715 | 70 087 | 91 768 |
| 2110 On a payroll basis | .. | 2 486 | 3 690 | 7 052 | 12 917 | 28 871 | 37 990 | 51 715 | 70 087 | 91 768 |
| 2120 On an income tax basis | .. | 0 | 0 | 0 | 0 | 0 | 0 | 0 | 0 | 0 |
| 2200 Employers | .. | 6 069 | 12 557 | 23 939 | 32 459 | 40 473 | 54 713 | 75 550 | 100 029 | 133 290 |
| 2210 On a payroll basis | .. | 6 069 | 12 557 | 23 939 | 32 459 | 40 473 | 54 713 | 75 550 | 100 029 | 133 290 |
| 2220 On an income tax basis | .. | 0 | 0 | 0 | 0 | 0 | 0 | 0 | 0 | 0 |
| 2300 Self-employed or non-employed | 98 | 1 115 | 1 153 | 5 615 | 7 189 | 7 886 | 9 757 | 9 922 | 9 661 | 11 014 |
| 2310 On a payroll basis | 98 | 1 115 | 1 153 | 5 615 | 7 189 | 7 886 | 9 757 | 9 922 | 9 661 | 11 014 |
| 2320 On an income tax basis | 0 | 0 | 0 | 0 | 0 | 0 | 0 | 0 | 0 | 0 |
| 2400 Unallocable between 2100, 2200 and 2300 | 2 485 | 0 | 0 | 0 | 0 | 0 | 0 | 0 | 0 | 0 |
| 2410 On a payroll basis | 2 485 | .. | .. | .. | .. | .. | .. | .. | .. | .. |
| 2420 On an income tax basis | 0 | .. | .. | .. | .. | .. | .. | .. | .. | .. |
| **3000 Taxes on payroll and workforce** | **0** | **0** | **0** | **0** | **0** | **0** | **0** | **0** | **0** | **0** |
| **4000 Taxes on property** | **1 302** | **3 896** | **15 997** | **23 977** | **30 859** | **33 167** | **43 539** | **57 521** | **72 431** | **96 390** |
| 4100 Recurrent taxes on immovable property | 412 | 1 809 | 2 836 | 3 025 | 3 929 | 4 170 | 5 035 | 6 092 | 9 814 | 14 038 |
| 4110 Households | 0 | 0 | 0 | 0 | 0 | 0 | 0 | 0 | 0 | 0 |
| 4120 Others | 412 | 1 809 | 2 836 | 3 025 | 3 929 | 4 170 | 5 035 | 6 092 | 9 814 | 14 038 |
| 4200 Recurrent taxes on net wealth | 235 | 1 084 | 1 868 | 2 557 | 3 446 | 4 123 | 5 248 | 6 018 | 7 408 | 10 471 |
| 4210 Individual | 232 | 1 024 | 1 813 | 2 492 | 3 375 | 4 041 | 5 147 | 5 892 | 7 263 | 10 296 |
| Personal assets | 232 | 1 024 | 1 813 | 2 492 | 3 375 | 4 041 | 5 147 | 5 892 | 7 263 | 10 296 |
| Recurrent taxes on net wealth | 0 | 0 | 0 | 0 | 0 | 0 | 0 | 0 | 0 | 0 |
| 4220 Corporate | 3 | 60 | 55 | 65 | 71 | 82 | 101 | 126 | 145 | 175 |
| 4300 Estate, inheritance and gift taxes | 0 | 0 | 0 | 0 | 0 | 0 | 0 | 0 | 0 | 0 |
| 4310 Estate and inheritance taxes | .. | .. | .. | .. | .. | .. | .. | .. | .. | .. |
| 4320 Gift taxes | .. | .. | .. | .. | .. | .. | .. | .. | .. | .. |
| 4400 Taxes on financial and capital transactions | 656 | 933 | 11 272 | 18 389 | 23 480 | 24 870 | 33 253 | 45 411 | 55 208 | 71 881 |
| Immovable property transfers | 0 | 54 | 116 | 382 | 439 | 372 | 539 | 775 | 721 | 734 |
| Movable property transfers | 0 | 0 | 0 | 0 | 0 | 0 | 0 | 0 | 0 | 0 |
| Bank accounts' credits and debits | 415 | 0 | 9 434 | 15 065 | 19 495 | 20 561 | 26 885 | 36 179 | 43 931 | 56 515 |
| Provincial taxes on financial and capital transactions | 160 | 833 | 1 722 | 2 942 | 3 546 | 3 937 | 5 829 | 8 457 | 10 556 | 14 632 |
| Stamp taxes | 81 | 46 | 0 | 0 | 0 | 0 | 0 | 0 | 0 | 0 |
| 4500 Non-recurrent taxes | 0 | 70 | 21 | 6 | 4 | 4 | 3 | 0 | 1 | 0 |
| 4510 On net wealth | .. | 0 | 0 | 0 | 0 | 0 | 0 | .. | 0 | .. |
| 4520 Other non-recurrent taxes | .. | 70 | 21 | 6 | 4 | 4 | 3 | .. | 1 | .. |
| 4600 Other recurrent taxes on property | 0 | 0 | 0 | 0 | 0 | 0 | 0 | 0 | 0 | 0 |
| **5000 Taxes on goods and services** | **5 692** | **34 510** | **77 960** | **128 333** | **175 234** | **188 345** | **253 092** | **327 003** | **408 457** | **516 688** |
| 5100 Taxes on production, sale, transfer, etc | 5 559 | 33 706 | 76 671 | 126 412 | 172 726 | 185 117 | 249 494 | 322 082 | 402 001 | 508 032 |
| 5110 General taxes | 2 437 | 24 541 | 49 581 | 84 890 | 110 212 | 124 407 | 164 478 | 220 074 | 280 298 | 375 736 |
| 5111 Value added taxes | 1 591 | 18 427 | 34 968 | 60 756 | 77 335 | 84 935 | 113 330 | 149 547 | 188 509 | 243 612 |
| 5112 Sales tax | 0 | 0 | 0 | 0 | 0 | 0 | 0 | 0 | 0 | 0 |
| 5113 Other | 846 | 6 114 | 14 613 | 24 134 | 32 877 | 39 472 | 51 148 | 70 527 | 91 789 | 132 124 |
| 5120 Taxes on specific goods and services | 3 122 | 9 165 | 27 090 | 41 522 | 62 514 | 60 710 | 85 016 | 102 008 | 121 703 | 132 296 |
| 5121 Excises | 2 082 | 5 850 | 10 611 | 13 168 | 16 439 | 19 522 | 26 207 | 30 851 | 40 799 | 49 680 |
| Alcoholic beverages | 0 | 36 | 73 | 95 | 116 | 169 | 238 | 322 | 422 | 525 |
| Non Alcoholic beverages | 0 | 90 | 189 | 312 | 411 | 441 | 501 | 654 | 912 | 1 195 |
| Beers | 0 | 50 | 131 | 149 | 228 | 226 | 212 | 210 | 332 | 650 |
| Tobacco products | 0 | 1 875 | 3 460 | 3 881 | 4 686 | 5 751 | 6 884 | 8 620 | 10 310 | 12 343 |
| Liquid fuel and gas | 1 068 | 3 478 | 6 019 | 7 469 | 9 701 | 11 593 | 15 269 | 18 131 | 25 785 | 31 010 |
| Electricity | 72 | 205 | 283 | 538 | 556 | 559 | 591 | 616 | 610 | 547 |
| Motor vehicles | 0 | 20 | 0 | 0 | 15 | 36 | 27 | 24 | 153 | 185 |
| Other | 942 | 96 | 456 | 724 | 726 | 747 | 2 485 | 2 274 | 2 275 | 3 225 |
| 5122 Profits of fiscal monopolies | 0 | 0 | 0 | 0 | 0 | 0 | 0 | 0 | 0 | 0 |

## Table 17. Argentina / Argentina *(cont.)*
Details of tax revenue / Ingresos tributarios detallados

*Million ARS*

| | 1990 | 2000 | 2005 | 2007 | 2008 | 2009 | 2010 | 2011 | 2012 | 2013 |
|---|---|---|---|---|---|---|---|---|---|---|
| 5123 Customs and import duties | 219 | 1 976 | 3 876 | 7 015 | 8 988 | 7 700 | 11 429 | 14 678 | 16 640 | 23 550 |
| Import duties | 166 | 1 938 | 3 780 | 6 859 | 8 803 | 7 526 | 11 183 | 14 373 | 16 313 | 23 134 |
| Export duties | 53 | 38 | 96 | 156 | 185 | 174 | 246 | 305 | 327 | 416 |
| 5124 Taxes on exports | 724 | 32 | 12 323 | 20 450 | 36 055 | 32 042 | 45 547 | 54 163 | 61 316 | 55 465 |
| 5125 Taxes on investment goods | 0 | 0 | 0 | 0 | 0 | 0 | 0 | 0 | 0 | 0 |
| 5126 Taxes on specific services | 0 | 1 233 | 151 | 675 | 769 | 1 191 | 1 429 | 1 819 | 2 227 | 2 677 |
| Insurance services | .. | 194 | 8 | 11 | 13 | 17 | 21 | 27 | 35 | 46 |
| Financial services | .. | 855 | 2 | 1 | 1 | 0 | 0 | 0 | 0 | 0 |
| Telephone services | .. | 33 | 110 | 417 | 480 | 779 | 936 | 1 163 | 1 391 | 1 605 |
| Other specific services | .. | 151 | 31 | 246 | 275 | 395 | 472 | 629 | 801 | 1 026 |
| 5127 Other taxes on internat. trade and transactions | 97 | 74 | 129 | 214 | 263 | 255 | 404 | 497 | 721 | 924 |
| 5128 Other taxes | 0 | 0 | 0 | 0 | 0 | 0 | 0 | 0 | 0 | 0 |
| 5130 Unallocable between 5110 and 5120 | 0 | 0 | 0 | 0 | 0 | 0 | 0 | 0 | 0 | 0 |
| 5200 Taxes on use of goods and perform activities | 133 | 804 | 1 289 | 1 921 | 2 508 | 3 228 | 3 598 | 4 921 | 6 456 | 8 656 |
| 5210 Recurrent taxes | 133 | 804 | 1 289 | 1 921 | 2 508 | 3 228 | 3 598 | 4 921 | 6 456 | 8 656 |
| 5211 Paid by households: motor vehicles | 0 | 0 | 0 | 0 | 0 | 0 | 0 | 0 | 0 | 0 |
| 5212 Paid by others: motor vehicles | 133 | 804 | 1 289 | 1 921 | 2 508 | 3 228 | 3 598 | 4 921 | 6 456 | 8 656 |
| 5213 Paid in respect of other goods | 0 | 0 | 0 | 0 | 0 | 0 | 0 | 0 | 0 | 0 |
| 5220 Non-recurrent taxes | 0 | 0 | 0 | 0 | 0 | 0 | 0 | 0 | 0 | 0 |
| 5300 Unallocable between 5100 and 5200 | 0 | 0 | 0 | 0 | 0 | 0 | 0 | 0 | 0 | 0 |
| **6000 Other taxes** | **258** | **1 705** | **2 346** | **3 370** | **4 205** | **5 322** | **5 496** | **6 526** | **8 075** | **8 210** |
| 6100 Paid solely by business | 0 | 354 | 757 | 1 063 | 1 355 | 1 550 | 2 093 | 2 983 | 3 825 | 4 423 |
| Simplified system for small taxpayers | .. | 354 | 757 | 1 063 | 1 355 | 1 550 | 2 093 | 2 983 | 3 825 | 4 423 |
| 6200 Other | 258 | 1 351 | 1 589 | 2 307 | 2 850 | 3 772 | 3 403 | 3 543 | 4 250 | 3 787 |
| Tax debt payments | 135 | 24 | 112 | 38 | 237 | 1 629 | 293 | 710 | 934 | -1 313 |
| Special payments | 80 | 6 | 1 | 0 | 0 | 0 | 0 | 0 | 0 | 0 |
| Other national level | 0 | 12 | 7 | 0 | 0 | 0 | 0 | 0 | 0 | 0 |
| Other provincial level | 43 | 1 309 | 1 469 | 2 269 | 2 613 | 2 143 | 3 110 | 2 833 | 3 316 | 5 100 |

*Note:* Year ending 31st December.
The data are on cash basis.
Figures exclude local government tax revenues as the data are not available.
Heading 5212: In ECLAC data, property tax on motor vehicles is classified in category 4000.
*Source:* Subsecretaría de Ingresos Públicos, Dirección Nacional de Coordinación Fiscal con las Provincias, Ministry of Economy and Production.

StatLink http://dx.doi.org/10.1787/888933190220

## Table 18. Barbados / Barbados
### Details of tax revenue / Ingresos tributarios detallados

*Million BAR*

| | 1990 | 2000 | 2005 | 2007 | 2008 | 2009 | 2010 | 2011 | 2012 | 2013 |
|---|---|---|---|---|---|---|---|---|---|---|
| **Total tax revenue** | **942 335** | **1 884 313** | **2 297 009** | **2 748 252** | **2 862 355** | **2 810 305** | **2 719 302** | **2 821 723** | **2 869 093** | **2 522 896** |
| **1000 Taxes on income, profits and capital gains** | **254 016** | **573 920** | **639 432** | **877 992** | **829 428** | **934 345** | **762 340** | **781 866** | **744 289** | **601 963** |
| 1100 Of individuals | 128 857 | 288 692 | 295 737 | 316 086 | 335 285 | 410 348 | 388 177 | 419 468 | 379 969 | 331 318 |
| 1110 On income and profits | 128 857 | 288 692 | 295 737 | 316 086 | 335 285 | 410 348 | 388 177 | 419 468 | 379 969 | 331 318 |
| 1120 On capital gains | .. | .. | .. | .. | .. | .. | .. | .. | .. | .. |
| 1200 Corporate | 111 111 | 252 291 | 294 320 | 499 054 | 419 233 | 457 825 | 327 471 | 298 535 | 276 296 | 191 330 |
| 1210 On profits | 111 111 | 252 291 | 294 320 | 499 054 | 419 233 | 457 825 | 327 471 | 298 535 | 276 296 | 191 330 |
| 1220 On capital gains | .. | .. | .. | .. | .. | .. | .. | .. | .. | .. |
| 1300 Unallocable between 1100 and 1200 | 14 048 | 32 937 | 49 375 | 62 852 | 74 910 | 66 172 | 46 692 | 63 863 | 88 024 | 79 315 |
| **2000 Social security contributions** | **133 866** | **295 268** | **408 109** | **487 062** | **527 999** | **523 444** | **525 467** | **525 706** | **529 263** | **512 521** |
| 2100 Employees | .. | .. | .. | .. | .. | .. | .. | .. | .. | .. |
| 2110 On a payroll basis | .. | .. | .. | .. | .. | .. | .. | .. | .. | .. |
| 2120 On an income tax basis | .. | .. | .. | .. | .. | .. | .. | .. | .. | .. |
| 2200 Employers | .. | .. | .. | .. | .. | .. | .. | .. | .. | .. |
| 2210 On a payroll basis | .. | .. | .. | .. | .. | .. | .. | .. | .. | .. |
| 2220 On an income tax basis | .. | .. | .. | .. | .. | .. | .. | .. | .. | .. |
| 2300 Self-employed or non-employed | .. | .. | .. | .. | .. | .. | .. | .. | .. | .. |
| 2310 On a payroll basis | .. | .. | .. | .. | .. | .. | .. | .. | .. | .. |
| 2320 On an income tax basis | .. | .. | .. | .. | .. | .. | .. | .. | .. | .. |
| 2400 Unallocable between 2100, 2200 and 2300 | 133 866 | 295 268 | 408 109 | 487 062 | 527 999 | 523 444 | 525 467 | 525 706 | 529 263 | 512 521 |
| 2410 On a payroll basis | .. | .. | .. | .. | .. | .. | .. | .. | .. | .. |
| 2420 On an income tax basis | .. | .. | .. | .. | .. | .. | .. | .. | .. | .. |
| **3000 Taxes on payroll and workforce** | **0** | **0** | **0** | **0** | **0** | **0** | **0** | **0** | **0** | **0** |
| **4000 Taxes on property** | **39 117** | **91 928** | **127 362** | **114 851** | **120 295** | **154 772** | **113 533** | **111 726** | **148 176** | **124 972** |
| 4100 Recurrent taxes on immovable property | 25 991 | 60 216 | 76 247 | 71 573 | 92 491 | 137 649 | 97 595 | 95 149 | 133 321 | 109 436 |
| 4110 Households | .. | .. | .. | .. | .. | .. | .. | .. | .. | .. |
| 4120 Others | .. | .. | .. | .. | .. | .. | .. | .. | .. | .. |
| 4200 Recurrent taxes on net wealth | 0 | 0 | 0 | 0 | 0 | 0 | 0 | 0 | 0 | 0 |
| 4210 Individual | .. | .. | .. | .. | .. | .. | .. | .. | .. | .. |
| 4220 Corporate | .. | .. | .. | .. | .. | .. | .. | .. | .. | .. |
| 4300 Estate, inheritance and gift taxes | 0 | 0 | 0 | 0 | 0 | 0 | 0 | 0 | 0 | 0 |
| 4310 Estate and inheritance taxes | .. | .. | .. | .. | .. | .. | .. | .. | .. | .. |
| 4320 Gift taxes | .. | .. | .. | .. | .. | .. | .. | .. | .. | .. |
| 4400 Taxes on financial and capital transactions | 0 | 0 | 0 | 0 | 0 | 0 | 0 | 0 | 0 | 0 |
| 4500 Non-recurrent taxes | 13 126 | 31 712 | 51 115 | 43 278 | 27 804 | 17 123 | 15 938 | 16 577 | 14 855 | 15 536 |
| 4510 On net wealth | .. | .. | .. | .. | .. | .. | .. | .. | .. | .. |
| 4520 Other non-recurrent taxes | .. | .. | .. | .. | .. | .. | .. | .. | .. | .. |
| 4600 Other recurrent taxes on property | 0 | 0 | 0 | 0 | 0 | 0 | 0 | 0 | 0 | 0 |
| **5000 Taxes on goods and services** | **422 259** | **897 092** | **1 101 319** | **1 233 167** | **1 310 038** | **1 124 028** | **1 242 416** | **1 366 659** | **1 420 525** | **1 252 138** |
| 5100 Taxes on production, sale, transfer, etc | 422 259 | 793 469 | 973 944 | 1 104 713 | 1 196 532 | 1 005 599 | 1 092 106 | 1 240 429 | 1 244 945 | 1 145 269 |
| 5110 General taxes | 196 817 | 501 399 | 609 915 | 765 950 | 817 511 | 677 415 | 753 003 | 897 020 | 907 255 | 821 305 |
| 5111 Value added taxes | 0 | 500 951 | 609 915 | 765 950 | 817 511 | 677 415 | 753 003 | 897 020 | 907 255 | 821 305 |
| 5112 Sales tax | 196 817 | 448 | 0 | 0 | 0 | 0 | 0 | 0 | 0 | 0 |
| 5113 Other | 0 | 0 | 0 | 0 | 0 | 0 | 0 | 0 | 0 | 0 |
| 5120 Taxes on specific goods and services | 225 442 | 292 069 | 364 029 | 338 763 | 379 021 | 328 184 | 339 103 | 343 409 | 337 690 | 323 964 |
| 5121 Excises | 4 767 | 158 803 | 172 377 | 149 054 | 162 696 | 144 895 | 148 191 | 158 864 | 137 286 | 133 297 |
| 5122 Profits of fiscal monopolies | 0 | 0 | 0 | 0 | 0 | 0 | 0 | 0 | 0 | 0 |
| 5123 Customs and import duties | 202 731 | 132 668 | 191 652 | 189 709 | 216 325 | 183 289 | 190 912 | 184 545 | 200 404 | 190 667 |
| 5124 Taxes on exports | 0 | 0 | 0 | 0 | 0 | 0 | 0 | 0 | 0 | 0 |
| 5125 Taxes on investment goods | 0 | 0 | 0 | 0 | 0 | 0 | 0 | 0 | 0 | 0 |
| 5126 Taxes on specific services | 17 944 | 598 | 0 | 0 | 0 | 0 | 0 | 0 | 0 | 0 |
| 5127 Other taxes on internat. trade and transactions | 0 | 0 | 0 | 0 | 0 | 0 | 0 | 0 | 0 | 0 |
| 5128 Other taxes | 0 | 0 | 0 | 0 | 0 | 0 | 0 | 0 | 0 | 0 |
| 5130 Unallocable between 5110 and 5120 | 0 | 0 | 0 | 0 | 0 | 0 | 0 | 0 | 0 | 0 |
| 5200 Taxes on use of goods and perform activities | 0 | 103 623 | 127 375 | 128 454 | 113 506 | 118 429 | 150 310 | 126 230 | 175 580 | 106 869 |
| 5210 Recurrent taxes | .. | 103 623 | 127 375 | 128 454 | 113 506 | 118 429 | 150 310 | 126 230 | 175 580 | 106 869 |
| 5211 Paid by households: motor vehicles | .. | 0 | 0 | 0 | 0 | 0 | 0 | 0 | 0 | 0 |
| 5212 Paid by others: motor vehicles | .. | 0 | 0 | 0 | 0 | 0 | 0 | 0 | 0 | 0 |
| 5213 Paid in respect of other goods | .. | 0 | 0 | 0 | 0 | 0 | 0 | 0 | 0 | 0 |
| 5220 Non-recurrent taxes | .. | 0 | 0 | 0 | 0 | 0 | 0 | 0 | 0 | 0 |
| 5300 Unallocable between 5100 and 5200 | 0 | 0 | 0 | 0 | 0 | 0 | 0 | 0 | 0 | 0 |
| **6000 Other taxes** | **93 077** | **26 105** | **20 787** | **35 180** | **74 594** | **73 716** | **75 546** | **35 766** | **26 840** | **31 302** |
| 6100 Paid solely by business | 0 | 0 | 0 | 0 | 0 | 0 | 0 | 0 | 0 | 0 |
| 6200 Other | 93 077 | 26 105 | 20 787 | 35 180 | 74 594 | 73 716 | 75 546 | 35 766 | 26 840 | 31 302 |

*Note:* Year ending 31st December.

The data are on cash basis.

The data exclude local government tax revenues as the data are not available.

*Source:* The Central Bank of Barbados and Inland Revenue Department.

StatLink http://dx.doi.org/10.1787/888933190239

# Table 19. Bolivia / Bolivia
## Details of tax revenue / Ingresos tributarios detallados

*Million BOB*

| | 1990 | 2000 | 2005 | 2007 | 2008 | 2009 | 2010 | 2011 | 2012 | 2013 |
|---|---|---|---|---|---|---|---|---|---|---|
| **Total tax revenue** | **1 088** | **7 616** | **14 553** | **23 017** | **24 264** | **27 172** | **28 073** | **39 490** | **47 670** | **58 282** |
| **1000 Taxes on income, profits and capital gains** | **123** | **967** | **2 058** | **3 118** | **4 540** | **4 700** | **5 326** | **6 331** | **7 556** | **8 246** |
| 1100 Of individuals | 0 | 0 | 0 | 0 | 0 | 0 | 0 | 0 | 0 | 0 |
| 1110 On income and profits | .. | .. | .. | .. | .. | .. | .. | .. | .. | .. |
| 1120 On capital gains | .. | .. | .. | .. | .. | .. | .. | .. | .. | .. |
| 1200 Corporate | 61 | 806 | 1 871 | 2 923 | 4 308 | 4 445 | 5 089 | 6 072 | 7 296 | 7 914 |
| 1210 On profits | 61 | 806 | 1 871 | 2 923 | 4 308 | 4 445 | 5 089 | 6 072 | 7 296 | 7 914 |
| Presume profit of enterprises | 60 | 2 | 0 | 0 | 0 | 0 | 0 | 0 | 0 | 0 |
| Mining profits | 0 | 0 | 75 | 153 | 80 | 61 | 473 | 616 | 322 | 283 |
| Tax regularization | 0 | 0 | 0 | 0 | 0 | 0 | 0 | 0 | 0 | 0 |
| Corporate tax | 0 | 546 | 1 481 | 2 251 | 3 657 | 3 761 | 3 874 | 4 724 | 6 256 | 6 824 |
| Corporate tax remittances | 0 | 258 | 315 | 519 | 571 | 623 | 742 | 732 | 718 | 806 |
| 1220 On capital gains | .. | .. | .. | .. | .. | .. | .. | .. | .. | .. |
| 1300 Unallocable between 1100 and 1200 | 62 | 161 | 187 | 195 | 232 | 255 | 237 | 260 | 260 | 333 |
| **2000 Social security contributions** | **0** | **666** | **936** | **1 109** | **1 347** | **1 515** | **1 645** | **2 665** | **2 878** | **3 000** |
| 2100 Employees | .. | .. | .. | .. | .. | .. | .. | .. | .. | .. |
| 2110 On a payroll basis | .. | .. | .. | .. | .. | .. | .. | .. | .. | .. |
| 2120 On an income tax basis | .. | .. | .. | .. | .. | .. | .. | .. | .. | .. |
| 2200 Employers | .. | .. | .. | .. | .. | .. | .. | .. | .. | .. |
| 2210 On a payroll basis | .. | .. | .. | .. | .. | .. | .. | .. | .. | .. |
| 2220 On an income tax basis | .. | .. | .. | .. | .. | .. | .. | .. | .. | .. |
| 2300 Self-employed or non-employed | .. | .. | .. | .. | .. | .. | .. | .. | .. | .. |
| 2310 On a payroll basis | .. | .. | .. | .. | .. | .. | .. | .. | .. | .. |
| 2320 On an income tax basis | .. | .. | .. | .. | .. | .. | .. | .. | .. | .. |
| 2400 Unallocable between 2100, 2200 and 2300 | .. | 666 | 936 | 1 109 | 1 347 | 1 515 | 1 645 | 2 665 | 2 878 | 3 000 |
| 2410 On a payroll basis | .. | 666 | 936 | 1 109 | 1 347 | 1 515 | 1 645 | 2 665 | 2 878 | 3 000 |
| 2420 On an income tax basis | .. | 0 | 0 | 0 | 0 | 0 | 0 | 0 | 0 | 0 |
| 2430 Unallocable | .. | 0 | 0 | 0 | 0 | 0 | 0 | 0 | 0 | 0 |
| **3000 Taxes on payroll and workforce** | **0** | **0** | **0** | **0** | **0** | **0** | **0** | **0** | **0** | **0** |
| **4000 Taxes on property** | **208** | **946** | **2 094** | **2 240** | **2 607** | **2 360** | **2 541** | **3 174** | **3 603** | **3 993** |
| 4100 Recurrent taxes on immovable property | 0 | 0 | 0 | 0 | 0 | 0 | 0 | 0 | 0 | 0 |
| 4110 Households | .. | .. | .. | .. | .. | .. | .. | .. | .. | .. |
| 4120 Others | .. | .. | .. | .. | .. | .. | .. | .. | .. | .. |
| 4200 Recurrent taxes on net wealth | 0 | 0 | 0 | 0 | 0 | 0 | 0 | 0 | 0 | 0 |
| 4210 Individual | .. | .. | .. | .. | .. | .. | .. | .. | .. | .. |
| 4220 Corporate | .. | .. | .. | .. | .. | .. | .. | .. | .. | .. |
| 4300 Estate, inheritance and gift taxes | 1 | 3 | 7 | 11 | 14 | 18 | 20 | 22 | 23 | 28 |
| 4310 Estate and inheritance taxes | 1 | 3 | 7 | 11 | 14 | 18 | 20 | 22 | 23 | 28 |
| 4320 Gift taxes | 0 | 0 | 0 | 0 | 0 | 0 | 0 | 0 | 0 | 0 |
| 4400 Taxes on financial and capital transactions | 136 | 943 | 2 087 | 2 229 | 2 593 | 2 342 | 2 521 | 3 152 | 3 580 | 3 965 |
| 4500 Non-recurrent taxes | 0 | 0 | 0 | 0 | 0 | 0 | 0 | 0 | 0 | 0 |
| 4510 On net wealth | .. | .. | .. | .. | .. | .. | .. | .. | .. | .. |
| 4520 Other non-recurrent taxes | .. | .. | .. | .. | .. | .. | .. | .. | .. | .. |
| 4600 Other recurrent taxes on property | 71 | 0 | 0 | 0 | 0 | 0 | 0 | 0 | 0 | 0 |
| **5000 Taxes on goods and services** | **786** | **5 206** | **9 674** | **16 981** | **19 816** | **17 142** | **20 011** | **27 300** | **31 762** | **39 817** |
| 5100 Taxes on production, sale, transfer, etc | 786 | 5 206 | 9 674 | 16 981 | 19 816 | 17 142 | 20 011 | 27 300 | 31 762 | 39 817 |
| 5110 General taxes | 497 | 2 649 | 4 574 | 6 734 | 8 393 | 7 705 | 9 293 | 12 109 | 14 245 | 16 514 |
| 5111 Value added taxes | 497 | 2 649 | 4 574 | 6 734 | 8 393 | 7 705 | 9 293 | 12 109 | 14 245 | 16 514 |
| 5112 Sales tax | 0 | 0 | 0 | 0 | 0 | 0 | 0 | 0 | 0 | 0 |
| 5113 Other | 0 | 0 | 0 | 0 | 0 | 0 | 0 | 0 | 0 | 0 |
| 5120 Taxes on specific goods and services | 289 | 2 557 | 5 100 | 10 247 | 11 423 | 9 437 | 10 718 | 15 191 | 17 517 | 23 303 |
| 5121 Excises | 83 | 1 930 | 4 274 | 9 111 | 9 986 | 8 220 | 9 126 | 13 077 | 14 992 | 19 410 |
| Excises (Internal) | 61 | 244 | 209 | 598 | 717 | 739 | 933 | 1 204 | 1 157 | 1 468 |
| Excises (Imports) | 22 | 298 | 208 | 485 | 594 | 367 | 379 | 642 | 580 | 719 |
| Special tax on hydrocarbons and derivatives | 0 | 1 387 | 1 529 | 2 073 | 2 031 | 650 | 1 070 | 2 236 | 1 144 | 1 681 |
| Excise tax on hydrocarbons | 0 | 0 | 2 328 | 5 954 | 6 644 | 6 465 | 6 744 | 8 996 | 12 111 | 15 543 |
| 5122 Profits of fiscal monopolies | 0 | 0 | 0 | 0 | 0 | 0 | 0 | 0 | 0 | 0 |
| 5123 Customs and import duties | 204 | 612 | 794 | 1 103 | 1 406 | 1 179 | 1 545 | 2 049 | 2 465 | 3 802 |
| 5124 Taxes on exports | 0 | 0 | 0 | 0 | 0 | 0 | 0 | 0 | 0 | 0 |
| 5125 Taxes on investment goods | 0 | 0 | 0 | 0 | 0 | 0 | 0 | 0 | 0 | 0 |
| 5126 Taxes on specific services | 2 | 15 | 32 | 33 | 31 | 38 | 47 | 65 | 60 | 91 |
| Air departure tax | 2 | 15 | 32 | 33 | 31 | 38 | 47 | 52 | 51 | 71 |
| Tax on gambling | 0 | 0 | 0 | 0 | 0 | 0 | 0 | 13 | 9 | 20 |
| 5127 Other taxes on internat. trade and transactions | 0 | 0 | 0 | 0 | 0 | 0 | 0 | 0 | 0 | 0 |
| 5128 Other taxes | 0 | 0 | 0 | 0 | 0 | 0 | 0 | 0 | 0 | 0 |
| 5130 Unallocable between 5110 and 5120 | 0 | 0 | 0 | 0 | 0 | 0 | 0 | 0 | 0 | 0 |
| 5200 Taxes on use of goods and perform activities | 0 | 0 | 0 | 0 | 0 | 0 | 0 | 0 | 0 | 0 |
| 5210 Recurrent taxes | .. | .. | .. | .. | .. | .. | .. | .. | .. | .. |

## **Table 19. Bolivia / Bolivia** *(cont.)*
Details of tax revenue / Ingresos tributarios detallados

*Million BOB*

| | 1990 | 2000 | 2005 | 2007 | 2008 | 2009 | 2010 | 2011 | 2012 | 2013 |
|---|---|---|---|---|---|---|---|---|---|---|
| 5211 Paid by households: motor vehicles | .. | .. | .. | .. | .. | .. | .. | .. | .. | .. |
| 5212 Paid by others: motor vehicles | .. | .. | .. | .. | .. | .. | .. | .. | .. | .. |
| 5213 Paid in respect of other goods | .. | .. | .. | .. | .. | .. | .. | .. | .. | .. |
| 5220 Non-recurrent taxes | .. | .. | .. | .. | .. | .. | .. | .. | .. | .. |
| 5300 Unallocable between 5100 and 5200 | 0 | 0 | 0 | 0 | 0 | 0 | 0 | 0 | 0 | 0 |
| **6000 Other taxes** | **-28** | **-170** | **-209** | **-431** | **-4 045** | **1 455** | **-1 451** | **19** | **1 872** | **3 226** |
| 6100 Paid solely by business | 4 | 6 | 4 | 8 | 11 | 12 | 12 | 13 | 14 | 17 |
| Simplified tax regim | 3 | 6 | 4 | 8 | 11 | 11 | 12 | 13 | 14 | 17 |
| Integrated tax system | 1 | 0 | 0 | 0 | 0 | 0 | 0 | 0 | 0 | 0 |
| 6200 Other | -33 | -176 | -214 | -439 | -4 056 | 1 443 | -1 463 | 6 | 1 858 | 3 209 |
| Rural property tax | 2 | 1 | 5 | 7 | 9 | 12 | 14 | 17 | 22 | 23 |
| Fiscal notes | 135 | 701 | 1 852 | 1 665 | 2 166 | 5 834 | 2 552 | 3 989 | 5 836 | 7 186 |
| Rebates | -169 | -878 | -2 071 | -2 111 | -6 231 | -4 403 | -4 029 | -4 000 | -4 000 | -4 000 |

*Note:* Year ending 31st December.
The data are on cash basis.
The data exclude local government tax revenues as the data are not available.
Heading 2000: The data for social security contributions are available from the year 2000 only and are estimated for 2013.
Heading 5121: In ECLAC data the excise tax on hydrocarbons (IDH) is treated as non tax revenues.
Heading 6200: The data for Rebates are available until 2010 and are estimated from 2011 onwards.
*Source:* Ministerio de Economía y Finanzas Públicas, Ministry of Economy and Public Finance.
Unidad de Análisis de Políticas Sociales y Económicas, Social and Economic Policy Analysis Unit.

StatLink http://dx.doi.org/10.1787/888933190248

## Table 20. Brazil / Brasil
Details of tax revenue / Ingresos tributarios detallados

*Million BRL*

| | 1990 | 2000 | 2005 | 2007 | 2008 | 2009 | 2010 | 2011 | 2012 | 2013 |
|---|---|---|---|---|---|---|---|---|---|---|
| **Total tax revenue** | **3** | **354 883** | **711 146** | **889 425** | **1 026 329** | **1 072 307** | **1 252 445** | **1 448 272** | **1 564 115** | **1 728 425** |
| **1000 Taxes on income, profits and capital gains** | **1** | **68 667** | **149 309** | **192 629** | **234 380** | **234 400** | **258 736** | **314 304** | **321 457** | **360 578** |
| 1100 Of individuals | 0 | 3 406 | 6 981 | 12 586 | 13 792 | 13 625 | 16 248 | 20 515 | 22 499 | 24 188 |
| 1110 On income and profits | 0 | 3 406 | 6 981 | 12 586 | 13 792 | 13 625 | 16 248 | 20 515 | 22 499 | 24 188 |
| 1120 On capital gains | .. | .. | .. | .. | .. | .. | .. | .. | .. | .. |
| 1200 Corporate | 0 | 25 430 | 73 071 | 98 788 | 120 184 | 120 767 | 128 255 | 153 652 | 148 423 | 171 003 |
| 1210 On profits | 0 | 25 430 | 73 071 | 98 788 | 120 184 | 120 767 | 128 255 | 153 652 | 148 423 | 171 003 |
| Corporate income tax | 0 | 16 680 | 47 832 | 65 605 | 78 521 | 77 343 | 82 474 | 94 958 | 92 589 | 109 316 |
| Social contribution on net profits (CSLL) | 0 | 8 750 | 25 239 | 33 183 | 41 664 | 43 424 | 45 780 | 58 694 | 55 834 | 61 687 |
| 1220 On capital gains | .. | .. | .. | .. | .. | .. | .. | .. | .. | .. |
| 1300 Unallocable between 1100 and 1200 | 0 | 39 831 | 69 257 | 81 255 | 100 403 | 100 007 | 114 233 | 140 137 | 150 534 | 165 386 |
| Withholding taxes | 0 | 39 831 | 69 257 | 81 255 | 100 403 | 100 007 | 114 233 | 140 137 | 150 534 | 165 386 |
| **2000 Social security contributions** | **1** | **83 469** | **168 226** | **215 190** | **246 502** | **273 596** | **314 868** | **362 716** | **404 667** | **444 278** |
| 2100 Employees | .. | .. | .. | .. | .. | .. | .. | .. | .. | .. |
| 2110 On a payroll basis | .. | .. | .. | .. | .. | .. | .. | .. | .. | .. |
| 2120 On an income tax basis | .. | .. | .. | .. | .. | .. | .. | .. | .. | .. |
| 2200 Employers | 0 | 18 709 | 32 248 | 43 602 | 50 518 | 57 183 | 64 271 | 74 979 | 85 813 | 98 045 |
| 2210 On a payroll basis | 0 | 18 709 | 32 248 | 43 602 | 50 518 | 57 183 | 64 271 | 74 979 | 85 813 | 98 045 |
| 2220 On an income tax basis | 0 | 0 | 0 | 0 | 0 | 0 | 0 | 0 | 0 | 0 |
| 2300 Self-employed or non-employed | .. | .. | .. | .. | .. | .. | .. | .. | .. | .. |
| 2310 On a payroll basis | .. | .. | .. | .. | .. | .. | .. | .. | .. | .. |
| 2320 On an income tax basis | .. | .. | .. | .. | .. | .. | .. | .. | .. | .. |
| 2400 Unallocable between 2100, 2200 and 2300 | 1 | 64 760 | 135 978 | 171 588 | 195 984 | 216 413 | 250 597 | 287 737 | 318 855 | 346 234 |
| 2410 On a payroll basis | 1 | 64 760 | 135 978 | 171 588 | 195 984 | 216 413 | 250 597 | 287 737 | 318 855 | 346 234 |
| Social security contributions (Federal) | 1 | 59 334 | 118 869 | 154 324 | 179 424 | 200 552 | 232 838 | 268 641 | 296 966 | 322 703 |
| Social security contributions (State) | 0 | 4 423 | 14 682 | 13 481 | 12 678 | 11 489 | 12 635 | 13 294 | 15 551 | 15 856 |
| Social security contributions (Municipal) | 0 | 1 003 | 2 427 | 3 783 | 3 882 | 4 372 | 5 124 | 5 802 | 6 337 | 7 674 |
| 2420 On an income tax basis | 0 | 0 | 0 | 0 | 0 | 0 | 0 | 0 | 0 | 0 |
| **3000 Taxes on payroll and workforce** | **0** | **6 749** | **14 469** | **19 310** | **23 309** | **20 108** | **23 173** | **27 246** | **30 771** | **34 596** |
| PASEP contributions | 0 | 1 312 | 2 864 | 4 039 | 4 894 | 0 | 0 | 0 | 0 | 0 |
| Payroll-based contribution to education | 0 | 2 791 | 5 906 | 7 089 | 8 776 | 9 589 | 11 049 | 13 115 | 14 775 | 16 561 |
| "S" System contributions | 0 | 2 646 | 4 397 | 6 592 | 7 826 | 8 524 | 9 887 | 11 663 | 13 519 | 15 332 |
| Other | 0 | 0 | 1 302 | 1 592 | 1 812 | 1 996 | 2 236 | 2 467 | 2 477 | 2 704 |
| **4000 Taxes on property** | **0** | **28 818** | **56 274** | **76 378** | **57 925** | **61 202** | **74 373** | **86 692** | **92 092** | **97 826** |
| 4100 Recurrent taxes on immovable property | 0 | 4 753 | 8 405 | 12 941 | 13 941 | 15 608 | 17 928 | 20 270 | 22 154 | 25 080 |
| 4110 Households | 0 | 0 | 0 | 0 | 0 | 0 | 0 | 0 | 0 | 0 |
| 4120 Others | 0 | 4 753 | 8 405 | 12 941 | 13 941 | 15 608 | 17 928 | 20 270 | 22 154 | 25 080 |
| Tax on rural land property (ITR) | 0 | 234 | 288 | 313 | 395 | 421 | 485 | 571 | 614 | 764 |
| Tax on urban land property (IPTU) | 0 | 4 519 | 8 117 | 12 628 | 13 546 | 15 187 | 17 443 | 19 699 | 21 540 | 24 316 |
| 4200 Recurrent taxes on net wealth | 0 | 0 | 0 | 0 | 0 | 0 | 0 | 0 | 0 | 0 |
| 4210 Individual | .. | .. | .. | .. | .. | .. | .. | .. | .. | .. |
| 4220 Corporate | .. | .. | .. | .. | .. | .. | .. | .. | .. | .. |
| 4300 Estate, inheritance and gift taxes | 0 | 329 | 821 | 1 208 | 1 489 | 1 678 | 2 518 | 2 768 | 3 409 | 4 142 |
| 4310 Estate and inheritance taxes | 0 | 329 | 821 | 1 208 | 1 489 | 1 678 | 2 518 | 2 768 | 3 409 | 4 142 |
| 4320 Gift taxes | 0 | 0 | 0 | 0 | 0 | 0 | 0 | 0 | 0 | 0 |
| 4400 Taxes on financial and capital transactions | 0 | 18 442 | 36 587 | 47 603 | 25 464 | 23 809 | 32 560 | 39 542 | 39 500 | 39 371 |
| Tax on financial operations (IOF) | 0 | 3 096 | 5 974 | 7 817 | 20 168 | 19 235 | 26 571 | 31 999 | 31 002 | 29 417 |
| Real estate property transfers (ITBI) | 0 | 950 | 1 593 | 3 467 | 4 324 | 4 610 | 6 007 | 7 464 | 8 498 | 9 954 |
| Other | 0 | 14 396 | 29 021 | 36 320 | 971 | -36 | -18 | 79 | 0 | 0 |
| 4500 Non-recurrent taxes | 0 | 0 | 0 | 0 | 0 | 0 | 0 | 0 | 0 | 0 |
| 4510 On net wealth | .. | .. | .. | .. | .. | .. | .. | .. | .. | .. |
| 4520 Other non-recurrent taxes | .. | .. | .. | .. | .. | .. | .. | .. | .. | .. |
| 4600 Other recurrent taxes on property | 0 | 5 294 | 10 460 | 14 626 | 17 031 | 20 107 | 21 367 | 24 112 | 27 030 | 29 232 |
| **5000 Taxes on goods and services** | **2** | **164 144** | **317 875** | **379 773** | **449 498** | **446 712** | **540 217** | **610 709** | **663 037** | **734 631** |
| 5100 Taxes on production, sale, transfer, etc | 2 | 162 575 | 312 503 | 372 728 | 441 310 | 446 712 | 540 217 | 610 709 | 663 037 | 734 631 |
| 5110 General taxes | 2 | 154 130 | 294 251 | 350 384 | 415 059 | 423 237 | 507 776 | 571 023 | 624 203 | 691 322 |
| 5111 Value added taxes | 1 | 100 978 | 177 589 | 207 303 | 246 178 | 247 821 | 293 489 | 324 761 | 358 323 | 395 077 |
| Tax on the circulation of goods and services (ICMS) | 1 | 82 279 | 153 437 | 186 681 | 221 213 | 227 830 | 268 117 | 297 419 | 327 369 | 364 525 |
| Tax on industrialized products (IPI) | 0 | 18 699 | 24 153 | 20 622 | 24 965 | 19 991 | 25 372 | 27 342 | 30 954 | 30 552 |
| 5112 Sales tax | 0 | 47 046 | 105 415 | 122 296 | 143 864 | 148 074 | 181 532 | 207 884 | 221 494 | 248 065 |
| Contribution to financing social security (COFINS) | 0 | 38 707 | 86 837 | 100 556 | 118 431 | 117 084 | 140 939 | 164 982 | 175 008 | 197 545 |
| PIS contribution | 0 | 8 339 | 18 578 | 21 741 | 25 433 | 30 990 | 40 594 | 42 902 | 46 486 | 50 520 |
| 5113 Other | 0 | 6 106 | 11 247 | 20 784 | 25 017 | 27 341 | 32 755 | 38 378 | 44 386 | 48 180 |
| 5120 Taxes on specific goods and services | 0 | 8 445 | 18 252 | 22 344 | 26 250 | 23 475 | 32 441 | 39 686 | 38 834 | 43 308 |
| 5121 Excises | .. | 0 | 7 683 | 7 943 | 5 927 | 4 912 | 7 761 | 8 950 | 2 883 | 734 |
| 5122 Profits of fiscal monopolies | .. | 0 | 0 | 0 | 0 | 0 | 0 | 0 | 0 | 0 |
| 5123 Customs and import duties | .. | 8 445 | 8 953 | 12 216 | 17 101 | 15 904 | 21 119 | 26 763 | 31 088 | 36 974 |
| 5124 Taxes on exports | .. | 0 | 0 | 0 | 0 | 0 | 0 | 0 | 0 | 0 |

## Table 20. Brazil / Brasil (cont.)
Details of tax revenue / Ingresos tributarios detallados

*Million BRL*

| | 1990 | 2000 | 2005 | 2007 | 2008 | 2009 | 2010 | 2011 | 2012 | 2013 |
|---|---|---|---|---|---|---|---|---|---|---|
| 5125 Taxes on investment goods | .. | 0 | 0 | 0 | 0 | 0 | 0 | 0 | 0 | 0 |
| 5126 Taxes on specific services | .. | 0 | 983 | 1 381 | 2 305 | 1 511 | 2 350 | 2 466 | 2 883 | 3 367 |
| 5127 Other taxes on internat. trade and transactions | .. | 0 | 0 | 0 | 0 | 0 | 0 | 0 | 0 | 0 |
| 5128 Other taxes | .. | 0 | 633 | 805 | 917 | 1 147 | 1 212 | 1 507 | 1 979 | 2 233 |
| 5130 Unallocable between 5110 and 5120 | .. | 0 | 0 | 0 | 0 | 0 | 0 | 0 | 0 | 0 |
| 5200 Taxes on use of goods and perform activities | 0 | 1 569 | 5 372 | 7 046 | 8 189 | 0 | 0 | 0 | 0 | 0 |
| 5210 Recurrent taxes | 0 | 1 569 | 5 372 | 7 046 | 8 189 | .. | .. | .. | .. | .. |
| 5211 Paid by households: motor vehicles | 0 | 1 569 | 5 372 | 7 046 | 8 189 | .. | .. | .. | .. | .. |
| 5212 Paid by others: motor vehicles | 0 | 0 | 0 | 0 | 0 | .. | .. | .. | .. | .. |
| 5213 Paid in respect of other goods | 0 | 0 | 0 | 0 | 0 | .. | .. | .. | .. | .. |
| 5220 Non-recurrent taxes | 0 | 0 | 0 | 0 | 0 | .. | .. | .. | .. | .. |
| 5300 Unallocable between 5100 and 5200 | 0 | 0 | 0 | 0 | 0 | 0 | 0 | 0 | 0 | 0 |
| **6000 Other taxes** | **0** | **3 036** | **4 993** | **6 145** | **14 716** | **36 289** | **41 078** | **46 605** | **52 091** | **56 517** |
| 6100 Paid solely by business | 0 | 0 | 277 | 307 | 186 | 0 | 0 | 0 | 0 | 0 |
| Revenue service development fund (FUNDAF) | .. | .. | 277 | 307 | 186 | 0 | 0 | 0 | 0 | 0 |
| 6200 Other | 0 | 3 036 | 4 715 | 5 839 | 14 530 | 36 289 | 41 078 | 46 605 | 52 091 | 56 517 |
| Other federal taxes | 0 | 941 | 36 | 39 | 45 | 6 752 | 7 772 | 8 661 | 9 491 | 9 538 |
| Other social contributions | 0 | 1 273 | 1 725 | 1 935 | 5 850 | 6 752 | 7 772 | 8 661 | 9 491 | 9 538 |
| Other state taxes | 0 | 322 | 1 551 | 1 498 | 1 716 | 15 429 | 17 135 | 19 825 | 22 980 | 26 645 |
| Other municipal taxes | 0 | 377 | 1 404 | 2 367 | 6 919 | 7 356 | 8 399 | 9 458 | 10 128 | 10 795 |

*Note:* Year ending 31 st December.

The data are on cash basis.

Headings 3000, 5112 and 6200: For years prior to 2000 and from 2009 onwards the PASEP (Program of Formation of the Patrimony of the Public Servants) contributions are combined with PIS (Social Integration Program) contributions in heading 5112.

Headings 5111 and 5121: From 2007 to 2011, a portion of the IPI (Industrial Products Tax) is levied separately as an excise tax on automobiles, beverages, and tobacco products.

Heading 6100: From 2008 FUNDAF (Special Fund for Development and Improvement of Auditing Activities) contributions are included in heading 6200.

Heading 5200: From 2009 Taxes paid by households: motor vehicles are included in heading 6200.

*Source:* Secretaria da Receita Federal (Ministry of Finance) in Carga Tributária no Brasil.

StatLink http://dx.doi.org/10.1787/888933190258

## Table 21. Chile / Chile
Details of tax revenue / Ingresos tributarios detallados

*Million CLP*

| | 1990 | 2000 | 2005 | 2007 | 2008 | 2009 | 2010 | 2011 | 2012 | 2013 |
|---|---|---|---|---|---|---|---|---|---|---|
| **Total tax revenue** | **1 777 218** | **7 901 998** | **14 265 204** | **20 599 131** | **20 081 681** | **16 595 349** | **21 678 481** | **25 762 449** | **27 714 772** | **27 755 439** |
| **1000 Taxes on income, profits and capital gains** | **412 974** | **1 841 630** | **5 171 293** | **9 412 056** | **7 536 172** | **5 162 043** | **8 329 060** | **10 322 824** | **10 803 031** | **9 945 910** |
| 1100 Of individuals | 99 154 | 604 100 | 738 620 | 989 348 | 1 146 546 | 1 252 672 | 1 492 837 | 1 690 230 | 1 893 620 | 1 964 172 |
| Second category tax | 65 552 | 490 980 | 700 150 | 993 129 | 1 110 643 | 1 239 815 | 1 449 099 | 1 663 293 | 1 917 675 | 1 981 699 |
| Global complementary tax | 33 603 | 113 120 | 38 470 | -3 781 | 35 903 | 12 857 | 43 738 | 26 936 | -24 055 | -17 527 |
| 1110 On income and profits | .. | .. | .. | .. | .. | .. | .. | .. | .. | .. |
| 1120 On capital gains | .. | .. | .. | .. | .. | .. | .. | .. | .. | .. |
| 1200 Corporate | 219 586 | 882 896 | 3 155 480 | 6 054 487 | 4 805 522 | 4 110 485 | 4 448 745 | 6 021 408 | 7 560 906 | 6 466 289 |
| First category tax | 200 891 | 815 747 | 3 040 875 | 5 084 996 | 4 252 551 | 3 729 488 | 3 913 870 | 5 254 907 | 6 770 329 | 5 878 569 |
| Surtax on state owned enterprises | 16 074 | 47 634 | 78 267 | 113 334 | 92 949 | 44 974 | 194 203 | 116 725 | 80 084 | 124 220 |
| Mining tax | 0 | 0 | 0 | 835 452 | 417 214 | 312 473 | 298 558 | 598 790 | 619 150 | 344 563 |
| Other | 2 621 | 19 516 | 36 338 | 20 705 | 42 808 | 23 550 | 42 114 | 50 987 | 91 343 | 118 937 |
| 1210 On profits | .. | .. | .. | .. | .. | .. | .. | .. | .. | .. |
| 1220 On capital gains | .. | .. | .. | .. | .. | .. | .. | .. | .. | .. |
| 1300 Unallocable between 1100 and 1200 | 94 233 | 354 634 | 1 277 193 | 2 368 221 | 1 584 104 | -201 113 | 2 387 478 | 2 611 186 | 1 348 506 | 1 515 449 |
| Adicionel tax | 59 082 | 350 301 | 799 648 | 1 462 715 | 1 363 357 | 1 023 497 | 1 414 057 | 1 187 866 | 1 178 917 | 1 337 721 |
| Other | 35 151 | 4 332 | 477 545 | 905 507 | 220 747 | -1 224 610 | 973 421 | 1 423 320 | 169 589 | 177 727 |
| **2000 Social security contributions** | **159 559** | **576 758** | **931 717** | **1 148 647** | **1 289 225** | **1 371 750** | **1 493 987** | **1 623 818** | **1 802 468** | **1 968 973** |
| 2100 Employees | 154 021 | 553 937 | 893 821 | 1 098 620 | 1 229 912 | 1 312 793 | 1 433 159 | 1 565 828 | 1 742 526 | 1 906 340 |
| 2110 On a payroll basis | 154 021 | 553 937 | 893 821 | 1 098 620 | 1 229 912 | 1 312 793 | 1 433 159 | 1 565 828 | 1 742 526 | 1 906 340 |
| 2120 On an income tax basis | 0 | 0 | 0 | 0 | 0 | 0 | 0 | 0 | 0 | 0 |
| 2200 Employers | 5 538 | 22 821 | 37 896 | 50 027 | 59 313 | 58 957 | 60 828 | 57 990 | 59 942 | 62 633 |
| 2210 On a payroll basis | 5 538 | 22 821 | 37 896 | 50 027 | 59 313 | 58 957 | 60 828 | 57 990 | 59 942 | 62 633 |
| 2220 On an income tax basis | 0 | 0 | 0 | 0 | 0 | 0 | 0 | 0 | 0 | 0 |
| 2300 Self-employed or non-employed | 0 | 0 | 0 | 0 | 0 | 0 | 0 | 0 | 0 | 0 |
| 2310 On a payroll basis | .. | .. | .. | .. | .. | .. | .. | .. | .. | .. |
| 2320 On an income tax basis | .. | .. | .. | .. | .. | .. | .. | .. | .. | .. |
| 2400 Unallocable between 2100, 2200 and 2300 | 0 | 0 | 0 | 0 | 0 | 0 | 0 | 0 | 0 | 0 |
| 2410 On a payroll basis | .. | .. | .. | .. | .. | .. | .. | .. | .. | .. |
| 2420 On an income tax basis | .. | .. | .. | .. | .. | .. | .. | .. | .. | .. |
| **3000 Taxes on payroll and workforce** | **0** | **0** | **0** | **0** | **0** | **0** | **0** | **0** | **0** | **0** |
| **4000 Taxes on property** | **109 319** | **554 037** | **901 776** | **1 013 571** | **1 080 090** | **795 084** | **785 364** | **1 027 627** | **1 180 307** | **1 114 322** |
| 4100 Recurrent taxes on immovable property | 59 968 | 302 244 | 416 565 | 496 311 | 541 268 | 532 279 | 549 125 | 731 191 | 788 919 | 821 399 |
| 4110 Households | .. | .. | .. | .. | .. | .. | .. | .. | .. | .. |
| 4120 Others | .. | .. | .. | .. | .. | .. | .. | .. | .. | .. |
| 4200 Recurrent taxes on net wealth | 0 | 0 | 0 | 0 | 0 | 0 | 0 | 0 | 0 | 0 |
| 4210 Individual | .. | .. | .. | .. | .. | .. | .. | .. | .. | .. |
| 4220 Corporate | .. | .. | .. | .. | .. | .. | .. | .. | .. | .. |
| 4300 Estate, inheritance and gift taxes | 3 444 | 10 906 | 23 184 | 28 501 | 35 554 | 200 203 | 39 338 | 30 876 | 66 719 | 45 550 |
| 4310 Estate and inheritance taxes | .. | .. | .. | .. | .. | .. | .. | .. | .. | .. |
| 4320 Gift taxes | .. | .. | .. | .. | .. | .. | .. | .. | .. | .. |
| 4400 Taxes on financial and capital transactions | 45 907 | 240 886 | 462 027 | 488 759 | 503 269 | 62 602 | 196 901 | 265 560 | 324 669 | 247 373 |
| 4500 Non-recurrent taxes | 0 | 0 | 0 | 0 | 0 | 0 | 0 | 0 | 0 | 0 |
| 4510 On net wealth | .. | .. | .. | .. | .. | .. | .. | .. | .. | .. |
| 4520 Other non-recurrent taxes | .. | .. | .. | .. | .. | .. | .. | .. | .. | .. |
| 4600 Other recurrent taxes on property | 0 | 0 | 0 | 0 | 0 | 0 | 0 | 0 | 0 | 0 |
| **5000 Taxes on goods and services** | **1 118 722** | **5 041 769** | **7 346 373** | **9 023 834** | **10 166 189** | **9 271 910** | **11 131 188** | **12 700 180** | **13 873 611** | **14 747 910** |
| 5100 Taxes on production, sale, transfer, etc | 1 074 009 | 4 789 827 | 6 952 031 | 8 578 804 | 9 650 260 | 8 724 696 | 10 514 822 | 11 963 914 | 13 052 989 | 13 856 246 |
| 5110 General taxes | 664 421 | 3 306 350 | 5 391 285 | 6 781 501 | 7 912 009 | 7 051 079 | 8 399 926 | 9 536 786 | 10 447 374 | 11 170 794 |
| 5111 Value added taxes | 664 421 | 3 306 350 | 5 391 285 | 6 781 501 | 7 912 009 | 7 051 079 | 8 399 926 | 9 536 786 | 10 447 374 | 11 170 794 |
| 5112 Sales tax | 0 | 0 | 0 | 0 | 0 | 0 | 0 | 0 | 0 | 0 |
| 5113 Other | 0 | 0 | 0 | 0 | 0 | 0 | 0 | 0 | 0 | 0 |
| 5120 Taxes on specific goods and services | 409 588 | 1 483 477 | 1 560 746 | 1 797 303 | 1 738 251 | 1 673 617 | 2 114 896 | 2 427 128 | 2 605 615 | 2 685 452 |
| 5121 Excises | 166 050 | 816 160 | 1 107 642 | 1 300 012 | 1 190 726 | 1 248 243 | 1 561 205 | 1 750 916 | 1 892 713 | 1 987 475 |
| Cigarettes and tobacco | 60 604 | 283 275 | 382 090 | 455 595 | 504 480 | 556 651 | 647 637 | 744 302 | 783 995 | 815 991 |
| Gasolene and diesel | 105 445 | 532 885 | 724 803 | 844 249 | 661 380 | 684 698 | 913 568 | 1 006 614 | 1 108 718 | 1 171 483 |
| Oil stabilisation fund | 0 | 0 | 149 | 168 | 24 866 | 6 894 | 0 | 0 | 0 | 0 |
| 5122 Profits of fiscal monopolies | 0 | 0 | 0 | 0 | 0 | 0 | 0 | 0 | 0 | 0 |
| 5123 Customs and import duties | 222 486 | 548 571 | 286 044 | 300 416 | 307 265 | 162 987 | 267 331 | 301 828 | 314 441 | 303 393 |
| 5124 Taxes on exports | 0 | 0 | 0 | 0 | 0 | 0 | 0 | 0 | 0 | 0 |
| 5125 Taxes on investment goods | 0 | 0 | 0 | 0 | 0 | 0 | 0 | 0 | 0 | 0 |
| 5126 Taxes on specific services | 21 052 | 118 746 | 167 060 | 196 875 | 240 260 | 262 387 | 286 360 | 374 384 | 398 461 | 394 584 |
| 5127 Other taxes on internat. trade and transactions | 0 | 0 | 0 | 0 | 0 | 0 | 0 | 0 | 0 | 0 |
| 5128 Other taxes | 0 | 0 | 0 | 0 | 0 | 0 | 0 | 0 | 0 | 0 |
| 5130 Unallocable between 5110 and 5120 | 0 | 0 | 0 | 0 | 0 | 0 | 0 | 0 | 0 | 0 |
| 5200 Taxes on use of goods and perform activities | 44 714 | 251 942 | 394 343 | 445 030 | 515 929 | 547 214 | 616 366 | 736 266 | 820 622 | 891 664 |
| 5210 Recurrent taxes | 44 714 | 251 942 | 394 343 | 445 030 | 515 929 | 547 214 | 616 366 | 736 266 | 820 622 | 891 664 |
| Motor vehicles | 24 469 | 93 880 | 139 174 | 155 158 | 177 167 | 171 141 | 197 145 | 267 116 | 301 895 | 325 076 |

## Table 21. Chile / Chile *(cont.)*
Details of tax revenue / Ingresos tributarios detallados

*Million CLP*

| | 1990 | 2000 | 2005 | 2007 | 2008 | 2009 | 2010 | 2011 | 2012 | 2013 |
|---|---|---|---|---|---|---|---|---|---|---|
| 5211 Paid by households: motor vehicles | 0 | 0 | 0 | 0 | 0 | 0 | 0 | 0 | 0 | 0 |
| 5212 Paid by others: motor vehicles | 0 | 0 | 0 | 0 | 0 | 0 | 0 | 0 | 0 | 0 |
| 5213 Paid in respect of other goods | 20 245 | 158 062 | 255 169 | 289 872 | 338 762 | 376 073 | 419 221 | 469 150 | 518 727 | 566 588 |
| Municipal permits | 18 401 | 136 138 | 234 460 | 263 996 | 307 349 | 342 861 | 382 245 | 425 138 | 468 938 | 514 939 |
| Mining patents | 3 374 | 34 730 | 20 094 | 25 184 | 30 391 | 32 690 | 36 213 | 42 944 | 47 899 | 50 094 |
| Other | -1 530 | -12 806 | 615 | 692 | 1 022 | 522 | 763 | 1 068 | 1 890 | 1 555 |
| 5220 Non-recurrent taxes | 0 | 0 | 0 | 0 | 0 | 0 | 0 | 0 | 0 | 0 |
| 5300 Unallocable between 5100 and 5200 | 0 | 0 | 0 | 0 | 0 | 0 | 0 | 0 | 0 | 0 |
| **6000 Other taxes** | **-23 356** | **-112 195** | **-85 954** | **1 023** | **10 005** | **-5 438** | **-61 117** | **88 000** | **55 355** | **-21 676** |
| 6100 Paid solely by business | 0 | 0 | 0 | 0 | 0 | 0 | 0 | 0 | 0 | 0 |
| 6200 Other | -23 356 | -112 195 | -85 954 | 1 023 | 10 005 | -5 438 | -61 117 | 88 000 | 55 355 | -21 676 |

*Note:* Year ending 31st December.

The data are on cash basis.

Heading 5121: In ECLAC data, figures from the Oil Prices Stabilisation Fund (FEPP) are considered as non tax revenues.

*Source:* Servicio de Impuestos Internos (Chile's Tax Service).

StatLink http://dx.doi.org/10.1787/888933190265

## Table 22. Colombia / Colombia
Details of tax revenue / Ingresos tributarios detallados

*Million COP*

| | 1990 | 2000 | 2005 | 2007 | 2008 | 2009 | 2010 | 2011 | 2012 | 2013 |
|---|---|---|---|---|---|---|---|---|---|---|
| **Total tax revenue** | **2 579 426** | **30 512 910** | **61 455 845** | **82 309 367** | **90 247 961** | **93 898 231** | **98 035 191** | **116 983 509** | **130 708 822** | **142 322 742** |
| **1000 Taxes on income, profits and capital gains** | **771 694** | **7 103 525** | **17 348 618** | **24 010 404** | **24 448 371** | **28 116 564** | **26 218 852** | **33 453 048** | **43 671 856** | **47 743 096** |
| 1100 Of individuals | 47 210 | 127 908 | 619 066 | 813 650 | 583 411 | 571 952 | 741 826 | 795 278 | 916 458 | 1 074 542 |
| 1110 On income and profits | 47 210 | 127 908 | 619 066 | 813 650 | 583 411 | 571 952 | 741 826 | 795 278 | 916 458 | 1 074 542 |
| 1120 On capital gains | .. | .. | .. | .. | .. | .. | .. | .. | .. | .. |
| 1200 Corporate | 359 758 | 1 180 627 | 7 453 811 | 10 534 870 | 8 910 177 | 11 134 039 | 7 799 486 | 11 372 600 | 20 273 545 | 19 677 250 |
| 1210 On profits | 359 758 | 1 180 627 | 7 453 811 | 10 534 870 | 8 910 177 | 11 134 039 | 7 799 486 | 11 372 600 | 20 273 545 | 19 677 250 |
| Ecopetrol | 359 758 | 1 180 627 | 7 453 811 | 10 534 870 | 8 910 177 | 11 134 039 | 7 799 486 | 11 372 600 | 20 273 545 | 19 677 250 |
| Other | 0 | 0 | 0 | 0 | 0 | 0 | 0 | 0 | 0 | 0 |
| 1220 On capital gains | .. | .. | .. | .. | .. | .. | .. | .. | .. | .. |
| 1300 Unallocable between 1100 and 1200 | 364 726 | 5 794 990 | 9 275 740 | 12 661 884 | 14 954 783 | 16 410 573 | 17 677 540 | 21 285 170 | 22 481 854 | 26 991 303 |
| **2000 Social security contributions** | **203 596** | **4 989 000** | **7 845 000** | **9 694 000** | **9 631 000** | **10 335 748** | **11 478 085** | **10 303 830** | **11 815 723** | **16 645 000** |
| 2100 Employees | .. | .. | .. | .. | .. | .. | .. | .. | .. | .. |
| 2110 On a payroll basis | .. | .. | .. | .. | .. | .. | .. | .. | .. | .. |
| 2120 On an income tax basis | .. | .. | .. | .. | .. | .. | .. | .. | .. | .. |
| 2200 Employers | .. | .. | .. | .. | .. | .. | .. | .. | .. | .. |
| 2210 On a payroll basis | .. | .. | .. | .. | .. | .. | .. | .. | .. | .. |
| 2220 On an income tax basis | .. | .. | .. | .. | .. | .. | .. | .. | .. | .. |
| 2300 Self-employed or non-employed | .. | .. | .. | .. | .. | .. | .. | .. | .. | .. |
| 2310 On a payroll basis | .. | .. | .. | .. | .. | .. | .. | .. | .. | .. |
| 2320 On an income tax basis | .. | .. | .. | .. | .. | .. | .. | .. | .. | .. |
| 2400 Unallocable between 2100, 2200 and 2300 | 203 596 | 4 989 000 | 7 845 000 | 9 694 000 | 9 631 000 | 10 335 748 | 11 478 085 | 10 303 830 | 11 815 723 | 16 645 000 |
| 2410 On a payroll basis | 203 596 | 4 989 000 | 7 845 000 | 9 694 000 | 9 631 000 | 10 335 748 | 11 478 085 | 10 303 830 | 11 815 723 | 16 645 000 |
| 2420 On an income tax basis | 0 | 0 | 0 | 0 | 0 | 0 | 0 | 0 | 0 | 0 |
| **3000 Taxes on payroll and workforce** | **0** | **1 286 803** | **2 179 842** | **2 798 906** | **3 178 259** | **3 587 147** | **4 022 503** | **4 479 886** | **4 775 034** | **3 527 459** |
| **4000 Taxes on property** | **56 160** | **2 027 654** | **4 838 158** | **6 459 259** | **8 932 264** | **8 220 499** | **8 359 387** | **13 017 198** | **13 569 680** | **15 130 482** |
| 4100 Recurrent taxes on immovable property | 56 160 | 991 070 | 1 974 213 | 2 298 829 | 2 532 996 | 3 076 434 | 3 163 084 | 3 707 079 | 3 917 577 | 4 957 894 |
| 4110 Households | 0 | 0 | 0 | 0 | 0 | 0 | 0 | 0 | 0 | 0 |
| 4120 Others | 56 160 | 991 070 | 1 974 213 | 2 298 829 | 2 532 996 | 3 076 434 | 3 163 084 | 3 707 079 | 3 917 577 | 4 957 894 |
| 4200 Recurrent taxes on net wealth | 0 | 0 | 462 720 | 1 170 908 | 3 199 668 | 2 022 787 | 1 970 530 | 4 240 512 | 4 183 752 | 4 274 832 |
| 4210 Individual | .. | .. | 462 720 | 1 170 908 | 3 199 668 | 2 022 787 | 1 970 530 | 4 240 512 | 4 183 752 | 4 274 832 |
| 4220 Corporate | .. | .. | 0 | 0 | 0 | 0 | 0 | 0 | 0 | 0 |
| 4300 Estate, inheritance and gift taxes | 0 | 0 | 0 | 0 | 0 | 0 | 0 | 0 | 0 | 0 |
| 4310 Estate and inheritance taxes | .. | .. | .. | .. | .. | .. | .. | .. | .. | .. |
| 4320 Gift taxes | .. | .. | .. | .. | .. | .. | .. | .. | .. | .. |
| 4400 Taxes on financial and capital transactions | 0 | 1 036 584 | 2 401 226 | 2 989 522 | 3 199 600 | 3 121 278 | 3 225 773 | 5 069 606 | 5 468 351 | 5 897 755 |
| 4500 Non-recurrent taxes | .. | .. | .. | .. | .. | .. | .. | .. | .. | .. |
| 4510 On net wealth | .. | .. | .. | .. | .. | .. | .. | .. | .. | .. |
| 4520 Other non-recurrent taxes | .. | .. | .. | .. | .. | .. | .. | .. | .. | .. |
| 4600 Other recurrent taxes on property | .. | .. | .. | .. | .. | .. | .. | .. | .. | .. |
| **5000 Taxes on goods and services** | **1 388 653** | **13 367 908** | **25 866 553** | **34 750 053** | **39 194 218** | **38 090 163** | **42 063 441** | **48 790 355** | **50 261 388** | **51 844 491** |
| 5100 Taxes on production, sale, transfer, etc | 1 388 653 | 13 367 908 | 25 866 553 | 34 750 053 | 39 194 218 | 38 090 163 | 42 063 441 | 48 790 355 | 50 261 388 | 51 844 491 |
| 5110 General taxes | 672 368 | 9 585 866 | 19 934 400 | 26 910 512 | 31 074 221 | 30 185 624 | 33 118 301 | 39 941 309 | 41 731 826 | 40 473 562 |
| 5111 Value added taxes | 583 078 | 8 445 776 | 17 427 948 | 23 377 821 | 27 064 094 | 25 910 469 | 28 811 682 | 35 093 071 | 36 324 330 | 34 642 822 |
| 5112 Sales tax | 89 290 | 1 140 090 | 2 506 452 | 3 532 691 | 4 010 127 | 4 275 155 | 4 306 620 | 4 848 238 | 5 407 497 | 5 830 740 |
| Industry and commerce tax (State) | 89 290 | 1 140 090 | 2 506 452 | 3 532 691 | 4 010 127 | 4 275 155 | 4 306 620 | 4 848 238 | 5 407 497 | 5 830 740 |
| 5113 Other | 0 | 0 | 0 | 0 | 0 | 0 | 0 | 0 | 0 | 0 |
| 5120 Taxes on specific goods and services | 716 285 | 3 782 042 | 5 932 153 | 7 839 541 | 8 119 997 | 7 904 539 | 8 945 140 | 8 849 045 | 8 529 561 | 11 370 929 |
| 5121 Excises | 404 699 | 2 037 944 | 3 109 633 | 3 579 755 | 3 828 119 | 3 903 697 | 4 293 141 | 4 768 330 | 5 006 241 | 7 473 746 |
| Petrol | 141 270 | 833 004 | 1 143 308 | 1 211 511 | 1 287 969 | 1 291 493 | 1 418 766 | 1 603 227 | 1 735 062 | 2 883 410 |
| Tobacco (State) | 52 898 | 213 410 | 287 379 | 330 016 | 333 170 | 317 317 | 391 852 | 471 441 | 447 731 | 472 360 |
| Beer (State) | 85 722 | 471 137 | 867 569 | 1 203 838 | 1 268 054 | 1 381 248 | 1 434 560 | 1 444 067 | 1 565 738 | 1 673 211 |
| Liquors (State) | 124 808 | 520 393 | 811 377 | 834 390 | 938 925 | 913 640 | 1 047 963 | 1 249 595 | 1 257 711 | 1 262 767 |
| 5122 Profits of fiscal monopolies | 0 | 0 | 0 | 0 | 0 | 0 | 0 | 0 | 0 | 0 |
| 5123 Customs and import duties | 311 586 | 1 744 097 | 2 822 520 | 4 259 786 | 4 291 878 | 4 000 842 | 4 651 999 | 4 080 716 | 3 523 320 | 3 897 184 |
| Custom duties | 180 989 | 1 744 097 | 2 822 520 | 4 259 786 | 4 291 878 | 4 000 842 | 4 651 999 | 4 080 716 | 3 523 320 | 3 897 184 |
| Imports surcharge | 130 597 | 0 | 0 | 0 | 0 | 0 | 0 | 0 | 0 | 0 |
| 5124 Taxes on exports | 0 | 0 | 0 | 0 | 0 | 0 | 0 | 0 | 0 | 0 |
| 5125 Taxes on investment goods | 0 | 0 | 0 | 0 | 0 | 0 | 0 | 0 | 0 | 0 |
| 5126 Taxes on specific services | 0 | 0 | 0 | 0 | 0 | 0 | 0 | 0 | 0 | 0 |
| 5127 Other taxes on internat. trade and transactions | 0 | 0 | 0 | 0 | 0 | 0 | 0 | 0 | 0 | 0 |
| 5128 Other taxes | 0 | 0 | 0 | 0 | 0 | 0 | 0 | 0 | 0 | 0 |
| 5130 Unallocable between 5110 and 5120 | 0 | 0 | 0 | 0 | 0 | 0 | 0 | 0 | 0 | 0 |
| 5200 Taxes on use of goods and perform activities | 0 | 0 | 0 | 0 | 0 | 0 | 0 | 0 | 0 | 0 |
| 5210 Recurrent taxes | .. | .. | .. | .. | .. | .. | .. | .. | .. | .. |
| 5211 Paid by households: motor vehicles | .. | .. | .. | .. | .. | .. | .. | .. | .. | .. |
| 5212 Paid by others: motor vehicles | .. | .. | .. | .. | .. | .. | .. | .. | .. | .. |
| 5213 Paid in respect of other goods | .. | .. | .. | .. | .. | .. | .. | .. | .. | .. |

## Table 22. Colombia / Colombia (cont.)
Details of tax revenue / Ingresos tributarios detallados

*Million COP*

| | 1990 | 2000 | 2005 | 2007 | 2008 | 2009 | 2010 | 2011 | 2012 | 2013 |
|---|---|---|---|---|---|---|---|---|---|---|
| 5220 Non-recurrent taxes | .. | .. | .. | .. | .. | .. | .. | .. | .. | .. |
| 5300 Unallocable between 5100 and 5200 | 0 | 0 | 0 | 0 | 0 | 0 | 0 | 0 | 0 | 0 |
| **6000 Other taxes** | **159 323** | **1 738 020** | **3 377 674** | **4 596 744** | **4 863 849** | **5 548 110** | **5 892 923** | **6 939 193** | **6 615 141** | **7 432 215** |
| 6100 Paid solely by business | 0 | 0 | 0 | 0 | 0 | 0 | 0 | 0 | 0 | 0 |
| 6200 Other | 159 323 | 1 738 020 | 3 377 674 | 4 596 744 | 4 863 849 | 5 548 110 | 5 892 923 | 6 939 193 | 6 615 141 | 7 432 215 |
| Stamp tax | 0 | 401 497 | 633 586 | 759 787 | 768 580 | 611 832 | 357 160 | 123 923 | 58 973 | 58 378 |
| Other | 78 306 | 79 287 | 48 498 | 86 297 | 88 790 | 120 721 | 126 602 | 143 770 | 174 845 | 200 465 |
| Other (sub-national) | 81 017 | 1 257 236 | 2 695 589 | 3 750 660 | 4 006 478 | 4 815 557 | 5 409 160 | 6 671 500 | 6 381 323 | 7 173 372 |

*Note:* Year ending 31st December.

The data are on cash basis.

Includes the reported consolidated revenues of the territorial entities (departments and municipalities).

Before 2013, social security contributions did not include all the contributions entering FOSYGA (Solidarity and Guarantee Fund) Only the portion of the contributions used to finance the subsidized regime (up to 1.5 pp of the 12.5% of the monthly wage paid by employers and employees as an obligatory health contribution) was included. The part of the contributions entering Fosyga to finance the contributory regime was classified in the social security sector as "other incomes". From 2013 on, all of the health contributions entering Fosyga are classified as Social Security Contributions. The portion of the contributions not entering Fosyga that is both collected and spent by the health insurers –EPS- is not part of the fiscal accounts).

*Source:* Ministry of Finance and Central Bank of Colombia.

StatLink http://dx.doi.org/10.1787/888933190277

## Table 23. Costa Rica / Costa Rica
Details of tax revenue / Ingresos tributarios detallados

*Million CRC*

| | 1990 | 2000 | 2005 | 2007 | 2008 | 2009 | 2010 | 2011 | 2012 | 2013 |
|---|---|---|---|---|---|---|---|---|---|---|
| **Total tax revenue** | **106 778** | **893 812** | **1 915 942** | **2 989 427** | **3 565 410** | **3 564 323** | **3 979 101** | **4 438 852** | **4 846 611** | **5 563 744** |
| **1000 Taxes on income, profits and capital gains** | **11 820** | **128 805** | **324 224** | **531 552** | **689 225** | **687 420** | **748 093** | **828 691** | **891 669** | **1 014 440** |
| 1100 Of individuals | .. | .. | 16 438 | 123 194 | 104 536 | 156 936 | 202 849 | 233 486 | 307 489 | 316 894 |
| 1110 On income and profits | .. | .. | 16 438 | 123 194 | 104 536 | 156 936 | 202 849 | 233 486 | 307 489 | 316 894 |
| 1120 On capital gains | .. | .. | .. | .. | .. | .. | .. | .. | .. | .. |
| 1200 Corporate | .. | .. | 288 355 | 348 826 | 481 736 | 444 242 | 450 312 | 486 001 | 461 481 | 545 183 |
| 1210 On profits | .. | .. | 288 355 | 348 826 | 481 736 | 444 242 | 450 312 | 486 001 | 461 481 | 545 183 |
| 1220 On capital gains | .. | .. | 0 | 0 | 0 | 0 | 0 | 0 | 0 | 0 |
| 1300 Unallocable between 1100 and 1200 | 11 820 | 128 805 | 19 430 | 59 531 | 102 953 | 86 241 | 94 932 | 109 204 | 122 699 | 152 363 |
| **2000 Social security contributions** | **29 065** | **249 886** | **528 132** | **773 450** | **927 932** | **1 044 617** | **1 204 995** | **1 354 199** | **1 482 847** | **1 874 010** |
| 2100 Employees | .. | 3 405 | 5 354 | 6 964 | 7 465 | 8 777 | 9 649 | 11 014 | 12 936 | 12 774 |
| 2110 On a payroll basis | .. | 3 405 | 5 354 | 6 964 | 7 465 | 8 777 | 9 649 | 11 014 | 12 936 | 12 774 |
| 2120 On an income tax basis | .. | .. | .. | .. | .. | .. | .. | .. | .. | .. |
| 2200 Employers | .. | .. | 24 481 | 31 335 | 38 126 | 47 925 | 56 332 | 63 094 | 68 092 | 344 622 |
| 2210 On a payroll basis | .. | .. | .. | .. | .. | .. | .. | .. | .. | .. |
| 2220 On an income tax basis | .. | .. | .. | .. | .. | .. | .. | .. | .. | .. |
| 2300 Self-employed or non-employed | .. | 5 858 | 16 414 | 20 987 | 24 555 | 30 656 | 33 778 | 36 733 | 39 462 | 21 090 |
| 2310 On a payroll basis | .. | 5 858 | 16 414 | 20 987 | 24 555 | 30 656 | 33 778 | 36 733 | 39 462 | 21 090 |
| 2320 On an income tax basis | .. | .. | .. | .. | .. | .. | .. | .. | .. | .. |
| 2400 Unallocable between 2100, 2200 and 2300 | 29 065 | 240 623 | 481 883 | 714 164 | 857 787 | 957 260 | 1 105 236 | 1 243 358 | 1 362 357 | 1 495 525 |
| 2410 On a payroll basis | .. | .. | .. | .. | .. | .. | .. | .. | .. | .. |
| 2420 On an income tax basis | .. | .. | .. | .. | .. | .. | .. | .. | .. | .. |
| **3000 Taxes on payroll and workforce** | **7 054** | **41 918** | **81 290** | **120 254** | **147 785** | **163 991** | **182 529** | **201 667** | **226 575** | **247 775** |
| **4000 Taxes on property** | **366** | **12 681** | **25 110** | **42 658** | **46 610** | **48 040** | **63 663** | **70 927** | **81 868** | **99 771** |
| 4100 Recurrent taxes on immovable property | 0 | 5 310 | 14 245 | 21 568 | 27 700 | 34 233 | 47 607 | 50 279 | 60 918 | 71 526 |
| Land tax | .. | 0 | 0 | 0 | 0 | 0 | 0 | 0 | 0 | 0 |
| Additional land tax | .. | 0 | 0 | 0 | 0 | 0 | 0 | 0 | 0 | 0 |
| Tax on sumptuary constructions | .. | 0 | 0 | 0 | 0 | 0 | 0 | 0 | 0 | 0 |
| Immovable property tax | .. | 0 | 0 | 0 | 0 | 55 | 3 527 | 2 475 | 2 638 | 3 998 |
| Municipal immovable property tax | .. | 5 310 | 14 245 | 21 568 | 27 700 | 34 178 | 44 080 | 47 804 | 58 280 | 67 528 |
| 4110 Households | .. | .. | .. | .. | .. | .. | .. | .. | .. | .. |
| 4120 Others | .. | .. | .. | .. | .. | .. | .. | .. | .. | .. |
| 4200 Recurrent taxes on net wealth | 0 | 4 284 | 0 | 0 | 0 | 0 | 0 | 0 | 0 | 0 |
| 4210 Individual | .. | 0 | .. | .. | .. | .. | .. | .. | .. | .. |
| 4220 Corporate | .. | 4 284 | .. | .. | .. | .. | .. | .. | .. | .. |
| Tax on corporate assets | .. | 4 284 | .. | .. | .. | .. | .. | .. | .. | .. |
| 4300 Estate, inheritance and gift taxes | 0 | 0 | 0 | 0 | 0 | 0 | 0 | 0 | 0 | 0 |
| 4310 Estate and inheritance taxes | .. | .. | .. | .. | .. | .. | .. | .. | .. | .. |
| 4320 Gift taxes | .. | .. | .. | .. | .. | .. | .. | .. | .. | .. |
| 4400 Taxes on financial and capital transactions | 366 | 3 007 | 10 846 | 19 366 | 17 204 | 12 734 | 14 743 | 19 053 | 20 950 | 28 245 |
| 4500 Non-recurrent taxes | 0 | 0 | 0 | 0 | 0 | 0 | 0 | 0 | 0 | 0 |
| 4510 On net wealth | .. | .. | .. | .. | .. | .. | .. | .. | .. | .. |
| 4520 Other non-recurrent taxes | .. | .. | .. | .. | .. | .. | .. | .. | .. | .. |
| 4600 Other recurrent taxes on property | 0 | 80 | 19 | 1 724 | 1 706 | 1 072 | 1 313 | 1 595 | 0 | 0 |
| **5000 Taxes on goods and services** | **52 360** | **456 707** | **946 970** | **1 505 545** | **1 737 642** | **1 606 222** | **1 762 591** | **1 963 833** | **2 122 589** | **2 268 536** |
| 5100 Taxes on production, sale, transfer, etc | 49 980 | 437 334 | 914 200 | 1 449 974 | 1 665 700 | 1 524 363 | 1 664 652 | 1 872 449 | 2 015 909 | 2 149 169 |
| 5110 General taxes | 21 326 | 222 775 | 485 168 | 797 850 | 936 721 | 830 538 | 920 298 | 1 029 811 | 1 122 978 | 1 176 758 |
| 5111 Value added taxes | 21 326 | 222 775 | 485 168 | 797 850 | 936 721 | 830 538 | 920 298 | 1 029 811 | 1 122 978 | 1 176 758 |
| 5112 Sales tax | 0 | 0 | 0 | 0 | 0 | 0 | 0 | 0 | 0 | 0 |
| 5113 Other | 0 | 0 | 0 | 0 | 0 | 0 | 0 | 0 | 0 | 0 |
| 5120 Taxes on specific goods and services | 28 654 | 213 499 | 423 486 | 648 428 | 722 432 | 688 697 | 739 494 | 837 573 | 813 013 | 880 232 |
| 5121 Excises | 11 096 | 157 204 | 296 222 | 447 168 | 485 696 | 481 147 | 523 617 | 596 268 | 629 423 | 689 528 |
| Fuels and energy | 0 | 0 | 172 028 | 250 577 | 268 070 | 308 274 | 320 638 | 359 425 | 354 149 | 404 210 |
| Alcohol beverages | 0 | 8 229 | 20 219 | 23 802 | 29 413 | 29 639 | 28 035 | 32 936 | 35 620 | 35 254 |
| Non alcoholic beverages | 0 | 0 | 12 491 | 18 263 | 22 710 | 24 420 | 26 566 | 27 804 | 30 205 | 32 519 |
| Soaps | 0 | 0 | 573 | 883 | 1 009 | 1 110 | 1 317 | 1 425 | 1 487 | 1 989 |
| Cement | 0 | 0 | 0 | 0 | 220 | 253 | 227 | 250 | 247 | 291 |
| Tobacco | 0 | 0 | 0 | 0 | 0 | 0 | 0 | 0 | 19 852 | 38 860 |
| Abolished specific taxes on production and consumption | 0 | 31 756 | 0 | 0 | 0 | 0 | 0 | 0 | 0 | 0 |
| Other specific taxes on consumption | 11 096 | 117 219 | 90 913 | 153 643 | 164 268 | 117 444 | 146 834 | 174 428 | 187 863 | 176 405 |
| Transfers of exempted vehicles | 0 | 0 | 0 | 0 | 0 | 0 | 0 | 0 | 0 | .. |
| 5122 Profits of fiscal monopolies | 0 | 0 | 0 | 0 | 0 | 0 | 0 | 0 | 0 | 0 |
| 5123 Customs and import duties | 15 053 | 40 485 | 82 446 | 134 576 | 156 816 | 117 256 | 126 135 | 146 511 | 152 275 | 154 576 |
| Import duties | 13 977 | 32 336 | 66 598 | 107 565 | 124 550 | 97 001 | 103 851 | 122 355 | 128 358 | 130 634 |
| Custom duties | 1 076 | 8 149 | 15 848 | 27 011 | 32 266 | 20 255 | 22 284 | 24 156 | 23 917 | 23 942 |

## Table 23. Costa Rica / Costa Rica (cont.)
Details of tax revenue / Ingresos tributarios detallados

*Million CRC*

| | 1990 | 2000 | 2005 | 2007 | 2008 | 2009 | 2010 | 2011 | 2012 | 2013 |
|---|---|---|---|---|---|---|---|---|---|---|
| 5124 Taxes on exports | 2 226 | 2 238 | 969 | 2 432 | 4 667 | 4 677 | 3 973 | 3 990 | 3 823 | 4 877 |
| Export duties | 2 226 | 1 835 | 830 | 2 260 | 4 508 | 4 534 | 3 816 | 3 827 | 3 663 | 4 104 |
| Export duties Law 133 | 0 | 0 | 0 | 0 | 0 | 0 | 0 | 0 | 0 | 0 |
| Export duties Law 5519 | 0 | 253 | 0 | 0 | 0 | 0 | 0 | 0 | 0 | 0 |
| Tax on banana exports | 0 | 150 | 139 | 172 | 160 | 143 | 157 | 163 | 160 | 168 |
| Export duties on flora and fauna | 0 | 0 | 0 | 0 | 0 | 0 | 0 | 0 | 0 | 605 |
| 5125 Taxes on investment goods | 0 | 0 | 0 | 0 | 0 | 0 | 0 | 0 | 0 | 0 |
| 5126 Taxes on specific services | 280 | 13 488 | 43 755 | 63 419 | 74 376 | 84 619 | 84 270 | 88 744 | 25 579 | 28 571 |
| Casinos and gambling | 0 | 225 | 519 | 442 | 458 | 411 | 445 | 288 | 213 | 1 000 |
| Electronic betting business | 0 | 0 | 0 | 0 | 0 | 0 | 0 | 0 | 0 | 19 |
| Port cargo movements | 0 | 6 | 13 | 0 | 0 | 12 | 0 | 0 | 0 | 0 |
| Overseas departure tax | 0 | 0 | 19 022 | 22 799 | 24 939 | 24 794 | 24 322 | 23 902 | 25 366 | 27 552 |
| 10% on public shows | 0 | 26 | 0 | 0 | 0 | 0 | 0 | 0 | 0 | 0 |
| Pro-national airport's stamp tax | 0 | 6 | 0 | 0 | 0 | 0 | 0 | 0 | 0 | 0 |
| Stamp tax on the use of borders and ports | 280 | 2 697 | 0 | 0 | 0 | 0 | 0 | 0 | 0 | 0 |
| Municipal licences and permits | 0 | 8 692 | 19 974 | 31 888 | 39 841 | 52 492 | 52 637 | 55 606 | 0 | 0 |
| Municipal tax on construction | 0 | 1 836 | 4 226 | 8 290 | 9 137 | 6 910 | 6 866 | 8 948 | 0 | 0 |
| 5127 Other taxes on internat. trade and transactions | 0 | 83 | 94 | 832 | 877 | 998 | 1 499 | 2 060 | 1 913 | 2 680 |
| 5128 Other taxes | 0 | 0 | 0 | 0 | 0 | 0 | 0 | 0 | 0 | 0 |
| 5130 Unallocable between 5110 and 5120 | 0 | 1 061 | 5 546 | 3 696 | 6 547 | 5 128 | 4 860 | 5 065 | 79 918 | 92 179 |
| 5200 Taxes on use of goods and perform activities | 2 380 | 19 357 | 32 758 | 55 536 | 71 871 | 81 705 | 97 803 | 91 266 | 106 557 | 119 235 |
| 5210 Recurrent taxes | 2 380 | 19 357 | 32 758 | 55 536 | 71 871 | 81 705 | 97 803 | 91 266 | 106 557 | 119 235 |
| 5211 Paid by households: motor vehicles | 0 | 0 | 0 | 0 | 0 | 0 | 0 | 0 | 0 | 0 |
| 5212 Paid by others: motor vehicles | 1 425 | 15 487 | 30 918 | 52 511 | 68 299 | 77 924 | 94 101 | 85 152 | 101 903 | 113 727 |
| Property tax on vehicles, aircraft and boats | 1 425 | 15 374 | 30 918 | 52 511 | 68 299 | 77 924 | 94 101 | 85 152 | 101 903 | 113 727 |
| Special tax on the use of public roads | 0 | 113 | 0 | 0 | 0 | 0 | 0 | 0 | 0 | 0 |
| 5213 Paid in respect of other goods | 955 | 3 870 | 1 841 | 3 025 | 3 572 | 3 781 | 3 702 | 6 114 | 4 654 | 5 508 |
| Hunting and fishing licences | 0 | 0 | 0 | 0 | 0 | 0 | 0 | 0 | 0 | 0 |
| Hunting and fishing licences (Ministry of Natural Resources, Energy and Mines) | 0 | 4 | 0 | 0 | 0 | 0 | 0 | 0 | 0 | 0 |
| Spirits license | 0 | 0 | 0 | 0 | 0 | 0 | 0 | 0 | 0 | 0 |
| Revenue stamps | 955 | 3 866 | 1 841 | 3 025 | 3 572 | 3 781 | 3 702 | 6 114 | 4 654 | 5 508 |
| Sport stamp tax | 0 | 0 | 0 | 0 | 0 | 0 | 0 | 0 | 0 | 0 |
| 5220 Non-recurrent taxes | 0 | 0 | 0 | 0 | 0 | 0 | 0 | 0 | 0 | 0 |
| 5300 Unallocable between 5100 and 5200 | 0 | 15 | 12 | 35 | 71 | 153 | 136 | 118 | 123 | 132 |
| **6000 Other taxes** | **6 113** | **3 816** | **10 216** | **15 968** | **16 216** | **14 034** | **17 230** | **19 535** | **41 063** | **59 212** |
| 6100 Paid solely by business | 0 | 15 | 624 | 1 629 | 1 068 | 521 | 459 | 526 | 22 724 | 36 125 |
| 6200 Other | 6 113 | 3 801 | 9 592 | 14 339 | 15 148 | 13 513 | 16 771 | 19 009 | 18 339 | 23 087 |
| Transfers of vehicles, aircraft and boat | 497 | 2 530 | 6 357 | 9 937 | 10 554 | 9 612 | 12 311 | 13 672 | 12 947 | 17 177 |

*Note:* Year ending 31st December.

The data are on cash basis.

The figures for years up to and including 1997 exclude local government tax revenues as the data are not available.

Heading 2000: In ECLAC data, social security contributions include INA (National Institute of Apprenticeship), IMAS (Joint Social Aid Institute) and FODESAF (Social Development and Family Allowances Fund).

Heading 3000: In ECLAC data, social security contributions from decentralized institutions are considered in category 2000.

Heading 5121: In ECLAC data, the tax on transfers of vehicles is classified as a property tax 4000.

Heading 5212: In ECLAC data, Property tax on vehicles, aircraft and boats is classified in category 4000.

Heading 6000: In ECLAC data, the tax on the transfer of used vehicles Law No. 7088 of 30/11/87 is classified as a property tax (4000).

*Source:* Secretaría Técnica de la Autoridad Presupuestaria, Ministry of Finance and Contraloría General de la República.

StatLink http://dx.doi.org/10.1787/888933190289

## Table 24. Dominican Republic / República Dominicana
Details of tax revenue / Ingresos tributarios detallados

*Million DOP*

| | 1990 | 2000 | 2005 | 2007 | 2008 | 2009 | 2010 | 2011 | 2012 | 2013 |
|---|---|---|---|---|---|---|---|---|---|---|
| **Total tax revenue** | **6 416** | **48 310** | **149 637** | **217 965** | **236 166** | **220 373** | **243 943** | **273 132** | **312 064** | **355 314** |
| **1000 Taxes on income, profits and capital gains** | **1 670** | **7 060** | **23 907** | **45 293** | **47 614** | **42 379** | **40 558** | **49 421** | **75 404** | **88 979** |
| 1100 Of individuals | .. | 366 | 1 454 | 4 725 | 5 661 | 3 688 | 4 002 | 4 889 | 4 861 | 5 658 |
| 1110 On income and profits | .. | 348 | 1 375 | 4 638 | 5 467 | 3 451 | 3 815 | 4 437 | 4 562 | 5 234 |
| 1120 On capital gains | .. | 18 | 79 | 87 | 194 | 237 | 187 | 453 | 299 | 424 |
| 1200 Corporate | .. | 4 679 | 16 222 | 29 203 | 26 999 | 22 546 | 21 475 | 25 083 | 46 624 | 50 782 |
| 1210 On profits | .. | 4 605 | 16 147 | 29 063 | 26 853 | 22 414 | 21 325 | 24 900 | 46 411 | 50 595 |
| 1220 On capital gains | .. | 74 | 75 | 140 | 146 | 132 | 151 | 182 | 213 | 187 |
| Casinos | .. | 59 | 73 | 140 | 146 | 132 | 151 | 182 | 213 | 187 |
| Racetracks | .. | 15 | 2 | 0 | 0 | 0 | 0 | 0 | 0 | 0 |
| 1300 Unallocable between 1100 and 1200 | 1 670 | 2 015 | 6 232 | 11 365 | 14 954 | 16 145 | 15 080 | 19 450 | 23 919 | 32 539 |
| **2000 Social security contributions** | **53** | **490** | **35** | **860** | **860** | **1 009** | **1 845** | **1 328** | **1 250** | **1 552** |
| 2100 Employees | .. | .. | .. | .. | .. | .. | .. | .. | .. | .. |
| 2110 On a payroll basis | .. | .. | .. | .. | .. | .. | .. | .. | .. | .. |
| 2120 On an income tax basis | .. | .. | .. | .. | .. | .. | .. | .. | .. | .. |
| 2200 Employers | .. | .. | .. | .. | .. | .. | .. | .. | .. | .. |
| 2210 On a payroll basis | .. | .. | .. | .. | .. | .. | .. | .. | .. | .. |
| 2220 On an income tax basis | .. | .. | .. | .. | .. | .. | .. | .. | .. | .. |
| 2300 Self-employed or non-employed | .. | .. | .. | .. | .. | .. | .. | .. | .. | .. |
| 2310 On a payroll basis | .. | .. | .. | .. | .. | .. | .. | .. | .. | .. |
| 2320 On an income tax basis | .. | .. | .. | .. | .. | .. | .. | .. | .. | .. |
| 2400 Unallocable between 2100, 2200 and 2300 | 53 | 490 | 35 | 860 | 860 | 1 009 | 1 845 | 1 328 | 1 250 | 1 552 |
| 2410 On a payroll basis | 53 | 490 | 35 | 860 | 860 | 1 009 | 1 845 | 1 328 | 1 250 | 1 552 |
| 2420 On an income tax basis | 0 | 0 | 0 | 0 | 0 | 0 | 0 | 0 | 0 | 0 |
| **3000 Taxes on payroll and workforce** | **0** | **3 722** | **6 134** | **9 940** | **10 921** | **11 749** | **13 086** | **15 784** | **16 871** | **19 270** |
| **4000 Taxes on property** | **46** | **505** | **6 555** | **9 713** | **11 441** | **11 127** | **12 738** | **15 306** | **18 867** | **22 333** |
| 4100 Recurrent taxes on immovable property | 9 | 115 | 1 710 | 1 875 | 2 567 | 2 702 | 3 004 | 5 235 | 8 351 | 10 183 |
| 4110 Households | 9 | 115 | 1 710 | 594 | 552 | 473 | 555 | 629 | 686 | 1 518 |
| 4120 Others | 0 | 0 | 0 | 1 281 | 2 016 | 2 230 | 2 449 | 4 605 | 7 665 | 8 666 |
| Tax on assets | .. | .. | .. | 1 281 | 2 016 | 2 230 | 2 449 | 2 790 | 3 044 | 3 337 |
| Tax on financial assets (Law 139-11) | .. | .. | .. | 0 | 0 | 0 | 0 | 1 816 | 4 620 | 5 329 |
| 4200 Recurrent taxes on net wealth | 0 | 0 | 0 | 0 | 0 | 0 | 0 | 0 | 0 | 0 |
| 4210 Individual | .. | .. | .. | .. | .. | .. | .. | .. | .. | .. |
| 4220 Corporate | .. | .. | .. | .. | .. | .. | .. | .. | .. | .. |
| 4300 Estate, inheritance and gift taxes | 11 | 96 | 84 | 143 | 221 | 199 | 231 | 237 | 227 | 315 |
| 4310 Estate and inheritance taxes | 0 | 0 | 0 | 0 | 0 | 0 | 0 | 0 | 0 | 0 |
| 4320 Gift taxes | 0 | 0 | 0 | 0 | 0 | 0 | 0 | 0 | 0 | 0 |
| 4400 Taxes on financial and capital transactions | 22 | 217 | 4 546 | 7 123 | 7 876 | 7 181 | 8 125 | 8 255 | 8 723 | 10 404 |
| Tax on checks | 0 | 0 | 3 133 | 3 833 | 4 472 | 3 919 | 4 262 | 4 492 | 4 852 | 5 168 |
| Real estate operations | 22 | 217 | 1 413 | 3 291 | 3 404 | 3 262 | 3 864 | 3 763 | 3 872 | 5 236 |
| 4500 Non-recurrent taxes | 3 | 32 | 89 | 270 | 324 | 282 | 488 | 578 | 609 | 412 |
| 4510 On net wealth | 3 | 32 | 89 | 270 | 324 | 282 | 488 | 578 | 609 | 412 |
| 4520 Other non-recurrent taxes | 0 | 0 | 0 | 0 | 0 | 0 | 0 | 0 | 0 | 0 |
| 4600 Other recurrent taxes on property | 1 | 45 | 127 | 302 | 452 | 763 | 891 | 1 002 | 957 | 1 019 |
| **5000 Taxes on goods and services** | **4 488** | **36 038** | **111 344** | **150 604** | **165 306** | **154 105** | **175 716** | **191 294** | **199 673** | **223 181** |
| 5100 Taxes on production, sale, transfer, etc | 4 410 | 35 281 | 109 602 | 148 276 | 163 286 | 151 840 | 173 403 | 188 560 | 196 473 | 219 939 |
| 5110 General taxes | 973 | 10 195 | 41 368 | 66 982 | 74 319 | 69 877 | 81 871 | 89 610 | 92 819 | 113 345 |
| 5111 Value added taxes | 973 | 10 195 | 41 368 | 66 982 | 74 319 | 69 877 | 81 871 | 89 610 | 92 819 | 113 345 |
| 5112 Sales tax | 0 | 0 | 0 | 0 | 0 | 0 | 0 | 0 | 0 | 0 |
| 5113 Other | 0 | 0 | 0 | 0 | 0 | 0 | 0 | 0 | 0 | 0 |
| 5120 Taxes on specific goods and services | 3 437 | 25 086 | 68 234 | 81 294 | 88 966 | 81 964 | 91 531 | 98 950 | 103 654 | 106 595 |
| 5121 Excises | 500 | 6 474 | 27 158 | 51 906 | 57 192 | 52 445 | 60 144 | 67 174 | 71 033 | 72 581 |
| Vehicle registration | 0 | 0 | 0 | 4 140 | 4 798 | 3 163 | 4 234 | 4 268 | 4 505 | 4 595 |
| Transfer tax | 18 | 160 | 170 | 251 | 386 | 507 | 533 | 572 | 682 | 805 |
| Alcoholic beverages | 251 | 2 451 | 0 142 | 13 101 | 13 030 | 13 343 | 15 054 | 16 240 | 17 089 | 17 969 |
| Tobacco products | 102 | 469 | 2 879 | 3 283 | 4 180 | 4 131 | 4 529 | 4 241 | 4 470 | 4 356 |
| Petroleum products | 105 | 3 143 | 14 712 | 29 985 | 33 905 | 30 373 | 34 598 | 40 303 | 42 460 | 42 222 |
| Other | 24 | 251 | 1 255 | 1 145 | 894 | 927 | 1 197 | 1 549 | 1 827 | 2 634 |
| 5122 Profits of fiscal monopolies | 0 | 0 | 0 | 0 | 0 | 0 | 0 | 0 | 0 | 0 |
| 5123 Customs and import duties | 1 194 | 13 469 | 14 403 | 19 425 | 21 182 | 18 293 | 19 492 | 18 850 | 18 920 | 19 076 |
| Custom duties | 615 | 13 456 | 14 293 | 19 336 | 21 141 | 18 264 | 19 455 | 18 801 | 18 776 | 18 916 |
| Other | 579 | 13 | 110 | 89 | 41 | 29 | 37 | 49 | 144 | 160 |
| 5124 Taxes on exports | 6 | 4 | 46 | 83 | 128 | 132 | 146 | 181 | 264 | 34 |
| 5125 Taxes on investment goods | 0 | 0 | 0 | 0 | 0 | 0 | 0 | 0 | 0 | 0 |

## Table 24. Dominican Republic / República Dominicana (cont.)
### Details of tax revenue / Ingresos tributarios detallados

*Million DOP*

| | 1990 | 2000 | 2005 | 2007 | 2008 | 2009 | 2010 | 2011 | 2012 | 2013 |
|---|---|---|---|---|---|---|---|---|---|---|
| 5126 Taxes on specific services | 347 | 1 593 | 5 620 | 9 215 | 10 017 | 10 799 | 11 407 | 12 404 | 13 128 | 14 501 |
| Telecommunications | 85 | 0 | 3 193 | 3 867 | 4 100 | 4 592 | 4 886 | 4 947 | 5 124 | 5 897 |
| Insurance premiums | 33 | 584 | 0 | 2 211 | 2 796 | 2 978 | 3 088 | 3 238 | 3 437 | 3 674 |
| Travel tickets | 204 | 809 | 2 414 | 3 131 | 3 073 | 3 222 | 3 428 | 3 632 | 3 951 | 4 283 |
| Hotels | 22 | 191 | 0 | 0 | 0 | 0 | 0 | 0 | 0 | 0 |
| Others | 4 | 9 | 12 | 7 | 48 | 6 | 5 | 588 | 616 | 647 |
| 5127 Other taxes on internat. trade and transactions | 1 390 | 3 546 | 21 008 | 665 | 447 | 295 | 342 | 340 | 309 | 402 |
| Exchange commission | 857 | 0 | 0 | 0 | 0 | 0 | 0 | 0 | 0 | 0 |
| Consular fees | 77 | 32 | 271 | 342 | 143 | 138 | 132 | 138 | 130 | 143 |
| Other | 457 | 3 514 | 20 737 | 323 | 304 | 156 | 210 | 202 | 179 | 259 |
| 5128 Other taxes | 0 | 0 | 0 | 0 | 0 | 0 | 0 | 0 | 0 | 0 |
| 5130 Unallocable between 5110 and 5120 | 0 | 0 | 0 | 0 | 0 | 0 | 0 | 0 | 0 | 0 |
| 5200 Taxes on use of goods and perform activities | 77 | 757 | 1 742 | 2 329 | 2 020 | 2 265 | 2 313 | 2 733 | 3 199 | 3 242 |
| 5210 Recurrent taxes | 77 | 757 | 1 742 | 2 329 | 2 020 | 2 265 | 2 313 | 2 733 | 3 199 | 3 242 |
| 5211 Paid by households: motor vehicles | 45 | 268 | 977 | 1 391 | 1 183 | 1 225 | 1 277 | 1 300 | 1 271 | 1 073 |
| 5212 Paid by others: motor vehicles | 0 | 0 | 0 | 0 | 0 | 0 | 0 | 0 | 0 | 0 |
| 5213 Paid in respect of other goods | 33 | 489 | 766 | 938 | 837 | 1 040 | 1 036 | 1 433 | 1 929 | 2 169 |
| Licenses to carry firearms | 17 | 237 | 244 | 316 | 214 | 346 | 296 | 253 | 194 | 240 |
| Licenses to operate gambling houses | 0 | 114 | 155 | 217 | 187 | 199 | 211 | 571 | 1 076 | 1 229 |
| Licenses to operate slot machines | 4 | 60 | 102 | 371 | 385 | 409 | 457 | 528 | 567 | 598 |
| Other | 12 | 78 | 264 | 34 | 51 | 86 | 72 | 82 | 92 | 102 |
| 5220 Non-recurrent taxes | 0 | 0 | 0 | 0 | 0 | 0 | 0 | 0 | 0 | 0 |
| 5300 Unallocable between 5100 and 5200 | 0 | 0 | 0 | 0 | 0 | 0 | 0 | 0 | 0 | 0 |
| **6000 Other taxes** | **159** | **495** | **1 661** | **1 555** | **25** | **5** | **0** | **0** | **0** | **0** |
| 6100 Paid solely by business | 0 | 0 | 0 | 0 | 0 | 0 | .. | .. | 0 | 0 |
| 6200 Other | 159 | 495 | 1 661 | 1 555 | 25 | 5 | .. | .. | 0 | 0 |

*Note:* Year ending 31st December.

The data are on cash basis.

The data exclude local government tax revenues as the data are not available.

Heading 2000: The data exclude social security contributions to general government managed by the private sector.

Heading 5121: In ECLAC data, the tax on transfer of movable goods is classified as a propety tax (4000).

Heading 6000: In ECLAC data, the Vehicle transfer tax is classified as a property tax (4000).

*Source:* Ministerio de Hacienda, Ministry of Finance.

StatLink http://dx.doi.org/10.1787/888933190299

## Table 25. Ecuador / Ecuador
Details of tax revenue / Ingresos tributarios detallados

*Million USD*

| | 1990 | 2000 | 2005 | 2007 | 2008 | 2009 | 2010 | 2011 | 2012 | 2013 |
|---|---|---|---|---|---|---|---|---|---|---|
| **Total tax revenue** | **1 076** | **1 851** | **4 850** | **6 545** | **8 667** | **9 318** | **11 343** | **13 736** | **17 007** | **18 214** |
| **1000 Taxes on income, profits and capital gains** | **138** | **293** | **937** | **1 268** | **2 339** | **2 518** | **2 353** | **3 030** | **3 313** | **3 847** |
| 1100 Of individuals | .. | .. | .. | .. | .. | .. | .. | .. | .. | .. |
| 1110 On income and profits | .. | .. | .. | .. | .. | .. | .. | .. | .. | .. |
| 1120 On capital gains | .. | .. | .. | .. | .. | .. | .. | .. | .. | .. |
| 1200 Corporate | .. | .. | .. | .. | .. | .. | .. | .. | .. | .. |
| 1210 On profits | .. | .. | .. | .. | .. | .. | .. | .. | .. | .. |
| 1220 On capital gains | .. | .. | .. | .. | .. | .. | .. | .. | .. | .. |
| 1300 Unallocable between 1100 and 1200 | 138 | 293 | 937 | 1 268 | 2 339 | 2 518 | 2 353 | 3 030 | 3 313 | 3 847 |
| **2000 Social security contributions** | **243** | **228** | **1 109** | **1 795** | **2 097** | **2 061** | **2 549** | **3 971** | **4 752** | **4 547** |
| 2100 Employees | .. | .. | .. | .. | .. | .. | .. | .. | .. | .. |
| 2110 On a payroll basis | .. | .. | .. | .. | .. | .. | .. | .. | .. | .. |
| 2120 On an income tax basis | .. | .. | .. | .. | .. | .. | .. | .. | .. | .. |
| 2200 Employers | .. | .. | .. | .. | .. | .. | .. | .. | .. | .. |
| 2210 On a payroll basis | .. | .. | .. | .. | .. | .. | .. | .. | .. | .. |
| 2220 On an income tax basis | .. | .. | .. | .. | .. | .. | .. | .. | .. | .. |
| 2300 Self-employed or non-employed | .. | .. | .. | .. | .. | .. | .. | .. | .. | .. |
| 2310 On a payroll basis | .. | .. | .. | .. | .. | .. | .. | .. | .. | .. |
| 2320 On an income tax basis | .. | .. | .. | .. | .. | .. | .. | .. | .. | .. |
| 2400 Unallocable between 2100, 2200 and 2300 | 243 | 228 | 1 109 | 1 795 | 2 097 | 2 061 | 2 549 | 3 971 | 4 752 | 4 547 |
| 2410 On a payroll basis | .. | .. | .. | .. | .. | .. | .. | .. | .. | .. |
| 2420 On an income tax basis | .. | .. | .. | .. | .. | .. | .. | .. | .. | .. |
| **3000 Taxes on payroll and workforce** | **0** | **0** | **0** | **0** | **0** | **0** | **0** | **0** | **0** | **0** |
| **4000 Taxes on property** | **0** | **0** | **0** | **0** | **0** | **0** | **0** | **0** | **0** | **0** |
| 4100 Recurrent taxes on immovable property | .. | .. | .. | .. | .. | .. | .. | .. | .. | .. |
| 4110 Households | .. | .. | .. | .. | .. | .. | .. | .. | .. | .. |
| 4120 Others | .. | .. | .. | .. | .. | .. | .. | .. | .. | .. |
| 4200 Recurrent taxes on net wealth | .. | .. | .. | .. | .. | .. | .. | .. | .. | .. |
| 4210 Individual | .. | .. | .. | .. | .. | .. | .. | .. | .. | .. |
| 4220 Corporate | .. | .. | .. | .. | .. | .. | .. | .. | .. | .. |
| 4300 Estate, inheritance and gift taxes | .. | .. | .. | .. | .. | .. | .. | .. | .. | .. |
| 4310 Estate and inheritance taxes | .. | .. | .. | .. | .. | .. | .. | .. | .. | .. |
| 4320 Gift taxes | .. | .. | .. | .. | .. | .. | .. | .. | .. | .. |
| 4400 Taxes on financial and capital transactions | .. | .. | .. | .. | .. | .. | .. | .. | .. | .. |
| 4500 Non-recurrent taxes | .. | .. | .. | .. | .. | .. | .. | .. | .. | .. |
| 4510 On net wealth | .. | .. | .. | .. | .. | .. | .. | .. | .. | .. |
| 4520 Other non-recurrent taxes | .. | .. | .. | .. | .. | .. | .. | .. | .. | .. |
| 4600 Other recurrent taxes on property | .. | .. | .. | .. | .. | .. | .. | .. | .. | .. |
| **5000 Taxes on goods and services** | **668** | **1 330** | **2 802** | **3 479** | **4 183** | **4 508** | **6 152** | **6 707** | **8 830** | **9 688** |
| 5100 Taxes on production, sale, transfer, etc | 665 | 1 319 | 2 742 | 3 407 | 4 088 | 4 390 | 5 997 | 6 533 | 8 636 | 9 474 |
| 5110 General taxes | 302 | 836 | 1 975 | 2 509 | 2 825 | 3 019 | 3 886 | 4 200 | 5 415 | 6 056 |
| 5111 Value added taxes | 302 | 836 | 1 975 | 2 509 | 2 825 | 3 019 | 3 886 | 4 200 | 5 415 | 6 056 |
| 5112 Sales tax | 0 | 0 | 0 | 0 | 0 | 0 | 0 | 0 | 0 | 0 |
| 5113 Other | 0 | 0 | 0 | 0 | 0 | 0 | 0 | 0 | 0 | 0 |
| 5120 Taxes on specific goods and services | 363 | 483 | 767 | 898 | 1 263 | 1 372 | 2 110 | 2 332 | 3 221 | 3 418 |
| 5121 Excises | 90 | 75 | 221 | 220 | 474 | 448 | 530 | 618 | 685 | 744 |
| Alcohol products | .. | 30 | 89 | 70 | .. | .. | .. | .. | .. | .. |
| Soft drinks and mineral water | .. | 9 | 15 | 15 | .. | .. | .. | .. | .. | .. |
| Cigarettes | .. | 24 | 71 | 74 | .. | .. | .. | .. | .. | .. |
| Luxury goods and vehicles | .. | 11 | 46 | 61 | .. | .. | .. | .. | .. | .. |
| 5122 Profits of fiscal monopolies | 0 | 0 | 0 | 0 | 0 | 0 | 0 | 0 | 0 | 0 |
| 5123 Customs and import duties | 227 | 217 | 547 | 679 | 789 | 923 | 1 152 | 1 156 | 1 261 | 1 352 |
| 5124 Taxes on exports | 0 | 0 | 0 | 0 | 0 | 0 | 0 | 0 | 0 | 0 |
| 5125 Taxes on investment goods | 0 | 0 | 0 | 0 | 0 | 0 | 0 | 0 | 0 | 0 |
| 5126 Taxes on specific services | 7 | 17 | 0 | 0 | 0 | 0 | 428 | 558 | 1 275 | 1 322 |
| Exit taxes | 7 | 17 | 0 | 0 | 0 | 0 | 428 | 558 | 1 275 | 1 322 |
| 5127 Other taxes on internat. trade and transactions | 40 | 175 | 0 | 0 | 0 | 0 | 0 | 0 | 0 | 0 |
| On capital movements | 0 | 169 | .. | .. | .. | .. | .. | .. | .. | .. |
| On purchase of foreign exchange | 22 | 4 | .. | .. | .. | .. | .. | .. | .. | .. |
| On credit operations in national currency | 18 | 2 | .. | .. | .. | .. | .. | .. | .. | .. |
| 5128 Other taxes | 0 | 0 | 0 | 0 | 0 | 0 | 0 | 0 | 0 | 0 |
| 5130 Unallocable between 5110 and 5120 | 0 | 0 | 0 | 0 | 0 | 0 | 0 | 0 | 0 | 0 |
| 5200 Taxes on use of goods and perform activities | 3 | 11 | 60 | 72 | 95 | 118 | 156 | 174 | 194 | 214 |
| 5210 Recurrent taxes | 3 | 11 | 60 | 72 | 95 | 118 | 156 | 174 | 194 | 214 |
| 5211 Paid by households: motor vehicles | 0 | 0 | 0 | 0 | 0 | 0 | 0 | 0 | 0 | 0 |
| 5212 Paid by others: motor vehicles | 3 | 11 | 60 | 72 | 95 | 118 | 156 | 174 | 194 | 214 |
| Annual tax on motor vehicles | 3 | 11 | 60 | 72 | 95 | 118 | 156 | 174 | 194 | 214 |
| 5213 Paid in respect of other goods | 0 | 0 | 0 | 0 | 0 | 0 | 0 | 0 | 0 | 0 |

## Table 25. Ecuador / Ecuador (cont.)
### Details of tax revenue / Ingresos tributarios detallados

*Million USD*

| | 1990 | 2000 | 2005 | 2007 | 2008 | 2009 | 2010 | 2011 | 2012 | 2013 |
|---|---|---|---|---|---|---|---|---|---|---|
| 5220 Non-recurrent taxes | 0 | 0 | 0 | 0 | 0 | 0 | 0 | 0 | 0 | 0 |
| 5300 Unallocable between 5100 and 5200 | 0 | 0 | 0 | 0 | 0 | 0 | 0 | 0 | 0 | 0 |
| **6000 Other taxes** | **27** | **0** | **2** | **3** | **48** | **231** | **289** | **28** | **111** | **132** |
| 6100 Paid solely by business | 0 | .. | 0 | 0 | 0 | 0 | 0 | 0 | 0 | 0 |
| 6200 Other | 27 | .. | 2 | 3 | 48 | 231 | 289 | 28 | 111 | 132 |

*Note:* Year ending 31st December.

The data are on cash basis.

The data exclude local government tax revenues as the data are not available.

Social security data is recorded at the non-financial public sector level.

Heading 5212: In ECLAC data, the annual tax on motor vehicles is classified as a property tax (4000).

*Source:* Banco Central del Ecuador, Central Bank of Ecuador.

StatLink http://dx.doi.org/10.1787/888933190307

## Table 26. El Salvador / El Salvador
Details of tax revenue / Ingresos tributarios detallados

*Million USD*

| | 1990 | 2000 | 2005 | 2007 | 2008 | 2009 | 2010 | 2011 | 2012 | 2013 |
|---|---|---|---|---|---|---|---|---|---|---|
| **Total tax revenue** | **506** | **1 607** | **2 414** | **3 056** | **3 240** | **2 966** | **3 180** | **3 445** | **3 762** | **4 003** |
| **1000 Taxes on income, profits and capital gains** | **95** | **429** | **668** | **933** | **1 004** | **948** | **940** | **1 020** | **1 184** | **1 344** |
| 1100 Of individuals | .. | .. | 312 | 395 | 536 | 444 | 571 | 456 | 697 | 578 |
| 1110 On income and profits | .. | .. | 312 | 395 | 536 | 444 | 571 | 456 | 697 | 578 |
| 1120 On capital gains | .. | .. | .. | .. | .. | .. | .. | .. | .. | .. |
| 1200 Corporate | .. | .. | 356 | 573 | 518 | 559 | 423 | 631 | 555 | 793 |
| 1210 On profits | .. | .. | 356 | 573 | 518 | 559 | 423 | 631 | 555 | 793 |
| 1220 On capital gains | .. | .. | .. | .. | .. | .. | .. | .. | .. | .. |
| 1300 Unallocable between 1100 and 1200 | 95 | 429 | 0 | -35 | -49 | -55 | -55 | -66 | -68 | -27 |
| Income tax | 95 | 429 | .. | 0 | 0 | 0 | 0 | 0 | 0 | 0 |
| Income tax refunds | 0 | 0 | .. | -35 | -49 | -55 | -55 | -66 | -68 | -27 |
| **2000 Social security contributions** | **67** | **263** | **282** | **331** | **356** | **358** | **369** | **382** | **404** | **425** |
| 2100 Employees | .. | 75 | 76 | 88 | 96 | 96 | 99 | 100 | 106 | 112 |
| 2110 On a payroll basis | .. | 75 | 76 | 88 | 96 | 96 | 99 | 100 | 106 | 112 |
| 2120 On an income tax basis | .. | 0 | 0 | 0 | 0 | 0 | 0 | 0 | 0 | 0 |
| 2200 Employers | .. | 176 | 181 | 214 | 230 | 230 | 238 | 245 | 260 | 273 |
| 2210 On a payroll basis | .. | 176 | 181 | 214 | 230 | 230 | 238 | 245 | 260 | 273 |
| 2220 On an income tax basis | .. | 0 | 0 | 0 | 0 | 0 | 0 | 0 | 0 | 0 |
| 2300 Self-employed or non-employed | .. | 13 | 25 | 29 | 29 | 31 | 33 | 36 | 38 | 40 |
| 2310 On a payroll basis | .. | 13 | 25 | 29 | 29 | 31 | 33 | 36 | 38 | 40 |
| 2320 On an income tax basis | .. | 0 | 0 | 0 | 0 | 0 | 0 | 0 | 0 | 0 |
| 2400 Unallocable between 2100, 2200 and 2300 | 67 | 0 | 0 | 0 | 0 | 0 | 0 | 0 | 0 | 0 |
| 2410 On a payroll basis | 67 | 0 | 0 | 0 | 0 | 0 | 0 | 0 | 0 | 0 |
| 2420 On an income tax basis | 0 | 0 | 0 | 0 | 0 | 0 | 0 | 0 | 0 | 0 |
| **3000 Taxes on payroll and workforce** | **0** | **0** | **0** | **0** | **0** | **0** | **0** | **0** | **0** | **0** |
| **4000 Taxes on property** | **26** | **12** | **16** | **21** | **18** | **13** | **16** | **16** | **20** | **21** |
| 4100 Recurrent taxes on immovable property | 0 | 0 | 0 | 0 | 0 | 0 | 0 | 0 | 0 | 0 |
| 4110 Households | .. | .. | .. | .. | .. | .. | .. | .. | .. | .. |
| 4120 Others | .. | .. | .. | .. | .. | .. | .. | .. | .. | .. |
| 4200 Recurrent taxes on net wealth | 16 | 0 | 0 | 0 | 0 | 0 | 0 | 0 | 0 | 0 |
| 4210 Individual | 16 | .. | .. | .. | .. | .. | .. | .. | .. | .. |
| 4220 Corporate | 0 | .. | .. | .. | .. | .. | .. | .. | .. | .. |
| 4300 Estate, inheritance and gift taxes | 0 | 0 | 0 | 0 | 0 | 0 | 0 | 0 | 0 | 0 |
| 4310 Estate and inheritance taxes | .. | .. | .. | .. | .. | .. | .. | .. | .. | .. |
| 4320 Gift taxes | .. | .. | .. | .. | .. | .. | .. | .. | .. | .. |
| 4400 Taxes on financial and capital transactions | 10 | 12 | 16 | 21 | 18 | 13 | 16 | 16 | 20 | 21 |
| 4500 Non-recurrent taxes | 0 | 0 | 0 | 0 | 0 | 0 | 0 | 0 | 0 | 0 |
| 4510 On net wealth | .. | .. | .. | .. | .. | .. | .. | .. | .. | .. |
| 4520 Other non-recurrent taxes | .. | .. | .. | .. | .. | .. | .. | .. | .. | .. |
| 4600 Other recurrent taxes on property | 0 | 0 | 0 | 0 | 0 | 0 | 0 | 0 | 0 | 0 |
| **5000 Taxes on goods and services** | **259** | **903** | **1 447** | **1 770** | **1 863** | **1 646** | **1 855** | **2 027** | **2 155** | **2 213** |
| 5100 Taxes on production, sale, transfer, etc | 259 | 903 | 1 447 | 1 770 | 1 863 | 1 646 | 1 855 | 2 027 | 2 155 | 2 213 |
| 5110 General taxes | 133 | 714 | 1 104 | 1 389 | 1 461 | 1 251 | 1 433 | 1 574 | 1 677 | 1 731 |
| 5111 Value added taxes | 0 | 714 | 1 104 | 1 389 | 1 461 | 1 251 | 1 433 | 1 574 | 1 677 | 1 731 |
| 5112 Sales tax | 0 | 0 | 0 | 0 | 0 | 0 | 0 | 0 | 0 | 0 |
| 5113 Other | 133 | 0 | 0 | 0 | 0 | 0 | 0 | 0 | 0 | 0 |
| 5120 Taxes on specific goods and services | 127 | 189 | 344 | 381 | 402 | 395 | 422 | 453 | 478 | 483 |
| 5121 Excises | 65 | 49 | 162 | 169 | 194 | 202 | 218 | 238 | 262 | 249 |
| Consumption of products | 65 | 49 | 0 | 0 | 0 | 0 | 0 | 0 | 0 | 0 |
| Consumption of products | 0 | 0 | 39 | 40 | 43 | 44 | 44 | 52 | 64 | 60 |
| Cigarettes | 0 | 0 | 23 | 30 | 27 | 31 | 31 | 38 | 40 | 27 |
| Soft drinks | 0 | 0 | 33 | 27 | 24 | 24 | 31 | 35 | 40 | 42 |
| Beer | 0 | 0 | 1 | 1 | 0 | 1 | 1 | 1 | 1 | 1 |
| Weapons, ammunition and explosives | 0 | 0 | 1 | 1 | 1 | 1 | 1 | 1 | 1 | 1 |
| Special Contribution- Sugar | 0 | 0 | 0 | 0 | 33 | 34 | 35 | 35 | 36 | 36 |
| Special Contribution- Public transportation | 0 | 0 | 66 | 70 | 65 | 68 | 69 | 69 | 71 | 72 |
| Special Contribution- FOVIAL | 0 | 0 | 0 | 0 | 0 | 0 | 7 | 8 | 9 | 11 |
| 5122 Profits of fiscal monopolies | 0 | 0 | 0 | 0 | 0 | 0 | 0 | 0 | 0 | 0 |
| 5123 Customs and import duties | 61 | 141 | 181 | 204 | 179 | 138 | 148 | 167 | 180 | 199 |
| 5124 Taxes on exports | 0 | 0 | 0 | 0 | 0 | 0 | 0 | 0 | 0 | 0 |
| 5125 Taxes on investment goods | 0 | 0 | 0 | 0 | 0 | 0 | 0 | 0 | 0 | 0 |
| 5126 Taxes on specific services | 0 | 0 | 0 | 8 | 30 | 55 | 56 | 48 | 36 | 34 |
| 5127 Other taxes on internat. trade and transactions | 0 | 0 | 0 | 0 | 0 | 0 | 0 | 0 | 0 | 0 |
| 5128 Other taxes | 0 | 0 | 0 | 0 | 0 | 0 | 0 | 0 | 0 | 0 |
| 5130 Unallocable between 5110 and 5120 | 0 | 0 | 0 | 0 | 0 | 0 | 0 | 0 | 0 | 0 |
| 5200 Taxes on use of goods and perform activities | 0 | 0 | 0 | 0 | 0 | 0 | 0 | 0 | 0 | 0 |
| 5210 Recurrent taxes | .. | .. | .. | .. | .. | .. | .. | .. | .. | .. |
| 5211 Paid by households: motor vehicles | .. | .. | .. | .. | .. | .. | .. | .. | .. | .. |

## Table 26. El Salvador / El Salvador (cont.)
Details of tax revenue / Ingresos tributarios detallados

*Million USD*

| | 1990 | 2000 | 2005 | 2007 | 2008 | 2009 | 2010 | 2011 | 2012 | 2013 |
|---|---|---|---|---|---|---|---|---|---|---|
| 5212 Paid by others: motor vehicles | .. | .. | .. | .. | .. | .. | .. | .. | .. | .. |
| 5213 Paid in respect of other goods | .. | .. | .. | .. | .. | .. | .. | .. | .. | .. |
| 5220 Non-recurrent taxes | .. | .. | .. | .. | .. | .. | .. | .. | .. | .. |
| 5300 Unallocable between 5100 and 5200 | 0 | 0 | 0 | 0 | 0 | 0 | 0 | 0 | 0 | 0 |
| **6000 Other taxes** | **58** | **0** | **0** | **0** | **0** | **0** | **0** | **0** | **0** | **0** |
| 6100 Paid solely by business | 0 | 0 | .. | .. | .. | .. | .. | .. | .. | .. |
| 6200 Other | 58 | 0 | .. | .. | .. | .. | .. | .. | .. | .. |

*Note:* Year ending 31st December.

The data are on cash basis.

The figures exclude local government tax revenues as the data are not available.

Heading 1000: For 2002 and from 2006 onwards sub-headings 1100 and 1200 are presented on a gross basis (i.e. not including income tax refunds. The latter is classified under heading 1300).

Heading 2000: Corresponds to social security contributions paid to the Salvadoran Institute of Social Security.

Heading 2000: Data on public pension contributions are not available for 2011 to 2013.

*Source:* Dirección General de Tesorería, Ministry of Finance (for national taxes). Central Reserve Bank of El Salvador from 1990 to 1996 and Salvadoran Institute of Social Security for subsequent years (for social security contribution figures).

StatLink http://dx.doi.org/10.1787/888933190314

## Table 27. Guatemala / Guatemala
Details of tax revenue / Ingresos tributarios detallados

*Million GTQ*

| | 1990 | 2000 | 2005 | 2007 | 2008 | 2009 | 2010 | 2011 | 2012 | 2013 |
|---|---|---|---|---|---|---|---|---|---|---|
| **Total tax revenue** | **2 801** | **16 531** | **27 187** | **36 406** | **38 206** | **37 661** | **41 189** | **46 984** | **50 441** | **54 954** |
| **1000 Taxes on income, profits and capital gains** | **507** | **3 295** | **6 049** | **8 654** | **9 698** | **9 706** | **10 319** | **12 696** | **13 445** | **16 041** |
| 1100 Of individuals | 25 | 143 | 645 | 877 | 945 | 1 060 | 1 225 | 1 462 | 1 477 | 1 246 |
| 1110 On income and profits | 25 | 143 | 645 | 877 | 945 | 1 060 | 1 225 | 1 462 | 1 477 | 1 246 |
| Personal income tax | 25 | 137 | 642 | 877 | 945 | 1 060 | 1 225 | 1 462 | 1 476 | 1 246 |
| Income from financial products | 0 | 6 | 4 | 0 | 0 | 0 | 0 | 0 | 1 | 0 |
| 1120 On capital gains | .. | .. | .. | .. | .. | .. | .. | .. | .. | .. |
| 1200 Corporate | 482 | 3 149 | 3 756 | 5 729 | 6 417 | 6 141 | 6 520 | 8 609 | 9 119 | 11 532 |
| 1210 On profits | 482 | 3 149 | 3 756 | 5 729 | 6 417 | 6 141 | 6 520 | 8 609 | 9 119 | 11 532 |
| Corporate income tax | 482 | 1 610 | 3 495 | 5 408 | 6 085 | 5 768 | 6 132 | 8 198 | 8 656 | 11 477 |
| Income from financial products | 0 | 248 | 235 | 312 | 322 | 371 | 386 | 403 | 463 | 52 |
| Commercial and agricultural enterprises | 0 | 1 291 | 26 | 9 | 11 | 2 | 2 | 8 | 0 | 3 |
| 1220 On capital gains | .. | .. | .. | .. | .. | .. | .. | .. | .. | .. |
| 1300 Unallocable between 1100 and 1200 | 0 | 2 | 1 647 | 2 048 | 2 336 | 2 505 | 2 574 | 2 625 | 2 849 | 3 263 |
| Extraordinary and temporary solidarity tax in support of peace agreements | .. | 0 | 1 647 | 2 047 | 2 336 | 677 | 44 | 54 | 4 | 21 |
| Solidarity tax | .. | 0 | 0 | 0 | 0 | 1 829 | 2 530 | 2 571 | 2 845 | 3 243 |
| Extraordinary and temporary solidarity tax | .. | 2 | 0 | 1 | 0 | 0 | 0 | 0 | 0 | 0 |
| **2000 Social security contributions** | **436** | **2 569** | **4 072** | **5 155** | **5 516** | **5 801** | **6 408** | **7 125** | **7 858** | **8 617** |
| 2100 Employees | .. | .. | .. | .. | .. | .. | .. | .. | .. | .. |
| 2110 On a payroll basis | .. | .. | .. | .. | .. | .. | .. | .. | .. | .. |
| 2120 On an income tax basis | .. | .. | .. | .. | .. | .. | .. | .. | .. | .. |
| 2200 Employers | .. | .. | .. | .. | .. | .. | .. | .. | .. | .. |
| 2210 On a payroll basis | .. | .. | .. | .. | .. | .. | .. | .. | .. | .. |
| 2220 On an income tax basis | .. | .. | .. | .. | .. | .. | .. | .. | .. | .. |
| 2300 Self-employed or non-employed | .. | .. | .. | .. | .. | .. | .. | .. | .. | .. |
| 2310 On a payroll basis | .. | .. | .. | .. | .. | .. | .. | .. | .. | .. |
| 2320 On an income tax basis | .. | .. | .. | .. | .. | .. | .. | .. | .. | .. |
| 2400 Unallocable between 2100, 2200 and 2300 | 436 | 2 569 | 4 072 | 5 155 | 5 516 | 5 801 | 6 408 | 7 125 | 7 858 | 8 617 |
| 2410 On a payroll basis | 436 | 2 569 | 4 072 | 5 155 | 5 516 | 5 801 | 6 408 | 7 125 | 7 858 | 8 617 |
| 2420 On an income tax basis | 0 | 0 | 0 | 0 | 0 | 0 | 0 | 0 | 0 | 0 |
| **3000 Taxes on payroll and workforce** | **0** | **0** | **0** | **0** | **0** | **0** | **0** | **0** | **0** | **0** |
| **4000 Taxes on property** | **45** | **165** | **350** | **440** | **496** | **578** | **631** | **648** | **743** | **791** |
| 4100 Recurrent taxes on immovable property | 0 | 153 | 341 | 426 | 481 | 569 | 621 | 635 | 735 | 780 |
| 4110 Households | .. | 0 | 0 | 0 | 0 | 0 | 0 | 0 | 0 | 0 |
| 4120 Others | .. | 153 | 341 | 426 | 481 | 569 | 621 | 635 | 735 | 780 |
| Property tax | .. | 6 | 1 | 1 | 1 | 1 | 1 | 1 | 1 | 1 |
| Property tax (municipal) | .. | 147 | 341 | 426 | 480 | 568 | 620 | 634 | 734 | 779 |
| 4200 Recurrent taxes on net wealth | 0 | 0 | 0 | 0 | 0 | 0 | 0 | 0 | 0 | 0 |
| 4210 Individual | .. | .. | .. | .. | .. | .. | .. | .. | .. | .. |
| 4220 Corporate | .. | .. | .. | .. | .. | .. | .. | .. | .. | .. |
| 4300 Estate, inheritance and gift taxes | 0 | 0 | 0 | 0 | 0 | 0 | 0 | 0 | 0 | 0 |
| 4310 Estate and inheritance taxes | .. | .. | .. | .. | .. | .. | .. | .. | .. | .. |
| 4320 Gift taxes | .. | .. | .. | .. | .. | .. | .. | .. | .. | .. |
| 4400 Taxes on financial and capital transactions | 45 | 12 | 8 | 14 | 15 | 9 | 10 | 13 | 8 | 10 |
| 4500 Non-recurrent taxes | 0 | 0 | 0 | 0 | 0 | 0 | 0 | 0 | 0 | 0 |
| 4510 On net wealth | .. | .. | .. | .. | .. | .. | .. | .. | .. | .. |
| 4520 Other non-recurrent taxes | .. | .. | .. | .. | .. | .. | .. | .. | .. | .. |
| 4600 Other recurrent taxes on property | 0 | 0 | 0 | 0 | 0 | 0 | 0 | 0 | 0 | 0 |
| **5000 Taxes on goods and services** | **1 709** | **10 317** | **16 402** | **21 764** | **22 118** | **20 980** | **23 259** | **25 876** | **27 518** | **29 075** |
| 5100 Taxes on production, sale, transfer, etc | 1 681 | 10 131 | 16 083 | 21 411 | 21 716 | 20 513 | 22 754 | 25 317 | 26 614 | 27 545 |
| 5110 General taxes | 762 | 6 259 | 10 753 | 15 382 | 16 155 | 15 015 | 16 980 | 19 472 | 20 913 | 21 874 |
| 5111 Value added taxes | 762 | 6 259 | 10 753 | 15 382 | 16 155 | 15 015 | 16 980 | 19 472 | 20 913 | 21 874 |
| 5112 Sales tax | 0 | 0 | 0 | 0 | 0 | 0 | 0 | 0 | 0 | 0 |
| 5113 Other | 0 | 0 | 0 | 0 | 0 | 0 | 0 | 0 | 0 | 0 |
| 5120 Taxes on specific goods and services | 919 | 3 872 | 5 330 | 6 029 | 5 561 | 5 497 | 5 773 | 5 845 | 5 701 | 5 671 |
| 5121 Excises | 258 | 1 797 | 1 262 | 2 946 | 2 822 | 3 058 | 3 101 | 3 013 | 3 072 | 3 372 |
| Tobacco and derivatives | 76 | 205 | 312 | 355 | 342 | 340 | 347 | 259 | 312 | 385 |
| Beer | 0 | 97 | 122 | 144 | 147 | 143 | 159 | 176 | 191 | 217 |
| Alcoholic beverages | 0 | 77 | 76 | 87 | 91 | 90 | 98 | 101 | 100 | 90 |
| Soft drinks | 0 | 15 | 172 | 195 | 196 | 200 | 220 | 245 | 263 | 282 |
| Other beverages | 77 | 12 | 2 | 1 | 2 | 1 | 2 | 2 | 1 | 1 |
| Cement | 0 | 0 | 93 | 117 | 105 | 99 | 99 | 104 | 102 | 100 |
| Oil and derivatives | 105 | 1 389 | 485 | 2 047 | 1 938 | 2 184 | 2 179 | 2 125 | 2 103 | 2 297 |
| 5122 Profits of fiscal monopolies | 0 | 0 | 0 | 0 | 0 | 0 | 0 | 0 | 0 | 0 |
| 5123 Customs and import duties | 506 | 1 806 | 3 715 | 2 654 | 2 427 | 2 139 | 2 368 | 2 533 | 2 311 | 1 965 |
| 5124 Taxes on exports | 0 | 0 | 0 | 0 | 0 | 0 | 0 | 0 | 0 | 0 |
| 5125 Taxes on investment goods | 0 | 0 | 0 | 0 | 0 | 0 | 0 | 0 | 0 | 0 |

## Table 27. Guatemala / Guatemala *(cont.)*
Details of tax revenue / Ingresos tributarios detallados

*Million GTQ*

| | 1990 | 2000 | 2005 | 2007 | 2008 | 2009 | 2010 | 2011 | 2012 | 2013 |
|---|---|---|---|---|---|---|---|---|---|---|
| 5126 Taxes on specific services | 155 | 269 | 354 | 429 | 311 | 301 | 304 | 300 | 318 | 334 |
| 5127 Other taxes on internat. trade and transactions | 0 | 0 | 0 | 0 | 0 | 0 | 0 | 0 | 0 | 0 |
| 5128 Other taxes | 0 | 0 | 0 | 0 | 0 | 0 | 0 | 0 | 0 | 0 |
| 5130 Unallocable between 5110 and 5120 | 0 | 0 | 0 | 0 | 0 | 0 | 0 | 0 | 0 | 0 |
| 5200 Taxes on use of goods and perform activities | 28 | 186 | 319 | 353 | 402 | 468 | 505 | 558 | 904 | 1 530 |
| 5210 Recurrent taxes | 28 | 186 | 319 | 353 | 402 | 468 | 505 | 558 | 904 | 1 530 |
| 5211 Paid by households: motor vehicles | 0 | 0 | 0 | 0 | 0 | 0 | 0 | 0 | 331 | 694 |
| 5212 Paid by others: motor vehicles | 28 | 186 | 319 | 353 | 402 | 468 | 505 | 558 | 573 | 836 |
| 5213 Paid in respect of other goods | 0 | 0 | 0 | 0 | 0 | 0 | 0 | 0 | 0 | 0 |
| 5220 Non-recurrent taxes | 0 | 0 | 0 | 0 | 0 | 0 | 0 | 0 | 0 | 0 |
| 5300 Unallocable between 5100 and 5200 | 0 | 0 | 0 | 0 | 0 | 0 | 0 | 0 | 0 | 0 |
| **6000 Other taxes** | **104** | **186** | **315** | **393** | **378** | **596** | **572** | **639** | **878** | **430** |
| 6100 Paid solely by business | 0 | 0 | 0 | 0 | 0 | 0 | 0 | 0 | 0 | 0 |
| 6200 Other | 104 | 186 | 315 | 393 | 378 | 596 | 572 | 639 | 878 | 430 |
| Revenue stamps and stamped paper | 104 | 182 | 313 | 392 | 376 | 595 | 572 | 638 | 877 | 430 |
| Other indirect taxes | 0 | 4 | 1 | 1 | 2 | 1 | 1 | 1 | 1 | 1 |

*Note:* Year ending 31st December.

The data are on cash basis.

The figures exclude some local government tax revenues as the data are not available. Revenues from the municipal property tax (IUSI) are included.

Heading 2000: Corresponds to social security contributions paid to the Guatemalan Social Security Institute (IGSS) and payments by public employees to the government's pension fund.

Headings 4120 and 4400: For years prior to 2000 the property tax under heading 4120 is included in the total under heading 4400.

Heading 5121: Up to 1999 "Other beverages" contains all alcoholic and non-alcoholic beverages.

*Source:* Superintendencia de Administración Tributaria, Ministry of Finance (for national and local taxes). Guatemalan Social Security Institute. (IGSS) from 1990 to 1994 and Superintendencia de Administración Tributaria for subsequent years (for social security contribution figures).

StatLink http://dx.doi.org/10.1787/888933190326

## Table 28. Honduras / Honduras
### Details of tax revenue / Ingresos tributarios detallados

*Million HNL*

| | 1990 | 2000 | 2005 | 2007 | 2008 | 2009 | 2010 | 2011 | 2012 | 2013 |
|---|---|---|---|---|---|---|---|---|---|---|
| **Total tax revenue** | **2 032** | **16 347** | **31 123** | **44 307** | **49 637** | **47 157** | **51 844** | **56 479** | **63 332** | **68 152** |
| **1000 Taxes on income, profits and capital gains** | **431** | **2 985** | **7 498** | **11 982** | **13 443** | **12 658** | **13 972** | **16 979** | **17 531** | **19 597** |
| 1100 Of individuals | 157 | 991 | 2 312 | 3 919 | 4 259 | 4 067 | 4 528 | 5 232 | 5 745 | 6 478 |
| 1110 On income and profits | 157 | 991 | 2 312 | 3 919 | 4 259 | 4 067 | 4 528 | 5 232 | 5 745 | 6 478 |
| 1120 On capital gains | .. | .. | .. | .. | .. | .. | .. | .. | .. | .. |
| 1200 Corporate | 274 | 1 916 | 4 725 | 7 915 | 8 904 | 8 424 | 8 705 | 11 437 | 11 556 | 12 875 |
| 1210 On profits | 274 | 1 916 | 4 725 | 7 915 | 8 904 | 8 424 | 8 705 | 11 437 | 11 556 | 12 875 |
| Corporate income tax | 274 | 1 916 | 4 121 | 6 877 | 7 572 | 7 230 | 7 400 | 9 447 | 10 088 | 11 523 |
| Income tax surcharge | 0 | 0 | 604 | 1 038 | 1 332 | 1 194 | 1 305 | 1 990 | 1 468 | 1 352 |
| 1220 On capital gains | .. | .. | .. | .. | .. | .. | .. | .. | .. | .. |
| 1300 Unallocable between 1100 and 1200 | 0 | 78 | 461 | 148 | 279 | 167 | 740 | 310 | 230 | 245 |
| Tax on net assets | .. | 78 | 144 | 148 | 279 | 167 | 359 | 310 | 230 | 245 |
| Revaluation of assets | .. | 0 | 316 | 0 | 0 | 0 | 381 | 0 | 0 | 0 |
| **2000 Social security contributions** | **179** | **1 727** | **4 416** | **6 037** | **7 308** | **8 122** | **8 671** | **6 955** | **10 854** | **12 529** |
| 2100 Employees | .. | .. | .. | .. | .. | .. | .. | .. | .. | .. |
| 2110 On a payroll basis | .. | .. | .. | .. | .. | .. | .. | .. | .. | .. |
| 2120 On an income tax basis | .. | .. | .. | .. | .. | .. | .. | .. | .. | .. |
| 2200 Employers | .. | .. | .. | .. | .. | .. | .. | .. | .. | .. |
| 2210 On a payroll basis | .. | .. | .. | .. | .. | .. | .. | .. | .. | .. |
| 2220 On an income tax basis | .. | .. | .. | .. | .. | .. | .. | .. | .. | .. |
| 2300 Self-employed or non-employed | .. | .. | .. | .. | .. | .. | .. | .. | .. | .. |
| 2310 On a payroll basis | .. | .. | .. | .. | .. | .. | .. | .. | .. | .. |
| 2320 On an income tax basis | .. | .. | .. | .. | .. | .. | .. | .. | .. | .. |
| 2400 Unallocable between 2100, 2200 and 2300 | 179 | 1 727 | 4 416 | 6 037 | 7 308 | 8 122 | 8 671 | 6 955 | 10 854 | 12 529 |
| 2410 On a payroll basis | 179 | 1 727 | 4 416 | 6 037 | 7 308 | 8 122 | 8 671 | 6 955 | 10 854 | 12 529 |
| 2420 On an income tax basis | 0 | 0 | 0 | 0 | 0 | 0 | 0 | 0 | 0 | 0 |
| **3000 Taxes on payroll and workforce** | **0** | **0** | **0** | **0** | **0** | **0** | **0** | **0** | **0** | **0** |
| **4000 Taxes on property** | **16** | **189** | **170** | **291** | **265** | **224** | **254** | **290** | **327** | **298** |
| 4100 Recurrent taxes on immovable property | 0 | 0 | 0 | 0 | 0 | 0 | 0 | 0 | 0 | 0 |
| 4110 Households | .. | .. | .. | .. | .. | .. | .. | .. | .. | .. |
| 4120 Others | .. | .. | .. | .. | .. | .. | .. | .. | .. | .. |
| 4200 Recurrent taxes on net wealth | 0 | 0 | 0 | 0 | 0 | 0 | 0 | 0 | 0 | 0 |
| 4210 Individual | .. | .. | .. | .. | .. | .. | .. | .. | .. | .. |
| 4220 Corporate | .. | .. | .. | .. | .. | .. | .. | .. | .. | .. |
| 4300 Estate, inheritance and gift taxes | 0 | 0 | 0 | 0 | 0 | 0 | 0 | 0 | 0 | 0 |
| 4310 Estate and inheritance taxes | .. | .. | .. | .. | .. | .. | .. | .. | .. | .. |
| 4320 Gift taxes | .. | .. | .. | .. | .. | .. | .. | .. | .. | .. |
| 4400 Taxes on financial and capital transactions | 0 | 0 | 0 | 0 | 0 | 0 | 0 | 0 | 0 | 0 |
| 4500 Non-recurrent taxes | 0 | 0 | 0 | 0 | 0 | 0 | 0 | 0 | 0 | 0 |
| 4510 On net wealth | .. | .. | .. | .. | .. | .. | .. | .. | .. | .. |
| 4520 Other non-recurrent taxes | .. | .. | .. | .. | .. | .. | .. | .. | .. | .. |
| 4600 Other recurrent taxes on property | 16 | 189 | 170 | 291 | 265 | 224 | 254 | 290 | 327 | 298 |
| **5000 Taxes on goods and services** | **1 405** | **11 445** | **19 032** | **25 985** | **28 608** | **26 141** | **28 937** | **32 247** | **34 610** | **35 720** |
| 5100 Taxes on production, sale, transfer, etc | 1 405 | 11 445 | 19 032 | 25 985 | 28 608 | 26 141 | 28 937 | 32 247 | 34 610 | 35 720 |
| 5110 General taxes | 344 | 5 146 | 9 565 | 14 170 | 16 464 | 14 396 | 16 050 | 18 967 | 20 150 | 20 637 |
| 5111 Value added taxes | 344 | 5 146 | 9 565 | 14 170 | 16 464 | 14 396 | 16 050 | 18 967 | 20 150 | 20 637 |
| 5112 Sales tax | 0 | 0 | 0 | 0 | 0 | 0 | 0 | 0 | 0 | 0 |
| 5113 Other | 0 | 0 | 0 | 0 | 0 | 0 | 0 | 0 | 0 | 0 |
| 5120 Taxes on specific goods and services | 1 061 | 6 299 | 9 468 | 11 815 | 12 145 | 11 746 | 12 887 | 13 279 | 14 460 | 15 082 |
| 5121 Excises | 256 | 3 600 | 6 322 | 7 606 | 7 581 | 8 022 | 8 458 | 8 670 | 9 490 | 10 119 |
| Beer | 71 | 376 | 338 | 358 | 373 | 344 | 376 | 466 | 503 | 503 |
| Soft drinks | 25 | 240 | 268 | 419 | 413 | 415 | 514 | 632 | 675 | 725 |
| Liquors | 32 | 48 | 69 | 80 | 79 | 76 | 121 | 164 | 165 | 165 |
| Petroleum products | 43 | 347 | 0 | 0 | 0 | 0 | 0 | 0 | 0 | 0 |
| Cigarettes | 57 | 369 | 437 | 502 | 560 | 646 | 607 | 660 | 633 | 495 |
| Fuel tax | 0 | 1 962 | 4 916 | 5 578 | 5 570 | 6 032 | 6 288 | 6 177 | 6 868 | 7 613 |
| Other | 28 | 258 | 295 | 589 | 577 | 509 | 551 | 572 | 646 | 618 |
| 5122 Profits of fiscal monopolies | 0 | 0 | 0 | 0 | 0 | 0 | 0 | 0 | 0 | 0 |
| 5123 Customs and import duties | 498 | 2 083 | 2 174 | 2 870 | 2 975 | 2 065 | 2 505 | 2 626 | 2 933 | 2 651 |
| Petroleum | 0 | 297 | 0 | 0 | 0 | 0 | 0 | 0 | 0 | 0 |
| Other | 498 | 1 786 | 2 174 | 2 870 | 2 975 | 2 065 | 2 505 | 2 626 | 2 933 | 2 651 |
| 5124 Taxes on exports | 217 | 6 | 0 | 0 | 0 | 0 | 0 | 0 | 0 | 0 |
| Bananas | 39 | 5 | 0 | 0 | 0 | 0 | 0 | 0 | 0 | 0 |
| Coffee | 1 | 0 | 0 | 0 | 0 | 0 | 0 | 0 | 0 | 0 |
| Temporary export tax | 163 | 0 | 0 | 0 | 0 | 0 | 0 | 0 | 0 | 0 |
| Other | 15 | 1 | 0 | 0 | 0 | 0 | 0 | 0 | 0 | 0 |
| 5125 Taxes on investment goods | 0 | 0 | 0 | 0 | 0 | 0 | 0 | 0 | 0 | 0 |
| 5126 Taxes on specific services | 0 | 0 | 0 | 0 | 0 | 0 | 0 | 0 | 0 | 0 |

## Table 28. Honduras / Honduras (cont.)
Details of tax revenue / Ingresos tributarios detallados

*Million HNL*

| | 1990 | 2000 | 2005 | 2007 | 2008 | 2009 | 2010 | 2011 | 2012 | 2013 |
|---|---|---|---|---|---|---|---|---|---|---|
| 5127 Other taxes on internat. trade and transactions | 0 | 0 | 0 | 0 | 0 | 0 | 0 | 0 | 0 | 0 |
| 5128 Other taxes | 90 | 610 | 971 | 1 340 | 1 589 | 1 659 | 1 924 | 1 983 | 2 038 | 2 312 |
| 5130 Unallocable between 5110 and 5120 | 0 | 0 | 0 | 0 | 0 | 0 | 0 | 0 | 0 | 0 |
| 5200 Taxes on use of goods and perform activities | 0 | 0 | 0 | 0 | 0 | 0 | 0 | 0 | 0 | 0 |
| 5210 Recurrent taxes | .. | .. | .. | .. | .. | .. | .. | .. | .. | .. |
| 5211 Paid by households: motor vehicles | .. | .. | .. | .. | .. | .. | .. | .. | .. | .. |
| 5212 Paid by others: motor vehicles | .. | .. | .. | .. | .. | .. | .. | .. | .. | .. |
| 5213 Paid in respect of other goods | .. | .. | .. | .. | .. | .. | .. | .. | .. | .. |
| 5220 Non-recurrent taxes | .. | .. | .. | .. | .. | .. | .. | .. | .. | .. |
| 5300 Unallocable between 5100 and 5200 | 0 | 0 | 0 | 0 | 0 | 0 | 0 | 0 | 0 | 0 |
| **6000 Other taxes** | **1** | **2** | **7** | **12** | **13** | **12** | **9** | **9** | **10** | **8** |
| 6100 Paid solely by business | 0 | 0 | 0 | 0 | 0 | 0 | 0 | 0 | 0 | 0 |
| 6200 Other | 1 | 2 | 7 | 12 | 13 | 12 | 9 | 9 | 10 | 8 |

*Note:* Year ending 31st December.
The data are on cash basis.
The data exclude local government tax revenues as the data are not available.
*Source:* Secretaria de Finanzas, Ministry of Finance.

StatLink http://dx.doi.org/10.1787/888933190331

# Table 29. Jamaica / Jamaica
## Details of tax revenue / Ingresos tributarios detallados

*Million JAM*

| | 1990 | 2000 | 2005 | 2007 | 2008 | 2009 | 2010 | 2011 | 2012 | 2013 |
|---|---|---|---|---|---|---|---|---|---|---|
| **Total tax revenue** | **7 748** | **87 713** | **163 359** | **220 209** | **249 330** | **264 389** | **288 380** | **303 947** | **322 948** | **357 979** |
| **1000 Taxes on income, profits and capital gains** | **3 944** | **39 277** | **69 894** | **97 924** | **114 481** | **124 475** | **118 708** | **122 752** | **126 441** | **129 951** |
| 1100 Of individuals | 1 687 | 17 441 | 36 043 | 48 220 | 59 802 | 62 043 | 54 798 | 62 792 | 64 315 | 66 283 |
| 1110 On income and profits | 1 687 | 17 441 | 36 043 | 48 220 | 59 802 | 62 043 | 54 798 | 62 792 | 64 315 | 66 283 |
| 1120 On capital gains | .. | .. | .. | .. | .. | .. | .. | .. | .. | .. |
| 1200 Corporate | 1 280 | 7 627 | 13 134 | 19 758 | 24 510 | 25 463 | 33 091 | 31 858 | 32 706 | 34 539 |
| 1210 On profits | 1 280 | 7 627 | 13 134 | 19 758 | 24 510 | 25 463 | 33 091 | 31 858 | 32 706 | 34 539 |
| 1220 On capital gains | .. | .. | .. | .. | .. | .. | .. | .. | .. | .. |
| 1300 Unallocable between 1100 and 1200 | 977 | 14 209 | 20 718 | 29 946 | 30 169 | 36 969 | 30 820 | 28 103 | 29 419 | 29 130 |
| **2000 Social security contributions** | **0** | **0** | **5 110** | **7 052** | **7 014** | **6 820** | **9 248** | **11 628** | **11 689** | **14 559** |
| 2100 Employees | .. | .. | .. | .. | .. | .. | .. | .. | .. | .. |
| 2110 On a payroll basis | .. | .. | .. | .. | .. | .. | .. | .. | .. | .. |
| 2120 On an income tax basis | .. | .. | .. | .. | .. | .. | .. | .. | .. | .. |
| 2200 Employers | .. | .. | .. | .. | .. | .. | .. | .. | .. | .. |
| 2210 On a payroll basis | .. | .. | .. | .. | .. | .. | .. | .. | .. | .. |
| 2220 On an income tax basis | .. | .. | .. | .. | .. | .. | .. | .. | .. | .. |
| 2300 Self-employed or non-employed | .. | .. | .. | .. | .. | .. | .. | .. | .. | .. |
| 2310 On a payroll basis | .. | .. | .. | .. | .. | .. | .. | .. | .. | .. |
| 2320 On an income tax basis | .. | .. | .. | .. | .. | .. | .. | .. | .. | .. |
| 2400 Unallocable between 2100, 2200 and 2300 | .. | .. | 5 110 | 7 052 | 7 014 | 6 820 | 9 248 | 11 628 | 11 689 | 14 559 |
| 2410 On a payroll basis | .. | .. | .. | .. | .. | .. | .. | .. | .. | .. |
| 2420 On an income tax basis | .. | .. | .. | .. | .. | .. | .. | .. | .. | .. |
| **3000 Taxes on payroll and workforce** | **0** | **0** | **0** | **0** | **0** | **0** | **0** | **0** | **0** | **0** |
| **4000 Taxes on property** | **67** | **639** | **1 474** | **1 859** | **2 286** | **1 831** | **2 792** | **2 531** | **2 805** | **5 842** |
| 4100 Recurrent taxes on immovable property | 67 | 639 | 1 474 | 1 859 | 2 286 | 1 831 | 2 792 | 2 531 | 2 805 | 5 842 |
| 4110 Households | 67 | 639 | 1 474 | 1 859 | 2 286 | 1 831 | 2 792 | 2 531 | 2 805 | 5 842 |
| 4120 Others | 0 | 0 | 0 | 0 | 0 | 0 | 0 | 0 | 0 | 0 |
| 4200 Recurrent taxes on net wealth | 0 | 0 | 0 | 0 | 0 | 0 | 0 | 0 | 0 | 0 |
| 4210 Individual | .. | .. | .. | .. | .. | .. | .. | .. | .. | .. |
| 4220 Corporate | .. | .. | .. | .. | .. | .. | .. | .. | .. | .. |
| 4300 Estate, inheritance and gift taxes | 0 | 0 | 0 | 0 | 0 | 0 | 0 | 0 | 0 | 0 |
| 4310 Estate and inheritance taxes | .. | .. | .. | .. | .. | .. | .. | .. | .. | .. |
| 4320 Gift taxes | .. | .. | .. | .. | .. | .. | .. | .. | .. | .. |
| 4400 Taxes on financial and capital transactions | 0 | 0 | 0 | 0 | 0 | 0 | 0 | 0 | 0 | 0 |
| 4500 Non-recurrent taxes | 0 | 0 | 0 | 0 | 0 | 0 | 0 | 0 | 0 | 0 |
| 4510 On net wealth | .. | .. | .. | .. | .. | .. | .. | .. | .. | .. |
| 4520 Other non-recurrent taxes | .. | .. | .. | .. | .. | .. | .. | .. | .. | .. |
| 4600 Other recurrent taxes on property | 0 | 0 | 0 | 0 | 0 | 0 | 0 | 0 | 0 | 0 |
| **5000 Taxes on goods and services** | **3 294** | **44 638** | **78 147** | **101 704** | **113 423** | **121 928** | **148 894** | **156 308** | **171 332** | **195 021** |
| 5100 Taxes on production, sale, transfer, etc | 3 230 | 43 838 | 77 036 | 100 383 | 111 569 | 119 749 | 146 850 | 154 208 | 168 940 | 192 167 |
| 5110 General taxes | 4 | 13 059 | 27 274 | 35 995 | 40 111 | 40 825 | 45 152 | 47 788 | 50 963 | 57 474 |
| 5111 Value added taxes | 0 | 13 059 | 27 274 | 35 995 | 40 111 | 40 825 | 45 152 | 47 788 | 50 963 | 57 474 |
| 5112 Sales tax | 4 | 0 | 0 | 0 | 0 | 0 | 0 | 0 | 0 | 0 |
| 5113 Other | 0 | 0 | 0 | 0 | 0 | 0 | 0 | 0 | 0 | 0 |
| 5120 Taxes on specific goods and services | 3 226 | 30 779 | 49 762 | 64 388 | 71 458 | 78 925 | 101 698 | 106 419 | 117 977 | 134 693 |
| 5121 Excises | 1 158 | 5 344 | 3 536 | 4 496 | 3 626 | 5 272 | 9 168 | 9 403 | 11 216 | 12 149 |
| 5122 Profits of fiscal monopolies | 0 | 0 | 0 | 0 | 0 | 0 | 0 | 0 | 0 | 0 |
| 5123 Customs and import duties | 1 545 | 22 932 | 43 260 | 56 534 | 64 650 | 70 608 | 87 510 | 90 180 | 97 497 | 103 747 |
| 5124 Taxes on exports | 0 | 0 | 0 | 0 | 0 | 0 | 0 | 0 | 0 | 0 |
| 5125 Taxes on investment goods | 0 | 0 | 0 | 0 | 0 | 0 | 0 | 0 | 0 | 0 |
| 5126 Taxes on specific services | 523 | 2 503 | 2 966 | 3 359 | 3 183 | 3 044 | 5 020 | 6 837 | 9 264 | 18 798 |
| 5127 Other taxes on internat. trade and transactions | 0 | 0 | 0 | 0 | 0 | 0 | 0 | 0 | 0 | 0 |
| 5128 Other taxes | 0 | 0 | 0 | 0 | 0 | 0 | 0 | 0 | 0 | 0 |
| 5130 Unallocable between 5110 and 5120 | 0 | 0 | 0 | 0 | 0 | 0 | 0 | 0 | 0 | 0 |
| 5200 Taxes on use of goods and perform activities | 64 | 800 | 1 111 | 1 322 | 1 854 | 2 179 | 2 045 | 2 100 | 2 393 | 2 854 |
| 5210 Recurrent taxes | 64 | 800 | 1 111 | 1 322 | 1 854 | 2 179 | 2 045 | 2 100 | 2 393 | 2 854 |
| 5211 Paid by households: motor vehicles | 47 | 751 | 935 | 1 012 | 1 486 | 1 734 | 1 775 | 1 748 | 2 043 | 2 493 |
| 5212 Paid by others: motor vehicles | 0 | 0 | 0 | 0 | 0 | 0 | 0 | 0 | 0 | 0 |
| 5213 Paid in respect of other goods | 17 | 49 | 176 | 310 | 368 | 445 | 270 | 352 | 350 | 361 |
| 5220 Non-recurrent taxes | 0 | 0 | 0 | 0 | 0 | 0 | 0 | 0 | 0 | 0 |
| 5300 Unallocable between 5100 and 5200 | 0 | 0 | 0 | 0 | 0 | 0 | 0 | 0 | 0 | 0 |
| **6000 Other taxes** | **444** | **3 159** | **8 733** | **11 670** | **12 127** | **9 336** | **8 738** | **10 729** | **10 680** | **12 606** |
| 6100 Paid solely by business | 0 | 0 | 0 | 0 | 0 | 0 | 0 | 0 | 0 | 0 |
| 6200 Other | 444 | 3 159 | 8 733 | 11 670 | 12 127 | 9 336 | 8 738 | 10 729 | 10 680 | 12 606 |

*Note:* Data collected by fiscal year (1 April - 31 March) for 1990-2003, then by calendar year (year ending 31st December).
The data are on cash basis.
The data exclude local government tax revenues as the data are not available.
The data for social security contributions are available from the year 2003 only.

*Source:* Ministry of Finance and Planning.

StatLink http://dx.doi.org/10.1787/888933190348

# Table 30. Mexico / México
## Details of tax revenue / Ingresos tributarios detallados

*Million MXN*

| | 1990 | 2000 | 2005 | 2007 | 2008 | 2009 | 2010 | 2011 | 2012 | 2013 |
|---|---|---|---|---|---|---|---|---|---|---|
| **Total tax revenue** | **127 959** | **1 014 625** | **1 667 424** | **2 002 846** | **2 539 615** | **2 071 854** | **2 458 249** | **2 830 477** | **3 048 560** | **3 028 137** |
| **1000 Taxes on income, profits and capital gains** | **34 673** | **276 548** | **402 036** | **554 099** | **629 135** | **591 942** | **683 604** | **772 704** | **803 071** | **957 213** |
| 1100 Of individuals | .. | .. | 195 869 | 238 938 | 285 270 | 280 230 | 313 473 | 352 386 | 397 701 | 425 621 |
| Tax on income of individuals | .. | .. | 195 869 | 238 938 | 285 270 | 280 230 | 313 473 | 352 386 | 397 701 | 425 621 |
| 1110 On income and profits | .. | .. | .. | .. | .. | .. | .. | .. | .. | .. |
| 1120 On capital gains | .. | .. | .. | .. | .. | .. | .. | .. | .. | .. |
| 1200 Corporate | .. | .. | 135 840 | 217 790 | 214 611 | 191 685 | 246 745 | 303 176 | 288 360 | 392 199 |
| Tax on income of corporations | .. | .. | 135 840 | 217 790 | 214 611 | 191 685 | 246 745 | 303 176 | 288 360 | 392 199 |
| 1210 On profits | .. | .. | .. | .. | .. | .. | .. | .. | .. | .. |
| 1220 On capital gains | .. | .. | .. | .. | .. | .. | .. | .. | .. | .. |
| 1300 Unallocable between 1100 and 1200 | 34 673 | 276 548 | 70 327 | 97 370 | 129 254 | 120 027 | 123 386 | 117 143 | 117 010 | 139 393 |
| Tax on income of other individuals and corporations | .. | 244 841 | 40 780 | 54 785 | 61 208 | 64 816 | 66 937 | 66 004 | 74 042 | 89 028 |
| Tax on asset | .. | 13 913 | 12 033 | 15 670 | 1 134 | -2 540 | -624 | -1 120 | -1 192 | -1 325 |
| Credit on salary | .. | 17 794 | 17 514 | 23 177 | 15 886 | 12 113 | 9 708 | 2 076 | 1 387 | 1 274 |
| Oil yields tax | .. | 0 | 0 | 3 738 | 4 441 | 921 | 2 296 | 3 019 | 573 | 3 210 |
| IETU | .. | 0 | 0 | 0 | 46 586 | 44 718 | 45 069 | 47 165 | 42 199 | 47 205 |
| **2000 Social security contributions** | **17 165** | **167 292** | **261 673** | **307 026** | **321 843** | **346 031** | **378 006** | **411 289** | **454 778** | **490 918** |
| 2100 Employees | .. | .. | .. | .. | .. | .. | .. | .. | .. | .. |
| 2110 On a payroll basis | .. | .. | .. | .. | .. | .. | .. | .. | .. | .. |
| 2120 On an income tax basis | .. | .. | .. | .. | .. | .. | .. | .. | .. | .. |
| 2200 Employers | .. | .. | .. | .. | .. | .. | .. | .. | .. | .. |
| 2210 On a payroll basis | .. | .. | .. | .. | .. | .. | .. | .. | .. | .. |
| 2220 On an income tax basis | .. | .. | .. | .. | .. | .. | .. | .. | .. | .. |
| 2300 Self-employed or non-employed | .. | .. | .. | .. | .. | .. | .. | .. | .. | .. |
| 2310 On a payroll basis | .. | .. | .. | .. | .. | .. | .. | .. | .. | .. |
| 2320 On an income tax basis | .. | .. | .. | .. | .. | .. | .. | .. | .. | .. |
| 2400 Unallocable between 2100, 2200 and 2300 | 17 165 | 167 292 | 261 673 | 307 026 | 321 843 | 346 031 | 378 006 | 411 289 | 454 778 | 490 918 |
| 2410 On a payroll basis | .. | 167 292 | 261 673 | 307 026 | 321 843 | 346 031 | 378 006 | 411 289 | 454 778 | 490 918 |
| 2420 On an income tax basis | .. | 0 | 0 | 0 | 0 | 0 | 0 | 0 | 0 | 0 |
| **3000 Taxes on payroll and workforce** | **1 797** | **11 217** | **20 461** | **28 071** | **31 123** | **31 965** | **36 911** | **41 980** | **48 033** | **0** |
| Substitute tax on salary | .. | 0 | 0 | 0 | 0 | 0 | 0 | 0 | 0 | .. |
| Payroll tax | .. | 11 101 | 15 746 | 20 277 | 22 919 | 23 530 | 27 813 | 31 817 | 35 480 | .. |
| Tax on remuneration to the personal work | .. | 65 | 4 562 | 7 578 | 7 992 | 8 180 | 8 841 | 9 990 | 12 333 | .. |
| Tax on professions and fees | .. | 36 | 53 | 68 | 72 | 70 | 71 | 58 | 48 | .. |
| Tax on operations by contract | .. | 15 | 100 | 148 | 140 | 186 | 186 | 116 | 173 | .. |
| **4000 Taxes on property** | **1 914** | **13 964** | **26 796** | **33 161** | **35 847** | **35 484** | **38 955** | **41 186** | **45 185** | **0** |
| 4100 Recurrent taxes on immovable property | 1 036 | 9 948 | 16 641 | 19 425 | 21 394 | 22 862 | 25 724 | 28 728 | 31 543 | .. |
| 4110 Households | 0 | 0 | 0 | 0 | 0 | 0 | 0 | 0 | 0 | .. |
| 4120 Others | 1 036 | 9 948 | 16 641 | 19 425 | 21 394 | 22 862 | 25 724 | 28 728 | 31 543 | .. |
| Property tax | .. | 9 948 | 16 641 | 19 425 | 21 394 | 22 862 | 25 724 | 28 728 | 31 543 | .. |
| 4200 Recurrent taxes on net wealth | 0 | 0 | 0 | 0 | 0 | 0 | 0 | 0 | 0 | .. |
| 4210 Individual | .. | .. | .. | .. | .. | .. | .. | .. | .. | .. |
| 4220 Corporate | .. | .. | .. | .. | .. | .. | .. | .. | .. | .. |
| 4300 Estate, inheritance and gift taxes | 8 | 0 | 0 | 0 | 0 | 0 | 0 | 0 | 0 | .. |
| 4310 Estate and inheritance taxes | 8 | .. | .. | .. | .. | .. | .. | .. | .. | .. |
| 4320 Gift taxes | 0 | .. | .. | .. | .. | .. | .. | .. | .. | .. |
| 4400 Taxes on financial and capital transactions | 870 | 4 017 | 10 155 | 13 736 | 14 452 | 12 622 | 13 231 | 12 458 | 13 642 | .. |
| Alienation of immovable property | .. | 1 763 | 984 | 1 076 | 1 310 | 1 163 | 1 122 | 1 379 | 1 341 | .. |
| Transfer of ownership of real estate | .. | 2 236 | 5 528 | 8 147 | 5 825 | 5 005 | 5 027 | 3 923 | 4 575 | .. |
| Purchasing property | .. | 18 | 3 643 | 4 513 | 7 318 | 6 454 | 7 082 | 7 157 | 7 725 | .. |
| 4500 Non-recurrent taxes | 0 | 0 | 0 | 0 | 0 | 0 | 0 | 0 | 0 | .. |
| 4510 On net wealth | .. | .. | .. | .. | .. | .. | .. | .. | .. | .. |
| 4520 Other non-recurrent taxes | .. | .. | .. | .. | .. | .. | .. | .. | .. | .. |
| 4600 Other recurrent taxes on property | 0 | 0 | 0 | 0 | 0 | 0 | 0 | 0 | 0 | .. |
| **5000 Taxes on goods and services** | **70 791** | **537 953** | **944 766** | **1 063 584** | **1 502 941** | **1 039 344** | **1 293 373** | **1 530 906** | **1 660 413** | **1 553 087** |
| 5100 Taxes on production, sale, transfer, etc | 70 125 | 528 666 | 928 979 | 1 042 372 | 1 480 972 | 1 017 627 | 1 271 581 | 1 508 269 | 1 643 337 | 1 552 680 |
| 5110 General taxes | 26 635 | 189 606 | 318 432 | 409 013 | 457 248 | 407 795 | 504 509 | 537 143 | 579 988 | 556 794 |
| 5111 Value added taxes | 26 635 | 189 606 | 318 432 | 409 013 | 457 248 | 407 795 | 504 509 | 537 143 | 579 988 | 556 794 |
| 5112 Sales tax | 0 | 0 | 0 | 0 | 0 | 0 | 0 | 0 | 0 | 0 |
| 5113 Other | 0 | 0 | 0 | 0 | 0 | 0 | 0 | 0 | 0 | 0 |
| 5120 Taxes on specific goods and services | 43 473 | 339 060 | 610 547 | 633 359 | 1 023 723 | 609 832 | 767 072 | 971 126 | 1 063 349 | 995 886 |
| 5121 Excises | 10 072 | 86 163 | 55 286 | 47 008 | 60 462 | 69 770 | 86 098 | 94 623 | 98 490 | 104 111 |
| Special tax on production and services | .. | 81 544 | 49 627 | 41 532 | 55 391 | 65 708 | 81 427 | 89 544 | 92 620 | 97 860 |
| Tax on new automobiles | .. | 4 619 | 5 659 | 5 476 | 5 071 | 4 063 | 4 671 | 5 079 | 5 870 | 6 252 |
| Tax on luxury goods and services | .. | 0 | 0 | 0 | 0 | 0 | 0 | 0 | 0 | 0 |
| 5122 Profits of fiscal monopolies | 0 | 0 | 0 | 0 | 0 | 0 | 0 | 0 | 0 | 0 |

## Table 30. Mexico / México *(cont.)*
### Details of tax revenue / Ingresos tributarios detallados

*Million MXN*

| | 1990 | 2000 | 2005 | 2007 | 2008 | 2009 | 2010 | 2011 | 2012 | 2013 |
|---|---|---|---|---|---|---|---|---|---|---|
| 5123 Customs and import duties | 6 998 | 33 285 | 27 512 | 33 344 | 37 831 | 31 732 | 26 602 | 29 946 | 31 161 | 32 324 |
| Step customs officer | .. | 423 | 692 | 1 156 | 2 048 | 1 535 | 2 071 | 3 065 | 3 255 | 3 065 |
| Import taxes | .. | 32 861 | 26 820 | 32 188 | 35 783 | 30 196 | 24 531 | 26 881 | 27 906 | 29 260 |
| 5124 Taxes on exports | 75 | 4 | 0 | 3 | 1 | 1 | 0 | 2 | 1 | 1 |
| Taxes on exports | .. | 4 | 0 | 3 | 1 | 1 | 0 | 2 | 1 | 1 |
| 5125 Taxes on investment goods | 0 | 0 | 0 | 0 | 0 | 0 | 0 | 0 | 0 | 0 |
| 5126 Taxes on specific services | 132 | 1 042 | 1 578 | 2 146 | 20 097 | 18 461 | 10 958 | -5 610 | 7 169 | -5 988 |
| IDE | .. | 0 | 0 | 0 | 17 700 | 15 888 | 8 022 | -8 442 | 2 786 | -5 988 |
| Tax on lodging | .. | 504 | 798 | 1 059 | 1 178 | 1 147 | 1 384 | 1 375 | 1 702 | 0 |
| Public entertainment tax | .. | 240 | 349 | 365 | 383 | 486 | 462 | 360 | 625 | 0 |
| Tax on lotteries, raffles and gambling | .. | 267 | 417 | 705 | 717 | 789 | 923 | 952 | 1 329 | 0 |
| Tax on commercials | .. | 4 | 15 | 17 | 118 | 150 | 166 | 145 | 16 | 0 |
| Various indirect taxes | .. | 28 | 0 | 0 | 0 | 0 | 1 | 0 | 711 | 0 |
| 5127 Other taxes on internat. trade and transactions | 0 | 0 | 0 | 0 | 0 | 0 | 0 | 0 | 0 | 0 |
| 5128 Other taxes | 26 196 | 218 567 | 526 171 | 550 858 | 905 332 | 489 869 | 643 414 | 852 166 | 926 528 | 865 438 |
| Ordinary fee on oil production | .. | 125 329 | 334 784 | 0 | 0 | 0 | 0 | 0 | 0 | 0 |
| Extraordinary fee on oil production | .. | 68 235 | 129 967 | 0 | 0 | 0 | 0 | 0 | 0 | 0 |
| Additional fee on oil production | .. | 2 576 | 6 772 | 3 233 | 3 715 | 149 | 0 | 0 | 0 | 0 |
| Tax on oil yields | .. | 22 201 | 54 298 | 1 255 | 0 | 0 | 0 | 0 | 0 | 0 |
| Mining fees | .. | 226 | 350 | 414 | 68 | 1 782 | 1 956 | 2 858 | 3 243 | 3 886 |
| Ordinary | .. | 0 | 0 | 478 609 | 794 030 | 410 437 | 543 895 | 721 209 | 769 489 | 721 790 |
| Stabilization Fund | .. | 0 | 0 | 55 402 | 71 536 | 63 839 | 77 071 | 81 247 | 106 151 | 106 401 |
| Extraordinary on crude petroleum export | .. | 0 | 0 | 11 517 | 33 640 | -556 | 6 644 | 24 152 | 19 594 | 10 313 |
| Scientific research and technologica Fund in the matter of energy | .. | 0 | 0 | 403 | 1 583 | 2 046 | 3 616 | 5 635 | 8 441 | 8 422 |
| For oil control | .. | 0 | 0 | 24 | 37 | 23 | 29 | 35 | 42 | 39 |
| Rights on the extraction of mineral oils | .. | 0 | 0 | 0 | 158 | 2 663 | 3 533 | 5 601 | 7 185 | 6 178 |
| Special rights on mineral oils for fields in the "Paleoncanal icontepec" | .. | 0 | 0 | 0 | 565 | 7 676 | 2 494 | 6 117 | 7 521 | 5 450 |
| Special rights on hydrocarbons | .. | 0 | 0 | 0 | 0 | 1 813 | 4 032 | 1 308 | 0 | 0 |
| Special right on hydrocarbons in deep water fields | .. | 0 | 0 | 0 | 0 | 0 | 143 | 4 003 | 4 493 | 2 574 |
| Right to register for exploration and exploitation of hydrocarbons | .. | 0 | 0 | 0 | 0 | 0 | 0 | 0 | 370 | 385 |
| 5130 Unallocable between 5110 and 5120 | 17 | 0 | 0 | 0 | 0 | 0 | 0 | 0 | 0 | 0 |
| 5200 Taxes on use of goods and perform activities | 666 | 9 287 | 15 787 | 21 212 | 21 970 | 21 717 | 21 792 | 22 637 | 17 076 | 408 |
| 5210 Recurrent taxes | 666 | 9 287 | 15 787 | 21 212 | 21 970 | 21 717 | 21 792 | 22 637 | 17 076 | 408 |
| 5211 Paid by households: motor vehicles | 567 | 8 878 | 15 237 | 20 692 | 21 492 | 21 301 | 21 319 | 22 186 | 16 464 | 0 |
| Tax on motor vehicules | .. | 8 878 | 15 237 | 20 692 | 21 492 | 21 301 | 21 319 | 22 186 | 16 464 | 0 |
| 5212 Paid by others: motor vehicles | 0 | 301 | 357 | 275 | 311 | 270 | 281 | 296 | 370 | 357 |
| Tax on federal auto transport | .. | 301 | 357 | 275 | 311 | 270 | 281 | 296 | 370 | 357 |
| 5213 Paid in respect of other goods | 99 | 108 | 193 | 246 | 166 | 147 | 193 | 155 | 242 | 50 |
| Sport fishing | .. | 40 | 80 | 98 | 85 | 68 | 59 | 50 | 55 | 50 |
| Sport hunting | .. | 3 | 0 | 0 | 1 | 0 | 0 | 0 | 0 | 0 |
| Tax on commercial activities | .. | 63 | 113 | 147 | 33 | 42 | 50 | 66 | 42 | 0 |
| Trade in books and magazines | .. | 0 | 0 | 0 | 0 | 0 | 0 | 0 | 0 | 0 |
| Tax on industrial activities | .. | 2 | 0 | 0 | 47 | 35 | 82 | 38 | 145 | 0 |
| 5220 Non-recurrent taxes | 0 | 0 | 0 | 0 | 0 | 0 | 0 | 0 | 0 | 0 |
| 5300 Unallocable between 5100 and 5200 | 0 | 0 | 0 | 0 | 0 | 0 | 0 | 0 | 0 | 0 |
| **6000 Other taxes** | **1 619** | **7 651** | **11 693** | **16 906** | **18 726** | **27 087** | **27 399** | **32 412** | **37 080** | **26 919** |
| 6100 Paid solely by business | 0 | 0 | 0 | 0 | 0 | 0 | 0 | 0 | 0 | 0 |
| 6200 Other | 1 619 | 7 651 | 11 693 | 16 906 | 18 726 | 27 087 | 27 399 | 32 412 | 37 080 | 26 919 |
| Accessories | .. | 5 504 | 9 543 | 12 403 | 13 744 | 21 710 | 22 206 | 24 059 | 24 077 | 25 301 |
| Unallocable between 1000 and 5000 caused in exercices fiscal previous liquidation slopes or of payment | .. | 374 | -927 | 222 | 58 | 7 | 30 | -118 | 2 260 | 1 618 |
| Additional state and local taxes | .. | 1 773 | 3 077 | 4 280 | 4 924 | 5 361 | 5 162 | 8 471 | 10 743 | 0 |
| **Total tax revenue** | **127 959** | **1 014 625** | **1 667 424** | **2 002 846** | **2 539 615** | **2 071 854** | **2 458 249** | **2 830 477** | **3 048 560** | **3 028 137** |
| **Fees levied on hydrocarbon production** | **-26 196** | **-218 567** | **-526 171** | **-550 858** | **-905 332** | **-489 869** | **-643 414** | **-852 166** | **-926 528** | **-865 438** |
| **Total tax revenue (net of fees on hydrocarbons)** | **101 763** | **796 059** | **1 141 254** | **1 451 988** | **1 634 282** | **1 581 985** | **1 814 835** | **1 978 312** | **2 122 032** | **2 162 699** |

*Note:* Year ending 31st December.

The data are on cash basis.

The 2013 data for tax revenues of the State and Local levels of government are not available. They comprise revenues in categories 3000, 4000, 5000, and 6000.

Heading 1000: In ECLAC data, income taxes are presented net of credit on salary figures.

Heading 2000: In ECLAC data, social security contributions are presented net of transfers from the Federal government for the payment of IMSS (Mexican Social Security Institute) pensions.

Heading 5128: In ECLAC and CIAT data, fees levied on hydrocarbon production are treated as non tax revenues. As a result they publish tax revenues net of these fees. The final three rows of the table display the impact of this.

*Source:* Ministry of Finance, Economic Department.

StatLink http://dx.doi.org/10.1787/888933190358

## Table 31. Nicaragua / Nicaragua
Details of tax revenue / Ingresos tributarios detallados

*Million NIO*

| | 1990 | 2000 | 2005 | 2007 | 2008 | 2009 | 2010 | 2011 | 2012 | 2013 |
|---|---|---|---|---|---|---|---|---|---|---|
| **Total tax revenue** | .. | **8 418** | **17 009** | **23 847** | **27 697** | **28 863** | **33 620** | **41 185** | **48 131** | **53 486** |
| **1000 Taxes on income, profits and capital gains** | .. | **1 144** | **3 902** | **5 752** | **7 002** | **7 818** | **8 351** | **11 144** | **13 107** | **14 521** |
| 1100 Of individuals | .. | .. | .. | .. | .. | .. | .. | .. | .. | .. |
| 1110 On income and profits | .. | .. | .. | .. | .. | .. | .. | .. | .. | .. |
| 1120 On capital gains | .. | .. | .. | .. | .. | .. | .. | .. | .. | .. |
| 1200 Corporate | .. | .. | .. | .. | .. | .. | .. | .. | .. | .. |
| 1210 On profits | .. | .. | .. | .. | .. | .. | .. | .. | .. | .. |
| Income tax | .. | .. | .. | .. | .. | .. | .. | .. | .. | .. |
| 1220 On capital gains | .. | .. | .. | .. | .. | .. | .. | .. | .. | .. |
| 1300 Unallocable between 1100 and 1200 | .. | 1 144 | 3 902 | 5 752 | 7 002 | 7 818 | 8 351 | 11 144 | 13 107 | 14 521 |
| **2000 Social security contributions** | .. | **1 678** | **3 363** | **4 921** | **6 023** | **6 804** | **8 090** | **9 433** | **11 007** | **12 805** |
| 2100 Employees | .. | .. | .. | .. | .. | .. | .. | .. | .. | .. |
| 2110 On a payroll basis | .. | .. | .. | .. | .. | .. | .. | .. | .. | .. |
| 2120 On an income tax basis | .. | .. | .. | .. | .. | .. | .. | .. | .. | .. |
| 2200 Employers | .. | .. | .. | .. | .. | .. | .. | .. | .. | .. |
| 2210 On a payroll basis | .. | .. | .. | .. | .. | .. | .. | .. | .. | .. |
| 2220 On an income tax basis | .. | .. | .. | .. | .. | .. | .. | .. | .. | .. |
| 2300 Self-employed or non-employed | .. | .. | .. | .. | .. | .. | .. | .. | .. | .. |
| 2310 On a payroll basis | .. | .. | .. | .. | .. | .. | .. | .. | .. | .. |
| 2320 On an income tax basis | .. | .. | .. | .. | .. | .. | .. | .. | .. | .. |
| 2400 Unallocable between 2100, 2200 and 2300 | .. | 1 678 | 3 363 | 4 921 | 6 023 | 6 804 | 8 090 | 9 433 | 11 007 | 12 805 |
| 2410 On a payroll basis | .. | 1 678 | 3 363 | 4 921 | 6 023 | 6 804 | 8 090 | 9 433 | 11 007 | 12 805 |
| 2420 On an income tax basis | .. | 0 | 0 | 0 | 0 | 0 | 0 | 0 | 0 | 0 |
| **3000 Taxes on payroll and workforce** | .. | **0** | **0** | **0** | **0** | **0** | **0** | **0** | **0** | **0** |
| **4000 Taxes on property** | .. | **0** | **2** | **0** | **0** | **48** | **130** | **191** | **239** | **311** |
| 4100 Recurrent taxes on immovable property | .. | .. | 0 | 0 | 0 | 0 | 0 | 0 | 0 | 0 |
| 4110 Households | .. | .. | .. | .. | .. | .. | .. | .. | .. | .. |
| 4120 Others | .. | .. | .. | .. | .. | .. | .. | .. | .. | .. |
| 4200 Recurrent taxes on net wealth | .. | .. | 2 | 0 | 0 | 48 | 130 | 191 | 239 | 311 |
| 4210 Individual | .. | .. | 2 | 0 | 0 | 48 | 130 | 191 | 239 | 311 |
| 4220 Corporate | .. | .. | 0 | 0 | 0 | 0 | 0 | 0 | 0 | 0 |
| 4300 Estate, inheritance and gift taxes | .. | .. | 0 | 0 | 0 | 0 | 0 | 0 | 0 | 0 |
| 4310 Estate and inheritance taxes | .. | .. | .. | .. | .. | .. | .. | .. | .. | .. |
| 4320 Gift taxes | .. | .. | .. | .. | .. | .. | .. | .. | .. | .. |
| 4400 Taxes on financial and capital transactions | .. | .. | 0 | 0 | 0 | 0 | 0 | 0 | 0 | 0 |
| 4500 Non-recurrent taxes | .. | .. | 0 | 0 | 0 | 0 | 0 | 0 | 0 | 0 |
| 4510 On net wealth | .. | .. | .. | .. | .. | .. | .. | .. | .. | .. |
| 4520 Other non-recurrent taxes | .. | .. | 0 | 0 | 0 | 0 | 0 | 0 | 0 | 0 |
| 4600 Other recurrent taxes on property | .. | .. | 0 | 0 | 0 | 0 | 0 | 0 | 0 | 0 |
| **5000 Taxes on goods and services** | .. | **5 584** | **9 725** | **13 153** | **14 650** | **14 170** | **17 029** | **20 395** | **23 754** | **25 771** |
| 5100 Taxes on production, sale, transfer, etc | .. | 5 584 | 9 725 | 13 153 | 14 650 | 14 170 | 17 029 | 20 395 | 23 754 | 25 771 |
| 5110 General taxes | .. | 2 931 | 5 599 | 8 025 | 9 009 | 8 871 | 10 353 | 12 876 | 15 151 | 16 736 |
| 5111 Value added taxes | .. | 2 931 | 5 599 | 8 025 | 9 009 | 8 871 | 10 353 | 12 876 | 15 151 | 16 736 |
| 5112 Sales tax | .. | 0 | 0 | 0 | 0 | 0 | 0 | 0 | 0 | 0 |
| 5113 Other | .. | 0 | 0 | 0 | 0 | 0 | 0 | 0 | 0 | 0 |
| 5120 Taxes on specific goods and services | .. | 2 653 | 4 126 | 5 128 | 5 641 | 5 299 | 6 676 | 7 519 | 8 603 | 9 035 |
| 5121 Excises | .. | 2 034 | 3 227 | 4 099 | 4 518 | 4 392 | 5 541 | 6 070 | 6 884 | 7 254 |
| Liquor | .. | 84 | 102 | 144 | 189 | 147 | 198 | 240 | 214 | 253 |
| Beer | .. | 203 | 340 | 480 | 561 | 556 | 645 | 781 | 915 | 1 047 |
| Cigarettes | .. | 70 | 143 | 158 | 177 | 171 | 45 | 0 | 0 | 174 |
| Soft drinks | .. | 123 | 128 | 146 | 194 | 188 | 248 | 292 | 351 | 389 |
| Petroleum products | .. | 1 359 | 1 756 | 2 108 | 2 162 | 2 277 | 2 699 | 2 700 | 3 045 | 3 418 |
| Excise taxes on imports | .. | 196 | 734 | 1 025 | 1 180 | 975 | 1 559 | 1 901 | 2 233 | 1 924 |
| Other specific excises on consumption | .. | -1 | 25 | 37 | 55 | 77 | 148 | 156 | 126 | 49 |
| 5122 Profits of fiscal monopolies | .. | 0 | 0 | 0 | 0 | 0 | 0 | 0 | 0 | 0 |
| 5123 Customs and import duties | .. | 619 | 856 | 1 030 | 1 123 | 908 | 1 135 | 1 449 | 1 719 | 1 782 |
| Custom duties | .. | 452 | 837 | 1 004 | 1 093 | 870 | 1 094 | 1 400 | 1 661 | 1 717 |
| Temporary protection duty | .. | 96 | 0 | 0 | 0 | 0 | 0 | 0 | 0 | 0 |
| On products originating in Colombia or Honduras | .. | 72 | 18 | 26 | 29 | 38 | 41 | 49 | 58 | 64 |
| 5124 Taxes on exports | .. | 0 | 0 | 0 | 0 | 0 | 0 | 0 | 0 | 0 |
| 5125 Taxes on investment goods | .. | 0 | 0 | 0 | 0 | 0 | 0 | 0 | 0 | 0 |
| 5126 Taxes on specific services | .. | 0 | 0 | 0 | 0 | 0 | 0 | 0 | 0 | 0 |
| 5127 Other taxes on internat. trade and transactions | .. | 0 | 43 | 0 | 0 | 0 | 0 | 0 | 0 | 0 |
| 5128 Other taxes | .. | 0 | 0 | 0 | 0 | 0 | 0 | 0 | 0 | 0 |
| 5130 Unallocable between 5110 and 5120 | .. | 0 | 0 | 0 | 0 | 0 | 0 | 0 | 0 | 0 |
| 5200 Taxes on use of goods and perform activities | .. | 0 | 0 | 0 | 0 | 0 | 0 | 0 | 0 | 0 |
| 5210 Recurrent taxes | .. | .. | .. | .. | .. | .. | .. | .. | .. | .. |
| 5211 Paid by households: motor vehicles | .. | .. | .. | .. | .. | .. | .. | .. | .. | .. |

## Table 31. Nicaragua / Nicaragua (*cont.*)
Details of tax revenue / Ingresos tributarios detallados

*Million NIO*

| | 1990 | 2000 | 2005 | 2007 | 2008 | 2009 | 2010 | 2011 | 2012 | 2013 |
|---|---|---|---|---|---|---|---|---|---|---|
| 5212 Paid by others: motor vehicles | .. | .. | .. | .. | .. | .. | .. | .. | .. | .. |
| 5213 Paid in respect of other goods | .. | .. | .. | .. | .. | .. | .. | .. | .. | .. |
| 5220 Non-recurrent taxes | .. | .. | .. | .. | .. | .. | .. | .. | .. | .. |
| 5300 Unallocable between 5100 and 5200 | .. | 0 | 0 | 0 | 0 | 0 | 0 | 0 | 0 | 0 |
| **6000 Other taxes** | **..** | **11** | **17** | **20** | **21** | **24** | **20** | **22** | **24** | **77** |
| 6100 Paid solely by business | .. | 0 | 0 | 0 | 0 | 0 | 0 | 0 | 0 | 0 |
| 6200 Other | .. | 11 | 17 | 20 | 21 | 24 | 20 | 22 | 24 | 77 |
| Stamp tax | .. | 11 | 17 | 20 | 21 | 24 | 20 | 22 | 24 | 77 |

*Note:* Year ending 31st December.
The data are on cash basis.
Comparable statistics for 1990 cannot be shown due to the devaluation of the Nicaraguan cordoba.
*Source:* Banco Central de Nicaragua, Central Bank of Nicaragua. Ministerio de Hacienda y Crédito Público, Ministry of Finance.

StatLink http://dx.doi.org/10.1787/888933190360

# Table 32. Panama / Panamá
## Details of tax revenue / Ingresos tributarios detallados

*Million PAB*

| | 1990 | 2000 | 2005 | 2007 | 2008 | 2009 | 2010 | 2011 | 2012 | 2013 |
|---|---|---|---|---|---|---|---|---|---|---|
| **Total tax revenue** | **892 837** | **1 941 623** | **2 256 604** | **3 297 911** | **3 883 852** | **4 193 049** | **4 814 829** | **5 665 638** | **6 703 099** | **7 650 394** |
| **1000 Taxes on income, profits and capital gains** | **216 950** | **484 872** | **562 852** | **921 831** | **1 097 062** | **1 285 649** | **1 317 028** | **1 349 792** | **1 985 220** | **2 199 534** |
| 1100 Of individuals | 14 155 | 20 343 | 24 395 | 27 927 | 30 098 | 38 811 | 35 456 | 28 458 | 37 825 | 51 598 |
| 1110 On income and profits | 14 155 | 20 343 | 24 395 | 27 927 | 30 098 | 38 811 | 35 456 | 28 458 | 37 825 | 51 598 |
| 1120 On capital gains | .. | .. | .. | .. | .. | .. | .. | .. | .. | .. |
| 1200 Corporate | 72 413 | 186 351 | 255 073 | 459 321 | 544 752 | 731 493 | 749 818 | 701 364 | 1 257 178 | 1 182 374 |
| 1210 On profits | 72 413 | 186 351 | 255 073 | 459 321 | 544 752 | 731 493 | 749 818 | 701 364 | 1 257 178 | 1 182 374 |
| 1220 On capital gains | .. | .. | .. | .. | .. | .. | .. | .. | .. | .. |
| 1300 Unallocable between 1100 and 1200 | 130 382 | 278 178 | 283 384 | 434 583 | 522 212 | 515 345 | 531 754 | 619 970 | 690 217 | 965 562 |
| Payroll | 115 138 | 222 025 | 226 563 | 303 233 | 370 755 | 394 854 | 352 550 | 420 411 | 455 553 | 568 026 |
| Panama Canal commissio | 10 225 | 52 774 | 52 325 | 62 068 | 62 899 | 62 109 | 52 398 | 65 377 | 60 246 | 59 325 |
| Colón Free Zone | 5 019 | 3 379 | 4 496 | 11 909 | 21 323 | 17 855 | 19 666 | 24 074 | 50 735 | 38 903 |
| Other | 0 | 0 | 0 | 57 373 | 67 235 | 40 527 | 107 140 | 110 108 | 123 682 | 299 308 |
| **2000 Social security contributions** | **271 300** | **742 000** | **827 300** | **1 104 000** | **1 330 200** | **1 383 300** | **1 637 100** | **2 041 500** | **2 168 500** | **2 676 700** |
| 2100 Employees | .. | .. | .. | .. | .. | .. | .. | .. | .. | .. |
| 2110 On a payroll basis | .. | .. | .. | .. | .. | .. | .. | .. | .. | .. |
| 2120 On an income tax basis | .. | .. | .. | .. | .. | .. | .. | .. | .. | .. |
| 2200 Employers | .. | .. | .. | .. | .. | .. | .. | .. | .. | .. |
| 2210 On a payroll basis | .. | .. | .. | .. | .. | .. | .. | .. | .. | .. |
| 2220 On an income tax basis | .. | .. | .. | .. | .. | .. | .. | .. | .. | .. |
| 2300 Self-employed or non-employed | .. | .. | .. | .. | .. | .. | .. | .. | .. | .. |
| 2310 On a payroll basis | .. | .. | .. | .. | .. | .. | .. | .. | .. | .. |
| 2320 On an income tax basis | .. | .. | .. | .. | .. | .. | .. | .. | .. | .. |
| 2400 Unallocable between 2100, 2200 and 2300 | 271 300 | 742 000 | 827 300 | 1 104 000 | 1 330 200 | 1 383 300 | 1 637 100 | 2 041 500 | 2 168 500 | 2 676 700 |
| 2410 On a payroll basis | .. | .. | .. | .. | .. | .. | .. | .. | .. | .. |
| 2420 On an income tax basis | .. | .. | .. | .. | .. | .. | .. | .. | .. | .. |
| **3000 Taxes on payroll and workforce** | **0** | **36 400** | **36 243** | **39 842** | **45 248** | **50 962** | **58 844** | **65 200** | **70 400** | **82 400** |
| Education insurance | 0 | 36 400 | 36 243 | 39 842 | 45 248 | 50 962 | 58 844 | 65 200 | 70 400 | 82 400 |
| **4000 Taxes on property** | **43 443** | **62 090** | **109 086** | **154 699** | **160 530** | **175 370** | **212 194** | **229 398** | **261 033** | **337 721** |
| 4100 Recurrent taxes on immovable property | 28 330 | 33 898 | 56 424 | 74 092 | 80 919 | 104 522 | 107 791 | 109 986 | 119 964 | 180 621 |
| 4110 Households | 28 330 | 33 898 | 56 424 | 74 092 | 80 919 | 104 522 | 107 791 | 109 986 | 119 964 | 180 621 |
| 4120 Others | 0 | 0 | 0 | 0 | 0 | 0 | 0 | 0 | 0 | 0 |
| 4200 Recurrent taxes on net wealth | 0 | 0 | 0 | 0 | 0 | 0 | 0 | 0 | 0 | 0 |
| 4210 Individual | .. | .. | .. | .. | .. | .. | .. | .. | .. | .. |
| 4220 Corporate | .. | .. | .. | .. | .. | .. | .. | .. | .. | .. |
| 4300 Estate, inheritance and gift taxes | 154 | 0 | 0 | 0 | 0 | 0 | 0 | 0 | 0 | 0 |
| 4310 Estate and inheritance taxes | .. | .. | .. | .. | .. | .. | .. | .. | .. | .. |
| 4320 Gift taxes | .. | .. | .. | .. | .. | .. | .. | .. | .. | .. |
| 4400 Taxes on financial and capital transactions | 3 419 | 9 343 | 21 049 | 45 383 | 40 528 | 24 456 | 29 810 | 36 195 | 40 998 | 49 391 |
| 4500 Non-recurrent taxes | 0 | 0 | 0 | 0 | 0 | 0 | 0 | 0 | 0 | 0 |
| 4510 On net wealth | .. | .. | .. | .. | .. | .. | .. | .. | .. | .. |
| 4520 Other non-recurrent taxes | .. | .. | .. | .. | .. | .. | .. | .. | .. | .. |
| 4600 Other recurrent taxes on property | 11 540 | 18 849 | 31 613 | 35 224 | 39 083 | 46 392 | 74 593 | 83 218 | 100 071 | 107 709 |
| Commercial licences | 11 540 | 18 849 | 31 613 | 35 224 | 39 083 | 46 392 | 74 593 | 83 218 | 100 071 | 107 709 |
| **5000 Taxes on goods and services** | **335 470** | **573 374** | **692 339** | **1 021 558** | **1 212 812** | **1 261 432** | **1 513 066** | **1 893 533** | **2 124 349** | **2 253 273** |
| 5100 Taxes on production, sale, transfer, etc | 331 758 | 530 329 | 641 713 | 960 450 | 1 143 757 | 1 191 097 | 1 472 515 | 1 845 207 | 2 067 189 | 2 193 455 |
| 5110 General taxes | 80 303 | 69 013 | 137 585 | 205 080 | 526 710 | 557 166 | 766 154 | 1 042 213 | 1 183 878 | 1 269 055 |
| 5111 Value added taxes | 80 303 | 69 013 | 137 585 | 205 080 | 526 710 | 557 166 | 766 154 | 1 042 213 | 1 183 878 | 1 269 055 |
| 5112 Sales tax | 0 | 0 | 0 | 0 | 0 | 0 | 0 | 0 | 0 | 0 |
| 5113 Other | 0 | 0 | 0 | 0 | 0 | 0 | 0 | 0 | 0 | 0 |
| 5120 Taxes on specific goods and services | 138 623 | 461 316 | 504 128 | 755 370 | 617 047 | 633 931 | 706 360 | 802 993 | 883 311 | 924 401 |
| 5121 Excises | 0 | 141 348 | 106 469 | 140 362 | 158 821 | 188 411 | 238 728 | 310 441 | 355 717 | 397 055 |
| Gasoline products | .. | 108 783 | 69 400 | 89 584 | 85 824 | 111 404 | 96 518 | 90 136 | 100 903 | 117 377 |
| Beer | .. | 18 249 | 22 317 | 25 272 | 28 459 | 30 635 | 31 025 | 32 715 | 34 572 | 35 641 |
| Wine and liquor | .. | 11 971 | 10 741 | 11 124 | 12 279 | 11 071 | 10 775 | 10 769 | 10 486 | 15 751 |
| Soft drinks | .. | 2 292 | 2 935 | 3 753 | 4 404 | 4 951 | 5 646 | 6 207 | 6 622 | 6 773 |
| Various products | .. | 0 | 821 | 10 580 | 27 760 | 30 302 | 94 726 | 170 595 | 45 285 | 53 248 |
| Automobiles | .. | 0 | 0 | 0 | 0 | 0 | 0 | 0 | 132 880 | 141 220 |
| Other | .. | 53 | 255 | 49 | 95 | 48 | 38 | 19 | 24 969 | 27 045 |
| 5122 Profits of fiscal monopolies | 0 | 0 | 0 | 0 | 0 | 0 | 0 | 0 | 0 | 0 |
| 5123 Customs and import duties | 124 914 | 298 323 | 363 687 | 573 841 | 411 586 | 390 129 | 390 024 | 393 668 | 420 448 | 408 901 |
| 5124 Taxes on exports | 12 621 | 158 | 0 | 0 | 283 | 104 | 104 | 0 | 0 | 0 |
| 5125 Taxes on investment goods | 0 | 0 | 0 | 0 | 0 | 0 | 0 | 0 | 0 | 0 |
| 5126 Taxes on specific services | 0 | 16 637 | 26 554 | 32 543 | 37 492 | 45 323 | 65 110 | 80 484 | 86 146 | 96 144 |
| Insurance premiums | 0 | 16 637 | 19 482 | 23 577 | 26 929 | 34 514 | 47 056 | 51 664 | 54 188 | 60 483 |
| Cable and telecommunications | 0 | 0 | 5 987 | 8 306 | 9 645 | 9 870 | 17 015 | 27 827 | 30 507 | 33 729 |
| Gambling | 0 | 0 | 1 085 | 660 | 918 | 939 | 1 039 | 993 | 1 451 | 1 932 |

## Table 32. Panama / Panamá (cont.)
Details of tax revenue / Ingresos tributarios detallados

*Million PAB*

| | 1990 | 2000 | 2005 | 2007 | 2008 | 2009 | 2010 | 2011 | 2012 | 2013 |
|---|---|---|---|---|---|---|---|---|---|---|
| 5127 Other taxes on internat. trade and transactions | 1 088 | 4 850 | 7 418 | 8 624 | 8 865 | 9 964 | 12 395 | 18 400 | 21 000 | 22 300 |
| Banks, financial institutions, and currency exchange | 0 | 2 005 | 7 418 | 8 623 | 8 865 | 9 964 | 12 395 | 18 400 | 21 000 | 22 300 |
| Other | 1 088 | 2 845 | 0 | 1 | 0 | 0 | 0 | 0 | 0 | 0 |
| 5128 Other taxes | 0 | 0 | 0 | 0 | 0 | 0 | 0 | 0 | 0 | 0 |
| 5130 Unallocable between 5110 and 5120 | 112 832 | 0 | 0 | 0 | 0 | 0 | 0 | 0 | 0 | 0 |
| 5200 Taxes on use of goods and perform activities | 3 712 | 43 045 | 50 626 | 61 108 | 69 055 | 70 335 | 40 551 | 48 327 | 57 160 | 59 817 |
| 5210 Recurrent taxes | 0 | 38 758 | 43 177 | 48 000 | 53 373 | 55 807 | 40 551 | 48 327 | 57 160 | 59 817 |
| 5211 Paid by households: motor vehicles | 0 | 7 042 | 8 423 | 10 327 | 10 863 | 11 332 | 0 | 0 | 0 | 0 |
| 5212 Paid by others: motor vehicles | 0 | 4 682 | 4 387 | 4 731 | 4 924 | 5 173 | 0 | 0 | 0 | 0 |
| 5213 Paid in respect of other goods | 0 | 27 033 | 30 367 | 32 942 | 37 586 | 39 302 | 40 551 | 48 327 | 57 160 | 59 817 |
| On commercial activities | 0 | 25 405 | 28 685 | 31 052 | 35 547 | 37 184 | 38 367 | 45 723 | 54 382 | 56 739 |
| On industrial activities | 0 | 1 628 | 1 682 | 1 891 | 2 039 | 2 118 | 2 184 | 2 604 | 2 778 | 3 078 |
| 5220 Non-recurrent taxes | 3 712 | 4 287 | 7 449 | 13 107 | 15 682 | 14 528 | 0 | 0 | 0 | 0 |
| Building and construction | .. | .. | .. | .. | .. | .. | .. | .. | .. | .. |
| Ship registration | .. | .. | .. | .. | .. | .. | .. | .. | .. | .. |
| 5300 Unallocable between 5100 and 5200 | 0 | 0 | 0 | 0 | 0 | 0 | 0 | 0 | 0 | 0 |
| **6000 Other taxes** | **25 674** | **42 887** | **28 784** | **55 981** | **38 000** | **36 336** | **76 597** | **86 214** | **93 598** | **100 766** |
| 6100 Paid solely by business | 0 | 11 | 0 | 0 | 27 | 0 | 0 | 0 | 0 | 0 |
| 6200 Other | 25 674 | 42 876 | 28 784 | 55 981 | 37 973 | 36 336 | 76 597 | 86 214 | 93 598 | 100 766 |
| Legal services | 16 691 | 42 330 | 27 684 | 37 689 | 37 912 | 36 278 | 41 064 | 47 000 | 44 900 | 46 200 |

*Note:* Year ending 31st December.

The data are on cash basis.

Heading 3000: In ECLAC data, Education insurance is classified as "Other taxes" (6000).

Heading 5127: In CIAT and ECLAC data, the tax on banks, financial institutions, and currency exchange is classified as a property tax.

Heading 6000: From 2011 the figures for local government taxes have been estimated and is included in heading 6200. It includes some revenues that would otherwise be shown under 4000 and 5000.

*Source:* Contraloría General de la Republica, General Controller of the Republic of Panama.

StatLink http://dx.doi.org/10.1787/888933190377

## Table 33. Paraguay / Paraguay
### Details of tax revenue / Ingresos tributarios detallados

*Million PYG*

| | 1990 | 2000 | 2005 | 2007 | 2008 | 2009 | 2010 | 2011 | 2012 | 2013 |
|---|---|---|---|---|---|---|---|---|---|---|
| **Total tax revenue** | **348 889** | **3 587 451** | **7 434 024** | **9 669 213** | **11 749 612** | **12 725 017** | **15 637 675** | **17 724 559** | **19 261 951** | **19 906 372** |
| **1000 Taxes on income, profits and capital gains** | **73 726** | **470 388** | **938 886** | **1 228 454** | **1 571 467** | **2 187 607** | **2 096 498** | **2 607 282** | **2 902 725** | **3 100 223** |
| 1100 Of individuals | .. | .. | .. | 766 | 318 | 574 | 1 150 | 154 | 507 | 13 375 |
| 1110 On income and profits | .. | .. | .. | 766 | 318 | 574 | 1 150 | 154 | 507 | 13 375 |
| 1120 On capital gains | .. | .. | .. | .. | .. | .. | .. | .. | .. | .. |
| 1200 Corporate | .. | 4 238 | 6 091 | 14 432 | 11 535 | 11 315 | 13 405 | 8 855 | 10 651 | 12 532 |
| 1210 On profits | .. | 4 238 | 6 091 | 14 432 | 11 535 | 11 315 | 13 405 | 8 855 | 10 651 | 12 532 |
| Income tax on small businesses | .. | 0 | 0 | 4 620 | 9 128 | 8 838 | 9 380 | 5 129 | 5 764 | 7 831 |
| Simplified tax on small businesses | .. | 4 238 | 5 802 | 8 411 | 1 181 | 644 | 715 | 544 | 317 | 32 |
| Simplified tax on maquiladoras | .. | 0 | 289 | 1 401 | 1 226 | 1 833 | 3 310 | 3 182 | 4 570 | 4 669 |
| 1220 On capital gains | .. | .. | .. | .. | .. | .. | .. | .. | .. | .. |
| 1300 Unallocable between 1100 and 1200 | 73 726 | 466 150 | 932 795 | 1 213 256 | 1 559 614 | 2 175 718 | 2 081 943 | 2 598 273 | 2 891 567 | 3 074 316 |
| Income tax on agricultural activities | 0 | 15 042 | 22 477 | 11 200 | 16 227 | 22 651 | 30 113 | 59 788 | 66 108 | 71 813 |
| Tax on industrial, commercial, and service activities | 0 | 451 108 | 910 318 | 1 202 056 | 1 543 387 | 2 153 067 | 2 051 830 | 2 538 485 | 2 825 459 | 3 002 503 |
| Other | 73 726 | 0 | 0 | 0 | 0 | 0 | 0 | 0 | 0 | 0 |
| **2000 Social security contributions** | **28 882** | **919 533** | **1 591 980** | **2 265 097** | **2 784 731** | **3 118 645** | **3 552 640** | **3 976 795** | **4 844 111** | **5 158 072** |
| 2100 Employees | .. | .. | .. | .. | .. | .. | .. | .. | .. | .. |
| 2110 On a payroll basis | .. | .. | .. | .. | .. | .. | .. | .. | .. | .. |
| 2120 On an income tax basis | .. | .. | .. | .. | .. | .. | .. | .. | .. | .. |
| 2200 Employers | .. | .. | .. | .. | .. | .. | .. | .. | .. | .. |
| 2210 On a payroll basis | .. | .. | .. | .. | .. | .. | .. | .. | .. | .. |
| 2220 On an income tax basis | .. | .. | .. | .. | .. | .. | .. | .. | .. | .. |
| 2300 Self-employed or non-employed | .. | .. | .. | .. | .. | .. | .. | .. | .. | .. |
| 2310 On a payroll basis | .. | .. | .. | .. | .. | .. | .. | .. | .. | .. |
| 2320 On an income tax basis | .. | .. | .. | .. | .. | .. | .. | .. | .. | .. |
| 2400 Unallocable between 2100, 2200 and 2300 | 28 882 | 919 533 | 1 591 980 | 2 265 097 | 2 784 731 | 3 118 645 | 3 552 640 | 3 976 795 | 4 844 111 | 5 158 072 |
| 2410 On a payroll basis | 28 882 | 919 533 | 1 591 980 | 2 265 097 | 2 784 731 | 3 118 645 | 3 552 640 | 3 976 795 | 4 844 111 | 5 158 072 |
| 2420 On an income tax basis | 0 | 0 | 0 | 0 | 0 | 0 | 0 | 0 | 0 | 0 |
| **3000 Taxes on payroll and workforce** | **0** | **0** | **0** | **0** | **0** | **0** | **0** | **0** | **0** | **0** |
| **4000 Taxes on property** | **17 162** | **0** | **0** | **203 605** | **255 333** | **253 821** | **272 385** | **289 456** | **310 237** | **0** |
| 4100 Recurrent taxes on immovable property | 17 162 | .. | .. | 194 246 | 239 680 | 240 217 | 254 306 | 266 371 | 289 493 | .. |
| 4110 Households | 17 162 | .. | .. | 194 246 | 239 680 | 240 217 | 254 306 | 266 371 | 289 493 | .. |
| Real estate tax | 0 | .. | .. | 190 796 | 230 570 | 233 423 | 249 697 | 261 051 | 285 034 | .. |
| Tax on vacant lots | 0 | .. | .. | 2 046 | 3 855 | 2 953 | 2 925 | 3 212 | 3 472 | .. |
| Other | 17 162 | .. | .. | 1 404 | 5 256 | 3 841 | 1 684 | 2 109 | 987 | .. |
| 4120 Others | 0 | .. | .. | 0 | 0 | 0 | 0 | 0 | 0 | .. |
| 4200 Recurrent taxes on net wealth | 0 | .. | .. | 0 | 0 | 0 | 0 | 0 | 0 | .. |
| 4210 Individual | .. | .. | .. | .. | .. | .. | .. | .. | .. | .. |
| 4220 Corporate | .. | .. | .. | .. | .. | .. | .. | .. | .. | .. |
| 4300 Estate, inheritance and gift taxes | .. | .. | .. | .. | .. | .. | .. | .. | .. | .. |
| 4310 Estate and inheritance taxes | .. | .. | .. | .. | .. | .. | .. | .. | .. | .. |
| 4320 Gift taxes | .. | .. | .. | .. | .. | .. | .. | .. | .. | .. |
| 4400 Taxes on financial and capital transactions | 0 | .. | .. | 9 294 | 15 170 | 13 391 | 16 316 | 22 406 | 20 061 | .. |
| Real estate transfer tax | .. | .. | .. | 6 412 | 11 275 | 9 675 | 11 766 | 16 362 | 14 704 | .. |
| Other | .. | .. | .. | 2 882 | 3 895 | 3 716 | 4 551 | 6 044 | 5 357 | .. |
| 4500 Non-recurrent taxes | 0 | .. | .. | 0 | 0 | 0 | 0 | 0 | 0 | .. |
| 4510 On net wealth | .. | .. | .. | .. | .. | .. | .. | .. | .. | .. |
| 4520 Other non-recurrent taxes | .. | .. | .. | .. | .. | .. | .. | .. | .. | .. |
| 4600 Other recurrent taxes on property | 0 | .. | .. | 65 | 482 | 213 | 1 762 | 679 | 682 | .. |
| **5000 Taxes on goods and services** | **179 312** | **2 080 878** | **4 309 832** | **5 808 675** | **7 039 349** | **7 068 556** | **9 460 962** | **10 749 735** | **11 081 105** | **11 524 523** |
| 5100 Taxes on production, sale, transfer, etc | 179 312 | 2 080 878 | 4 309 832 | 5 687 532 | 6 887 675 | 6 928 055 | 9 249 698 | 10 501 464 | 10 849 519 | 11 524 523 |
| 5110 General taxes | 0 | 1 150 496 | 2 478 998 | 3 496 787 | 4 409 140 | 4 399 503 | 5 991 694 | 6 887 685 | 7 126 623 | 7 843 002 |
| 5111 Value added taxes | .. | 1 150 496 | 2 478 998 | 3 496 787 | 4 409 140 | 4 399 503 | 5 991 694 | 6 887 685 | 7 126 623 | 7 843 002 |
| 5112 Sales tax | .. | 0 | 0 | 0 | 0 | 0 | 0 | 0 | 0 | 0 |
| 5113 Other | .. | 0 | 0 | 0 | 0 | 0 | 0 | 0 | 0 | 0 |
| 5120 Taxes on specific goods and services | 179 312 | 930 382 | 1 830 834 | 2 190 745 | 2 478 535 | 2 528 552 | 3 258 004 | 3 613 779 | 3 722 896 | 3 681 521 |
| 5121 Excises | 41 087 | 456 561 | 949 962 | 1 335 033 | 1 411 846 | 1 532 365 | 1 710 531 | 1 892 587 | 2 063 020 | 2 048 143 |
| Fuels | 41 087 | 316 694 | 688 773 | 1 000 727 | 1 027 042 | 1 093 058 | 1 126 143 | 1 328 213 | 1 455 820 | 1 427 769 |
| Other excises | 0 | 136 194 | 249 239 | 309 383 | 347 467 | 399 940 | 537 887 | 564 374 | 607 200 | 620 374 |
| Animal health and quality service | 0 | 3 673 | 11 950 | 24 923 | 37 337 | 39 367 | 46 501 | 0 | 0 | 0 |
| Livestock trade | 0 | 0 | 0 | 0 | 0 | 0 | 0 | 0 | 0 | 0 |
| 5122 Profits of fiscal monopolies | 0 | 0 | 0 | 0 | 0 | 0 | 0 | 0 | 0 | 0 |
| 5123 Customs and import duties | 138 225 | 473 821 | 880 872 | 838 494 | 1 045 788 | 975 487 | 1 524 252 | 1 696 945 | 1 637 588 | 1 633 378 |
| 5124 Taxes on exports | 0 | 0 | 0 | 0 | 0 | 0 | 0 | 0 | 0 | 0 |
| 5125 Taxes on investment goods | 0 | 0 | 0 | 0 | 0 | 0 | 0 | 0 | 0 | 0 |

## Table 33. Paraguay / Paraguay (cont.)
Details of tax revenue / Ingresos tributarios detallados

*Million PYG*

| | 1990 | 2000 | 2005 | 2007 | 2008 | 2009 | 2010 | 2011 | 2012 | 2013 |
|---|---|---|---|---|---|---|---|---|---|---|
| 5126 Taxes on specific services | 0 | 0 | 0 | 17 218 | 20 900 | 20 700 | 23 221 | 24 247 | 22 288 | 0 |
| Advertising | .. | .. | .. | 3 613 | 5 109 | 4 555 | 5 249 | 6 047 | 6 560 | .. |
| Public transport | .. | .. | .. | 4 173 | 4 508 | 4 245 | 4 363 | 4 649 | 4 121 | .. |
| Other | .. | .. | .. | 9 432 | 11 284 | 11 900 | 13 609 | 13 551 | 11 607 | .. |
| 5127 Other taxes on internat. trade and transactions | 0 | 0 | 0 | 0 | 0 | 0 | 0 | 0 | 0 | 0 |
| 5128 Other taxes | 0 | 0 | 0 | 0 | 0 | 0 | 0 | 0 | 0 | 0 |
| 5130 Unallocable between 5110 and 5120 | 0 | 0 | 0 | 0 | 0 | 0 | 0 | 0 | 0 | 0 |
| 5200 Taxes on use of goods and perform activities | 0 | 0 | 0 | 119 834 | 151 211 | 140 466 | 211 027 | 208 542 | 230 890 | 0 |
| 5210 Recurrent taxes | 0 | 0 | 0 | 119 834 | 151 211 | 140 466 | 211 027 | 208 542 | 230 890 | .. |
| 5211 Paid by households: motor vehicles | .. | .. | .. | 0 | 0 | 0 | 0 | 0 | 0 | .. |
| 5212 Paid by others: motor vehicles | .. | .. | .. | 28 343 | 27 174 | 41 701 | 52 365 | 64 667 | 67 399 | .. |
| Motor vehicle licences | .. | .. | .. | 28 343 | 27 174 | 41 701 | 52 365 | 64 667 | 67 399 | .. |
| 5213 Paid in respect of other goods | .. | .. | .. | 91 492 | 124 037 | 98 765 | 158 662 | 143 875 | 163 491 | .. |
| Tax on construction | .. | .. | .. | 16 168 | 20 362 | 24 476 | 31 696 | 38 891 | 50 337 | .. |
| Licencing fees | .. | .. | .. | 75 323 | 103 675 | 74 289 | 126 965 | 104 983 | 113 153 | .. |
| 5220 Non-recurrent taxes | .. | .. | .. | .. | .. | .. | .. | .. | .. | .. |
| 5300 Unallocable between 5100 and 5200 | 0 | 0 | 0 | 1 309 | 463 | 35 | 237 | 39 730 | 696 | .. |
| **6000 Other taxes** | **49 807** | **116 652** | **593 326** | **163 383** | **98 733** | **96 388** | **255 190** | **101 291** | **123 774** | **123 554** |
| 6100 Paid solely by business | 0 | 0 | 0 | 0 | 0 | 0 | 0 | 0 | 0 | 0 |
| 6200 Other | 49 807 | 116 652 | 593 326 | 163 383 | 98 733 | 96 388 | 255 190 | 101 291 | 123 774 | 123 554 |
| Registration and stamp duties | 0 | 71 777 | 192 393 | 70 954 | 6 825 | 319 | 332 | 159 | 168 | 179 |
| Luxury automobile tax | 0 | 0 | 3 897 | 2 750 | 839 | 118 | 91 | 129 | 153 | 218 |
| Other | 49 807 | 44 875 | 397 036 | 89 679 | 91 069 | 95 951 | 254 767 | 101 003 | 123 453 | 123 157 |

*Note:* Year ending 31st December.

The data are on cash basis.

The figures for years up to and including 2004, as well as for 2013, exclude local government tax revenues as the data are not available.This affects data in categories 4000, 5000, and 6000.

Heading 2000:. Data on social security contributions collected by decentralized institutions are not available for 2011 to 2013, with the exception of the contributions made to the Instituto de Previsión Social (Social Security Institute).

Heading 5121: Data for Animal health and quality service are not available for 2011, 2012 and 2013.

*Source:* Ministry of Finance.

StatLink http://dx.doi.org/10.1787/888933190381

## Table 34. Peru / Perú
Details of tax revenue / Ingresos tributarios detallados

*Million PEN*

| | 1990 | 2000 | 2005 | 2007 | 2008 | 2009 | 2010 | 2011 | 2012 | 2013 |
|---|---|---|---|---|---|---|---|---|---|---|
| **Total tax revenue** | **645** | **25 851** | **41 281** | **59 800** | **67 533** | **62 198** | **75 646** | **86 702** | **95 542** | **100 111** |
| **1000 Taxes on income, profits and capital gains** | **37** | **5 130** | **12 283** | **24 357** | **26 464** | **22 645** | **28 357** | **36 640** | **40 650** | **39 982** |
| 1100 Of individuals | 3 | 2 117 | 3 349 | 4 671 | 6 141 | 6 438 | 7 286 | 8 869 | 9 953 | 10 927 |
| First category | .. | 167 | 181 | 217 | 241 | 145 | 160 | 196 | 253 | 310 |
| Second category | .. | 7 | 250 | 611 | 712 | 661 | 869 | 1 291 | 1 136 | 1 275 |
| Fourth category | .. | 234 | 395 | 408 | 437 | 473 | 521 | 567 | 637 | 744 |
| Fifth category | .. | 1 641 | 2 369 | 3 241 | 3 966 | 4 329 | 4 735 | 5 877 | 7 054 | 7 820 |
| Solidarity contribution for pension plan | .. | 0 | 23 | 26 | 557 | 577 | 768 | 661 | 491 | 357 |
| Tax debt payments | .. | 68 | 130 | 168 | 228 | 254 | 233 | 277 | 382 | 421 |
| 1110 On income and profits | .. | 0 | 0 | 0 | 0 | 0 | 0 | 0 | 0 | 0 |
| 1120 On capital gains | .. | .. | .. | .. | .. | .. | .. | .. | .. | .. |
| 1200 Corporate | 32 | 3 012 | 8 933 | 19 685 | 20 322 | 16 207 | 21 071 | 27 712 | 30 255 | 28 718 |
| 1210 On profits | 32 | 3 012 | 8 933 | 19 685 | 20 322 | 16 207 | 21 071 | 27 712 | 30 255 | 28 718 |
| Third category | .. | 2 023 | 5 316 | 13 258 | 14 921 | 10 691 | 14 652 | 19 321 | 20 744 | 19 633 |
| Income tax on non-residents | .. | 487 | 542 | 961 | 1 204 | 1 391 | 1 511 | 1 735 | 2 244 | 2 848 |
| Income tax special regime | .. | 47 | 55 | 60 | 79 | 89 | 118 | 153 | 202 | 246 |
| Other incomes corporate | .. | 18 | 41 | 95 | 110 | 98 | 148 | 224 | 229 | 187 |
| Tax debt payments | .. | 438 | 1 908 | 3 829 | 2 248 | 2 216 | 2 856 | 3 987 | 4 397 | 3 029 |
| Temporary tax on net assets | .. | 0 | 1 073 | 1 483 | 1 761 | 1 722 | 1 788 | 2 293 | 2 439 | 2 776 |
| 1220 On capital gains | .. | .. | .. | .. | .. | .. | .. | .. | .. | .. |
| 1300 Unallocable between 1100 and 1200 | 1 | 0 | 0 | 0 | 0 | 0 | 0 | 59 | 442 | 337 |
| **2000 Social security contributions** | **50** | **3 184** | **4 000** | **5 219** | **6 211** | **6 667** | **7 189** | **8 319** | **9 694** | **10 946** |
| 2100 Employees | .. | 541 | 644 | 914 | 1 209 | 1 401 | 1 618 | 1 997 | 2 389 | 2 786 |
| 2110 On a payroll basis | .. | 541 | 644 | 914 | 1 209 | 1 401 | 1 618 | 1 997 | 2 389 | 2 786 |
| 2120 On an income tax basis | .. | 0 | 0 | 0 | 0 | 0 | 0 | 0 | 0 | 0 |
| 2200 Employers | .. | 2 447 | 3 207 | 4 092 | 4 774 | 5 015 | 5 283 | 6 099 | 7 075 | 7 928 |
| 2210 On a payroll basis | .. | 2 447 | 3 207 | 4 092 | 4 774 | 5 015 | 5 283 | 6 099 | 7 075 | 7 928 |
| 2220 On an income tax basis | .. | 0 | 0 | 0 | 0 | 0 | 0 | 0 | 0 | 0 |
| 2300 Self-employed or non-employed | .. | 95 | 36 | 34 | 38 | 38 | 42 | 46 | 51 | 55 |
| 2310 On a payroll basis | .. | 95 | 36 | 34 | 38 | 38 | 42 | 46 | 51 | 55 |
| 2320 On an income tax basis | .. | 0 | 0 | 0 | 0 | 0 | 0 | 0 | 0 | 0 |
| 2400 Unallocable between 2100, 2200 and 2300 | 50 | 102 | 113 | 178 | 190 | 213 | 246 | 177 | 179 | 177 |
| 2410 On a payroll basis | 50 | 102 | 113 | 178 | 190 | 213 | 246 | 177 | 179 | 177 |
| 2420 On an income tax basis | 0 | 0 | 0 | 0 | 0 | 0 | 0 | 0 | 0 | 0 |
| **3000 Taxes on payroll and workforce** | **0** | **1 038** | **27** | **9** | **7** | **6** | **3** | **1** | **2** | **1** |
| **4000 Taxes on property** | **99** | **0** | **1 332** | **1 929** | **2 173** | **2 042** | **2 237** | **1 876** | **1 897** | **1 905** |
| 4100 Recurrent taxes on immovable property | 0 | 0 | 453 | 552 | 615 | 676 | 864 | 856 | 958 | 1 770 |
| 4110 Households | .. | .. | 0 | 0 | 0 | 0 | 0 | 0 | 0 | 0 |
| 4120 Others | .. | .. | 0 | 0 | 0 | 0 | 0 | 0 | 0 | 0 |
| 4200 Recurrent taxes on net wealth | 61 | 0 | 0 | 0 | 0 | 0 | 0 | 0 | 0 | 0 |
| 4210 Individual | 60 | 0 | 0 | 0 | .. | .. | .. | .. | .. | .. |
| 4220 Corporate | 1 | 0 | 0 | 0 | .. | .. | .. | .. | .. | .. |
| Revaluation of fixed assets | 1 | .. | 0 | 0 | .. | .. | .. | .. | .. | .. |
| 4300 Estate, inheritance and gift taxes | 0 | 0 | 0 | 0 | 0 | 0 | 0 | 0 | 0 | 0 |
| 4310 Estate and inheritance taxes | .. | .. | .. | .. | .. | .. | .. | .. | .. | .. |
| 4320 Gift taxes | .. | .. | .. | .. | .. | .. | .. | .. | .. | .. |
| 4400 Taxes on financial and capital transactions | 38 | 0 | 802 | 1 377 | 1 559 | 1 366 | 1 373 | 1 020 | 939 | 134 |
| Financial transactions tax | 0 | .. | 706 | 1 031 | 1 138 | 968 | 944 | 395 | 126 | 134 |
| Real Estate Transfer Tax | 0 | .. | 96 | 347 | 421 | 398 | 429 | 625 | 813 | 0 |
| Tax Law Decree 519 | 38 | .. | 0 | 0 | 0 | 0 | 0 | 0 | 0 | 0 |
| 4500 Non-recurrent taxes | 0 | 0 | 0 | 0 | 0 | 0 | 0 | 0 | 0 | 0 |
| 4510 On net wealth | .. | .. | .. | .. | .. | .. | .. | .. | .. | .. |
| 4520 Other non-recurrent taxes | .. | .. | .. | .. | .. | .. | .. | .. | .. | .. |
| 4600 Other recurrent taxes on property | 0 | 0 | 76 | 0 | 0 | 0 | 0 | 0 | 0 | 0 |
| **5000 Taxes on goods and services** | **423** | **15 739** | **21 852** | **26 235** | **30 456** | **28 172** | **34 855** | **37 804** | **40 522** | **44 586** |
| 5100 Taxes on production, sale, transfer, etc | 423 | 15 739 | 21 852 | 26 235 | 30 456 | 28 172 | 34 855 | 37 804 | 40 522 | 44 586 |
| 5110 General taxes | 78 | 9 519 | 14 779 | 19 865 | 25 109 | 22 918 | 28 693 | 31 535 | 33 881 | 37 052 |
| 5111 Value added taxes | 78 | 9 472 | 14 732 | 19 865 | 25 109 | 22 918 | 28 693 | 31 535 | 33 881 | 37 052 |
| 5112 Sales tax | 0 | 0 | 0 | 0 | 0 | 0 | 0 | 0 | 0 | 0 |
| 5113 Other | 0 | 47 | 47 | 0 | 0 | 0 | 0 | 0 | 0 | 0 |
| 5120 Taxes on specific goods and services | 345 | 6 220 | 7 073 | 6 370 | 5 347 | 5 254 | 6 161 | 6 269 | 6 641 | 7 534 |
| 5121 Excises | 232 | 3 521 | 4 205 | 4 465 | 3 682 | 4 288 | 4 879 | 5 001 | 5 243 | 5 814 |
| Fuels | 151 | 2 120 | 2 607 | 2 419 | 1 457 | 2 255 | 2 410 | 2 231 | 2 149 | 2 502 |
| Gasoline sales tax | 3 | 97 | 140 | 174 | 222 | 143 | 210 | 282 | 325 | 335 |
| Other | 78 | 1 304 | 1 459 | 1 872 | 2 003 | 1 890 | 2 258 | 2 487 | 2 769 | 2 978 |
| 5122 Profits of fiscal monopolies | 0 | 0 | 0 | 0 | 0 | 0 | 0 | 0 | 0 | 0 |
| 5123 Customs and import duties | 64 | 2 698 | 2 695 | 1 625 | 1 281 | 576 | 855 | 810 | 901 | 1 135 |
| 5124 Taxes on exports | 2 | 0 | 0 | 0 | 0 | 0 | 0 | 0 | 0 | 0 |

## Table 34. Peru / Perú (cont.)
### Details of tax revenue / Ingresos tributarios detallados

*Million PEN*

| | 1990 | 2000 | 2005 | 2007 | 2008 | 2009 | 2010 | 2011 | 2012 | 2013 |
|---|---|---|---|---|---|---|---|---|---|---|
| 5125 Taxes on investment goods | 0 | 0 | 0 | 0 | 0 | 0 | 0 | 0 | 0 | 0 |
| 5126 Taxes on specific services | 0 | 0 | 172 | 281 | 385 | 390 | 428 | 459 | 497 | 585 |
| Casinos and slot machines | .. | .. | 49 | 109 | 170 | 163 | 187 | 195 | 219 | 269 |
| Tourism tax | .. | .. | 74 | 87 | 93 | 104 | 105 | 116 | 115 | 118 |
| Municipal taxes on services | .. | .. | 49 | 85 | 122 | 123 | 136 | 148 | 163 | 198 |
| 5127 Other taxes on internat. trade and transactions | 48 | 0 | 0 | 0 | 0 | 0 | 0 | 0 | 0 | 0 |
| 5128 Other taxes | 0 | 0 | 0 | 0 | 0 | 0 | 0 | 0 | 0 | 0 |
| 5130 Unallocable between 5110 and 5120 | 0 | 0 | 0 | 0 | 0 | 0 | 0 | 0 | 0 | 0 |
| 5200 Taxes on use of goods and perform activities | 0 | 0 | 0 | 0 | 0 | 0 | 0 | 0 | 0 | 0 |
| 5210 Recurrent taxes | .. | .. | .. | .. | .. | .. | .. | .. | .. | .. |
| 5211 Paid by households: motor vehicles | .. | .. | .. | .. | .. | .. | .. | .. | .. | .. |
| 5212 Paid by others: motor vehicles | .. | .. | .. | .. | .. | .. | .. | .. | .. | .. |
| 5213 Paid in respect of other goods | .. | .. | .. | .. | .. | .. | .. | .. | .. | .. |
| 5220 Non-recurrent taxes | .. | .. | .. | .. | .. | .. | .. | .. | .. | .. |
| 5300 Unallocable between 5100 and 5200 | 0 | 0 | 0 | 0 | 0 | 0 | 0 | 0 | 0 | 0 |
| **6000 Other taxes** | **36** | **761** | **1 786** | **2 051** | **2 223** | **2 665** | **3 005** | **2 061** | **2 777** | **2 691** |
| 6100 Paid solely by business | 0 | 84 | 73 | 82 | 91 | 98 | 108 | 118 | 133 | 147 |
| Single simplified regime | .. | 84 | 73 | 82 | 91 | 98 | 108 | 118 | 133 | 147 |
| University Development Fund | .. | 0 | 0 | 0 | 0 | 0 | 0 | 0 | 0 | 0 |
| 6200 Other | 36 | 678 | 1 714 | 1 969 | 2 131 | 2 567 | 2 897 | 1 944 | 2 644 | 2 544 |
| Tax debt payments | 9 | 543 | 397 | 510 | 515 | 735 | 714 | 709 | 857 | 893 |
| Penalties | 0 | 114 | 159 | 263 | 268 | 287 | 330 | 453 | 937 | 1 001 |
| Municipal fees | 0 | 0 | 951 | 1 021 | 1 166 | 1 260 | 1 562 | 710 | 775 | 568 |
| Other national level | 28 | 20 | 171 | 148 | 146 | 234 | 238 | 0 | 0 | 0 |
| Other local level | 0 | 0 | 35 | 27 | 36 | 51 | 54 | 72 | 76 | 82 |

*Note:* Year ending 31st December.
The data are on cash basis.
The figures for years up to and including 2004 exclude local government tax revenues as the data are not available.

*Source:* Banco Central de Reserva del Perú, Reserve Bank of Peru. Superintendencia Nacional de Aduanas y de Administración Tributaria, National Superintendency of Tax Administration.

StatLink http://dx.doi.org/10.1787/888933190394

## Table 35. Uruguay / Uruguay
Details of tax revenue / Ingresos tributarios detallados

*Million UYU*

| | 1990 | 2000 | 2005 | 2007 | 2008 | 2009 | 2010 | 2011 | 2012 | 2013 |
|---|---|---|---|---|---|---|---|---|---|---|
| **Total tax revenue** | **2 352** | **59 656** | **101 306** | **137 545** | **166 284** | **184 547** | **210 191** | **244 433** | **278 182** | **308 660** |
| **1000 Taxes on income, profits and capital gains** | **114** | **5 620** | **11 969** | **18 683** | **34 366** | **38 457** | **44 573** | **50 957** | **58 291** | **71 398** |
| 1100 Of individuals | 0 | 0 | 44 | 4 869 | 14 823 | 16 431 | 19 654 | 24 429 | 30 071 | 34 611 |
| 1110 On income and profits | .. | .. | 44 | 607 | 2 441 | 3 990 | 5 011 | 6 007 | 7 537 | 8 564 |
| First category | .. | .. | 0 | 581 | 1 781 | 1 921 | 2 358 | 2 946 | 3 764 | 4 278 |
| Social security assistance | .. | .. | 0 | 0 | 660 | 2 066 | 2 651 | 3 061 | 3 773 | 4 285 |
| 1120 On capital gains | .. | .. | .. | 4 262 | 12 381 | 12 441 | 14 643 | 18 422 | 22 534 | 26 048 |
| Second category | .. | .. | .. | 4 262 | 12 381 | 12 441 | 14 643 | 18 422 | 22 534 | 26 048 |
| 1200 Corporate | 114 | 5 620 | 11 925 | 13 464 | 18 518 | 20 240 | 23 257 | 23 940 | 26 166 | 34 108 |
| 1210 On profits | 114 | 5 620 | 11 925 | 13 464 | 18 518 | 20 240 | 23 257 | 23 940 | 26 166 | 34 108 |
| Corporate income tax (IRAE) | 0 | 0 | 0 | 709 | 11 724 | 16 512 | 21 280 | 21 719 | 23 937 | 31 812 |
| Corporate income tax (IRIC) | 97 | 5 096 | 10 516 | 11 055 | 5 313 | 2 355 | 491 | 469 | 414 | 387 |
| Small firms (minimum VAT) | 0 | 296 | 457 | 563 | 573 | 596 | 586 | 600 | 631 | 686 |
| Other | 17 | 228 | 952 | 1 138 | 907 | 777 | 900 | 1 151 | 1 185 | 1 222 |
| 1220 On capital gains | .. | .. | .. | .. | .. | .. | .. | .. | .. | .. |
| 1300 Unallocable between 1100 and 1200 | 0 | 0 | 0 | 349 | 1 025 | 1 785 | 1 662 | 2 588 | 2 053 | 2 679 |
| Non resident taxpayers | .. | .. | .. | 349 | 1 025 | 1 785 | 1 662 | 2 588 | 2 053 | 2 679 |
| **2000 Social security contributions** | **717** | **17 679** | **21 425** | **28 473** | **34 778** | **42 922** | **49 742** | **59 930** | **72 601** | **86 012** |
| 2100 Employees | .. | .. | .. | .. | .. | .. | .. | .. | .. | .. |
| 2110 On a payroll basis | .. | .. | .. | .. | .. | .. | .. | .. | .. | .. |
| 2120 On an income tax basis | .. | .. | .. | .. | .. | .. | .. | .. | .. | .. |
| 2200 Employers | .. | .. | .. | .. | .. | .. | .. | .. | .. | .. |
| 2210 On a payroll basis | .. | .. | .. | .. | .. | .. | .. | .. | .. | .. |
| 2220 On an income tax basis | .. | .. | .. | .. | .. | .. | .. | .. | .. | .. |
| 2300 Self-employed or non-employed | .. | .. | .. | .. | .. | .. | .. | .. | .. | .. |
| 2310 On a payroll basis | .. | .. | .. | .. | .. | .. | .. | .. | .. | .. |
| 2320 On an income tax basis | .. | .. | .. | .. | .. | .. | .. | .. | .. | .. |
| 2400 Unallocable between 2100, 2200 and 2300 | 717 | 17 679 | 21 425 | 28 473 | 34 778 | 42 922 | 49 742 | 59 930 | 72 601 | 86 012 |
| 2410 On a payroll basis | 717 | 17 679 | 21 425 | 28 473 | 34 778 | 42 922 | 49 742 | 59 930 | 72 601 | 86 012 |
| 2420 On an income tax basis | 0 | 0 | 0 | 0 | 0 | 0 | 0 | 0 | 0 | 0 |
| **3000 Taxes on payroll and workforce** | **0** | **0** | **0** | **0** | **0** | **0** | **0** | **0** | **0** | **0** |
| **4000 Taxes on property** | **197** | **6 077** | **12 039** | **13 966** | **15 213** | **16 581** | **16 935** | **18 960** | **20 447** | **21 388** |
| 4100 Recurrent taxes on immovable property | 72 | 2 521 | 4 639 | 6 098 | 6 780 | 6 622 | 6 308 | 6 941 | 7 500 | 7 500 |
| 4110 Households | .. | .. | .. | .. | .. | .. | .. | .. | .. | .. |
| 4120 Others | .. | .. | .. | .. | .. | .. | .. | .. | .. | .. |
| 4200 Recurrent taxes on net wealth | 94 | 2 076 | 4 943 | 5 392 | 6 939 | 8 634 | 8 948 | 10 030 | 11 067 | 11 892 |
| 4210 Individual | 64 | 108 | 336 | 340 | 325 | 371 | 382 | 422 | 445 | 491 |
| 4220 Corporate | 30 | 1 968 | 4 607 | 5 052 | 6 614 | 8 263 | 8 567 | 9 607 | 10 622 | 11 401 |
| Corporate wealth | 28 | 1 661 | 4 383 | 4 805 | 6 380 | 8 056 | 8 354 | 9 413 | 10 609 | 11 390 |
| Other | 1 | 307 | 224 | 247 | 234 | 207 | 213 | 194 | 13 | 11 |
| 4300 Estate, inheritance and gift taxes | 0 | 0 | 0 | 0 | 0 | 0 | 0 | 0 | 0 | 0 |
| 4310 Estate and inheritance taxes | .. | .. | .. | .. | .. | .. | .. | .. | .. | .. |
| 4320 Gift taxes | .. | .. | .. | .. | .. | .. | .. | .. | .. | .. |
| 4400 Taxes on financial and capital transactions | 0 | 372 | 933 | 1 455 | 1 206 | 1 027 | 1 350 | 1 545 | 1 414 | 1 516 |
| Capital transfers | .. | 372 | 886 | 1 268 | 1 202 | 1 027 | 1 347 | 1 545 | 1 413 | 1 516 |
| Capital transfers (additional) | .. | 0 | 0 | 0 | 0 | 0 | 0 | 0 | 0 | 0 |
| 4500 Non-recurrent taxes | 0 | 0 | 0 | 0 | 0 | 0 | 0 | 0 | 0 | 0 |
| 4510 On net wealth | .. | .. | .. | .. | .. | .. | .. | .. | .. | .. |
| 4520 Other non-recurrent taxes | .. | .. | .. | .. | .. | .. | .. | .. | .. | .. |
| 4600 Other recurrent taxes on property | 31 | 1 107 | 1 524 | 1 021 | 288 | 299 | 328 | 445 | 466 | 480 |
| **5000 Taxes on goods and services** | **1 334** | **30 877** | **55 798** | **76 359** | **81 919** | **86 505** | **98 942** | **114 586** | **126 844** | **129 648** |
| 5100 Taxes on production, sale, transfer, etc | 1 270 | 28 301 | 52 727 | 72 607 | 77 784 | 82 657 | 94 990 | 110 473 | 122 310 | 125 048 |
| 5110 General taxes | 660 | 18 009 | 34 641 | 50 943 | 58 277 | 61 469 | 69 365 | 79 672 | 88 338 | 98 071 |
| 5111 Value added taxes | 660 | 17 995 | 34 601 | 50 923 | 58 277 | 61 469 | 69 365 | 79 672 | 88 338 | 98 071 |
| 5112 Sales tax | 1 | 14 | 40 | 20 | 0 | 0 | 0 | 0 | 0 | 0 |
| 5113 Other | 0 | 0 | 0 | 0 | 0 | 0 | 0 | 0 | 0 | 0 |
| 5120 Taxes on specific goods and services | 610 | 10 291 | 18 086 | 21 664 | 19 507 | 21 188 | 25 625 | 30 801 | 33 972 | 26 977 |
| 5121 Excises | 393 | 7 673 | 10 524 | 12 336 | 11 560 | 13 312 | 16 401 | 19 401 | 21 417 | 13 064 |
| Fuels | 203 | 4 067 | 4 900 | 5 694 | 4 437 | 5 462 | 6 551 | 8 447 | 9 147 | 10 269 |
| Tobacco products | 80 | 1 741 | 2 705 | 3 085 | 2 948 | 3 248 | 4 236 | 4 925 | 4 768 | 4 755 |
| Alcoholic beverages | 24 | 229 | 375 | 448 | 533 | 657 | 602 | 622 | 800 | 840 |
| Beer | 8 | 205 | 308 | 372 | 402 | 480 | 602 | 895 | 895 | 1 024 |
| Non-alcoholic beverages | 19 | 464 | 532 | 804 | 990 | 1 240 | 1 172 | 1 451 | 1 518 | 1 718 |
| Motor vehicles | 20 | 656 | 977 | 1 333 | 1 616 | 1 662 | 2 289 | 2 710 | 3 025 | 3 388 |
| Sales of agricultural goods (MEVIR and INIA) | 4 | 76 | 260 | 323 | 417 | 414 | 451 | 538 | 648 | 648 |
| Other | 35 | 235 | 468 | 277 | 217 | 148 | 497 | -188 | 616 | 689 |
| 5122 Profits of fiscal monopolies | 0 | 0 | 0 | 0 | 0 | 0 | 0 | 0 | 0 | 0 |
| 5123 Customs and import duties | 214 | 1 967 | 5 195 | 7 077 | 7 103 | 7 042 | 8 478 | 10 543 | 11 670 | 13 020 |

## Table 35. Uruguay / Uruguay *(cont.)*
### Details of tax revenue / Ingresos tributarios detallados

*Million UYU*

| | 1990 | 2000 | 2005 | 2007 | 2008 | 2009 | 2010 | 2011 | 2012 | 2013 |
|---|---|---|---|---|---|---|---|---|---|---|
| 5124 Taxes on exports | 1 | 92 | 287 | 311 | 371 | 349 | 371 | 446 | 432 | 422 |
| 5125 Taxes on investment goods | 0 | 0 | 0 | 0 | 0 | 0 | 0 | 0 | 0 | 0 |
| 5126 Taxes on specific services | 3 | 293 | 1 590 | 1 419 | 472 | 484 | 376 | 411 | 454 | 470 |
| 5127 Other taxes on internat. trade and transactions | 0 | 265 | 489 | 520 | 0 | 0 | 0 | 0 | 0 | 0 |
| 5128 Other taxes | 0 | 0 | 0 | 0 | 0 | 0 | 0 | 0 | 0 | 0 |
| 5130 Unallocable between 5110 and 5120 | 0 | 0 | 0 | 0 | 0 | 0 | 0 | 0 | 0 | 0 |
| 5200 Taxes on use of goods and perform activities | 64 | 2 576 | 3 071 | 3 753 | 4 135 | 3 848 | 3 952 | 4 113 | 4 534 | 4 600 |
| 5210 Recurrent taxes | 64 | 2 576 | 3 071 | 3 753 | 4 135 | 3 848 | 3 952 | 4 113 | 4 534 | 4 600 |
| 5211 Paid by households: motor vehicles | 0 | 0 | 0 | 0 | 0 | 0 | 0 | 0 | 0 | 0 |
| 5212 Paid by others: motor vehicles | 64 | 2 576 | 3 071 | 3 753 | 4 135 | 3 848 | 3 952 | 4 113 | 4 534 | 4 600 |
| 5213 Paid in respect of other goods | 0 | 0 | 0 | 0 | 0 | 0 | 0 | 0 | 0 | 0 |
| 5220 Non-recurrent taxes | 0 | 0 | 0 | 0 | 0 | 0 | 0 | 0 | 0 | 0 |
| 5300 Unallocable between 5100 and 5200 | 0 | 0 | 0 | 0 | 0 | 0 | 0 | 0 | 0 | 0 |
| **6000 Other taxes** | **-10** | **-596** | **76** | **63** | **8** | **82** | **0** | **0** | **0** | **214** |
| 6100 Paid solely by business | -10 | -596 | 76 | 63 | 8 | 82 | 0 | 0 | 0 | 214 |
| 6200 Other | 0 | 0 | 0 | 0 | 0 | 0 | 0 | 0 | 0 | 0 |

*Note:* Year ending 31st December.

The data are on cash basis.

Data on the following taxes are not available for 2013: Property tax (municipal), Rural property tax and Vehicle licences (municipal). This affects data in categories 4100 and 5200.

Heading 2000: Figures for 1990-1998 are reconstructed estimates, as the current methodology used to calculate social security contributions was not employed until 1999.

Headings 4000 and 5000: In ECLAC data, the tax on sales in public auctions is classified in category 4000.

Heading 5112: In ECLAC data, the tax on the sale of goods by public auctions is classified in category 4000.

*Source:* Dirección General Impositiva, Ministry of Economy and Finance. Banco de Previsión Social, Social Welfare Bank. Insituto Nacional de Estadistica, National Institute of Statistics.

StatLink http://dx.doi.org/10.1787/888933190400

## Table 36. Venezuela / Venezuela
Details of tax revenue / Ingresos tributarios detallados

*Million VEF*

| | 1990 | 2000 | 2005 | 2007 | 2008 | 2009 | 2010 | 2011 | 2012 | 2013 |
|---|---|---|---|---|---|---|---|---|---|---|
| **Total tax revenue** | **412** | **10 849** | **48 285** | **83 163** | **95 791** | **101 014** | **116 311** | **178 217** | **227 255** | **314 647** |
| **1000 Taxes on income, profits and capital gains** | **344** | **4 686** | **18 529** | **37 564** | **39 632** | **38 966** | **36 836** | **53 280** | **70 739** | **93 694** |
| 1100 Of individuals | .. | .. | .. | .. | .. | .. | .. | .. | .. | .. |
| 1110 On income and profits | .. | .. | .. | .. | .. | .. | .. | .. | .. | .. |
| 1120 On capital gains | .. | .. | .. | .. | .. | .. | .. | .. | .. | .. |
| 1200 Corporate | 315 | 3 368 | 11 184 | 19 959 | 17 834 | 12 944 | 8 700 | 16 510 | 22 879 | 25 270 |
| 1210 On profits | 315 | 3 368 | 11 184 | 19 959 | 17 834 | 12 944 | 8 700 | 16 510 | 22 879 | 25 270 |
| Oil | 315 | 3 368 | 11 184 | 19 959 | 17 834 | 12 944 | 8 700 | 16 510 | 22 879 | 25 270 |
| 1220 On capital gains | .. | .. | .. | .. | .. | .. | .. | .. | .. | .. |
| 1300 Unallocable between 1100 and 1200 | 30 | 1 317 | 7 345 | 17 606 | 21 798 | 26 022 | 28 137 | 36 770 | 47 859 | 68 424 |
| **2000 Social security contributions** | **20** | **591** | **1 890** | **4 218** | **5 085** | **6 740** | **5 547** | **7 405** | **9 435** | **10 000** |
| 2100 Employees | .. | .. | .. | .. | .. | .. | .. | .. | .. | .. |
| 2110 On a payroll basis | .. | .. | .. | .. | .. | .. | .. | .. | .. | .. |
| 2120 On an income tax basis | .. | .. | .. | .. | .. | .. | .. | .. | .. | .. |
| 2200 Employers | .. | .. | .. | .. | .. | .. | .. | .. | .. | .. |
| 2210 On a payroll basis | .. | .. | .. | .. | .. | .. | .. | .. | .. | .. |
| 2220 On an income tax basis | .. | .. | .. | .. | .. | .. | .. | .. | .. | .. |
| 2300 Self-employed or non-employed | .. | .. | .. | .. | .. | .. | .. | .. | .. | .. |
| 2310 On a payroll basis | .. | .. | .. | .. | .. | .. | .. | .. | .. | .. |
| 2320 On an income tax basis | .. | .. | .. | .. | .. | .. | .. | .. | .. | .. |
| 2400 Unallocable between 2100, 2200 and 2300 | 20 | 591 | 1 890 | 4 218 | 5 085 | 6 740 | 5 547 | 7 405 | 9 435 | 10 000 |
| 2410 On a payroll basis | .. | .. | .. | .. | .. | .. | .. | .. | .. | .. |
| 2420 On an income tax basis | .. | .. | .. | .. | .. | .. | .. | .. | .. | .. |
| **3000 Taxes on payroll and workforce** | **0** | **0** | **0** | **0** | **0** | **0** | **0** | **0** | **0** | **0** |
| **4000 Taxes on property** | **1** | **400** | **2 834** | **2 715** | **6 250** | **175** | **222** | **273** | **346** | **530** |
| 4100 Recurrent taxes on immovable property | 0 | 0 | 0 | 0 | 0 | 0 | 0 | 0 | 0 | 0 |
| 4110 Households | .. | .. | .. | .. | .. | .. | .. | .. | .. | .. |
| 4120 Others | .. | .. | .. | .. | .. | .. | .. | .. | .. | .. |
| 4200 Recurrent taxes on net wealth | 0 | 0 | 0 | 0 | 0 | 0 | 0 | 0 | 0 | 0 |
| 4210 Individual | .. | .. | .. | .. | .. | .. | .. | .. | .. | .. |
| 4220 Corporate | .. | .. | .. | .. | .. | .. | .. | .. | .. | .. |
| 4300 Estate, inheritance and gift taxes | 1 | 19 | 55 | 105 | 119 | 175 | 222 | 273 | 346 | 530 |
| 4310 Estate and inheritance taxes | .. | .. | .. | .. | .. | .. | .. | .. | .. | .. |
| 4320 Gift taxes | .. | .. | .. | .. | .. | .. | .. | .. | .. | .. |
| 4400 Taxes on financial and capital transactions | 0 | 381 | 2 779 | 2 610 | 6 132 | 0 | 0 | 0 | 0 | 0 |
| Bank debits | 0 | 292 | 2 743 | 2 610 | 6 132 | .. | .. | .. | .. | .. |
| Registration of immovable property rights | 0 | 89 | 36 | 0 | 0 | .. | .. | .. | .. | .. |
| 4500 Non-recurrent taxes | 0 | 0 | 0 | 0 | 0 | .. | .. | .. | .. | .. |
| 4510 On net wealth | .. | .. | .. | .. | .. | .. | .. | .. | .. | .. |
| 4520 Other non-recurrent taxes | .. | .. | .. | .. | .. | .. | .. | .. | .. | .. |
| 4600 Other recurrent taxes on property | 0 | 0 | 0 | 0 | 0 | 0 | 0 | 0 | 0 | 0 |
| **5000 Taxes on goods and services** | **46** | **5 173** | **25 032** | **38 667** | **44 824** | **55 134** | **73 707** | **108 268** | **141 505** | **205 423** |
| 5100 Taxes on production, sale, transfer, etc | 46 | 5 173 | 25 032 | 38 667 | 44 824 | 55 134 | 73 707 | 108 268 | 141 505 | 205 423 |
| 5110 General taxes | 0 | 3 272 | 19 513 | 27 895 | 31 396 | 41 611 | 56 101 | 84 348 | 111 102 | 164 737 |
| 5111 Value added taxes | .. | 3 272 | 19 513 | 27 895 | 31 396 | 41 611 | 56 101 | 84 348 | 111 102 | 164 737 |
| 5112 Sales tax | .. | 0 | 0 | 0 | 0 | 0 | 0 | 0 | 0 | 0 |
| 5113 Other | .. | 0 | 0 | 0 | 0 | 0 | 0 | 0 | 0 | 0 |
| 5120 Taxes on specific goods and services | 46 | 1 901 | 5 519 | 10 772 | 13 428 | 13 523 | 17 606 | 23 920 | 30 403 | 40 686 |
| 5121 Excises | 16 | 774 | 1 604 | 2 978 | 5 744 | 6 727 | 8 872 | 8 774 | 11 247 | 16 371 |
| Oil | 6 | 468 | 472 | 704 | 1 174 | 756 | 1 280 | 0 | 0 | 0 |
| Alcoholic beverages | 6 | 85 | 427 | 908 | 1 323 | 1 765 | 2 192 | 2 762 | 3 542 | 5 975 |
| Tobacco | 4 | 220 | 704 | 1 364 | 3 246 | 4 205 | 5 401 | 6 011 | 7 706 | 10 397 |
| Matches | 0 | 1 | 1 | 2 | 1 | 2 | 0 | 0 | 0 | 0 |
| 5122 Profits of fiscal monopolies | 0 | 0 | 0 | 0 | 0 | 0 | 0 | 0 | 0 | 0 |
| 5123 Customs and import duties | 30 | 972 | 3 652 | 7 573 | 7 267 | 6 409 | 8 504 | 15 017 | 19 052 | 24 185 |
| 5124 Taxes on exports | 0 | 0 | 0 | 0 | 0 | 0 | 0 | 0 | 0 | 0 |
| 5125 Taxes on investment goods | 0 | 0 | 0 | 0 | 0 | 0 | 0 | 0 | 0 | 0 |
| 5126 Taxes on specific services | 0 | 155 | 263 | 220 | 417 | 386 | 230 | 129 | 104 | 130 |
| Telecommunications | 0 | 151 | 237 | 166 | 247 | 183 | 0 | 0 | 0 | 0 |
| Casinos, bingo and slot machines | 0 | 5 | 26 | 55 | 171 | 203 | 230 | 129 | 104 | 130 |
| 5127 Other taxes on internat. trade and transactions | 0 | 0 | 0 | 0 | 0 | 0 | 0 | 0 | 0 | 0 |
| 5128 Other taxes | 0 | 0 | 0 | 0 | 0 | 0 | 0 | 0 | 0 | 0 |
| 5130 Unallocable between 5110 and 5120 | 0 | 0 | 0 | 0 | 0 | 0 | 0 | 0 | 0 | 0 |
| 5200 Taxes on use of goods and perform activities | 0 | 0 | 0 | 0 | 0 | 0 | 0 | 0 | 0 | 0 |
| 5210 Recurrent taxes | .. | .. | .. | .. | .. | .. | .. | .. | .. | .. |
| 5211 Paid by households: motor vehicles | .. | .. | .. | .. | .. | .. | .. | .. | .. | .. |
| 5212 Paid by others: motor vehicles | .. | .. | .. | .. | .. | .. | .. | .. | .. | .. |
| 5213 Paid in respect of other goods | .. | .. | .. | .. | .. | .. | .. | .. | .. | .. |

## Table 36. Venezuela / Venezuela *(cont.)*
### Details of tax revenue / Ingresos tributarios detallados

*Million VEF*

| | 1990 | 2000 | 2005 | 2007 | 2008 | 2009 | 2010 | 2011 | 2012 | 2013 |
|---|---|---|---|---|---|---|---|---|---|---|
| 5220 Non-recurrent taxes | .. | .. | .. | .. | .. | .. | .. | .. | .. | .. |
| 5300 Unallocable between 5100 and 5200 | 0 | 0 | 0 | 0 | 0 | 0 | 0 | 0 | 0 | 0 |
| **6000 Other taxes** | **0** | **0** | **0** | **0** | **0** | **0** | **0** | **8 991** | **5 230** | **5 000** |
| 6100 Paid solely by business | .. | .. | .. | .. | .. | .. | .. | 0 | 0 | 0 |
| 6200 Other | .. | .. | .. | .. | .. | .. | .. | 8 991 | 5 230 | 5 000 |

*Note:* Year ending 31st December.
The data are on cash basis.
The figures exclude state and local government tax revenues as the data are not available.
Heading 2000: The data on social security contributions were estimated for 2011 to 2013.
Heading 5121: Data oil excises are not available from 2011.
Heading 6000: The data on other taxes were estimated for 2013.
*Source:* Servicio Nacional Integrado de Administración Aduanera y Tributaria, Ministry of Finance.

StatLink http://dx.doi.org/10.1787/888933190414

# PART IV

# TAX REVENUES BY SUB-SECTORS OF GENERAL GOVERNMENT

# PARTE IV

# INGRESOS TRIBUTARIOS POR SUB-SECTORES DE GOBIERNO GENERAL

## Table 37. Attribution of tax revenues to sub-sectors of general government as percentage of total tax revenue[1]

## Cuadro 37. Atribución de los ingresos tributarios en los sub-sectores del gobierno general como porcentaje del ingreso tributario total[1]

| | Central government | | | State or regional government | | | Local government | | | Social security funds | | | |
|---|---|---|---|---|---|---|---|---|---|---|---|---|---|
| | 1995 | 2000 | 2012 | 1995 | 2000 | 2012 | 1995 | 2000 | 2012 | 1995 | 2000 | 2012 | |
| **Federal countries** | | | | | | | | | | | | | **Países federales** |
| Argentina | 59.0 | 66.4 | 62.7 | 17.5 | 17.8 | 15.1 | .. | .. | .. | 23.4 | 15.8 | 22.2 | Argentina |
| Brazil | 44.7 | 47.8 | 45.1 | 26.8 | 25.3 | 24.3 | 3.7 | 3.4 | 5.4 | 24.8 | 23.5 | 25.9 | Brasil |
| Mexico | 80.1 | 80.7 | 81.0 | 2.1 | 2.0 | 2.9 | 1.1 | 0.8 | 1.2 | 16.6 | 16.5 | 14.9 | México |
| Venezuela | 94.6 | 94.6 | 95.8 | .. | .. | .. | .. | .. | .. | 5.4 | 5.4 | 4.2 | Venezuela |
| OECD[2,3] | 53.3 | 56.5 | 54.5 | 15.9 | 15.3 | 16.5 | 7.7 | 6.9 | 7.6 | 22.9 | 21.1 | 21.3 | OCDE[2,3] |
| **Regional countries** | | | | | | | | | | | | | **Países regionales** |
| Colombia[4] | 63.2 | 68.6 | 76.4 | 5.5 | 5.6 | 4.2 | 8.6 | 9.4 | 10.3 | 22.7 | 16.4 | 9.0 | Colombia[4] |
| OECD[5] | 50.4 | 49.0 | 22.3 | 4.8 | 7.6 | 32.2 | 8.5 | 9.1 | 9.9 | 35.8 | 33.8 | 35.1 | OCDE[5] |
| **Unitary countries** | | | | | | | | | | | | | **Países unitarios** |
| Barbados | 85.3 | 84.3 | 81.6 | | | | .. | .. | .. | 14.7 | 15.7 | 18.4 | Barbados |
| Bolivia | 100.0 | 91.2 | 94.0 | | | | .. | .. | .. | .. | 8.7 | 6.0 | Bolivia |
| Chile | 89.9 | 87.8 | 88.2 | | | | 6.5 | 7.9 | 6.7 | 3.6 | 4.4 | 5.1 | Chile |
| Costa Rica | 66.2 | 65.3 | 61.7 | | | | .. | 2.1 | 3.0 | 33.8 | 32.6 | 35.3 | Costa Rica |
| Dominican Republic | 99.3 | 99.0 | 99.6 | | | | .. | .. | .. | 0.7 | 1.0 | 0.4 | República Dominicana |
| Ecuador | 73.9 | 87.7 | 72.1 | | | | .. | .. | .. | 26.1 | 12.3 | 27.9 | Ecuador |
| El Salvador | 85.9 | 83.6 | 89.3 | | | | .. | .. | .. | 14.1 | 16.4 | 10.7 | El Salvador |
| Guatemala | 83.8 | 83.6 | 83.0 | | | | 0.6 | 0.9 | 1.5 | 15.6 | 15.5 | 15.6 | Guatemala |
| Honduras | 90.1 | 89.4 | 82.9 | | | | .. | .. | .. | 9.9 | 10.6 | 17.1 | Honduras |
| Jamaica | 100.0 | 99.3 | 95.5 | | | | .. | 0.7 | 0.9 | .. | .. | 3.6 | Jamaica |
| Nicaragua | 84.0 | 80.1 | 77.1 | | | | .. | .. | .. | 16.0 | 19.9 | 22.9 | Nicaragua |
| Panama | 62.0 | 59.6 | 66.1 | | | | .. | 2.2 | 1.6 | 38.0 | 38.2 | 32.4 | Panamá |
| Paraguay | 100.0 | 82.7 | 80.6 | | | | .. | .. | 3.0 | .. | 17.3 | 16.4 | Paraguay[6] |
| Peru | 88.2 | 87.7 | 86.7 | | | | .. | .. | 3.1 | 11.8 | 12.3 | 10.1 | Perú |
| Uruguay | 62.0 | 62.5 | 70.0 | | | | 7.8 | 7.9 | 3.9 | 30.1 | 29.6 | 26.1 | Uruguay |
| OECD[2,6] | 65.8 | 66.4 | 62.9 | | | | 10.7 | 11.0 | 12.0 | 23.2 | 22.3 | 24.8 | OCDE[2,6] |

1. The figures exclude local government revenues for Argentina (but include provincial revenues), Barbados, Bolivia, Costa Rica (up to 1997), Dominican Republic, Ecuador, El Salvador, Honduras, Jamaica, Nicaragua, Panama (up to 1998), Paraguay (up to 2004 and 2013), Peru (up to 2004), Uruguay (2013) and Venezuela as the data are not available.
1. Las cifras excluyen los ingresos de gobiernos locales en Argentina (pero incluye ingresos de las provincias), Barbados, Bolivia, Costa Rica (hasta 1997), República Dominicana, Ecuador, El Salvador, Honduras, Jamaica, Nicaragua, Panamá (hasta 1998), Paraguay (hasta 2004 y 2013), Perú (hasta 2004), Uruguay (2013) y Venezuela dado que los datos no están disponibles.
2. Chile and Mexico are also part of the OECD group.
2. Chile y México son también parte del grupo OCDE.
3. Represents the unweighted average for OECD federal member countries.
3. Representa el promedio no ponderado para los países federales miembros de la OCDE.
4. Colombia is constitutionally a unitary country with high autonomy of its territorial entities.
4. Colombia es constitucionalmente un país unitario con una estructura política descentralizada.
5. Represents Spain, which is constitutionally a non-federal country with a highly decentralised political structure.
5. Representa a España, que es constitucionalmente un país no federal con una estructura política altamente descentralizada.
6. Represents the unweighted average for OECD unitary countries.
6. Representa el promedio no ponderado para los países unitarios miembros de la OCDE.

StatLink http://dx.doi.org/10.1787/888933190589

## Table 38. Argentina, tax revenues by sub-sectors of government

*Million ARS*

| | Federal government | | | | | State/Regional | | | | |
|---|---|---|---|---|---|---|---|---|---|---|
| | 1990 | 2000 | 2005 | 2010 | 2013 | 1990 | 2000 | 2005 | 2010 | 2013 |
| **1000 Taxes on income, profits and capital gains** | **382** | **11 304** | **29 202** | **78 428** | **185 688** | **0** | **0** | **0** | **0** | **0** |
| 1100 Of individuals | 12 | 3 937 | 8 192 | 23 981 | 79 582 | .. | .. | .. | .. | .. |
| 1200 Corporate | .. | 6 575 | 19 601 | 50 664 | 99 470 | .. | .. | .. | .. | .. |
| 1300 Unallocable between 1100 and 1200 | 371 | 792 | 1 409 | 3 783 | 6 636 | .. | .. | .. | .. | .. |
| **2000 Social security contributions** | **0** | **0** | **0** | **0** | **0** | **0** | **0** | **0** | **0** | **0** |
| 2100 Employees | .. | .. | .. | .. | .. | .. | .. | .. | .. | .. |
| 2200 Employers | .. | .. | .. | .. | .. | .. | .. | .. | .. | .. |
| 2300 Self-employed or non-employed | .. | .. | .. | .. | .. | .. | .. | .. | .. | .. |
| 2400 Unallocable between 2100, 2200 and 2300 | .. | .. | .. | .. | .. | .. | .. | .. | .. | .. |
| **3000 Taxes on payroll and workforce** | **0** | **0** | **0** | **0** | **0** | **0** | **0** | **0** | **0** | **0** |
| **4000 Taxes on property** | **730** | **1 254** | **11 439** | **32 675** | **67 720** | **572** | **2 642** | **4 558** | **10 864** | **28 670** |
| 4100 Recurrent taxes on immovable property | 0 | 0 | 0 | 0 | 0 | 412 | 1 809 | 2 836 | 5 035 | 14 038 |
| 4200 Recurrent taxes on net wealth | 235 | 1 084 | 1 868 | 5 248 | 10 471 | 0 | 0 | 0 | 0 | 0 |
| 4300 Estate, inheritance and gift taxes | 0 | 0 | 0 | 0 | 0 | 0 | 0 | 0 | 0 | 0 |
| 4400 Taxes on financial and capital transactions | 496 | 100 | 9 550 | 27 424 | 57 249 | 160 | 833 | 1 722 | 5 829 | 14 632 |
| 4500 Non-recurrent taxes | 0 | 70 | 21 | 3 | 0 | 0 | 0 | 0 | 0 | 0 |
| 4600 Other recurrent taxes on property | 0 | 0 | 0 | 0 | 0 | 0 | 0 | 0 | 0 | 0 |
| **5000 Taxes on goods and services** | **4 713** | **27 592** | **62 058** | **198 346** | **375 908** | **979** | **6 918** | **15 902** | **54 746** | **140 780** |
| 5100 Taxes on production, sale, transfer, etc | 4 713 | 27 592 | 62 058 | 198 346 | 375 908 | 846 | 6 114 | 14 613 | 51 148 | 132 124 |
| 5110 General taxes | 1 591 | 18 427 | 34 968 | 113 330 | 243 612 | 846 | 6 114 | 14 613 | 51 148 | 132 124 |
| 5120 Taxes on specific goods and services | 3 122 | 9 165 | 27 090 | 85 016 | 132 296 | 0 | 0 | 0 | 0 | 0 |
| 5130 Unallocable between 5110 and 5120 | 0 | 0 | 0 | 0 | 0 | 0 | 0 | 0 | 0 | 0 |
| 5200 Taxes on use of goods and perform activities[1] | 0 | 0 | 0 | 0 | 0 | 133 | 804 | 1 289 | 3 598 | 8 656 |
| 5300 Unallocable between 5100 and 5200 | 0 | 0 | 0 | 0 | 0 | 0 | 0 | 0 | 0 | 0 |
| **6000 Other taxes** | **215** | **396** | **877** | **2 386** | **3 110** | **43** | **1 309** | **1 469** | **3 110** | **5 100** |
| 6100 Paid solely by business | 0 | 354 | 757 | 2 093 | 4 423 | 0 | 0 | 0 | 0 | 0 |
| 6200 Other | 215 | 42 | 120 | 293 | -1 313 | 43 | 1 309 | 1 469 | 3 110 | 5 100 |
| **Total tax revenue** | **6 041** | **40 546** | **103 576** | **311 835** | **632 426** | **1 594** | **10 869** | **21 929** | **68 720** | **174 550** |

*Million ARS*

| | Local government[2] | | | | | Social Security Funds | | | | |
|---|---|---|---|---|---|---|---|---|---|---|
| | 1990 | 2000 | 2005 | 2010 | 2013 | 1990 | 2000 | 2005 | 2010 | 2013 |
| **1000 Taxes on income, profits and capital gains** | .. | .. | .. | .. | .. | **0** | **0** | **0** | **0** | **0** |
| 1100 Of individuals | .. | .. | .. | .. | .. | .. | .. | .. | .. | .. |
| 1200 Corporate | .. | .. | .. | .. | .. | .. | .. | .. | .. | .. |
| 1300 Unallocable between 1100 and 1200 | .. | .. | .. | .. | .. | .. | .. | .. | .. | .. |
| **2000 Social security contributions** | .. | .. | .. | .. | .. | **2 583** | **9 670** | **17 400** | **102 460** | **236 072** |
| 2100 Employees | .. | .. | .. | .. | .. | .. | 2 486 | 3 690 | 37 990 | 91 768 |
| 2200 Employers | .. | .. | .. | .. | .. | .. | 6 069 | 12 557 | 54 713 | 133 290 |
| 2300 Self-employed or non-employed | .. | .. | .. | .. | .. | 98 | 1 115 | 1 153 | 9 757 | 11 014 |
| 2400 Unallocable between 2100, 2200 and 2300 | .. | .. | .. | .. | .. | 2 485 | 0 | 0 | 0 | 0 |
| **3000 Taxes on payroll and workforce** | .. | .. | .. | .. | .. | **0** | **0** | **0** | **0** | **0** |
| **4000 Taxes on property** | .. | .. | .. | .. | .. | **0** | **0** | **0** | **0** | **0** |
| 4100 Recurrent taxes on immovable property | .. | .. | .. | .. | .. | .. | .. | .. | .. | .. |
| 4200 Recurrent taxes on net wealth | .. | .. | .. | .. | .. | .. | .. | .. | .. | .. |
| 4300 Estate, inheritance and gift taxes | .. | .. | .. | .. | .. | .. | .. | .. | .. | .. |
| 4400 Taxes on financial and capital transactions | .. | .. | .. | .. | .. | .. | .. | .. | .. | .. |
| 4500 Non-recurrent taxes | .. | .. | .. | .. | .. | .. | .. | .. | .. | .. |
| 4600 Other recurrent taxes on property | .. | .. | .. | .. | .. | .. | .. | .. | .. | .. |
| **5000 Taxes on goods and services** | .. | .. | .. | .. | .. | **0** | **0** | **0** | **0** | **0** |
| 5100 Taxes on production, sale, transfer, etc | .. | .. | .. | .. | .. | .. | .. | .. | .. | .. |
| 5110 General taxes | .. | .. | .. | .. | .. | .. | .. | .. | .. | .. |
| 5120 Taxes on specific goods and services | .. | .. | .. | .. | .. | .. | .. | .. | .. | .. |
| 5130 Unallocable between 5110 and 5120 | .. | .. | .. | .. | .. | .. | .. | .. | .. | .. |
| 5200 Taxes on use of goods and perform activities[1] | .. | .. | .. | .. | .. | .. | .. | .. | .. | .. |
| 5300 Unallocable between 5100 and 5200 | .. | .. | .. | .. | .. | .. | .. | .. | .. | .. |
| **6000 Other taxes** | .. | .. | .. | .. | .. | **0** | **0** | **0** | **0** | **0** |
| 6100 Paid solely by business | .. | .. | .. | .. | .. | .. | .. | .. | .. | .. |
| 6200 Other | .. | .. | .. | .. | .. | .. | .. | .. | .. | .. |
| **Total tax revenue** | .. | .. | .. | .. | .. | **2 583** | **9 670** | **17 400** | **102 460** | **236 072** |

1. In ECLAC data, property tax on motor vehicles is classified in category 4000.
2. The figures exclude local government tax revenues as the data are not available.

StatLink http://dx.doi.org/10.1787/888933190026

## Table 39. Barbados, tax revenues by sub-sectors of government

*Million BAR*

| | Federal government | | | | | State/Regional | | | | |
|---|---|---|---|---|---|---|---|---|---|---|
| | 1990 | 2000 | 2005 | 2010 | 2013 | 1990 | 2000 | 2005 | 2010 | 2013 |
| **1000 Taxes on income, profits and capital gains** | **254 016** | **573 920** | **639 432** | **762 340** | **601 963** | .. | .. | .. | .. | .. |
| 1100 Of individuals | 128 857 | 288 692 | 295 737 | 388 177 | 331 318 | .. | .. | .. | .. | .. |
| 1200 Corporate | 111 111 | 252 291 | 294 320 | 327 471 | 191 330 | .. | .. | .. | .. | .. |
| 1300 Unallocable between 1100 and 1200 | 14 048 | 32 937 | 49 375 | 46 692 | 79 315 | .. | .. | .. | .. | .. |
| **2000 Social security contributions** | **0** | **0** | **0** | **0** | **0** | .. | .. | .. | .. | .. |
| 2100 Employees | .. | .. | .. | .. | .. | .. | .. | .. | .. | .. |
| 2200 Employers | .. | .. | .. | .. | .. | .. | .. | .. | .. | .. |
| 2300 Self-employed or non-employed | .. | .. | .. | .. | .. | .. | .. | .. | .. | .. |
| 2400 Unallocable between 2100, 2200 and 2300 | .. | .. | .. | .. | .. | .. | .. | .. | .. | .. |
| **3000 Taxes on payroll and workforce** | **0** | **0** | **0** | **0** | **0** | .. | .. | .. | .. | .. |
| **4000 Taxes on property** | **39 117** | **91 928** | **127 362** | **113 533** | **124 972** | .. | .. | .. | .. | .. |
| 4100 Recurrent taxes on immovable property | 25 991 | 60 216 | 76 247 | 97 595 | 109 436 | .. | .. | .. | .. | .. |
| 4200 Recurrent taxes on net wealth | 0 | 0 | 0 | 0 | 0 | .. | .. | .. | .. | .. |
| 4300 Estate, inheritance and gift taxes | 0 | 0 | 0 | 0 | 0 | .. | .. | .. | .. | .. |
| 4400 Taxes on financial and capital transactions | 0 | 0 | 0 | 0 | 0 | .. | .. | .. | .. | .. |
| 4500 Non-recurrent taxes | 13 126 | 31 712 | 51 115 | 15 938 | 15 536 | .. | .. | .. | .. | .. |
| 4600 Other recurrent taxes on property | 0 | 0 | 0 | 0 | 0 | .. | .. | .. | .. | .. |
| **5000 Taxes on goods and services** | **422 259** | **897 092** | **1 101 319** | **1 242 416** | **1 252 138** | .. | .. | .. | .. | .. |
| 5100 Taxes on production, sale, transfer, etc | 422 259 | 793 469 | 973 944 | 1 092 106 | 1 145 269 | .. | .. | .. | .. | .. |
| 5110 General taxes | 196 817 | 501 399 | 609 915 | 753 003 | 821 305 | .. | .. | .. | .. | .. |
| 5120 Taxes on specific goods and services | 225 442 | 292 069 | 364 029 | 339 103 | 323 964 | .. | .. | .. | .. | .. |
| 5130 Unallocable between 5110 and 5120 | 0 | 0 | 0 | 0 | 0 | .. | .. | .. | .. | .. |
| 5200 Taxes on use of goods and perform activities | 0 | 103 623 | 127 375 | 150 310 | 106 869 | .. | .. | .. | .. | .. |
| 5300 Unallocable between 5100 and 5200 | 0 | 0 | 0 | 0 | 0 | .. | .. | .. | .. | .. |
| **6000 Other taxes** | **93 077** | **26 105** | **20 787** | **75 546** | **31 302** | .. | .. | .. | .. | .. |
| 6100 Paid solely by business | 0 | 0 | 0 | 0 | 0 | .. | .. | .. | .. | .. |
| 6200 Other | 93 077 | 26 105 | 20 787 | 75 546 | 31 302 | .. | .. | .. | .. | .. |
| **Total tax revenue** | **808 469** | **1 589 045** | **1 888 901** | **2 193 835** | **2 010 375** | .. | .. | .. | .. | .. |

*Million BAR*

| | Local government[1] | | | | | Social Security Funds | | | | |
|---|---|---|---|---|---|---|---|---|---|---|
| | 1990 | 2000 | 2005 | 2010 | 2013 | 1990 | 2000 | 2005 | 2010 | 2013 |
| **1000 Taxes on income, profits and capital gains** | .. | .. | .. | .. | .. | **0** | **0** | **0** | **0** | **0** |
| 1100 Of individuals | .. | .. | .. | .. | .. | .. | .. | .. | .. | .. |
| 1200 Corporate | .. | .. | .. | .. | .. | .. | .. | .. | .. | .. |
| 1300 Unallocable between 1100 and 1200 | .. | .. | .. | .. | .. | .. | .. | .. | .. | .. |
| **2000 Social security contributions** | .. | .. | .. | .. | .. | **133 866** | **295 268** | **408 109** | **525 467** | **512 521** |
| 2100 Employees | .. | .. | .. | .. | .. | .. | .. | .. | .. | .. |
| 2200 Employers | .. | .. | .. | .. | .. | .. | .. | .. | .. | .. |
| 2300 Self-employed or non-employed | .. | .. | .. | .. | .. | .. | .. | .. | .. | .. |
| 2400 Unallocable between 2100, 2200 and 2300 | .. | .. | .. | .. | .. | 133 866 | 295 268 | 408 109 | 525 467 | 512 521 |
| **3000 Taxes on payroll and workforce** | .. | .. | .. | .. | .. | **0** | **0** | **0** | **0** | **0** |
| **4000 Taxes on property** | .. | .. | .. | .. | .. | **0** | **0** | **0** | **0** | **0** |
| 4100 Recurrent taxes on immovable property | .. | .. | .. | .. | .. | .. | .. | .. | .. | .. |
| 4200 Recurrent taxes on net wealth | .. | .. | .. | .. | .. | .. | .. | .. | .. | .. |
| 4300 Estate, inheritance and gift taxes | .. | .. | .. | .. | .. | .. | .. | .. | .. | .. |
| 4400 Taxes on financial and capital transactions | .. | .. | .. | .. | .. | .. | .. | .. | .. | .. |
| 4500 Non-recurrent taxes | .. | .. | .. | .. | .. | .. | .. | .. | .. | .. |
| 4600 Other recurrent taxes on property | .. | .. | .. | .. | .. | .. | .. | .. | .. | .. |
| **5000 Taxes on goods and services** | .. | .. | .. | .. | .. | **0** | **0** | **0** | **0** | **0** |
| 5100 Taxes on production, sale, transfer, etc | .. | .. | .. | .. | .. | .. | .. | .. | .. | .. |
| 5110 General taxes | .. | .. | .. | .. | .. | .. | .. | .. | .. | .. |
| 5120 Taxes on specific goods and services | .. | .. | .. | .. | .. | .. | .. | .. | .. | .. |
| 5130 Unallocable between 5110 and 5120 | .. | .. | .. | .. | .. | .. | .. | .. | .. | .. |
| 5200 Taxes on use of goods and perform activities | .. | .. | .. | .. | .. | .. | .. | .. | .. | .. |
| 5300 Unallocable between 5100 and 5200 | .. | .. | .. | .. | .. | .. | .. | .. | .. | .. |
| **6000 Other taxes** | .. | .. | .. | .. | .. | **0** | **0** | **0** | **0** | **0** |
| 6100 Paid solely by business | .. | .. | .. | .. | .. | .. | .. | .. | .. | .. |
| 6200 Other | .. | .. | .. | .. | .. | .. | .. | .. | .. | .. |
| **Total tax revenue** | .. | .. | .. | .. | .. | **133 866** | **295 268** | **408 109** | **525 467** | **512 521** |

1. The figures exclude local government tax revenues as the data are not available.

StatLink http://dx.doi.org/10.1787/888933190034

## Table 40. Bolivia, tax revenues by sub-sectors of government

*Million BOB*

| | Federal government | | | | | State/Regional | | | | |
|---|---|---|---|---|---|---|---|---|---|---|
| | 1990 | 2000 | 2005 | 2010 | 2013 | 1990 | 2000 | 2005 | 2010 | 2013 |
| **1000 Taxes on income, profits and capital gains** | **123** | **967** | **2 058** | **5 326** | **8 246** | .. | .. | .. | .. | .. |
| 1100 Of individuals | .. | .. | .. | .. | .. | .. | .. | .. | .. | .. |
| 1200 Corporate | 61 | 806 | 1 871 | 5 089 | 7 914 | .. | .. | .. | .. | .. |
| 1300 Unallocable between 1100 and 1200 | 62 | 161 | 187 | 237 | 333 | .. | .. | .. | .. | .. |
| **2000 Social security contributions[1]** | **0** | **0** | **0** | **0** | **0** | .. | .. | .. | .. | .. |
| 2100 Employees | .. | .. | .. | .. | .. | .. | .. | .. | .. | .. |
| 2200 Employers | .. | .. | .. | .. | .. | .. | .. | .. | .. | .. |
| 2300 Self-employed or non-employed | .. | .. | .. | .. | .. | .. | .. | .. | .. | .. |
| 2400 Unallocable between 2100, 2200 and 2300 | .. | .. | .. | .. | .. | .. | .. | .. | .. | .. |
| **3000 Taxes on payroll and workforce** | **0** | **0** | **0** | **0** | **0** | .. | .. | .. | .. | .. |
| **4000 Taxes on property** | **208** | **946** | **2 094** | **2 541** | **3 993** | .. | .. | .. | .. | .. |
| 4100 Recurrent taxes on immovable property | 0 | 0 | 0 | 0 | 0 | .. | .. | .. | .. | .. |
| 4200 Recurrent taxes on net wealth | 0 | 0 | 0 | 0 | 0 | .. | .. | .. | .. | .. |
| 4300 Estate, inheritance and gift taxes | 1 | 3 | 7 | 20 | 28 | .. | .. | .. | .. | .. |
| 4400 Taxes on financial and capital transactions | 136 | 943 | 2 087 | 2 521 | 3 965 | .. | .. | .. | .. | .. |
| 4500 Non-recurrent taxes | 0 | 0 | 0 | 0 | 0 | .. | .. | .. | .. | .. |
| 4600 Other recurrent taxes on property | 71 | 0 | 0 | 0 | 0 | .. | .. | .. | .. | .. |
| **5000 Taxes on goods and services** | **786** | **5 206** | **9 674** | **20 011** | **39 817** | .. | .. | .. | .. | .. |
| 5100 Taxes on production, sale, transfer, etc | 786 | 5 206 | 9 674 | 20 011 | 39 817 | .. | .. | .. | .. | .. |
| 5110 General taxes | 497 | 2 649 | 4 574 | 9 293 | 16 514 | .. | .. | .. | .. | .. |
| 5120 Taxes on specific goods and services | 289 | 2 557 | 5 100 | 10 718 | 23 303 | .. | .. | .. | .. | .. |
| 5130 Unallocable between 5110 and 5120 | 0 | 0 | 0 | 0 | 0 | .. | .. | .. | .. | .. |
| 5200 Taxes on use of goods and perform activities | 0 | 0 | 0 | 0 | 0 | .. | .. | .. | .. | .. |
| 5300 Unallocable between 5100 and 5200 | 0 | 0 | 0 | 0 | 0 | .. | .. | .. | .. | .. |
| **6000 Other taxes** | **-28** | **-170** | **-209** | **-1 451** | **3 226** | .. | .. | .. | .. | .. |
| 6100 Paid solely by business | 4 | 6 | 4 | 12 | 17 | .. | .. | .. | .. | .. |
| 6200 Other[2] | -33 | -176 | -214 | -1 463 | 3 209 | .. | .. | .. | .. | .. |
| **Total tax revenue** | **1 088** | **6 949** | **13 617** | **26 428** | **55 282** | .. | .. | .. | .. | .. |

*Million BOB*

| | Local government[3] | | | | | Social Security Funds | | | | |
|---|---|---|---|---|---|---|---|---|---|---|
| | 1990 | 2000 | 2005 | 2010 | 2013 | 1990 | 2000 | 2005 | 2010 | 2013 |
| **1000 Taxes on income, profits and capital gains** | .. | .. | .. | .. | .. | .. | **0** | **0** | **0** | **0** |
| 1100 Of individuals | .. | .. | .. | .. | .. | .. | .. | .. | .. | .. |
| 1200 Corporate | .. | .. | .. | .. | .. | .. | .. | .. | .. | .. |
| 1300 Unallocable between 1100 and 1200 | .. | .. | .. | .. | .. | .. | .. | .. | .. | .. |
| **2000 Social security contributions[1]** | .. | .. | .. | .. | .. | .. | **666** | **936** | **1 645** | **3 000** |
| 2100 Employees | .. | .. | .. | .. | .. | .. | .. | .. | .. | .. |
| 2200 Employers | .. | .. | .. | .. | .. | .. | .. | .. | .. | .. |
| 2300 Self-employed or non-employed | .. | .. | .. | .. | .. | .. | .. | .. | .. | .. |
| 2400 Unallocable between 2100, 2200 and 2300 | .. | .. | .. | .. | .. | .. | 666 | 936 | 1 645 | 3 000 |
| **3000 Taxes on payroll and workforce** | .. | .. | .. | .. | .. | .. | **0** | **0** | **0** | **0** |
| **4000 Taxes on property** | .. | .. | .. | .. | .. | .. | **0** | **0** | **0** | **0** |
| 4100 Recurrent taxes on immovable property | .. | .. | .. | .. | .. | .. | .. | .. | .. | .. |
| 4200 Recurrent taxes on net wealth | .. | .. | .. | .. | .. | .. | .. | .. | .. | .. |
| 4300 Estate, inheritance and gift taxes | .. | .. | .. | .. | .. | .. | .. | .. | .. | .. |
| 4400 Taxes on financial and capital transactions | .. | .. | .. | .. | .. | .. | .. | .. | .. | .. |
| 4500 Non-recurrent taxes | .. | .. | .. | .. | .. | .. | .. | .. | .. | .. |
| 4600 Other recurrent taxes on property | .. | .. | .. | .. | .. | .. | .. | .. | .. | .. |
| **5000 Taxes on goods and services** | .. | .. | .. | .. | .. | .. | **0** | **0** | **0** | **0** |
| 5100 Taxes on production, sale, transfer, etc | .. | .. | .. | .. | .. | .. | .. | .. | .. | .. |
| 5110 General taxes | .. | .. | .. | .. | .. | .. | .. | .. | .. | .. |
| 5120 Taxes on specific goods and services | .. | .. | .. | .. | .. | .. | .. | .. | .. | .. |
| 5130 Unallocable between 5110 and 5120 | .. | .. | .. | .. | .. | .. | .. | .. | .. | .. |
| 5200 Taxes on use of goods and perform activities | .. | .. | .. | .. | .. | .. | .. | .. | .. | .. |
| 5300 Unallocable between 5100 and 5200 | .. | .. | .. | .. | .. | .. | .. | .. | .. | .. |
| **6000 Other taxes** | .. | .. | .. | .. | .. | .. | **0** | **0** | **0** | **0** |
| 6100 Paid solely by business | .. | .. | .. | .. | .. | .. | .. | .. | .. | .. |
| 6200 Other[2] | .. | .. | .. | .. | .. | .. | .. | .. | .. | .. |
| **Total tax revenue** | .. | .. | .. | .. | .. | .. | **666** | **936** | **1 645** | **3 000** |

1. The data for social security contributions are available from the year 2000 only and are estimated for 2013.
2. The data are estimated from 2011 onwards.
3. The figures exclude local government tax revenues as the data are not available.

StatLink http://dx.doi.org/10.1787/888933190040

## Table 41. Brazil, tax revenues by sub-sectors of government

*Million BRL*

| | Federal government | | | | | State/Regional | | | | |
|---|---|---|---|---|---|---|---|---|---|---|
| | 1990 | 2000 | 2005 | 2010 | 2013 | 1990 | 2000 | 2005 | 2010 | 2013 |
| **1000 Taxes on income, profits and capital gains** | **1** | **68 667** | **149 309** | **258 736** | **360 578** | **0** | **0** | **0** | **0** | **0** |
| 1100 Of individuals | 0 | 3 406 | 6 981 | 16 248 | 24 188 | .. | .. | .. | .. | .. |
| 1200 Corporate | 0 | 25 430 | 73 071 | 128 255 | 171 003 | .. | .. | .. | .. | .. |
| 1300 Unallocable between 1100 and 1200 | 0 | 39 831 | 69 257 | 114 233 | 165 386 | .. | .. | .. | .. | .. |
| **2000 Social security contributions** | **0** | **0** | **0** | **0** | **0** | **0** | **0** | **0** | **0** | **0** |
| 2100 Employees | .. | .. | .. | .. | .. | .. | .. | .. | .. | .. |
| 2200 Employers | .. | .. | .. | .. | .. | .. | .. | .. | .. | .. |
| 2300 Self-employed or non-employed | .. | .. | .. | .. | .. | .. | .. | .. | .. | .. |
| 2400 Unallocable between 2100, 2200 and 2300 | .. | .. | .. | .. | .. | .. | .. | .. | .. | .. |
| **3000 Taxes on payroll and workforce[1]** | **0** | **6 749** | **14 469** | **23 173** | **34 596** | **0** | **0** | **0** | **0** | **0** |
| **4000 Taxes on property** | **0** | **17 726** | **35 282** | **27 038** | **30 181** | **0** | **5 623** | **11 282** | **23 885** | **33 374** |
| 4100 Recurrent taxes on immovable property | 0 | 234 | 288 | 485 | 764 | 0 | 0 | 0 | 0 | 0 |
| 4200 Recurrent taxes on net wealth | 0 | 0 | 0 | 0 | 0 | 0 | 0 | 0 | 0 | 0 |
| 4300 Estate, inheritance and gift taxes | 0 | 0 | 0 | 0 | 0 | 0 | 329 | 821 | 2 518 | 4 142 |
| 4400 Taxes on financial and capital transactions | 0 | 17 492 | 34 994 | 26 553 | 29 417 | 0 | 0 | 0 | 0 | 0 |
| 4500 Non-recurrent taxes | 0 | 0 | 0 | 0 | 0 | 0 | 0 | 0 | 0 | 0 |
| 4600 Other recurrent taxes on property | 0 | 0 | 0 | 0 | 0 | 0 | 5 294 | 10 460 | 21 367 | 29 232 |
| **5000 Taxes on goods and services** | **1** | **74 190** | **147 819** | **251 267** | **334 296** | **1** | **83 848** | **158 809** | **268 117** | **364 525** |
| 5100 Taxes on production, sale, transfer, etc | 1 | 74 190 | 147 819 | 251 267 | 334 296 | 1 | 82 279 | 153 437 | 268 117 | 364 525 |
| 5110 General taxes[1] | 1 | 65 745 | 129 567 | 206 904 | 278 617 | 1 | 82 279 | 153 437 | 268 117 | 364 525 |
| 5120 Taxes on specific goods and services | 0 | 8 445 | 18 252 | 44 363 | 55 679 | 0 | 0 | 0 | 0 | 0 |
| 5130 Unallocable between 5110 and 5120 | .. | 0 | 0 | 0 | 0 | 0 | 0 | 0 | 0 | 0 |
| 5200 Taxes on use of goods and perform activities | 0 | 0 | 0 | 0 | 0 | 0 | 1 569 | 5 372 | 0 | 0 |
| 5300 Unallocable between 5100 and 5200 | 0 | 0 | 0 | 0 | 0 | 0 | 0 | 0 | 0 | 0 |
| **6000 Other taxes[2]** | **0** | **2 337** | **2 039** | **15 545** | **19 076** | **0** | **322** | **1 551** | **17 135** | **26 645** |
| 6100 Paid solely by business | 0 | 0 | 277 | 0 | 0 | 0 | 0 | 0 | 0 | 0 |
| 6200 Other[1] | 0 | 2 337 | 1 761 | 15 545 | 19 076 | 0 | 322 | 1 551 | 17 135 | 26 645 |
| **Total tax revenue** | **1** | **169 669** | **348 918** | **575 759** | **778 728** | **1** | **89 793** | **171 641** | **309 137** | **424 544** |

*Million BRL*

| | Local government | | | | | Social Security Funds | | | | |
|---|---|---|---|---|---|---|---|---|---|---|
| | 1990 | 2000 | 2005 | 2010 | 2013 | 1990 | 2000 | 2005 | 2010 | 2013 |
| **1000 Taxes on income, profits and capital gains** | **0** | **0** | **0** | **0** | **0** | **0** | **0** | **0** | **0** | **0** |
| 1100 Of individuals | .. | .. | .. | .. | .. | .. | .. | .. | .. | .. |
| 1200 Corporate | .. | .. | .. | .. | .. | .. | .. | .. | .. | .. |
| 1300 Unallocable between 1100 and 1200 | .. | .. | .. | .. | .. | .. | .. | .. | .. | .. |
| **2000 Social security contributions** | **0** | **0** | **0** | **0** | **0** | **1** | **83 469** | **168 226** | **314 868** | **444 278** |
| 2100 Employees | .. | .. | .. | .. | .. | .. | .. | .. | .. | .. |
| 2200 Employers | .. | .. | .. | .. | .. | 0 | 18 709 | 32 248 | 64 271 | 98 045 |
| 2300 Self-employed or non-employed | .. | .. | .. | .. | .. | .. | .. | .. | .. | .. |
| 2400 Unallocable between 2100, 2200 and 2300 | .. | .. | .. | .. | .. | 1 | 64 760 | 135 978 | 250 597 | 346 234 |
| **3000 Taxes on payroll and workforce[1]** | **0** | **0** | **0** | **0** | **0** | **0** | **0** | **0** | **0** | **0** |
| **4000 Taxes on property** | **0** | **5 469** | **9 710** | **23 450** | **34 270** | **0** | **0** | **0** | **0** | **0** |
| 4100 Recurrent taxes on immovable property | 0 | 4 519 | 8 117 | 17 443 | 24 316 | .. | .. | .. | .. | .. |
| 4200 Recurrent taxes on net wealth | 0 | 0 | 0 | 0 | 0 | .. | .. | .. | .. | .. |
| 4300 Estate, inheritance and gift taxes | 0 | 0 | 0 | 0 | 0 | .. | .. | .. | .. | .. |
| 4400 Taxes on financial and capital transactions | 0 | 950 | 1 593 | 6 007 | 9 954 | .. | .. | .. | .. | .. |
| 4500 Non-recurrent taxes | 0 | 0 | 0 | 0 | 0 | .. | .. | .. | .. | .. |
| 4600 Other recurrent taxes on property | 0 | 0 | 0 | 0 | 0 | .. | .. | .. | .. | .. |
| **5000 Taxes on goods and services** | **0** | **6 106** | **11 247** | **32 755** | **48 180** | **0** | **0** | **0** | **0** | **0** |
| 5100 Taxes on production, sale, transfer, etc | 0 | 6 106 | 11 247 | 32 755 | 48 180 | .. | .. | .. | .. | .. |
| 5110 General taxes[1] | 0 | 6 106 | 11 247 | 32 755 | 48 180 | .. | .. | .. | .. | .. |
| 5120 Taxes on specific goods and services | 0 | 0 | 0 | 0 | 0 | .. | .. | .. | .. | .. |
| 5130 Unallocable between 5110 and 5120 | 0 | 0 | 0 | 0 | 0 | .. | .. | .. | .. | .. |
| 5200 Taxes on use of goods and perform activities | 0 | 0 | 0 | 0 | 0 | .. | .. | .. | .. | .. |
| 5300 Unallocable between 5100 and 5200 | 0 | 0 | 0 | 0 | 0 | .. | .. | .. | .. | .. |
| **6000 Other taxes[2]** | **0** | **377** | **1 404** | **8 399** | **10 795** | **0** | **0** | **0** | **0** | **0** |
| 6100 Paid solely by business | 0 | 0 | 0 | 0 | 0 | .. | .. | .. | .. | .. |
| 6200 Other[1] | 0 | 377 | 1 404 | 8 399 | 10 795 | .. | .. | .. | .. | .. |
| **Total tax revenue** | **0** | **11 952** | **22 360** | **64 603** | **93 246** | **1** | **83 469** | **168 226** | **314 868** | **444 278** |

1. For years prior to 2000 and from 2009 onwards the PASEP (Program of Formation of the Patrimony of the Public Servants) contributions are combined with PIS (Social Integration Program) contributions in heading 5110.
2. From 2008 FUNDAF (Special Fund for Development and Improvement of Auditing Activities) contributions are included in heading 6200.

StatLink http://dx.doi.org/10.1787/888933190051

## Table 42. Chile, tax revenues by sub-sectors of government

*Million CLP*

| | Federal government | | | | | State/Regional | | | | |
|---|---|---|---|---|---|---|---|---|---|---|
| | 1990 | 2000 | 2005 | 2010 | 2013 | 1990 | 2000 | 2005 | 2010 | 2013 |
| **1000 Taxes on income, profits and capital gains** | **412 974** | **1 841 630** | **5 171 293** | **8 329 060** | **9 945 910** | .. | .. | .. | .. | .. |
| 1100 Of individuals | 99 154 | 604 100 | 738 620 | 1 492 837 | 1 964 172 | .. | .. | .. | .. | .. |
| 1200 Corporate | 219 586 | 882 896 | 3 155 480 | 4 448 745 | 6 466 289 | .. | .. | .. | .. | .. |
| 1300 Unallocable between 1100 and 1200 | 94 233 | 354 634 | 1 277 193 | 2 387 478 | 1 515 449 | .. | .. | .. | .. | .. |
| **2000 Social security contributions** | **66 738** | **232 728** | **287 422** | **371 386** | **406 360** | .. | .. | .. | .. | .. |
| 2100 Employees | 61 200 | 209 907 | 249 526 | 310 558 | 343 727 | .. | .. | .. | .. | .. |
| 2200 Employers | 5 538 | 22 821 | 37 896 | 60 828 | 62 633 | .. | .. | .. | .. | .. |
| 2300 Self-employed or non-employed | 0 | 0 | 0 | 0 | 0 | .. | .. | .. | .. | .. |
| 2400 Unallocable between 2100, 2200 and 2300 | 0 | 0 | 0 | 0 | 0 | .. | .. | .. | .. | .. |
| **3000 Taxes on payroll and workforce** | **0** | **0** | **0** | **0** | **0** | .. | .. | .. | .. | .. |
| **4000 Taxes on property** | **59 682** | **255 371** | **490 120** | **245 044** | **305 330** | .. | .. | .. | .. | .. |
| 4100 Recurrent taxes on immovable property | 10 331 | 3 578 | 4 909 | 8 805 | 12 407 | .. | .. | .. | .. | .. |
| 4200 Recurrent taxes on net wealth | 0 | 0 | 0 | 0 | 0 | .. | .. | .. | .. | .. |
| 4300 Estate, inheritance and gift taxes | 3 444 | 10 906 | 23 184 | 39 338 | 45 550 | .. | .. | .. | .. | .. |
| 4400 Taxes on financial and capital transactions | 45 907 | 240 886 | 462 027 | 196 901 | 247 373 | .. | .. | .. | .. | .. |
| 4500 Non-recurrent taxes | 0 | 0 | 0 | 0 | 0 | .. | .. | .. | .. | .. |
| 4600 Other recurrent taxes on property | 0 | 0 | 0 | 0 | 0 | .. | .. | .. | .. | .. |
| **5000 Taxes on goods and services** | **1 063 677** | **4 719 255** | **6 831 421** | **10 330 378** | **13 598 329** | .. | .. | .. | .. | .. |
| 5100 Taxes on production, sale, transfer, etc | 1 060 304 | 4 684 525 | 6 811 328 | 10 294 165 | 13 548 235 | .. | .. | .. | .. | .. |
| 5110 General taxes | 664 421 | 3 306 350 | 5 391 285 | 8 399 926 | 11 170 794 | .. | .. | .. | .. | .. |
| 5120 Taxes on specific goods and services[1] | 395 883 | 1 378 175 | 1 420 043 | 1 894 239 | 2 377 441 | .. | .. | .. | .. | .. |
| 5130 Unallocable between 5110 and 5120 | 0 | 0 | 0 | 0 | 0 | .. | .. | .. | .. | .. |
| 5200 Taxes on use of goods and perform activities | 3 374 | 34 730 | 20 094 | 36 213 | 50 094 | .. | .. | .. | .. | .. |
| 5300 Unallocable between 5100 and 5200 | 0 | 0 | 0 | 0 | 0 | .. | .. | .. | .. | .. |
| **6000 Other taxes** | **-23 356** | **-112 195** | **-85 954** | **-61 117** | **-21 676** | .. | .. | .. | .. | .. |
| 6100 Paid solely by business | 0 | 0 | 0 | 0 | 0 | .. | .. | .. | .. | .. |
| 6200 Other | -23 356 | -112 195 | -85 954 | -61 117 | -21 676 | .. | .. | .. | .. | .. |
| **Total tax revenue** | **1 579 715** | **6 936 788** | **12 694 301** | **19 214 751** | **24 234 253** | .. | .. | .. | .. | .. |

*Million CLP*

| | Local government | | | | | Social Security Funds | | | | |
|---|---|---|---|---|---|---|---|---|---|---|
| | 1990 | 2000 | 2005 | 2010 | 2013 | 1990 | 2000 | 2005 | 2010 | 2013 |
| **1000 Taxes on income, profits and capital gains** | **0** | **0** | **0** | **0** | **0** | **0** | **0** | **0** | **0** | **0** |
| 1100 Of individuals | 0 | 0 | 0 | 0 | 0 | 0 | 0 | 0 | 0 | 0 |
| 1200 Corporate | 0 | 0 | 0 | 0 | 0 | 0 | 0 | 0 | 0 | 0 |
| 1300 Unallocable between 1100 and 1200 | 0 | 0 | 0 | 0 | 0 | 0 | 0 | 0 | 0 | 0 |
| **2000 Social security contributions** | **0** | **0** | **0** | **0** | **0** | **92 821** | **344 030** | **644 295** | **1 122 601** | **1 562 613** |
| 2100 Employees | .. | .. | .. | .. | .. | 92 821 | 344 030 | 644 295 | 1 122 601 | 1 562 613 |
| 2200 Employers | .. | .. | .. | .. | .. | 0 | 0 | 0 | 0 | 0 |
| 2300 Self-employed or non-employed | .. | .. | .. | .. | .. | 0 | 0 | 0 | 0 | 0 |
| 2400 Unallocable between 2100, 2200 and 2300 | .. | .. | .. | .. | .. | 0 | 0 | 0 | 0 | 0 |
| **3000 Taxes on payroll and workforce** | **0** | **0** | **0** | **0** | **0** | **0** | **0** | **0** | **0** | **0** |
| **4000 Taxes on property** | **49 637** | **298 666** | **411 656** | **540 320** | **808 992** | **0** | **0** | **0** | **0** | **0** |
| 4100 Recurrent taxes on immovable property | 49 637 | 298 666 | 411 656 | 540 320 | 808 992 | .. | .. | .. | .. | .. |
| 4200 Recurrent taxes on net wealth | 0 | 0 | 0 | 0 | 0 | .. | .. | .. | .. | .. |
| 4300 Estate, inheritance and gift taxes | 0 | 0 | 0 | 0 | 0 | .. | .. | .. | .. | .. |
| 4400 Taxes on financial and capital transactions | 0 | 0 | 0 | 0 | 0 | .. | .. | .. | .. | .. |
| 4500 Non-recurrent taxes | 0 | 0 | 0 | 0 | 0 | .. | .. | .. | .. | .. |
| 4600 Other recurrent taxes on property | 0 | 0 | 0 | 0 | 0 | .. | .. | .. | .. | .. |
| **5000 Taxes on goods and services** | **55 045** | **322 514** | **514 952** | **800 810** | **1 149 581** | **0** | **0** | **0** | **0** | **0** |
| 5100 Taxes on production, sale, transfer, etc | 13 705 | 105 302 | 140 703 | 220 657 | 308 011 | .. | .. | .. | .. | .. |
| 5110 General taxes | 0 | 0 | 0 | 0 | 0 | .. | .. | .. | .. | .. |
| 5120 Taxes on specific goods and services[1] | 13 705 | 105 302 | 140 703 | 220 657 | 308 011 | .. | .. | .. | .. | .. |
| 5130 Unallocable between 5110 and 5120 | 0 | 0 | 0 | 0 | 0 | .. | .. | .. | .. | .. |
| 5200 Taxes on use of goods and perform activities | 41 340 | 217 212 | 374 249 | 580 153 | 841 570 | .. | .. | .. | .. | .. |
| 5300 Unallocable between 5100 and 5200 | 0 | 0 | 0 | 0 | 0 | .. | .. | .. | .. | .. |
| **6000 Other taxes** | **0** | **0** | **0** | **0** | **0** | **0** | **0** | **0** | **0** | **0** |
| 6100 Paid solely by business | .. | .. | .. | .. | .. | .. | .. | .. | .. | .. |
| 6200 Other | .. | .. | .. | .. | .. | .. | .. | .. | .. | .. |
| **Total tax revenue** | **104 682** | **621 180** | **926 608** | **1 341 129** | **1 958 573** | **92 821** | **344 030** | **644 295** | **1 122 601** | **1 562 613** |

1. In ECLAC data, figures from the Oil Prices Stabilisation Fund (FEPP) are considered as non tax revenues.

StatLink http://dx.doi.org/10.1787/888933190061

# Table 43. Colombia, tax revenues by sub-sectors of government

*Million COP*

| | Federal government | | | | | State/Regional[1] | | | | |
|---|---|---|---|---|---|---|---|---|---|---|
| | 1990 | 2000 | 2005 | 2010 | 2013 | 1990 | 2000 | 2005 | 2010 | 2013 |
| **1000 Taxes on income, profits and capital gains** | **771 694** | **7 103 525** | **17 348 618** | **26 218 852** | **47 743 096** | **0** | **0** | **0** | **0** | **0** |
| 1100 Of individuals | 47 210 | 127 908 | 619 066 | 741 826 | 1 074 542 | .. | .. | .. | .. | .. |
| 1200 Corporate | 359 758 | 1 180 627 | 7 453 811 | 7 799 486 | 19 677 250 | .. | .. | .. | .. | .. |
| 1300 Unallocable between 1100 and 1200 | 364 726 | 5 794 990 | 9 275 740 | 17 677 540 | 26 991 303 | .. | .. | .. | .. | .. |
| **2000 Social security contributions** | **0** | **0** | **0** | **0** | **0** | **0** | **0** | **0** | **0** | **0** |
| 2100 Employees | .. | .. | .. | .. | .. | .. | .. | .. | .. | .. |
| 2200 Employers | .. | .. | .. | .. | .. | .. | .. | .. | .. | .. |
| 2300 Self-employed or non-employed | .. | .. | .. | .. | .. | .. | .. | .. | .. | .. |
| 2400 Unallocable between 2100, 2200 and 2300 | .. | .. | .. | .. | .. | .. | .. | .. | .. | .. |
| **3000 Taxes on payroll and workforce** | **0** | **1 286 803** | **2 179 842** | **4 022 503** | **3 527 459** | **0** | **0** | **0** | **0** | **0** |
| **4000 Taxes on property** | **0** | **1 036 584** | **2 863 946** | **5 196 303** | **10 172 587** | **0** | **0** | **0** | **0** | **0** |
| 4100 Recurrent taxes on immovable property | .. | 0 | 0 | 0 | .. | .. | .. | .. | .. | .. |
| 4200 Recurrent taxes on net wealth | .. | 0 | 462 720 | 1 970 530 | 4 274 832 | .. | .. | .. | .. | .. |
| 4300 Estate, inheritance and gift taxes | .. | 0 | 0 | 0 | 0 | .. | .. | .. | .. | .. |
| 4400 Taxes on financial and capital transactions | .. | 1 036 584 | 2 401 226 | 3 225 773 | 5 897 755 | .. | .. | .. | .. | .. |
| 4500 Non-recurrent taxes | .. | 0 | 0 | 0 | 0 | .. | .. | .. | .. | .. |
| 4600 Other recurrent taxes on property | .. | 0 | 0 | 0 | 0 | .. | .. | .. | .. | .. |
| **5000 Taxes on goods and services** | **1 035 934** | **11 022 878** | **21 393 776** | **34 882 447** | **42 605 413** | **263 429** | **1 204 940** | **1 966 325** | **2 874 375** | **4 590 336** |
| 5100 Taxes on production, sale, transfer, etc | 1 035 934 | 11 022 878 | 21 393 776 | 34 882 447 | 42 605 413 | 263 429 | 1 204 940 | 1 966 325 | 2 874 375 | 4 590 336 |
| 5110 General taxes | 583 078 | 8 445 776 | 17 427 948 | 28 811 682 | 34 642 822 | 0 | 0 | 0 | 0 | 0 |
| 5120 Taxes on specific goods and services | 452 856 | 2 577 102 | 3 965 828 | 6 070 765 | 7 962 591 | 263 429 | 1 204 940 | 1 966 325 | 2 874 375 | 4 590 336 |
| 5130 Unallocable between 5110 and 5120 | 0 | 0 | 0 | 0 | 0 | 0 | 0 | 0 | 0 | 0 |
| 5200 Taxes on use of goods and perform activities | 0 | 0 | 0 | 0 | 0 | 0 | 0 | 0 | 0 | 0 |
| 5300 Unallocable between 5100 and 5200 | 0 | 0 | 0 | 0 | 0 | 0 | 0 | 0 | 0 | 0 |
| **6000 Other taxes** | **78 306** | **480 784** | **682 084** | **483 762** | **258 843** | **0** | **518 253** | **1 117 016** | **2 005 277** | **2 577 463** |
| 6100 Paid solely by business | 0 | 0 | 0 | 0 | 0 | .. | 0 | 0 | 0 | 0 |
| 6200 Other | 78 306 | 480 784 | 682 084 | 483 762 | 258 843 | .. | 518 253 | 1 117 016 | 2 005 277 | 2 577 463 |
| **Total tax revenue** | **1 885 934** | **20 930 574** | **44 468 266** | **70 803 867** | **104 307 398** | **263 429** | **1 723 193** | **3 083 341** | **4 879 652** | **7 167 800** |

*Million COP*

| | Local government[1] | | | | | Social Security Funds[2] | | | | |
|---|---|---|---|---|---|---|---|---|---|---|
| | 1990 | 2000 | 2005 | 2010 | 2013 | 1990 | 2000 | 2005 | 2010 | 2013 |
| **1000 Taxes on income, profits and capital gains** | **0** | **0** | **0** | **0** | **0** | **0** | **0** | **0** | **0** | **0** |
| 1100 Of individuals | .. | .. | .. | .. | .. | .. | .. | .. | .. | .. |
| 1200 Corporate | .. | .. | .. | .. | .. | .. | .. | .. | .. | .. |
| 1300 Unallocable between 1100 and 1200 | .. | .. | .. | .. | .. | .. | .. | .. | .. | .. |
| **2000 Social security contributions** | **0** | **0** | **0** | **0** | **0** | **203 596** | **4 989 000** | **7 845 000** | **11 478 085** | **16 645 000** |
| 2100 Employees | .. | .. | .. | .. | .. | .. | .. | .. | .. | .. |
| 2200 Employers | .. | .. | .. | .. | .. | .. | .. | .. | .. | .. |
| 2300 Self-employed or non-employed | .. | .. | .. | .. | .. | .. | .. | .. | .. | .. |
| 2400 Unallocable between 2100, 2200 and 2300 | .. | .. | .. | .. | .. | 203 596 | 4 989 000 | 7 845 000 | 11 478 085 | 16 645 000 |
| **3000 Taxes on payroll and workforce** | **0** | **0** | **0** | **0** | **0** | **0** | **0** | **0** | **0** | **0** |
| **4000 Taxes on property** | **56 160** | **991 070** | **1 974 213** | **3 163 084** | **4 957 894** | **0** | **0** | **0** | **0** | **0** |
| 4100 Recurrent taxes on immovable property | 56 160 | 991 070 | 1 974 213 | 3 163 084 | 4 957 894 | .. | .. | .. | .. | .. |
| 4200 Recurrent taxes on net wealth | 0 | 0 | 0 | 0 | 0 | .. | .. | .. | .. | .. |
| 4300 Estate, inheritance and gift taxes | 0 | 0 | 0 | 0 | 0 | .. | .. | .. | .. | .. |
| 4400 Taxes on financial and capital transactions | 0 | 0 | 0 | 0 | 0 | .. | .. | .. | .. | .. |
| 4500 Non-recurrent taxes | 0 | 0 | 0 | 0 | 0 | .. | .. | .. | .. | .. |
| 4600 Other recurrent taxes on property | 0 | 0 | 0 | 0 | 0 | .. | .. | .. | .. | .. |
| **5000 Taxes on goods and services** | **89 290** | **1 140 090** | **2 506 452** | **4 306 620** | **5 830 740** | **0** | **0** | **0** | **0** | **0** |
| 5100 Taxes on production, sale, transfer, etc | 89 290 | 1 140 090 | 2 506 452 | 4 306 620 | 5 830 740 | .. | .. | .. | .. | .. |
| 5110 General taxes | 89 290 | 1 140 090 | 2 506 452 | 4 306 620 | 5 830 740 | .. | .. | .. | .. | .. |
| 5120 Taxes on specific goods and services | 0 | 0 | 0 | 0 | 0 | .. | .. | .. | .. | .. |
| 5130 Unallocable between 5110 and 5120 | 0 | 0 | 0 | 0 | 0 | .. | .. | .. | .. | .. |
| 5200 Taxes on use of goods and perform activities | 0 | 0 | 0 | 0 | 0 | .. | .. | .. | .. | .. |
| 5300 Unallocable between 5100 and 5200 | 0 | 0 | 0 | 0 | 0 | .. | .. | .. | .. | .. |
| **6000 Other taxes** | **81 017** | **738 983** | **1 578 573** | **3 403 883** | **4 595 908** | **0** | **0** | **0** | **0** | **0** |
| 6100 Paid solely by business | 0 | 0 | 0 | 0 | 0 | .. | .. | .. | .. | .. |
| 6200 Other | 81 017 | 738 983 | 1 578 573 | 3 403 883 | 4 595 908 | .. | .. | .. | .. | .. |
| **Total tax revenue** | **226 467** | **2 870 144** | **6 059 238** | **10 873 586** | **15 384 542** | **203 596** | **4 989 000** | **7 845 000** | **11 478 085** | **16 645 000** |

1. Corresponds to the reported consolidated revenues of the territorial entities (departments and municipalities).
2. For 2013, all of the health contributions entering FOSYGA (Solidarity and Guarantee Fund) are classified as Social Security Contributions. Previously only the portion of the contributions used to finance the subsidized regime was included and the part to finance the contributory regime was classified in the social security sector as "other incomes". A more detailed explanation is shown in table 22 in the country tables.

StatLink http://dx.doi.org/10.1787/888933190070

## Table 44. Costa Rica, tax revenues by sub-sectors of government

*Million CRC*

| | Federal government | | | | | State/Regional | | | | |
|---|---|---|---|---|---|---|---|---|---|---|
| | 1990 | 2000 | 2005 | 2010 | 2013 | 1990 | 2000 | 2005 | 2010 | 2013 |
| **1000 Taxes on income, profits and capital gains** | **11 820** | **128 805** | **324 224** | **748 093** | **1 014 440** | .. | .. | .. | .. | .. |
| 1100 Of individuals | .. | .. | 16 438 | 202 849 | 316 894 | .. | .. | .. | .. | .. |
| 1200 Corporate | .. | .. | 288 355 | 450 312 | 545 183 | .. | .. | .. | .. | .. |
| 1300 Unallocable between 1100 and 1200 | 11 820 | 128 805 | 19 430 | 94 932 | 152 363 | .. | .. | .. | .. | .. |
| **2000 Social security contributions[1]** | **0** | **0** | **0** | **0** | **0** | .. | .. | .. | .. | .. |
| 2100 Employees | .. | .. | .. | .. | .. | .. | .. | .. | .. | .. |
| 2200 Employers | .. | .. | .. | .. | .. | .. | .. | .. | .. | .. |
| 2300 Self-employed or non-employed | .. | .. | .. | .. | .. | .. | .. | .. | .. | .. |
| 2400 Unallocable between 2100, 2200 and 2300 | .. | .. | .. | .. | .. | .. | .. | .. | .. | .. |
| **3000 Taxes on payroll and workforce** | **0** | **0** | **0** | **0** | **0** | .. | .. | .. | .. | .. |
| **4000 Taxes on property** | **366** | **7 291** | **10 846** | **18 270** | **32 243** | .. | .. | .. | .. | .. |
| 4100 Recurrent taxes on immovable property | 0 | 0 | 0 | 3 527 | 3 998 | .. | .. | .. | .. | .. |
| 4200 Recurrent taxes on net wealth | 0 | 4 284 | 0 | 0 | 0 | .. | .. | .. | .. | .. |
| 4300 Estate, inheritance and gift taxes | 0 | 0 | 0 | 0 | 0 | .. | .. | .. | .. | .. |
| 4400 Taxes on financial and capital transactions | 366 | 3 007 | 10 846 | 14 743 | 28 245 | .. | .. | .. | .. | .. |
| 4500 Non-recurrent taxes | 0 | 0 | 0 | 0 | 0 | .. | .. | .. | .. | .. |
| 4600 Other recurrent taxes on property | 0 | 0 | 0 | 0 | 0 | .. | .. | .. | .. | .. |
| **5000 Taxes on goods and services** | **52 360** | **444 726** | **920 160** | **1 696 729** | **2 173 664** | .. | .. | .. | .. | .. |
| 5100 Taxes on production, sale, transfer, etc | 49 980 | 425 353 | 887 390 | 1 598 790 | 2 054 297 | .. | .. | .. | .. | .. |
| 5110 General taxes | 21 326 | 222 775 | 485 168 | 920 298 | 1 176 745 | .. | .. | .. | .. | .. |
| 5120 Taxes on specific goods and services[2] | 28 654 | 202 887 | 399 192 | 678 492 | 877 552 | .. | .. | .. | .. | .. |
| 5130 Unallocable between 5110 and 5120 | 0 | -308 | 3 031 | 0 | 0 | .. | .. | .. | .. | .. |
| 5200 Taxes on use of goods and perform activities | 2 380 | 19 357 | 32 758 | 97 803 | 119 235 | .. | .. | .. | .. | .. |
| 5300 Unallocable between 5100 and 5200 | 0 | 15 | 12 | 136 | 132 | .. | .. | .. | .. | .. |
| **6000 Other taxes[3]** | **6 113** | **2 573** | **7 009** | **12 864** | **53 432** | .. | .. | .. | .. | .. |
| 6100 Paid solely by business | 0 | 15 | 624 | 459 | 36 125 | .. | .. | .. | .. | .. |
| 6200 Other | 6 113 | 2 558 | 6 385 | 12 405 | 17 307 | .. | .. | .. | .. | .. |
| **Total tax revenue** | **70 660** | **583 395** | **1 262 240** | **2 475 956** | **3 273 779** | .. | .. | .. | .. | .. |

*Million CRC*

| | Local government[4] | | | | | Social Security Funds | | | | |
|---|---|---|---|---|---|---|---|---|---|---|
| | 1990 | 2000 | 2005 | 2010 | 2013 | 1990 | 2000 | 2005 | 2010 | 2013 |
| **1000 Taxes on income, profits and capital gains** | .. | **0** | **0** | **0** | **0** | **0** | **0** | **0** | **0** | **0** |
| 1100 Of individuals | .. | .. | .. | .. | .. | .. | .. | .. | .. | .. |
| 1200 Corporate | .. | .. | .. | .. | .. | .. | .. | .. | .. | .. |
| 1300 Unallocable between 1100 and 1200 | .. | .. | .. | .. | .. | .. | .. | .. | .. | .. |
| **2000 Social security contributions[1]** | .. | **0** | **0** | **0** | **0** | **29 065** | **249 886** | **528 132** | **1 204 995** | **1 874 010** |
| 2100 Employees | .. | .. | .. | .. | .. | .. | 3 405 | 5 354 | 9 649 | 12 774 |
| 2200 Employers | .. | .. | .. | .. | .. | .. | 0 | 24 481 | 56 332 | 344 622 |
| 2300 Self-employed or non-employed | .. | .. | .. | .. | .. | .. | 5 858 | 16 414 | 33 778 | 21 090 |
| 2400 Unallocable between 2100, 2200 and 2300 | .. | .. | .. | .. | .. | 29 065 | 240 623 | 481 883 | 1 105 236 | 1 495 525 |
| **3000 Taxes on payroll and workforce** | .. | **0** | **0** | **0** | **0** | **7 054** | **41 918** | **81 290** | **182 529** | **247 775** |
| **4000 Taxes on property** | .. | **5 390** | **14 264** | **45 393** | **67 528** | **0** | **0** | **0** | **0** | **0** |
| 4100 Recurrent taxes on immovable property | .. | 5 310 | 14 245 | 44 080 | 67 528 | .. | .. | .. | .. | .. |
| 4200 Recurrent taxes on net wealth | .. | 0 | 0 | 0 | 0 | .. | .. | .. | .. | .. |
| 4300 Estate, inheritance and gift taxes | .. | 0 | 0 | 0 | 0 | .. | .. | .. | .. | .. |
| 4400 Taxes on financial and capital transactions | .. | 0 | 0 | 0 | 0 | .. | .. | .. | .. | .. |
| 4500 Non-recurrent taxes | .. | 0 | 0 | 0 | 0 | .. | .. | .. | .. | .. |
| 4600 Other recurrent taxes on property | .. | 80 | 19 | 1 313 | 0 | .. | .. | .. | .. | .. |
| **5000 Taxes on goods and services** | .. | **11 981** | **26 810** | **65 862** | **94 872** | **0** | **0** | **0** | **0** | **0** |
| 5100 Taxes on production, sale, transfer, etc | .. | 11 981 | 26 810 | 65 862 | 94 872 | .. | .. | .. | .. | .. |
| 5110 General taxes | .. | 0 | 0 | 0 | 13 | .. | .. | .. | .. | .. |
| 5120 Taxes on specific goods and services[2] | .. | 10 612 | 24 294 | 61 002 | 2 680 | .. | .. | .. | .. | .. |
| 5130 Unallocable between 5110 and 5120 | .. | 1 369 | 2 515 | 4 860 | 92 179 | .. | .. | .. | .. | .. |
| 5200 Taxes on use of goods and perform activities | .. | 0 | 0 | 0 | 0 | .. | .. | .. | .. | .. |
| 5300 Unallocable between 5100 and 5200 | .. | 0 | 0 | 0 | 0 | .. | .. | .. | .. | .. |
| **6000 Other taxes[3]** | .. | **1 242** | **3 207** | **4 366** | **5 780** | **0** | **0** | **0** | **0** | **0** |
| 6100 Paid solely by business | .. | 0 | 0 | 0 | 0 | .. | .. | .. | .. | .. |
| 6200 Other | .. | 1 242 | 3 207 | 4 366 | 5 780 | .. | .. | .. | .. | .. |
| **Total tax revenue** | .. | **18 613** | **44 280** | **115 621** | **168 180** | **36 119** | **291 804** | **609 422** | **1 387 524** | **2 121 785** |

1. In ECLAC data, social security contributions include INA (National Institute of Apprenticeship), IMAS (Joint Social Aid Institute), and FODESAF (Social Development and Family Allowances Fund).
2. In ECLAC data, the property tax on vehicles, aircraft and boats is classified in category 4000.
3. In ECLAC data, the tax on the transfer of used vehicles Law No. 7088 of 30/11/87 is classified as a property tax (4000).
4. The figures for years up to an including 1997 exclude local government tax revenues as the data are not available.

StatLink http://dx.doi.org/10.1787/888933190087

## Table 45. Dominican Republic, tax revenues by sub-sectors of government

*Million DOP*

| | Federal government | | | | | State/Regional | | | | |
|---|---|---|---|---|---|---|---|---|---|---|
| | 1990 | 2000 | 2005 | 2010 | 2013 | 1990 | 2000 | 2005 | 2010 | 2013 |
| **1000 Taxes on income, profits and capital gains** | **1 670** | **7 060** | **23 907** | **40 558** | **88 979** | .. | .. | .. | .. | .. |
| 1100 Of individuals | .. | 366 | 1 454 | 4 002 | 5 658 | .. | .. | .. | .. | .. |
| 1200 Corporate | .. | 4 679 | 16 222 | 21 475 | 50 782 | .. | .. | .. | .. | .. |
| 1300 Unallocable between 1100 and 1200 | 1 670 | 2 015 | 6 232 | 15 080 | 32 539 | .. | .. | .. | .. | .. |
| **2000 Social security contributions** | **0** | **0** | **0** | **0** | **0** | .. | .. | .. | .. | .. |
| 2100 Employees | .. | .. | .. | .. | .. | .. | .. | .. | .. | .. |
| 2200 Employers | .. | .. | .. | .. | .. | .. | .. | .. | .. | .. |
| 2300 Self-employed or non-employed | .. | .. | .. | .. | .. | .. | .. | .. | .. | .. |
| 2400 Unallocable between 2100, 2200 and 2300 | .. | .. | .. | .. | .. | .. | .. | .. | .. | .. |
| **3000 Taxes on payroll and workforce** | **0** | **3 722** | **6 134** | **13 086** | **19 270** | .. | .. | .. | .. | .. |
| **4000 Taxes on property** | **46** | **505** | **6 555** | **12 738** | **22 333** | .. | .. | .. | .. | .. |
| 4100 Recurrent taxes on immovable property | 9 | 115 | 1 710 | 3 004 | 10 183 | .. | .. | .. | .. | .. |
| 4200 Recurrent taxes on net wealth | 0 | 0 | 0 | 0 | 0 | .. | .. | .. | .. | .. |
| 4300 Estate, inheritance and gift taxes | 11 | 96 | 84 | 231 | 315 | .. | .. | .. | .. | .. |
| 4400 Taxes on financial and capital transactions | 22 | 217 | 4 546 | 8 125 | 10 404 | .. | .. | .. | .. | .. |
| 4500 Non-recurrent taxes | 3 | 32 | 89 | 488 | 412 | .. | .. | .. | .. | .. |
| 4600 Other recurrent taxes on property | 1 | 45 | 127 | 891 | 1 019 | .. | .. | .. | .. | .. |
| **5000 Taxes on goods and services** | **4 488** | **36 038** | **111 344** | **175 716** | **223 181** | .. | .. | .. | .. | .. |
| 5100 Taxes on production, sale, transfer, etc | 4 410 | 35 281 | 109 602 | 173 403 | 219 939 | .. | .. | .. | .. | .. |
| 5110 General taxes | 973 | 10 195 | 41 368 | 81 871 | 113 345 | .. | .. | .. | .. | .. |
| 5120 Taxes on specific goods and services[1] | 3 437 | 25 086 | 68 234 | 91 531 | 106 595 | .. | .. | .. | .. | .. |
| 5130 Unallocable between 5110 and 5120 | 0 | 0 | 0 | 0 | 0 | .. | .. | .. | .. | .. |
| 5200 Taxes on use of goods and perform activities | 77 | 757 | 1 742 | 2 313 | 3 242 | .. | .. | .. | .. | .. |
| 5300 Unallocable between 5100 and 5200 | 0 | 0 | 0 | 0 | 0 | .. | .. | .. | .. | .. |
| **6000 Other taxes[2]** | **159** | **495** | **1 661** | **0** | **0** | .. | .. | .. | .. | .. |
| 6100 Paid solely by business | 0 | 0 | 0 | .. | 0 | .. | .. | .. | .. | .. |
| 6200 Other | 159 | 495 | 1 661 | .. | 0 | .. | .. | .. | .. | .. |
| **Total tax revenue** | **6 362** | **47 820** | **149 602** | **242 097** | **353 762** | .. | .. | .. | .. | .. |

*Million DOP*

| | Local government[3] | | | | | Social Security Funds[4] | | | | |
|---|---|---|---|---|---|---|---|---|---|---|
| | 1990 | 2000 | 2005 | 2010 | 2013 | 1990 | 2000 | 2005 | 2010 | 2013 |
| **1000 Taxes on income, profits and capital gains** | .. | .. | .. | .. | .. | **0** | **0** | **0** | **0** | **0** |
| 1100 Of individuals | .. | .. | .. | .. | .. | .. | .. | .. | .. | .. |
| 1200 Corporate | .. | .. | .. | .. | .. | .. | .. | .. | .. | .. |
| 1300 Unallocable between 1100 and 1200 | .. | .. | .. | .. | .. | .. | .. | .. | .. | .. |
| **2000 Social security contributions** | .. | .. | .. | .. | .. | **53** | **490** | **35** | **1 845** | **1 552** |
| 2100 Employees | .. | .. | .. | .. | .. | .. | .. | .. | .. | .. |
| 2200 Employers | .. | .. | .. | .. | .. | .. | .. | .. | .. | .. |
| 2300 Self-employed or non-employed | .. | .. | .. | .. | .. | .. | .. | .. | .. | .. |
| 2400 Unallocable between 2100, 2200 and 2300 | .. | .. | .. | .. | .. | 53 | 490 | 35 | 1 845 | 1 552 |
| **3000 Taxes on payroll and workforce** | .. | .. | .. | .. | .. | **0** | **0** | **0** | **0** | **0** |
| **4000 Taxes on property** | .. | .. | .. | .. | .. | **0** | **0** | **0** | **0** | **0** |
| 4100 Recurrent taxes on immovable property | .. | .. | .. | .. | .. | .. | .. | .. | .. | .. |
| 4200 Recurrent taxes on net wealth | .. | .. | .. | .. | .. | .. | .. | .. | .. | .. |
| 4300 Estate, inheritance and gift taxes | .. | .. | .. | .. | .. | .. | .. | .. | .. | .. |
| 4400 Taxes on financial and capital transactions | .. | .. | .. | .. | .. | .. | .. | .. | .. | .. |
| 4500 Non-recurrent taxes | .. | .. | .. | .. | .. | .. | .. | .. | .. | .. |
| 4600 Other recurrent taxes on property | .. | .. | .. | .. | .. | .. | .. | .. | .. | .. |
| **5000 Taxes on goods and services** | .. | .. | .. | .. | .. | **0** | **0** | **0** | **0** | **0** |
| 5100 Taxes on production, sale, transfer, etc | .. | .. | .. | .. | .. | .. | .. | .. | .. | .. |
| 5110 General taxes | .. | .. | .. | .. | .. | .. | .. | .. | .. | .. |
| 5120 Taxes on specific goods and services[1] | .. | .. | .. | .. | .. | .. | .. | .. | .. | .. |
| 5130 Unallocable between 5110 and 5120 | .. | .. | .. | .. | .. | .. | .. | .. | .. | .. |
| 5200 Taxes on use of goods and perform activities | .. | .. | .. | .. | .. | .. | .. | .. | .. | .. |
| 5300 Unallocable between 5100 and 5200 | .. | .. | .. | .. | .. | .. | .. | .. | .. | .. |
| **6000 Other taxes[2]** | .. | .. | .. | .. | .. | **0** | **0** | **0** | **0** | **0** |
| 6100 Paid solely by business | .. | .. | .. | .. | .. | .. | .. | .. | .. | .. |
| 6200 Other | .. | .. | .. | .. | .. | .. | .. | .. | .. | .. |
| **Total tax revenue** | .. | .. | .. | .. | .. | **53** | **490** | **35** | **1 845** | **1 552** |

1. In ECLAC data, the tax on transfer of movable goods is classified as a property tax (4000).
2. In ECLAC data, the Vehicle transfer tax is classified as a property tax (4000).
3. The figures exclude local government tax revenues as the data are not available.
4. The figures exclude social security contributions to general government managed by the private sector.

StatLink http://dx.doi.org/10.1787/888933190095

## Table 46. Ecuador, tax revenues by sub-sectors of government

*Million USD*

| | Federal government | | | | | State/Regional | | | | |
|---|---|---|---|---|---|---|---|---|---|---|
| | 1990 | 2000 | 2005 | 2010 | 2013 | 1990 | 2000 | 2005 | 2010 | 2013 |
| **1000 Taxes on income, profits and capital gains** | **138** | **293** | **937** | **2 353** | **3 847** | .. | .. | .. | .. | .. |
| 1100 Of individuals | .. | .. | .. | .. | .. | .. | .. | .. | .. | .. |
| 1200 Corporate | .. | .. | .. | .. | .. | .. | .. | .. | .. | .. |
| 1300 Unallocable between 1100 and 1200 | 138 | 293 | 937 | 2 353 | 3 847 | .. | .. | .. | .. | .. |
| **2000 Social security contributions** | **0** | **0** | **0** | **0** | **0** | .. | .. | .. | .. | .. |
| 2100 Employees | .. | .. | .. | .. | .. | .. | .. | .. | .. | .. |
| 2200 Employers | .. | .. | .. | .. | .. | .. | .. | .. | .. | .. |
| 2300 Self-employed or non-employed | .. | .. | .. | .. | .. | .. | .. | .. | .. | .. |
| 2400 Unallocable between 2100, 2200 and 2300 | .. | .. | .. | .. | .. | .. | .. | .. | .. | .. |
| **3000 Taxes on payroll and workforce** | **0** | **0** | **0** | **0** | **0** | .. | .. | .. | .. | .. |
| **4000 Taxes on property** | **0** | **0** | **0** | **0** | **0** | .. | .. | .. | .. | .. |
| 4100 Recurrent taxes on immovable property | .. | .. | .. | .. | .. | .. | .. | .. | .. | .. |
| 4200 Recurrent taxes on net wealth | .. | .. | .. | .. | .. | .. | .. | .. | .. | .. |
| 4300 Estate, inheritance and gift taxes | .. | .. | .. | .. | .. | .. | .. | .. | .. | .. |
| 4400 Taxes on financial and capital transactions | .. | .. | .. | .. | .. | .. | .. | .. | .. | .. |
| 4500 Non-recurrent taxes | .. | .. | .. | .. | .. | .. | .. | .. | .. | .. |
| 4600 Other recurrent taxes on property | .. | .. | .. | .. | .. | .. | .. | .. | .. | .. |
| **5000 Taxes on goods and services** | **668** | **1 330** | **2 802** | **6 152** | **9 688** | .. | .. | .. | .. | .. |
| 5100 Taxes on production, sale, transfer, etc | 665 | 1 319 | 2 742 | 5 997 | 9 474 | .. | .. | .. | .. | .. |
| 5110 General taxes | 302 | 836 | 1 975 | 3 886 | 6 056 | .. | .. | .. | .. | .. |
| 5120 Taxes on specific goods and services | 363 | 483 | 767 | 2 110 | 3 418 | .. | .. | .. | .. | .. |
| 5130 Unallocable between 5110 and 5120 | 0 | 0 | 0 | 0 | 0 | .. | .. | .. | .. | .. |
| 5200 Taxes on use of goods and perform activities[1] | 3 | 11 | 60 | 156 | 214 | .. | .. | .. | .. | .. |
| 5300 Unallocable between 5100 and 5200 | 0 | 0 | 0 | 0 | 0 | .. | .. | .. | .. | .. |
| **6000 Other taxes** | **27** | **0** | **2** | **289** | **132** | .. | .. | .. | .. | .. |
| 6100 Paid solely by business | 0 | 0 | 0 | 0 | 0 | .. | .. | .. | .. | .. |
| 6200 Other | 27 | 0 | 2 | 289 | 132 | .. | .. | .. | .. | .. |
| **Total tax revenue** | **833** | **1 623** | **3 741** | **8 794** | **13 668** | .. | .. | .. | .. | .. |

*Million USD*

| | Local government[2] | | | | | Social Security Funds[3] | | | | |
|---|---|---|---|---|---|---|---|---|---|---|
| | 1990 | 2000 | 2005 | 2010 | 2013 | 1990 | 2000 | 2005 | 2010 | 2013 |
| **1000 Taxes on income, profits and capital gains** | .. | .. | .. | .. | .. | **0** | **0** | **0** | **0** | **0** |
| 1100 Of individuals | .. | .. | .. | .. | .. | .. | .. | .. | .. | .. |
| 1200 Corporate | .. | .. | .. | .. | .. | .. | .. | .. | .. | .. |
| 1300 Unallocable between 1100 and 1200 | .. | .. | .. | .. | .. | .. | .. | .. | .. | .. |
| **2000 Social security contributions** | .. | .. | .. | .. | .. | **243** | **228** | **1 109** | **2 549** | **4 547** |
| 2100 Employees | .. | .. | .. | .. | .. | .. | .. | .. | .. | .. |
| 2200 Employers | .. | .. | .. | .. | .. | .. | .. | .. | .. | .. |
| 2300 Self-employed or non-employed | .. | .. | .. | .. | .. | .. | .. | .. | .. | .. |
| 2400 Unallocable between 2100, 2200 and 2300 | .. | .. | .. | .. | .. | 243 | 228 | 1 109 | 2 549 | 4 547 |
| **3000 Taxes on payroll and workforce** | .. | .. | .. | .. | .. | **0** | **0** | **0** | **0** | **0** |
| **4000 Taxes on property** | .. | .. | .. | .. | .. | **0** | **0** | **0** | **0** | **0** |
| 4100 Recurrent taxes on immovable property | .. | .. | .. | .. | .. | .. | .. | .. | .. | .. |
| 4200 Recurrent taxes on net wealth | .. | .. | .. | .. | .. | .. | .. | .. | .. | .. |
| 4300 Estate, inheritance and gift taxes | .. | .. | .. | .. | .. | .. | .. | .. | .. | .. |
| 4400 Taxes on financial and capital transactions | .. | .. | .. | .. | .. | .. | .. | .. | .. | .. |
| 4500 Non-recurrent taxes | .. | .. | .. | .. | .. | .. | .. | .. | .. | .. |
| 4600 Other recurrent taxes on property | .. | .. | .. | .. | .. | .. | .. | .. | .. | .. |
| **5000 Taxes on goods and services** | .. | .. | .. | .. | .. | **0** | **0** | **0** | **0** | **0** |
| 5100 Taxes on production, sale, transfer, etc | .. | .. | .. | .. | .. | .. | .. | .. | .. | .. |
| 5110 General taxes | .. | .. | .. | .. | .. | .. | .. | .. | .. | .. |
| 5120 Taxes on specific goods and services | .. | .. | .. | .. | .. | .. | .. | .. | .. | .. |
| 5130 Unallocable between 5110 and 5120 | .. | .. | .. | .. | .. | .. | .. | .. | .. | .. |
| 5200 Taxes on use of goods and perform activities[1] | .. | .. | .. | .. | .. | .. | .. | .. | .. | .. |
| 5300 Unallocable between 5100 and 5200 | .. | .. | .. | .. | .. | .. | .. | .. | .. | .. |
| **6000 Other taxes** | .. | .. | .. | .. | .. | **0** | **0** | **0** | **0** | **0** |
| 6100 Paid solely by business | .. | .. | .. | .. | .. | .. | .. | .. | .. | .. |
| 6200 Other | .. | .. | .. | .. | .. | .. | .. | .. | .. | .. |
| **Total tax revenue** | .. | .. | .. | .. | .. | **243** | **228** | **1 109** | **2 549** | **4 547** |

1. In ECLAC data, the annual tax on motor vehicles is classified as a property tax (4000).
2. The figures exclude local government tax revenues as the data are not available.
3. Social security data is recorded at the non-financial public sector level.

StatLink http://dx.doi.org/10.1787/888933190102

## Table 47. El Salvador, tax revenues by sub-sectors of government

*Million USD*

| | Federal government | | | | | State/Regional | | | | |
|---|---|---|---|---|---|---|---|---|---|---|
| | 1990 | 2000 | 2005 | 2010 | 2013 | 1990 | 2000 | 2005 | 2010 | 2013 |
| **1000 Taxes on income, profits and capital gains** | **95** | **429** | **668** | **940** | **1 344** | .. | .. | .. | .. | .. |
| 1100 Of individuals | .. | .. | 312 | 571 | 578 | .. | .. | .. | .. | .. |
| 1200 Corporate | .. | .. | 356 | 423 | 793 | .. | .. | .. | .. | .. |
| 1300 Unallocable between 1100 and 1200 | 95 | 429 | 0 | -55 | -27 | .. | .. | .. | .. | .. |
| **2000 Social security contributions** | **0** | **0** | **0** | **0** | **0** | .. | .. | .. | .. | .. |
| 2100 Employees | .. | .. | .. | .. | .. | .. | .. | .. | .. | .. |
| 2200 Employers | .. | .. | .. | .. | .. | .. | .. | .. | .. | .. |
| 2300 Self-employed or non-employed | .. | .. | .. | .. | .. | .. | .. | .. | .. | .. |
| 2400 Unallocable between 2100, 2200 and 2300 | .. | .. | .. | .. | .. | .. | .. | .. | .. | .. |
| **3000 Taxes on payroll and workforce** | **0** | **0** | **0** | **0** | **0** | .. | .. | .. | .. | .. |
| **4000 Taxes on property** | **26** | **12** | **16** | **16** | **21** | .. | .. | .. | .. | .. |
| 4100 Recurrent taxes on immovable property | 0 | 0 | 0 | 0 | 0 | .. | .. | .. | .. | .. |
| 4200 Recurrent taxes on net wealth | 16 | 0 | 0 | 0 | 0 | .. | .. | .. | .. | .. |
| 4300 Estate, inheritance and gift taxes | 0 | 0 | 0 | 0 | 0 | .. | .. | .. | .. | .. |
| 4400 Taxes on financial and capital transactions | 10 | 12 | 16 | 16 | 21 | .. | .. | .. | .. | .. |
| 4500 Non-recurrent taxes | 0 | 0 | 0 | 0 | 0 | .. | .. | .. | .. | .. |
| 4600 Other recurrent taxes on property | 0 | 0 | 0 | 0 | 0 | .. | .. | .. | .. | .. |
| **5000 Taxes on goods and services** | **259** | **903** | **1 447** | **1 855** | **2 213** | .. | .. | .. | .. | .. |
| 5100 Taxes on production, sale, transfer, etc | 259 | 903 | 1 447 | 1 855 | 2 213 | .. | .. | .. | .. | .. |
| 5110 General taxes | 133 | 714 | 1 104 | 1 433 | 1 731 | .. | .. | .. | .. | .. |
| 5120 Taxes on specific goods and services | 127 | 189 | 344 | 422 | 483 | .. | .. | .. | .. | .. |
| 5130 Unallocable between 5110 and 5120 | 0 | 0 | 0 | 0 | 0 | .. | .. | .. | .. | .. |
| 5200 Taxes on use of goods and perform activities | 0 | 0 | 0 | 0 | 0 | .. | .. | .. | .. | .. |
| 5300 Unallocable between 5100 and 5200 | 0 | 0 | 0 | 0 | 0 | .. | .. | .. | .. | .. |
| **6000 Other taxes** | **58** | **0** | **0** | **0** | **0** | .. | .. | .. | .. | .. |
| 6100 Paid solely by business | 0 | 0 | .. | .. | .. | .. | .. | .. | .. | .. |
| 6200 Other | 58 | 0 | .. | .. | .. | .. | .. | .. | .. | .. |
| **Total tax revenue** | **438** | **1 344** | **2 131** | **2 810** | **3 578** | .. | .. | .. | .. | .. |

*Million USD*

| | Local government[1] | | | | | Social Security Funds[2,3] | | | | |
|---|---|---|---|---|---|---|---|---|---|---|
| | 1990 | 2000 | 2005 | 2010 | 2013 | 1990 | 2000 | 2005 | 2010 | 2013 |
| **1000 Taxes on income, profits and capital gains** | .. | .. | .. | .. | .. | **0** | **0** | **0** | **0** | **0** |
| 1100 Of individuals | .. | .. | .. | .. | .. | .. | .. | .. | .. | .. |
| 1200 Corporate | .. | .. | .. | .. | .. | .. | .. | .. | .. | .. |
| 1300 Unallocable between 1100 and 1200 | .. | .. | .. | .. | .. | .. | .. | .. | .. | .. |
| **2000 Social security contributions** | .. | .. | .. | .. | .. | **67** | **263** | **282** | **369** | **425** |
| 2100 Employees | .. | .. | .. | .. | .. | .. | 75 | 76 | 99 | 112 |
| 2200 Employers | .. | .. | .. | .. | .. | .. | 176 | 181 | 238 | 273 |
| 2300 Self-employed or non-employed | .. | .. | .. | .. | .. | .. | 13 | 25 | 33 | 40 |
| 2400 Unallocable between 2100, 2200 and 2300 | .. | .. | .. | .. | .. | 67 | 0 | 0 | 0 | 0 |
| **3000 Taxes on payroll and workforce** | .. | .. | .. | .. | .. | **0** | **0** | **0** | **0** | **0** |
| **4000 Taxes on property** | .. | .. | .. | .. | .. | **0** | **0** | **0** | **0** | **0** |
| 4100 Recurrent taxes on immovable property | .. | .. | .. | .. | .. | .. | .. | .. | .. | .. |
| 4200 Recurrent taxes on net wealth | .. | .. | .. | .. | .. | .. | .. | .. | .. | .. |
| 4300 Estate, inheritance and gift taxes | .. | .. | .. | .. | .. | .. | .. | .. | .. | .. |
| 4400 Taxes on financial and capital transactions | .. | .. | .. | .. | .. | .. | .. | .. | .. | .. |
| 4500 Non-recurrent taxes | .. | .. | .. | .. | .. | .. | .. | .. | .. | .. |
| 4600 Other recurrent taxes on property | .. | .. | .. | .. | .. | .. | .. | .. | .. | .. |
| **5000 Taxes on goods and services** | .. | .. | .. | .. | .. | **0** | **0** | **0** | **0** | **0** |
| 5100 Taxes on production, sale, transfer, etc | .. | .. | .. | .. | .. | .. | .. | .. | .. | .. |
| 5110 General taxes | .. | .. | .. | .. | .. | .. | .. | .. | .. | .. |
| 5120 Taxes on specific goods and services | .. | .. | .. | .. | .. | .. | .. | .. | .. | .. |
| 5130 Unallocable between 5110 and 5120 | .. | .. | .. | .. | .. | .. | .. | .. | .. | .. |
| 5200 Taxes on use of goods and perform activities | .. | .. | .. | .. | .. | .. | .. | .. | .. | .. |
| 5300 Unallocable between 5100 and 5200 | .. | .. | .. | .. | .. | .. | .. | .. | .. | .. |
| **6000 Other taxes** | .. | .. | .. | .. | .. | **0** | **0** | **0** | **0** | **0** |
| 6100 Paid solely by business | .. | .. | .. | .. | .. | .. | .. | .. | .. | .. |
| 6200 Other | .. | .. | .. | .. | .. | .. | .. | .. | .. | .. |
| **Total tax revenue** | .. | .. | .. | .. | .. | **67** | **263** | **282** | **369** | **425** |

1. The figures exclude local government tax revenues as the data are not available.
2. Corresponds to social security contributions paid to the Salvadoran Institute of Social Security.
3. Data on public pension contributions are not available for 2011 to 2013.

StatLink http://dx.doi.org/10.1787/888933190112

## Table 48. Guatemala, tax revenues by sub-sectors of government

*Million GTQ*

| | Federal government | | | | | State/Regional | | | | |
|---|---|---|---|---|---|---|---|---|---|---|
| | 1990 | 2000 | 2005 | 2010 | 2013 | 1990 | 2000 | 2005 | 2010 | 2013 |
| **1000 Taxes on income, profits and capital gains** | **507** | **3 295** | **6 049** | **10 319** | **16 041** | .. | .. | .. | .. | .. |
| 1100 Of individuals | 25 | 143 | 645 | 1 225 | 1 246 | .. | .. | .. | .. | .. |
| 1200 Corporate | 482 | 3 149 | 3 756 | 6 520 | 11 532 | .. | .. | .. | .. | .. |
| 1300 Unallocable between 1100 and 1200 | 0 | 2 | 1 647 | 2 574 | 3 263 | .. | .. | .. | .. | .. |
| **2000 Social security contributions** | **0** | **0** | **0** | **0** | **0** | .. | .. | .. | .. | .. |
| 2100 Employees | .. | .. | .. | .. | .. | .. | .. | .. | .. | .. |
| 2200 Employers | .. | .. | .. | .. | .. | .. | .. | .. | .. | .. |
| 2300 Self-employed or non-employed | .. | .. | .. | .. | .. | .. | .. | .. | .. | .. |
| 2400 Unallocable between 2100, 2200 and 2300 | .. | .. | .. | .. | .. | .. | .. | .. | .. | .. |
| **3000 Taxes on payroll and workforce** | **0** | **0** | **0** | **0** | **0** | .. | .. | .. | .. | .. |
| **4000 Taxes on property** | **45** | **17** | **9** | **11** | **12** | .. | .. | .. | .. | .. |
| 4100 Recurrent taxes on immovable property | 0 | 6 | 1 | 1 | 1 | .. | .. | .. | .. | .. |
| 4200 Recurrent taxes on net wealth | 0 | 0 | 0 | 0 | 0 | .. | .. | .. | .. | .. |
| 4300 Estate, inheritance and gift taxes | 0 | 0 | 0 | 0 | 0 | .. | .. | .. | .. | .. |
| 4400 Taxes on financial and capital transactions | 45 | 12 | 8 | 10 | 10 | .. | .. | .. | .. | .. |
| 4500 Non-recurrent taxes | 0 | 0 | 0 | 0 | 0 | .. | .. | .. | .. | .. |
| 4600 Other recurrent taxes on property | 0 | 0 | 0 | 0 | 0 | .. | .. | .. | .. | .. |
| **5000 Taxes on goods and services** | **1 709** | **10 317** | **16 402** | **23 259** | **29 075** | .. | .. | .. | .. | .. |
| 5100 Taxes on production, sale, transfer, etc | 1 681 | 10 131 | 16 083 | 22 754 | 27 545 | .. | .. | .. | .. | .. |
| 5110 General taxes | 762 | 6 259 | 10 753 | 16 980 | 21 874 | .. | .. | .. | .. | .. |
| 5120 Taxes on specific goods and services | 919 | 3 872 | 5 330 | 5 773 | 5 671 | .. | .. | .. | .. | .. |
| 5130 Unallocable between 5110 and 5120 | 0 | 0 | 0 | 0 | 0 | .. | .. | .. | .. | .. |
| 5200 Taxes on use of goods and perform activities | 28 | 186 | 319 | 505 | 1 530 | .. | .. | .. | .. | .. |
| 5300 Unallocable between 5100 and 5200 | 0 | 0 | 0 | 0 | 0 | .. | .. | .. | .. | .. |
| **6000 Other taxes** | **104** | **186** | **315** | **572** | **430** | .. | .. | .. | .. | .. |
| 6100 Paid solely by business | 0 | 0 | 0 | 0 | 0 | .. | .. | .. | .. | .. |
| 6200 Other | 104 | 186 | 315 | 572 | 430 | .. | .. | .. | .. | .. |
| **Total tax revenue** | **2 365** | **13 816** | **22 775** | **34 161** | **45 558** | .. | .. | .. | .. | .. |

*Million GTQ*

| | Local government[1] | | | | | Social Security Funds[2] | | | | |
|---|---|---|---|---|---|---|---|---|---|---|
| | 1990 | 2000 | 2005 | 2010 | 2013 | 1990 | 2000 | 2005 | 2010 | 2013 |
| **1000 Taxes on income, profits and capital gains** | .. | **0** | **0** | **0** | **0** | **0** | **0** | **0** | **0** | **0** |
| 1100 Of individuals | .. | .. | .. | .. | .. | .. | .. | .. | .. | .. |
| 1200 Corporate | .. | .. | .. | .. | .. | .. | .. | .. | .. | .. |
| 1300 Unallocable between 1100 and 1200 | .. | .. | .. | .. | .. | .. | .. | .. | .. | .. |
| **2000 Social security contributions** | .. | **0** | **0** | **0** | **0** | **436** | **2 569** | **4 072** | **6 408** | **8 617** |
| 2100 Employees | .. | .. | .. | .. | .. | .. | .. | .. | .. | .. |
| 2200 Employers | .. | .. | .. | .. | .. | .. | .. | .. | .. | .. |
| 2300 Self-employed or non-employed | .. | .. | .. | .. | .. | .. | .. | .. | .. | .. |
| 2400 Unallocable between 2100, 2200 and 2300 | .. | .. | .. | .. | .. | 436 | 2 569 | 4 072 | 6 408 | 8 617 |
| **3000 Taxes on payroll and workforce** | .. | **0** | **0** | **0** | **0** | **0** | **0** | **0** | **0** | **0** |
| **4000 Taxes on property** | .. | **147** | **341** | **620** | **779** | **0** | **0** | **0** | **0** | **0** |
| 4100 Recurrent taxes on immovable property | .. | 147 | 341 | 620 | 779 | .. | .. | .. | .. | .. |
| 4200 Recurrent taxes on net wealth | .. | 0 | 0 | 0 | 0 | .. | .. | .. | .. | .. |
| 4300 Estate, inheritance and gift taxes | .. | 0 | 0 | 0 | 0 | .. | .. | .. | .. | .. |
| 4400 Taxes on financial and capital transactions | .. | 0 | 0 | 0 | 0 | .. | .. | .. | .. | .. |
| 4500 Non-recurrent taxes | .. | 0 | 0 | 0 | 0 | .. | .. | .. | .. | .. |
| 4600 Other recurrent taxes on property | .. | 0 | 0 | 0 | 0 | .. | .. | .. | .. | .. |
| **5000 Taxes on goods and services** | .. | **0** | **0** | **0** | **0** | **0** | **0** | **0** | **0** | **0** |
| 5100 Taxes on production, sale, transfer, etc | .. | .. | .. | .. | .. | .. | .. | .. | .. | .. |
| 5110 General taxes | .. | .. | .. | .. | .. | .. | .. | .. | .. | .. |
| 5120 Taxes on specific goods and services | .. | .. | .. | .. | .. | .. | .. | .. | .. | .. |
| 5130 Unallocable between 5110 and 5120 | .. | .. | .. | .. | .. | .. | .. | .. | .. | .. |
| 5200 Taxes on use of goods and perform activities | .. | .. | .. | .. | .. | .. | .. | .. | .. | .. |
| 5300 Unallocable between 5100 and 5200 | .. | .. | .. | .. | .. | .. | .. | .. | .. | .. |
| **6000 Other taxes** | .. | **0** | **0** | **0** | **0** | **0** | **0** | **0** | **0** | **0** |
| 6100 Paid solely by business | .. | .. | .. | .. | .. | .. | .. | .. | .. | .. |
| 6200 Other | .. | .. | .. | .. | .. | .. | .. | .. | .. | .. |
| **Total tax revenue** | .. | **147** | **341** | **620** | **779** | **436** | **2 569** | **4 072** | **6 408** | **8 617** |

1. The figures exclude some local government tax revenues as the data are not available. Revenues from the municipal property tax (IUSI) are included.
2. Corresponds to social security contributions to the Guatemalan Social Security Institute (IGSS) and payments by public employees to the government's pension fund.

StatLink http://dx.doi.org/10.1787/888933190125

## Table 49. Honduras, tax revenues by sub-sectors of government

*Million HNL*

| | Federal government | | | | | State/Regional | | | | |
|---|---|---|---|---|---|---|---|---|---|---|
| | 1990 | 2000 | 2005 | 2010 | 2013 | 1990 | 2000 | 2005 | 2010 | 2013 |
| **1000 Taxes on income, profits and capital gains** | **431** | **2 985** | **7 498** | **13 972** | **19 597** | .. | .. | .. | .. | .. |
| 1100 Of individuals | 157 | 991 | 2 312 | 4 528 | 6 478 | .. | .. | .. | .. | .. |
| 1200 Corporate | 274 | 1 916 | 4 725 | 8 705 | 12 875 | .. | .. | .. | .. | .. |
| 1300 Unallocable between 1100 and 1200 | 0 | 78 | 461 | 740 | 245 | .. | .. | .. | .. | .. |
| **2000 Social security contributions** | **0** | **0** | **0** | **0** | **0** | .. | .. | .. | .. | .. |
| 2100 Employees | .. | .. | .. | .. | .. | .. | .. | .. | .. | .. |
| 2200 Employers | .. | .. | .. | .. | .. | .. | .. | .. | .. | .. |
| 2300 Self-employed or non-employed | .. | .. | .. | .. | .. | .. | .. | .. | .. | .. |
| 2400 Unallocable between 2100, 2200 and 2300 | .. | .. | .. | .. | .. | .. | .. | .. | .. | .. |
| **3000 Taxes on payroll and workforce** | **0** | **0** | **0** | **0** | **0** | .. | .. | .. | .. | .. |
| **4000 Taxes on property** | **16** | **189** | **170** | **254** | **298** | .. | .. | .. | .. | .. |
| 4100 Recurrent taxes on immovable property | 0 | 0 | 0 | 0 | 0 | .. | .. | .. | .. | .. |
| 4200 Recurrent taxes on net wealth | 0 | 0 | 0 | 0 | 0 | .. | .. | .. | .. | .. |
| 4300 Estate, inheritance and gift taxes | 0 | 0 | 0 | 0 | 0 | .. | .. | .. | .. | .. |
| 4400 Taxes on financial and capital transactions | 0 | 0 | 0 | 0 | 0 | .. | .. | .. | .. | .. |
| 4500 Non-recurrent taxes | 0 | 0 | 0 | 0 | 0 | .. | .. | .. | .. | .. |
| 4600 Other recurrent taxes on property | 16 | 189 | 170 | 254 | 298 | .. | .. | .. | .. | .. |
| **5000 Taxes on goods and services** | **1 405** | **11 445** | **19 032** | **28 937** | **35 720** | .. | .. | .. | .. | .. |
| 5100 Taxes on production, sale, transfer, etc | 1 405 | 11 445 | 19 032 | 28 937 | 35 720 | .. | .. | .. | .. | .. |
| 5110 General taxes | 344 | 5 146 | 9 565 | 16 050 | 20 637 | .. | .. | .. | .. | .. |
| 5120 Taxes on specific goods and services | 1 061 | 6 299 | 9 468 | 12 887 | 15 082 | .. | .. | .. | .. | .. |
| 5130 Unallocable between 5110 and 5120 | 0 | 0 | 0 | 0 | 0 | .. | .. | .. | .. | .. |
| 5200 Taxes on use of goods and perform activities | 0 | 0 | 0 | 0 | 0 | .. | .. | .. | .. | .. |
| 5300 Unallocable between 5100 and 5200 | 0 | 0 | 0 | 0 | 0 | .. | .. | .. | .. | .. |
| **6000 Other taxes** | **1** | **2** | **7** | **9** | **8** | .. | .. | .. | .. | .. |
| 6100 Paid solely by business | 0 | 0 | 0 | 0 | 0 | .. | .. | .. | .. | .. |
| 6200 Other | 1 | 2 | 7 | 9 | 8 | .. | .. | .. | .. | .. |
| **Total tax revenue** | **1 853** | **14 620** | **26 708** | **43 173** | **55 622** | .. | .. | .. | .. | .. |

*Million HNL*

| | Local government[1] | | | | | Social Security Funds | | | | |
|---|---|---|---|---|---|---|---|---|---|---|
| | 1990 | 2000 | 2005 | 2010 | 2013 | 1990 | 2000 | 2005 | 2010 | 2013 |
| **1000 Taxes on income, profits and capital gains** | .. | .. | .. | .. | .. | **0** | **0** | **0** | **0** | **0** |
| 1100 Of individuals | .. | .. | .. | .. | .. | .. | .. | .. | .. | .. |
| 1200 Corporate | .. | .. | .. | .. | .. | .. | .. | .. | .. | .. |
| 1300 Unallocable between 1100 and 1200 | .. | .. | .. | .. | .. | .. | .. | .. | .. | .. |
| **2000 Social security contributions** | .. | .. | .. | .. | .. | **179** | **1 727** | **4 416** | **8 671** | **12 529** |
| 2100 Employees | .. | .. | .. | .. | .. | .. | .. | .. | .. | .. |
| 2200 Employers | .. | .. | .. | .. | .. | .. | .. | .. | .. | .. |
| 2300 Self-employed or non-employed | .. | .. | .. | .. | .. | .. | .. | .. | .. | .. |
| 2400 Unallocable between 2100, 2200 and 2300 | .. | .. | .. | .. | .. | 179 | 1 727 | 4 416 | 8 671 | 12 529 |
| **3000 Taxes on payroll and workforce** | .. | .. | .. | .. | .. | **0** | **0** | **0** | **0** | **0** |
| **4000 Taxes on property** | .. | .. | .. | .. | .. | **0** | **0** | **0** | **0** | **0** |
| 4100 Recurrent taxes on immovable property | .. | .. | .. | .. | .. | .. | .. | .. | .. | .. |
| 4200 Recurrent taxes on net wealth | .. | .. | .. | .. | .. | .. | .. | .. | .. | .. |
| 4300 Estate, inheritance and gift taxes | .. | .. | .. | .. | .. | .. | .. | .. | .. | .. |
| 4400 Taxes on financial and capital transactions | .. | .. | .. | .. | .. | .. | .. | .. | .. | .. |
| 4500 Non-recurrent taxes | .. | .. | .. | .. | .. | .. | .. | .. | .. | .. |
| 4600 Other recurrent taxes on property | .. | .. | .. | .. | .. | .. | .. | .. | .. | .. |
| **5000 Taxes on goods and services** | .. | .. | .. | .. | .. | **0** | **0** | **0** | **0** | **0** |
| 5100 Taxes on production, sale, transfer, etc | .. | .. | .. | .. | .. | .. | .. | .. | .. | .. |
| 5110 General taxes | .. | .. | .. | .. | .. | .. | .. | .. | .. | .. |
| 5120 Taxes on specific goods and services | .. | .. | .. | .. | .. | .. | .. | .. | .. | .. |
| 5130 Unallocable between 5110 and 5120 | .. | .. | .. | .. | .. | .. | .. | .. | .. | .. |
| 5200 Taxes on use of goods and perform activities | .. | .. | .. | .. | .. | .. | .. | .. | .. | .. |
| 5300 Unallocable between 5100 and 5200 | .. | .. | .. | .. | .. | .. | .. | .. | .. | .. |
| **6000 Other taxes** | .. | .. | .. | .. | .. | **0** | **0** | **0** | **0** | **0** |
| 6100 Paid solely by business | .. | .. | .. | .. | .. | .. | .. | .. | .. | .. |
| 6200 Other | .. | .. | .. | .. | .. | .. | .. | .. | .. | .. |
| **Total tax revenue** | .. | .. | .. | .. | .. | **179** | **1 727** | **4 416** | **8 671** | **12 529** |

1. The figures exclude local government tax revenues as the data are not available.

StatLink http://dx.doi.org/10.1787/888933190132

## Table 50. Jamaica, tax revenues by sub-sectors of government

*Million JAM*

| | Federal government | | | | | State/Regional[1] | | | | |
|---|---|---|---|---|---|---|---|---|---|---|
| | 1990 | 2000 | 2005 | 2010 | 2013 | 1990 | 2000 | 2005 | 2010 | 2013 |
| **1000 Taxes on income, profits and capital gains** | **3 944** | **39 277** | **69 894** | **118 708** | **129 951** | .. | .. | .. | .. | .. |
| 1100 Of individuals | 1 687 | 17 441 | 36 043 | 54 798 | 66 283 | .. | .. | .. | .. | .. |
| 1200 Corporate | 1 280 | 7 627 | 13 134 | 33 091 | 34 539 | .. | .. | .. | .. | .. |
| 1300 Unallocable between 1100 and 1200 | 977 | 14 209 | 20 718 | 30 820 | 29 130 | .. | .. | .. | .. | .. |
| **2000 Social security contributions** | **0** | **0** | **0** | **0** | **0** | .. | .. | .. | .. | .. |
| 2100 Employees | .. | .. | .. | .. | .. | .. | .. | .. | .. | .. |
| 2200 Employers | .. | .. | .. | .. | .. | .. | .. | .. | .. | .. |
| 2300 Self-employed or non-employed | .. | .. | .. | .. | .. | .. | .. | .. | .. | .. |
| 2400 Unallocable between 2100, 2200 and 2300 | .. | .. | .. | .. | .. | .. | .. | .. | .. | .. |
| **3000 Taxes on payroll and workforce** | **0** | **0** | **0** | **0** | **0** | .. | .. | .. | .. | .. |
| **4000 Taxes on property** | **67** | **0** | **0** | **0** | **0** | .. | .. | .. | .. | .. |
| 4100 Recurrent taxes on immovable property | 67 | .. | .. | .. | .. | .. | .. | .. | .. | .. |
| 4200 Recurrent taxes on net wealth | 0 | .. | .. | .. | .. | .. | .. | .. | .. | .. |
| 4300 Estate, inheritance and gift taxes | 0 | .. | .. | .. | .. | .. | .. | .. | .. | .. |
| 4400 Taxes on financial and capital transactions | 0 | .. | .. | .. | .. | .. | .. | .. | .. | .. |
| 4500 Non-recurrent taxes | 0 | .. | .. | .. | .. | .. | .. | .. | .. | .. |
| 4600 Other recurrent taxes on property | 0 | .. | .. | .. | .. | .. | .. | .. | .. | .. |
| **5000 Taxes on goods and services** | **3 294** | **44 638** | **78 147** | **148 894** | **195 021** | .. | .. | .. | .. | .. |
| 5100 Taxes on production, sale, transfer, etc | 3 230 | 43 838 | 77 036 | 146 850 | 192 167 | .. | .. | .. | .. | .. |
| 5110 General taxes | 4 | 13 059 | 27 274 | 45 152 | 57 474 | .. | .. | .. | .. | .. |
| 5120 Taxes on specific goods and services | 3 226 | 30 779 | 49 762 | 101 698 | 134 693 | .. | .. | .. | .. | .. |
| 5130 Unallocable between 5110 and 5120 | 0 | 0 | 0 | 0 | 0 | .. | .. | .. | .. | .. |
| 5200 Taxes on use of goods and perform activities | 64 | 800 | 1 111 | 2 045 | 2 854 | .. | .. | .. | .. | .. |
| 5300 Unallocable between 5100 and 5200 | 0 | 0 | 0 | 0 | 0 | .. | .. | .. | .. | .. |
| **6000 Other taxes** | **444** | **3 159** | **8 733** | **8 738** | **12 606** | .. | .. | .. | .. | .. |
| 6100 Paid solely by business | 0 | 0 | 0 | 0 | 0 | .. | .. | .. | .. | .. |
| 6200 Other | 444 | 3 159 | 8 733 | 8 738 | 12 606 | .. | .. | .. | .. | .. |
| **Total tax revenue** | **7 748** | **87 074** | **156 775** | **276 340** | **337 578** | .. | .. | .. | .. | .. |

*Million JAM*

| | Local government | | | | | Social Security Funds | | | | |
|---|---|---|---|---|---|---|---|---|---|---|
| | 1990 | 2000 | 2005 | 2010 | 2013 | 1990 | 2000 | 2005 | 2010 | 2013 |
| **1000 Taxes on income, profits and capital gains** | **0** | **0** | **0** | **0** | **0** | **0** | **0** | **0** | **0** | **0** |
| 1100 Of individuals | .. | .. | .. | .. | .. | .. | .. | .. | .. | .. |
| 1200 Corporate | .. | .. | .. | .. | .. | .. | .. | .. | .. | .. |
| 1300 Unallocable between 1100 and 1200 | .. | .. | .. | .. | .. | .. | .. | .. | .. | .. |
| **2000 Social security contributions** | **0** | **0** | **0** | **0** | **0** | **0** | **0** | **5 110** | **9 248** | **14 559** |
| 2100 Employees | .. | .. | .. | .. | .. | .. | .. | .. | .. | .. |
| 2200 Employers | .. | .. | .. | .. | .. | .. | .. | .. | .. | .. |
| 2300 Self-employed or non-employed | .. | .. | .. | .. | .. | .. | .. | .. | .. | .. |
| 2400 Unallocable between 2100, 2200 and 2300 | .. | .. | .. | .. | .. | .. | .. | 5 110 | 9 248 | 14 559 |
| **3000 Taxes on payroll and workforce** | **0** | **0** | **0** | **0** | **0** | **0** | **0** | **0** | **0** | **0** |
| **4000 Taxes on property** | **0** | **639** | **1 474** | **2 792** | **5 842** | **0** | **0** | **0** | **0** | **0** |
| 4100 Recurrent taxes on immovable property | .. | 639 | 1 474 | 2 792 | 5 842 | .. | .. | .. | .. | .. |
| 4200 Recurrent taxes on net wealth | .. | 0 | 0 | 0 | 0 | .. | .. | .. | .. | .. |
| 4300 Estate, inheritance and gift taxes | .. | 0 | 0 | 0 | 0 | .. | .. | .. | .. | .. |
| 4400 Taxes on financial and capital transactions | .. | 0 | 0 | 0 | 0 | .. | .. | .. | .. | .. |
| 4500 Non-recurrent taxes | .. | 0 | 0 | 0 | 0 | .. | .. | .. | .. | .. |
| 4600 Other recurrent taxes on property | .. | 0 | 0 | 0 | 0 | .. | .. | .. | .. | .. |
| **5000 Taxes on goods and services** | **0** | **0** | **0** | **0** | **0** | **0** | **0** | **0** | **0** | **0** |
| 5100 Taxes on production, sale, transfer, etc | .. | .. | .. | .. | .. | .. | .. | .. | .. | .. |
| 5110 General taxes | .. | .. | .. | .. | .. | .. | .. | .. | .. | .. |
| 5120 Taxes on specific goods and services | .. | .. | .. | .. | .. | .. | .. | .. | .. | .. |
| 5130 Unallocable between 5110 and 5120 | .. | .. | .. | .. | .. | .. | .. | .. | .. | .. |
| 5200 Taxes on use of goods and perform activities | .. | .. | .. | .. | .. | .. | .. | .. | .. | .. |
| 5300 Unallocable between 5100 and 5200 | .. | .. | .. | .. | .. | .. | .. | .. | .. | .. |
| **6000 Other taxes** | **0** | **0** | **0** | **0** | **0** | **0** | **0** | **0** | **0** | **0** |
| 6100 Paid solely by business | .. | .. | .. | .. | .. | .. | .. | .. | .. | .. |
| 6200 Other | .. | .. | .. | .. | .. | .. | .. | .. | .. | .. |
| **Total tax revenue** | **0** | **639** | **1 474** | **2 792** | **5 842** | **0** | **0** | **5 110** | **9 248** | **14 559** |

1. The figures exclude state/regional government tax revenues as the data are not available.

StatLink http://dx.doi.org/10.1787/888933190142

## Table 51. Mexico, tax revenues by sub-sectors of government

*Million MXN*

| | Federal government[3] | | | | | State/Regional[3] | | | | |
|---|---|---|---|---|---|---|---|---|---|---|
| | 1990 | 2000 | 2005 | 2010 | 2013 | 1990 | 2000 | 2005 | 2010 | 2013 |
| **1000 Taxes on income, profits and capital gains[1]** | **34 668** | **276 548** | **402 036** | **683 604** | **957 213** | **3** | **0** | **0** | **0** | **0** |
| 1100 Of individuals | .. | .. | 195 869 | 313 473 | 425 621 | .. | .. | .. | .. | .. |
| 1200 Corporate | .. | .. | 135 840 | 246 745 | 392 199 | .. | .. | .. | .. | .. |
| 1300 Unallocable between 1100 and 1200 | 34 668 | 276 548 | 70 327 | 123 386 | 139 393 | 3 | .. | .. | .. | .. |
| **2000 Social security contributions[2]** | **0** | **0** | **0** | **0** | **0** | **0** | **0** | **0** | **0** | **0** |
| 2100 Employees | .. | .. | .. | .. | .. | .. | .. | .. | .. | .. |
| 2200 Employers | .. | .. | .. | .. | .. | .. | .. | .. | .. | .. |
| 2300 Self-employed or non-employed | .. | .. | .. | .. | .. | .. | .. | .. | .. | .. |
| 2400 Unallocable between 2100, 2200 and 2300 | .. | .. | .. | .. | .. | .. | .. | .. | .. | .. |
| **3000 Taxes on payroll and workforce** | **818** | **0** | **0** | **0** | **0** | **972** | **11 215** | **20 429** | **36 818** | .. |
| **4000 Taxes on property** | **3** | **0** | **0** | **0** | **0** | **894** | **7 018** | **10 905** | **13 137** | .. |
| 4100 Recurrent taxes on immovable property | 0 | .. | .. | .. | .. | 482 | 5 238 | 6 544 | 8 522 | .. |
| 4200 Recurrent taxes on net wealth | 0 | .. | .. | .. | .. | 0 | 0 | 0 | 0 | .. |
| 4300 Estate, inheritance and gift taxes | 0 | .. | .. | .. | .. | 7 | 0 | 0 | 0 | .. |
| 4400 Taxes on financial and capital transactions | 3 | .. | .. | .. | .. | 405 | 1 781 | 4 361 | 4 615 | .. |
| 4500 Non-recurrent taxes | 0 | .. | .. | .. | .. | 0 | 0 | 0 | 0 | .. |
| 4600 Other recurrent taxes on property | 0 | .. | .. | .. | .. | 0 | 0 | 0 | 0 | .. |
| **5000 Taxes on goods and services** | **70 559** | **536 406** | **942 354** | **1 287 081** | **1 553 087** | **118** | **1 346** | **2 124** | **5 805** | .. |
| 5100 Taxes on production, sale, transfer, etc | 69 983 | 527 624 | 927 401 | 1 268 645 | 1 552 680 | 45 | 910 | 1 364 | 2 470 | .. |
| 5110 General taxes | 26 635 | 189 606 | 318 432 | 504 509 | 556 794 | 0 | 0 | 0 | 0 | .. |
| 5120 Taxes on specific goods and services | 43 348 | 338 018 | 608 969 | 764 136 | 995 886 | 30 | 910 | 1 364 | 2 470 | .. |
| 5130 Unallocable between 5110 and 5120 | 0 | 0 | 0 | 0 | 0 | 15 | 0 | 0 | 0 | .. |
| 5200 Taxes on use of goods and perform activities | 576 | 8 782 | 14 953 | 18 436 | 408 | 73 | 436 | 760 | 3 335 | .. |
| 5300 Unallocable between 5100 and 5200 | 0 | 0 | 0 | 0 | 0 | 0 | 0 | 0 | 0 | .. |
| **6000 Other taxes** | **1 340** | **5 878** | **8 616** | **22 236** | **26 919** | **165** | **907** | **1 537** | **2 547** | .. |
| 6100 Paid solely by business | 0 | 0 | 0 | 0 | 0 | 0 | 0 | 0 | 0 | .. |
| 6200 Other | 1 340 | 5 878 | 8 616 | 22 236 | 26 919 | 165 | 907 | 1 537 | 2 547 | .. |
| **Total tax revenue** | **107 388** | **818 832** | **1 353 007** | **1 992 921** | **2 537 219** | **2 152** | **20 485** | **34 995** | **58 307** | .. |

*Million MXN*

| | Local government[3] | | | | | Social Security Funds | | | | |
|---|---|---|---|---|---|---|---|---|---|---|
| | 1990 | 2000 | 2005 | 2010 | 2013 | 1990 | 2000 | 2005 | 2010 | 2013 |
| **1000 Taxes on income, profits and capital gains[1]** | **2** | **0** | **0** | **0** | **0** | **0** | **0** | **0** | **0** | **0** |
| 1100 Of individuals | .. | .. | .. | .. | .. | .. | .. | .. | .. | .. |
| 1200 Corporate | .. | .. | .. | .. | .. | .. | .. | .. | .. | .. |
| 1300 Unallocable between 1100 and 1200 | 2 | .. | .. | .. | .. | .. | .. | .. | .. | .. |
| **2000 Social security contributions[2]** | **0** | **0** | **0** | **0** | **0** | **17 165** | **167 292** | **261 673** | **378 006** | **490 918** |
| 2100 Employees | .. | .. | .. | .. | .. | .. | .. | .. | .. | .. |
| 2200 Employers | .. | .. | .. | .. | .. | .. | .. | .. | .. | .. |
| 2300 Self-employed or non-employed | .. | .. | .. | .. | .. | .. | .. | .. | .. | .. |
| 2400 Unallocable between 2100, 2200 and 2300 | .. | .. | .. | .. | .. | 17 165 | 167 292 | 261 673 | 378 006 | 490 918 |
| **3000 Taxes on payroll and workforce** | **7** | **2** | **32** | **93** | .. | **0** | **0** | **0** | **0** | **0** |
| **4000 Taxes on property** | **1 017** | **6 946** | **15 891** | **25 818** | .. | **0** | **0** | **0** | **0** | **0** |
| 4100 Recurrent taxes on immovable property | 554 | 4 710 | 10 098 | 17 202 | .. | .. | .. | .. | .. | .. |
| 4200 Recurrent taxes on net wealth | 0 | 0 | 0 | 0 | .. | .. | .. | .. | .. | .. |
| 4300 Estate, inheritance and gift taxes | 1 | 0 | 0 | 0 | .. | .. | .. | .. | .. | .. |
| 4400 Taxes on financial and capital transactions | 462 | 2 236 | 5 793 | 8 616 | .. | .. | .. | .. | .. | .. |
| 4500 Non-recurrent taxes | 0 | 0 | 0 | 0 | .. | .. | .. | .. | .. | .. |
| 4600 Other recurrent taxes on property | 0 | 0 | 0 | 0 | .. | .. | .. | .. | .. | .. |
| **5000 Taxes on goods and services** | **114** | **202** | **288** | **487** | .. | **0** | **0** | **0** | **0** | **0** |
| 5100 Taxes on production, sale, transfer, etc | 97 | 133 | 214 | 466 | .. | .. | .. | .. | .. | .. |
| 5110 General taxes | 0 | 0 | 0 | 0 | .. | .. | .. | .. | .. | .. |
| 5120 Taxes on specific goods and services | 95 | 133 | 214 | 466 | .. | .. | .. | .. | .. | .. |
| 5130 Unallocable between 5110 and 5120 | 2 | 0 | 0 | 0 | .. | .. | .. | .. | .. | .. |
| 5200 Taxes on use of goods and perform activities | 17 | 69 | 74 | 21 | .. | .. | .. | .. | .. | .. |
| 5300 Unallocable between 5100 and 5200 | 0 | 0 | 0 | 0 | .. | .. | .. | .. | .. | .. |
| **6000 Other taxes** | **114** | **866** | **1 539** | **2 616** | .. | **0** | **0** | **0** | **0** | **0** |
| 6100 Paid solely by business | 0 | 0 | 0 | 0 | .. | .. | .. | .. | .. | .. |
| 6200 Other | 114 | 866 | 1 539 | 2 616 | .. | .. | .. | .. | .. | .. |
| **Total tax revenue** | **1 254** | **8 016** | **17 750** | **29 014** | .. | **17 165** | **167 292** | **261 673** | **378 006** | **490 918** |

*Note:* The 2013 data for tax revenues of the State and Local levels of government are not available. They comprise revenues in categories 3000, 4000,5000, and 6000.

1. In ECLAC data, income taxes are presented net of credit on salary figures.
2. In ECLAC data, social security contributions are presented net of transfers from the Federal government for the payment of IMSS (Mexican Social Security Institute) pensions.
3. This adjustment for taxes collected by Federal government in which states and local governments have a share. Sub-central government's shares cannot be identified by type of tax.

StatLink http://dx.doi.org/10.1787/888933190152

## Table 52. Nicaragua, tax revenues by sub-sectors of government

*Million NIO*

| | Federal government | | | | | State/Regional | | | | |
|---|---|---|---|---|---|---|---|---|---|---|
| | 1990 | 2000 | 2005 | 2010 | 2013 | 1990 | 2000 | 2005 | 2010 | 2013 |
| **1000 Taxes on income, profits and capital gains** | .. | **1 144** | **3 902** | **8 351** | **14 521** | .. | .. | .. | .. | .. |
| 1100 Of individuals | .. | .. | .. | .. | .. | .. | .. | .. | .. | .. |
| 1200 Corporate | .. | .. | .. | .. | .. | .. | .. | .. | .. | .. |
| 1300 Unallocable between 1100 and 1200 | .. | 1 144 | 3 902 | 8 351 | 14 521 | .. | .. | .. | .. | .. |
| **2000 Social security contributions** | .. | **0** | **0** | **0** | **0** | .. | .. | .. | .. | .. |
| 2100 Employees | .. | .. | .. | .. | .. | .. | .. | .. | .. | .. |
| 2200 Employers | .. | .. | .. | .. | .. | .. | .. | .. | .. | .. |
| 2300 Self-employed or non-employed | .. | .. | .. | .. | .. | .. | .. | .. | .. | .. |
| 2400 Unallocable between 2100, 2200 and 2300 | .. | .. | .. | .. | .. | .. | .. | .. | .. | .. |
| **3000 Taxes on payroll and workforce** | .. | **0** | **0** | **0** | **0** | .. | .. | .. | .. | .. |
| **4000 Taxes on property** | .. | **0** | **2** | **130** | **311** | .. | .. | .. | .. | .. |
| 4100 Recurrent taxes on immovable property | .. | .. | 0 | 0 | 0 | .. | .. | .. | .. | .. |
| 4200 Recurrent taxes on net wealth | .. | .. | 2 | 130 | 311 | .. | .. | .. | .. | .. |
| 4300 Estate, inheritance and gift taxes | .. | .. | 0 | 0 | 0 | .. | .. | .. | .. | .. |
| 4400 Taxes on financial and capital transactions | .. | .. | 0 | 0 | 0 | .. | .. | .. | .. | .. |
| 4500 Non-recurrent taxes | .. | .. | 0 | 0 | 0 | .. | .. | .. | .. | .. |
| 4600 Other recurrent taxes on property | .. | .. | 0 | 0 | 0 | .. | .. | .. | .. | .. |
| **5000 Taxes on goods and services** | .. | **5 584** | **9 725** | **17 029** | **25 771** | .. | .. | .. | .. | .. |
| 5100 Taxes on production, sale, transfer, etc | .. | 5 584 | 9 725 | 17 029 | 25 771 | .. | .. | .. | .. | .. |
| 5110 General taxes | .. | 2 931 | 5 599 | 10 353 | 16 736 | .. | .. | .. | .. | .. |
| 5120 Taxes on specific goods and services | .. | 2 653 | 4 126 | 6 676 | 9 035 | .. | .. | .. | .. | .. |
| 5130 Unallocable between 5110 and 5120 | .. | 0 | 0 | 0 | 0 | .. | .. | .. | .. | .. |
| 5200 Taxes on use of goods and perform activities | .. | 0 | 0 | 0 | 0 | .. | .. | .. | .. | .. |
| 5300 Unallocable between 5100 and 5200 | .. | 0 | 0 | 0 | 0 | .. | .. | .. | .. | .. |
| **6000 Other taxes** | .. | **11** | **17** | **20** | **77** | .. | .. | .. | .. | .. |
| 6100 Paid solely by business | .. | 0 | 0 | 0 | 0 | .. | .. | .. | .. | .. |
| 6200 Other | .. | 11 | 17 | 20 | 77 | .. | .. | .. | .. | .. |
| **Total tax revenue** | .. | **6 739** | **13 646** | **25 530** | **40 681** | .. | .. | .. | .. | .. |

*Million NIO*

| | Local government[1] | | | | | Social Security Funds | | | | |
|---|---|---|---|---|---|---|---|---|---|---|
| | 1990 | 2000 | 2005 | 2010 | 2013 | 1990 | 2000 | 2005 | 2010 | 2013 |
| **1000 Taxes on income, profits and capital gains** | .. | .. | .. | .. | .. | .. | **0** | **0** | **0** | **0** |
| 1100 Of individuals | .. | .. | .. | .. | .. | .. | .. | .. | .. | .. |
| 1200 Corporate | .. | .. | .. | .. | .. | .. | .. | .. | .. | .. |
| 1300 Unallocable between 1100 and 1200 | .. | .. | .. | .. | .. | .. | .. | .. | .. | .. |
| **2000 Social security contributions** | .. | .. | .. | .. | .. | .. | **1 678** | **3 363** | **8 090** | **12 805** |
| 2100 Employees | .. | .. | .. | .. | .. | .. | .. | .. | .. | .. |
| 2200 Employers | .. | .. | .. | .. | .. | .. | .. | .. | .. | .. |
| 2300 Self-employed or non-employed | .. | .. | .. | .. | .. | .. | .. | .. | .. | .. |
| 2400 Unallocable between 2100, 2200 and 2300 | .. | .. | .. | .. | .. | .. | 1 678 | 3 363 | 8 090 | 12 805 |
| **3000 Taxes on payroll and workforce** | .. | .. | .. | .. | .. | .. | **0** | **0** | **0** | **0** |
| **4000 Taxes on property** | .. | .. | .. | .. | .. | .. | **0** | **0** | **0** | **0** |
| 4100 Recurrent taxes on immovable property | .. | .. | .. | .. | .. | .. | .. | .. | .. | .. |
| 4200 Recurrent taxes on net wealth | .. | .. | .. | .. | .. | .. | .. | .. | .. | .. |
| 4300 Estate, inheritance and gift taxes | .. | .. | .. | .. | .. | .. | .. | .. | .. | .. |
| 4400 Taxes on financial and capital transactions | .. | .. | .. | .. | .. | .. | .. | .. | .. | .. |
| 4500 Non-recurrent taxes | .. | .. | .. | .. | .. | .. | .. | .. | .. | .. |
| 4600 Other recurrent taxes on property | .. | .. | .. | .. | .. | .. | .. | .. | .. | .. |
| **5000 Taxes on goods and services** | .. | .. | .. | .. | .. | .. | **0** | **0** | **0** | **0** |
| 5100 Taxes on production, sale, transfer, etc | .. | .. | .. | .. | .. | .. | .. | .. | .. | .. |
| 5110 General taxes | .. | .. | .. | .. | .. | .. | .. | .. | .. | .. |
| 5120 Taxes on specific goods and services | .. | .. | .. | .. | .. | .. | .. | .. | .. | .. |
| 5130 Unallocable between 5110 and 5120 | .. | .. | .. | .. | .. | .. | .. | .. | .. | .. |
| 5200 Taxes on use of goods and perform activities | .. | .. | .. | .. | .. | .. | .. | .. | .. | .. |
| 5300 Unallocable between 5100 and 5200 | .. | .. | .. | .. | .. | .. | .. | .. | .. | .. |
| **6000 Other taxes** | .. | .. | .. | .. | .. | .. | **0** | **0** | **0** | **0** |
| 6100 Paid solely by business | .. | .. | .. | .. | .. | .. | .. | .. | .. | .. |
| 6200 Other | .. | .. | .. | .. | .. | .. | .. | .. | .. | .. |
| **Total tax revenue** | .. | .. | .. | .. | .. | .. | **1 678** | **3 363** | **8 090** | **12 805** |

*Note:* Comparable statistics for 1990 cannot be shown due to the devaluation of the Nicaraguan cordoba.

1. The figures exclude local government tax revenues as the data are not available.

StatLink http://dx.doi.org/10.1787/888933190168

## Table 53. Panama, tax revenues by sub-sectors of government

*Million PAB*

| | Federal government | | | | | State/Regional | | | | |
|---|---|---|---|---|---|---|---|---|---|---|
| | 1990 | 2000 | 2005 | 2010 | 2013 | 1990 | 2000 | 2005 | 2010 | 2013 |
| **1000 Taxes on income, profits and capital gains** | **216 950** | **484 872** | **562 852** | **1 317 028** | **2 199 534** | .. | .. | .. | .. | .. |
| 1100 Of individuals | 14 155 | 20 343 | 24 395 | 35 456 | 51 598 | .. | .. | .. | .. | .. |
| 1200 Corporate | 72 413 | 186 351 | 255 073 | 749 818 | 1 182 374 | .. | .. | .. | .. | .. |
| 1300 Unallocable between 1100 and 1200 | 130 382 | 278 178 | 283 384 | 531 754 | 965 562 | .. | .. | .. | .. | .. |
| **2000 Social security contributions** | **0** | **0** | **0** | **0** | **0** | .. | .. | .. | .. | .. |
| 2100 Employees | .. | .. | .. | .. | .. | .. | .. | .. | .. | .. |
| 2200 Employers | .. | .. | .. | .. | .. | .. | .. | .. | .. | .. |
| 2300 Self-employed or non-employed | .. | .. | .. | .. | .. | .. | .. | .. | .. | .. |
| 2400 Unallocable between 2100, 2200 and 2300 | .. | .. | .. | .. | .. | .. | .. | .. | .. | .. |
| **3000 Taxes on payroll and workforce[1]** | **0** | **36 400** | **36 243** | **58 844** | **82 400** | .. | .. | .. | .. | .. |
| **4000 Taxes on property** | **43 443** | **62 090** | **109 086** | **212 194** | **337 721** | .. | .. | .. | .. | .. |
| 4100 Recurrent taxes on immovable property | 28 330 | 33 898 | 56 424 | 107 791 | 180 621 | .. | .. | .. | .. | .. |
| 4200 Recurrent taxes on net wealth | 0 | 0 | 0 | 0 | 0 | .. | .. | .. | .. | .. |
| 4300 Estate, inheritance and gift taxes | 154 | 0 | 0 | 0 | 0 | .. | .. | .. | .. | .. |
| 4400 Taxes on financial and capital transactions | 3 419 | 9 343 | 21 049 | 29 810 | 49 391 | .. | .. | .. | .. | .. |
| 4500 Non-recurrent taxes | 0 | 0 | 0 | 0 | 0 | .. | .. | .. | .. | .. |
| 4600 Other recurrent taxes on property | 11 540 | 18 849 | 31 613 | 74 593 | 107 709 | .. | .. | .. | .. | .. |
| **5000 Taxes on goods and services** | **335 470** | **530 276** | **641 708** | **1 472 515** | **2 193 455** | .. | .. | .. | .. | .. |
| 5100 Taxes on production, sale, transfer, etc | 331 758 | 530 276 | 641 708 | 1 472 515 | 2 193 455 | .. | .. | .. | .. | .. |
| 5110 General taxes | 80 303 | 69 013 | 137 585 | 766 154 | 1 269 055 | .. | .. | .. | .. | .. |
| 5120 Taxes on specific goods and services[2] | 138 623 | 461 263 | 504 123 | 706 360 | 924 401 | .. | .. | .. | .. | .. |
| 5130 Unallocable between 5110 and 5120 | 112 832 | 0 | 0 | 0 | 0 | .. | .. | .. | .. | .. |
| 5200 Taxes on use of goods and perform activities | 3 712 | 0 | 0 | 0 | 0 | .. | .. | .. | .. | .. |
| 5300 Unallocable between 5100 and 5200 | 0 | 0 | 0 | 0 | 0 | .. | .. | .. | .. | .. |
| **6000 Other taxes[3]** | **25 674** | **42 876** | **28 784** | **41 064** | **46 200** | .. | .. | .. | .. | .. |
| 6100 Paid solely by business | 0 | 0 | 0 | 0 | 0 | .. | .. | .. | .. | .. |
| 6200 Other | 25 674 | 42 876 | 28 784 | 41 064 | 46 200 | .. | .. | .. | .. | .. |
| **Total tax revenue** | **621 537** | **1 156 514** | **1 378 673** | **3 101 645** | **4 859 310** | .. | .. | .. | .. | .. |

*Million PAB*

| | Local government[3] | | | | | Social Security Funds | | | | |
|---|---|---|---|---|---|---|---|---|---|---|
| | 1990 | 2000 | 2005 | 2010 | 2013 | 1990 | 2000 | 2005 | 2010 | 2013 |
| **1000 Taxes on income, profits and capital gains** | **0** | **0** | **0** | **0** | **0** | **0** | **0** | **0** | **0** | **0** |
| 1100 Of individuals | .. | .. | .. | .. | .. | .. | .. | .. | .. | .. |
| 1200 Corporate | .. | .. | .. | .. | .. | .. | .. | .. | .. | .. |
| 1300 Unallocable between 1100 and 1200 | .. | .. | .. | .. | .. | .. | .. | .. | .. | .. |
| **2000 Social security contributions** | **0** | **0** | **0** | **0** | **0** | **271 300** | **742 000** | **827 300** | **1 637 100** | **2 676 700** |
| 2100 Employees | .. | .. | .. | .. | .. | .. | .. | .. | .. | .. |
| 2200 Employers | .. | .. | .. | .. | .. | .. | .. | .. | .. | .. |
| 2300 Self-employed or non-employed | .. | .. | .. | .. | .. | .. | .. | .. | .. | .. |
| 2400 Unallocable between 2100, 2200 and 2300 | .. | .. | .. | .. | .. | 271 300 | 742 000 | 827 300 | 1 637 100 | 2 676 700 |
| **3000 Taxes on payroll and workforce[1]** | **0** | **0** | **0** | **0** | **0** | **0** | **0** | **0** | **0** | **0** |
| **4000 Taxes on property** | **0** | **0** | **0** | **0** | **0** | **0** | **0** | **0** | **0** | **0** |
| 4100 Recurrent taxes on immovable property | .. | 0 | 0 | .. | .. | .. | .. | .. | .. | .. |
| 4200 Recurrent taxes on net wealth | .. | 0 | 0 | .. | .. | .. | .. | .. | .. | .. |
| 4300 Estate, inheritance and gift taxes | .. | 0 | 0 | .. | .. | .. | .. | .. | .. | .. |
| 4400 Taxes on financial and capital transactions | .. | 0 | 0 | .. | .. | .. | .. | .. | .. | .. |
| 4500 Non-recurrent taxes | .. | 0 | 0 | .. | .. | .. | .. | .. | .. | .. |
| 4600 Other recurrent taxes on property | .. | 0 | 0 | .. | .. | .. | .. | .. | .. | .. |
| **5000 Taxes on goods and services** | **0** | **43 098** | **50 631** | **40 551** | **59 817** | **0** | **0** | **0** | **0** | **0** |
| 5100 Taxes on production, sale, transfer, etc | .. | 53 | 5 | 0 | 0 | .. | .. | .. | .. | .. |
| 5110 General taxes | .. | 0 | 0 | 0 | 0 | .. | .. | .. | .. | .. |
| 5120 Taxes on specific goods and services[2] | .. | 53 | 5 | 0 | 0 | .. | .. | .. | .. | .. |
| 5130 Unallocable between 5110 and 5120 | .. | 0 | 0 | 0 | 0 | .. | .. | .. | .. | .. |
| 5200 Taxes on use of goods and perform activities | .. | 43 045 | 50 626 | 40 551 | 59 817 | .. | .. | .. | .. | .. |
| 5300 Unallocable between 5100 and 5200 | .. | 0 | 0 | 0 | 0 | .. | .. | .. | .. | .. |
| **6000 Other taxes[3]** | **0** | **11** | **0** | **35 533** | **54 566** | **0** | **0** | **0** | **0** | **0** |
| 6100 Paid solely by business | .. | 0 | 0 | 0 | 0 | .. | .. | .. | .. | .. |
| 6200 Other | .. | 11 | 0 | 35 533 | 54 566 | .. | .. | .. | .. | .. |
| **Total tax revenue** | **0** | **43 109** | **50 631** | **76 085** | **114 383** | **271 300** | **742 000** | **827 300** | **1 637 100** | **2 676 700** |

1. In ECLAC data, Education insurance is classified as "Other taxes" (6000).
2. In CIAT and ECLAC data, the tax on banks, financial institutions, and currency exchange is classified as a property tax.
3. From 2011, figures for local government taxes have been estimated as shown under heading 6000. It includes some revenues that would otherwise be shown under 4000 and 5000.

StatLink http://dx.doi.org/10.1787/888933190173

## Table 54. Paraguay, tax revenues by sub-sectors of government

*Million PYG*

| | Federal government | | | | | State/Regional | | | | |
|---|---|---|---|---|---|---|---|---|---|---|
| | 1990 | 2000 | 2005 | 2010 | 2013 | 1990 | 2000 | 2005 | 2010 | 2013 |
| **1000 Taxes on income, profits and capital gains** | **73 726** | **470 388** | **938 886** | **2 096 498** | **3 100 223** | .. | .. | .. | .. | .. |
| 1100 Of individuals | .. | .. | .. | 1 150 | 13 375 | .. | .. | .. | .. | .. |
| 1200 Corporate | .. | 4 238 | 6 091 | 13 405 | 12 532 | .. | .. | .. | .. | .. |
| 1300 Unallocable between 1100 and 1200 | 73 726 | 466 150 | 932 795 | 2 081 943 | 3 074 316 | .. | .. | .. | .. | .. |
| **2000 Social security contributions[1]** | **28 882** | **300 451** | **541 310** | **1 140 654** | **1 607 065** | .. | .. | .. | .. | .. |
| 2100 Employees | .. | .. | .. | .. | .. | .. | .. | .. | .. | .. |
| 2200 Employers | .. | .. | .. | .. | .. | .. | .. | .. | .. | .. |
| 2300 Self-employed or non-employed | .. | .. | .. | .. | .. | .. | .. | .. | .. | .. |
| 2400 Unallocable between 2100, 2200 and 2300 | 28 882 | 300 451 | 541 310 | 1 140 654 | 1 607 065 | .. | .. | .. | .. | .. |
| **3000 Taxes on payroll and workforce** | **0** | **0** | **0** | **0** | **0** | .. | .. | .. | .. | .. |
| **4000 Taxes on property** | **17 162** | **0** | **0** | **0** | **0** | .. | .. | .. | .. | .. |
| 4100 Recurrent taxes on immovable property | 17 162 | .. | .. | .. | .. | .. | .. | .. | .. | .. |
| 4200 Recurrent taxes on net wealth | 0 | .. | .. | .. | .. | .. | .. | .. | .. | .. |
| 4300 Estate, inheritance and gift taxes | 0 | .. | .. | .. | .. | .. | .. | .. | .. | .. |
| 4400 Taxes on financial and capital transactions | 0 | .. | .. | .. | .. | .. | .. | .. | .. | .. |
| 4500 Non-recurrent taxes | 0 | .. | .. | .. | .. | .. | .. | .. | .. | .. |
| 4600 Other recurrent taxes on property | 0 | .. | .. | .. | .. | .. | .. | .. | .. | .. |
| **5000 Taxes on goods and services** | **179 312** | **2 080 878** | **4 309 832** | **9 226 477** | **11 524 523** | .. | .. | .. | .. | .. |
| 5100 Taxes on production, sale, transfer, etc | 179 312 | 2 080 878 | 4 309 832 | 9 226 477 | 11 524 523 | .. | .. | .. | .. | .. |
| 5110 General taxes | 0 | 1 150 496 | 2 478 998 | 5 991 694 | 7 843 002 | .. | .. | .. | .. | .. |
| 5120 Taxes on specific goods and services | 179 312 | 930 382 | 1 830 834 | 3 234 783 | 3 681 521 | .. | .. | .. | .. | .. |
| 5130 Unallocable between 5110 and 5120 | 0 | 0 | 0 | 0 | 0 | .. | .. | .. | .. | .. |
| 5200 Taxes on use of goods and perform activities | 0 | 0 | 0 | 0 | 0 | .. | .. | .. | .. | .. |
| 5300 Unallocable between 5100 and 5200 | 0 | 0 | 0 | 0 | 0 | .. | .. | .. | .. | .. |
| **6000 Other taxes** | **49 807** | **116 652** | **238 134** | **109 424** | **123 554** | .. | .. | .. | .. | .. |
| 6100 Paid solely by business | 0 | 0 | 0 | 0 | 0 | .. | .. | .. | .. | .. |
| 6200 Other | 49 807 | 116 652 | 238 134 | 109 424 | 123 554 | .. | .. | .. | .. | .. |
| **Total tax revenue** | **348 889** | **2 968 370** | **6 028 162** | **12 573 052** | **16 355 365** | .. | .. | .. | .. | .. |

*Million PYG*

| | Local government[2] | | | | | Social Security Funds[3] | | | | |
|---|---|---|---|---|---|---|---|---|---|---|
| | 1990 | 2000 | 2005 | 2010 | 2013 | 1990 | 2000 | 2005 | 2010 | 2013 |
| **1000 Taxes on income, profits and capital gains** | .. | .. | **0** | **0** | .. | .. | **0** | **0** | **0** | **0** |
| 1100 Of individuals | .. | .. | .. | .. | .. | .. | .. | .. | .. | .. |
| 1200 Corporate | .. | .. | .. | .. | .. | .. | .. | .. | .. | .. |
| 1300 Unallocable between 1100 and 1200 | .. | .. | .. | .. | .. | .. | .. | .. | .. | .. |
| **2000 Social security contributions[1]** | .. | .. | **0** | **0** | .. | .. | **619 082** | **1 050 670** | **2 411 987** | **3 551 007** |
| 2100 Employees | .. | .. | .. | .. | .. | .. | .. | .. | .. | .. |
| 2200 Employers | .. | .. | .. | .. | .. | .. | .. | .. | .. | .. |
| 2300 Self-employed or non-employed | .. | .. | .. | .. | .. | .. | .. | .. | .. | .. |
| 2400 Unallocable between 2100, 2200 and 2300 | .. | .. | .. | .. | .. | .. | 619 082 | 1 050 670 | 2 411 987 | 3 551 007 |
| **3000 Taxes on payroll and workforce** | .. | .. | **0** | **0** | .. | .. | **0** | **0** | **0** | **0** |
| **4000 Taxes on property** | .. | .. | **0** | **272 385** | .. | .. | **0** | **0** | **0** | **0** |
| 4100 Recurrent taxes on immovable property | .. | .. | .. | 254 306 | .. | .. | .. | .. | .. | .. |
| 4200 Recurrent taxes on net wealth | .. | .. | .. | 0 | .. | .. | .. | .. | .. | .. |
| 4300 Estate, inheritance and gift taxes | .. | .. | .. | 0 | .. | .. | .. | .. | .. | .. |
| 4400 Taxes on financial and capital transactions | .. | .. | .. | 16 316 | .. | .. | .. | .. | .. | .. |
| 4500 Non-recurrent taxes | .. | .. | .. | 0 | .. | .. | .. | .. | .. | .. |
| 4600 Other recurrent taxes on property | .. | .. | .. | 1 762 | .. | .. | .. | .. | .. | .. |
| **5000 Taxes on goods and services** | .. | .. | .. | **234 485** | .. | .. | **0** | **0** | **0** | **0** |
| 5100 Taxes on production, sale, transfer, etc | .. | .. | .. | 23 221 | .. | .. | .. | .. | .. | .. |
| 5110 General taxes | .. | .. | .. | 0 | .. | .. | .. | .. | .. | .. |
| 5120 Taxes on specific goods and services | .. | .. | .. | 23 221 | .. | .. | .. | .. | .. | .. |
| 5130 Unallocable between 5110 and 5120 | .. | .. | .. | 0 | .. | .. | .. | .. | .. | .. |
| 5200 Taxes on use of goods and perform activities | .. | .. | .. | 211 027 | .. | .. | .. | .. | .. | .. |
| 5300 Unallocable between 5100 and 5200 | .. | .. | .. | 237 | .. | .. | .. | .. | .. | .. |
| **6000 Other taxes** | .. | .. | **355 192** | **145 766** | .. | .. | **0** | **0** | **0** | **0** |
| 6100 Paid solely by business | .. | .. | 0 | 0 | .. | .. | .. | .. | .. | .. |
| 6200 Other | .. | .. | 355 192 | 145 766 | .. | .. | .. | .. | .. | .. |
| **Total tax revenue** | .. | .. | **355 192** | **652 636** | .. | .. | **619 082** | **1 050 670** | **2 411 987** | **3 551 007** |

1. Data on social security contributions collected by decentralized institutions are not available for 2011 to 2013, with the exception of the contributions made to the Instituto de Previsión Social (Social Security Institute).
2. The figures for years up to and including 2004, as well as for 2013, exclude local government tax revenues as the data are not available.
3. The figures for years up to and including 1998, as well as 2013, exclude decentralized institutions as the data are not available.

StatLink http://dx.doi.org/10.1787/888933190181

## Table 55. Peru, tax revenues by sub-sectors of government

*Million PEN*

| | Federal government | | | | | State/Regional | | | | |
|---|---|---|---|---|---|---|---|---|---|---|
| | 1990 | 2000 | 2005 | 2010 | 2013 | 1990 | 2000 | 2005 | 2010 | 2013 |
| **1000 Taxes on income, profits and capital gains** | **37** | **5 130** | **12 283** | **28 357** | **39 982** | .. | .. | .. | .. | .. |
| 1100 Of individuals | 3 | 2 117 | 3 349 | 7 286 | 10 927 | .. | .. | .. | .. | .. |
| 1200 Corporate | 32 | 3 012 | 8 933 | 21 071 | 28 718 | .. | .. | .. | .. | .. |
| 1300 Unallocable between 1100 and 1200 | 1 | 0 | 0 | 0 | 337 | .. | .. | .. | .. | .. |
| **2000 Social security contributions** | **0** | **0** | **0** | **0** | **0** | .. | .. | .. | .. | .. |
| 2100 Employees | .. | .. | .. | .. | .. | .. | .. | .. | .. | .. |
| 2200 Employers | .. | .. | .. | .. | .. | .. | .. | .. | .. | .. |
| 2300 Self-employed or non-employed | .. | .. | .. | .. | .. | .. | .. | .. | .. | .. |
| 2400 Unallocable between 2100, 2200 and 2300 | .. | .. | .. | .. | .. | .. | .. | .. | .. | .. |
| **3000 Taxes on payroll and workforce** | **0** | **1 038** | **27** | **3** | **1** | .. | .. | .. | .. | .. |
| **4000 Taxes on property** | **99** | **0** | **783** | **944** | **134** | .. | .. | .. | .. | .. |
| 4100 Recurrent taxes on immovable property | 0 | 0 | 0 | 0 | 0 | .. | .. | .. | .. | .. |
| 4200 Recurrent taxes on net wealth | 61 | 0 | 0 | 0 | 0 | .. | .. | .. | .. | .. |
| 4300 Estate, inheritance and gift taxes | 0 | 0 | 0 | 0 | 0 | .. | .. | .. | .. | .. |
| 4400 Taxes on financial and capital transactions | 38 | 0 | 706 | 944 | 134 | .. | .. | .. | .. | .. |
| 4500 Non-recurrent taxes | 0 | 0 | 0 | 0 | 0 | .. | .. | .. | .. | .. |
| 4600 Other recurrent taxes on property | 0 | 0 | 76 | 0 | 0 | .. | .. | .. | .. | .. |
| **5000 Taxes on goods and services** | **423** | **15 739** | **21 748** | **34 565** | **44 154** | .. | .. | .. | .. | .. |
| 5100 Taxes on production, sale, transfer, etc | 423 | 15 739 | 21 748 | 34 565 | 44 154 | .. | .. | .. | .. | .. |
| 5110 General taxes | 78 | 9 519 | 14 779 | 28 693 | 37 052 | .. | .. | .. | .. | .. |
| 5120 Taxes on specific goods and services | 345 | 6 220 | 6 969 | 5 871 | 7 102 | .. | .. | .. | .. | .. |
| 5130 Unallocable between 5110 and 5120 | 0 | 0 | 0 | 0 | 0 | .. | .. | .. | .. | .. |
| 5200 Taxes on use of goods and perform activities | 0 | 0 | 0 | 0 | 0 | .. | .. | .. | .. | .. |
| 5300 Unallocable between 5100 and 5200 | 0 | 0 | 0 | 0 | 0 | .. | .. | .. | .. | .. |
| **6000 Other taxes** | **36** | **761** | **800** | **1 389** | **2 041** | .. | .. | .. | .. | .. |
| 6100 Paid solely by business | 0 | 84 | 73 | 108 | 147 | .. | .. | .. | .. | .. |
| 6200 Other | 36 | 678 | 727 | 1 281 | 1 894 | .. | .. | .. | .. | .. |
| **Total tax revenue** | **595** | **22 667** | **35 640** | **65 258** | **86 313** | .. | .. | .. | .. | .. |

*Million PEN*

| | Local government[1] | | | | | Social Security Funds | | | | |
|---|---|---|---|---|---|---|---|---|---|---|
| | 1990 | 2000 | 2005 | 2010 | 2013 | 1990 | 2000 | 2005 | 2010 | 2013 |
| **1000 Taxes on income, profits and capital gains** | .. | .. | **0** | **0** | **0** | **0** | **0** | **0** | **0** | **0** |
| 1100 Of individuals | .. | .. | .. | .. | .. | .. | .. | .. | .. | .. |
| 1200 Corporate | .. | .. | .. | .. | .. | .. | .. | .. | .. | .. |
| 1300 Unallocable between 1100 and 1200 | .. | .. | .. | .. | .. | .. | .. | .. | .. | .. |
| **2000 Social security contributions** | .. | .. | **0** | **0** | **0** | **50** | **3 184** | **4 000** | **7 189** | **10 946** |
| 2100 Employees | .. | .. | .. | .. | .. | .. | 541 | 644 | 1 618 | 2 786 |
| 2200 Employers | .. | .. | .. | .. | .. | .. | 2 447 | 3 207 | 5 283 | 7 928 |
| 2300 Self-employed or non-employed | .. | .. | .. | .. | .. | .. | 95 | 36 | 42 | 55 |
| 2400 Unallocable between 2100, 2200 and 2300 | .. | .. | .. | .. | .. | 50 | 102 | 113 | 246 | 177 |
| **3000 Taxes on payroll and workforce** | .. | .. | **0** | **0** | **0** | **0** | **0** | **0** | **0** | **0** |
| **4000 Taxes on property** | .. | .. | **549** | **1 293** | **1 770** | **0** | **0** | **0** | **0** | **0** |
| 4100 Recurrent taxes on immovable property | .. | .. | 453 | 864 | 1 770 | .. | .. | .. | .. | .. |
| 4200 Recurrent taxes on net wealth | .. | .. | 0 | 0 | 0 | .. | .. | .. | .. | .. |
| 4300 Estate, inheritance and gift taxes | .. | .. | 0 | 0 | 0 | .. | .. | .. | .. | .. |
| 4400 Taxes on financial and capital transactions | .. | .. | 96 | 429 | 0 | .. | .. | .. | .. | .. |
| 4500 Non-recurrent taxes | .. | .. | 0 | 0 | 0 | .. | .. | .. | .. | .. |
| 4600 Other recurrent taxes on property | .. | .. | .. | .. | .. | .. | .. | .. | .. | .. |
| **5000 Taxes on goods and services** | .. | .. | **104** | **290** | **431** | **0** | **0** | **0** | **0** | **0** |
| 5100 Taxes on production, sale, transfer, etc | .. | .. | 104 | 290 | 431 | .. | .. | .. | .. | .. |
| 5110 General taxes | .. | .. | 0 | 0 | 0 | .. | .. | .. | .. | .. |
| 5120 Taxes on specific goods and services | .. | .. | 104 | 290 | 431 | .. | .. | .. | .. | .. |
| 5130 Unallocable between 5110 and 5120 | .. | .. | 0 | 0 | 0 | .. | .. | .. | .. | .. |
| 5200 Taxes on use of goods and perform activities | .. | .. | 0 | 0 | 0 | .. | .. | .. | .. | .. |
| 5300 Unallocable between 5100 and 5200 | .. | .. | 0 | 0 | 0 | .. | .. | .. | .. | .. |
| **6000 Other taxes** | .. | .. | **987** | **1 616** | **650** | **0** | **0** | **0** | **0** | **0** |
| 6100 Paid solely by business | .. | .. | 0 | 0 | 0 | .. | .. | .. | .. | .. |
| 6200 Other | .. | .. | 987 | 1 616 | 650 | .. | .. | .. | .. | .. |
| **Total tax revenue** | .. | .. | **1 640** | **3 199** | **2 852** | **50** | **3 184** | **4 000** | **7 189** | **10 946** |

1. The figures for years up to and including 2004 exclude local government tax revenues as the data are not available.

StatLink http://dx.doi.org/10.1787/888933190195

## Table 56. Uruguay, tax revenues by sub-sectors of government

*Million UYU*

| | Federal government | | | | | State/Regional | | | | |
|---|---|---|---|---|---|---|---|---|---|---|
| | 1990 | 2000 | 2005 | 2010 | 2013 | 1990 | 2000 | 2005 | 2010 | 2013 |
| **1000 Taxes on income, profits and capital gains** | **114** | **5 620** | **11 969** | **44 573** | **71 398** | .. | .. | .. | .. | .. |
| 1100 Of individuals | 0 | 0 | 44 | 19 654 | 34 611 | .. | .. | .. | .. | .. |
| 1200 Corporate | 114 | 5 620 | 11 925 | 23 257 | 34 108 | .. | .. | .. | .. | .. |
| 1300 Unallocable between 1100 and 1200 | 0 | 0 | 0 | 1 662 | 2 679 | .. | .. | .. | .. | .. |
| **2000 Social security contributions[1]** | **0** | **0** | **0** | **0** | **0** | .. | .. | .. | .. | .. |
| 2100 Employees | .. | .. | .. | .. | .. | .. | .. | .. | .. | .. |
| 2200 Employers | .. | .. | .. | .. | .. | .. | .. | .. | .. | .. |
| 2300 Self-employed or non-employed | .. | .. | .. | .. | .. | .. | .. | .. | .. | .. |
| 2400 Unallocable between 2100, 2200 and 2300 | .. | .. | .. | .. | .. | .. | .. | .. | .. | .. |
| **3000 Taxes on payroll and workforce** | **0** | **0** | **0** | **0** | **0** | .. | .. | .. | .. | .. |
| **4000 Taxes on property[2]** | **125** | **3 935** | **8 252** | **11 690** | **15 126** | .. | .. | .. | .. | .. |
| 4100 Recurrent taxes on immovable property[3] | 0 | 378 | 852 | 1 064 | 1 238 | .. | .. | .. | .. | .. |
| 4200 Recurrent taxes on net wealth | 94 | 2 076 | 4 943 | 8 948 | 11 892 | .. | .. | .. | .. | .. |
| 4300 Estate, inheritance and gift taxes | 0 | 0 | 0 | 0 | 0 | .. | .. | .. | .. | .. |
| 4400 Taxes on financial and capital transactions | 0 | 372 | 933 | 1 350 | 1 516 | .. | .. | .. | .. | .. |
| 4500 Non-recurrent taxes | 0 | 0 | 0 | 0 | 0 | .. | .. | .. | .. | .. |
| 4600 Other recurrent taxes on property | 31 | 1 107 | 1 524 | 328 | 480 | .. | .. | .. | .. | .. |
| **5000 Taxes on goods and services[2]** | **1 270** | **28 301** | **52 727** | **94 990** | **125 048** | .. | .. | .. | .. | .. |
| 5100 Taxes on production, sale, transfer, etc | 1 270 | 28 301 | 52 727 | 94 990 | 125 048 | .. | .. | .. | .. | .. |
| 5110 General taxes[2] | 660 | 18 009 | 34 641 | 69 365 | 98 071 | .. | .. | .. | .. | .. |
| 5120 Taxes on specific goods and services | 610 | 10 291 | 18 086 | 25 625 | 26 977 | .. | .. | .. | .. | .. |
| 5130 Unallocable between 5110 and 5120 | 0 | 0 | 0 | 0 | 0 | .. | .. | .. | .. | .. |
| 5200 Taxes on use of goods and perform activities[3] | 0 | 0 | 0 | 0 | 0 | .. | .. | .. | .. | .. |
| 5300 Unallocable between 5100 and 5200 | 0 | 0 | 0 | 0 | 0 | .. | .. | .. | .. | .. |
| **6000 Other taxes** | **-10** | **-596** | **76** | **0** | **214** | .. | .. | .. | .. | .. |
| 6100 Paid solely by business | -10 | -596 | 76 | 0 | 214 | .. | .. | .. | .. | .. |
| 6200 Other | 0 | 0 | 0 | 0 | 0 | .. | .. | .. | .. | .. |
| **Total tax revenue** | **1 500** | **37 259** | **73 023** | **151 253** | **211 787** | .. | .. | .. | .. | .. |

*Million UYU*

| | Local government | | | | | Social Security Funds | | | | |
|---|---|---|---|---|---|---|---|---|---|---|
| | 1990 | 2000 | 2005 | 2010 | 2013 | 1990 | 2000 | 2005 | 2010 | 2013 |
| **1000 Taxes on income, profits and capital gains** | **0** | **0** | **0** | **0** | **0** | **0** | **0** | **0** | **0** | **0** |
| 1100 Of individuals | .. | .. | .. | .. | .. | .. | .. | .. | .. | .. |
| 1200 Corporate | .. | .. | .. | .. | .. | .. | .. | .. | .. | .. |
| 1300 Unallocable between 1100 and 1200 | .. | .. | .. | .. | .. | .. | .. | .. | .. | .. |
| **2000 Social security contributions[1]** | **0** | **0** | **0** | **0** | **0** | **717** | **17 679** | **21 425** | **49 742** | **86 012** |
| 2100 Employees | .. | .. | .. | .. | .. | .. | .. | .. | .. | .. |
| 2200 Employers | .. | .. | .. | .. | .. | .. | .. | .. | .. | .. |
| 2300 Self-employed or non-employed | .. | .. | .. | .. | .. | .. | .. | .. | .. | .. |
| 2400 Unallocable between 2100, 2200 and 2300 | .. | .. | .. | .. | .. | 717 | 17 679 | 21 425 | 49 742 | 86 012 |
| **3000 Taxes on payroll and workforce** | **0** | **0** | **0** | **0** | **0** | **0** | **0** | **0** | **0** | **0** |
| **4000 Taxes on property[2]** | **72** | **2 142** | **3 787** | **5 245** | **6 262** | **0** | **0** | **0** | **0** | **0** |
| 4100 Recurrent taxes on immovable property[3] | 72 | 2 142 | 3 787 | 5 245 | 6 262 | .. | .. | .. | .. | .. |
| 4200 Recurrent taxes on net wealth | 0 | 0 | 0 | 0 | 0 | .. | .. | .. | .. | .. |
| 4300 Estate, inheritance and gift taxes | 0 | 0 | 0 | 0 | 0 | .. | .. | .. | .. | .. |
| 4400 Taxes on financial and capital transactions | 0 | 0 | 0 | 0 | 0 | .. | .. | .. | .. | .. |
| 4500 Non-recurrent taxes | 0 | 0 | 0 | 0 | 0 | .. | .. | .. | .. | .. |
| 4600 Other recurrent taxes on property | 0 | 0 | 0 | 0 | 0 | .. | .. | .. | .. | .. |
| **5000 Taxes on goods and services[2]** | **64** | **2 576** | **3 071** | **3 952** | **4 600** | **0** | **0** | **0** | **0** | **0** |
| 5100 Taxes on production, sale, transfer, etc | 0 | 0 | 0 | 0 | 0 | .. | .. | .. | .. | .. |
| 5110 General taxes[2] | .. | .. | .. | .. | .. | .. | .. | .. | .. | .. |
| 5120 Taxes on specific goods and services | .. | .. | .. | .. | .. | .. | .. | .. | .. | .. |
| 5130 Unallocable between 5110 and 5120 | .. | .. | .. | .. | .. | .. | .. | .. | .. | .. |
| 5200 Taxes on use of goods and perform activities[3] | 64 | 2 576 | 3 071 | 3 952 | 4 600 | .. | .. | .. | .. | .. |
| 5300 Unallocable between 5100 and 5200 | 0 | 0 | 0 | 0 | 0 | .. | .. | .. | .. | .. |
| **6000 Other taxes** | **0** | **0** | **0** | **0** | **0** | **0** | **0** | **0** | **0** | **0** |
| 6100 Paid solely by business | .. | .. | .. | .. | .. | .. | .. | .. | .. | .. |
| 6200 Other | .. | .. | .. | .. | .. | .. | .. | .. | .. | .. |
| **Total tax revenue** | **136** | **4 718** | **6 858** | **9 196** | **10 862** | **717** | **17 679** | **21 425** | **49 742** | **86 012** |

1. Figures for 1990-1998 are reconstructed estimates, as the current methodology used to calculate social security contributions was not employed until 1999.
2. In ECLAC data, the tax on the sale of goods by public auction is classified in category 4000.
3. Data on the following taxes are not available for 2013: Property tax (municipal), Rural property tax and Vehicle licences (municipal).

StatLink http://dx.doi.org/10.1787/888933190205

## Table 57. Venezuela, tax revenues by sub-sectors of government

*Million VEF*

| | Federal government | | | | | State/Regional[3] | | | | |
|---|---|---|---|---|---|---|---|---|---|---|
| | 1990 | 2000 | 2005 | 2010 | 2013 | 1990 | 2000 | 2005 | 2010 | 2013 |
| **1000 Taxes on income, profits and capital gains** | **344** | **4 686** | **18 529** | **36 836** | **93 694** | .. | .. | .. | .. | .. |
| 1100 Of individuals | .. | .. | .. | .. | .. | .. | .. | .. | .. | .. |
| 1200 Corporate | 315 | 3 368 | 11 184 | 8 700 | 25 270 | .. | .. | .. | .. | .. |
| 1300 Unallocable between 1100 and 1200 | 30 | 1 317 | 7 345 | 28 137 | 68 424 | .. | .. | .. | .. | .. |
| **2000 Social security contributions[1]** | **0** | **0** | **0** | **0** | **0** | .. | .. | .. | .. | .. |
| 2100 Employees | .. | .. | .. | .. | .. | .. | .. | .. | .. | .. |
| 2200 Employers | .. | .. | .. | .. | .. | .. | .. | .. | .. | .. |
| 2300 Self-employed or non-employed | .. | .. | .. | .. | .. | .. | .. | .. | .. | .. |
| 2400 Unallocable between 2100, 2200 and 2300 | .. | .. | .. | .. | .. | .. | .. | .. | .. | .. |
| **3000 Taxes on payroll and workforce** | **0** | **0** | **0** | **0** | **0** | .. | .. | .. | .. | .. |
| **4000 Taxes on property** | **1** | **400** | **2 834** | **222** | **530** | .. | .. | .. | .. | .. |
| 4100 Recurrent taxes on immovable property | 0 | 0 | 0 | 0 | 0 | .. | .. | .. | .. | .. |
| 4200 Recurrent taxes on net wealth | 0 | 0 | 0 | 0 | 0 | .. | .. | .. | .. | .. |
| 4300 Estate, inheritance and gift taxes | 1 | 19 | 55 | 222 | 530 | .. | .. | .. | .. | .. |
| 4400 Taxes on financial and capital transactions | 0 | 381 | 2 779 | 0 | 0 | .. | .. | .. | .. | .. |
| 4500 Non-recurrent taxes | 0 | 0 | 0 | 0 | 0 | .. | .. | .. | .. | .. |
| 4600 Other recurrent taxes on property | 0 | 0 | 0 | 0 | 0 | .. | .. | .. | .. | .. |
| **5000 Taxes on goods and services** | **46** | **5 173** | **25 032** | **73 707** | **205 423** | .. | .. | .. | .. | .. |
| 5100 Taxes on production, sale, transfer, etc | 46 | 5 173 | 25 032 | 73 707 | 205 423 | .. | .. | .. | .. | .. |
| 5110 General taxes | 0 | 3 272 | 19 513 | 56 101 | 164 737 | .. | .. | .. | .. | .. |
| 5120 Taxes on specific goods and services | 46 | 1 901 | 5 519 | 17 606 | 40 686 | .. | .. | .. | .. | .. |
| 5130 Unallocable between 5110 and 5120 | 0 | 0 | 0 | 0 | 0 | .. | .. | .. | .. | .. |
| 5200 Taxes on use of goods and perform activities | 0 | 0 | 0 | 0 | 0 | .. | .. | .. | .. | .. |
| 5300 Unallocable between 5100 and 5200 | 0 | 0 | 0 | 0 | 0 | .. | .. | .. | .. | .. |
| **6000 Other taxes[2]** | **0** | **0** | **0** | **0** | **5 000** | .. | .. | .. | .. | .. |
| 6100 Paid solely by business | .. | .. | .. | .. | 0 | .. | .. | .. | .. | .. |
| 6200 Other | .. | .. | .. | .. | 5 000 | .. | .. | .. | .. | .. |
| **Total tax revenue** | **391** | **10 258** | **46 395** | **110 765** | **304 647** | .. | .. | .. | .. | .. |

*Million VEF*

| | Local government[3] | | | | | Social Security Funds | | | | |
|---|---|---|---|---|---|---|---|---|---|---|
| | 1990 | 2000 | 2005 | 2010 | 2013 | 1990 | 2000 | 2005 | 2010 | 2013 |
| **1000 Taxes on income, profits and capital gains** | .. | .. | .. | .. | .. | **0** | **0** | **0** | **0** | **0** |
| 1100 Of individuals | .. | .. | .. | .. | .. | .. | .. | .. | .. | .. |
| 1200 Corporate | .. | .. | .. | .. | .. | .. | .. | .. | .. | .. |
| 1300 Unallocable between 1100 and 1200 | .. | .. | .. | .. | .. | .. | .. | .. | .. | .. |
| **2000 Social security contributions[1]** | .. | .. | .. | .. | .. | **20** | **591** | **1 890** | **5 547** | **10 000** |
| 2100 Employees | .. | .. | .. | .. | .. | .. | .. | .. | .. | .. |
| 2200 Employers | .. | .. | .. | .. | .. | .. | .. | .. | .. | .. |
| 2300 Self-employed or non-employed | .. | .. | .. | .. | .. | .. | .. | .. | .. | .. |
| 2400 Unallocable between 2100, 2200 and 2300 | .. | .. | .. | .. | .. | 20 | 591 | 1 890 | 5 547 | 10 000 |
| **3000 Taxes on payroll and workforce** | .. | .. | .. | .. | .. | **0** | **0** | **0** | **0** | **0** |
| **4000 Taxes on property** | .. | .. | .. | .. | .. | **0** | **0** | **0** | **0** | **0** |
| 4100 Recurrent taxes on immovable property | .. | .. | .. | .. | .. | .. | .. | .. | .. | .. |
| 4200 Recurrent taxes on net wealth | .. | .. | .. | .. | .. | .. | .. | .. | .. | .. |
| 4300 Estate, inheritance and gift taxes | .. | .. | .. | .. | .. | .. | .. | .. | .. | .. |
| 4400 Taxes on financial and capital transactions | .. | .. | .. | .. | .. | .. | .. | .. | .. | .. |
| 4500 Non-recurrent taxes | .. | .. | .. | .. | .. | .. | .. | .. | .. | .. |
| 4600 Other recurrent taxes on property | .. | .. | .. | .. | .. | .. | .. | .. | .. | .. |
| **5000 Taxes on goods and services** | .. | .. | .. | .. | .. | **0** | **0** | **0** | **0** | **0** |
| 5100 Taxes on production, sale, transfer, etc | .. | .. | .. | .. | .. | .. | .. | .. | .. | .. |
| 5110 General taxes | .. | .. | .. | .. | .. | .. | .. | .. | .. | .. |
| 5120 Taxes on specific goods and services | .. | .. | .. | .. | .. | .. | .. | .. | .. | .. |
| 5130 Unallocable between 5110 and 5120 | .. | .. | .. | .. | .. | .. | .. | .. | .. | .. |
| 5200 Taxes on use of goods and perform activities | .. | .. | .. | .. | .. | .. | .. | .. | .. | .. |
| 5300 Unallocable between 5100 and 5200 | .. | .. | .. | .. | .. | .. | .. | .. | .. | .. |
| **6000 Other taxes[2]** | .. | .. | .. | .. | .. | **0** | **0** | **0** | **0** | **0** |
| 6100 Paid solely by business | .. | .. | .. | .. | .. | .. | .. | .. | .. | .. |
| 6200 Other | .. | .. | .. | .. | .. | .. | .. | .. | .. | .. |
| **Total tax revenue** | .. | .. | .. | .. | .. | **20** | **591** | **1 890** | **5 547** | **10 000** |

1. The data on social security contributions are unavailable for 2011 to 2013 and were estimated.
2. The data on other taxes were estimated for 2013.
3. The figures exclude state and local government tax revenues as the data are not available.

StatLink http://dx.doi.org/10.1787/888933190211

## Chart 3. **Attribution of tax revenues to sub-sectors of general government, 2012**

Receipts as percentage of total tax revenue

## Gráfico 3. **Atribución de los ingresos tributarios en los sub-sectores del gobierno general, 2012**

Ingresos como porcentaje de los ingresos tributarios totales

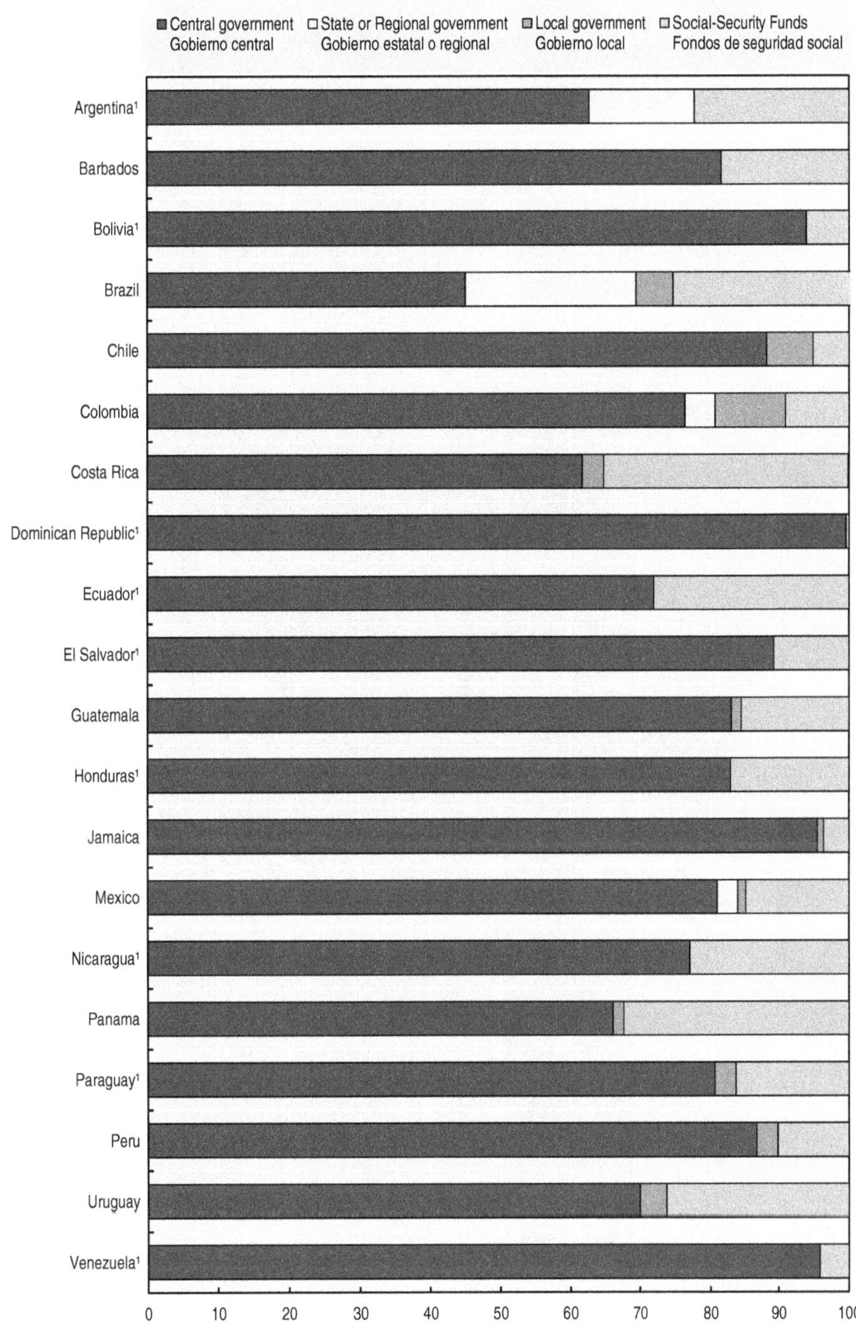


1. The figures exclude local government revenues for Argentina, Barbados, Bolivia, Dominican Republic, Ecuador, El Salvador, Honduras, Jamaica, Nicaragua, Paraguay and Venezuela as the data are not available.

1. Las cifras excluyen los ingresos de gobiernos locales en Argentina, Barbados, Bolivia, Ecuador, El Salvador, Honduras, Jamaica, Nicaragua, Paraguay, República Dominicana y Venezuela dado que los datos no están disponibles.

*Source*: Table 37 in Part IV/Cuadro 37 en Parte IV.

StatLink http://dx.doi.org/10.1787/888933189860

# ANNEX A

## *The OECD classification of taxes and Interpretative Guide*

## *Table of contents*


| | Page |
|---|---|
| The OECD classification of taxes | 174 |
| The OECD Interpretative Guide | 176 |
| A. Coverage | 176 |
| B. Basis of reporting | 178 |
| C. General classification criteria | 179 |
| D. Commentaries on items of the list | 181 |
| E. Conciliation with National Accounts | 191 |
| F. Memorandum item on the financing of social security benefits | 191 |
| G. Memorandum item on identifiable taxes paid by government | 191 |
| H. Relation of OECD classification of taxes to national accounting systems | 191 |
| I. The OECD classification of taxes and the International Monetary Fund system | 192 |
| J. Comparison of the OECD classification of taxes with other international classifications | 192 |
| K. Attribution of tax revenues by subsectors of general government | 194 |
| L. Provisional classification of revenues from bank levies and payments to deposit insurance and financial stability schemes | 197 |
| Notes | 198 |

# The OECD classification of taxes

1000 *Taxes on income, profits and capital gains*

- 1100 Individuals
  - 1110 Income and profits
  - 1120 Capital gains
- 1200 Corporates
  - 1210 Income and profits
  - 1220 Capital gains
- 1300 Unallocable as between 1100 and 1200

2000 *Social security contributions*

- 2100 Employees
- 2200 Employers
- 2300 Self-employed, non-employed
- 2400 Unallocable as between 2100, 2200 and 2300

3000 *Taxes on payroll and workforce*

4000 *Taxes on property*

- 4100 Recurrent taxes on immovable property
  - 4110 Households
  - 4120 Other
- 4200 Recurrent net wealth taxes
  - 4210 Individuals
  - 4220 Corporates
- 4300 Estate, inheritance and gift taxes
  - 4310 Estate and inheritance taxes
  - 4320 Gift taxes
- 4400 Taxes on financial and capital transactions
- 4500 Other non-recurrent taxes on property
- 4600 Other recurrent taxes on property

5000 *Taxes on goods and services*

- 5100 Taxes on production, sale and transfer of goods and services
  - 5110 General sales taxes
    - 5111 Value-added taxes
    - 5112 Sales taxes
    - 5113 Other general taxes
  - 5120 Taxes on specific goods and services
    - 5121 Excises
    - 5122 Profits of fiscal monopolies
    - 5123 Customs and import duties
    - 5124 On exports
    - 5125 On investment goods
    - 5126 On specific services
    - 5127 Other taxes on international trade and transactions
    - 5128 Other taxes on specific goods and services
  - 5130 Unallocable as between 5110 and 5120
- 5200 Taxes on use of goods
  - 5210 Recurrent taxes
    - 5211 Motor vehicles taxes households
    - 5212 Motor vehicles taxes others
    - 5213 Other recurrent taxes
  - 5220 Non-recurrent taxes
- 5300 Unallocable as between 5100 and 5200

6000 *Other taxes*

- 6100 Paid solely by business
- 6200 Paid by other than business, or unidentifiable

# The OECD Interpretative Guide[1]

## A. Coverage

*General criteria*

1. In the OECD classification the term "taxes" is confined to compulsory unrequited payments to general government. Taxes are unrequited in the sense that benefits provided by government to taxpayers are not normally in proportion to their payments.

2. The term 'tax' does not include fines unrelated to tax offences and compulsory loans paid to government. Borderline cases between tax and non-tax revenues in relation to certain fees and charges are discussed in §9–13.

3. General government consists of the central administration, agencies whose operations are under its effective control, state and local governments and their administrations, certain social security schemes and autonomous governmental entities, excluding public enterprises. This definition of government follows that of the 2008 System of National Accounts (SNA).[2] In that publication, the general government sector and its sub-sectors are defined in chapter 4, section F, pages 80-84.

4. Compulsory payments to supra-national bodies and their agencies are no longer included as taxes as from 1998, with some exceptions. However, custom duties collected by EU member states on behalf of the European Union are still identified as memorandum items and included in overall tax revenue amounts in the country tables (Part III) of the country in which they are collected. (See §95). In countries where the church forms part of general government church taxes are included, provided they meet the criteria set out in §1 above. As the data refer to receipts of general government, levies paid to non-government bodies, welfare agencies or social insurance schemes outside general government, trade unions or trade associations, even where such levies are compulsory, are excluded. Compulsory payments to general government earmarked for such bodies are, however, included, provided that the government is not simply acting in an agency capacity.[3] Profits from fiscal monopolies are distinguished from those of other public enterprises and are treated as taxes because they reflect the exercise of the taxing power of the state by the use of monopoly powers (see §62–64), as are profits received by the government from the purchase and sale of foreign exchange at different rates (see §70).

5. Taxes paid by governments (e.g. social security contributions and payroll taxes paid by governments in their capacity as an employer, consumption taxes on their purchases or taxes on their property) are not excluded from the data provided. However, where it is possible to identify the amounts of revenue involved,[4] they are shown in section III.C of this Report.

6. The relationship between this classification and that of the System of National Accounts (SNA) is set out in Sections H and J below. Because of the differences between the two classifications, the data shown in national accounts are sometimes calculated or classified differently from the practice set out in this guide. These and other differences are mentioned where appropriate (e.g. in §13 and §26 below) but it is not possible to refer to all of them. There may also be some differences between this classification and that employed domestically by certain national administrations (e.g. see §10 below), so that OECD and national statistics data may not always be consistent: any such differences, however, are likely to be very slight in terms of amounts of revenues involved.

*Social security contributions*

7. Compulsory social security contributions, as defined in §35 below, paid to general government, are treated here as tax revenues. Being compulsory payments to general government they clearly resemble taxes. They may, however, differ from other taxes in that the receipt of social security benefits depends, in most countries, upon appropriate contributions having been made, although the size of the benefits is not necessarily related to the amount of the contributions. Better comparability between countries is obtained by treating social security contributions as taxes, but they are listed under a separate heading so that they can be distinguished in any analysis.

8. Social security contributions which are either voluntary or not payable to general government (see §1) are not treated as taxes, though in some countries, as indicated in the country footnotes, there are difficulties in eliminating voluntary contributions and certain compulsory payments to the private sector.

*Fees, user charges and licence fees*

9. Apart from vehicle licence fees, which are universally regarded as taxes, it is not easy to distinguish between those fees and user charges which are to be treated as taxes and those which are not, since, whilst a fee or charge is levied in connection with a specific service or activity, the strength of the link between the fee and the service provided may vary considerably, as may the relation between the amount of the fee and the cost of providing the service. Where the recipient of a service pays a fee clearly related to the cost of providing the service, the levy may be regarded as requited and under the definition of §1 would not be considered as a tax. In the following cases, however, a levy could be considered as 'unrequited':

a) where the charge greatly exceeds the cost of providing the service;

b) where the payer of the levy is not the receiver of the benefit (e.g. a fee collected from slaughterhouses to finance a service which is provided to farmers);

c) where government is not providing a specific service in return for the levy which it receives even though a licence may be issued to the payer (e.g. where the government grants a hunting, fishing or shooting licence which is not accompanied by the right to use a specific area of government land);

d) where benefits are received only by those paying the levy but the benefits received by each individual are not necessarily in proportion to his payments (e.g. a milk marketing levy paid by dairy farmers and used to promote the consumption of milk).

10. In marginal cases, however, the application of the criteria set out in §1 can be particularly difficult. The solution adopted – given the desirability of international uniformity and the relatively small amounts of revenue usually involved – is to follow the predominant practice among tax administrations rather than to allow each country to adopt its own view as to whether such levies are regarded as taxes or as non-tax revenue.[5]

11. A list of the main fees and charges in question and their normal[6] treatment in this publication is as follows:

| | |
|---|---|
| Non-tax revenues: | court fees; driving licence fees; harbour fees; passport fees; radio and television licence fees where public authorities provide the service. |
| Taxes within heading 5200: | permission to perform such activities as distributing films; hunting, fishing and shooting; providing entertainment or gambling facilities; selling alcohol or tobacco; permission to own dogs or to use or own motor vehicles or guns; severance taxes. |

12. In practice it may not always be possible to isolate tax receipts from non-tax revenue receipts when they are recorded together. If it is estimated that the bulk of the receipts derive from non-tax revenues, the whole amount involved is treated as a non-tax revenue; otherwise, such government receipts are included and classified according to the rules provided in §28 below.

13. Two differences between the OECD classification and SNA regarding the borderline between tax and non-tax revenues are:

a) SNA classifies a number of levies as indirect taxes if paid by enterprises, but as non-tax revenues if paid by households, a distinction which is regarded as irrelevant in this classification for distinguishing between tax and non-tax revenues.[7]

b) Predominant practice among most OECD tax administrations, which is occasionally used in this classification for distinguishing between tax and non-tax revenues, is not a relevant criterion for SNA purposes.

### *Royalties*

14. Royalty payments for the right to extract oil and gas or to exploit other mineral resources are normally regarded as non-tax revenues since they are property income from government-owned land or resources.

### *Fines and penalties*

15. Receipts from fines and penalties paid for infringement of regulations identified as relating to a particular tax and interest on payments overdue in respect of a particular tax are recorded together with receipts from that tax. Other kinds of fines identifiable as relating to tax offences are classified in the residual heading 6000. Fines not relating to tax offences (e.g. for parking offences), or not identifiable as relating to tax offences, are not treated as taxes.

## B. Basis of reporting

### *Accrual reporting*

16. The data reported in this publication for recent years are predominantly recorded on an accrual basis, i.e. recorded at the time that the tax liability was created. Further information is provided in the footnotes to the country table in Part III of the Report.

17. However, data for earlier years are still predominantly recorded on a cash basis, i.e. at the time at which the payment was received by government. Thus, for example, taxes withheld by employers in one year but paid to the government in the following year and taxes due in one year but actually paid in the following year are both included in the receipts of the second year. Corrective transactions, such as refunds, repayments and drawbacks, are deducted from gross revenues of the period in which they are made.

18. Data on tax revenues are recorded without offsets for the administrative expenses connected with tax collection. Similarly, where the proceeds of tax are used to subsidise particular members of the community, the subsidy is not deducted from the yield of the tax, though the tax may be shown net of subsidies in the national records of some countries.

19. As regards fiscal monopolies (heading 5122), only the amount actually transferred to the government is included in government revenues. However, if any expenditures of fiscal monopolies are considered to be government expenditures (e.g. social expenditures undertaken by fiscal monopolies at the direction of the government) they are added back for the purpose of arriving at tax revenue figures (see §62 below).

*The distinction between tax and expenditure provisions*[8]

20. Because this publication is concerned only with the revenue side of government operations, no account being taken of the expenditure side, a distinction has to be made between tax and expenditure provisions. Normally there is no difficulty in making this distinction as expenditures are made outside the tax system and the tax accounts and under legislation separate from the tax legislation. In borderline cases, cash flow is used to distinguish between tax provisions and expenditure provisions. Insofar as a provision affects the flow of tax payments from the taxpayer to the government, it is regarded as a tax provision and is taken into account in the data shown in this publication. A provision which does not affect this flow is seen as an expenditure provision and is disregarded in the data recorded in this publication.

21. Tax allowances, exemptions and deductions against the tax base clearly affect the amount of tax paid to the government and are therefore considered as tax provisions. At the other extreme, those subsidies which cannot be offset against tax liability and which are clearly not connected with the assessment process, do not reduce tax revenues as recorded in this publication. Tax credits are amounts deductible from tax payable (as distinct from deductions from the tax base). Two types of tax credits are distinguished, those (referred to here as wastable tax credits) which are limited to the amount of the tax liability and therefore cannot give rise to a payment by the authorities to the taxpayer, and those (referred to as non-wastable tax credits) which are not so limited, so that the excess of the credit over the tax liability can be paid to the taxpayer.[9] A wastable tax credit, like a tax allowance, clearly affects the amount of tax paid to the government, and is therefore considered as a tax provision. The practice followed for non-wastable tax credits[10] is to distinguish between the "tax expenditure component",[11] which is that portion of the credit that is used to reduce or eliminate a taxpayer's liability, and the 'transfer component', which is the portion that exceeds the taxpayer's liability and is paid to that taxpayer. Reported tax revenues should be reduced by the amount of the tax expenditure component but not by the amount of the transfer component. In addition, the amounts of the tax expenditure and transfer components should be reported as memorandum items in the country tables. Countries that are unable to distinguish between the tax expenditure and transfer components should indicate whether or not the tax revenues have been reduced by the total of these components, and provide any available estimates of the amounts of the two components. Further information is given in section C of Part I of the Report, which illustrates the effect of alternative treatments of non-wastable tax credits on Tax to GDP.

*Calendar and fiscal years*

22. National authorities whose fiscal years do not correspond to the calendar year show data, where possible, on a calendar year basis to permit maximum comparability with the data of other countries. There remain a few countries where data refer to fiscal years. For these the GDP data used in the comparative tables also correspond to the fiscal years.

## C. General classification criteria

*The main classification criteria*

23. The classification of receipts among the main headings (1000, 2000, 3000, 4000, 5000 and 6000) is generally governed by the base on which the tax is levied: 1000 income, profits and capital gains; 2000 and 3000 earnings, payroll or number of employees; 4000 property; 5000 goods and services; 6000 multiple bases, other bases or unidentifiable bases. Where a tax is calculated on more than one base, the receipts are, where possible, split among the various headings (see §28 and §78). The headings 4000 and 5000 cover

not only taxes where the tax base is the property, goods or services themselves but also certain related taxes. Thus, taxes on the transfer of property are included in 4400[12] and taxes on the use of goods or on permission to perform activities in 5200. In headings 4000 and 5000 a distinction is made in certain sub-headings between recurrent and non-recurrent taxes: recurrent taxes are defined as those levied at regular intervals (usually annually) and non-recurrent taxes are levied once and for all (see also §43 to §46, §49, §50 and §76 for particular applications of this distinction).

24. Earmarking of a tax for specific purposes does not affect the classification of tax receipts. However, as explained in §35 on the classification of social security contributions, the conferment of an entitlement to social benefits is crucial to the definition of the 2000 main heading.

25. The way that a tax is levied or collected (e.g. by use of stamps) does not affect classification.

*Classification of taxpayers*

26. In certain sub-headings distinctions are made between different categories of taxpayers. These distinctions vary from tax to tax:

*a) Between individuals and corporations in relation to income and net wealth taxes*

The basic distinction is that corporation income taxes, as distinct from individual income taxes, are levied on the corporation as an entity, not on the individuals who own it, and without regard to the personal circumstances of these individuals. The same distinction applies to net wealth taxes on corporations and those on individuals. Taxes paid on the profits of partnerships and the income of institutions, such as life insurance or pension funds, are classified according to the same rule. They are classified as corporate taxes (1200) if they are charged on the partnership or institution as an entity without regard to the personal circumstances of the owners. Otherwise, they are treated as individual taxes (1100). Usually, there is different legislation for the corporation taxes and for the individual taxes.[13] The distinction made here between individuals and corporations does not follow the sector classification between households, enterprises, and so on of the System of National Accounts for income and outlay accounts. The SNA classification requires certain unincorporated businesses[14] to be excluded from the household sector and included with non-financial enterprises and financial institutions. The tax on the profits of these businesses, however, cannot always be separated from the tax on the other income of their owners, or can be separated only on an arbitrary basis. No attempt at this separation is made here and the whole of the individual income tax is shown together without regard to the nature of the income chargeable.

*b) Between households and others in relation to taxes on immovable property*

Here the distinction is that adopted by the SNA for the production and consumption expenditure accounts. The distinction is between households as consumers (i.e. excluding non-incorporated business) on the one hand and producers on the other hand. However, taxes on dwellings occupied by households, whether paid by owner-occupiers, tenants or landlords, are classified under households. This follows the common distinction made between taxes on domestic property versus taxes on business property. Some countries are not, however, in a position to make this distinction.

*c) Between households and others in relation to motor vehicle licences*

Here the distinction is between households as consumers on the one hand and producers on the other, as in the production and consumption expenditure accounts of the SNA.

*d) Between business and others in relation to the residual taxes (6000)*

The distinction is the same as in c) above between producers on the one hand and households as consumers on the other hand. Taxes which are included under the heading 6000 because they involve more than one tax base or because the tax base does not fall within any of the previous categories but which are identifiable as levyable only on producers and not on households are included under "business". The rest of the taxes which are included under the heading 6000 are shown as "other" or non-identified.

*Surcharges*

27. Receipts from surcharges in respect of particular taxes are usually classified with the receipts from the relevant tax whether or not the surcharge is temporary. If, however, the surcharge has a characteristic which would render it classifiable in a different heading of the OECD list, receipts from the surcharge are classified under that heading separately from the relevant tax.

***Unidentifiable tax receipts and residual sub-headings***

28. A number of cases arise where taxes cannot be identified as belonging entirely to a heading or sub-heading of the OECD classification and the following practices are applied in such cases:

a) The heading is known, but it is not known how receipts should be allocated between sub-headings: receipts are classified in the appropriate residual sub-heading (1300, 2400, 4520, 4600, 5130, 5300 or 6200).

b) It is known that the bulk of receipts from a group of taxes (usually local taxes) is derived from taxes within a particular heading or sub-heading, but some of the taxes in the group whose amount cannot be precisely ascertained may be classifiable in other headings or sub-headings: receipts are shown in the heading or sub-heading under which most of the receipts fall.

c) Neither the heading nor sub-heading of a tax (usually local) can be identified: the tax is classified in 6200 unless it is known that it is a tax on business in which case it is classified in 6100.

## D. Commentaries on items of the list

**1000 – *Taxes on income, profits and capital gains***

29. This heading covers taxes levied on the net income or profits (i.e. gross income minus allowable tax reliefs) of individuals and enterprises. Also covered are taxes levied on the capital gains of individuals and enterprises, and gains from gambling.

30. Included in the heading are:

a) taxes levied predominantly on income or profits, though partially on other bases. Taxes on various bases which are not predominantly income or profits are classified according to the principles laid down in §28 and §78;

b) taxes on property, which are levied on a presumed or estimated income as part of an income tax (see also §43(a), (c) and (d));

c) compulsory payments to social security fund contributions that are levied on income but do not confer an entitlement to social benefits. When such contributions do confer an entitlement to social benefits, they are included in heading 2000 (see §35);

d) receipts from integrated scheduler income tax systems are classified as a whole in this heading, even though certain of the scheduler taxes may be based upon gross income and may not take into account the personal circumstances of the taxpayer.

31. The main subdivision of this heading is between levies on individuals (1100) and those on corporate enterprises (1200). Under each subdivision a distinction is made between taxes on income and profits (1110 and 1210), and taxes on capital gains (1120 and 1220). If certain receipts cannot be identified as appropriate to either 1100 or 1200, or if in practice this distinction cannot be made (e.g., because there are no reliable data on the recipients of payments from which withholding taxes are deducted) they are classified in 1300 as not-allocable.

*Treatment of credits under imputation systems*

32. Under imputation systems of corporate income tax, a company's shareholders are wholly or partly relieved of their liability to income tax on dividends paid by the company out of income or profits liable to corporate income tax. In countries with such systems,[15] part of the tax on the company's profits is available to provide relief against the shareholders' own tax liability. The relief to the shareholder takes the form of a tax credit, the amount of which may be less than, equal to, or more than the shareholder's overall tax liability. If the tax credit exceeds this tax liability the excess may be payable to the shareholder. As this type of tax credit is an integral part of the imputation system of corporate income tax, any payment to the shareholders is treated as a repayment of tax and not as expenditure (compare the treatment of other tax credits described in §21).

33. As the tax credit under imputation systems (even when exceeding tax liability) is to be regarded as a tax provision, the question arises whether it should be deducted from individual income tax receipts (1110) or corporate income tax receipts (1210). In this Report, the full amount of corporate income tax paid is shown under 1210 and no imputed tax is included under 1110. Thus, the full amount of the credit reduces the amount of 1110 whether the credit results in a reduction of personal income tax liability or whether an actual refund is made because the credit exceeds the income tax liability. (Where, however, such tax credits are deducted from corporation tax in respect of dividends paid to corporations the amounts are deducted from the receipts of 1210.)

**1120 and 1220 – *Taxes on capital gains***

34. These sub-headings comprise taxes imposed on capital gains, 1120 covering those levied on the gains of individuals and 1220 those levied on the gains of corporate enterprises, where receipts from such taxes can be separately identified. In many countries this is not the case and the receipts from such taxes are then classified with those from the income tax. Heading 1120 also includes taxes on gains from gambling.

**2000 – *Social security contributions***

35. Classified here are all compulsory payments that confer an entitlement to receive a (contingent) future social benefit. Such payments are usually earmarked to finance social benefits and are often paid to institutions of general government that provide such benefits. However, such earmarking is not part of the definition of social security contributions and is not required for a tax to be classified here. However, conferment of an entitlement is required for a tax to be classified under this heading. So, levies on income or payroll that are earmarked for social security funds but do not confer an entitlement to benefit are excluded from this heading and shown under personal income taxes (1100) or taxes on payroll and workforce (3000). Taxes on other bases, such as goods and services, which are earmarked for social security benefits are not shown

here but are classified according to their respective bases because they generally confer no entitlement to social security benefits.

36. Contributions for the following types of social security benefits would, *inter alia*, be included: unemployment insurance benefits and supplements, accident, injury and sickness benefits, old-age, disability and survivors' pensions, family allowances, reimbursements for medical and hospital expenses or provision of hospital or medical services. Contributions may be levied on both employees and employers.

37. Contributions may be based on earnings or payroll ("on a payroll basis") or on net income after deductions and exemptions for personal circumstances ("on an income tax basis"), and the revenues from the two bases should be separately identified if possible. However, where contributions to a general social security scheme are on a payroll basis, but the contributions of particular groups (such as the self-employed) cannot be assessed on this basis and net income is used as a proxy for gross earnings, the receipts may still be classified as being on a payroll basis. In principle, this heading excludes voluntary contributions paid to social security schemes. When separately identifiable these are shown in the memorandum item on the financing of social security benefits. In practice, however, they cannot always be separately identified from compulsory contributions, in which case they are included in this heading.

38. Contributions to social insurance schemes which are not institutions of general government and to other types of insurance schemes, provident funds, pension funds, friendly societies or other saving schemes are not considered as social security contributions. Provident funds are arrangements under which the contributions of each employee and of the corresponding employer on his/her behalf are kept in a separate account earning interest and withdrawable under specific circumstances. Pension funds are separately organised schemes negotiated between employees and employers and carry provisions for different contributions and benefits, sometimes more directly tied to salary levels and length of service than under social security schemes. When contributions to these schemes are compulsory or quasi-compulsory (e.g. by virtue of agreement with professional and union organisations) they are shown in the memorandum item (refer to Section III.B of the Report).

39. Contributions by government employees and by governments in respect of their employees, to social security schemes classified within general government are included in this heading. Contributions to separate schemes for government employees, which can be regarded as replacing general social security schemes, are also regarded as taxes.[16] Where, however, a separate scheme is not seen as replacing a general scheme and has been negotiated between the government, in its role as an employer, and its employees, it is not regarded as social security and contributions to it are not regarded as taxes, even though the scheme may have been established by legislation.

40. This heading excludes 'imputed' contributions, which correspond to social benefits paid directly by employers to their employees or former employees or to their representatives (e.g. when employers are legally obliged to pay sickness benefits for a certain period).

41. Contributions are divided into those of employees (2100), employers (2200), and self-employed or non-employed (2300), and then further sub-divided according to the basis on which they are levied. Employees are defined for this purpose as all persons engaged in activities of business units, government bodies, private non-profit institutions, or other paid employment, except the proprietors and their unpaid family members in the case of unincorporated businesses. Members of the armed forces are included, irrespective of the duration and type of their service, if they contribute to social security schemes. The

contributions of employers are defined as their payments on account of their employees to social security schemes. Where employees or employers are required to continue the payment of social security contributions when the employee becomes unemployed these contributions, data permitting, are shown in 2100 and 2200 respectively. Accordingly, the sub-heading 2300 is confined to contributions paid by the self-employed and by those outside of the labour force (e.g. disabled or retired individuals).

3000 – *Taxes on payroll and workforce*

42. This heading covers taxes paid by employers, employees or the self-employed either as a proportion of payroll or as a fixed amount per person, and which do not confer entitlement to social benefits. Examples of taxes classified here are the United Kingdom national insurance surcharge (introduced in 1977), the Swedish payroll tax (1969–1979), and the Austrian Contribution to the Family Burden Equalisation Fund and Community Tax.

4000 – *Taxes on property*

43. This heading covers recurrent and non-recurrent taxes on the use, ownership or transfer of property. These include taxes on immovable property or net wealth, taxes on the change of ownership of property through inheritance or gift and taxes on financial and capital transactions. The following kinds of tax are excluded from this heading:

a) taxes on capital gains resulting from the sale of a property (1120 or 1220);

b) taxes on the use of goods or on permission to use goods or perform activities (5200); see §73;

c) taxes on immovable property levied on the basis of a presumed net income which take into account the personal circumstances of the taxpayer. They are classified as income taxes along with taxes on income and capital gains derived from property (1100);

d) taxes on the use of property for residence, where the tax is payable by either proprietor or tenant and the amount payable is a function of the user's personal circumstances (pay, dependants, and so on). They are classified as taxes on income (1100);

e) taxes on building in excess of permitted maximum density, taxes on the enlargement, construction or alteration of certain buildings beyond a permitted value and taxes on building construction. They are classified as taxes on permission to perform activities (5200);

f) taxes on the use of one's own property for special trading purposes like selling alcohol, tobacco, meat or for exploitation of land resources (e.g. United States severance taxes). They are classified as taxes on permission to perform activities (5200).

4100 – *Recurrent taxes on immovable property*

44. This sub-heading covers taxes levied regularly in respect of the use or ownership of immovable property.

- these taxes are levied on land and buildings;
- they can be in the form of a percentage of an assessed property value based on a national rental income, sales price, or capitalised yield; or in terms of other characteristics of real property, (for example size or location) from which a presumed rent or capital value can be derived.

- such taxes can be levied on proprietors, tenants, or both. They can also be paid by one level of government to another level of government in respect of property under the jurisdiction of the latter.
- debts are not taken into account in the assessment of these taxes, and they differ from taxes on net wealth in this respect.

45. Taxes on immovable property are further sub-divided into those paid by households (4110) and those paid by other entities (4120), according to the criteria set out in §26(b) above.

**4200 – *Recurrent taxes on net wealth***

46. This sub-heading covers taxes levied regularly (in most cases annually) on net wealth, i.e. taxes on a wide range of movable and immovable property, net of debt. It is sub-divided into taxes paid by individuals (4210) and taxes paid by corporate enterprises (4220) according to the criteria set out in §26(a) above. If separate figures exist for receipts paid by institutions, the tax payments involved are added to those paid by corporations.

**4300 – *Estate, inheritance and gift taxes***

47. This sub-heading is divided into taxes on estates and inheritances (4310) and taxes on gifts (4320).[17] Estate taxes are charged on the amount of the total estate whereas inheritance taxes are charged on the shares of the individual recipients; in addition the latter may take into account the relationship of the individual recipients to the deceased.

**4400 – *Taxes on financial and capital transactions***

48. This sub-heading comprises, inter alia, taxes on the issue, transfer, purchase and sale of securities, taxes on cheques, and taxes levied on specific legal transactions such as validation of contracts and the sale of immovable property. The heading does not include:

a) taxes on the use of goods or property or permission to perform certain activities (5200);

b) fees paid to cover court charges, charges for birth, marriage or death certificates, which are normally regarded as non-tax revenues (see §9);

c) taxes on capital gains (1000);

d) recurrent taxes on immovable property (4100);

e) recurrent taxes on net wealth (4200);

f) once-and-for-all levies on property or wealth (4500).

**4500 – *Other non-recurrent taxes on property***[17]

49. This sub-heading covers once-and-for-all, as distinct from recurrent, levies on property. It is divided into taxes on net wealth (4510) and other non-recurrent taxes on property (4520). Heading 4510 would include taxes levied to meet emergency expenditures, or for redistribution purposes. Heading 4520 would cover taxes levied to take account of increases in land value due to permission given to develop or provision of additional local facilities by general government, any taxes on the revaluation of capital and once-and-for-all taxes on particular items of property.

**4600 – *Other recurrent taxes on property***

50. These rarely exist in OECD member countries, but the heading would include taxes on goods such as cattle, jewellery, windows, and other external signs of wealth.

**5000 – *Taxes on goods and services***

51. All taxes and duties levied on the production, extraction, sale, transfer, leasing or delivery of goods, and the rendering of services (5100), or in respect of the use of goods or permission to use goods or to perform activities (5200) are included here. The heading thus covers:

a) multi-stage cumulative taxes;

b) general sales taxes – whether levied at manufacture/production, wholesale or retail level;

c) value-added taxes;

d) excises;

e) taxes levied on the import and export of goods;

f) taxes levied in respect of the use of goods and taxes on permission to use goods, or perform certain activities;

g) taxes on the extraction, processing or production of minerals and other products.

52. Borderline cases between this heading and heading 4000 (taxes on property) and 6100 (other taxes on business) are referred to in §43, §48 and §75. Residual sub-headings (5300) and (5130) cover tax receipts which cannot be allocated between 5100 and 5200 and between 5110 and 5120, respectively; see §28.

**5100 – *Taxes on the production, sale, transfer, leasing and delivery of goods and rendering of services***

53. This sub-heading consists of all taxes, levied on transactions in goods and services on the basis of their intrinsic characteristics (e.g. value, weight of tobacco, strength of alcohol, and so on) as distinct from taxes imposed on the use of goods, or permission to use goods or perform activities, which fall under 5200.

**5110 – *General taxes on goods and services***

54. This sub-heading includes all taxes, other than import and export duties (5123 and 5124), levied on the production, leasing, transfer, delivery or sales of a wide range of goods and/or the rendering of a wide range of services, irrespective of whether they are domestically produced or imported and irrespective of the stage of production or distribution at which they are levied. It thus covers value-added taxes, sales taxes and multi-stage cumulative taxes. Receipts from border adjustments in respect of such taxes when goods are imported are added to gross receipts for this category, and repayments of such taxes when goods are exported are deducted. These taxes are subdivided into 5111 value-added taxes, 5112 sales taxes, 5113 other general taxes on goods and services.

55. Borderline cases arise between this heading and taxes on specific goods (5120) when taxes are levied on a large number of goods, for example, the United Kingdom purchase tax (repealed in 1973) and the Japanese commodity tax (repealed in 1988). In conformity with national views, the former United Kingdom purchase tax is classified as a general tax (5112) and the former Japanese commodity tax as excises (5121).

**5111 – *Value-added taxes***

56. All general consumption taxes charged on value-added are classified in this sub-heading, irrespective of the method of deduction and the stages at which the taxes are levied. In practice, all OECD countries with value-added taxes normally allow immediate deduction of taxes on purchases by all but the final consumer and impose

tax at all stages. In some countries the heading may include certain taxes, such as those on financial and insurance activities, either because receipts from them cannot be identified separately from those from the value-added tax, or because they are regarded as an integral part of the value-added tax, even though similar taxes in other countries might be classified elsewhere (e.g. 5126 as taxes on services or 4400 as taxes on financial and capital transactions).

**5112 – *Sales taxes***

57. All general taxes levied at one stage only, whether at manufacturing or production, wholesale or retail stage are classified here.

**5113 – *Other general taxes on goods and services***

58. This sub-heading covers multi-stage cumulative taxes (also know as 'cascade taxes') where tax is levied each time a transaction takes place without deduction for tax paid on inputs, and also those general consumption taxes where elements of value-added, sales or cascade taxes are combined.

**5120 – *Taxes on specific goods and services***

59. Excises, profits generated and transferred from fiscal monopolies, and customs and imports duties as well as taxes on exports, foreign exchange transactions, investment goods and betting stakes and special taxes on services, which do not form part of a general tax of 5110, are included in this category.

**5121 – *Excises***

60. Excises are taxes levied on particular products, or on a limited range of products, which are not classifiable under 5110 (general taxes), 5123 (import duties) and 5124 (export duties). They may be imposed at any stage of production or distribution and are usually assessed by reference to the weight or strength or quantity of the product, but sometimes by reference to value. Thus, special taxes on, for example, sugar, beetroot, matches, chocolates, and taxes at varying rates on a certain range of goods, as well as those levied in most countries on tobacco goods, alcoholic drinks and hydrocarbon oils and other energy sources, are included in this sub-heading.

61. Excises are distinguished from:

a) 5110 (general taxes). This is discussed in §54-55;

b) 5123 (import duties). If a tax collected principally on imported goods also applies, or would apply, under the law by which the tax is imposed to comparable home-produced goods, the receipts there from would be classified as excises (5121). This principle applies even if there is no comparable home production or no possibility of it (see also §65);

c) 5126 (taxes on services). The problem here arises in respect of taxes on electricity, gas and energy. All of these are regarded as taxes on goods and are included under 5121.

**5122 – *Profits of fiscal monopolies***

62. This sub-heading covers that part of the profits of fiscal monopolies which is transferred to general government or which is used to finance any expenditures considered to be government expenditures (see §19). Amounts are shown when they are transferred to general government or used to make expenditures considered to be government expenditures

63. Fiscal monopolies reflect the exercise of the taxing power of government by the use of monopoly powers. Fiscal monopolies are non-financial public enterprises exercising a monopoly in most cases over the production or distribution of tobacco,

alcoholic beverages, salt, matches, playing cards and petroleum or agricultural products (i.e. on the kind of products which are likely to be, alternatively or additionally, subject to the excises of 5121), to raise the government revenues which in other countries are gathered through taxes on dealings in such commodities by private business units. The government monopoly may be at the production stage or, as in the case of government-owned and controlled liquor stores, at the distribution stage.

64. Fiscal monopolies are distinguished from public utilities such as rail transport, electricity, post offices, and other communications, which may enjoy a monopoly or quasi-monopoly position but where the primary purpose is normally to provide basic services rather than to raise revenue for government. Transfers from such other public enterprises to the government are considered as non-tax revenues. The traditional concept of fiscal monopoly has not been extended to include state lotteries, the profits of which are accordingly regarded as non-tax revenues. Fiscal monopoly profits are distinguished from export and import monopoly profits (5127) transferred from marketing boards or other enterprises dealing with international trade.

**5123 – *Customs and other import duties***

65. Taxes, stamp duties and surcharges restricted by law to imported products are included here. Also included are levies on imported agricultural products which are imposed in member countries of the European Union and amounts paid by certain of these countries under the Monetary Compensation Accounts (MCA) system.[18] Starting from 1998, customs duties collected by European Union member states on behalf of the European Union are no longer reported under this heading in the country tables (in Part III of the Report). Excluded here are taxes collected on imports as part of a general tax on goods and services, or an excise applicable to both imported and domestically produced goods.

**5124 – *Taxes on exports***

66. In the 1970s, export duties were levied in Australia, Canada and Portugal as a regular measure and they have been used in Finland for counter-cyclical purposes. Some member countries of the European Union pay, as part of the MCA system, a levy on exports (see note 18 to §65). Where these amounts are identifiable, they are shown in this heading. This heading does not include repayments of general consumption taxes or excises or customs duties on exported goods, which should be deducted from the gross receipts under 5110, 5121 or 5123, as appropriate.

**5125 – *Taxes on investment goods***

67. This sub-heading covers taxes on investment goods, such as machinery. These taxes may be imposed for a number of years or temporarily for counter-cyclical purposes. Taxes on industrial inputs which are also levied on consumers [e.g., the Swedish energy tax which is classified under (5121)] are not included here.

**5126 – *Taxes on specific services***

68. All taxes assessed on the payment for specific services, such as taxes on insurance premiums, banking services, gambling and betting stakes (e.g., from horse races, football pools, lottery tickets), transport, entertainment, restaurant and advertising charges, fall into this category. Taxes levied on the gross income of companies providing the service (e.g. gross insurance premiums or gambling stakes received by the company) are also classified under this heading. Tax revenues from bank levies and payments to deposit insurance and financial stability schemes are provisionally included here for the 2012 edition. The detailed classification is set out in paragraph 105.

69. Excluded from this sub-heading are:

a) taxes on services forming part of a general tax on goods and services (5110);

b) taxes on electricity, gas and energy (5121 as excises);

c) taxes on individual gains from gambling (1120 as taxes on capital gains of individuals and non-corporate enterprises) and lump-sum taxes on the transfer of private lotteries or on the permission to set up lotteries (5200);[19]

d) taxes on cheques and on the issue, transfer or redemption of securities (4400 as taxes on financial and capital transactions).

**5127 – *Other taxes on international trade and transactions***

70. This sub-heading covers revenue received by the government from the purchase and sale of foreign exchange at different rates. When the government exercises monopoly powers to extract a margin between the purchase and sales price of foreign exchange, other than to cover administrative costs, the revenue derived constitutes a compulsory levy exacted in indeterminate proportions from both purchaser and seller of foreign exchange. It is the common equivalent of an import duty and export duty levied in a single exchange rate system or of a tax on the sale or purchase of foreign exchange. Like the profits of fiscal monopolies and import or export monopolies transferred to government, it represents the exercise of monopoly powers for tax purposes and is included in tax revenues.

71. The sub-heading covers also the profits of export or import monopolies, which do not however exist in OECD countries, taxes on purchase or sale of foreign exchange, and any other taxes levied specifically on international trade or transactions.

**5128 – *Other taxes on specific goods and services***

72. This item includes taxes on the extraction of minerals, fossil fuels and other exhaustible resources from deposits owned privately or by another government together with any other unidentifiable receipts from taxes on specific goods and services. Taxes on the extraction of exhaustible resources are usually a fixed amount per unit of quality or weight, but can be a percentage of value. The taxes are recorded when the resources are extracted. Payments from the extraction of exhaustible resources from deposits owned by the government unit receiving the payment are classified as rent.

**5200 – *Taxes on use of goods or on permission to use goods or perform activities***

73. This sub-heading covers taxes which are levied in respect of the use of goods as distinct from taxes on the goods themselves. Unlike the latter taxes – reported under 5100 –, they are not assessed on the value of the goods but usually as fixed amounts. Taxes on permission to use goods or to perform activities are also included here, as are pollution taxes not based upon the value of particular goods. It is sometimes difficult to distinguish between compulsory user charges and licence fees which are regarded as taxes and those which are excluded as non-tax revenues. The criteria which are employed are noted in §9-10.

74. Although the sub-heading refers to the 'use' of goods, registration of ownership rather than use may be what generates liability to tax, so that the taxes of this heading may apply to the ownership of animals or goods rather than their use (e.g. race horses, dogs and motor vehicles) and may apply even to unusable goods (e.g. unusable motor vehicles or guns).

75. Borderline cases arise with:

a) taxes on the permission to perform business activities which are levied on a combined income, payroll or turnover base and, accordingly, are classified following the rules in §78;

b) taxes on the ownership or use of property of headings 4100, 4200 and 4600. The heading 4100 is confined to taxes on the ownership or tenancy of immovable property and – unlike the taxes of 5200 – they are related to the value of the property. The net wealth taxes and taxes on chattels of 4200 and 4600 respectively are confined to the ownership rather than the use of assets, apply to groups of assets rather than particular goods and again are related to the value of the assets.

5210 – *Recurrent taxes on use of goods and on permission to use goods or perform activities*

76. The principal characteristic of taxes classified here is that they are levied at regular intervals and that they are usually fixed amounts. The most important item in terms of revenue receipts is vehicle licence taxes. This sub-heading also covers taxes on permission to hunt, shoot, fish or to sell certain products and taxes on the ownership of dogs and on the performance of certain services, provided that they meet the criteria set out in §9–10. The sub-divisions of 5210 are user taxes on motor vehicles paid by households (5211) and those paid by others (5212).[20] Sub-heading 5213 covers dog licences and user charges for permission to perform activities such as selling meat or liquor when the levies are on a recurring basis. It also covers recurrent general licences for hunting, shooting and fishing where the right to carry out these activities is not granted as part of a normal commercial transaction (e.g. the granting of the licence is not accompanied by the right to use a specific area which is owned by government).

5220 – *Non-recurrent taxes on use of goods and on permission to use goods or perform activities*

77. This section covers non-recurrent taxes levied on the use of goods or on permission to use goods or perform activities and taxes levied each time goods are used. It includes taxes levied on the emission or discharge into the environment of noxious gases, liquids or other harmful substances.

- Payments for tradable emission permits issued by governments under cap and trade schemes should be recorded here at the time the emissions occur. No revenue should be recorded for permits that governments issue free of charge. The accrual basis of recording means that there can be a timing difference between the cash being received by government for the permits and the time the emission occurs. In the national accounts, this timing gives rise to a financial liability for government during the period.
- Payments made for the collection and disposal of waste or noxious substances by public authorities should be excluded as they constitute a sale of services to enterprises.

78. Other taxes falling under heading 5200 that are not levied recurrently are also included here. Thus, once-and-for-all payments for permission to sell liquor or tobacco or to set up betting shops are included provided they meet the criteria set out in §9–10.

6000 – *Other taxes*

79. Taxes levied on a base, or bases, other than those described under headings 1000, 3000, 4000 and 5000, or on bases of which none could be regarded as being predominantly the same as that of any one of these headings, are covered here. As regards taxes levied on a multiple base, if it is possible to estimate receipts related to each base (e.g. the Austrian and German 'Gewerbesteuer') this is done and the separate amounts included under the appropriate headings. If the separate amounts cannot be estimated, but it is known that most of the receipts are derived from one base, the whole of the receipts are classified according to that base. If neither of these procedures can be followed, they are classified here. The sub-headings may also include receipts from taxes which

governments are unable to identify or isolate (see §28). Included here also are fines and penalties paid for infringement of regulations relating to taxes but not identifiable as relating to a particular category of taxes (see §15). A subdivision is made between taxes levied wholly or predominantly on business (6100) and those levied on others (6200).

## E. Conciliation with National Accounts

80. This section of the tables provides a re-conciliation between the OECD calculation of total tax revenues and the total of all taxes and social contributions paid to general government as recorded in the country's National Accounts. Where the country is a member of the European Union (EU), the comparison is between the OECD calculation of total tax revenues and the sum of tax revenues and social contributions recorded in the combination of the general government and the institutions of the EU sectors of the National Accounts.

## F. Memorandum item on the financing of social security benefits

81. In view of the varying relationship between taxation and social security contributions and the cases referred to in §35 to §41, a memorandum item collects together all payments earmarked for social security-type benefits, other than voluntary payments to the private sector. Data are presented as follows (refer section III.B of the Report):

a) Taxes of 2000 series.

b) Taxes earmarked for social security benefits.

c) Voluntary contributions to the government.

d) Compulsory contributions to the private sector.

Guidance on the breakdown of (a) to (d) above is provided in §35 to §41.

## G. Memorandum item on identifiable taxes paid by government

82. Identifiable taxes actually paid by government are presented in a memorandum item classified by the main headings of the OECD classification of taxes. In the vast majority of countries, only social security contributions and payroll taxes paid by government can be identified. These are, however, usually the most important taxes paid by governments (refer section III.C of the Report).

## H. Relation of OECD classification of taxes to national accounting systems

83. A system of national accounts (SNA) seeks to provide a coherent framework for recording and presenting the main flows relating respectively to production, consumption, accumulation and external transactions of a given economic area, usually a country or a major region within a country. Government revenues are an important part of the transactions recorded in SNA. The final version of the 2008 SNA was jointly published by five international organisations: the United Nations, the International Monetary Fund, the European Union, the Organisation for Economic Co-operation and Development, and the World Bank in August 2009. The System is a comprehensive, consistent and flexible set of macroeconomic accounts. It is designed for use in countries with market economies, whatever their stage of economic development, and also in countries in transition to market economies. The important parts of the SNA's conceptual framework and its definitions of the various sectors of the economy have been reflected in the OECD's classification of taxes.

84. There are, however, some differences between the OECD classification of taxes and SNA concepts that are listed below. They arise because the aim of the former is to provide the maximum disaggregation of statistical data on what are generally regarded as taxes by tax administrations.

a) OECD includes social security contributions in total tax revenues (§7 and §8 above);

b) there are different points of view on whether or not some levies and fees are classified as taxes (§9 and §10 above);

c) OECD excludes imputed taxes or subsidies resulting from the operation of official multiple exchange rates;

d) there are differences in the treatment of non-wastable tax credits

85. As noted in §1 and §2, headings 1000 to 6000 of the OECD list of taxes cover all unrequited payments to general government, other than compulsory loans and fines. Such unrequited payments including fines, but excluding compulsory loans can be obtained from adding together the following figures in the 2008 SNA

- value-added type taxes (D.211);
- taxes and duties on imports, excluding VAT (D.212);
- export taxes (D.213);
- taxes on products, excluding VAT, import and export taxes (D.214);
- other taxes on production (D.29);
- taxes on income (D.51);
- other current taxes (D.59);
- social contributions (D.61), excluding voluntary contributions;
- capital taxes (D.91).

## I. The OECD classification of taxes and the International Monetary Fund (GFS) system

86. The coverage and valuation of tax revenues in the GFS system and the 2008 SNA are very similar. Therefore, with the exception of the treatment of non-wastable tax credits, the differences between the OECD classification and that of the 2008 SNA (see §84 above) also apply to the GFS. In addition the International Monetary Fund subdivides the OECD 5000 heading into section IV (Domestic Taxes on Goods and Services) and section V (Taxes on International Trade and Transactions). This reflects the fact that while the latter usually yield insignificant amounts of revenue in OECD countries, this is not the case in many non-OECD countries.

## J. Comparison of the OECD classification of taxes with other international classifications

87. The table below describes an item by item comparison of the OECD classification of taxes and the classifications used in the following:

i) System of National Accounts (2008 SNA);

ii) European System of Accounts (1995 ESA);

iii) IMF *Government Finance Statistics Manual* (GFSM2001).

88. These comparisons represent those that would be expected to apply in the majority of cases. However in practice some flexibility should be used in their application. This is because in particular cases, countries can adopt varying approaches to the classification of revenues in National Accounts.

| OECD Classification | | 2008 SNA | 1995 ESA | GFSM2001 |
|---|---|---|---|---|
| 1000 | Taxes on income, profits and capital gains | | | |
| | 1100 Individuals | | | |
| | 1110 Income/profits | D51-8.61a | D51A | 1111 |
| | 1120 Capital gains | D51-8.61c,d | D51C,D | 1111 |
| | 1200 Corporations | | | |
| | 1210 Income/profits | D51-8.61b | D51B | 1112 |
| | 1220 Capital gains | D51-8.61c | D51C | 1112 |
| | 1300 Unallocable as between 1100 and 1200 | | | 1113 |
| 2000 | Social security contributions | | | |
| | 2100 Employees | D613-8.85 | D61111 | 1211 |
| | 2200 Employers | D611-8.83 | D61121 | 1212 |
| | 2300 Self-employed, non-employed | D613-8.85 | D61131 | 1213 |
| | 2400 Unallocable as between 2100, 2200 and 2300 | | | 1214 |
| 3000 | Taxes on payroll and workforce | D29-7.97a | D29C | 112 |
| 4000 | Taxes on property | | | |
| | 4100 Recurrent taxes on immovable property | | | |
| | 4110 Households | D59-8.63a | D59A | 1131 |
| | 4120 Other | D29-7.97b | D29A | 1131 |
| | 4200 Recurrent net wealth taxes | | | |
| | 4210 Individual | D59-8.63b | D59A | 1132 |
| | 4220 Corporations | D59-8.63b | D59A | 1132 |
| | 4300 Estate, inheritance and gift taxes | | | |
| | 4310 Estate and inheritance taxes | D91-10.207b | D91A | 1133 |
| | 4320 Gift taxes | D91-10.207b | D91A | 1133 |
| | 4400 Taxes on financial and capital transactions | D59-7.96d;<br>D29-7.97e | D214B,C | 1134:1161 |
| | 4500 Other non-recurrent taxes on property | D91-10.207a | D91B | 1135 |
| | 4600 Other recurrent taxes on property | D59-8.63c | D59A | 1136 |
| 5000 | Taxes on goods and services | | | |
| | 5100 Taxes on production, sale and transfer of goods and services | | | |
| | 5110 General sales taxes | | | |
| | 5111 Value-added taxes | D211-7.89 | D211; D29G | 11411 |
| | 5112 Sales taxes | D2122-7.94a;<br>D214-7.96a | D2122D;<br>D214I | 11412 |
| | 5113 Other general taxes | D214-7.96a | D214I | 11413 |
| | 5120 Taxes on specific goods and services | | | |
| | 5121 Excises | D2122-7.94b;<br>D214-7.96b | D2122C;<br>D214A,B,D | 1142 |
| | 5122 Profits of fiscal monopolies | D214-7.96e | D214J | 1143 |
| | 5123 Customs/import duties | D2121-7.93 | D2121; D2122A,B | 1151 |
| | 5124 On exports | D213-7.95a | D214K | 1152-4 |
| | 5125 On investment goods | | | |
| | 5126 On specific services | D2122-7.94c;<br>D214-7.96c | D2122E;<br>D214E,F,G;<br>D29F | 1144; 1156 |
| | 5127 Other taxes on international trade and transactions | D2122-7.94d<br>D29-7.95b<br>D29-7.97g<br>D59-8.64d | D2122F;<br>D29D;<br>D59E | 1153<br>1155-6 |
| | 5128 Other taxes on specific goods and services | | | 1146 |
| | 5130 Unallocable as between 5110 and 5120 | | | |
| | 5200 Taxes on use of goods | | | |
| | 5210 Recurrent taxes | | | |
| | 5211 Motor vehicle taxes households | D59-8.64c | D59D | 11451 |
| | 5212 Motor vehicles taxes others | D29-7.97d | D214D; D29B | 11451 |
| | 5213 Other recurrent taxes | D29-7.97c,d,f<br>D59-8.64c | D29B,E,F;<br>D59D | 11452 |
| | 5220 Non-recurrent taxes | | | |
| | 5300 Unallocable as between 5100 and 5200 | | | |
| 6000 | Other taxes | | | |
| | 6100 Paid solely by business | | | |
| | 6200 Paid by other than business, or unidentifiable | D59-8.64a,b | D59B,C | 1162 |

## K. Attribution of tax revenues by sub-sectors of general government

89. The OECD classification requires a breakdown of tax revenues by sub-sectors of government. The definition of each sub-sector and the criteria to be used to attribute tax revenues between these sub-sectors are set out below. They follow the guidance of the 2008 SNA and GFSM2001.

***Sub-sectors of general government to be identified***

*a) Central government*

90. The central government sub-sector includes all governmental departments, offices, establishments and other bodies which are agencies or instruments of the central authority whose competence extends over the whole territory, with the exception of the administration of social security funds.Central government therefore has the authority to impose taxes on all resident and non-resident units engaged in economic activities within the country.

*b) State, provincial or regional government*

91. This sub-sector consists of intermediate units of government exercising a competence at a level below that of central government. It includes all such units operating independently of central government in a part of a country's territory encompassing a number of smaller localities, with the exception of the administration of social security funds. In unitary countries, regional governments may be considered to have a separate existence where they have substantial autonomy to raise a significant proportion of their revenues from sources within their control and their officers are independent of external administrative control in the actual operation of the unit's activities.

92. At present, federal countries comprise the majority of cases where revenues attributed to intermediate units of government are identified separately. Spain is the only unitary country in this position. In the remaining unitary countries, regional revenues are included with those of local governments.

*c) Local government*

93. This sub-sector includes all other units of government exercising an independent competence in part of the territory of a country, with the exception of the administration of social security funds. It encompasses various urban and/or rural jurisdictions (e.g. local authorities, municipalities, cities, boroughs, districts).

*d) Social security funds*

94. Social security funds form a separate sub-sector of general government. The social security sub-sector is defined in the 2008 SNA by the following extracts from paragraphs 4.124 to 4.126 and 4.147:

"Social security schemes are social insurance schemes covering the community as a whole or large section of the community that are imposed and controlled by government units. The schemes cover a wide variety of programmes, providing benefits in cash or in kind for old age, invalidity or death, survivors, sickness and maternity, work injury, unemployment, family allowance, health care, etc. There is not necessarily a direct link between the amount of the contribution paid by an individual and the benefits he or she may receive." (Paragraph 4.124).

"When social security schemes are separately organised from the other activities of government units and hold their assets and liabilities separately from the latter and engage in financial transactions on their own account they qualify as institutional units that are described as social security funds." (Paragraph 4.125).

"The amounts raised, and paid out, in social security contributions and benefits may be deliberately varied in order to achieve objectives of government policy that have no direct connection with the concept of social security as a scheme to provide social benefits to members of the community. They may be raised or lowered in order to influence the level of aggregate demand in the economy, for example. Nevertheless, so long as they remain separately constituted funds, they must be treated as separate institutional units in the SNA." (Paragraph 4.126).

"The social security funds sub-sector (of general government) consists of the social security funds operating at all levels of government. Such funds are social insurance schemes covering the community as a whole or large section of the community that are imposed by government units." (Paragraph 4.147).

95. This definition of social security funds is followed in the OECD classification with the two following exceptions which are excluded:

- Schemes imposed by government and operated by bodies outside the general government sector, as defined in §3 of this manual; and
- Schemes to which all contributions are voluntary.

***Supra-national authorities***

96. This sub-sector covers the revenue-raising operations of supra-national authorities within a country. In practice, the only relevant supra-national authority in the OECD area is that of the institutions of the European Union (EU). As from 1998, supra-national authorities are no longer included in the *Revenue Statistics*, to achieve consistency with the SNA definition of general government which excludes them. For example, income taxes and social security contributions collected by European Institutions and paid by European civil servants who are resident of EU member countries should not be included. However the specific levies paid by the member states of the EU continue to be included in total tax revenues and they are shown under this heading.

*Criteria to be used for the attribution of tax revenues*

97. When a government collects taxes and pays them over in whole or in part to other governments, it is necessary to determine whether the revenues should be considered to be those of the collecting government which it distributes to others as grants, or those of the beneficiary governments which the collecting government receives and passes on only as their agent. The criteria to be used in the attribution of revenues are set out in §98 to §101 which replicate paragraphs 3.70 to 3.73 from the 2008 SNA.

98. In general, a tax is attributed to the government unit that:

a) exercises the authority to impose the tax (either as a principal or through the delegated authority of the principal);

b) has final discretion to set and vary the rate of the tax.

99. Where an amount is collected by one government for and on behalf of another government, and the latter government has the authority to impose the tax, and set and vary its rate, then the former is acting as an agent for the latter and the tax is reassigned. Any amount retained by the collecting government as a collection charge should be treated as a payment for a service. Any other amount retained by the collecting

government, such as under a tax-sharing arrangement, should be treated as a current grant. If the collecting government was delegated the authority to set and vary the rate, then the amount collected should be treated as tax revenue of this government.

100. Where different governments jointly and equally set the rate of a tax and jointly and equally decide on the distribution of the proceeds, with no individual government having ultimate overriding authority, then the tax revenues are attributed to each government according to its respective share of the proceeds. If an arrangement allows one government unit to exercise ultimate overriding authority, then all of the tax revenue is attributed to that unit.

101. There may also be the circumstance where a tax is imposed under the constitutional or other authority of one government, but other governments individually set the tax rate in their jurisdictions. The proceeds of the tax generated in each respective government's jurisdiction are attributed as tax revenues of that government.

*Levies paid by member states of the European Union*

102. The levies paid by the member states of the EU take the form:

- VAT own resources; and
- Specific levies which include:

a) custom duties and levies on agricultural goods (5123);

b) gross monetary compensation accounts (5123 if relating to imports and 5124 if relating to exports); and

c) Steel, coal, sugar and milk levies (5128).

103. The custom duties collected by member states on behalf of the EU are recorded:

- on a gross of collection fee basis;
- using figures adjusted so that duties are shown on a 'final destination' as opposed to a 'country of first entry' basis where such adjustments can be made. These adjustments concern in particular duties collected at important (sea) ports. Although the EU duties are collected by the authorities of the country of first entry, when possible these duties should be excluded from the revenue of the collecting country and be included in the revenue of the country of final destination.

This is the specific EU levy that most clearly conforms to the attribution criterion described in §96 above. Consequently as from 1998, these amounts are footnoted as a memorandum item to the EU member state country tables (in Part III) and no longer shown under heading 5123. However the figures are included in the total tax revenue figures on the top line for all the relevant years shown in the tables.

104. The VAT own resources, which are determined by applying a rate not exceeding 1% to an assessment basis specified in the Sixth Directive,[21] are more of a borderline case. They have some of the characteristics of a transfer (they are not derived from a clearly identifiable source of funds that are actually collected) and some of a tax (the amount of the transfer is determined by the receiving sub-sector of government). In this publication they are not shown as a tax of the European Union (but as a tax of the EU member states), though the amounts involved are footnoted in the tables contained in Part IV.

## L. Provisional classification of revenues from bank levies and payments to deposit insurance and financial stability schemes

105. The OECD have adopted the following interim approach to reporting revenue from bank levies plus deposit insurance and stability fees for the 2012 edition of *OECD Revenue Statistics*; The amounts should be recorded under category 5126.

- Compulsory payments of stability fees, bank levies and deposit insurance should generally be treated as tax revenues where the payments are made to General Government and allocated to the governments' consolidated or general funds so that the Government is free to make immediate use of the money for the purposes that it chooses. This principle would apply regardless of whether the Government is promising to make payments to guarantee the banks' customer deposits in some future contingency.
- If the compulsory payments are made to general government and placed in funds that are earmarked to be entirely channelled back to the sector of the economy that comprises the companies that are subject to the payment, they would still generally be treated as tax revenues on the grounds that the funds would be available for the government and would reduce its budget deficit, the fee is unrequited for an individual entity and the amounts raised could be unrelated to any eventual pay out to depositors or expenditure on wider support for the financial sector.
- Payments to made to the smaller long-standing schemes for insuring 'retail' deposits, where the payment levels are consistent with the costs of insurance should be classified as fee for service.
- Any payments which involve governments realising the assets of a failed institution or receiving a priority claim on its assets in liquidation in order to fund payments of compensation to customers for their lost deposits would be treated as a fee for a service as opposed to tax revenues.
- Compulsory payments that are made to funds operated outside the government sector and non-state institutions backed by the deposit takers and all payments to voluntary schemes should not be treated as tax revenues.

### Notes

1. References in the OECD Guide to Sections or Parts of "this Annex" refer to OECD (2014), *Revenue Statistics* 1965-2013, OECD Publishing, Paris.
2. All references to SNA are to the 2008 edition.
3. See section K of this guide for a discussion of the concept of agency capacity.
4. It is usually possible to identify amounts of social security contributions and payroll taxes, but not other taxes paid by government.
5. If, however, a levy which is considered as non-tax revenue by most countries is regarded as a tax – or raises substantial revenue – in one or more countries, the amounts collected are footnoted at the end of the relevant country tables, even though the amounts are not included in total tax revenues.
6. Names, however, can frequently be misleading. For example, though a passport fee would normally be considered a non-tax revenue, if a supplementary levy on passports (as is the case in Portugal) were imposed in order to raise substantial amounts of revenue relative to the cost of providing the passport, the levy would be regarded as a tax under 5200.
7. There are practical difficulties in operating the distinction made by 1993 SNA.
8. A more detailed explanation of this distinction can be found in the special feature, "Current issues in reporting tax revenues", in the 2001 edition of the *Revenue Statistics*.
9. Sometimes the terms "non-refundable" and "refundable" are used, but it may be considered illogical to talk of "refundable" when nothing has been paid.
10. A different treatment, however, is accorded to non-wastable tax credits under imputation systems of corporate income tax (§32–34).
11. This is not strictly a true tax expenditure in the formal sense. Such tax expenditures require identification of a benchmark tax system for each country or, preferably, a common international benchmark. In practice it has not been possible to reach agreement on a common international benchmark.
12. Unless based on the profit made on a sale, in which case they would be classified as capital gains taxes under 1120 or 1220.
13. In some countries the same legislation applies to both individual and corporate enterprises for particular taxes on income.However, the receipts from such taxes are usually allocable between individuals and enterprises and can therefore be shown in the appropriate sub-heading.
14. For example, "...sufficiently self-contained and independent that they behave in the same way as corporations.......(including) keeping a complete set of accounts" (2008SNA, section 4.44).
15. In Canada – a country also referred to as having an imputation system – the (wastable) tax credit for the shareholder is in respect of domestic corporation tax deemed to have been paid whether or not a corporation tax liability has arisen.As there is no integral connection between the corporation tax liability and the credit given against income tax under such systems, these credits for dividends are treated, along with other tax credits, on the lines described in §21.
16. This may also apply where a scheme for government employees existed prior to the introduction of a general social security scheme.
17. In the 2008 SNA these are regarded as capital transfers and not as taxes (see section G).
18. This is the system by which the European Union adjusts for differences between the exchange rates used to determine prices under the Common Market Agricultural Policy and actual exchange rates. Payments under the system may relate to imports or exports and where these amounts are separately identifiable they are shown under the appropriate heading (5123 or 5124). In this Report, these amounts are shown gross (i.e. without deducting any subsidies paid out under the MCA system).
19. Transfers of profits of State lotteries are regarded as non-tax revenues (see also §64).
20. See §26(c) as regards this distinction.
21. At the Edinburgh Summit (1992) EU Member countries have decided to gradually reduce this percentage from 1.4 to 1, and to effectuate this reduction between years 1995 and 1999. During the period 1970–1983 this percentage also amounted to 1.

# ANEXO A

## *Clasificación de impuestos y Guía de interpretación de la OCDE*

## *Índice*

Página


Clasificación de impuestos de la OCDE ... 200

Guía de interpretación de la OCDE ... 202

A. Cobertura ... 202

B. Principios de registro ... 205

C. Criterios generales de clasificación ... 206

D. Comentarios sobre ítems de la lista ... 208

E. Conciliación con las cuentas nacionales ... 219

F. Partida informativa sobre el financiamiento de las prestaciones sociales ... 220

G. Partida informativa sobre impuestos identificables pagados por el gobierno ... 220

H. Relación de la clasificación de impuestos de la OCDE con el Sistema de Cuentas Nacionales ... 220

I. Relación de la clasificación de impuestos de la OCDE con el sistema de estadísticas de finanzas públicas del Fondo Monetario Internacional ... 221

J. Comparación de la clasificación de impuestos de la OCDE con otras clasificaciones internacionales ... 221

K. Atribución de ingresos tributarios por subsectores del gobierno general ... 223

L. Clasificación provisional de los ingresos tributarios procedentes de gravámenes bancarios y pagos a sistemas de seguro de depósitos y de estabilidad financiera ... 226

Notas ... 227

# Clasificación de impuestos de la OCDE

1000 *Impuestos sobre la renta, las utilidades y las ganancias de capital*

- 1100 Personas físicas
  - 1110 Renta y utilidades
  - 1120 Ganancias de capital
- 1200 Sociedades
  - 1210 Renta y utilidades
  - 1220 Ganancias de capital
- 1300 No clasificables entre 1100 y 1200

2000 *Contribuciones a la seguridad social*

- 2100 Empleados
- 2200 Empleadores
- 2300 Trabajadores por cuenta propia o no empleados
- 2400 No clasificables entre 2100, 2200 y 2300

3000 *Impuestos sobre la nómina y la fuerza de trabajo*

4000 *Impuestos sobre la propiedad*

- 4100 Impuestos recurrentes sobre la propiedad inmueble
  - 4110 Hogares
  - 4120 Otros
- 4200 Impuestos recurrentes sobre la riqueza neta
  - 4210 Personas físicas
  - 4220 Sociedades
- 4300 Impuestos sobre sucesiones, herencias y donaciones
  - 4310 Impuestos sobre sucesiones y herencias
  - 4320 Impuestos sobre donaciones
- 4400 Impuestos sobre transacciones financieras y de capital
- 4500 Otros impuestos no recurrentes sobre la propiedad
- 4600 Otros impuestos recurrentes sobre la propiedad

5000 *Impuestos sobre los bienes y servicios*

5100 Impuestos sobre la producción, venta y transmisión de bienes y prestación de servicios

5110 Impuestos generales

5111 Impuestos sobre el valor agregado

5112 Impuestos sobre las ventas

5113 Otros impuestos generales sobre los bienes y servicios

5120 Impuestos sobre bienes y servicios específicos

5121 Impuestos selectivos

5122 Utilidades de los monopolios fiscales

5123 Derechos de aduanas y otros derechos de importación

5124 Sobre las exportaciones

5125 Sobre los bienes de inversión

5126 Sobre servicios específicos

5127 Otros impuestos sobre el comercio y las transacciones internacionales

5128 Otros impuestos sobre bienes y servicios específicos

5130 No clasificables entre 5110 y 5120

5200 Impuestos sobre el uso de bienes y sobre el permiso para usar bienes y realizar actividades

5210 Impuestos recurrentes

5211 Sobre vehículos automotores: hogares

5212 Sobre vehículos automotores: otros

5213 Otros impuestos recurrentes

5220 Impuestos no recurrentes

5300 No clasificables entre 5100 y 5200

6000 *Otros impuestos*

6100 Pagados únicamente por empresas

6200 Pagados por otros distintos de las empresas o no identificables

# Guía de interpretación de la OCDE[1]

## A. Cobertura

### *Criterios generales*

1. En la clasificación de la OCDE, el término "impuestos" se circunscribe exclusivamente a los pagos sin contraprestación efectuados al gobierno general. Los impuestos carecen de contraprestación en el sentido en que, normalmente, las prestaciones proporcionadas por el gobierno a los contribuyentes no guardan relación directa con los pagos realizados por estos.

2. El término "impuestos" no incluye las multas o sanciones pecuniarias no relacionadas con infracciones tributarias ni los préstamos obligatorios pagados al gobierno. La delimitación entre ingresos tributarios y no tributarios en relación con ciertas tasas y cargos se abordan en los §§ 9–13.

3. El gobierno general comprende la Administración central y los organismos que se hallan bajo su control efectivo, los gobiernos estatales y locales y sus respectivas administraciones, y ciertos regímenes de seguridad social y entidades gubernamentales autónomas, excluidas las empresas públicas. Esta definición del gobierno proviene del Sistema de Cuentas Nacionales (SCN) 2008;[2] en esa publicación, el sector del gobierno general y sus subsectores se hallan definidos en el capítulo 4, sección F, páginas 80-84 de la versión inglesa.

4. Los pagos obligatorios a autoridades supranacionales y a los organismos vinculados a ellas no se incluyen como impuestos desde 1998, con contadas excepciones; sin embargo, los derechos de aduana recaudados por los estados miembros de la Unión Europea en nombre de esta siguen registrándose como partidas informativas y se incluyen en los cuadros de países (parte III de la publicación Revenue Statistics de la OCDE), concretamente en la recaudación tributaria total del país en el que se cobran (véase el § 95). Por otra parte, en los países en los que la Iglesia forma parte del gobierno general, se computan los impuestos eclesiásticos, siempre que reúnan los criterios establecidos en el § 1. Además, habida cuenta de que los datos hacen referencia a las entradas que recibe el gobierno general, quedan excluidos los gravámenes abonados a órganos no gubernamentales, organismos de bienestar o regímenes de seguro social externos al gobierno general, y sindicatos u organizaciones profesionales, aun cuando dichos gravámenes sean obligatorios; sin embargo, los pagos obligatorios al gobierno general asignados a esos entes sí están incluidos aquí siempre que el gobierno no actúe como mero agente de estos.[3] Las utilidades de los monopolios fiscales se diferencian de las de otras empresas públicas, y se tratan como impuestos porque reflejan el ejercicio del poder tributario del Estado mediante el uso de prerrogativas monopolísticas (véanse los §§ 62–64), al igual que las utilidades percibidas por el gobierno por la compra y la venta de divisas a diferentes tipos de cambio (véase el § 70).

5. Los impuestos pagados por el gobierno (p. ej., contribuciones a la seguridad social e impuestos sobre la nómina pagados por el gobierno en su calidad de empleador, impuestos sobre el consumo en sus compras o impuestos sobre sus propiedades) no se han excluido de los datos presentados. Sin embargo, cuando ha sido posible identificar las cantidades de ingreso implicadas,[4] se han mostrado en la parte III, sección C, de la publicación Revenue Statistics de la OCDE.

6. La relación entre esta clasificación y la del Sistema de Cuentas Nacionales (SCN) se aclara en los apartados H y J infra.; dado que estas dos clasificaciones no coinciden en todos sus aspectos, en ocasiones, los datos presentados en las cuentas nacionales se calculan o clasifican de forma diferente a lo establecido en la presente guía y, aunque esas y otras diferencias se han mencionado en determinados casos (p. ej., en los §§ 13 y 26), no ha sido posible hacer referencia a todas ellas. Por otra parte, pueden darse asimismo ciertas disparidades entre la presente clasificación y la empleada internamente por algunas administraciones nacionales (véase el § 10), por lo que quizá las estadísticas de la OCDE y las nacionales no siempre concuerden; sin embargo, es más que probable que esas diferencias sean mínimas en lo que a la cuantía de ingresos se refiere.

*Contribuciones a la seguridad social*

7. Las contribuciones obligatorias a la seguridad social, tal y como se definen en el § 35, abonadas al gobierno general, se tratan aquí como ingresos tributarios, ya que, al tratarse de pagos preceptivos al gobierno general, se asemejan claramente a los impuestos. No obstante, pueden diferir de otros impuestos por el hecho de que la recepción de prestaciones de la seguridad social depende, en numerosos países, de que se hayan aportado las debidas contribuciones, aunque la magnitud de dichas prestaciones no tiene por qué estar supeditada obligatoriamente al importe de las contribuciones. Al tratar las contribuciones sociales como impuestos, se obtiene un mayor grado de comparabilidad entre países, aunque se han consignado en una categoría separada para poder distinguirlas en cualquier análisis.

8. Por el contrario, las contribuciones a la seguridad social voluntarias o no pagaderas al gobierno general (véase el § 1) no se tratan como impuestos, aunque en ciertos países, tal y como se indica debidamente en cada caso en las notas que figuran al pie de los cuadros, plantea dificultades el eliminar tanto las contribuciones voluntarias como algunos pagos obligatorios al sector privado.

*Tasas, cargos a usuarios y licencias*

9. Aparte de las tasas por licencia de vehículos, universalmente consideradas como impuestos, no resulta fácil distinguir entre las tasas y cargos a usuarios que deben tratarse como impuestos y las que no, ya que, aunque toda tasa o cargo se impone en conexión con un servicio o una actividad específicos, la intensidad del vínculo entre el derecho cobrado y el servicio prestado puede variar considerablemente, al igual que puede hacerlo la relación entre la cuantía de la tasa y el costo que supone proporcionar el servicio en cuestión. En todo caso, cuando el beneficiario del servicio pague una tasa claramente relacionada con el costo que supone prestar un servicio, puede inferirse que el gravamen tiene contraprestación y, de acuerdo con la definición reseñada en el § 1, no se considerará como impuesto. En sentido contrario, puede estimarse que el gravamen "carece de contraprestación" cuando:

a) el cargo exceda con creces el costo que supone prestar el servicio;

b) el pagador o sujeto pasivo del gravamen no sea el beneficiario del servicio (p. ej., tasas recaudadas de los mataderos para financiar un servicio proporcionado a los titulares de explotaciones agropecuarias);

c) el gobierno no proporcione un servicio específico a cambio del pago del gravamen, aun y cuando se emita un permiso en beneficio del sujeto pasivo (p. ej., cuando el gobierno concede licencias de caza, pesca o tiro que no otorgan el derecho a usar una zona específica propiedad del gobierno);

d) los servicios beneficien únicamente a los pagadores del gravamen, pero las utilidades recibidas por cada persona no guarden necesariamente proporción con sus pagos (p. ej., el gravamen sobre la comercialización de la leche que recae en los criadores de ganado lechero y que se utiliza para fomentar el consumo de la leche).

10. Pese a las anteriores consideraciones, en ciertos casos excepcionales la aplicación de los criterios plasmados en el § 1 puede resultar particularmente compleja. La solución adoptada –dada la conveniencia de uniformidad internacional y las cantidades de ingreso relativamente bajas implicadas por lo general– ha consistido en seguir la práctica dominante en la mayoría de las administraciones, en lugar de permitir que cada país aplique su propia visión sobre si estos gravámenes deben considerarse como ingresos tributarios o no tributarios.[5]

11. Seguidamente, se ofrece una lista de las principales tasas y cargos en cuestión, y su tratamiento normal[6] en esta publicación:

| | |
|---|---|
| Ingresos no tributarios: | tasas procesales, permisos de conducir, tasas portuarias, tasas por expedición de pasaportes, licencias de radio y televisión cuando las autoridades públicas proporcionan el servicio de difusión. |
| Impuestos de la partida 5200: | permiso para realizar actividades tales como distribución cinematográfica; caza, pesca o tiro; suministro de instalaciones para actividades recreativas o de ocio o juegos de azar; venta de bebidas alcohólicas o tabaco; posesión de animales domésticos o uso de vehículos automotores; derechos sobre la extracción. |

12. En la práctica, puede que no siempre resulte posible aislar las entradas tributarias de las no tributarias cuando estas se registran conjuntamente. En ese caso, si se considera que la mayoría de las entradas proviene de ingresos no tributarios, se tratará el importe total como tal; de lo contrario, esas entradas del gobierno se incluirán y clasificarán según las normas recogidas en el § 28.

13. En relación con la delimitación de los ingresos tributarios y no tributarios, se observan las dos siguientes diferencias entre la clasificación de la OCDE y la del SCN:

- El SCN considera un cierto número de gravámenes como impuestos indirectos si los abonan las empresas y como ingresos no tributarios si los satisfacen los hogares, una distinción obviada en la presente clasificación a la hora diferenciar entre ingresos tributarios y no tributarios.[7]
- La práctica dominante en la mayoría de las administraciones tributarias de la OCDE, un criterio empleado ocasionalmente en la presente clasificación para distinguir entre ingresos tributarios y no tributarios, no resulta pertinente a efectos del SCN.

*Regalías*

14. Las regalías percibidas por el derecho a extraer petróleo o gas, o a explotar otros recursos minerales, se consideran normalmente ingresos no tributarios, ya que son rentas de la propiedad procedentes de tierras o recursos del gobierno.

*Multas y sanciones pecuniarias*

15. Las entradas procedentes de multas y sanciones pecuniarias impuestas por el incumplimiento de normas vinculadas a un impuesto determinado, así como los intereses devengados por los pagos adeudados en relación con ese impuesto, se registrarán junto

con las entradas derivadas de dicho impuesto. Otros tipos de multas vinculadas a infracciones tributarias se clasificarán en la partida residual 6000. Las multas que no deriven de infracciones tributarias (p. ej., infracción de aparcamiento) o que no puedan vincularse a una infracción tributaria concreta no se tratan como impuestos.

## B. Principios de registro

### *Criterio de devengo*

16. Los datos recogidos en esta publicación relativos a los últimos años se han registrado predominantemente según el criterio de devengo, esto es, se han computado en el momento en que nace la obligación. En las notas que figuran al pie de los cuadros de países de la parte III del informe, se ofrece más información al respecto.

17. Sin embargo, los datos relativos a años anteriores han seguido registrándose principalmente según el criterio de caja, es decir, en el momento en que el gobierno recibió el pago. Por lo tanto, por ejemplo, los impuestos descontados por los empleadores en un año pero pagados al gobierno al año siguiente y los impuestos debidos un año pero liquidados el año después constan ambos en las entradas del segundo año. Las transacciones correctoras, tales como devoluciones, reembolsos y reintegros, se deducen de los ingresos brutos del periodo en que se realizan.

18. Los datos sobre ingresos tributarios se registran sin deducción de los gastos administrativos propios de la recaudación impositiva. De igual modo, cuando los recursos generados por un impuesto se emplean para subvencionar a miembros particulares de la comunidad, el subsidio no se descuenta del producto impositivo, aunque puede que el impuesto aparezca sin los subsidios en los registros nacionales de algunos países.

19. En lo que a los monopolios fiscales se refiere (5122), únicamente se incluye en los ingresos del gobierno el importe realmente transferido a este. Sin embargo, si cualquier gasto de los monopolios fiscales se considera gasto del gobierno (p. ej., gastos sociales emprendidos por los monopolios fiscales en beneficio del gobierno), se añadirán posteriormente con el fin de llegar a cifras de ingreso tributario (véase el § 62 infra.).

### *Distinción entre disposiciones tributarias y disposiciones relativas al gasto*[8]

20. Dado que la presente publicación aborda únicamente la actividad del gobierno desde el punto de vista del ingreso, sin tener en cuenta los aspectos relacionados con el gasto, resulta preciso realizar una distinción entre las disposiciones que rigen estos dos elementos. Por lo general, no existe dificultad alguna en diferenciar ambos aspectos, ya que los gastos operan en un ámbito externo al sistema tributario y sus cuentas, y se rigen por una legislación separada de la impositiva. En los casos de difícil delimitación, se emplea el flujo de caja para distinguir entre disposiciones tributarias y disposiciones relativas al gasto. En la medida en que una disposición incida en el flujo de pagos tributarios del contribuyente al gobierno, se entenderá que reviste un carácter tributario y se tendrá en cuenta en los datos recogidos en esta publicación. Cualquier disposición que no afecte a ese flujo se reputará como relativa al gasto y no se tendrá en consideración en la información plasmada en la publicación.

21. Las desgravaciones, exenciones y deducciones tributarias sobre la base imponible afectan claramente a la cantidad transferida al gobierno y, por ende, se consideran disposiciones de naturaleza tributaria. En el extremo opuesto, los subsidios o exoneraciones que no compensen la obligación tributaria y que estén claramente desvinculados del proceso de evaluación, no reducen los ingresos tributarios consignados en esta publicación. De particular interés en este ámbito resultan los créditos fiscales,

que son cantidades deducibles del impuesto liquidable (lo que los diferencia de las deducciones sobre la base imponible). Cabe distinguir dos tipos de créditos fiscales: los créditos fiscales no exigibles (a veces denominados desaprovechables), limitados al importe de la obligación tributaria y que, por ende, no pueden generar un pago de las autoridades al contribuyente; y los créditos fiscales exigibles (o no desaprovechables), que no están sometidos a dicho límite, de forma que toda cantidad que exceda la obligación tributaria puede abonarse al contribuyente.[9] Al igual que las desgravaciones, un crédito fiscal no exigible afecta claramente a la cantidad transferida al gobierno y, por ende, se considerará como tributario. La práctica seguida para los créditos fiscales exigibles[10] consiste en distinguir entre "el componente de gasto tributario"[11] que es la porción del crédito empleada en reducir o eliminar la obligación del contribuyente" y el "componente de transferencia", constituido por la parte que excede la obligación del contribuyente y que se paga a este. Al registrar los ingresos tributarios deberá restarse la parte equivalente al componente de gasto tributario, pero no la correspondiente al componente de transferencia. Además, las cantidades de ambos componentes deberán figurar como partidas informativas en los cuadros de países. Los países que no puedan diferenciar entre estos dos componentes deberán indicar si se ha restado de los ingresos tributarios el total de ellos y presentar las evaluaciones disponibles del valor que ambos representan. Para mayor información, consúltese la sección C de la parte I de la publicación Revenue Statistics de la OCDE, que examina el efecto de los diversos tratamientos de los créditos fiscales exigibles en la relación impuestos sobre PIB.

#### *Calendario y ejercicio fiscal*

22. Las autoridades nacionales cuyos ejercicios fiscales no coinciden con el año calendario deben presentar los datos, siempre que sea posible, sobre la base del año calendario, a fin de permitir el mayor grado posible de comparación con la información de otros países. Subsisten algunos países en los que los datos hacen referencia a los ejercicios fiscales; para ellos, los datos relativos al PIB utilizados en los cuadros comparativos corresponden igualmente a los ejercicios fiscales.

## C. Criterios generales de clasificación

#### *Principales criterios de clasificación*

23. El desglose de las entradas fiscales en las diversas categorías (1000, 2000, 3000, 4000, 5000 y 6000) se rige en general por la base sobre la cual recae el impuesto: 1000, renta, utilidades y ganancias de capital; 2000 y 3000, remuneraciones, nómina o número de empleados (fuerza de trabajo); 4000, propiedad; 5000, bienes y servicios; 6000, bases múltiples, otras bases o bases no identificables. Cuando un impuesto se calcula sobre más de una base, las entradas que genera se distribuyen, en la medida de lo posible, entre las diversas categorías (véanse los §§ 28 y 78). Las categorías 4000 y 5000 no sólo cubren aquellos impuestos en los que la base tributaria está constituida por la propiedad, los bienes o los servicios en sí mismos, sino también ciertos impuestos afines; y así, por ejemplo, los impuestos sobre transmisiones patrimoniales se incluyen en la partida 4400,[12] y los impuestos sobre el uso de bienes y sobre el permiso para realizar actividades, en la 5200. En las categorías 4000 y 5000, se distingue en ocasiones entre impuestos recurrentes y no recurrentes: son impuestos recurrentes los que se recaudan a intervalos regulares (por lo general, anualmente), y no recurrentes, los que se imponen una sola vez (véanse los §§ 43 46, 49–50 y 76–77 para profundizar en las aplicaciones particulares de esta distinción).

24. La asignación de un impuesto a fines específicos no afecta a la clasificación de las entradas fiscales que genera. Sin embargo, tal y como se explica en el § 35 en relación con la clasificación de las contribuciones a la seguridad social, el hecho de que estas confieran un derecho a recibir prestaciones sociales es decisivo para la definición de la categoría 2000.

25. La forma en que se establece o recauda un impuesto (p.ej., mediante el uso de timbres) no afecta a su clasificación.

***Clasificación de los contribuyentes***

26. En ocasiones, se distingue entre diversas clases de contribuyentes. Esas distinciones dependen de cada impuesto.

*a) Entre personas físicas y sociedades en relación con los impuestos sobre la renta y sobre la riqueza neta*

La distinción básica aquí es que los impuestos sobre la renta de las sociedades (impuesto de sociedades), a diferencia de los impuestos sobre la renta de las personas físicas, gravan a la sociedad como entidad y no a sus propietarios, independientemente de las circunstancias personales de estos; la misma distinción se aplica a los impuestos sobre la riqueza neta de las sociedades y de las personas físicas. Los impuestos liquidados sobre las utilidades de las asociaciones y sobre la renta de las instituciones, tales como seguros de vida o fondos de pensiones, se clasifican siguiendo la misma regla, y así, se considerarán impuestos sobre las sociedades (1200) si se cargan a la asociación o institución como persona jurídica sin tener en cuenta las circunstancias personales de sus propietarios, o impuestos sobre las personas físicas en el caso contrario (1100). Por lo general, los impuestos aplicados a las sociedades y a las personas físicas se rigen por legislaciones diferentes.[13] La distinción realizada aquí entre personas físicas y sociedades no sigue la categorización por sectores entre hogares, empresas, etcétera, del Sistema de Cuentas Nacionales para las cuentas de ingresos y desembolsos. La clasificación del SCN requiere que ciertas empresas no constituidas en sociedad[14] se excluyan del sector de los hogares y vengan a sumarse a las empresas no financieras y las instituciones financieras. Sin embargo, el impuesto sobre las utilidades de esos negocios no siempre puede separarse del impuesto sobre la renta de sus propietarios o, como mucho, puede deslindarse sólo arbitrariamente. Por ello, no se ha intentado reproducir aquí esa separación, y la totalidad del impuesto sobre la renta de las personas físicas se ha recogido en un solo bloque, independientemente de la naturaleza del ingreso imponible.

*b) Entre hogares y otros en relación con los impuestos sobre la propiedad inmueble*

Esta distinción es la misma que la adoptada por el SCN para las cuentas de gasto del consumo final de los hogares y de producción. Se trata pues de diferenciar a los hogares como consumidores (esto es, excluidas las empresas no constituidas en sociedad), por una parte, y a los productores, por otra. Los impuestos sobre las viviendas ocupadas por los hogares, tanto a cargo de los propietarios-ocupantes como de los arrendatarios o de los arrendadores, se incluyen en los hogares, lo que coincide con la diferenciación que suele hacerse comúnmente entre los impuestos sobre la propiedad doméstica y los impuestos sobre la propiedad empresarial. No obstante, algunos países no se hallan en situación de operar esta distinción.

*c) Entre hogares y otros en relación con las licencias de vehículos automotores*

Se distingue aquí entre los hogares como consumidores, por una parte, y los productores, por otra, al igual que en las cuentas de gasto del consumo final de los hogares y de producción del SCN.

*d) Entre empresas y otros en relación con los impuestos residuales (6000)*

La distinción es la misma que en c), esta vez, entre los productores, por una parte, y los hogares como consumidores, por otra. Los impuestos recogidos en la categoría 6000 bien porque gravan más de una base tributaria, o bien porque su base no entra dentro del ámbito de ninguna de las categorías anteriores pero es identificable como imponible sobre los productores, y no sobre los hogares, se incluyen en "empresas". El resto de los impuestos de la categoría 6000 se imputan a "otros" o "no identificables".

***Recargos***

27. Las entradas procedentes de recargos relacionados con impuestos particulares se clasifican por lo general en base al impuesto correspondiente, ya sea el recargo temporal o no. Pero si el recargo posee una característica que lo califica para ser clasificada en una categoría diferente de la lista de la OCDE, las entradas generadas por el recargo se recogen en dicha categoría, separadas de las del correspondiente impuesto.

***Entradas tributarias no identificables y partidas residuales***

28. En un cierto número de casos, no logra determinarse que los impuestos pertenezcan enteramente a una categoría o partida de la clasificación de la OCDE y, en esos casos, se aplican las siguientes pautas:

a) Se conoce la categoría, pero no la forma de distribuir las entradas entre las diversas subdivisiones: las entradas se clasifican en la correspondiente partida o subpartida residual (1300, 2400, 4520, 4600, 5130, 5300 o 6200).

b) Se sabe que la mayor parte de las entradas procedentes de un grupo de impuestos (normalmente, impuestos locales) proviene de impuestos de una categoría o una partida particulares, pero algunos de los impuestos del grupo cuya cuantía no puede determinarse con exactitud pueden clasificarse en otras categorías o partidas: las entradas se consignan en la categoría o partida a la que pertenezca la mayoría de ellas.

c) No puede identificarse ni la categoría ni la partida correspondiente al impuesto (normalmente, local): el impuesto se incorpora a la partida 6200, a menos que se conozca que se trata de un impuesto sobre las empresas, en cuyo caso se incluye en la partida 6100.

## D. Comentarios sobre ítems de la lista

### 1000 – *Impuestos sobre la renta, las utilidades y las ganancias de capital*

29. Esta categoría cubre los impuestos aplicados a la renta o a las utilidades netas (esto es, la renta bruta menos las deducciones permitidas) de las personas físicas y las sociedades, así como los impuestos a los que se someten las ganancias de capital de esos mismos sujetos pasivos, y las ganancias obtenidas en juegos de azar.

30. Se incluyen en esta categoría:

a) los impuestos que gravan predominantemente la renta o las utilidades, aunque recaigan parcialmente sobre otras bases; los impuestos aplicados a varias bases que no sean mayoritariamente la renta o las utilidades se clasifican de acuerdo con los principios establecidos en los §§ 28 y 78;

b) los impuestos sobre la propiedad aplicados a un ingreso presunto o estimado como parte de un impuesto sobre la renta (véase el § 43(a), (c) y (d));

c) los pagos obligatorios al fondo de contribuciones de la seguridad social impuestos sobre la renta que no confieran un derecho a prestaciones sociales; si esas contribuciones otorgan derecho a prestaciones sociales, se incluyen en la categoría 2000 (véase el § 35);

d) el producto de los sistemas integrados de impuestos sobre la renta de régimen cedular se clasifican como un todo en esta categoría, aunque algunos de los impuestos cedulares puedan basarse en la renta bruta y no tener en cuenta las circunstancias personales del contribuyente.

31. La principal división de esta categoría se efectúa entre los gravámenes a personas físicas (1100) y aquellos a sociedades (1200). A su vez, en cada partida, se separa entre impuestos sobre la renta y las utilidades (1110 y 1210) e impuestos sobre las ganancias de capital (1120 y 1220). Si algunas entradas no pueden atribuirse pertinentemente a la partida 1100 o a la 1200, o si no puede realizarse esta distinción en la práctica (p. ej., por falta de datos fiables sobre los receptores de los pagos de los que se deducen los impuestos con retención en la fuente), las entradas se incorporan a la partida 1300 como "no clasificables".

*Tratamiento de los créditos fiscales en los sistemas de imputación*

32. En los sistemas de imputación del impuesto de sociedades, los accionistas están exentos, total o parcialmente, de responder en concepto del impuesto sobre la renta por los dividendos abonados por la compañía a partir de la renta o de las utilidades sometidas al impuesto de sociedades. En los países con este sistema,[15] una parte del impuesto sobre las utilidades de la sociedad está disponible para exonerar a los accionistas de su propia obligación tributaria. La exoneración del accionista reviste la forma de un crédito fiscal, cuyo importe puede ser inferior, igual o superior al pasivo tributario total del accionista. Si el crédito fiscal excede al pasivo tributario, puede que ese exceso sea pagadero al accionista. Dado que este tipo de crédito fiscal es parte integrante del sistema de imputación del impuesto sobre la renta de las sociedades, cualquier pago a los accionistas se trata como devolución tributaria, y no como gasto (compárese con el tratamiento de otros créditos fiscales descrito en el § 21).

33. Puesto que en los sistemas de imputación el crédito fiscal (incluso cuando excede la obligación tributaria) debe considerarse como disposición tributaria, se plantea la cuestión de determinar si deberá deducirse de las entradas en concepto de impuesto sobre la renta de las personas físicas (1110) o de las entradas atribuibles al impuesto sobre la renta de las sociedades (1210). En este informe, la cantidad total pagada a título del impuesto sobre la renta de las sociedades se recoge en la subpartida 1210, y el impuesto no imputado en la subpartida 1110. Por lo tanto, la cuantía total del crédito se resta de esta última subpartida, tanto si el crédito da lugar a una reducción de la obligación tributaria por renta personal, como si se realiza un reembolso porque el crédito fiscal excede el pasivo tributario por este concepto. (No obstante, si los créditos fiscales se deducen del impuesto de sociedades por dividendos repartidos a otras sociedades, las correspondientes cantidades se descuentan de las entradas registradas en la subpartida 1210.)

1120 y 1220 – *Impuestos sobre las ganancias de capital*

34. Como su nombre indica, estas subpartidas engloban los impuestos sobre las ganancias de capital, ya de las personas físicas (1120), ya de las sociedades (1220), siempre que las entradas procedentes de estos impuestos puedan identificarse por separado. Ese no es el caso en numerosos países, y las entradas de estos impuestos se clasifican junto con las del impuesto sobre la renta. La subpartida 1120 contiene asimismo los impuestos sobre las ganancias obtenidas en juegos de azar.

### 2000 – *Contribuciones a la seguridad social*

35. Entran en esta categoría todos los pagos obligatorios que confieran un derecho a recibir una prestación social futura (contingente). Esos pagos suelen estar asignados al financiamiento de prestaciones sociales y, a menudo, se pagan a las instituciones del gobierno general que proporcionan dichas prestaciones. Sin embargo, esa asignación no forma parte de la definición de las contribuciones a la seguridad social y no es necesaria para que un impuesto sea clasificado en esta categoría, pero, para que un impuesto se incluya aquí, sí será preciso que confiera un derecho. Y así, los gravámenes sobre la renta o la nómina asignados a los fondos de seguridad social pero que no confieran el derecho a recibir prestaciones sociales quedan excluidos de la presente categoría y se registran bien entre los impuestos sobre la renta de las personas físicas (1100), bien junto con los impuestos sobre la nómina y la fuerza de trabajo (3000). Los impuestos que reposen sobre otras bases, como los bienes y servicios, no se consignarán aquí aunque estén asignados a prestaciones de la seguridad social, sino que se catalogarán según sus respectivas bases, ya que por lo general no otorgarán derecho alguno a prestaciones sociales.

36. Entre otras, se incluirán aquí las contribuciones a los siguientes tipos de prestaciones de la seguridad social: prestaciones y suplementos por seguro de desempleo; prestaciones por accidente, lesión o enfermedad; pensiones por jubilación, invalidez y supervivencia; ayudas familiares; reembolsos de gastos médicos u hospitalarios o prestación de servicios médicos u hospitalarios. Las contribuciones pueden recaudarse tanto de los empleados como de los empleadores.

37. Las contribuciones pueden tener como base bien las remuneraciones o la nómina ("sobre la base de la nómina"), bien la renta neta tras deducciones y exenciones por circunstancias personales ("sobre la base del impuesto sobre la renta"), y el producto de ambas bases deberá identificarse separadamente en la medida de lo posible. Cuando las contribuciones al régimen general de la seguridad social se basen en la nómina, pero las de grupos particulares (tales como los trabajadores por cuenta propia) no puedan evaluarse en función de esta base y se emplee en ese caso la renta neta como una aproximación de las remuneraciones brutas, las entradas seguirán clasificándose sobre la base de la nómina. En principio, esta categoría excluye las contribuciones voluntarias aportadas a los regímenes de seguridad social, que, cuando sea posible identificarlas de forma separada, se recogerán en la partida informativa sobre el financiamiento de las prestaciones sociales; sin embargo, en la práctica, estas aportaciones no siempre pueden desvincularse de las contribuciones obligatorias, en cuyo caso se incluirán igualmente en esta categoría.

38. Las contribuciones a los regímenes de seguro social no vinculados a instituciones del gobierno general, así como las aportaciones a otros tipos de sistemas de seguro, tales como planes de previsión o planes de pensiones, mutualidades u otros planes de ahorro, no se consideran contribuciones a la seguridad social. Los planes de previsión son acuerdos por los que las contribuciones de cada empleado y la parte correspondiente del empleador en nombre de aquél se conservan en una cuenta separada que genera interés, de la que pueden retirarse en circunstancias específicas. Por su parte, los planes de pensiones son regímenes organizados separadamente, negociados entres empleados y empleadores, que conllevan disposiciones sobre diversas contribuciones y prestaciones, a veces más directamente vinculadas a los niveles salariales y a la duración del servicio que en otros esquemas sociales. Cuando las contribuciones a esos regímenes son obligatorias o cuasiobligatorias (p. ej., en virtud de un acuerdo con sindicatos u organizaciones profesionales), se hacen constar en la partida informativa (véase la parte III, sección B, de la publicación Revenue Statistics de la OCDE).

39. Las contribuciones de los empleados del gobierno y de este con respecto a sus empleados a los regímenes de seguridad social incluidos en el gobierno general se clasifican en esta categoría. También se consideran impuestos las contribuciones de los empleados del gobierno a regímenes diferentes que puedan reputarse sustitutivos de los regímenes generales de seguridad social.[16] Por el contrario, cuando un régimen diferente no pueda considerarse sustitutivo de uno general y haya sido negociado entre el gobierno, en su papel de empleador, y sus empleados, no se estimará como régimen de seguridad social y, por lo tanto, las contribuciones a él no se tendrán como impuestos, aunque el régimen haya sido instaurado por la legislación.

40. Esta categoría excluye las contribuciones "imputadas", que corresponden a las prestaciones sociales pagadas directamente por los empleadores a sus empleados, antiguos empleados o personas a cargo de estos (p. ej., cuando los empleadores están legalmente obligados a correr con las prestaciones por enfermedad durante cierto tiempo).

41. Las contribuciones se dividen en tres partidas principales –empleados (2100), empleadores (2200) y trabajadores por cuenta propia o no empleados (2300)– y se subdividen posteriormente en función de la base que gravan. A efectos de la presente publicación, se entiende por empleados todas las personas contratadas en actividades de unidades empresariales, órganos gubernamentales, instituciones privadas sin ánimo de lucro u otro tipo de empleo remunerado, con excepción de los dueños de empresas no constituidas en sociedad y de los miembros no remunerados de sus familias. También se consideran empleados los miembros de las Fuerzas Armadas, independientemente de la duración y del tipo de su servicio, siempre que coticen a regímenes de la seguridad social. Por su parte, las contribuciones de los empleadores se definen como las aportaciones que estos realizan por cuenta de sus empleados a los sistemas de seguridad social. Si los empleados o los empleadores tienen la obligación de continuar cotizando a la seguridad social en el caso de desempleo de un empleado, esas contribuciones se muestran en las partidas 2100 y 2200, respectivamente, siempre que los datos lo permitan. En consecuencia, la partida 2300 queda reservada a las contribuciones abonadas por los trabajadores por cuenta propia y por quienes no se hallan incluidos en la población activa (p. ej., incapacitados o jubilados).

#### 3000 – *Impuestos sobre la nómina y la fuerza de trabajo*

42. Esta categoría cubre los impuestos satisfechos por los empleadores, los empleados o los trabajadores por cuenta propia, ya como una proporción de la nómina, ya como una cantidad fija por persona, que no confieren derecho a prestaciones sociales. Como ejemplos de impuestos integrados en esta categoría, cabe citar la aportación al seguro nacional del Reino Unido (introducido en 1977), el impuesto sobre la nómina de Suecia (1969-1979) o la contribución al fondo de equiparación de la carga familiar e impuesto comunitario de Austria.

#### 4000 – *Impuestos sobre la propiedad*

43. Esta categoría engloba los impuestos, recurrentes y no recurrentes, sobre el uso, la titularidad o la transmisión de la propiedad, lo que incluye impuestos sobre la propiedad inmueble y la riqueza neta, sobre el cambio de titularidad en la propiedad por herencia o donación, y sobre transacciones financieras y de capital. Quedan excluidas de esta categoría los siguientes tipos de impuestos:

a) los impuestos sobre las ganancias de capital procedentes de la venta de propiedad (1120 o 1220);

b) los impuestos sobre el uso de bienes y sobre el permiso para usar bienes o realizar actividades (5200): véase el § 73;

c) los impuestos sobre los bienes inmuebles gravados sobre la base de un ingreso neto presunto que tiene en cuenta las circunstancias personales del contribuyente: se clasifican como impuestos sobre la renta junto con los impuestos sobre la renta y sobre las ganancias de capital derivadas de la propiedad (1100);

d) los impuestos sobre el uso de la propiedad con fines residenciales, tanto si debe responder del impuesto el propietario como el arrendatario, siempre que la cantidad debida tenga en cuenta las circunstancias personales del usuario (ingresos, personas a cargo, etcétera): se integran en los impuestos sobre la renta (1100);

e) los impuestos sobre los edificios con una densidad máxima superior a la permitida; sobre la ampliación, construcción o modificación de ciertos edificios más allá de un valor umbral; y sobre la construcción de edificios: todos ellos se integran en los impuestos sobre el permiso para realizar actividades (5200);

f) los impuestos sobre el uso de la propiedad propia para fines comerciales especiales, tales como la venta de bebidas alcohólicas, tabaco o carne, o para la explotación de tierras (p. ej., impuestos sobre la extracción en Estados Unidos): se integran en los impuestos sobre el permiso para realizar actividades (5200).

### 4100 – *Impuestos recurrentes sobre la propiedad inmueble*

44. Esta partida comprende los impuestos con que se grava de forma regular el uso o la titularidad de bienes inmuebles.

- Estos impuestos gravan las tierras y los edificios.
- Pueden consistir en un porcentaje del valor tasado de una propiedad, basado a su vez en un ingreso por alquiler hipotético, en el precio de venta, en un rendimiento capitalizado o en otras características de la propiedad inmueble (por ejemplo, el tamaño o la ubicación) de las que quepa inferir un alquiler o un valor de capital hipotéticos.
- Estos impuestos pueden aplicarse a los propietarios, a los arrendatarios o a ambos. También pueden pagarse de un nivel de gobierno a otro en relación con los bienes bajo jurisdicción de este último.
- Para la evaluación de estos impuestos, no se tienen en cuenta las deudas y, en ese sentido, difieren de los impuestos sobre la riqueza neta.

45. Los impuestos recurrentes sobre la propiedad inmueble se subdividen a su vez en los pagados por los hogares (4110) y los abonados por otros sujetos pasivos (4120), de acuerdo con los criterios establecidos en el § 26(b) supra.

### 4200 – *Impuestos recurrentes sobre la riqueza neta*

46. Esta partida abarca los impuestos con que se grava periódicamente (por lo general, anualmente) la riqueza neta, esto es, los impuestos sobre un amplio abanico de bienes muebles e inmuebles, descontadas sus deudas. Esta partida se subdivide a su vez en los impuestos pagados por las personas físicas (4210) y los abonados por las sociedades (4220), de acuerdo con los criterios establecidos en el § 26(a) supra. Si existen cifras separadas para las entradas correspondientes a pagos realizados por instituciones, se añaden a la subpartida de las sociedades.

### 4300 – *Impuestos sobre sucesiones, herencias y donaciones*

47. Esta partida se divide entre impuestos sobre sucesiones o herencias (4310) e impuestos sobre donaciones (4320).[17] Los impuestos sobre sucesiones gravan el valor total de la sucesión o del caudal hereditario, mientras los impuestos sobre herencias se aplican a las cuotas recibidas por los causahabientes individualmente considerados o en función de la relación de estos con el difunto.

### 4400 – *Impuestos sobre transacciones financieras y de capital*

48. Esta partida incluye, entre otros, los impuestos sobre la emisión, transmisión, compra y venta de valores, sobre los cheques, y sobre transacciones legales específicas, tales como la validación de contratos o la venta de bienes inmuebles. La partida no incluye:

a) los impuestos sobre el uso de bienes y sobre el permiso para realizar ciertas actividades (5200);

b) las tasas abonadas en concepto de costos procesales o expedición de actas de nacimiento, matrimonio o defunción, que suelen considerarse como ingresos no tributarios (véase el § 9);

c) los impuestos sobre ganancias de capital (1000);

d) los impuestos recurrentes sobre la propiedad inmueble (4100);

e) los impuestos recurrentes sobre la riqueza neta (4200);

f) otros impuestos no recurrentes sobre la propiedad o la riqueza (4500).

### 4500 – *Otros impuestos no recurrentes sobre la propiedad*[17]

49. Esta partida cubre los gravámenes sobre la propiedad que, a diferencia de los impuestos recurrentes, se recaudan una sola vez. Se divide en impuestos no recurrentes sobre la riqueza neta (4510) y otros impuestos no recurrentes sobre la propiedad (4520). La subpartida 4510 contiene los impuestos que se recaudan a fin de hacer frente a gastos excepcionales o de redistribuir la riqueza. Por su parte, la subpartida 4520 comprende los impuestos que gravan los incrementos de valor de la tierra, debido, por ejemplo, a permisos para su desarrollo concedidos por el gobierno general o a la provisión por parte de este de instalaciones locales adicionales; cualesquiera impuestos sobre la reevaluación del capital; y aquellos impuestos gravados una sola vez sobre determinados tipos de propiedad.

### 4600 – *Otros impuestos recurrentes sobre la propiedad*

50. Aunque este tipo de impuestos rara vez se dan en los países miembros de la OCDE, esta partida incluye los impuestos sobre bienes tales como ganado bovino, joyas, ventanas y otros signos externos de riqueza.

### 5000 – *Impuestos sobre los bienes y servicios*

51. Se incluyen en esta categoría todos los impuestos y derechos sobre la producción, extracción, venta, transmisión, arrendamiento y entrega de bienes, así como sobre la prestación de servicios (5100), y también los impuestos aplicados al uso de bienes y al permiso para usar bienes o realizar actividades (5200). Por lo tanto, esta categoría comprende:

a) los impuestos acumulativos de etapas múltiples;

b) los impuestos generales sobre las ventas aplicados, ya sea en la fabricación/producción, ya sea en la venta al por mayor o al por menor;

c) los impuestos sobre el valor agregado;

d) los impuestos selectivos;

e) los impuestos sobre las importaciones y exportaciones de bienes;

f) los impuestos sobre el uso de bienes y sobre el permiso para usar bienes o realizar ciertas actividades;

g) los impuestos sobre la extracción, el procesamiento o la producción de minerales y otros productos.

52. Los casos de difícil delimitación entre esta categoría y la categoría 4000 (impuestos sobre la propiedad) o la partida 6100 (otros impuestos pagados únicamente por empresas) se tratan en los §§ 43, 48 y 75. La partida 5300 y la subpartida 5130, ambas residuales, incluyen, respectivamente, las entradas tributarias que no hayan podido clasificarse entre las partidas 5100 y 5200 o entre las subpartidas 5110 y 5120.

### 5100 – *Impuestos sobre la producción, venta, transmisión, arrendamiento y entrega de bienes, y la prestación de servicios*

53. Esta partida comprende todos los impuestos aplicados a transacciones de bienes y servicios por las características intrínsecas de estos (p. ej., valor, peso del tabaco, graduación de las bebidas alcohólicas, etcétera) a diferencia de los impuestos determinados por el uso de bienes o por el permiso para usar bienes o realizar actividades, que entran dentro del ámbito de la partida 5200.

### 5110 – *Impuestos generales*

54. En esta subpartida, se incluyen todos los impuestos, aparte de los derechos de importación y exportación (5123 y 5124, respectivamente), que gravan la producción, el arrendamiento, la transmisión, la entrega o la venta de un amplio abanico de bienes o la prestación de una gran variedad de servicios, independientemente de que sean de producción nacional o importados, o de la etapa de producción o de distribución en la que recaigan. Por ende, comprende los impuestos sobre el valor agregado, los impuestos sobre las ventas y los impuestos acumulativos de etapas múltiples. A las entradas brutas generadas, se añaden las entradas por ajustes fronterizos en concepto de esos impuestos cuando se importan bienes, y se restan las devoluciones de dichos impuestos cuando se exportan bienes. Esta subpartida se divide a su vez en los epígrafes 5111, impuestos sobre el valor agregado; 5112, impuestos sobre las ventas; y 5113, otros impuestos generales sobre los bienes y servicios.

55. Suelen plantearse dificultades de delimitación entre esta subpartida y la dedicada a los impuestos sobre bienes y servicios específicos (5120) cuando los impuestos se aplican a un gran número de bienes, como, por ejemplo, en el caso del impuesto sobre las compras del Reino Unido (abolido en 1973) o el impuesto sobre mercancías de Japón (abolido en 1988). De acuerdo con las respectivas perspectivas nacionales, el antiguo impuesto sobre las compras británico se ha clasificado como impuesto general (5112), mientras el desaparecido impuesto sobre mercancías japonés se ha incluido entre los impuestos selectivos (5121).

### 5111 – *Impuestos sobre el valor agregado*

56. Todos los impuestos generales al consumo cargados sobre el valor agregado entran dentro de este epígrafe, independientemente del método de deducción y de las etapas en las que recaiga el impuesto. En la práctica, todos los países de la OCDE con este tipo de impuestos permiten que todos los intermediarios, excepto el consumidor final, se deduzcan inmediatamente los impuestos sobre las compras e imponen tributación en todas las etapas. Para algunos países, puede que se incluyan en este epígrafe otros impuestos, tales como los aplicados sobre actividades financieras y de seguros, o bien porque las entradas que generan no pueden identificarse separadamente de las procedentes del impuesto sobre el valor agregado, o bien porque se considera que forman parte de este último, aunque esos mismos impuestos puedan clasificarse diferentemente en terceros países (p. ej., como impuestos sobre servicios específicos (5126) o impuestos sobre transacciones financieras y de capital (4400).

### 5112 – *Impuestos sobre las ventas*

57. Se clasifican aquí todos los impuestos generales aplicados a una sola etapa, ya sea en la fabricación/producción, o en la venta al por mayor o al por menor.

### 5113 – *Otros impuestos generales sobre los bienes y servicios*

58. Este epígrafe comprende los impuestos acumulativos de etapas múltiples (también conocidos como "impuestos en cascada"), en los que el impuesto se aplica cada vez que se realiza una transacción sin deducción del valor del impuesto pagado sobre los insumos, así como los impuestos generales al consumo cuando estos combinan elementos de los impuestos sobre el valor agregado, sobre las ventas o en cascada.

### 5120 – *Impuestos sobre bienes y servicios específicos*

59. Se incluyen en esta subpartida los impuestos selectivos, las utilidades generadas y transferidas por los monopolios fiscales, y los derechos de aduana y otros derechos de importación, así como los impuestos sobre las exportaciones, las transacciones de divisas, los bienes de inversión y las apuestas, y los impuestos especiales sobre los servicios que no formen parte de uno de los impuestos generales de la subpartida 5110.

### 5121 – *Impuestos selectivos*

60. Los impuestos selectivos son impuestos que se aplican a productos particulares o a un abanico limitado de productos, que no pueden clasificarse ni en 5110 (impuestos generales) ni en 5123 (derechos de aduana y otros derechos de importación) ni en 5124 (impuestos sobre las exportaciones). Pueden imponerse en cualquier etapa de la producción o la distribución, y suelen determinarse por referencia al peso, la graduación o la cantidad del producto, aunque, en ocasiones, también en función del valor de éste. Se incluyen, por lo tanto, en este epígrafe, los impuestos especiales sobre, por ejemplo, el azúcar, la remolacha, los fósforos o el chocolate; los impuestos a tasas impositivas variables sobre una cierta gama de bienes; y los impuestos que gravan en la mayoría de los países los productos derivados del tabaco, las bebidas alcohólicas, y los aceites de hidrocarburos y otras fuentes de energía.

61. Los impuestos selectivos se distinguen de:

a) los impuestos generales (5110): abordado en los §§ 54 y 55;

b) los derechos de aduana y otros derechos de importación (5123): si un impuesto recaudado principalmente sobre los bienes importados también se aplica, o podría aplicarse, de conformidad con la misma ley que establece el impuesto, a bienes comparables producidos en el país, las entradas de dicho impuesto se clasifican como impuestos selectivos (5121); este principio rige incluso cuando no existan productos nacionales comparables ni la posibilidad de que se produzcan (véase el § 65);

c) los impuestos sobre servicios específicos (5126): el problema se plantea en relación con los impuestos sobre la electricidad, el gas y la energía, que se consideran impuestos sobre los bienes y se incluyen en el epígrafe 5121.

### 5122 – *Utilidades de los monopolios fiscales*

62. Este epígrafe comprende la parte de las utilidades de los monopolios fiscales transferida al gobierno general o usada para financiar gastos considerados como gastos del gobierno (véase el § 19). Las cantidades implicadas se registran cuando se transfieren al gobierno general o cuando se usan para gastos considerados como gastos del gobierno.

63. Los monopolios fiscales reflejan el ejercicio del poder tributario del gobierno mediante el uso de prerrogativas monopolísticas. Se trata de empresas públicas no financieras que ejercen un monopolio, en la mayoría de los casos sobre la producción o la distribución de tabaco, bebidas alcohólicas, sal, fósforos, cartas de juego, productos derivados del petróleo y productos agrícolas (es decir, sobre el tipo de productos susceptibles de estar sometidos, alternativa o adicionalmente, a los impuestos selectivos del epígrafe 5121), con el fin de recaudar ingresos para el gobierno que en otros países se obtienen gravando las operaciones que sobre dichos bienes efectúan las unidades empresariales privadas. El monopolio del gobierno puede intervenir en la etapa de producción o, en el caso de los establecimientos de licores propiedad del gobierno o bajo control de éste, en la etapa de distribución.

64. Cabe distinguir los monopolios fiscales de los servicios públicos, tales como el transporte ferroviario, la electricidad, los servicios de correos y otras comunicaciones, que pueden gozar también de una posición monopolística o cuasimonopolística, pero cuyo fin primero suele ser la prestación de servicios básicos y no la obtención de ingresos para el gobierno; las transferencias de esas otras empresas públicas al gobierno se consideran ingresos no tributarios. El concepto tradicional de monopolio fiscal no llega a abarcar las loterías estatales, cuyas utilidades se consideran, en consecuencia, ingresos no tributarios. Las utilidades de los monopolios fiscales se han separado de las de los monopolios de importación y exportación (5127) transferidas de juntas de comercialización u otras empresas dedicadas al comercio internacional.

#### 5123 – *Derechos de aduana y otros derechos de importación*

65. Se incluyen aquí los impuestos, derechos de timbre y sobrecargas limitados por ley a los productos importados, así como los gravámenes sobre los productos agrícolas importados impuestos en los países miembros de la Unión Europea y las cantidades satisfechas por algunos de esos países a tenor del sistema de montantes compensatorios monetarios (MCM).[18] Desde 1998, los derechos de aduana recaudados por los Estados miembros de la Unión Europea en nombre de ésta ya no se registran en este epígrafe en los cuadros de países (parte III de la publicación Revenue Statistics de la OCDE). Quedan excluidos aquí los impuestos recaudados de las importaciones como parte de un impuesto general sobre los bienes y servicios, así como los impuestos selectivos aplicables tanto a bienes importados como a bienes de producción nacional.

#### 5124 – *Impuestos sobre las exportaciones*

66. En los años 1970, los derechos de exportación se aplicaban en Australia, Canadá y Portugal como una medida de carácter regular, y en Finlandia se han utilizado con fines contracíclicos. Algunos países miembros de la Unión Europea pagan un gravamen sobre las exportaciones, en el marco del sistema MCM (véase la nota a pie de página 18 en el § 65). Cuando las cantidades recaudadas son identificables, se integran en este epígrafe, que no incluye, sin embargo, las devoluciones de impuestos generales al consumo, de impuestos selectivos o de derechos de aduana sobre los bienes exportados, que se deducirán de las entradas brutas de 5110, 5121 o 5123, según corresponda.

#### 5125 – *Impuestos sobre los bienes de inversión*

67. Este epígrafe cubre los impuestos sobre los bienes de inversión, tales como la maquinaria. Estos impuestos pueden cargarse por un cierto número de años o temporalmente con fines contracíclicos. No se incluyen aquí aquellos impuestos sobre los insumos industriales que recaen también en los consumidores (p. ej., el impuesto sobre la energía en Suecia, que se clasifica en 5121).

**5126 – *Impuestos sobre servicios específicos***

68. Todos los impuestos sobre el pago por servicios específicos, tales como los impuestos sobre las primas de seguro, los servicios bancarios, los juegos de azar y las apuestas (p. ej., carreras de caballos, quinielas de fútbol, lotería), el transporte, las actividades recreativas o de ocio, los restaurantes y la publicidad, entran dentro de este epígrafe. También se clasifican aquí los impuestos sobre el ingreso bruto de las empresas que prestan el servicio (p. ej., primas de seguro o apuestas brutas recibidas por una empresa). Los ingresos tributarios procedentes de gravámenes bancarios y pagos a sistemas de seguro de depósitos y de estabilidad financiera se han incluido provisionalmente en este epígrafe para la edición de 2012. La clasificación detallada figura en el Anexo A.

69. Se excluyen de este epígrafe:

a) los impuestos sobre servicios que formen parte de un impuesto general sobre los bienes y servicios (5110);

b) los impuestos sobre la electricidad, el gas y la energía (5121, impuestos selectivos);

c) los impuestos sobre las ganancias de las personas físicas en los juegos de azar (1120, impuestos sobre las ganancias de capital de las personas físicas o de las empresas no constituidas en sociedad) y los impuestos fijos sobre la transferencia de loterías privadas o sobre el permiso para crear loterías (5200);[19]

d) los impuestos sobre los cheques y sobre la emisión, transmisión o compra y venta de valores (4400, impuestos sobre transacciones financieras y de capital).

**5127 – *Otros impuestos sobre el comercio y las transacciones internacionales***

70. Este epígrafe abarca los ingresos percibidos por el gobierno por la compra y la venta de divisas a diferentes tipos de cambio. Cuando el gobierno ejerce poderes monopolísticos para obtener un margen entre los precios de compra y de venta de divisas superior al que sería necesario para cubrir los costos administrativos, el ingreso generado constituye un gravamen obligatorio impuesto en proporciones indeterminadas tanto sobre el comprador como sobre el vendedor de divisas. Es un equivalente común de los derechos de importación y exportación cargados en un sistema con tipo de cambio único o de un impuesto sobre la compraventa de divisas. Al igual que las utilidades de los monopolios fiscales o de los monopolios de importación y exportación transferidas al gobierno, representa el ejercicio de las prerrogativas monopolísticas con fines fiscales y, por lo tanto, se incluye en los ingresos tributarios.

71. El epígrafe engloba asimismo las utilidades de los monopolios de importación y exportación, que, sin embargo, son inexistentes en los países de la OCDE; los impuestos sobre la compraventa de divisas; y cualesquiera otros impuestos que recaigan sobre el comercio o las transacciones internacionales.

**5128 – *Otros impuestos sobre bienes y servicios específicos***

72. Este epígrafe incluye los impuestos sobre la extracción de minerales, combustibles fósiles y otros recursos agotables de yacimientos de propieddad privada o de otro nivel de gobierno, así como cualesquiera otras entradas no identificables procedentes de impuestos sobre bienes y servicios específicos. Los impuestos sobre la extracción de recursos agotables suelen traducirse en un importe fijo por cantidad o peso, pero también pueden adoptar un valor porcentual. Los impuestos se registran en el momento de extracción de los recursos. Los pagos por extracción de recursos agotables de yacimientos propiedad de la unidad de gobierno que recibe el pago se clasifican como alquiler.

**5200 – *Impuestos sobre el uso de bienes y sobre el permiso para usar bienes o realizar actividades***

73. Esta partida incluye los impuestos aplicados al uso de bienes a diferencia de los impuestos sobre los propios bienes. Al contrario que los impuestos de este último tipo (registrados en la partida 5100), los impuestos considerados aquí no se basan en el valor de los bienes, sino que suelen revestir la forma de importes fijos. Los impuestos sobre el permiso para usar bienes o realizar actividades entran asimismo en esta partida, como, por ejemplo, los impuestos sobre la contaminación que no se basan en el valor de bienes particulares. En ocasiones, resulta complejo distinguir entre cargos obligatorios a los usuarios y tasas de licencia que se consideran como impuestos y aquellos que quedan excluidos por reputarse como ingresos no tributarios; los criterios de deslinde empleados se explican en los §§ 9 y 10.

74. Aunque el título de esta partida menciona el "uso" de bienes, es posible que sea el registro de la propiedad, y no el uso, lo que dé lugar a la obligación tributaria, y que los impuestos contenidos aquí se apliquen más al hecho de ser titular de ciertos animales o bienes (p. ej., caballos de carreras, perros y vehículos automotores) que al uso que se hace de ellos, o que recaigan incluso en bienes inutilizables (p. ej., vehículos automotores o armas inservibles).

75. Se plantean casos de difícil delimitación con respecto a:

a) los impuestos sobre el permiso para realizar actividades empresariales que parten de una base combinada de renta, nómina o volumen de ventas, que se clasifican de acuerdo con las normas del § 78;

b) los impuestos sobre la propiedad o el uso de la propiedad de las partidas 4100, 4200 y 4600; la partida 4100 se dedica exclusivamente a los impuestos sobre la titularidad o la posesión de bienes inmuebles y, a diferencia de los impuestos de la partida 5200, recaen siempre sobre el valor de la propiedad; los impuestos sobre la riqueza neta (4200) y otros impuestos recurrentes sobre la propiedad (4600) se circunscriben al hecho de ser titular de propiedades, y no al uso de activos; se aplican a grupos de activos, y no a bienes particulares; y están en todo caso relacionados con el valor de los activos en cuestión.

**5210 – *Impuestos recurrentes***

76. La principal característica de los impuestos consignados aquí es que se recaudan a intervalos regulares y se cobran por lo general según una cantidad fija. En términos de ingresos, el elemento más importante está constituido por los impuestos por licencia de vehículos, aunque también integran esta subpartida los impuestos sobre los permisos de caza, pesca o tiro o sobre la venta de ciertos productos, así como los impuestos sobre la propiedad de animales domésticos y sobre la prestación de ciertos servicios siempre que estos reúnan los criterios establecidos en los §§ 9 y 10. Los epígrafes en que se divide la partida 5210 son: los impuestos sobre vehículos automotores pagados por los hogares (5211) y los satisfechos por otros sujetos pasivos (5212);[20] por su parte, el epígrafe 5213 abarca las licencias a propietarios de animales domésticos y los cargos a usuarios por el permiso de realizar actividades, tales como la venta de carne o de bebidas alcohólica cuando los gravámenes se imponen de forma recurrente, así como las licencias generales periódicas de caza, pesca y tiro cuando el derecho a emprender esas actividades no se otorga como parte de una transacción comercial normal (p. ej., la concesión de la licencia no implica el derecho a usar una zona específica propiedad del gobierno).

**5220 – *Impuestos no recurrentes***

77. Se incluyen aquí los impuestos no recurrentes aplicados sobre el uso de bienes y sobre el permiso para utilizar bienes o realizar actividades, así como los impuestos aplicados cada vez que se utilizan los bienes.

- Entran en esta subpartida los impuestos sobre la emisión o liberación en el medio ambiente de gases y líquidos nocivos y otras sustancias peligrosas. Los pagos por permisos negociables de emisión expedidos por los gobiernos en el marco de programas de límites máximos y comercio de emisiones deberán registrarse aquí en la fecha en que se produzcan las emisiones. No se computarán ingresos por los permisos que los gobiernos expidan a título gratuito.
- El registro según el criterio de devengo implica que habrá una diferencia temporal entre el momento en que el gobierno reciba el pago por los permisos y el momento en que se produzca la emisión. En las cuentas nacionales, esta diferencia genera un pasivo para el gobierno durante ese periodo.
- Se excluirán los pagos efectuados por la recogida y eliminación de desechos o sustancias nocivas por parte de los poderes públicos, ya que constituyen una venta de servicios a las empresas.

78. También se incluyen aquí otros impuestos que entren dentro del ámbito de aplicación de la partida 5200 y que no se recauden recurrentemente. Por lo tanto, quedarán comprendidos los pagos únicos por permisos para la venta de alcohol o tabaco o para la creación de centros de apuestas, siempre que cumplan los criterios de los §§ 9 y 10.

**6000 – *Otros impuestos***

79. Esta categoría recoge los impuestos que reposan en una o varias bases diferentes de las descritas en las categorías 1000, 3000, 4000 y 5000, o en bases que no puedan considerarse predominantemente las mismas que las incluidas en esas categorías. En relación con los impuestos de base múltiple, si es posible estimar las entradas relacionadas con cada base (p. ej., el impuesto Gewerbesteuer en Alemania y Austria), las cantidades desglosadas se repartirán en las correspondientes categorías. Si no pueden calcularse los valores por separado, pero se sabe que la mayoría de las entradas proceden de una base determinada, el total de estas se atribuirán de acuerdo con dicha base. Si no puede seguirse ninguno de estos procedimientos, las entradas se clasificarán aquí. Las diversas partidas de esta categoría podrán incluir asimismo el producto de impuestos que los gobiernos no puedan identificar o aislar (véase el § 28). Se incorporan asimismo aquí las multas y sanciones pecuniarias pagadas por el incumplimiento de normas tributarias, pero no imputables a una categoría particular de impuestos (véase el § 15). Esta categoría se subdivide entre los impuestos pagados completa o principalmente por las empresas (6100) y los abonados por otros sujetos pasivos (6200).

## E. Conciliación con las cuentas nacionales

80. Esta sección de los cuadros reconcilia el cálculo de la recaudación tributaria total realizado por la OCDE y el total de todos los impuestos y contribuciones sociales pagados al gobierno general tal y como figuran en el registro de las cuentas nacionales de cada país. Cuando el país es miembro de la Unión Europea (UE), la comparación se establece entre el cálculo de la recaudación tributaria total realizado por la OCDE y la suma de los ingresos tributarios y contribuciones sociales registrado en la combinación del gobierno general y de las instituciones de los sectores de la UE de las cuentas nacionales.

## F. Partida informativa sobre el financiamiento de las prestaciones sociales

81. A la vista de la variedad de relaciones entre la tributación y las contribuciones a la seguridad social y de los casos mencionados en los §§ 35–41, se ha previsto una partida informativa que recopile todos los pagos asignados a las prestaciones tipo de la seguridad social, aparte de los pagos voluntarios al sector privado. Los datos se presentan de la forma siguiente (véase la parte III, sección B, de la publicación *Revenue Statistics* de la OCDE):

a) Impuestos de la categoría 2000.

b) Impuestos asignados a las prestaciones de la seguridad social.

c) Contribuciones voluntarias al gobierno.

d) Contribuciones obligatorias al sector privado.

Los §§ 35–41 ofrecen las debidas orientaciones para efectuar el desglose entre las rúbricas (a) a (d).

## G. Partida informativa sobre impuestos identificables pagados por el gobierno

82. Los impuestos identificables realmente pagados por el gobierno se presentan en una partida informativa, desglosados según las principales categorías de la clasificación de impuestos de la OCDE. En la vasta mayoría de los países, sólo pueden identificarse las contribuciones a la seguridad social y los impuestos sobre la nómina satisfechos por el gobierno, que, sin embargo, suelen ser los gravámenes más importantes liquidados por los gobiernos (véase la parte III, sección C, de la publicación *Revenue Statistics* de la OCDE).

## H. Relación de la clasificación de impuestos de la OCDE con el Sistema de Cuentas Nacionales

83. El Sistema de Cuentas Nacionales (SCN) pretende proporcionar un marco coherente para registrar y presentar los principales flujos relacionados con la producción, el consumo, la acumulación y las transacciones con el exterior de una determinada zona económica, por lo general, un país o una región destacada de un país, y, en este sentido, los ingresos del gobierno constituyen una importante parte de las transacciones registradas en todo sistema de cuentas nacionales. En agosto de 2009, la versión final del SCN 2008 se publicó conjuntamente por cinco organizaciones internacionales: la Organización de las Naciones Unidas, el Fondo Monetario Internacional, la Unión Europea, la Organización para la Cooperación y el Desarrollo Económicos, y el Banco Mundial. La publicación está diseñada para ser empleada en países con economías de mercado, sea cual sea su estadio de desarrollo económico, así como en países en transición hacia economías de mercado. Las principales partes del marco conceptual y las definiciones de los diversos sectores económicos del SCN se han plasmado en la clasificación de impuestos de la OCDE.

84. Sin embargo, existen ciertas diferencias, reseñadas seguidamente, entre la clasificación de impuestos de la OCDE y los conceptos del SCN, debidas a que la finalidad de la clasificación de la OCDE consiste en lograr la máxima desagregación posible de los datos estadísticos en relación con lo que, por lo general, las Administraciones tributarias consideran como impuestos. Y así:

a) la OCDE incluye las contribuciones a la seguridad social en la recaudación tributaria total (véanse los §§ 7 y 8 *supra.*);

b) los puntos de vista sobre la calificación de algunos gravámenes y tasas como impuestos son diferentes (§§ 9 y 10 *supra.*);

c) la OCDE excluye los impuestos imputados o los subsidios procedentes de la aplicación de múltiples tipos de cambio oficiales;

d) los créditos fiscales exigibles se tratan de forma diferente.

85. Tal y como se ha apuntado en los §§ 1 y 2, las categorías 1000 a 6000 de la lista de impuestos de la OCDE cubren todos los pagos sin contraprestación al gobierno general, aparte de las multas y los préstamos obligatorios. Esos pagos sin contraprestación, incluidas las multas pero excluidos los préstamos obligatorios, pueden obtenerse añadiendo los siguientes valores del SCN 2008:

- impuestos sobre el valor agregado (D211);
- impuestos y derechos sobre las importaciones, IVA no incluido (D212);
- impuestos sobre las exportaciones (D213);
- impuestos sobre los productos, IVA e impuestos sobre las importaciones y exportaciones no incluidos (D214);
- otros impuestos sobre la producción (D29);
- impuestos sobre la renta (D51);
- otros impuestos corrientes (D59);
- contribuciones sociales (D61), excluidas las contribuciones voluntarias;
- impuestos sobre el capital (D91).

## I. Relación de la clasificación de impuestos de la OCDE con el sistema de estadísticas de finanzas públicas del Fondo Monetario Internacional

86. La cobertura y la valoración de los ingresos tributarios en el sistema de estadísticas de finanzas públicas (EFP) y en el SCN 2008 son muy similares. Por lo tanto, a excepción del tratamiento dado a los créditos fiscales exigibles, las diferencias entre la clasificación de la OCDE y la del SCN 2008 (véase el § 84 *supra.*) son de aplicación igualmente al sistema de EFP. Además, el Fondo Monetario Internacional (FMI) escinde la categoría única 5000 de la OCDE en dos categorías distintas dedicadas a los impuestos nacionales sobre bienes y servicios (114) y a los impuestos sobre el comercio y las transacciones internacionales (115). Esto refleja el hecho de que, mientras estos últimos impuestos suelen generar insignificantes cantidades de ingresos en la zona de la OCDE, ese no es el caso en la mayoría de los países no pertenecientes a la Organización.

## J. Comparación de la clasificación de impuestos de la OCDE con otras clasificaciones internacionales

87. El cuadro siguiente recoge una comparación ítem por ítem entre la clasificación de impuestos de la OCDE y las clasificaciones empleadas en:

i) el Sistema de Cuentas Nacionales (SCN 2008);

ii) el Sistema Europeo de Cuentas (SEC 1995);

iii) el *Manual de estadísticas de finanzas públicas* del FMI (MEFP 2001).

88. Estas comparaciones representan equivalencias que podrán aplicarse en la mayoría de los casos. Con todo, deberán emplearse con cierta flexibilidad, ya que, en casos particulares, los países pueden adoptar enfoques diferentes para la clasificación de los ingresos en las cuentas nacionales.

| Clasificación de la OCDE | | SCN 2008 | SEC 1995 | MEFP 2001 |
|---|---|---|---|---|
| 1000 | Impuestos sobre la renta, las utilidades y las ganancias de capital | | | |
| | 1100 Personas físicas | | | |
| | 1110 Renta/utilidades | D51-8.61a | D51A | 1111 |
| | 1120 Ganancias de capital | D51-8.61c,d | D51C,D | 1111 |
| | 1200 Sociedades | | | |
| | 1210 Renta/utilidades | D51-8.61b | D51B | 1112 |
| | 1220 Ganancias de capital | D51-8.61c | D51C | 1112 |
| | 1300 No clasificables entre 1100 y 1200 | | | 1113 |
| 2000 | Contribuciones a la seguridad social | | | |
| | 2100 Empleados | D613-8.85 | D61111 | 1211 |
| | 2200 Empleadores | D611-8.83 | D61121 | 1212 |
| | 2300 Trabajadores por cuenta propia o no empleados | D613-8.85 | D61131 | 1213 |
| | 2400 No clasificables entre 2100, 2200 y 2300 | | | 1214 |
| 3000 | Impuestos sobre la nómina y la fuerza de trabajo | D29-7.97a | D29C | 112 |
| 4000 | Impuestos sobre la propiedad | | | |
| | 4100 Impuestos recurrentes sobre la propiedad inmueble | | | |
| | 4110 Hogares | D59-8.63a | D59A | 1131 |
| | 4120 Otros | D29-7.97b | D29A | 1131 |
| | 4200 Impuestos recurrentes sobre la riqueza neta | | | |
| | 4210 Personas físicas | D59-8.63b | D59A | 1132 |
| | 4220 Sociedades | D59-8.63b | D59A | 1132 |
| | 4300 Impuestos sobre sucesiones, herencias y donaciones | | | |
| | 4310 Impuestos sobre sucesiones y herencias | D91-10.207b | D91A | 1133 |
| | 4320 Impuestos sobre donaciones | D91-10.207b | D91A | 1133 |
| | 4400 Impuestos sobre transacciones financieras y de capital | D59-7.96d; D29-7.97e | D214B,C | 1134:1161 |
| | 4500 Otros impuestos no recurrentes sobre la propiedad | D91-10.207a | D91B | 1135 |
| | 4600 Otros impuestos recurrentes sobre la propiedad | D59-8.63c | D59A | 1136 |
| 5000 | Impuestos sobre los bienes y servicios | | | |
| | 5100 Impuestos sobre la producción, venta y transmisión de bienes y prestación de servicios | | | |
| | 5110 Impuestos generales | | | |
| | 5111 Impuestos sobre el valor agregado | D211-7.89 | D211; D29G | 11411 |
| | 5112 Impuestos sobre las ventas | D2122-7.94a; D214-7.96a | D2122D; D214I | 11412 |
| | 5113 Otros impuestos generales sobre los bienes y servicios | D214-7.96a | D214I | 11413 |
| | 5120 Impuestos sobre bienes y servicios específicos | | | |
| | 5121 Impuestos selectivos | D2122-7.94b; D214-7.96b | D2122C; D214A,B,D | 1142 |
| | 5122 Utilidades de los monopolios fiscales | D214-7.65e | D214J | 143 |
| | 5123 Derechos de aduanas y otros derechos de importación | D2121-7.93 | D2121; D2122A,B | 1151 |
| | 5124 Sobre las exportaciones | D213-7.95a | D214K | 1152-4 |
| | 5125 Sobre los bienes de inversión | | | |
| | 5126 Sobre servicios específicos | D2122-7.94c; D214-7.96c | D2122E; D214E,F,G; D29F | 1144; 1156 |
| | 5127 Otros impuestos sobre el comercio y las transacciones internacionales | D2122-7.94d D29-7.95b D29-7.97g D59-8.64d | D2122F; D29D D59E | 1153 1155-6 |
| | 5128 Otros impuestos sobre bienes y servicios específicos | | | 1146 |
| | 5130 No clasificables entre 5110 y 5120 | | | |
| | 5200 Impuestos sobre el uso de bienes y sobre el permiso para usar bienes y realizar actividades | | | |
| | 5210 Impuestos recurrentes | | | |
| | 5211 Sobre vehículos automotores: hogares | D59-8.64c | D59D | 11451 |
| | 5212 Sobre vehículos automotores: otros | D29-7.97d | D214D; D29B | 11451 |
| | 5213 Otros impuestos recurrentes | D29-7.97c,d,f D59-8.64c | D29B,E,F; D59D | 11452 |
| | 5220 Impuestos no recurrentes | | | |
| | 5300 No clasificables entre 5100 y 5200 | | | |
| 6000 | Otros impuestos | | | |
| | 6100 Pagados únicamente por empresas | | | |
| | 6200 Pagados por otros distintos de las empresas o no identificables | D59-8.64a,b | D59B,C | 1162 |

## K. Atribución de ingresos tributarios por subsectores del gobierno general

89. La clasificación de la OCDE requiere un desglose de los ingresos tributarios por subsectores del gobierno general. Seguidamente, se establecen la definición de cada subsector y los criterios que deben emplearse para atribuir los ingresos tributarios entre ellos, que siguen las orientaciones del SCN 2008 y del MEFP 2001.

***Identificación de los subsectores del gobierno general***

*a) Gobierno central*

90. El subsector del gobierno central incluye todos los departamentos, oficinas y establecimientos del gobierno, así como otros órganos que constituyen organismos o instrumentos de la autoridad central, cuya competencia se extiende a todo el territorio, con excepción de la administración de los fondos de seguridad social. En consecuencia, el gobierno central tiene la facultad de someter a tributación a todas las unidades residentes y no residentes que emprendan actividades económicas en el país.

*b) Gobierno estatal, provincial o regional*

91. Este subsector está compuesto por unidades intermedias del gobierno que ejercen su competencia a un nivel inferior al del gobierno central. Incluye a todas las unidades que operan independientemente del gobierno central en una parte del territorio de un país que engloba numerosas pequeñas localidades, con la excepción de la administración de los fondos de seguridad social. En los países unitarios, puede considerarse que los gobiernos regionales tienen una existencia separada, en la que cuentan con la suficiente autonomía como para recaudar sus ingresos de fuentes bajo su control, y sus funcionarios son independientes del control administrativo externo en el ejercicio de las actividades de la unidad.

92. En la actualidad, los países federales representan la mayoría de los casos en los que los ingresos atribuidos a unidades intermedias del gobierno se identifican de forma separada. España es el único país unitario en ese caso; en el resto de los países unitarios, los ingresos regionales se computan junto con los de los gobiernos locales.

*c) Gobierno local*

93. Este subsector incluye todas las demás unidades del gobierno que ejercen una competencia independiente en parte del territorio de un país, con excepción de la administración de los fondos de seguridad social. Engloba varios entes urbanos o rurales (p. ej., autoridades locales, municipios, ciudades, delegaciones, distritos).

*d) Fondos de seguridad social*

94. Los fondos de seguridad social forman un subsector separado del gobierno general. El SCN 2008 define el subsector de la seguridad social según lo expuesto en sus puntos 4.124 a 4.126 y 4.147, citados seguidamente:

> "Los regímenes de seguridad social son sistemas de seguros sociales que cubren a la comunidad en su conjunto o a amplios sectores de la misma, y que son impuestos y controlados por unidades del gobierno. Los sistemas abarcan una gran variedad de programas, y ofrecen prestaciones en dinero o en especie por vejez, invalidez o muerte, supervivencia, enfermedad y maternidad, accidentes de trabajo, desempleo, ayudas familiares, asistencia sanitaria, etc. No existe necesariamente una relación directa entre la cuantía de la contribución pagada por un individuo y las prestaciones que este pueda recibir." (punto 4.124)

"Cuando los sistemas de seguridad social se organizan por separado de las demás actividades de las unidades del gobierno, mantienen sus activos y pasivos separados de estas últimas, y realizan operaciones financieras por cuenta propia, se califican de unidades institucionales, que reciben el nombre de fondos de seguridad social." (punto 4.125)

"Las cantidades recaudadas y pagadas por contribuciones y prestaciones de la seguridad social pueden modificarse deliberadamente con el fin de alcanzar determinados objetivos de la política del gobierno que no tengan relación directa con el concepto de la seguridad social como sistema destinado a ofrecer prestaciones sociales a los miembros de la comunidad. Pueden aumentarse o disminuirse, por ejemplo, con el fin de influir en el nivel de la demanda agregada de la economía. No obstante, mientras se mantengan como fondos constituidos por separado, han de ser tratados, en el SCN, como unidades institucionales diferentes." (punto 4.126)

"El subsector de los fondos de seguridad social [del gobierno general] está conformado por los fondos de seguridad social que operan en todos los niveles del gobierno. Dichos fondos son sistemas de seguros sociales que cubren a la comunidad en su conjunto o a amplios sectores de la misma, y que son impuestos por unidades del gobierno." (punto 4.147)

95. La clasificación de la OCDE sigue esta definición de los fondos de seguridad social con las dos siguientes excepciones, por las se excluyen:

- os sistemas impuestos por el gobierno pero administrados por órganos externos al sector del gobierno general, tal y como se ha definido en el § 3 de este manual, y
- los sistemas en los que todas las contribuciones son voluntarias.

***Autoridades supranacionales***

96. Este subsector engloba las operaciones de recaudación fiscal de autoridades supranacionales dentro de un país. En la práctica, la única autoridad supranacional que cabe tener en cuenta en la zona de la OCDE es la que conforman las instituciones de la Unión Europea (UE). Desde 1998, las autoridades supranacionales no se incluyen en *Revenue Statistics*, a fin de ser coherentes con la definición que el SCN da del gobierno general, que las excluye. Por ejemplo, los impuestos sobre la renta y las contribuciones a la seguridad social recaudados por instituciones europeas y pagados a empleados públicos europeos que residen en países miembros de la OCDE no deberían incluirse. Pese a todo, ciertos gravámenes específicos pagados por los Estados miembros de la UE siguen incorporándose a la recaudación tributaria total y, en ese caso, se muestran bajo esta denominación.

*Criterios de atribución de los ingresos tributarios*

97. Cuando un gobierno recauda impuestos y los transfiere, en todo o en parte, a otros gobiernos, es necesario determinar si esos ingresos se imputarán al gobierno recaudador que los distribuye a otros en forma de donaciones, o si se atribuirán a los gobiernos beneficiarios para los que el gobierno recaudador actúa como mero agente, recibiendo el producto de los impuestos y transfiriéndolos posteriormente. Los criterios de atribución de los ingresos se establecen en los §§ 98–102 siguientes, y siguen lo dispuesto en los puntos 3.70 a 3.73 del SCN 2008.

98. Por regla general, un impuesto se atribuye a la unidad de gobierno que:

a) ejerce la facultad de aplicar el impuesto (como entidad principal o a través de la autoridad delegada por la entidad principal), y

b) puede a su discreción establecer y modificar la tasa del impuesto.

99. Cuando un gobierno recauda impuestos para y en nombre de otro, y este último tiene la facultad de aplicar el impuesto y establecer y modificar su tasa impositiva, entonces el gobierno recaudador actúa como agente de este, y el impuesto se reasigna. Cualquier cantidad retenida por el gobierno recaudador como cargo por la recaudación deberá tratarse como pago por un servicio. Cualquier otra cantidad retenida por el gobierno recaudador, por ejemplo, en el marco de un arreglo de coparticipación de impuestos, deberá tratarse como una donación corriente. Si se delegó al gobierno recaudador la autoridad para establecer y modificar la tasa impositiva entonces las cantidades recaudadas deberán tratarse como ingresos tributarios de este gobierno.

100. Cuando diferentes gobiernos establecen conjuntamente y por igual la tasa de un impuesto y el uso de los recursos, sin que ninguno de ellos tengan la autoridad final y exclusiva, entonces los ingresos tributarios se atribuyen a cada gobierno según la proporción de recursos que le corresponda; si el acuerdo permite a una unidad del gobierno ejercer el control final y exclusivo, entonces todos los ingresos tributarios se atribuirán a dicha unidad.

101. También puede ocurrir que un gobierno tenga la autoridad constitucional o de otra índole de aplicar un impuesto, pero que otros gobiernos establezcan individualmente la tasa de ese impuesto en sus jurisdicciones; los recursos generados por el impuesto en cuestión en la jurisdicción de cada gobierno se atribuirán como ingresos tributarios a los respectivos gobiernos.

*Gravámenes satisfechos por los Estados miembros de la Unión Europea*

102. Los gravámenes satisfechos por los Estados miembros de la Unión Europea (UE) revisten la forma de:

- recursos propios por IVA, y
- gravámenes específicos, entre los que se incluyen:

a) derechos de aduana y gravámenes sobre los bienes agrícolas (5123),

b) montantes compensatorios monetarios brutos (5123 en relación con las importaciones y 5124 en relación con las exportaciones), y

c) gravámenes sobre el acero, el carbón, el azúcar y la leche (5128).

103. Los derechos de aduana recaudados por los Estados miembros de la UE en nombre de esta se registran de la siguiente forma:

- sobre la base de un coeficiente de recaudación bruta;
- ajustando los resultados, siempre que sea posible, de forma que esos derechos se muestren en relación con una base de "destino final", por oposición a la base de "país de primera entrada"; estos ajustes atañen particularmente a los derechos colectados en importantes puertos (marítimos), aunque los derechos de la UE se perciben por las autoridades del país de primera entrada, siempre que sea posible cabrá excluir esos derechos del ingreso del país recaudador e incluirlos en el ingreso del país de destino final.

Este es el gravamen específico de la UE que más claramente se ciñe al criterio de atribución consignado en el § 97. En consecuencia, desde 1998, las cantidades en relación con este gravamen se registran como partida informativa en los cuadros de países de los Estados miembros de la UE (en la parte III de la publicación Revenue Statistics de la OCDE) y no se integran ya en el epígrafe 5123. Sin embargo, se incluyen en las cifras de recaudación tributaria total de la línea superior para los años correspondientes mostrados en los cuadros.

104. En cuanto a los recursos propios por IVA, que se determinan aplicando una tasa no superior al 1 por ciento a una base cuya evaluación viene dada en la Sexta Directiva,[21] se trata ciertamente de un caso de más difícil delimitación, ya que estos recursos reúnen ciertas características de una transferencia (no nacen de una fuente claramente identificable de fondos realmente recaudados) y ciertas otras de un impuesto (la cantidad de la transferencia viene determinada por el subsector del gobierno receptor). En esta publicación, no se consideran un impuesto de la Unión Europea (sino un impuesto de los Estados miembros), aunque las cantidades implicadas se indican al pie de los cuadros de la parte IV de la publicación Revenue Statistics de la OCDE.

## L. Clasificación provisional de los ingresos tributarios procedentes de gravámenes bancarios y pagos a sistemas de seguro de depósitos y de estabilidad financiera

105. La OCDE ha adoptado el siguiente enfoque provisional para el registro de los ingresos procedentes de gravámenes bancarios, así como de seguro de depósitos y tasas de estabilidad para la edición 2012 de la publicación *Revenue Statistics* de la OCDE. Los importes deberán consignarse en el epígrafe 5126.

- Los pagos obligatorios de tasas de estabilidad, gravámenes bancarios y primas de seguro de depósitos se tratarán por lo general como ingresos tributarios cuando se abonen al gobierno general y se asignen a los fondos consolidados o generales de este, de forma que el gobierno pueda utilizar libre e inmediatamente el dinero para los fines que elija. Este principio se aplicará independientemente de que el gobierno prometa revertir esos pagos para garantizar los depósitos de los clientes de los bancos en caso de necesidad futura.
- Si los pagos obligatorios se abonan al gobierno general y se destinan a fondos afectados exclusivamente a volver al sector de la economía que engloba a las sociedades sujetas a dichos pagos, éstos seguirán considerándose ingresos tributarios dado que los fondos estarán disponibles para el gobierno y podrán reducir su déficit presupuestario, que la tasa no conlleva contraprestación para una entidad individual y que las cantidades recaudadas no tienen relación con cualquier pago posterior a los depositantes o cualquier gasto realizado como medio de respaldo más amplio al sector financiero.
- Se clasificarán como tasa por servicio los pagos que deban aportarse a sistemas permanentes más reducidos para garantizar los depósitos de "particulares" cuando los niveles de pago concuerden con el coste del seguro.
- También se clasificarán como tasa por servicio, y no como ingreso tributario, los pagos que impliquen que el gobierno ejecute los activos de una institución en quiebra o tenga un derecho prioritario sobre la liquidación de activos de esta con objeto de financiar los pagos de compensación a los clientes por la pérdida de sus depósitos.

No se tratarán como ingresos tributarios los pagos obligatorios destinados a fondos externos al sector de gobierno y a instituciones no estatales respaldadas por los tomadores de depósitos, ni los pagos hechos a sistemas voluntarios.

## Notas

1. Las referencias en la Guía a las secciones o partes de "este reporte" se refieren a OCDE (2014), *Revenue Statistics* 1965-2013 (Estadísticas tributarias 1965-2013), Publicaciones de la OCDE, París.
2. Todas las referencias al SCN deberán entenderse hechas a la edición de 2008.
3. Véase el apartado K de la presente guía para el análisis del concepto de agente.
4. Por lo general, es posible identificar la cuantía de las contribuciones a la seguridad social y de los impuestos sobre la nómina, pero no otros impuestos asumidos por el gobierno.
5. Sin embargo, si un gravamen considerado como ingreso no tributario en la mayoría de los países se califica de tributario –o permite recaudar sustanciales ingresos– en uno o más países, las entradas en concepto de dicho gravamen se indican en las notas que figuran al pie de los cuadros de países, pero no se incluyen en la recaudación tributaria total.
6. Obsérvese, no obstante, que los nombres pueden dar lugar a confusión. Por ejemplo, aunque una tasa sobre los pasaportes se trataría normalmente como ingreso no tributario, si se impone un gravamen suplementario sobre los pasaportes (como en el caso de Portugal) con el fin de conseguir un ingreso sustancialmente mayor que el costo que supone proporcionar el pasaporte, dicho gravamen deberá considerarse como un impuesto sobre el uso de bienes (5200).
7. Existen ciertas dificultades prácticas para llevar a cabo la distinción operada por el SCN 1993.
8. Para una explicación más detallada de esta distinción, consúltese el estudio especial sobre cuestiones de actualidad en relación con el registro de los ingresos tributarios Current issues in reporting tax revenues, en la edición 2001 de Revenue Statistics.
9. En ocasiones, se emplean asimismo los términos "no reembolsable" y "reembolsable", pero puede parecer ilógico hablar de "reembolsable" cuando no se ha pagado nada.
10. Con la excepción del diferente tratamiento dado a los créditos fiscales exigibles en los sistemas de imputación del impuesto sobre sociedades (§§ 32–34).
11. No se trata aquí de verdaderos gastos tributarios en sentido formal, ya que tales gastos requieren que se identifique un sistema tributario de referencia para cada país o, mejor si cabe, una referencia internacional común y, en la práctica, no se ha logrado acuerdo sobre esta última.
12. A menos que se basen en la plusvalía obtenida con la venta, en cuyo caso se clasificarían como impuestos sobre las ganancias de capital, en las subpartidas 1120 o 1220.
13. Con todo, algunos países aplican la misma legislación a ambos en impuestos particulares sobre la renta, aunque las entradas procedentes de dichos impuestos suelen ser fácilmente atribuibles a uno u otro caso y pueden, por lo tanto, consignarse en la debida partida.
14. Por ejemplo, "[...] que son suficientemente autónomas e independientes y se comportan como si fueran sociedades [...] (incluido en el hecho de llevar) conjuntos completos de cuentas" (SCN 2008, 4.44).
15. En Canadá, país en el que se considera que rige un sistema de imputación, el crédito fiscal (no exigible) para el accionista nace en relación con el impuesto nacional sobre sociedades que se reputa haber pagado, tanto si ha surgido una obligación tributaria para la sociedad como si no. Habida cuenta de que no existe una conexión íntegra entre la obligación tributaria de la sociedad y el crédito concedido en relación con el impuesto sobre la renta en esos sistemas, los créditos por dividendos se tratan, junto con otros créditos fiscales, según lo descrito en el § 21.
16. Esto puede darse, por ejemplo, cuando ya existía un régimen para los empleados del gobierno previo a la introducción de un régimen general de seguridad social.
17. En el SCN 2008, se consideran transferencias de capital y no impuestos (véase el apartado G).
18. Mediante este sistema, la Unión Europea ajusta las diferencias entre los tipos de cambio empleados para determinar los precios de la política agrícola común (PAC) y los tipos de cambio reales. Los pagos realizados en este sistema pueden estar relacionados con importaciones o exportaciones y, cuando ha sido posible identificar por separado las respectivas cantidades, se han mostrado en el correspondiente epígrafe (5123 o 5124). En el presente informe, esas cantidades se han consignado en valores brutos (esto es, sin deducir ningún subsidio otorgado en el marco del sistema MCM).
19. Las transferencias de las utilidades de las loterías del Estado se consideran ingresos no tributarios (véase el § 64).
20. Véase el § 26(c) en relación con esta distinción.
21. En la Cumbre de Edimburgo (1992), los países miembros de la UE decidieron reducir paulatinamente este porcentaje del 1.4 al 1, entre los años 1995 y 1999. Durante el periodo 1970-1983, este porcentaje también fue de 1.

## ORGANISATION FOR ECONOMIC CO-OPERATION AND DEVELOPMENT

The OECD is a unique forum where governments work together to address the economic, social and environmental challenges of globalisation. The OECD is also at the forefront of efforts to understand and to help governments respond to new developments and concerns, such as corporate governance, the information economy and the challenges of an ageing population. The Organisation provides a setting where governments can compare policy experiences, seek answers to common problems, identify good practice and work to co-ordinate domestic and international policies.

The OECD member countries are: Australia, Austria, Belgium, Canada, Chile, the Czech Republic, Denmark, Estonia, Finland, France, Germany, Greece, Hungary, Iceland, Ireland, Israel, Italy, Japan, Korea, Luxembourg, Mexico, the Netherlands, New Zealand, Norway, Poland, Portugal, the Slovak Republic, Slovenia, Spain, Sweden, Switzerland, Turkey, the United Kingdom and the United States. The European Union takes part in the work of the OECD.

OECD Publishing disseminates widely the results of the Organisation's statistics gathering and research on economic, social and environmental issues, as well as the conventions, guidelines and standards agreed by its members.

## ECONOMIC COMMISSION FOR LATIN AMERICA AND THE CARIBBEAN (ECLAC)

ECLAC is one of the five regional commissions of the United Nations. ECLAC was founded in 1948 for the purpose of contributing to the economic development of Latin America and the Caribbean, coordinating actions directed to this end and reinforcing economic ties among the region's countries and with other nations of the world.

Over the years, the institution's in-depth analysis of the region has taken the form of two main lines of action: economic and social research and the provision of technical cooperation to Governments. The Commission's ongoing concern for growth, technical progress, social justice and democracy has characterized the integral approach towards development that now forms part of the legacy of its rich intellectual tradition.

The 33 countries of Latin America and the Caribbean, together with several Asian, European and North American nations that have historical, economic and cultural ties with the region, comprise the 44 Member States of ECLAC. Thirteen non-independent territories in the Caribbean are Associate Members of the Commission.

## INTER-AMERICAN CENTER OF TAX ADMINISTRATIONS (CIAT IN SPANISH)

CIAT is an international public organization with a non-profit aim, which promotes international cooperation and the exchange of experiences and information related to tax administrations. It also delivers technical assistance services, studies and training.

It was founded in 1967 as an initiative of American countries to serve as a permanent forum to address the issues and concerns, first, of tax administrators, and then, of the tax administrations. Currently CIAT has 38 member countries and associate member countries from 4 continents: 31 countries of the Americas, 5 European countries, 1 African country and 1 Asian country.

CIAT is governed by a General Assembly consisting of representatives of member countries, an Executive Council composed of one President and 8 Council members, and an Executive Secretariat based in Panama City, Republic of Panama.

## INTER-AMERICAN DEVELOPMENT BANK (BID IN SPANISH)

Established in 1959, the IDB is the main source of multilateral financing and expertise for sustainable economic, social and institutional development in Latin America and the Caribbean. To help the region achieve greater economic and social progress, the IDB supports clients in the design of projects, and provides financing, technical assistance and knowledge services to support development interventions. In addition, the IDB draws on the expertise of specialists in a wide range of fields in order to conduct research and seminars addressing key challenges for the region and evidence of successful interventions.

The IDB has developed strategies for four sector priorities: Social policy for equity and productivity; institutions for growth and social welfare; competitive regional and global international integration; and climate change adaptation and mitigation and sustainable and renewable energy.

The IDB shareholders are 48 member countries, including 26 Latin American and Caribbean borrowing members, who hold a majority ownership.

OECD PUBLISHING, 2, rue André-Pascal, 75775 PARIS CEDEX 16
(23 2015 01 3 P) ISBN 978-92-64-22938-9 – 2015-02

www.ingramcontent.com/pod-product-compliance
Lightning Source LLC
Chambersburg PA
CBHW061208240926
51846CB00006B/1151